Radical Virtues

Radical Virtues

Moral Wisdom and the
Ethics of Contemporary Life

Richard White

ROWMAN & LITTLEFIELD PUBLISHERS, INC.
Lanham • Boulder • New York • Toronto • Plymouth, UK

ROWMAN & LITTLEFIELD PUBLISHERS, INC.

Published in the United States of America
by Rowman & Littlefield Publishers, Inc.
A wholly owned subsidiary of The Rowman & Littlefield Publishing Group, Inc.
4501 Forbes Boulevard, Suite 200, Lanham, Maryland 20706
www.rowmanlittlefield.com

Estover Road
Plymouth PL6 7PY
United Kingdom

British Library Cataloguing in Publication Information Available

Library of Congress Cataloging-in-Publication Data

White, Richard J. (Richard John), 1956–
    Radical virtues : moral wisdom and the ethics of contemporary life / Richard White.
        p. cm.
    Includes bibliographical references and index.
    ISBN-13: 978-0-7425-6099-4 (cloth : alk. paper)
    ISBN-10: 0-7425-6099-6 (cloth : alk. paper)
    ISBN-13: 978-0-7425-6100-7 (pbk. : alk. paper)
    ISBN-10: 0-7425-6100-3 (pbk. : alk. paper)
    1. Cardinal virtues. 2. Compassion. 3. Ethics, Modern. I. Title.
    BJ1531.W53 2008
    179'.9—dc22   2007046214

Printed in the United States of America

⊚™ The paper used in this publication meets the minimum requirements of
American National Standard for Information Sciences—Permanence of Paper
for Printed Library Materials, ANSI/NISO Z39.48-1992.

This book is for Adam White

Contents

~

Preface

Aristotle said that the real reason for studying ethics was not to learn about moral theories but to become a better person. He was surely right about this, but we need to be reminded of his point, for as philosophy becomes more abstract it also seems to withdraw from the immediate concerns of human existence. This book, written for philosophers and other students of life, is an attempt to illuminate moral experience by looking at five virtues that help to shape our moral understanding. The "return to virtue" has been a feature of contemporary thought, both in academic philosophy and in popular thinking about what it means to be good. In this book, I look at the virtues as measures of individual goodness. But I also show how the virtues can illuminate some broader themes of social life, leading to radical conclusions about how we should live and what we should strive for.

No one is ever really a "sole author," and quite apart from all of the thinkers and writers who are discussed or referred to in this book, I have benefited from many conversations or communications with others. I would especially like to acknowledge the support of my colleagues at Creighton University, including Patrick Murray and Jeanne Schuler for years of discussion; Ross Miller, my editor at Rowman & Littlefield, for his encouragement and expert guidance; Deborah Chaffin for many significant philosophical conversations; and my partner, Clarinda Karpov for all her support and love.

~

Introduction

How should I live? In recent years, many philosophers and other writers have grown skeptical of formal approaches to ethics that emphasize objective principles and universal rules.[1] At the same time, they have started to think in a more sustained way about the nature of virtue, which always was the focus for ancient philosophers, including Socrates, Plato, Aristotle, and followers of the Stoic tradition of thought. From the perspective of modern thinkers like Kant and Mill, the most important moral questions include *What is the right thing to do?* and *How do you decide what is the best way to act?* From the perspective of virtue, the most important ethical question is *What is a good life?* Or, more directly, *What does it mean to be a good person?* As the ancient philosophers realized, however, there is no simple formula for resolving this issue; but we can clarify what it means to be good by analyzing all the different virtues that we esteem—including compassion, wisdom, generosity, and courage—as the different aspects of a life that is well lived. Popular moral wisdom provides us with a basic understanding of these virtues and their role in everyday life. A more critical philosophical reflection, however, allows us to go beyond these received ideas to the underlying reality of virtue itself.

Let us begin with the basic idea that virtues, including justice, courage, and compassion, are the ways in which we typically grasp the nature of goodness. And if a good person is someone who is totally committed and oriented toward "the good"—as Plato might put it—then her commitment involves every aspect of her life. The goodness is expressed in actions, in judgments, and by appropriate emotional responses. It is more than just an intellectual commitment, and it goes beyond having good intentions. For example, a just person is someone who is fair to others; she will be able to judge wisely about what is fair and unfair, and she will think seriously about such issues. If an obvious injustice is committed, if a policy is grossly unfair, or an unjust war is pursued, she will be outraged or deeply affected in some way, and will do everything possible to effect a change. She will also want her children to be fair-minded and avoid people who have a reputation for being unscrupulous. It will be deeply disturbing to her if her friends do something underhanded. All of this clarifies a commitment of the whole person to justice over an extended period of time. As Aristotle comments, "Indeed, we may go further and assert that anyone who does not delight in fine actions is not even a good man; for nobody would say that a man is just unless he enjoys acting justly, nor liberal unless he enjoys liberal actions, and similarly in all other cases."[2] Good intentions by themselves are not enough; but neither are good actions, for obviously people sometimes do the right thing for the wrong reasons. You cannot be considered "just" on the basis of a few just decisions. But neither are you a completely just person if you obey good laws begrudgingly; or if you realize that something would be just but fail to support it with your actions; or if you deliberately avoid thinking about issues of justice or right and wrong because they are disturbing or unsettling to your peace of mind.

Justice is a model virtue in the sense that all of the virtues involve appropriate actions, reflections, and feelings. This may not be obvious in some cases. It seems impossible to fit wisdom into this schema, for example, since wisdom is primarily an intellectual virtue. Nevertheless, a wise person is one who lives and acts wisely. A wise person understands the limitations of all knowledge and wisdom (like Socrates, who claimed that the only thing he knew was that he didn't really know anything), and a wise person is one who experiences a profound sense of humility rather than satisfaction at the extent of her own understanding. In the *Nicomachean Ethics*, Aristotle argues along similar lines when he claims that virtues are dispositions to act, judge, *and* feel in accordance with right reason: "It is in the field of actions and feelings that virtue operates; and in them excess and deficiency are failings, whereas the mean is praised and recognized as a success."[3] And the mean is something to be achieved through the proper exercise of reason, "or as a prudent man would determine it."[4] The good person responds to the claims of the world, and the need for sincerity, justice, and courage. At a deep level, she identifies herself as the kind of person for whom goodness matters, and this means that every aspect of her character should be in accordance with this end.

It can hardly be denied that virtue is an achievement, and this is the reason we esteem those who are particularly courageous, generous, or just. If people were routinely courageous, generous, or just, then virtue would not be remarkable or exceptional in the same way. This does not imply anything about an underlying "human nature," but it does mean that for the most part, courage, generosity, and the other virtues can be viewed as qualities that must be actively cultivated within the individual soul because we are not predisposed to be that way. It is usually more comfortable and less threatening to avoid danger, to ignore those who are unjustly treated, and to keep your money for yourself. And hence the virtues are those qualities that express our reorientation away from narrow self-involvement and toward a higher good. They represent forms of self-overcoming for the sake of individual perfectibility, the community that we belong to, or goodness itself.

This book is more concerned with specific virtues, like courage and justice, than with the justification of "virtue ethics" as a particular philosophical viewpoint. But in focusing on the specific virtues, we are of course implying that the perspective of virtue ethics is a significant and valuable means of ethical inquiry that supplements, at least, an ethics that is based on principles, maxims, and rules. In what follows, I will use the work of philosophers like Plato, Aristotle, Hume, and Nietzsche who have thought profoundly about the nature of the virtues, although my interest is not so much in the technical arguments they develop as in the basic moral wisdom that each of them possesses. Limiting ourselves to the history of Western philosophy, there are at least four different ways of thinking about virtue that have been argued for in a sustained way, suggesting four distinctive accounts of the nature of virtue.

First, Aristotle claims that a life lived virtuously is the most complete expression of a flourishing human existence: "Let us assert, then, that any kind of excellence renders that of which it is the excellence *good*, and makes it perform its function *well*. For example, the excellence of the eye makes both the eye and its function good (because it is through the excellence of the eye that we see well). . . . If this rule holds good for all cases, then *human* excellence will be the disposition that makes one a good man and causes him to perform his function well."[5] Just as a good knife is one that is sharp and capable of cutting well, so also a good human being is one who lives and acts in accordance with virtue, and this means in accordance with our distinctive nature as rational beings living together within a community. In other words, the virtuous man is a "successful" human being, and in the *Nicomachean Ethics*, Aristotle describes the self-cultivation of virtue in terms of a reasonable standard. The strength of this account is that it closely coheres to a lot of ordinary thinking about the virtues: We do admire those who are virtuous, and we regard them as ideal exemplars of humanity we should strive to emulate ourselves. Likewise, a virtuous life must be a fulfilled life, and we certainly should not think of the virtues as so many constraints upon us. But Aristotle's account of the virtues is very culturally specific and describes the ideal gentleman of the Athenian polis. Women and non-citizens (slaves) make only a very brief appearance in his discussion, because he accepts from the outset that the Athenian gentleman is the true epitome of virtue. On the one hand, this is a very narrow and exclusive point of view that could never serve as a universal model of virtue for the present age. On the other hand, it suggests how sometimes a fixed model of human nature—whether it is Aristotelian, Thomist, or Marxist—can oppress human beings by foisting an ideal upon them that is coercive and intolerant of individual differences.

In *Utilitarianism*, John Stuart Mill argues for a purely functional account of virtue, claiming that the latter consists of whatever qualities or traits have served to enhance human life in the past. As he puts it:

> Virtue, according to the utilitarian conception, is a good of this description. There was no original desire of it, or motive to it, save its conduciveness to pleasure, and especially to protection from pain. But through the association thus formed, it may be felt a good in itself, and desired as such with as great intensity as any other good; and with this difference between it and the love of money, of power, or of fame, that all of these may, and often do, render the individual noxious to the other members of the society to which he belongs, whereas there is nothing which makes him so much a blessing to them as the cultivation of the disinterested love of virtue.[6]

Hence, sincerity is a virtue because, for the most part, telling the truth promotes happiness—even if a lie might occasionally help to soothe someone's feelings, we prefer to know where we stand. Likewise, courage is a virtue because it's what you need to uphold your moral commitments even if you are threatened with danger or death. Once again, there is much to be said in favor of this account, and it does seem to be supported by ordinary common sense. It's fairly obvious why dishonesty, fearfulness, and greed are not considered virtues but vices, and this supports a functional explanation of what society requires of its members in order to maintain itself and prosper. It's not clear, however, that Mill's account gives us the whole story. When Socrates speaks truth to power, for example, he is unsettling Athenian society, and in the aftermath of years of war with Sparta he realizes that his activity as a gadfly does not necessarily promote the stability of his city. But his life is definitely virtuous, even though he does challenge Athenian authority and convention, and in this respect at least we could argue that his virtue is not entirely "functional" in Mill's intended sense. Of course,

Socrates believes that his gadfly activity is a service that he owes to the state, but it is subversive and threatening, and for this he is sentenced to die.

The third perspective on virtue, Nietzsche's, explicitly disclaims this functional perspective. Nietzsche argues that, on the one hand, certain actions like keeping one's promises or turning the other cheek, and dispositions like humility and even self-contempt have been celebrated at some time or another as virtues that serve to keep populations under control: "The herd man in Europe today gives himself the appearance of being the only permissible kind of man, and glorifies his attributes, which make him tame, easy to get along with, and useful to the herd, as if they were the truly human virtues: namely, public spirit, benevolence, consideration, industriousness, moderation, modesty, indulgence and pity."[7] More positively, Nietzsche argues that an authentic virtue must be an expression of individual self-affirmation and strength, which thereby involves the consecration of life. The ideal individual, sometimes called the "overman," doesn't simply follow rules but actively creates himself, and in so doing he affirms his own virtues and his own way as the very model of individual sovereignty. But such an expression is unique and could never serve as a universal standard that would only depress and confine the life that was bounded by it: "for it is selfish to experience one's own judgment as a universal law; and this selfishness is blind, petty and frugal because it betrays that you have not discovered yourself nor created for yourself an ideal of your own."[8] Once again, there is something very powerful about Nietzsche's perspective on virtue, and he helps us to realize that a truly virtuous life must be an expression of strength rather than weakness—and this makes sense because we think that such a life is admirable. And yet, we might also wonder whether this particular account of virtue isn't too individualistic. Doesn't a virtue have to be recognized by others, or belong to an everyday social context that it illuminates and transfigures? A purely individual expression of virtue that took no notice of anyone else, even disdaining admiration, would be autistic and irrelevant. The point is that we need a recognized social context of shared values and virtues that allows us to cultivate our individual traits and powers, and it's only within this horizon that we can be esteemed as outstanding or virtuous in any way. Hence, Aristotle and Mill would be right to emphasize the contribution that virtue makes to a given community and individual well-being within that context; although Nietzsche is also correct to emphasize that virtue is not just a matter of following rules, but involves the self-affirmation of individual power and strength.

I have left Plato and Kant for last. Of course their moral theories are very different, but for both of them, virtue involves devotion to a basic moral principle that Plato calls "the good," and Kant "the moral law." For Plato, the good is out there, and we are required to make progress toward it; while for Kant, the good is "within us," in the sense that it depends upon the moral law, which is ultimately an expression of our own rational nature. In spite of the differences, however, their perspectives on the virtues are broadly comparable: Plato, like Socrates, insists on the unity of the virtues, and the virtues that we separate and distinguish are only separate aspects or manifestations of the good. In the *Republic*, Plato distinguishes the four cardinal virtues of justice, courage, temperance, and wisdom, assigning each to a particular class within the state or to the relationship between the classes. But in the end there is just one ideal society, or Republic, and this is meant as an analogy for the virtuous soul. In each case, the virtues described are different aspects of goodness, and there can be no final conflict between them because they all participate in the same ultimate Form. Plato emphasizes the otherworldly aspects of the good: In the *Republic*, the good is said to be "beyond being," or outside of space and time, and so virtue is ultimately related to something that is both transcendent and ideal.[9] In Kant, the good is secondary to the moral law and virtue is defined in terms of the latter. But the virtues that Kant describes in the *Metaphysics of Morals* and elsewhere are ultimately unified and supported by the good will that is orientated to the moral law. And by reducing all the virtues to a single underlying principle he also makes conflict between them impossible. As he writes, "Virtue is the strength of man's maxims in fulfilling his duty. We can recognize strength of any kind only by the obstacles it can overcome, and in the case of virtue these obstacles are the natural inclinations, which can come into conflict with man's moral resolution. . . . Virtue is . . . self-constraint according to a principle of inner freedom, and so by the mere thought of one's duty in accordance with its formal law."[10] In Kant as in Plato, virtue relates us to a higher reality that we ultimately belong to even if we cannot specify it further: the (noumenal) realm of freedom that is beyond all appearances. For Kant, moral activity is in this sense the only true metaphysics, since it allows us to participate in the higher realm of being; but Plato's account of our relation to the good is structured along similar lines insofar as it refers to the "ideal city" that true philosophers belong to regardless of where they happen to live.

In summary, we have at least four different accounts of virtue that emphasize, respectively: the model of a human flourishing within a community; a functional necessity of society itself; the achievement of individual sovereignty; and the strength of our connection to a basic moral principle, like the good or the moral law, that must be further described. There is no need to place these particular perspectives in any rank order. Virtue is not a unitary phenomenon but a very complex and overdetermined idea that cannot be grasped by any single formulation. But each of the four perspectives expresses important points about the overall nature of virtue, and they have endured because they illuminate a different aspect of the way things are. Elsewhere, David Hume offers a composite definition that seeks to incorporate different commonsense ideas about what virtue is: "It is the nature and indeed the definition of virtue," he writes, "that it is a quality of the mind agreeable to or approved of by everyone who considers or contemplates it. But some qualities produce pleasure because they are useful to society or useful or agreeable to the person himself; others produce it more immediately."[11] For Hume, a virtue can be a quality that is agreeable to ourselves, or agreeable to others, or useful to ourselves, or useful to others. Some may object that this is not nearly precise enough, but the truth is that virtue is not a precise idea, and Hume recognizes correctly that all of these different aspects may apply. Like Hume, I will work from our everyday understanding of the virtues: If there are contradictions at this level, then we will try to resolve them, but at the same time it would be a mistake to legislate a fixed definition of virtue that denies all ambiguity of meaning in advance; for the ambiguity of "virtue" is a creative ambiguity that helps us to think about virtue in a more authentic manner.

Reflection on the virtues helps to illuminate morality and what it means to be a good person, but there are some concerns about this approach that must be seriously considered before we begin our discussion of the particular virtues. First, it may be argued that virtue is not a proper basis for morality because the virtues are culturally relative, and it would be ethnocentric to come up with a single list of virtues that was supposedly appropriate for all human societies. Different societies esteem different virtues, and they rank these virtues differently. Humility, for example, is not a virtue that would be esteemed in Homeric society; indeed, if anything it would be a vice not to celebrate one's own powers. But humility is one of the central Christian virtues, and it is esteemed in traditional Chinese culture, while in modern Western society it is a more ambivalent ideal. In other ages, a woman's "virtue" was equivalent to her chastity or sexual purity. For a man, courage as true virility is the original, defining virtue that is still preserved in the etymology of "virtue," from *vir*, the Latin word for man. Today, we may not place as high a value on chastity, and we recognize courage as one of several important virtues that are equally available to women and men. In *After Virtue*, Alasdair MacIntyre argues that in Homeric Greece, one's arête (or virtue) was entirely derived from one's station in life—the virtue of a king was entirely different from the virtue of a woman or the virtue of a slave.[12] But *we* prefer to believe that all men and women are capable of practicing specific virtues and living virtuous lives.

Second, it may be argued that to focus on virtue is not really helpful for knowing how to act in the world. Of course, we can reflect on the nature of virtues like generosity or courage, and it may be inspiring to consider the lives of virtuous individuals like Socrates, the Buddha, or Jesus. But does this really help us to decide what we should do in any particular circumstance? "Virtue ethics" does not give us rules or procedures for moral action, and so it is apparently empty. It is edifying, but it may not be of any practical relevance for living in the world and making specific moral decisions. Putting this point differently, it can also be argued that understanding what it means to be virtuous is a completely separate question that has no bearing on the pressing moral issues that face us today, such as problems with the environment, issues like poverty and war, or the nature of the just society.

The third point is closely associated with the second. It may be held that a focus on individual virtue is actually selfish or self-involved in a morally distracting way. Surely the most important thing is just to do the right thing? But if we become more involved with cultivating our own goodness and living virtuous lives, we may lose track of what should be done. It cannot be denied that virtue is important, but isn't it ultimately a secondary consideration? This seems to be the attitude of moral philosophers like Kant and Mill who argue that the virtues have an instrumental value; the virtues are means to an end, since they may be defined as the qualities that enable us to do the right thing—like courage, which helps us to follow through, even when it is difficult or dangerous, or temperance, which allows us to perform our duty even when we could be tempted by the prospect of pleasure. In this regard, to focus on individual virtue may be a selfish distraction from what is more important; it is a secondary aspect of morality that should not be taken for the thing itself.

Finally, it could be said that a focus on virtue has troubling, "reactionary" connotations. If we are encouraged to return to Aristotle or Aquinas, for instance, then we may also be asked to endorse a world that is ordered around the adult freeborn male in which women and others are considered inferior, or a world in which everyone is supposed to know their place in the social hierarchy. Likewise, as we saw above, there is a sense in which an exclusive focus on the virtues, considered as timeless and self-contained ideals for living, detaches the individual from broader issues and concerns that shape human societies. This leads to the idea that ethics and politics are separate realms, and it seems to imply that a good person would live exactly the same kind of life regardless of the society in which she happened to be. In this way, individual character is made primary with questions of social ethics quite secondary and beside the point. But this is a reactionary perspective insofar as it ignores all the complexity of modern life and the reality that virtues are not just given but are themselves the product of the societies in which we live. We must be mindful of the respect to which our understanding of these virtues is often shaped and conditioned by broader cultural forces that are beyond our control. Take courage, for example: Why do we typically associate courage with the activity of soldiers? And why do we usually rank courage above patience in the list of virtues? Why is it that pacifists are often considered cowards? These are questions that require us to go beyond the simple horizon of the virtues themselves in order to reflect on the way that such ideals are shaped and conditioned by deeper social forces. But a fixed and exclusive focus on virtue ignores these issues by pretending that morality is unproblematic and does not require a more critical point of view.

Each of these objections deserves a response. In this book, we will of course accept from the outset that virtues can vary from one society to another, and even within the same society, people's ideas about virtue can differ from one age to the next. But we will also look for commonalities that may be transcultural. For example, could one even have a society in which courage was not a virtue? For courage simply implies a devotion to whatever is considered right, even when this might be dangerous. The same with justice, which implies a commitment to "being fair," however that may be construed. In the following chapters, I will pay particular attention to philosophical accounts of the virtues, since this is where a lot of profound reflection on the virtues has taken place. By including both ancient and modern perspectives and making cross-cultural comparisons, we should be able to clarify the nature of the virtues from a variety of different points of view. The fact that virtues are to some extent shaped and conditioned by particular cultures is by no means an objection to this project. By bringing different perspectives on the virtues together, it becomes easier to clarify what these virtues are, and we may even make some moral progress from our own more limited standpoint. Of course, the present book is written by someone who has a distinct history and situated in North American/European culture. But if this is a limitation, it also serves as a starting-point. I remain optimistic about the possibility of moral growth, and I believe that the intensive study of the virtues can only make one better.

Second, it cannot be said that reflection on virtue is irrelevant to the more pressing issue of what should be done. In this book, I particularly want to emphasize the connections between individual virtues and broader social issues and concerns. The clarification of temperance, for example, actually leads to a more specifically environmentalist philosophy that is itself a reflection of this virtue; the reflection on justice as an individual virtue leads to a correlative understanding of social justice and the nature of the just society; and the discussion of wisdom supports the movement toward multiculturalism as a more inclusive attitude toward knowledge and ultimate moral concerns. In this book, I look at five different virtues: courage, temperance, justice, compassion, and wisdom. In each case, one of the main aims of discussion is to show the connection between the virtue that is under consideration and a particular social movement that it clarifies in some way. Sometimes, as in the case of temperance or compassion, the respective connections to movements such as environmentalism and animal liberation are quite obvious and direct. In other cases, including courage and justice, the connection to pacifism and socialism may be more contentious, but I will show how these movements are also illuminated by the virtues they are derived from. In the *Republic*, Plato asks about the nature of justice as a quality of the individual soul, but he argues that in order to clarify this virtue it is first of all necessary to see justice writ large in the ideal city or the republic. The strategy in this book is to *begin* with the individual virtue and then use it to show the validity of the social movement as a fitting expression of that virtue in a broader social context. But this is not to assume that the individual virtue is any more fundamental than the social movement, since it is more than likely that these two different levels must enhance and illuminate each other.

In response to the third point, it is not obvious that the preoccupation with virtue or the focused attention on what it means to be a good person is somehow self-absorbed or a kind of escapism from the complexities of modern life. Presumably, a virtuous person is someone who wants to do the right thing and who is also very much concerned with the happiness and well-being of others. In fact, the focus on virtue actually gives us a more nuanced and deeper understanding of moral life than traditional philosophies like Kantianism or utilitarianism: The first of these reduces the ethical self to that part of the person that follows the imperative of the moral law; the second turns morality itself into a productive enterprise with the goal of producing as much happiness as possible, and with the moral agent becoming an indifferent means to this end. Far from being a marginal perspective, the focus on virtue may be the most inclusive moral horizon that there is, for the virtuous person is also bound to pay attention to principles and consequences, and the happiness and moral well-being of others.

Taking all of these ideas together, the response to the fourth point—that virtue ethics is inherently limited and reactionary—should now be apparent. Reflection on the virtues and the sheer variety of their forms across different ages and cultures can make us much more aware that our own virtues are neither obvious nor inevitable; they are also open to critical reflection and improvement. In fact, the study of the virtues leads to a progressive understanding of moral life, once it becomes clear that important social movements like multiculturalism or environmentalism are implicated and supported by particular virtues. The title of this book, *Radical Virtues* emphasizes this point. The study of virtue, and "virtue ethics," is not just a relic of ancient and medieval philosophy, but an ongoing possibility of thought that can help us to grasp some of the underlying movements of contemporary life. This book is called *Radical Virtues* because it tries to show the progressive aspect of the virtues, usually ignored, that can help us to bridge the gap between the moral life of the individual and the various social movements that are also expressions of the ethical good. It is an attempt to begin what has also been called a "virtue politics."

In what follows, then, we will use philosophical perspectives from Aristotle, Plato, Hume, Nietzsche and others to grasp the basic reality of the virtues, although our interest lies in the obvious moral wisdom of each of these philosophers and only to a lesser extent in their theories about the nature of virtue. We will also use non-Western thinkers and ideas, as well as literary examples. One important point that we need to emphasize is that the history of a virtue is really crucial for determining its true significance: In contemporary Western society, each of the specific virtues is associated with a fairly narrow range of ideas and representations, and there is nothing natural or inevitable about these privileged forms. They are historical determinations that may or may not endure. To give an obvious example, courage is often thought of as a soldier's virtue, or it is the defining virtue of a man and the index of manliness itself. As we will see in the next chapter, however, this makes it quite difficult even to consider the possibility of female courage (as opposed to patience) or the courage of those who refuse to fight. Perhaps by looking at the history of specific virtues and their favored paradigmatic forms, we may actually gain a critical distance from that history. Indeed, we will see that there could still be different ways of representing courage or any other virtue that would expand our understanding of that virtue and make it more consistent with itself. Clearly, what is required here is a sense of the historical aspect of the virtues, as well as a creative moral imagination that can rethink and revalue the virtues, and realign their focus by showing connections where none had appeared before.

I will not attempt an exhaustive account of the virtues. Instead, I will focus my attention on five specific examples: the traditional "cardinal" virtues, including courage, temperance, justice, and wisdom, which were esteemed in the ancient world and reaffirmed by medieval philosophers such as Thomas Aquinas, and compassion, which remains the dominant virtue in Buddhism and other Asian traditions. This book was originally envisioned as a longer and more detailed account of all the dominant virtues. But I now believe that there is something to be said for the privileged status of the cardinal virtues and compassion as the basic virtues on which all the others depend. Historically, at least, the attention paid to these particular virtues has helped to shape our moral life and our understanding of virtue. And this selective account of the virtues may prove to be more illuminating than any extended treatise that covers all of them in detail.

The goal of this work is not to reach a consistent theory of virtue or provide a systematic account of the virtues, along the lines of Aristotle or Aquinas. Nevertheless, each of the different chapters will work toward a cumulative effect that will make it clear how the individual virtues are socially relevant, not self-contained, and require a particular kind of involvement in the world. In each chapter I focus on a particular point of view: Aristotle on courage, Hume and Plato on justice, Lao Tzu on temperance, and so forth. The goal is not so much to be wide-ranging, but to bring a particular virtue into greater focus through the use of judicious comparisons. I will also look closely at moral exemplars and focus on some lives of individual virtue, such as Gandhi, the Buddha, or Orwell that suggest in a more compelling and obvious way how virtues may be embodied. My hope is that all of this will provoke discussion and continue the conversation this book begins, and so enhance the life of virtue.

One final word on the way this book is written. This is a work of philosophy that makes continual reference to important thinkers such as Plato, Aristotle, Kant, and the Buddha, as well as basic concepts and ideas that help us to think more clearly about the nature of virtue or goodness. In this regard, it is offered as a philosophical contribution. On the other hand, it is certainly not a technical work. As far as possible, I have tried to avoid all philosophical jargon, since I am interested in the moral understanding of Plato, Aristotle, the Buddha, and so forth, rather than arguments that later philosophers have sought to extrapolate from their basic views. In this book, I am interested in the possibility of moral wisdom—which is neither banal nor technically complex—and I illuminate moral wisdom through the discussion of five of the most important virtues that clarify what it means to be good. In this respect, I hope that this book will speak to all intelligent readers, regardless of their intellectual background or the extent of their previous involvement with philosophy.

CHAPTER ONE

~

Courage

Courage is an obvious virtue. It seems to be universally admired, and it would be impossible to imagine a society in which courageous actions were not very highly regarded. But this is not a contingent feature of human societies: courage just is a necessary condition for the other virtues regardless of what the other virtues are. Can we really say that we believe in justice if we do not have the courage to defend it? And can we say that we really care about other people if we abandon them once it becomes dangerous to help? Courage may be most recognizable as military valor on the field of battle, but it also involves the difficult effort of overcoming fear and remaining steadfast whenever goodness is threatened or called into question. In this respect, Kant argues that courage, or more particularly fortitude, is both a specific virtue as well as the fundamental principle of all the virtues, for without fortitude we could not remain in a state of virtuous resolve—and this would be true whatever we think goodness is like. As Kant puts it, "Now the capacity and considered resolve to withstand a strong but unjust opponent is fortitude (fortitudo) and, with respect to what opposes the moral disposition within us, *virtue* (virtus, fortitudo moralis)."[1]

Historically, courage also has a kind of priority over all the other virtues. As Montaigne and others have pointed out, the very word for "value" is itself derived from the word for "valor," which strongly suggests that in this culture at least, martial bravery and daring may be the original value from which all the others have subsequently derived.[2] A similar point can be made about the etymological origins of "virtue" from "virility" and other cognates of manliness, which suggests the originary nature of courage in a historical if not a conceptual sense.

On the face of it, then, the virtue of courage is self-evident, and it is distinguished as a condition for all the other virtues. But once we move beyond these more general considerations and reflect on specific examples, courage becomes more difficult to apprehend. There are at least two different kinds of issues that I shall briefly mention here. First, the problem of politics and interpretation: One long-standing question concerning courage is whether it is possible to speak of a "courageous villain," and whether his villainy is mitigated or exacerbated by his daring. In a famous passage in the *Foundations of the Metaphysics of Morals*, Kant asserts that only the good will is unconditionally good, and so the courageous villain is actually worse for being courageous because his courage makes him capable of more evildoing.[3] This may be right in theory, but the problem with this response is that it remains tied to the moral and political perspective of whoever is making that claim. In World War I, for example, the average British soldier had a grudging respect for the German soldiers who faced him in the trenches, and according to Robert Graves, this was in stark contrast to the very hostile attitude of politicians and the civilian population at home. The average British soldier recognized the courage of German soldiers even though they were the enemy. But in World War II, allied soldiers did not typically respect the extreme devotion of Japanese soldiers, whose refusal to surrender and willingness to die was not considered courage but a kind of fanaticism and mindless obedience to orders. Two more contemporary examples of this ethical ambiguity concerning courage would be the hunger striker and the suicide bomber, for whether we prefer to call these individuals courageous or fanatical largely depends upon our own political affiliation. In 1981, Bobby Sands, a prisoner and a member of the IRA who was protesting British policy in Northern Ireland died after a hunger strike that lasted 66 days. For many, he was a hero, a courageous man of principle who suffered and died for what he believed was right. But according to British public opinion of the time, he was just a misguided fanatic who foolishly threw his life away for a worthless cause. Presumably, the suicide bomber also considers himself to be a soldier at war, and he uses his own body as the ultimate weapon. Should we say that his actions can only be considered "courageous" after we have determined that his cause is just? But this seems odd. Aren't the soldiers who fight on different sides in a war both capable of courage and cowardice? And even if we do think that one side is justified—as in the case of World War II, for example—it hardly follows that by definition alone no courageous acts were committed by Japanese or German troops.

The second set of problems concerns the psychology of courage. We may decide to bracket out all political and historical considerations to argue that courageous persons and courageous actions exist independently of our own political views. This means that to understand courage we need to turn away from the goals of courageous action and focus instead upon the inner disposition of the courageous person. The difficulty here is that courage isn't usually a motivating force. I don't usually do things in order to be courageous (unless I want to prove something to myself or others), and I don't typically enjoy being courageous, in the same way that I might enjoy being generous or kind to others. Courage involves rising to the occasion and doing something that is inherently dangerous, and hence fearsome, that we would not ordinarily choose to do unless there was a very good reason.

Some have argued that courage is therefore a privative idea, in the sense that having courage means that we do whatever is required of us, even when we are threatened, because there are no inner obstacles, like fear, that would prevent us from doing what we should.[4] One concern here is whether we can really be considered courageous if we don't have any fear. Aristotle denies that the Celts are courageous people precisely because they appear incapable of fearing anything, making them more like brutes than human beings. The shell-shocked soldier who wanders into no-man's-land can hardly be considered courageous at that moment. The true believer, who thinks he is invulnerable or destined to survive, isn't courageous either. This is because we typically think that true courage must involve an awareness of personal risk and danger and the willingness to proceed in spite of everything. The awareness of personal risk and danger is experienced as fear, and so the courageous disposition must involve both the awareness of danger and the overcoming of fear. But there are problems with this formulation, because it includes too many possibilities. Even if we limit ourselves to the case of courage under fire, we would have to agree that the latter can be inspired by several different motives. In the case of the Homeric heroes, courageous actions are often motivated by the fear of disgrace or a competitive desire to show superior boldness. In Stephen Crane's novel *The Red Badge of Courage*, Henry Fleming is most eager to show courage on the battlefield because this would be a sign, both to himself and to others, that he really is a man. Sometimes a soldier will act out of fury when his comrade has just been killed, and sometimes he will endure danger and hardships and follow difficult orders, because the alternative is to be shot for desertion or disobedience. The point is that all of these can be viewed as examples of courageous action, but there is not a uniform psychological state, or a specific set of reasons for action, that underlies every example of courage. Things become even more complicated once we move away from the field of battle to consider examples of moral courage in everyday life. Is stubborn, unyielding determination for something a form of courage or just obstinacy? We are often told that we should have the courage of our convictions, but as Nietzsche commented, it is also important to have the courage to challenge our convictions and to admit on occasion that we could be wrong. The inherent complexity of courage must be kept in mind throughout this discussion.

In this chapter, I begin with the most influential philosophical account of courage found in Aristotle's *Nicomachean Ethics*. I emphasize the military paradigm that shapes Aristotle's own philosophical ideas and show how, in this way, courage is construed as the ultimate signifier of masculinity. I then discuss Aquinas's reformulation of Aristotle's position. These philosophical discussions provide us with a springboard for further reflection. I then consider some of their shortcomings: Most importantly, I argue that we need to separate the idea of courage as a moral virtue from its role as the ultimate signifier of masculinity, since this is the source of much of our confusion about the nature of courage. In the past and even today, men were supposed to prove their manliness by their valor in battle while the coward was usually loathed for being effeminate or un-manly. But to be authentically masculine in any accepted sense is not the same as being good, and so we need to distinguish the gender role from the virtue. I offer three examples, from Robert Graves, Ralph Waldo Emerson, and Stephen Crane, to show the problems of associating courage with the military ideal. The idea that courage is rooted in military manliness makes it difficult for us to comprehend women's courage; we cannot measure the courage of pacifists and others who refuse to fight, while we are often uncritical of those who fight bravely for an evil cause. So, even if bravery in battle is the original model of courage, and is upheld in different ways by Homer, Aristotle, and Aquinas, it is by no means obvious that our own understanding of courage must ultimately relate to this model. Moral courage may derive from the idea of physical courage, but it is no longer contained or defined by it and we must consider new models or examples of courage that can guide our thinking for the future. In the final part of this chapter, I look at pacifism which seems to be at odds with the military model of courage, although the life of the pacifist actually conforms to the outline of courage described by Aristotle and Aquinas. Pacifism is an appropriate end of virtue, and it surpasses a militarism that reduces courage to manliness and makes other aspects of courage invisible.

Greek and Christian Views of Courage

In *The Iliad*, Achilles is the most magnificent of all the Greek heroes. His goal is to win imperishable glory for himself, but he knows that he will have to pay for his renown with a life that is cut short in its prime. At first, Achilles stays out of the fighting, angry that he has been dishonored by Agamemnon, who has taken his concubine away from him. But after the death of Patroclus, he goes on a bloody rampage that Homer compares to the eruption of a force of nature: "On went Achilles: as a devouring conflagration rages through the valley, of a parched mountain height, and the thick forest blazes, while the wind rolls the flames to all sides in riotous confusion, so he stormed over the field like a fury, driving all before him, and killing until the earth was a river of blood."[5] Achilles is an ambivalent hero. His prowess and personal valor on the field of battle are unassailable. And when he sets out to avenge Patroclus by killing Hector he knows that he is advancing his own death. For it had already been prophesied that, "Quick after Hector fate is ready for you."[6] But he is also self-absorbed, and he has such an extreme sense of honor that he allows his rage at Agamemnon to take priority over the common project of the Greeks in the Trojan War.

Thus it is certainly possible to distinguish Achilles' contribution to the Greek cause from his personal valor as a soldier. David Hume discusses this aspect of courage in his *Inquiry Concerning the Principles of Morals*: Courage is virtuous, because it is a useful quality that contributes toward a final goal that is considered good; but, he adds that courage is also a personal quality that is completely admirable in itself, quite apart from whatever it may or may not achieve. Indeed, "to anyone who duly considers of this matter, it will appear that this quality [courage] has a peculiar luster, which it derives wholly from itself, and from that noble elevation inseparable from it. Its figure, drawn by painters and by poets, displays, in each feature, a sublimity and daring confidence; which catches the eye, engages the affections, and diffuses, by sympathy, a like sublimity of sentiment over every spectator."[7] Hume adds that even though some individuals may be completely steadfast and dazzling in personal bravery, it does not follow that this quality must be beneficial for others: for example, "The excessive bravery and resolute inflexibility of Charles the XIIth [the warrior king of Sweden] ruined his own country, and infested all his neighbours."[8] The point is that examples of courage and individual heroism may be lustrous and inspiring for a variety of different reasons, and in the case of Achilles it is surely because his actions expressed a supreme achievement of powerful self-assertion. But unless this quality is directed toward the good—however this is defined—it may be uncontrolled and self-serving. Achilles cannot be relied upon. His courage is magnificent, but he is self-involved insofar as he views combat as a forum for individual bravery rather than the means to a virtuous end. And even though Socrates and many other Greeks will continue to use him as an emblem of true courage and heroism, there is a sense in which the example of Achilles must be overcome.

All of which brings us to the philosophical perspective of Aristotle, and the discussion of courage that he offers in book two and three of the *Nicomachean Ethics*. Aristotle's ethics can be viewed as a response to the dominance of Homeric virtue in traditional Greek society and in particular, it seems to challenge the view that manliness embodied in the popular example of Achilles really is the highest expression of virtue. Following Socrates and Plato, Aristotle emphasizes the absolute necessity of linking virtue to reflection. We may think that personal qualities like daring, intelligence, and caution are natural endowments over which we have little control. But it is possible to cultivate these qualities and transform them into proper virtues by learning how to use them appropriately—which means, in accordance with the rational part of the soul. In general terms, Aristotle conceives of virtue as a habitual rational and emotional disposition to feel, choose, and act in the right way for the right ends. With regard to courage, this means, "The man who faces and fears (or similarly feels confident about) the right things for the right reason and in the right way and at the right time is courageous (for the courageous man feels and acts duly, and as principle directs)."[9]

In book two of the *Nicomachean Ethics*, Aristotle introduces the example of courage, as his first illustration of the doctrine of the mean, and how it is to be understood: "In the field of Fear and Confidence the mean is Courage; and of those who go to extremes the man who exceeds in fearlessness has no name to describe him (there are many nameless cases), the one who exceeds in confidence is called Rash, and the one who shows an excess of fear and a deficiency of confidence is called cowardly."[10] Much has been written about this definition of courage, which is later summarized in book three as a "mean state, in relation to feelings of fear and confidence."[11] The difficulty here is that Aristotle seems to be saying that courage is a complicated virtue—it is not simply the mean point of a single continuum that ranges between timidity and foolhardiness, but it involves a relationship to two different registers. On the one hand, it seems courage is a mean state between too much fear, or cowardice, and too little fear, or foolhardiness. While on the other hand, it can also be viewed as a mean between not enough confidence, or timidity, and excessive confidence, or rashness. Some commentators are content to read Aristotle as if he were speaking less precisely at this point, since timidity and excessive fear are the same in many contexts. But excessive caution is not the same thing as cowardice, and while they are related to each other, rashness is not the same thing as complete and utter fearlessness. Aristotle condemns the Celts for their fabled lack of fear in situations like a storm at sea or an earthquake, when he thinks that any rational person would have to be afraid. But this extreme form of fearlessness is not the same thing as recklessness or overconfidence, which might involve taking extreme risks for a trivial end: thrill-seeking just for the sake of it or attacking the enemy out of bravado when it's dangerous and it's clear that nothing will be gained. At the same time, it is not reasonable to prepare for every eventuality, and such excessive caution, while it is not exactly cowardice, is also negatively related to the proper nature of courage.

Later in his discussion, Aristotle does comment that while courage is concerned with the sentiments of fear and confidence, it is not concerned equally with both of these, but chiefly with the causes of fear. Confidence involves being cool and composed, though not overconfident, in difficult situations. Presumably, it is compatible with some degree of fear; indeed, to be without fear in dangerous situations would suggest that we were no longer in our right mind. By the same token, however, we might lack confidence and yet not be particularly afraid: like the general who is too cautious to attack but who will never yield when attacked himself. Aristotle's discussion is complicated, but things become a lot clearer when one bears in mind that for him the good soldier is the paradigm example of courage. For it makes sense to say that the good soldier must be confident *and* brave, and only if both qualities are present can he truly be said to have courage, or even be a good soldier.

Up to this point, then, we have considered the general background of Aristotle's discussion of courage and the formal definition of courage as a mean in regard to sentiments of fear and confidence. But as in any ethical account, the true sense of Aristotle's theory of courage only becomes clear once we go on to consider some examples and particularly his own paradigm example of courage, which is that of the soldier fighting in battle. At several points in the text, Aristotle makes the general claim that in learning how to be virtuous we must begin by imitating those who are considered virtuous: "It is therefore right to say that a man becomes just by the performance of the just, and temperate by the performance of temperate, acts; nor is there the smallest likelihood of any man's becoming good by not doing them."[12] Obviously, the same rule applies to how we become courageous, and in order to make sense of his specific comments on the nature of courage we need a concrete example of the courageous person who will act as the embodied expression of our theoretical account and offer a direction for moral cultivation. In Aristotle's ethics that guiding example is the soldier in battle. It is not enough to say that this is his favorite example of courage in action, for as we will see, the use of this particular paradigm is meant to shape all of our thinking about courage. It provides us with the template that influences, ahead of time, exactly what should be considered courageous, the nature of the truly courageous man, and what must be viewed as secondary and derived.

Aristotle argues that we prove our courage in the most decisive way by facing up to death, for of all the things that confront us, death is generally reckoned to be the most fearful of all: "Now the most fearful thing of all is death; for it is the end, and it is assumed that for the dead there is no good or evil any more."[13] Now there are of course, many situations that would make us face up to the immediate or eventual possibility of death and nonbeing, including a storm at sea or the onset of disease. But according to Aristotle, these situations do not testify to the highest achievement of courage, since they are not associated with a noble cause. Bravely facing the onslaught of a disease like AIDS takes courage, but for Aristotle it is less distinguished and certainly less magnificent than the soldier who faces death in battle and who is prepared to sacrifice his own personal existence for the sake of the community he belongs to. "So in the strict sense of the word the courageous man will be one who is fearless in the face of an honorable death, or of some sudden threat of death; and it is in war that such situations chiefly occur."[14] Aristotle implies that we can only grasp what it means to be truly courageous by reflecting on the example of the person who is willing to die for the sake of the good, and the example of the soldier in battle is supposed to epitomize this ideal of courage in different ways. First, the possibility of death is the greatest challenge to individual self-assertion. In everyday life, we strive to be good and to do the right thing in spite of all temptations to the contrary, but death is the absolute limit. So if we can remain true to ourselves and self-possessed in spite of the greatest threat of all, then we have demonstrated the most complete assertion of courage. Likewise, the nobler the cause, the more lustrous and glorious is the courage that is demonstrated on its behalf. This explains why bravery in battle is more obviously courageous than the bravery involved in personal crises, like disease or the prospect of death at sea: "This is true of the courageous man," he writes. "His courage is a noble thing, so its end is of the same kind, because the nature of any given thing is determined by its end. Thus it is for a right and noble motive that the courageous man faces the dangers and performs the actions appropriate to his courage."[15] We can add a third point: the experience of the soldier in battle is also intended as an image of pure activity and spontaneity. In this respect, it is the masculine ideal par excellence, for as Aristotle argues elsewhere, the masculine principle is active and form-creating, while the feminine principle is passive and literally informed. Following this line of thought, the suffering of women in childbirth could never epitomize courage, since it is only passive endurance—and this is secondary to the active principle of self-determination associated with men that achieves its highest expression in military valor.

In the final paragraphs of his discussion, Aristotle explains that the authentic form of courage exists in a very narrow range, and it should never be confused with actions that derive from other passions like anger, shamelessness, or exuberance. As we have seen, it is difficult to say exactly what courage is, but one thing we can do is to get the sense of the inner reality of courage by carefully distinguishing it from every other passion or motive that appears to resemble it. To begin with, there is political courage, which Aristotle says "has the closest resemblance of all to courage as described above." Significantly, in discussing this deficient mode of courage, he refers to Diomedes and Hector and other examples from the Homeric poems. In political courage, the citizens are inspired to act by the desire for honor and glory, and also by the desire to avoid punishment and censure. The motive here is not virtue for its own sake, as in the defense of one's homeland or the community one belongs to, but a selfish longing for individual recognition and honor or even worse, the desire to avoid personal reproach for appearing to be cowardly. Such courage is inferior, we might say, because it derives from a compulsion to do what is expected as opposed to acting this way because it is noble and the right thing to do.

The other spurious forms of courage that Aristotle goes on to consider are experience, passion, optimism, and ignorance. His treatment of passion, or spirit (thumos), is perhaps most significant, since here he returns to the Homeric heroes and denies that someone acting under the influence of passion is necessarily courageous. He comments, "Spirit is also referred to as courage, for those who act with spirit, like beasts charging those who have wounded them, are also considered dangerous, because the courageous too are spirited (for spirit is very bold in the face of danger)." Aristotle admits that the courageous are passionate, and at the end of the discussion he also allows that, "The quasi courage that is due to [passion or] spirit seems to be the most natural, and if it includes deliberate choice and purpose it is considered to be courage."[16] But at the same time, he quotes several passages from the Homeric poems, where the heroes have become wild with grief or anger, and he suggests that in these cases it is not so much courage, but an animal reaction—an emotional response—that inspires them, and this is no different from an animal goaded or terrified into action by pain. In *The Iliad*, Homer uses the metaphor of the lion to describe Achilles on the rampage. In an extraordinary passage he is described, "like some wild lion when a crowd of men have come out to destroy him, a whole village; at first he moves unheeding, but as soon as some bold lad casts a lance and wounds him, he crouches down with open jaws, foam gathers about his teeth, he growls in rage and flogs flanks and ribs with his tail to excite himself, glaring at his foes—then a leap and a furious charge upon the mass, either to kill or to die. So rage and fury stirred Achilles to meet his enemy face to face."[17] Aristotle does not mention this passage explicitly, but it clearly falls under the general principle that he has laid out. Once again, Achilles is rejected as the true exemplar of courage, and he is to be replaced by the citizen soldier who understands that he is fighting for the sake of virtue and what is fitting.

Clearly, Aristotle's discussion at the end of book three is an attempt to get at the elusive psychology of courage. There are so many bold actions that seem to be inspired by courage, or something very like it. But if we want to have a profound understanding of what courage is, it becomes very important to distinguish authentic courage from its deficient modes. Notice, however, how all of his examples relate to the military paradigm as the ideal that can be approximated more or less. In the course of this discussion, Aristotle offers us one instance of true courage that can be weighed against these spurious forms. The example is that of the Coronean citizens who were all killed while defending the temple of Hermes. Their Boeotian auxiliaries were professional soldiers, and presumably better trained, but they all fled in a panic as soon as defeat became obvious. The Coroneans continued fighting though death and defeat were imminent. Like real men, they remained self-possessed even in the face of death, when this had become inevitable. And they died fighting for the sake of virtue, and the defense of a holy shrine, although there was nothing else to be gained. As this example shows, the paradigm of courage involves a confrontation with death that tests one's mettle and whether one is really a man. But Aristotle insists that this is not the only important point about courage. Courageous display is not an end in itself; indeed, it only becomes courageous behavior once it is tied to a virtuous end that is sought for its own sake. Apart from that, he implies, it is a passionate response or a form of self-affirmation that may be astonishing and even sublime, but never virtue in the fullest sense.

Aristotle's philosophical reflections on courage may have a limited bearing on what we think about courage today. But the military model of courage that he describes and endorses still shapes and determines most of our ordinary ideas about the nature of courage. For in this culture, at least, we think of courage primarily in terms of the military example. We often assume without question that moral courage is something secondary and derivative of physical courage as displayed on the field of battle.[18] The very words we use seem to confirm this priority. In any context involving courageous resolve, we talk about standing firm in the face of difficulty, refusing to surrender our principles, and not laying down until we have finally prevailed. The military metaphor that is at work here, and which underlies much of our thinking about courage, makes our moral life into a series of contests and battles, with true virtue grasped as an absolute readiness to fight for whatever is right, and a refusal to compromise one's position. As we will see, this way of thinking about courage is profoundly problematic.

In the *Summa Theologiae*, Thomas Aquinas discusses courage and related virtues like patience, perseverance, magnanimity, and daring in quite considerable detail. Of course, St. Thomas is deeply influenced by Aristotle's discussion, but in the opening discussion of courage itself, Aquinas attempts a revaluation of Aristotle's position by proposing a new paradigm of courage in the Christian context. The function of courage, he argues, is to instill steadfastness of mind in those who are faced with the danger of death. Often, we think of this danger in the context of warfare, but of course there are many situations in which we may undergo the peril of death in the service of virtue—by visiting a sick friend who has a deadly infection, or not shrinking from a journey on some matter of duty because of the fear of shipwreck or bandits. Aquinas argues that in this respect it may be allowed that courage involves a steadfastness of mind in those who are faced with the danger of death, not only in an actual war, "but also in an individual assault which cannot be labeled 'war' in the usual sense."[19] From this redefinition of the meaning of war to cover both military and nonmilitary contexts, Aquinas goes on to argue that martyrdom is the highest example of courage, since it involves sacrifice for the highest good of all, which is to say, God. As he puts it, "The martyrs endure assaults on their persons for the highest good, which is God. Their courage accordingly wins especial praise. Nor is their courage different in kind from that concerned with war; hence martyrs are said to have been made valiant in war."[20] With all deference to Aristotle, Aquinas has apparently changed the paradigm example of courage from that of the soldier to that of the martyr. And in the lengthy discussion of courage that follows, he emphasizes the endurance of pain, perseverance, and patience as the most important aspects of courage, while the active and aggressive aspects of courage are now considered secondary. "For it is more difficult to suppress fear than to control an act of daring; since danger itself, which is the concern both of daring and of fear, provides some check to daring but increases fear. Now attack lies within the sphere of courage in so far as this regulates daring, whereas endurance is the outcome of suppressing fear. So the chief activity of courage is not so much attacking as enduring, or standing one's ground amid dangers."[21]

There are two important points to consider here. First, Aquinas clearly understands the importance of the example in clarifying the basic sense of what courage is. His break with Aristotle is not so much in terms of the formal definition of courage, but in his shift to martyrdom as the paradigm of courageous activity.[22] Aquinas is of course aware that not every Christian will be called upon to suffer physical martyrdom. And given the existence of Christendom, true martyrdom is typically a thing of the past. But he argues, against St. Jerome, Gregory, and others, that physical martyrdom remains the very apogee of courage precisely because it involves holding firm to the Christian faith and bearing witness to it even in the face of the greatest possible trial, which can be nothing other than death itself: "The merit of martyrdom does not come after death," he writes, "but lies in the voluntary endurance of death, in so far as one willingly endures his execution."[23] Shortly, I want to propose some new paradigms and guiding examples for thinking about courage, since by now it should be clear that the paradigm of courage is not just an illustrative example, but the pattern that helps to determine what courage is and to what extent any particular action should or should not be valued as courageous. And if we change the paradigm, as Aquinas attempted to do, then we also change the general understanding of what courage is.

The second point is that even though Aquinas does focus on martyrdom as the most exalted form of courage, he never breaks free of Aristotle's military metaphor; he just expands the meaning of warfare to cover nonmilitary situations and reframes the figure of the martyr as a soldier who is fighting for Christ. As in Aristotle, courage is measured by the ability to stand firm in the face of death. Aquinas is by no means exceptional, however, for accounts of the early Christian martyrs abound in martial language. And while the suffering of martyrdom seems primarily to involve patience and exceptional endurance as a witness for Christ, it is often presented as the ultimate form of self-assertion and personal heroism for the sake of the highest good of all. Thus at the end of the account of the martyrdom of Perpetua and Felicitas, probably written in the second century, the commentator writes: "Ah, most valiant and blessed martyrs! Truly are you called and chosen for the glory of Christ Jesus our Lord! And any man who exalts, honours, and worships his glory should read for the consolation of the church these new deeds of heroism which are no less significant than the tales of old. For these new manifestations of virtue will bear witness to one and the same Spirit who still operates, and to God the Father almighty, to his Son Jesus Christ our Lord, to whom is splendour and immeasurable power for all the ages. Amen."[24] Given that this particular narrative concerns the martyrdom of two women it is interesting to note that their extreme suffering is actually presented as the highest form of heroism and confers a kind of masculinity upon them. This is reflected in the story when Perpetua describes her dream of being prepared for the amphitheater: "My clothes were stripped off, and suddenly I was a man. My seconds began to rub me down with oil (as they are wont to do before a contest)."[25] The military metaphor that shapes our understanding of courage is clearly a very powerful and compelling one, and it will not be easy to think about courage in terms of any other examples and paradigms that may be available to us. In the next section, however, this is what we must try to do.

Rethinking the Masculine Ideal

Aristotle's ethics may be read as an attempt to challenge the traditional morality of ancient Greece, which emphasizes "military manliness" as the most important aspect of virtue.[26] In particular, Aristotle's discussion of courage is a response to the Homeric ideal of Achilles and the other warrior heroes who fought magnificently but didn't always subordinate the love of valor to reason or the greater good of the community itself. In Aristotle's philosophical account, courage is still viewed in terms of an encounter with death and the extremity of self-possession that is required by such a contest. At the same time, such valor is revalued in terms of its relationship to reason and the greater good of the community, while recklessness, passion, and the desire for honor or revenge are explicitly rejected as appropriate motives for the authentic display of courage as a virtue.

In spite of this philosophical transformation, however, it may be argued that the ethical distance between Homer and Aristotle really isn't so great. When Aristotle uses the example of the soldier in battle as the paradigm of what it is to be courageous, he is not just offering an illustration of his general definition. The discussion of courage as a mean between the emotions of fear and confidence remains rather indeterminate until Aristotle makes it concrete with the military examples that he provides. As we have already noted, Aristotle says that in order to become virtuous one must act in the way that a virtuous person would act. From this it follows that virtues are not so much grasped intellectually or philosophically, but through the concrete example of the virtuous type. And if our thoughts were focused on a different example of courage, such as the courage of a woman in childbirth, our basic understanding of courage would be quite different from what it is now. In this respect, Aquinas's account of courage is significant since the guiding example that he uses is the martyr rather than the soldier. Even so, it is still the military standard that he refers to, so Aquinas does not fundamentally change our perspective on courage.

The problem with this is that the virtue involved in military valor is completely entangled with the ideal of masculinity, and it is difficult to separate the one from the other or to know exactly what it is that we admire when we praise the soldier who fights heroically in battle. What, for instance, is the power of Achilles' appeal and the meaning of his heroism? Do we admire him as a champion of virtue, or is it because he is the embodiment of masculine self-assertion? Now it is probable that Achilles appeals to us on both counts, for he does the honorable thing in fighting to avenge the death of his companion Patroclus. At the same time, he shows himself to be a true man by remaining self-possessed and unflinching even in the face of death. But the fact that these two aspects are separable, even if they often go together, suggests that we may also confuse these two aspects and admire some examples of male valor not for their relationship to goodness, but for the image of masculine excellence that they convey. In this way, we may come to admire bravery, even when it's for an evil cause; or we may come to admire military manliness or masculine self-assertion for its own sake, while remaining oblivious to the overall context in which this is expressed. We may also be asked to support our troops and to recognize their bravery. But if we know nothing about the cause for which they are fighting, then it's more likely to be the luster of the masculine ideal that appeals to us and overshadows other ethical considerations.

I will now look at three different examples that should clarify this critical standpoint, and that derive from history, philosophy, and literature, respectively. First, at the outbreak of World War I, thousands of young men signed up to fight for their country. Most of them had absolutely no idea what the war was about, but they were prepared to die for their homeland. Those who hesitated to enlist before the advent of conscription were stigmatized as cowards and handed white feathers by patriotic women, who made it their business to shame all shirkers. Obviously, many men succumbed to this kind of emotional blackmail, but it was probably their anxiety about being real men that motivated them and not the desire to do what they considered right. In his autobiography, *Goodbye to All That*, Robert Graves describes the situation of the allied troops in France: "In the First and Second Battalions, throughout the war, not merely the officers and N.C.O.s knew their regimental history. The men had learned far more about Minden, Albuhera and Waterloo, and the battle of the Pyramids, than they had about the fighting on the other fronts, or the official causes of the war."[27] What was emphasized here was the masculine military ideal for which a venerable tradition had been established over the course of previous battles and campaigns and that was now perpetuated as an end in itself. Graves notes that after their initial enthusiasm had faded, all of his "old hands," men who had been in the regiment since the beginning, came to loathe the war and no longer believed in it. They even looked forward to the prospect of being wounded, so that they might be sent home with an honorable discharge. And while they would continue to fight and follow their officers anywhere, they had no enthusiasm for fighting; they lacked any deep sense of patriotism: "A new arrival who talked patriotism would soon be told to cut it out."[28] They came to admire the courage of their German counterparts, while they were contemptuous of the officers of their own high command, who sacrificed troops while staying out of the fighting themselves. Now given all of this disaffection in the ranks, one has to ask why these soldiers kept fighting even when they no longer believed in the virtue of their cause. And the obvious answer is the sense of personal honor and the masculine identity that was promoted by the camaraderie and the regimental tradition, but which was morally indifferent to the professed aims of the war. Hence the absurdity of the situation: Killing in war is presumably just as serious as any other kind of killing and should never be taken lightly. But here were thousands of men killing each other day after day, when they no longer believed in what they were fighting for but unwilling to stop, not just because of what might happen to them if they refused to fight but because they wanted to show that they were men who would rather face death than lose this sense of group belonging.

In such a situation of course it becomes more difficult to determine where true courage and cowardice lie. Robert Graves writes about his friend, the poet Siegfried Sassoon, one of the bravest men he knew who was decorated several times for heroic actions under fire. Eventually, Sassoon came to believe that the war was wrong. He even wrote a letter of protest, called "Finished with the War, a Soldier's Declaration," that was published in a national newspaper. Graves completely agreed with Sassoon's sentiments, and he also comments that under the circumstances Sassoon's action was "magnificently courageous." But at the same time, he thought the letter was a huge mistake; he became furious with the pacifists who encouraged him to write it, and he hoped that the letter would be put down to nervous collapse. A little later, Sassoon decided that even though he was still a convinced pacifist, he should go back to the front to be with his men, where he says, he trained them with complete military efficiency. All of this is quite puzzling to say the least. Both Graves and Sassoon had come to the conclusion that the war was wrong and a waste of human lives, but at different times they felt a conflicting commitment to remain with their men and do their duty as soldiers: "I reminded him," Graves writes, "that the regiment would either think him a coward, or regard his protest as a lapse from good form."[29]

Would it really be overstating things to suggest that Graves and Sassoon were deflected from the path of virtue (or at least what they thought to be right) by the allure of the military paradigm? I have tried to show how the latter can often become an end in itself because of its deep connection to the masculine ideal. And this can lead to moral blindness and incoherence on the part of people like Graves and Sassoon, who accept the evil of war, while still continuing to fight. It is not because they lacked courage—they were both extremely courageous under enemy fire—but because it was ultimately impossible for them to resist the paradigm of military manliness that constrained their view of virtue.

Almost as disturbing is Emerson's essay, "Heroism" (1841), which shows how the heroic conception of courage can lead one astray. In this essay—which may not be representative of his mature ethics—Emerson complains about the feeble state of contemporary human existence and the absence of what is "manly" and "daring" in character when compared to the heroic ages of the past. Emerson looks to *Plutarch's Lives* as a treasure house of heroic exemplars, and he celebrates Plutarch's accounts of heroism and courage as antidotes to the contemptible concern for comfort, prudence, and peace that appears to characterize modern sensibility: "Each of his 'Lives' is a refutation to the despondency and cowardice of our religious and political theorists. A wild courage, a stoicism not of the schools, but of the blood, shines in every anecdote, and has given that book its immense fame."[30] Thus Emerson, like Nietzsche, and a host of other modern discontents, calls for the reassertion of proper manliness, and he can only envisage this in military terms: "Our culture," he writes, "must not omit the arming of the man. Let him hear in season, that he is born into the state of war, and that the commonwealth and his own well-being require that he should not go dancing in the weeds of peace; but warned, self-collected, and neither defying nor dreading the thunder, let him take both reputation and life in his hand, and with perfect urbanity dare the gibbet and the mob by the absolute truth of his speech and the rectitude of his behavior." He continues, "Towards all this external evil the man within the breast assumes a warlike attitude of the soul we give the name of Heroism. Its rudest form is the contempt for safety and ease, which makes the attractiveness of war. It is a self-trust which slights the restraints of prudence."[31] Now Emerson may not be calling for an actual war as the only forum that would allow young men to prove their manhood, although he certainly comes quite close to this position, but at the very least, he celebrates this military attitude of soul as the proper expression of manhood that should be cultivated in every age. Thus for Emerson, courage is completely allied to the masculine ideal and detached from its relation to moral goodness and virtue. He is explicit about this when he separates courage from prudence and philosophy: "Heroism feels and never reasons, and therefore is always right; and although a different breeding, different religion, and greater intellectual activity, would have modified or even reversed the particular action, yet for the hero, that thing he does is the highest deed, and is not open to the censure of philosophers or divines."[32] Courage is reduced to masculine self-assertion and requires no justification, because it is reckoned as a glorious end in itself. But this, of course, is a very dangerous attitude and morally suspect on a variety of fronts. It is wildly romantic and self-involved, as well as elitist insofar as it seems to be lacking in compassion for ordinary men and women, or "the littleness of common life," which is spurned as wretched and contemptible. More significantly, it actively seeks out crises, which it also provokes in order to test itself. And it is finally unconcerned with matters of justification and right and wrong, while rejecting compromise and reconciliation as forms of personal failure. In this essay, Emerson returns us to the Homeric ideal, which Aristotle sought to humanize and place in the service of virtue or the community as the greater good. Emerson is taken by the military model of courage, and his essay demonstrates once again how our understanding of any other virtue is shaped and conditioned by the kinds of examples that we privilege. The military paradigm of courage emphasizes the necessity of conflict and opposition to compromise; it is sporadic and spontaneous (disdaining reflection), and is bound up with masculine self-assertion as a separate end in itself. It is also disturbing, to say the least, that this paradigm of courage is inconsistent with moral virtue in many contexts.

Finally, even though it is a work of fiction, Stephen Crane's novel, *The Red Badge of Courage* seems to make a similar point about war as the proving ground of masculine identity. *The Red Badge of Courage* has been interpreted both as a celebration of military valor and as an anti-war novel. In either case, it offers a compelling account of the soldier's motivations. Henry Fleming wanted to enlist, but not because he understood the causes of the war or felt any burning desire to do what was right. Instead, we are

told, "Tales of great movements shook the land. They might not be distinctly Homeric, but there seemed to be much glory in them. He had read
of marches, sieges, conflicts, and he had longed to see it all. His busy mind
had drawn for him large pictures extravagant in color, lurid with breathless
deeds."[33] It is significant that there are no discussions of the merits of the
Civil War in The Red Badge of Courage. What is apparently more important
to all the characters that we are given access to is the display of courage as
the sign of genuine masculinity. From the beginning of the story, Henry ag-
onizes over whether he will stand and fight when the battle begins or
whether he will flee. The thing is, he doesn't know how he will act, and
Crane describes his personal anxiety in some detail:

> But here, he was confronted with a thing of moment. It had suddenly appeared
> to him that perhaps in a battle he might run. He was forced to admit that as
> far as war was concerned he knew nothing of himself. . . . He must accumulate
> information of himself, and meanwhile he resolved to remain close upon his
> guard lest those qualities of which he knew nothing should everlastingly dis-
> grace him. "Good Lord!" he repeated in dismay.[34]

In the end, Henry Fleming realizes that he can only prove his manhood by
remaining self-possessed in the face of fighting and death. The Red Badge of
Courage may not be an anti-war novel in the classic sense, but it does emphasize the deep need for masculine self-assertion and the confirmation of
masculine gender identity that warfare is supposed to provide.

Of course Crane's novel is ultimately cynical of this kind of testing. In
his first real encounter with the enemy, Henry runs away. Later, when he
returns to fight with the regiment, he is struck by one of his own men, and
the bloody wound is recognized as the sign of his courage, even though it
was more of an accident than the result of standing firm in the face of enemy fire. Later without really knowing where he is or what he is doing, he
is swept back into the battle, and full of fury, he performs an act of unin-
tentional heroism when he seizes the Confederate flag from its falling
bearer. It seems that he has proved his masculinity once and for all and
Crane writes, "With the conviction came a store of assurance. He felt a
quiet manhood, non-assertive but of sturdy and strong blood. He knew
that he would no more quail before his guides wherever they should point.
He had been to touch the great death, and found that, after all, it was but
the great death. He was a man."[35] But from the reader's perspective, of
course, it is not at all clear that Henry Fleming is "master of his fate." He
is rather the victim of circumstances, and his final achievement of hero-

ism is somewhat accidental. Hence the red badge of courage is at best an equivocal sign of his masculinity. But it bears no connection to his virtue as a human being.

We typically emphasize the physical aspects of courage. The very word for courage directs attention toward our physical being, since it is literally a matter of having heart, or *coeur*. Likewise, courage has also been viewed as the masculine virtue—hence the connection that is frequently made between courage and self-assertion, or the distinction of masculine identity, even in the face of death. There is something popular and appealing about this connection of courage with military manliness. But in the previous pages, I have argued that it also has its limitations and requires us to think about courage in a very one-sided way. It's not that we need to rethink the meaning of courage. As I suggested at the outset, courage is the most obvious virtue and the definitions that Aristotle, Aquinas, and others have developed are at least reasonably helpful. The problem is that the military paradigm tends to make other kinds of courage invisible, and at best derivative, and so we are left with an inadequate understanding of what courage is. Hence to clarify and deepen our understanding of the nature of courage, I now propose three alternative paradigms, which supplement the military model and allow us to grasp its limitations.

First, courage in Homer or Aristotle is depicted as a magnificent form of self-assertion that holds firm, even in the face of death. But this emphasis on spectacular displays of courage makes it harder to appreciate everyday examples of courage—in ordinary or extraordinary situations—which may require an even greater moral effort to sustain. Primo Levi gives an example of this in his memoir of the Holocaust, *Survival in Auschwitz*. Levi describes the heroism of those who actively resisted the Nazis, even in the concentration camps, but he is most impressed by his fellow prisoner Steinlauf, and others like him, who didn't allow the appalling conditions to crush their spirit or destroy their moral well-being. Levi describes how the whole apparatus of the camp seemed specifically designed to obliterate every residue of human decency and personal life, beginning with the assembly line procedures that greeted the new arrivals who were processed, shorn, and tattooed with a number that replaced their name:

> It is not possible to sink lower than this; no human condition is more miserable than this, nor could it conceivably be so. Nothing belongs to us anymore; they have taken away our clothes, our shoes, even our hair; if we speak, they will not listen to us, and if they listen, they will not understand. They will even

take away our name; and if we want to keep it, we will have to find in ourselves the strength to do so, to manage somehow so that behind the name something of us, of us as we were, still remains.[36]

Steinlauf was one of those courageous individuals who sought to maintain their own personal dignity and decency in the face of this dehumanizing power. Now given the filthy conditions that existed, Levi was surprised that Steinlauf would even bother to go through the motions of washing and cleaning himself every day. But Steinlauf understood that this was the only possible response to the system that sought to dehumanize absolutely:

We are slaves, deprived of every right, exposed to every insult, condemned to certain death, but we still retain one power, and we must defend it with all our strength for it is the last—the power to refuse our consent. So we must certainly wash our faces without soap in dirty water and dry ourselves on our jackets. We must polish our shoes, not because the regulation states it, but for dignity and propriety. We must walk erect, without dragging our feet, not in homage to Prussian discipline but to remain alive, not to begin to die.[37]

Notice that in this case, it's not the grandiose gesture that defines Steinlauf's courage, but the smaller acts of personal regard that must be repeated one day after another, unlike the tumult of battle, which is sporadic and often short lived. Likewise, it's not exactly true that Steinlauf's courage involves the overcoming of fear. Presumably fear was a constant in the concentration camp, but the greatest moral danger was despair, which involved giving up on oneself and accepting the process of dehumanization that the Nazis had imposed. Steinlauf's courage must be understood as the refusal to despair even in the worst of all possible situations. It bears some resemblance to the military model of courage, but it is significantly different in its mundaneity, its persistence, and its opposition to despair, as opposed to fear. Someone with a terminal illness, or someone who faced harassment or prejudice on a daily basis but who refused to be beaten in spirit by it might also demonstrate such an everyday model of courage.

Courage is often considered the defining masculine virtue, and Aristotle is representative of many other male thinkers who appear to question the possibility of female courage or consider it secondary: "For a man would be thought a coward if he had no more courage than a courageous woman."[38] Unless we still want to argue chauvinistically that courage is the proper preserve of men, we should now consider the possibility of a different model of courage, or a female courage, which cannot be captured by the existing ideal of manliness. I am not suggesting that men and women display different kinds of courage that are appropriate to their gender; only that by thinking through the very idea of female courage, we may come to understand one of the neglected dimensions of courage itself.

Let us consider this more closely: Aristotle and Homer treat courage as a form of self-assertion, to be maintained even in the face of death itself. In this respect, it is the ultimate expression of independence and self-possession that supposedly defines the masculine ideal. But why do we assume that courage must involve this kind of heroic self-assertion? Or that self-assertion belongs to the highest if not the only kind of courage? Sometimes courage involves the refusal of self-assertion and the willingness to put all of one's projects and goals on hold for the sake of other people. And since this is the kind of self-sacrifice that frequently characterizes the lives of women, I think it is appropriate to call it female courage. One may argue, reasonably enough, that women are often *too* patient and *too* willing to sacrifice themselves for others, so that the very idea of "female courage" is in this sense itself a form of oppression. On the other hand, it is not inappropriate to contrast the masculine account of courage that we have so far considered with an alternative perspective; and *this* kind of courage is characterized by endurance and patience—rather than opposition—and accepting misfortune for the sake of what has to be. It doesn't seek to impose its will, but surrenders its will for the sake of what is good. There is courage in the mother's relationship to her child and in personal daily sacrifice for the sake of another, and in the persistence of that care and love in the face of disappointment and grief. There is also courage in the adult who looks after the sick or dying relative, but who refuses to despair or stop caring. By its very nature, heroism is excessive and demands our attention on the battlefield or the martyr's field of suffering. By contrast, the kind of courage that I have described withdraws from our focus and refuses to celebrate itself. Military manliness displays courage by affirming itself even in the face of death, but female courage goes one step further with the courage that refuses self-affirmation for the sake of someone else.

Finally, when courage is viewed along military lines it becomes very difficult to recognize or even understand the courage of those who oppose militarism and campaign instead for peace. The paradigm example of courage is supposed to be the soldier fighting in war. But if someone rejects war and the habitual recourse to physical violence, it seems to follow that he or she is outside the scope of courage and therefore cowardly. Pacifists, those who oppose war, or those who refuse to fight because they don't believe in the moral necessity of conflict, are routinely condemned as cowardly and selfish—even though it often takes considerable personal bravery to resist the weight of public opinion, the appeal to patriotism and duty, and the moral isolation involved in an unpopular cause.

In fact, moral courage is often more difficult to sustain than physical courage, and it is often what is most needed. As we have noted, Robert Graves displayed incredible courage on the field of battle. But even though he knew the war was wrong, he found it more difficult to speak out against it or to encourage his friend Siegfried Sassoon in campaigning for peace.

The military paradigm of courage also makes it difficult to understand the courage of someone like Gandhi who devoted his whole life to nonviolence and refused to view armed conflict as an acceptable way of achieving the goal of independence for India. Gandhi believed that violence only ever created more violence. At the same time, however, he recognized the limitation of rational discussion, and so he developed his idea of *satyagraha*, or soul force, to penetrate barriers of prejudice and dogmatism and transform the soul of the opponent. He writes:

> Satyagrahis bear no ill will, do not lay down their life in anger, but refuse rather to submit to their "enemy" or oppressor because the satyagrahis have the strength within to suffer. Satyagrahis should, therefore, have a courageous spirit and a forgiving and a compassionate nature. Satyagraha is the way of non-violence. It is therefore justified; indeed it is the right course, at all times and in all places. The power of arms is violence and condemned as such in all religions. Even those who advocate the use of arms put various limits on it. There are no limits on satyagraha, or rather, none except those placed by the satyagrahi's capacity for voluntary suffering.[39]

None of this was intended in the spirit of moral blackmail or personal confrontation. The forms of satyagraha were deliberately nonviolent and included fasting, strikes, civil resistance, and the acceptance of punishment, sometimes violent, as a way of bearing witness to the oppression and violence of the situation through the suffering of the satyagrahi. Gandhi suffered years of imprisonment by the authorities and frequent rejection by his own supporters, but he forged a courageous path for himself and achieved the goal of Indian independence without compromising his commitment to nonviolence. In the end, Gandhi's courage for peace is one of the most relevant and compelling models of courage in modern times. Like many others including Aung Sun Soong Kyi in Burma, Ken Sara-Wiwa in Nigeria, and Martin Luther King in America, he challenged the establishment in the spirit of peace and nonviolence, refusing to accept its moral authority and the oppressive ideas it supported. Gandhi devoted his whole life to peace, but he was not a "soldier for peace," and this way of thinking only confuses the issue. The essential point is that Gandhi eschewed militarism and violence, and his courage for peace must be understood as an authentic display of courage that cannot be captured by the military paradigm.

Reflection on these three possibilities, everyday courage, what I have called "female courage," and the courage for peace forces us to rethink many of our received ideas about the nature of courage. It is not simply that we should change our definition of courage, but the alternative models that we have used to explain it must deepen our understanding of what courage is. To conclude, I want to look more closely at the whole idea of a "courage for peace" by focusing on pacifism as a significant force in the modern world. Pacifism is under a distinct disadvantage because any opposition to militarism suggests a moral distance from the model of courageous action that is embodied by the soldier. I argue that pacifism is not only harmonious with the virtue of courage, but it is actually one of the most profound manifestations of courage that we have. And as such, it forces us to rethink the nature of courage.

From Courage to Pacifism

Pacifism is a broad social movement that includes a variety of different positions, ranging philosophically from absolute pacifism, which eschews every form of violence, to contingent pacifism, which at least admits the possibility of a justified war even if every war up until now has been disastrous for humankind. Similarly, pacifism is inspired, or we might say "overdetermined," by several different perspectives, including religion, feminism, and the desire for political change. Thus some contemporary Christians, including Quakers, would point out that the earliest Christians were pacifists and opposed to violence and every kind of killing including killing in war; Jesus himself commanded his followers to "turn the other cheek," and his last request to his disciples was to "put away the sword" and let the soldiers take him. Some feminists would argue that war is the ultimate expression of male violence, and as such it must be counteracted by feminine qualities of caring and nurturing; and this gives us another strong argument for the social and political advancement of women who have been excluded from positions of power. For, presumably, women would be less willing to resort to armed conflict since they are more disposed to values like connection and caring. Finally, in recent years, the peace movement has not only focused on conflicts between nations, but on all forms of injustice within a given society, which can be regarded as forms of violence. Hence, the boycotts against companies that use sweat-shops, or protests against employers who don't permit workers to join trade unions. All of this makes it difficult to define exactly what pacifism is, and it would not be hard to get bogged down in a debate concerning the meaning of terms. Nevertheless, we can look more closely at some of the most important strands within the pacifist movement that seem to characterize this outlook and distinguish it from other ways of thinking.

Historically speaking, pacifism involves a desire to promote peace rather than war and the abandonment of war as a way of settling disputes between peoples. Beginning with Thomas Aquinas and other medieval thinkers, the just war theorists argued that even though war is an evil, it can still be justified by a good cause: if going to war would actually save more lives than not going to war, for example, or if the war is conducted in self-defense, or for a good cause like spreading the word of God. By contrast, the typical pacifist would argue that war is seldom if ever justified and the individual's participation in war cannot be right since it only contributes to more violence and the implicit endorsement of war as a way of settling disputes. In the rest of this chapter, instead of surveying the whole of pacifism, its history, and the complex variety of positions it includes, I will focus on three significant aspects that distinguish pacifism as a broad social movement in the world today. I do not argue for the moral rightness or wrongness of any particular conflicts, although I believe that most wars in history have not been justified since they have typically been fought for very limited or selfish reasons.

First, the pacifist insists on the absolute value of human life and remains focused on the moral intuition that killing another person is wrong. The pacifist argues that war is an absolute evil, because the scale of killing and suffering involved in any war is usually so massive as to be practically beyond belief. Such killing involves soldiers on both sides, as well as the innocent civilian population. Likewise, the pacifist argues that killing in war is really no different from other kinds of killing and so it should elicit the same outrage that violence and murder produce within our community. All killing is wrong because every life is unique and valuable. The problem is, we tend to think of killing in war as somehow less serious than other kinds of killing. Indeed, the state sanctions this mass death, and it appears to take personal responsibility away from individual soldiers. But as pacifists have always pointed out, when we participate in a war, we don't lose any of our moral responsibilities. It is up to individuals to resist the military ambitions of their governments, for in this way, they create a tradition in which it becomes much more difficult for governments to contemplate war as a feasible option. It sometimes seems that war is one of the first resorts of governments intent on settling disputes. But a tradition of pacifist resistance makes it much less likely that war will be used as a means to an end.

The pacifist realizes, while others tend to forget, that the scale of killing in war makes it a very great moral evil, which is seldom if ever justified by the cause that one is fighting for. And it is a fact that war brutalizes people. The enemy dead become so many casualties, or a body count, and yet, they are basically the same as you and me, people engaged in living their own lives, planning their futures, and hoping for happiness and well-being—and their deaths should be viewed as an irreparable loss. In the context of war it is possible to create a moral distance that allows us to commit all kinds of terrible atrocities by ignoring the humanity of those we are fighting against. This can be achieved by physical distance, such as dropping bombs on an enemy without experiencing the devastation that this produces, or psychological distance, in which the enemy population is regarded as inhuman or morally worthless. One central goal of pacifism is to abolish this distance, to emphasize the absolute wrongness of all killing and especially killing in war, which is always on a massive scale. Finally, it can hardly be denied that the justifications offered in support of war are often paltry and self-serving; if we surveyed all the wars in history, we would probably have to conclude that most were fought for very feeble or selfish reasons.

The second point is the pacifist's recognition that violence can never be a means to peace, because typically violence only leads to more violence, and it's difficult to break this cycle of hatred and suffering once it has begun. For example, World War I was not a war to end all wars, as many people hoped and believed, since it created mutual hatred, leading to the German humiliation at Versailles, the rise of Hitler, and ultimately World War II, which was even more destructive than World War I had been. This is also the case even when the cause seems eminently justified. The Russian Revolution and the Chinese Revolution, for example, were enacted in the name of downtrodden people who suffered miserable conditions of poverty under their feudal lords. But the revolutionaries never abandoned their violence, and succeeding communist regimes of Lenin, Stalin, Mao, and others were notorious for their executions and the imprisonment or "re-education" of millions of so-called dissidents who were perceived as threats to the regime. Terrorism in Ireland, Palestine, and elsewhere may also be completely understandable as a response to unbearable and unjustified state violence, but the lesson of history shows that in the end all such violence is self-defeating because it only leads to more violence and a tradition in which violence is the accepted way of settling all disputes. Jonathan Glover uses the "cruel punishments" analogy to make this point: You can argue that any particular crime may be so heinous that the perpetrator deserves to be publicly hanged, drawn, and quartered, just as any war could be justified if the situation were bad enough. By resorting to such punishments—or war—we contribute to a tradition in which these are the accepted forms of response; and we may end with a nuclear holocaust in which we would somehow be justified in destroying everything that exists. Thus we should do everything in our power to create an alternative tradition in which war gradually becomes unthinkable, like the cruel punishments of old, rather than an easy option that is continually threatened and sometimes used as a first resort: "Every time we go to war, even in such a relatively clear-cut case as to defeat Hitler, we make a contribution to a tradition in which war is legitimate. But every time we refuse to continue politics by the 'other means' of war, we contribute to the establishment of the alternative tradition which may be the most important thing in the world."[40] Resistance to war helps to create this tradition, and so in the end humanity benefits from anti-war protests, which make governments more hesitant to declare war in the future.

The third point is this: Pacifism involves an attempt to change the world by promoting the conditions of peace, but this will never be achieved unless the individual is able to transform her own attitudes and her own life in a way that reflects this ultimate value. In earlier years, pacifists worked for peace in the world by appealing to the dictates of religion, or by supporting the efforts of bodies like the League of Nations and the United Nations to resolve international conflicts peacefully. But there is now much stronger awareness that pacifism, as a spiritual movement, also requires a profound transformation in the life of each individual who is concerned about the future of humankind. There is an analogy between the inner and outer expressions of hostility and the one is profoundly related to the other. This also involves the recognition that war is not just about armed hostilities between nations, since an underlying relationship of violence exists whenever any individual or group oppresses another and denies its fundamental rights or its possibilities of well-being. Once again, Gandhi is an obvious point of reference: In India under the British Raj, mistreatment and exploitation of the civilian population was common and culminated with the Amritsar massacre of 1919, in which over 400 peaceful protesters were gunned down by British troops. This was the event that radicalized Gandhi and made him realize the inherent violence of all colonialism. But at the same time, Gandhi saw the pointlessness of using violence to end violence, and so he led a campaign of nonviolent resistance against British rule. This included fasting and vows of silence, boycotts of British-made goods, and peaceful demonstrations that were conducted even when they were forbidden and continued peacefully even when they were met with a violent response. Through this exercise of satyagraha, people were able to bear witness to the inherent violence of the situation by accepting suffering, but without contributing to the cycle of violence by attacking other people. As Gandhi himself discovered, however, and as he admits in his autobiography, this is often incredibly difficult since one's first response is typically one of hatred and hostility even if this doesn't always issue in violent action. It takes a great spiritual effort and a sustained mindfulness, cultivated over a long period of time, to overcome such violent feelings to create in oneself the transformation that one wishes to see in the world: "Nonviolence is the greatest and most active force in the world," Gandhi wrote. "One person who can express nonviolence in life exercises a force superior to all the forces of brutality. My optimism rests on my belief in the infinite possibilities of the individual to develop nonviolence. The more you develop it in your own being, the more infectious it becomes till it overwhelms your surroundings and by and by might oversweep the world."[41] In contemporary society, protesters against war and nuclear proliferation, environmental activists and consumer advocates all use the principles of nonviolent direct action: The point is to reject the violent response, and the spiral of violence that is thereby created, but also to acknowledge the violence and the injustice of the situation, by boycotting companies that use sweatshops and other unfair labor practices, demonstrating in the streets, and suffering the pain that is involved in bearing witness to injustice, through arrest or even worse. In this way, pacifism has affirmed itself as a creative political praxis, and a kind of spiritual politics, that bypasses the traditional impasse of conflict between individual protest and the violence of the state.

The earlier discussion of courage in Aristotle, Aquinas, and other traditional texts noted three significant features that seemed to frame the understanding of what courage is, quite apart from any formal definition. First, courage is directed toward the highest good, whether this is reckoned to be the community, or God, or some other ultimate goal; and this means that the equivalent daring for selfish or ridiculous ends is not really virtuous at all. Second, courage involves self-affirmation even in the face of death. Of course one can be courageous in less challenging situations, but the confrontation with death is the ultimate test of courage since it takes self-possession and endurance to its absolute limit. Third, the paradigm example of courage is typically associated with the martial bravery of the soldier or the martyr as the soldier of Christ. In conclusion, I want to suggest another model of courage, closely related to this one, which suggests the priority of pacifism over militarism as the fulfillment of this virtue. I will clarify this alternative model by considering pacifism in relation to each of the above three points.

First, peace and justice are the explicit goals of pacifism, and many would say they are the highest goals of all. Indeed, peace and justice are much broader goals than the particular goals of the community that underlie Aristotle's own account of courage as a virtue. Putting one's whole life on the line for the sake of justice and peace is surely a valid end of courageous activity. And while peace is not a specifically religious ideal, it is certainly consistent with religion, and should appeal to those of all faiths or no faith at all.

Second, to be willing to die for one's beliefs suggests an extreme in courageous devotion and virtue that cannot be surpassed, since it seems to confirm that there is something that I value even more highly than my own selfish life. Without diminishing anything about the courage that faces up to death, however, I think there is a lot to be said for the courage that is oriented toward life. This would be courage in refusing to despair or lose hope, the courage of individuals like Gandhi, the Dalai Lama, or Martin Luther King, who continue with their efforts for justice and reform when others might be totally discouraged or prepared to accept things as they are. Once again, this is the kind of courage that involves standing firm, but not in regard to death, which leads to the heroic pose, but against the background of life and the future possibility of success. Now certainly, we could say that Gandhi was courageous because of the punishments he was prepared to endure and the death that he risked on a daily basis and that ultimately came in the form of an assassin's bullet. But even more courageously, in spite of every setback and every temptation to despair or abandon his path, Gandhi did all he could for the sake of peace and justice, and his whole life was a continual affirmation of these values. Thomas Aquinas emphasizes endurance rather than confidence as the most important aspect of courage. But it is still endurance in the face of death as undergone by the martyr. What I am suggesting here is that the courage that endures over the course of a whole lifetime is actually more profound and exemplary. There are many individuals who have lived such lives, including Gandhi, Martin Luther King, and Frederick Douglass, who fought against slavery, the unequal treatment of women, and oppression wherever he found it. Although some of these people were killed, and all were ready to die for their beliefs, the final measure of their courage actually lies in their enduring affirmation of life against the evil of violence and injustice.

Finally, the soldier is often presented as the paradigm example of courageous activity. But the soldier is also the absolute expression of masculine achievement, and there is an ongoing confusion between these two aspects:

courage as a sign of manhood and courage as a virtue. We are often deeply impressed by the magnificence of military valor, but it isn't always clear which of these two aspects is the most alluring to us. The military model is suspect because it makes courage a matter of self-assertion and it tends to promote an oppositional attitude toward life and all its difficulties. It leads us to think that a courageous person is someone who "sticks to his guns" and refuses to compromise. And it sometimes seems that all negotiation and willingness to discuss or to admit that one could be wrong are tainted by the military paradigm as so many forms of moral weakness. Probably because of the military model, we tend to associate courage with self-possession to the very end, and it becomes difficult even to imagine that the courage to change, the courage to abandon one's own path for others, or the courage to endure sufferings patiently and without rancor or defiance, may actually be important aspects of courage. The military paradigm of courage also suggests the superiority of physical courage over moral courage, since the latter must be derived from the first. By contrast, the pacifist model of courage does not involve self-assertion, or self-sacrifice for the sake of something greater, but a quiet self-overcoming for the sake of what is good. Indeed, it focuses upon the other—the weak, the oppressed, future generations, and so forth—who are regarded as more important than the subject's own life. Hence the ongoing devotion of some individuals to the cause of peace and justice even beyond the explicit context of war; but such people are courageous in quite different ways than soldiers who are mainly concerned with the immediate physical threat.

In summary, the explicit goal of pacifism is the survival and well-being of humanity, and it involves the recognition that this is under threat. The standpoint of pacifism supports a sustained affirmation of life in spite of whatever obstacles and causes for despair and resignation may exist. The pacifist works tirelessly for the promotion of peace and justice, and tries to shape her own life in accordance with the principle she espouses. In this respect, pacifism is an expression of courage, and the animus against pacifism as a cowardly option is shown to be wrong. At the same time, pacifism helps to clarify and deepen our understanding of courage, and it leads to the disengagement of militarism as the most appropriate example of what courage is.

CHAPTER TWO

~

Temperance

Different cultures have different virtues or at least prioritize the forms of human excellence in different ways, and even within the same society the nature of virtues and vices may change periodically, from one age to the next. There are some virtues like courage or justice that seem to be universal. On the other hand, there are some virtues that become more, or less, important as time goes by. Temperance is one of these. Plato, like other Greeks, considered it one of the four cardinal virtues, but in modern times its standing has diminished. This should prompt us to examine temperance from a historical and a philosophical perspective; for we cannot grasp the significance of any particular virtue unless we understand its historical filiation as well as its ethical point.

Like temperance, chastity was also considered a great virtue in classical antiquity. In the sense of sexual purity it was one of the defining virtues for women, as opposed to courage, which was the definitive virtue for men. With the advent of Christianity, chastity and a commitment to virginity became a sign of the most complete devotion to religious life. In a famous passage, which is often misquoted, St. Paul comments, "To the unmarried and widows I say that it is well for them to remain single as I do. But if they cannot exercise self-control, they should marry. For it is better to marry, than to be aflame with passion."[1] This passage implies that sexual continence within marriage is an acceptable option, but that celibacy, for men and women, is a much greater virtue since it represents a sacrifice of worldly desire and complete devotion to the will of God. But chastity is not so highly regarded in contemporary Western society, and for the most part virginity seems to be viewed as a lifestyle choice that should be respected but not a virtue that everyone is bound to affirm. A similar point can be made about humility, which, as Nietzsche says, the Romans scorned and the Christians exalted. Humility has strong undertones of self-abnegation, and it may be inspired by a fear of anything exceptional. And so today we are ambivalent about humility, and while there are some contexts in which we may think of it as a virtue, there are situations in which it is definitely a vice.

Nietzsche writes about the revaluation of values that occurred when the achievements of the ancient world were reconstrued by the early Christians in terms of sinfulness and pride. "The whole labor of the ancient world in vain," he complains. "I have no word to express my feelings about something so tremendous. And considering that its labor was a preliminary labor that only the foundations for the labors of thousands of years had been laid with granite self-confidence—the whole meaning of the ancient world in vain! Wherefore Greeks? Wherefore Romans?"[2] Nietzsche argues that Christianity made us despise our physical nature, leading to self-hatred and the mortification of the will through guilt. At the same time, he argues that Christianity revalued the secondary qualities of passivity—including humility, obedience, and turning the other cheek—as the primary forms of goodness, making virtue a matter of passivity and negative self-denial. Presumably, the Christian would respond that many of the values and practices of the ancient world, including its apparent joy in cruelty and contempt for the unfortunate, were seriously flawed, and hence the triumph of Christian ideals implies the exhaustion of the previous worldview that was alien to human flourishing. In a self-consciously religious society, self-denial, obedience, temperance, and humility are more highly valued as individual virtues; but in contemporary Western society, these virtues are not so highly esteemed because they seem to conflict with popular values such as personal fulfillment and the enjoyment of life. All of this shows the real difficulty of tracing the progress of any particular virtue, even if we remain within the same cultural horizons. And it is even more difficult to follow a particular virtue—like temperance—from one culture to another, as if it were a separate, self-contained form of goodness that remains the same regardless of context.[3]

With these warnings in place, we can now focus more closely on the virtue of temperance, as moderation and self-control. Temperance involves elements of humility, and it also concerns the proper relationship to our physical or "animal" nature, which St. Paul, St. Augustine, and other Christian thinkers were most concerned about. Temperance is derived from the Greek ideal of *sophrosyne*, which means having a sound mind, or "mental health," but it can also be understood as calmness of soul, self-control, or the awareness of human limitation and the refusal of overreaching pride. Cicero was apparently the first to translate sophrosyne into temperantia when he opposed the latter virtue to all the forms of self-indulgence and excess that he railed against in his moral writings.[4] And hence, while the translation isn't perfect, especially since temperance often implies a negative attitude toward personal enjoyment, there is both a conceptual and a historical warrant for using sophrosyne and temperance as if they were more or less equivalent to each other. At the very least, we would have to say that the two ideals are closely linked because they illuminate a common area of moral concern, and they respond to the same basic questions concerning what it means to live according to (our) nature.

In her important study, Helen North points out how many of the Greek tragedies are really focused on the ideal of sophrosyne.[5] But this is also an essential theme in Greek philosophy. Socrates is portrayed as the very image and epitome of temperance; while in the *Republic*, the tyrant is presented as an immoderate man completely lacking in self-control. He cannot rule himself, and so he is the worst possible person to rule over others. Aristotle's discussion of temperance is framed within the context of our animal desires and pleasures, and he shows how the achievement of temperance is also the achievement of a proper relationship to our physical nature. Aristotle argues that whoever has to struggle against their impulses is not in possession of true temperance. The soul at war with itself may achieve continence through strict self-discipline and control; but this is not the same thing as temperance, which involves the harmonious attunement of the self.

Finally, the virtue of temperance was appropriated by Christianity. As Foucault has shown, temperance under Christianity is identified with purity, and the importance of virginity or chastity even within marriage is among its obvious aspects. Many of the early Christians thought that they could root out the promptings of sexual desire and overcome ordinary human nature to become the perfect servants of God. For St. Augustine, like many of the Church Fathers, sexual desire resisted our conscious control, and so it was the sign of our inherent rebelliousness against God. In this way, temperance becomes more closely associated with self-denial. In recent times, the growth of temperance movements against alcohol and other forms of intoxication seems to continue this very particular view that temperance involves the refusal of everything associated with self-indulgence. Today, temperance is practically equivalent to moderation. It is opposed to all the exuberance of life, and it emphasizes the importance of self-restraint.

We want to be small, Nietzsche might say; we are afraid of anything exceptional or extreme, and so we praise temperance because we are mediocre and comfortable only with the virtues of mediocrity.

But what does all of this signify? Are we to say that the contemporary decline and fall of temperance as a virtue is just the unraveling of its own internal contradictions and a sign of its irrelevance? That temperance, along with chastity and humility, is an outmoded ideal? Or do we need to rehabilitate temperance as a virtue, because we have lost a sense of its original importance, and it is precisely this that we need now? In this chapter I want to argue for the latter position, for I think that the ancient estimation of temperance, as one of the most significant virtues, is the expression of a profound moral understanding. And I want to reclaim a meaningful version of temperance that articulates a space of moral goodness that is associated with our relationship to nature. We have seen how Nietzsche criticizes the way in which virtues like temperance have been appropriated and made small. This criticism derives from the standpoint that the virtues should be an expression of strength. In what follows, however, I will show how temperance can involve the achievement of personal sovereignty and the attunement of the self with the world, which entails individual strength and well-being.

I begin with the genealogy of sophrosyne, or the origins of temperance from Plato and Aristotle to Christianity and beyond. This sequence suggests the philosophical decline of temperance, which reflects the popular decline of temperance as a virtue in the modern Western world. Next, Taoism provides us with a different perspective, and we can examine the *Tao te Ching* insofar as it suggests another version of temperance. Of course, Taoism represents a very different cultural standpoint that originated in China well over 2000 years ago; but the parallels between Taoism and other accounts of temperance are significant, and they show how cross-cultural perspectives can illuminate the virtues even when they derive from very different contexts. Indeed, this suggests the need for a revaluation of temperance in terms of our attunement with nature that emphasizes self-cultivation, a sense of proper measure, and the awareness of limits. It also leads to a discussion of environmentalism as the fulfillment of temperance on a global scale. Now it is true that the current state of pollution, species-endangerment, and overdevelopment in the world may require massive forms of intervention, and only a general environmental policy can be deduced from the outline of a virtue. But we can still return to temperance as the underlying concern for nature that promotes a sense of belonging to the world and a sense of the interrelationship of everything that exists. And whether we think of ecology as a form of extended self-interest or virtuous self-denial, temperance can guide our actions, judgments, and feelings about the natural world.

Greeks and Christians: On Temperance

Sophrosyne, or temperance, is a major theme in many of the Greek tragedies, for even a cursory reading of these plays makes it clear that for the Greeks there was a natural order to things, and human beings must learn to accept their place within the cosmos: such is the virtue of sophrosyne. But ignoring human limitations or meddling in divine matters are expressions of hubris that are bound to end in disaster. In Aeschylus's play *The Persians*, Xerxes shows hubris and a lack of sophrosyne in his overweening ambition to conquer all of Greece, destroying Greek temples and attempting, as the chorus puts it, to master the gods. Because of this, Xerxes must be humbled, and his force is utterly destroyed at the Battle of Plataea, which is "payment for his pride and godless arrogance."[6] Likewise in Euripides' play *The Bacchae*, Pentheus is the strict proponent of rational self-control; he is outraged by the new Dionysian cult and the challenge to the social order that it seems to entail, with women abandoning their place in the household to worship a strange new god in the mountains. From one perspective, Pentheus seems to be the perfect model of temperance as rational self-constraint; and yet as Euripides shows, authentic temperance goes much deeper than this. Pentheus is unbalanced because he refuses to acknowledge the divinity of nature. By moving against Dionysus the god and his followers, he shows a complete lack of temperance and a willful self-assertion that leads to his own humiliation and death.

The same preoccupation with temperance is also a major theme in Greek philosophy. In several dialogues, Plato portrays Socrates as the model of temperance that we should all strive to emulate. The *Symposium*, for example, is about love, and in it Aristophanes articulates the popular view that love involves an absolute yearning for the beloved up to the point of self-abandonment: "and everybody would regard it as the precise expression of the desire which he had long felt but had been unable to formulate, that he should melt into his beloved, and that henceforth they should be one being instead of two."[7] When Socrates speaks about love, he describes a force that is first revealed through the physical attractiveness of a particular individual who wrenches us out of our self-containment. But then he describes a progress in the different forms of love that finally culminates in the love of the Good and the total self-containment and self-sufficiency of the philosopher who seems to need nothing and no one beyond himself: "And having brought forth and nurtured true goodness he will have the privilege of being beloved of God, and becoming, if ever a man can, immortal himself."[8] At this point, Alcibiades enters with some other drunken revelers and makes it clear that Socrates himself is the epitome of the self-contained philosopher that has just been described. Alcibiades disdains philosophical argument, and he doesn't speak in general praise of love, but in the space of a few pages he offers us a compelling portrait of Socrates as someone who exemplifies the virtue of temperance.

What fascinates Alcibiades is the allure of self-possession that Socrates projects: Socrates has complete control over all his desires, and he seems to be in touch with a higher wisdom that others around him can sense and are also attracted to. It's not that he has eradicated all of his desires and lives at a minimal level of intensity. Indeed, Alcibiades compares Socrates to the figure of Silenus sold in statuary shops—he looks like the satyr but when you look inside his soul you glimpse something divine: "But this is exactly the point in which he resembles Silenus; he wears these characteristics superficially, like the carved figure, but once you see beneath the surface you will discover a degree of self-control of which you can hardly form a notion."[9] Alcibiades describes all of his attempts to get Socrates to sleep with him. He thinks that somehow he will gain access to Socrates' secret wisdom through a physical relationship with him. But Socrates rebuffs him, not because he is cold and without desire, but because he doesn't need Alcibiades to be complete. The point is that Socrates has achieved sophrosyne, and so he is able to keep all of his desires and appetites in their proper place. As Alcibiades comments, "On the one hand I realized that I had been slighted, but on the other I felt a reverence for Socrates' character, his self-control and courage; I had met a man whose like for wisdom and fortitude I could never have expected to encounter."[10]

Further evidence is given of Socrates' ability to endure hardship without complaint and his indifference to physical conditions. In the military campaign, he endured the icy cold, lack of sleep, and lack of food better than anyone else; though when supplies were abundant, "no one enjoyed them more; at drinking especially, though he drank only when he was forced to do so, he was invincible, and yet, what is most remarkable of all, no human being has ever seen Socrates drunk."[11] Once again, the point is not that he was indifferent to his physical well-being, but his temperance involved the achievement of personal sovereignty and the harmonious arrangement of all the different aspects of his life. At the end of the *Symposium*, we are left with the image of Socrates still awake and alert, long after everyone else has succumbed to alcohol and fatigue. "Then Socrates, having put both his inter-locutors to sleep, got up and went away. . . . He went to the Lyceum and washed, and spent the day as he would any other, and finally towards evening went home to bed."[12] What is so striking about this description is the effort-lessness of Socrates' behavior. He is not a heroic soul who struggles against temptation to achieve virtue by self-mastery; and even though temperance may require self-restraint and resistance to temptation, he is by now so well-ordered that whatever unruly impulses he has are immediately set aside.

In contrast to this portrait of Socrates, Plato also gives us the figure of the tyrant as the unhappiest man who is totally subject to his own desires. Earlier in the *Republic*, the tyrant is praised as the most fortunate of men who is able to gratify whatever desires he has whenever they occur to him. But in book nine, Socrates argues that such a life is ultimately wretched. Since there is no need to practice self-restraint, the tyrant is not prone to possess temperance, and he loses whatever self-control he might have had once he comes into office. Numerous examples come to mind in support of Plato's analysis: Stalin had most of his revolutionary comrades purged be-cause he couldn't trust them, and he was especially fearful of any colleagues who approached him in popularity. Hitler, Mao, and Pol Pot thought they could only maintain their rule through the continual threat of violence that would keep people obedient through fear. But in these circumstances all genuine friendship becomes impossible, and the ruler is himself a pris-oner of his own oppressive regime. As Plato puts it: "Isn't the tyrant bound in such a prison, he who has a nature such as we described, full of many fears and loves of all kinds? And he, whose soul is so gourmand, alone of the men in the city can't go anywhere abroad or see all the things the other free men desire to see: but stuck in his house for the most part, he lives like a woman, envying any of the other citizens who travel abroad and see any-thing good."[13] In sum, the tyrant is the least self-sufficient man, and he is full of anxiety.

The tyrant has no self-control, he is subject to whatever passion arises within his soul, and in this respect he is the opposite of the strong masculine personality who is self-controlled and therefore capable of ruling over others. For the Greeks, temperance does not involve weak desires, and it is actually the sign of ethical virility. As Foucault puts it: "In the full meaning of the word, moderation was a man's virtue."[14] Self-mastery was "a way of being a man with respect to oneself; that is, a way of commanding what needed com-manding, of coercing what was not capable of self-direction, of imposing prin-ciples of reason on what was wanting in reason; in short it was a way of being active in relation to what was by nature passive and ought to remain so. In this ethics of men made for men, the development of the self as an ethical subject consisted in setting up a structure of virility that related oneself to oneself."[15] Hence in the *Republic* the choice is finally between the immoderate and effeminate life of the tyrant, which is so seductive and alluring, and the life of temperance, which is embodied by the philosopher and more particularly in the person of Socrates himself. The philosopher king achieves this self-moderation, and so he is the most appropriate individual to rule the state.

We can briefly consider the explicit theoretical discussions of temperance in Plato's philosophy. The most important passages are the discussion of temperance as one of the four cardinal virtues in book four of the *Republic*, and Socrates' reflection on temperance in the *Gorgias*. In the *Republic*, Socrates argues that true temperance involves the rule of the better part, the rational part, over the spirited and competitive aspects of the soul that should be obedient. And the well-ordered and harmonious soul that Socrates describes is mirrored in the *Republic* by the unanimity of the rulers and the ruled as to who should rule: "So we would quite rightly claim that this unanimity is moderation, an accord of worse and better, according to nature, as to which must rule in the city and in each one."[16] In this discussion, temperance is defined by the two aspects of self-restraint and self-knowledge: not only should the better part control the worse in the individual as well as in the city, but this is something that should be understood by all the different parties involved. Socrates has been at pains to point out that in the "ideal city," the best rule because the others recognize their right to rule. It is a harmonious regime in this respect, which parallels the harmonious soul that is cultivated in the education of the guardians. Temperance involves the proper harmony, balance, and order of the soul. It is completely opposed to the tyrannical soul that allows desire to take over, but it is also opposed to the view of the passions as "mad masters" that must be ignored or even destroyed. But the cultivation of this internal harmony is not an easy business, and once temperance has been achieved, it must be carefully maintained through the proper exercise of the soul lest we are corrupted by desire or the love of power or money.

Temperance involves self-discipline and a harmonious adjustment to the good society but also to the cosmos itself. Plato makes this point clearest in the *Gorgias*, at a point in the dialogue when Callicles is still present but refuses to discuss anything further, and Socrates has to assert these conclusions as if they were revealed truth:

> Then the goodness of anything is due to order and arrangement? I should agree. It is then the presence in each thing of the order appropriate to it that

makes everything good? So it appears to me. The soul then that has its own appropriate order is better than that which has none? Necessarily. But further, the soul possessed of order is orderly? Of course. And the orderly is the temperate? Most necessarily. Then the temperate soul is the good.[17]

Socrates goes on to assert that the idea of temperance is an essential aspect of the universe itself, and so the one who possesses a harmonious or temperate soul is in accordance with the basic order of the cosmos and most available to himself, his city, and others:

> Wise men, Callicles, say that the heavens and the earth, gods and men, are bound together by fellowship and friendship, and order and temperance and justice, and for this reason they call the sum of things the "ordered" universe, my friend, not the world of disorder or riot. But it seems to me that you pay no attention to these things in spite of your wisdom, but you are unaware that geometric equality is of great importance among gods and men alike, and you think we should practice overreaching others, for you neglect geometry.[18]

Callicles had argued for the life of the tyrant as the best life of all and he rejected justice and temperance as a fraud perpetrated by the weak. Socrates' argument brings out the limitation of this perspective and again the total isolation and misery of those who are completely self-involved. In the end, we are impressed by temperance as the virtue that connects the inner being with outer reality and allows us to live harmoniously within the world.

In Aristotle, the discussion of temperance is organized through the idea of the mean. Temperance is a virtue that concerns our relationship to bodily pleasures: if we are prone to indulge ourselves by feasting, drinking, or sexual excess then we miss the mark of virtue and may be considered self-indulgent. But if we are totally insensible to physical pleasures and make it our practice to avoid every kind of physical enjoyment, we also miss the mark of virtue by refusing to honor the physical side of our nature. Hence temperance is the calm state of soul that lies between self-indulgence and total self-denial. But not only is the virtue of temperance organized in terms of the mean, the mean as the organizing principle of virtue is itself an expression of the principle of temperance. Thus Aristotle views temperance both as a specific virtue like self-control and as the harmonious condition of soul that involves a fundamental attunement with ourselves and the world; and this is the precondition for all virtue.

According to Aristotle, the specific virtue of temperance is concerned with pleasures and to a lesser extent with pains. But what kind of pleasures? Not the pleasures of the soul, like philosophy or mathematics—although even here it is possible to be excessive and live an unbalanced life. Aristotle relates temperance to physical pleasure, and he even specifies that it is concerned more narrowly with the pleasures of touch and taste. This is an interesting decision on his part for it means that he specifies temperance in terms of the relationship to our animal nature: "Thus temperance and licentiousness are concerned with such pleasures as are shared by animals too (which makes them regarded as low and brutish)."[19] Clearly what we share with animals is the desire for food and drink and sex. As human beings though we should be aware that some of our desires and pleasures are inappropriate or excessive: "Some of those who are called 'lovers' of this or that go wrong in enjoying the wrong objects, others in enjoying things with abnormal intensity, or in the wrong way; and the licentious display excess in every form. They enjoy some things that it is wrong to enjoy, because they are odious; and where it is right to enjoy something, they enjoy it more than is right, or more than is normal."[20] At the end of book three, Aristotle compares the intemperate person to a child who is still fixated on whatever it desires or gives it pleasure. Aristotle might say that such a person has not grown up or become morally mature, since he still allows his desire for pleasure to drive out reason. For Aristotle, temperance is a distinctive human achievement, and his discussion of temperance is focused on our animal nature and the anxiety that we should relate properly to this aspect of ourselves.

Aristotle advances the discussion of temperance in book seven of the *Nicomachean Ethics* when he considers the distinction between continence, incontinence, and temperance. The incontinent person (akrasis) is someone who knows what is right but who lacks the strength of will to do what is right or is swayed by the possibility of more immediate gratification. Aristotle says that Socrates denied the very possibility of such akratic actions: Since Socrates believed that one cannot resist the power of the good, evildoing was only possible because of ignorance and a faulty understanding of what the good was like. Aristotle then spends a considerable part of book seven trying to unravel the riddle of akratic actions, and to show how weakness of the will is possible. But he forgets the example of Alcibiades in Plato's *Symposium*. As we have noted, Alcibiades is in awe of Socrates and when he is with Socrates, he admits he is ashamed of himself. In his pursuit of fame and political success, Alcibiades has ignored the most important needs of his soul, but when he is around Socrates he knows that he is not living his life in the right way:

> He is the only person in whose presence I experience a sensation of which I
> might be thought incapable, a sensation of shame; he and he alone positively

makes me ashamed of myself. The reason is that I am conscious that there is no arguing against the conclusion that one should do as he bids, and yet that, whenever I am away from him, I succumb to the temptations of popularity. So I behave like a runaway slave and take to my heels, and when I see him the conclusions which he has forced upon me make me ashamed.[21]

Presumably, Alcibiades is able to ignore Socrates because even though he recognizes that Socrates is right this is not a truth he has been able to incorporate at the deepest level of his being. He both knows and yet doesn't know the truth of Socrates' philosophy and in this sense he embodies Aristotle's own philosophical position on incontinence: "Nor does the incontinent man *know* what is right in the sense of actively contemplating it; only as a person asleep or drunk can be said to know a thing . . . the incontinent man is like a state which passes all the right decrees and has good laws, but makes no use of them."[22]

Whereas the incontinent man is weak-willed and allows himself to be overwhelmed by desire, the continent man is one who successfully resists the contrary desires and emerges from temptation as the captain of his soul. In terms of their actions there is no difference between the continent and the temperate man. But while the continent man continues to struggle, albeit successfully, against his unruly desires, the temperate man has successfully tamed these desires and is no longer troubled by them. It is not that temperance involves passivity and feebleness of soul. The temperate man is not insensible; on the contrary, "the temperate man desires the right things in the right way and at the right time, and this also is prescribed by rational principle."[23] Finally, as in Plato, the relationship between individual mastery and the rule of the city is always close to the surface of things: Temperance is an important political virtue and only the man who can rule himself can effectively rule over others.

Aristotle comments briefly and in passing on the very few people who seem to be opposed to physical enjoyment or even incapable of physical pleasure. Of course the great majority of people are prone to self-indulgence, but Aristotle does mention the insensibility to pleasure as a vice that as yet has no name. Given what he knew of human nature, Aristotle didn't think that insensibility to pleasure could ever be a serious problem. The irony is that at the end of classical antiquity Christianity emerged as a popular movement that emphasized asceticism, the denial of the flesh, and self-mortification for the sake of the world to come. As we have seen, Nietzsche himself was outraged by Christianity's revaluation of pagan values, and he viewed its attack upon the physical body and all of its instincts as the sign of its ultimate nihilism.

There is a huge difference in Plato and Aristotle's views on temperance, physical pleasure, and desire, and the way that Christians of different perspectives have experienced the same complex of issues. Of course, if we use examples from the early Church Fathers it would be quite easy to show how Christianity has promoted a very negative attitude to the body. The early Christians in particular seemed to cultivate an exceptional sexual discipline that signified their distinction from the rest of the pagan world. Many early Christians pledged themselves to virginity and chastity even within marriage; they rejected divorce and disapproved of remarriage. The leaders of the early Church practiced celibacy and sought to overcome sexual desire to achieve a singleness of mind that would allow them to be devoted to God. As Peter Brown writes, "In such a way celibacy demarcated quite unmistakably the existence of a class of persons who were central to the public life of the church, precisely because they were permanently removed from what was considered most private in the life of the average Christian layman in the world."[24] For many of the early Christians, the goal was to achieve supremacy over this world by renouncing physical pleasure, especially sexual pleasure, and becoming indifferent to physical pain. Hence the much-criticized Tertullian, who called for the public veiling of women and girls, who railed against public entertainments, and who insisted that the sin of the fallen angels was a lack of chastity. Hence the extreme case of the ascetic desert fathers, or the pillar-squatting saints like St. Simeon Stylites, who lived for years at the top of a 60-foot platform in the desert, fasting, praying, and experiencing extreme physical hardship while at the same time he achieved immense fame. Such examples exalt an ideal that involves repudiation of worldly pleasure and scorn for personal pain and suffering. For in this way, the individual is supposedly made pure from the corruption of the world. Of course, Tertullian was later considered a heretic, and the desert saints can be seen as fanatics, while more mainstream Christian writers like St. Augustine and St. Thomas Aquinas accept the necessity of marriage and sexual activity. But even in St. Augustine and Aquinas there is still a sense that the sensual is something to be resisted since it is the inferior element of creation. This implies a dualism of spirit and matter, and the path to perfection involves the renunciation of our lower nature, insofar as this is possible in this world.

There are many different sins that one could be guilty of. But for Augustine, the sins of the flesh remain central and paradigmatic of our own fallen nature, and the persistence of unlawful sexual desire becomes the privileged marker of our own progress toward salvation. In book XIV of the

City of God, Augustine explains that sexual desire and orgasm are the deepest symptoms of our own fallen nature. Lust is born with original sin and through it the original disobedience of the will is fulfilled in the body's disobedience to the soul. Sexual orgasm did not exist before the Fall, because it is a consequence of the new dichotomy between the body and soul. It is a violent and discordant state in which everything is commingled and the mind is overwhelmed:

> Human nature then is, without any doubt, ashamed about lust, and rightly ashamed. For in its disobedience, which subjected the sexual organs solely to its own impulses and snatched them from the will's authority, we see a proof of the retribution imposed on man for that first disobedience. And it was entirely fitting that this retribution should show itself in that part which effects the procreation of the very nature that was changed for the worse through that first great sin.[25]

Men and women bear in their own unruly bodies the fatal symptom of the Fall of Adam and Eve. Before the Fall, Adam and Eve had a harmonious sexual union, but now sexual desire comes and goes when it wants and not when it is ordered. Thus our sexual being shows the radical dislocation of our life and our separation from God. There is no way out here, except to put ourselves completely in the power of God, which means to accept God's will and completely deny our own. As Augustine celebrates, "Lord, I am your servant, born of your own handmaid. You have broken the chains that bound me. . . . At last my mind was free from the gnawing anxieties of ambition and gain, from wallowing in filth and scratching the itching sore of lust. I began to talk to you freely, O You who are my God, my Light, my Wealth, and my Salvation."[26] Paradoxically, self-denial leads to fulfillment and that death in our own life when the will of God is entirely present within us.

Augustine is the presiding genius of Christian theology, who responds to underlying themes and anxieties of the Christian mind at the same time as he clarifies and organizes Christian doctrines. The *Confessions* and the *City of God* reflect the Christian preoccupation with physical desire as the basis of our sinful nature. Clearly for Augustine, as well as for other Christian thinkers, the essential task is the purification of all that offends against the spiritual will. It would be best if we could live without it, but given our sinful nature, we must remain suspicious of our physical being. We must confine it to the proper forms of heterosexual monogamy and (as confessors were instructed) we should be on the lookout for every manifestation of improper thought and act. "It is right, therefore, to be ashamed of this lust, and it is right that the members which it moves or fails to move by its own right, so to speak, and not in complete conformity to our decision, should be called pudenda ('parts of shame'), which they were not called before man's sin; for, as scripture tells us, 'they were naked and yet they felt no embarrassment.'"27

Clearly this is a very different account of temperance than the one we examined in ancient Greek philosophy. But in one way or another, it informs most of the thinkers in the Christian tradition including those thinkers who are critical in rejecting some of the excesses of the "monkish" virtues. In the *Summa Theologiae*, for example, Aquinas gives an extended and thoughtful account of temperance that attempts to realign Christianity within an Aristotelian frame. Temperance concerns the desires that are most necessary to the life of the individual and the continuation of the species. Aquinas doesn't call for the suppression of these desires and yet he declares that chastity and virginity are the purest forms of temperance: "We have explained how the final and essential touch to virginity is the purpose of renouncing the pleasures of sex, which purpose is rendered praiseworthy because adopted for the sake of being free to be devoted to divine things: the immunity of the flesh from all sex-experience is but the material of virginity."28 Marriage, he says, is for the body's good whereas virginity is for the good of the soul in the life of contemplation. Hence, "without doubt," he concludes "virginity is to be esteemed more highly than conjugal continence." Aquinas argues that some people serve the community through marriage and bearing children while others serve the community through their religious devotion. This seems like a statement of equality: in this respect, bearing children is a good thing for without it the community would perish, and Aquinas is certainly not one of the radical deniers of the flesh who calls for complete self-mortification. And yet, he has to agree with Augustine in the end that marriage is a necessary evil, and virginity for the sake of Christian service is a more exalted state than marriage itself: "It is thus that virginity dedicated to God is ranked higher than bodily fruitfulness. And so Augustine writes, 'It must be confessed that fruitfulness of the flesh, even for women of our day who want children for no other reason than to make them children of Christ, cannot compensate for the virginity that has been lost.'"29 Following this, Aquinas contends that any form of sexuality that doesn't fall within the natural goal of the species—including homosexuality, incest, masturbation, or even improper sexual practices within marriage—are against God's law. Once again, Aquinas and Augustine agree on this point. Aquinas writes, "The developed plan of living according to reason comes from man; the plan of nature comes from God, and therefore a violation of

this plan, as by unnatural sins, is an affront to God, the ordainer of nature."[30]
And again he quotes Augustine:

> Those foul offences against nature should be detested and punished every-
> where and at all times, such as were those of the people of Sodom, which,
> should all nations commit, then would all stand guilty of the same crime by
> God's law, which has not made men that they should so abuse one another. For
> then even the very intercourse which should be between God and us is vio-
> lated when that same nature, of which he is the author, is polluted by the per-
> versity of lust.[31]

Now we may have freed ourselves from the long regime of sexual repression
endorsed by Augustine and Aquinas and others, but as Foucault points out,
we still live in a culture that focuses on sex and makes it a source of extreme
anxiety. Sexuality suffuses this culture, and we are incited at every turn to determine ourselves as sexual beings. In this respect, we are still in the orbit of
repression, and "temperance" remains an ambivalent virtue.

In the end, I think we can say that temperance is largely equivalent to
what has also been called "the care of the self." In Plato and Aristotle, this
involves the promotion of an inner harmony and balance that is equivalent
to the spiritual health of the soul. The inner regime of the soul bears some
analogy to the political order of the state, and it is crucial that the rational
part be in control while the other parts of the soul acknowledge reason's rule.
With Christianity, the idea of temperance is more closely associated with
spiritual purity; but self-control is emphasized as an ultimate goal. Some of
the early Church Fathers, such as Tertullian, seemed intent on punishing the
body and extirpating the passions as the vile remnant of our fallen nature.
For Augustine and Aquinas, on the other hand, the physical desires are an
undeniable aspect of human nature, and they have an important part to play
in our overall well-being. But in their comments on original sin and the significance of chastity and virginity, there remains a deep suspicion of our
physical being and especially carnal desire, which is viewed as the index of
our sinful nature. Christianity takes this tendency to an extreme, but even in
Aristotle, the discussion of temperance is directed by anxiety concerning the
proper distance that we should keep from the pleasures and desires that derive from our animal nature.

What this brief survey shows is that there are at least two different ways
of going wrong with temperance. First, a lack of temperance involves a lack
of personal sovereignty and the inability to rule over oneself or others. Like
the tyrant who cannot control his desires and who is incapable of enjoying

what he has: Complete satiety only produces disgust and signifies an inability to feel at home or at peace in the world. But the other way of going wrong with temperance involves too much self-control, which leads to self-hatred for whatever resists the will's commandment over itself, and the ultimate rejection of our physical nature. With Christianity especially, the split between our physical and our spiritual nature is often emphatic and extreme—the physical is opposed to the spiritual and the very idea of a spirituality of the body is literally inconceivable.[32] We cannot accept ourselves as we are, and for as long as we don't identify with our physical nature, it means that we don't have a strong connection to the natural world we belong to. Perhaps this is why temperance is a more ambivalent virtue today: Of course we know that it *should* be a virtue because there is something wrong with self-abandonment, but at the same time we sense that the meaning it has acquired (as self-control and even self-denial) is quite impoverished and says nothing about our place in the world around us.

Taoism and Nature

It is certainly true that temperance requires an inner harmony and self-control, but the relationship to whatever is within us is always at the same time a relationship to whatever is outside of us. Temperance is not just self-fashioning for the sake of it. We are embedded in the world—this much is inescapable—and our sense of who we are is completely bound up with our sense of belonging to the world around us. Hence, as Socrates recognized, we need to stay mindful of our limitations, our lack of knowledge, and our mortality; we must not overreach ourselves or set ourselves up as if we were above nature or use it as a thing; and we should be able to enjoy what we have been given, while avoiding the excessive pleasures and desires that lead to disgust or inner turmoil. In the end, this may also involve a sense of the sacred character of the world around us, which must be respected and cared for. All of this is contained in the ideal of temperance, but it certainly cannot be extrapolated from the imperative of self-control. Thinking of temperance as self-control only implies an inner turmoil that has just been overcome. Hence, I think it would be preferable to say that the deepest aspect of temperance involves an attunement to the natural order of the world. And this is reflected by the profound inner calm, or serenity, of whoever has achieved the proper harmony of the soul—like Socrates, as Plato describes him.

This way of thinking helps to clarify the sense in which temperance belongs to the very basis of ecology since it concerns our relationship to the world around us. It emphasizes the need to cultivate attitudes like frugality, a sense of limits, and antipathy to waste, gratitude for whatever is given, and even a sense of the sacred, as the proper attunement to the world that expresses our own sense of belonging to it. But before we turn explicitly to environmentalism in the final part of this chapter, we will look at the philosophy of Taoism, which offers another way of thinking about our relationship to the natural world and another perspective on temperance. In fact, Taoism offers a new paradigm for temperance that is close enough to the Western account we have just considered to suggest that temperance is a more universal theme, and the proper relationship to nature is something that cannot be ignored without incurring spiritual and material distress.

There is growing interest in Taoism amongst environmental philosophers for Taoism seems to offer an ecological foundation that gives a much better account of the relationship between human beings and the natural world than the one that has usually prevailed. The world is in the throes of a profound environmental crisis: as we pollute the atmosphere and allow different species to disappear, we are also threatening the well-being of future generations and putting our own species at risk. But how has this happened? What led us to the current environmental catastrophe, and can we still save ourselves? One response to such questions is to show how our basic relationship to the natural world is conditioned by an underlying paradigm that shapes all thinking and our actions in advance. In the West it is perhaps the "dominion" theory of creation, expressed in the Book of Genesis, that seems to encapsulate and justify our historical attitude toward the natural world: as when God directs Adam to "increase, multiply, fill the earth and bring it into subjection." But if we are dissatisfied with this way of thinking and dismayed by the consequences it seems to entail, we should try to articulate another basic paradigm that would guide our relationship to nature in more meaningful and beneficial ways. Lynn White writes: "What people do about their ecology depends upon what they think about themselves in relation to the world around them. Human ecology is deeply conditioned by beliefs about our nature and destiny."[33] In response, J. Callicott argues that Taoism offers the most promising ecological foundation:

> Taoism could help environmentalists express the emergent order of nature, which is the outcome of a process of mutual adjustment among plants, animals, the earth and the atmosphere over many millennia. Just as important, the contemporary evolutionary and ecological worldview might be welcomed in modern China—and better appreciated than here in the west—as a scientific expression and confirmation of a classical Chinese insight.[34]

At the same time, as I will show, Taoism is focused on temperance as a fundamental virtue.

Now there is a major difficulty with any attempt to appropriate another tradition and use it for your own ends. Presumably Taoism does not exist to solve the problems of the West, and it is a form of cultural imperialism to approach Taoism with a specific agenda to ask what it can do for us. If Taoism is supposed to promote a harmonious relationship with nature, then one might expect that it would have some effect on environmental attitudes in China where it has remained a popular philosophy. But environmental destruction is rampant in China too. Indeed a close examination of the classic *Tao te Ching* suggests that this work was originally written as a manual for rulers; the intended audience seems to be members of the male aristocracy while the common people are dismissed as "straw dogs" to be handled and put aside. Supporters of the popular version of Taoism subscribed to in the West may ignore unsettling passages like these or claim they are metaphorically intended, in order to avoid the challenging aspects of this tradition in favor of a diluted version of it. But of course there is no authentic encounter with another culture as long as one determines the terms of engagement in advance. We might conclude that the whole idea of a Taoist environmental ethics is misguided and involves the selfish misappropriation of a tradition that has a trajectory of its own.

And yet it may be argued that Taoist texts like the *Tao te Ching* and the *Chuang Tzu* give evidence of a more positive attitude toward nature than comparable works in the Judeo-Christian tradition. The Tao is something like the underlying principle of change and the original movement of the world that is manifest in nature as well as human affairs, which also belong to the natural world. In the *Tao te Ching*, the basic imperative for the ruler, or the reader, is to revere and follow the way of the Tao. Self-assertion is accordingly condemned, and the ultimate goal is to harmonize one's own nature with the Tao, which supports individual existence. In this respect, Taoism is all about the need to achieve a harmonious relationship with the natural order. And while the text may actually be addressed to the ruler, it also elaborates an image of personal sovereignty that may be characterized in terms of yielding and self-overcoming—as opposed to self-assertion—and the harmonious integration of different aspects of one's own existence with the natural order of things. I will discuss these themes in more detail in what follows. But even at this point, it must be conceded that Taoism does not provide us with an explicit environmental philosophy. For one thing, environmental awareness and the perspective of "deep ecology" seem to require an active intervention in nature in order to prevent or reverse environmental difficulties, such as the threatened extinction of whales or the massive pollution that can be caused by oil tankers that are built with a single hull. Environmentalism requires activism and legislation that is apparently at odds with the Taoist emphasis on letting go or letting things be—which is affirmed by the high priority given to the concept of wu-wei, or "acting by not acting." This is not to say that Taoism encourages passivity and fatalism. The point is that even while it does promote a harmonious attitude toward the natural world, Taoism has complete trust in the power of heaven to control and curtail human activities, so to use it in support of radical intervention on behalf of nature would be problematic.

The precise relationship between Taoism and ecology is therefore difficult to define, and perhaps it is optimistic to think that Taoism could provide us with a coherent paradigm for an appropriate environmental involvement. What I would argue, however, is that Taoism does offer a very significant account of temperance, in works like the *Tao te Ching* and especially in the model of the Taoist sage that is sketched out both in the *Tao te Ching* and in the *Chuang Tzu*. In these works, we encounter the same cluster of ideas and values that we have come to associate with temperance in the corresponding Western tradition, including frugality and contentment, the awareness of limits, and attunement to both the inner and the outer realms of nature. Through this discussion, the significance of temperance may now be illuminated as a transcultural value that is deeply rooted in human nature itself.

I will focus on the *Tao te Ching* as the central text of Taoism and certainly its most well-known work. There is considerable dispute about who wrote the *Tao te Ching* and when, and whether the surviving text is complete or a corruption of the original. By most accounts, however, the *Tao te Ching* was composed sometime in the fourth century BCE, and so it may be roughly contemporaneous with the life of Socrates. It is not a systematic metaphysical text although it may be said to contain and endorse a particular perspective on the world, and in a series of figures and oracular pronouncements it suggests a model of sagacity—the ideal perspective of the sage whose attunement to the Tao and its manifestation in nature is the basis of his virtue. In this respect it could be held that something very much like "temperance" is the underlying condition of all virtue in the Taoist philosophical scheme. The following discussion is brief and sketches out only four basic aspects of the Taoist standpoint in the *Tao te Ching*. The danger with any limited account of the text is that it is bound to oversimplify or even falsify important ideas for the sake of its own ends. But in this discussion my goal is to specify some significant points of comparison that will suggest continuity between the Western ideal of temperance and the corresponding Taoist account that seems to dominate this text.

The *Tao te Ching* may be read as a work of philosophy that seeks to describe the way the world is, but it is also an attempt to inspire and transform the reader by instilling a particular attitude toward nature or the cosmos that may fairly be characterized as "temperance" or something very like it. By constant repetition and reflection on each chapter, the reader of the *Tao te Ching* must eventually shape her own thinking in conformity with this framework. It is a descriptive account, but at the same time it is also a performative text that provokes the responsive soul. Hence reading this book involves acquiring a basic orientation toward the world rather than accepting a list of teachings: "He who knows has no wide learning; he who has wide learning does not know. / The sage does not hoard. / Having bestowed all he has on others, he has yet more."[35] More specifically, the *Tao te Ching* addresses the individual by dwelling on at least four significant themes: 1) An insistence on the priority of process and change that the idea of the Tao upholds, 2) The theory of letting-alone and letting-be (wu-wei) that allows us to follow the model of nature as an expression of the Tao, 3) The project of integrating each human life within its particular horizon of meaning and relationship to others as the working of the Tao in human life, and 4) The experience of serenity and fullness of being as the achievement of the Tao within us; this is shown in the *Tao te Ching* and elsewhere by the model of the Taoist sage.[36]

First of all, the most basic and insistent claim in the *Tao te Ching* is the reality of process and change and the very limited and temporary character of substantial forms and independent beings. As we read in the first chapter: "The nameless was the beginning of heaven and earth; / The named was the mother of the myriad creatures. /.../ These two are the same / But diverge in name as they issue forth." Likewise, in chapter 25, the ineffable character of the Tao is described as that which supports and animates all things; it is not itself a thing and cannot be considered as one object among others. Even though the Tao can be referred to in this way as "the mother of the world" or "the great," or even "the way," it is not itself a substantial reality, and the claim that the Tao does not change is therefore self-canceling: "There is a thing confusedly formed, / Born before heaven and earth / Silent and void / It stands alone and does not change. / Goes round and does not weary. / It is capable of being the mother of the world. / I know not its name / So I style it 'the way.'" As it becomes clear in other chapters, the Tao is itself the principle of change that animates everything that is. In chapter 32, for example, it is compared to the river that all the rivulets and streams belong to. That is, it is not something that is independent and separate from the rest of the world but the animating principle of everything that is. The Tao is not an ideal substratum or a fixed substance that somehow avoids flux. Indeed it would be better to characterize it as nothing. Hence in chapter 40: "The myriad creatures in the world are born from / Something, and Something from Nothing." The Tao exceeds every attempt to describe it or give it a name. It is not a thing and it cannot be appropriated by language, and in this sense it is "nothing." Finally, however, it is important to note that the Tao is celebrated as a benign principle, indeed it is the very principle of goodness and everything succeeds insofar as it is in accordance with the Tao. It is therefore referred to as the mother (in chapter 25 above), and described as the principle of pure benevolence in chapter 41: "The way conceals itself in being nameless / It is the way alone that excels in bestowing and in accomplishing." Hence to live in accordance with the Tao, by cooperating with the unconscious principles of nature, is to live in accordance with what is good.

Nothing is substantial or enduring, and the fundamental character of the world is one of perpetual flux. But this is neither the unfolding of a particular plan that brings us closer to some final goal, nor a chaotic flow that proceeds quite randomly. To put it in positive terms, the Tao is the expression of the fundamental harmony that underlies nature and the world, and it includes all creatures in its sway. Hence the second point, that in order to follow the Tao, we must avoid all self-assertion and embrace the unfolding of nature by deliberately refraining from any active intervention that seeks the immediate transformation of the world. In chapter 3, for example: "Do that which consists in taking no action, and order will prevail," and in chapter 55 we are warned against subverting the natural order of things: "A creature in its prime doing harm to the old / Is known as going against the way. / That which goes against the way will come to an early end." In the *Tao de Ching*, the principle of wu-wei is given an important place. It means acting without taking action, and it is a characteristic of the sage. In chapter 63, for example: "Do that which consists in taking no action; pursue that which is not meddlesome; savor that which has no flavor." Again in chapter 64: "Whoever does anything to it will ruin it; whoever lays hold of it will lose it. / Therefore the sage, because he does nothing, never ruins anything; and, because he does not lay hold of anything, loses nothing." Wu-wei involves an extreme restraint of physical action and forbearance in not interfering or ordering things according to one's own fixed ideas, as well as the internal restraint that involves shaping one's emotional responses so that they accord harmoniously with the unfolding of the Tao. For it's no real achievement to refrain from action if at the same time we rant and rail against perceived misfortunes like old age and death. Since we belong to the natural order we should cultivate a harmonious attunement to it.

In other chapters, the same point is made by emphasizing the superiority and stronger power of the female principle over that of the male; in chapter 28, for example, the advice is: "Know the male / But keep to the role of the female / And be a ravine to the empire. / If you are a ravine to the empire, / Then the constant virtue will not desert you / And you will again return to being a babe." Likewise, the text emphasizes the power of water that defeats every solid obstacle through patience and self-effacing withdrawal. In chapter 8 we are told: "Highest good is like water. Because water excels in benefiting the myriad creatures without contending with them and settles where none would like to be, it comes close to the way." And more dramatically in chapter 78: "In the world there is nothing more submissive and weak than water. Yet for attacking that which is hard and strong nothing can surpass it. This is because there is nothing that can take its place. / That the weak overcomes the strong, / And the submissive overcomes the hard, / Everyone in the world knows yet no one can put this knowledge into practice." Finally, in chapter 43 we are told that submission and compliance with the unfolding of the Tao achieves far more than self-assertion and foolish railing against fate. "That is why I know the benefit of resorting to no action. The teaching that uses no words, the benefit of resorting to no action, these are beyond the understanding of all but a very few in the world." But all of this is more than just a vague principle of exhortation, and it must affect whoever is prepared to take it seriously, while failure to accept it may be disastrous. In modern China, for example, more than 30 million people ultimately died because of Mao's attempt to reorganize food production in the Great Leap Forward of the 1950s. Even if his intentions were good, the fact is he denied the spirit of the Tao by imposing his will on the land. Traditional farming methods that had developed over the course of centuries were summarily abolished, and the result was an unmitigated disaster.

According to the *Tao te Ching*, the ruler accepts and understands the workings of all things and so he does not resist their essential unfolding. He doesn't assert his will but allows things to be what they must be, and he lets go of his own selfish desires. In chapter 48, for example: "It is always through not meddling that the empire is won. Should you meddle, then you are not equal to the task of winning the empire." At a more abstract level, the point here is that action in accordance with the Tao should be harmonious, and even effortless since it doesn't move against the essential flow of things. In this respect we can understand chapter 46: "When the way prevails in the empire, fleet-footed horses are relegated to ploughing the fields; when the way does not prevail in the empire, war horses breed on the border. There is no crime greater than having too many desires." The point is that war, understood as an obvious mode of antagonistic self-assertion, is entirely opposed to the Tao which relates things together and brings them into their essential harmony. In chapter 76: "Thus the hard and the strong are the comrades of death; the supple and the weak are the comrades of life."

The third point is that human beings are themselves a part of nature—as the *Tao te Ching* frequently insists—and so it would be a mistake to think of an absolute opposition between nature and culture or to see our own particular human actions as somehow separate from the natural context in which they emerge. And since we belong to nature and form a significant part of it, we should not think of ourselves as passive and simply bound to accept whatever happens in a fatalistic way. Again, wu-wei does not involve self-abandonment but an intuitive cooperation with the natural order. This is an important point because there is a big difference between Taoist wisdom and Stoicism: the first, unlike the second, does not require acceptance of whatever life brings. But rather, it enjoins the creative appropriation of one's own personal horizon and the aesthetic cultivation of the local context in which one lives. For this is how the Tao works itself out in us. Chapter 54 for example describes a progression from individual cultivation to family, hamlet, state, and empire: "Cultivate it in your person / And its virtue will be genuine; / Cultivate it in the family / And its virtue will be more than sufficient; / Cultivate it in the hamlet / And its virtue will endure; / Cultivate it in the state / And its virtue will abound; / Cultivate it in the empire / And its virtue will be pervasive." Each level reflects and harmonizes with every other level, so that the self-cultivation of the sage must ultimately have an effect on all the people that he is surrounded by. Or in chapter 37, "The way never acts yet nothing is left undone. / Should lords and princes be able to hold fast to it, / The myriad creatures will be transformed of their own accord." In chapter 47, the Taoist wisdom is not identified with any secret knowledge that requires complete self-denial, or leaving the cave of everyday life to encounter profound or abstract truths. Instead it is revealed to be a matter of harmonizing with one's lived world and surroundings. The truth is not to be found through excessive scholarship but in the profound cultivation and appreciation of whatever is here and now: "Without stirring abroad / One can know the whole world; / Without looking out of the window / One can see the way of heaven. / The further one goes / The less one knows." It is not about leaving home or mundane existence behind you, but as T. S. Eliot puts it: "We shall not cease from exploration / And the end of all our exploring / Will be to arrive where we started / And know the place for the first time."[37]

Finally we are told that the Taoist sage lives in a state of serenity and contentment. From chapter 46, "There is no crime greater than having too many desires; / There is no disaster greater than not being content; / There is no misfortune greater than being covetous. / Hence in being content, one will always have enough." It seems the sage has no private desires; he doesn't really care about personal success and so he doesn't experience misfortunes either. In fact, he subordinates all of his own desires to the requirements of the situation, and in following the Tao rather than his own personal agenda, he is described as a "model for the Empire." From chapter 22: "He does not show himself, and so is conspicuous; / He does not consider himself right, and so is illustrious; / He does not brag, and so has merit; He does not boast, and so endures. / It is because he does not contend that no one in the empire is in a position to contend with him." In chapter 57, the sage speaks, and he appears to be the embodiment of temperance: "I take no action and the people are transformed of themselves; / I prefer stillness and the people are rectified of themselves; I am not meddlesome and the people prosper of themselves; / I am free from desire and the people of themselves become simple like the uncarved block." Likewise, in chapter 67, he talks of "the three treasures" that order the principle of his life: compassion, frugality, and a refusal to take the lead in the empire, which suggests the lack of any personal ambition. But as the *Tao te Ching* comments, these qualities are precisely those that make him the best person to rule. In chapter 29: "Therefore the sage avoids excess, extravagance, and arrogance." This brief sketch reminds us of Socrates as the individual embodiment of temperance described by Plato in dialogues like the *Symposium* or the *Phaedo*, where he demonstrates a singular unconcern with his own life and so he achieves an absolute distinction. It is significant that there are such obvious parallels between the image of the Chinese sage as sketched in the *Tao te Ching* and the model of temperance described by Plato and Aristotle and revised by Augustine and Aquinas. For all of these different strands help to illuminate a single virtue that has different manifestations, but also seems to have a substantial core that is valued across different cultures. The Greek, Christian, and Taoist conceptions of temperance are mutually illuminating, and they confirm and contest each other; in this way, a deeper understanding of temperance begins to emerge, as the virtue that connects us to the natural world, and of which our inner nature is itself a constituent part.

From Temperance to Environmentalism

Scientists all over the world have recognized for some time that species extinctions are now occurring on a massive scale. Indeed, the rate of these extinctions seems to rival that of the Cretaceous period of about 65 million years ago when many species, including the dinosaur, also became extinct. But while every other case of mass extinction in global history has come about as a result of climatic change or some cataclysmic event, the present crisis is entirely the result of human influence, and has been caused by pollution, overdevelopment, and overpopulation, and an underlying lack of concern for the natural environment that all of these factors manifest. Some scientists and activists are now working to preserve the biological diversity of different local habitats, and environmental issues such as deforestation, overdevelopment, pollution, and global warming have been brought into public focus. More than ever before, we are asked to live mindfully and responsibly in the natural world, and to practice a policy of sustainable development that would keep the world in good condition for our children and for future generations of human beings who are as yet unborn. In very broad terms, this is environmentalism; and it is profoundly associated with the virtue of temperance insofar as it involves a harmonious attunement to the world around us, which reflects the same harmonious attunement that temperance achieves within the individual soul.

The environmental movement has emerged in response to a growing sense of a crisis in the natural world. It is not the expression of a "special interest," since it is concerned with the maintenance of biodiversity as an end in itself and as a necessary condition for the health and well-being of all present and future human beings. In fact, environmentalism forces us to change our focus from a purely anthropocentric point of view to the consideration of nature as a whole. As Aldo Leopold puts it in his famous formulation, "A thing is right when it tends to preserve the integrity, stability and beauty of the biotic community; it is wrong when it tends to do otherwise."[38] Lying behind this is the idea that all the different aspects of the environment are ultimately interconnected: anything that happens in one place eventually has some kind of an effect on everything else; while the natural world, both in its details and taken as a whole, is not an indifferent space but a place of beauty and spiritual possibility that our attunement to nature allows us to celebrate; in the end, the whole of nature is an ecological community that we ourselves belong to. We already know this on a personal level—the food that I eat is food that someone else doesn't eat, even though they may be starving; any fuel that I use now depletes supplies for future generations; and the way that I leave my city, my garbage, or my world may have a marked effect on those who come to these things after I have gone. But we lose sight of this when we emphasize our domination and control over the natural world, and we assume that the world is just an object that is subject to us. With other cultural perspectives such as Taoism or the Native American view, there is profound wisdom in the claim that the world does not belong to us, and we should assume an attitude of reverence toward the natural world as our home. This entails not harming it, cultivating a sense of gratitude for what we have been given, and recognizing the extent to which we are embedded in the world as one species amongst thousands of others.

There are of course countless examples we could choose to illustrate the point that nature is an interconnected realm. But there are three basic issues that seem to recur over and over again—pollution, overdevelopment, and species endangerment or extinction. This is not to say that environmentalism involves only these three issues, but insofar as we can distinguish them from each other, pollution, overdevelopment, and species endangerment or extinction seem to be the most common features of the environmental crisis we are facing.

As an example of what happens when a species is endangered and undermines the ecological balance we can take the recent decline of the vulture population in India. Once they were a common sight all over India, but since at least 1999, the number of vultures has collapsed and many scientists think they are facing extinction. Pesticides are blamed, but there is also a consensus that vultures are dying because the corpses of cattle they traditionally feed upon now contain hormone additives that are given to the cattle in order to boost their milk production. The vultures are poisoned by these additives. As a result the population of wild dogs has markedly increased as they feed on the carrion that is now available to them. Many of these dogs are infected with rabies, however, so the number of Indians who die of rabies each year has greatly increased. Similarly, pollution off the coast of Florida and global warming are killing coral reefs along the Florida Keys. But the latter serve as the habitat for hundreds of different species of fish, including schools of sharks, lobsters, and eels, while they also give the coastline a protective barrier. Many coastal communities depend upon the reefs for their livelihood, through fishing and tourism, but now the numbers of fish have started to decline, and by some estimates up to 90% of the reefs are dying.

Next, consider the problem of waste, including industrial waste, smog, and perhaps most dangerous of all, nuclear waste. Industrial production creates jobs, consumer goods, and other benefits, but in the long term, it is also destroying the stability, integrity, and beauty of the natural environment and endangering future generations of human beings. One significant example would be the enormous amount of waste dumped into the Rio Grande River from the U.S.-owned chemical plants operating in Mexico. Most of the residents of the Rio Grande area obtain their drinking water from the river. But there is a lot of unexplained sickness in this region, and the rate of anencephaly in border cities like Brownsville and Matamoros is four times the national average. Despite legal suits against the companies, however, the pollution continues since residents have to be able to prove the specific linkage between the pollution and these conditions to shut the factories down.[39] In the case of nuclear waste, the problem is even more alarming. Since nuclear waste will remain radioactive for thousands of years, any short-term measures for dealing with it—such as putting it in the ocean or burying it in a mountain—are quite problematic given the possibility of earthquakes and other disasters. Environmental concerns like this that affect the well-being of many future generations—or the problem of human debris, spread over billions of miles in space—tend to affirm a strong sense of our place in nature and even in the universe as a whole.

Finally, there is the urgent threat of global warming. There is now a considerable measure of agreement among scientists that global warming is caused by the erosion of the ozone layer surrounding the earth, while this in turn is caused by the massive scale of pollution from toxic emissions released into the atmosphere by exhaust systems and other kinds of waste that are the consequence of industrial activity and human overdevelopment. As a result of global warming the seas will rise as the ice caps begin to melt; huge numbers of people and animal populations will be displaced or die in resultant flooding. Global warning will most likely affect the Gulf Stream and may even make it change direction if the warming is significant enough, and this could produce a global catastrophe as traditional ecosystems are suddenly altered or destroyed. These three examples, out of thousands that could have been mentioned, show the extent of interconnections in nature and how damage to one part ultimately affects the whole of the eco-system. They show the importance of our attunement to the natural world both on an individual level and at the level of humankind itself. Human beings may gain a short-term advantage by disregarding their place in the natural order, by promoting overdevelopment that leads to pollution and environmental desolation; but in the long run they are bound to come to grief.

In this respect, then, temperance leads to environmentalism as the harmonious adjustment to the natural world; for even if one person's actions may not have a significant impact, the combined effect of millions of people acting responsibly will. Now there is still considerable dispute about the extent to which intervention in the natural world is necessary and exactly which environmental policies should be followed in the world today. Environmentalism includes a variety of different perspectives ranging from deep ecology to ecological feminism and different versions of humanism. Nevertheless, all of these views presuppose temperance as an underlying virtue that promotes a harmonious relationship to the world around us as something we should be concerned about in our desire to be good. There are three important aspects to consider here, and we can summarize them as the basis of our environmental philosophy. First, temperance promotes environmentally friendly attitudes and behaviors like frugality, antipathy to waste, and humility; it also involves enjoyment of the earth—not overindulgence, or the refusal of pleasure that would entail ingratitude—but the appreciation of simple pleasures that testify to our appreciation of the world around us. Next, temperance emphasizes the importance of attunement and a harmonious adjustment to the natural world and even the cosmos itself. In both a local and a global sense, it involves cultivating a sense of belonging and responding to one's place in nature—and we have seen that this is the Taoist ideal. Finally, temperance also involves a nonappropriative relationship to the world: the world is not there to be dominated or controlled, it is to be appreciated for its own sake. This implies a sense of wonder, or an aesthetic appreciation of the natural world, as a basic response that we may cultivate to affirm our sense of belonging. I will consider this point in more detail.

In the history of philosophy, Kant is one thinker who writes thoughtfully about our relationship to the natural world, and this is especially evident in his discussion of the sublime. Of course, Kant's focus is on the power and the immensity of nature—the massive overhanging cliffs or the storm at sea or the starry sky at night that remind us of the power or the magnitude of the universe. But I think that what he says about the sublime is true for our experience of nature in general, that in various ways it promotes a sense of wonder that reinforces the strength of our connection to it. As Kant puts it:

> Bold, overhanging, and as it were, threatening rocks, thunderclouds piled up the vault of heaven, borne along with flashes and peals, volcanoes in all their violence of destruction, hurricanes leaving desolation in their track, the boundless ocean rising with rebellious force, the high waterfall of some mighty river, and the like, make our power of resistance of trifling moment in comparison with their might.

But then he adds:

> Provided our position is secure, their aspect is all the more attractive for its fearfulness; and we readily call these objects sublime, because they raise the

forces of the soul above the height of vulgar commonplace, and discover within us a power of resistance of quite another kind, which gives us courage to be able to measure ourselves against the seeming omnipotence of nature.[40]

Here, Kant emphasizes the triumphant reassertion of the self that follows the impact of the overpowering object of the sublime. Initially, our physical self is threatened, and even overwhelmed, by the immensity or the power of nature. But there is a second moment of recuperation; the experience of the sublime is ultimately uplifting as it makes us realize that even though our physical existence is threatened, we transcend the physical realm, and our existence has an infinite significance and worth. Leaving aside Kant's own interpretation of this experience, I think that what he recognized in the sublime is the sense of being in relation to something much greater than ourselves. As Kant writes, "This thrusting aside of the sensible barriers gives it a feeling of being unbounded; and that removal is thus a presentation of the infinite."[41] Another way of explaining the experience of the sublime, however, is just to say that it is a very powerful and affirmative experience because it gives us a strong sense of belonging to the natural world around us, even while it humbles whatever pretensions we might have as "the lords and possessors of nature." The experience of the sublime is a dramatic manifestation of our experience of nature in general, but it suggests that it is always possible to experience nature with a sense of wonder, even with a sense of the sacred. And even though it may ultimately be in our own best interests, environmentalism cannot finally be based on calculation or purely pragmatic considerations, for the sense of reverence and awe is what leads us to care about nature in the first place.

In the end, most of the typical criticisms of environmentalism are unfounded. It is said, for example, that environmentalism is only a recent development, implying that it is shallow and not an enduring theme; some have claimed that environmentalism is an exclusively Western preoccupation, and so it remains a luxury and irrelevant to the rest of the world; while others have argued that environmentalism is selfish, and our concern for the environment is ultimately bound up with our own prestige and survival as the dominant species on the planet. But none of these points are valid.

The first claim holds that environmentalism is only a recent development, which suggests that it does not belong to a profound stream of moral wisdom; it is just the response to a perceived crisis, and so it won't endure as an abiding concern. Now in a sense, it would be true to say that environmentalism as a broad social movement is something that has only emerged quite recently. Indeed the history of modern environmental philosophy probably begins with pioneering texts like *A Sand County Almanac* by Aldo Leopold (1949) or Rachel Carson's *Silent Spring* (1962). On the other hand, it is also the case that obliviousness to nature has been a feature of modern life, and we are now suffering the consequences of our unconcern. As we have seen, temperance is a fundamental virtue in Plato and Aristotle, and it is manifest in other ancient traditions like Taoism. So the recovery of environmental concern is not so much an innovation but the return to a more original perspective that recognized the importance of a harmonious attunement to the natural world.

Likewise, the claim that environmentalism is a specifically Western concern is also false, as Taoism, the Native American standpoint, and African tribal views all celebrate our connection with nature and the need to cultivate a harmonious sense of belonging to it. Of course, it may be argued that underdeveloped countries are the least able to afford environmental safeguards and pollution controls that impede their economic growth. And yet the people in these countries are usually the ones who suffer most from pollution and in the long term, they are the victims of environmental disaster. The tragedy of Bhopal is an obvious case in point: Union Carbide, who owned the factory in Bhopal, India, took advantage of cheap local labor and less stringent environmental safeguards; indeed they would not have been allowed to build such a facility in the United States. When a cloud of poisonous gas escaped from the factory in 1984, the whole community was devastated, more than 400 people were killed, and thousands more were made invalids for the rest of their lives. It is simply false to say that the poor—wherever they live—have no interest in environmental issues.

Finally, we have already considered the claim that environmentalism is basically a selfish or self-regarding policy. Perhaps environmentalism could be viewed as a form of extended humanism, for environmentalism is certainly in our own best interests and promotes the future well-being of the earth for succeeding generations. But at the same time, environmentalism forces us to challenge the self-other or subject-object distinction that underlies this whole way of thinking. As we have seen, the goal of temperance is to harmonize inner and outer nature in such a way that the well-being of the one becomes completely integrated with the well-being of the other. Temperance and environmentalism undermine the sense of an independent self that holds itself against nature as an object that is to be dominated and controlled. Putting this more positively, we could say, in conclusion, that temperance and environmentalism promote spiritual renewal both in the life of the individual and in the human community itself.

CHAPTER THREE

~

Justice

On the night that Macbeth murders his king, the whole balance of nature is undone and the most terrible happenings are observed in the kingdom of Scotland. Macbeth must be punished for his crimes. Only then is the natural order restored, and Malcolm can be crowned as the rightful king of Scotland. There are similar themes in Greek tragedy: Although he is completely unaware of what he has done, Oedipus must be made to suffer for killing his father and marrying his mother, for the Furies demand retribution for these unnatural deeds. And because of the crimes of Atreus, who killed his brother's children, a whole sequence of murders and calamities is unleashed, which Aeschylus describes in the *Oresteia*: "Blood is the rule when its drops have spilled / on the ground; a fresh request for blood. / Slaughter screams for the Spirit of Vengeance / to fetch from the first the death it will lay / on the death it has brought to another."[1] After a trial before the gods, it is decided that justice has been served, and the bloody cycle of retribution comes to an end. In each case, justice is a matter of redressing the balance and returning the world to its original condition. The crime is an affront to heaven, and it must be expiated with the death or extreme suffering of those who have disordered the world. In this respect, justice is the master virtue, and even though we may believe that justice and the laws are human creations, we are still drawn by this idea that to bring about justice is to restore the natural order of things that had been undermined.

Macbeth is also guilty of overreaching; he doesn't accept the place that he occupies in the social hierarchy and covets being king. Likewise, Orestes and

Electra abandon their filial positions when they murder their mother even though they were seeking vengeance for the death of their father. Over-reaching and the refusal to play one's part can be disastrous for the entire community, and so they epitomize wrongdoing. This leads to the idea that injustice is evidenced in not fulfilling the duties of one's station, and a correlative sense of justice as doing what you are supposed to do. In Plato's formulation, justice is "minding your own business." Plato also says that justice means having a healthy soul, in which all the faculties are well ordered and know their place; in this respect, justice is the highest personal virtue, and it leads to living well and doing whatever is required of you. We no longer believe in the divine right of kings, and the limitation of "my station and its duties" is confining and may even be a form of injustice itself. But there is something appealing about this formulation that requires that everyone play their part to preserve the well-being of the community, and something like this is the core meaning of justice as a personal virtue.

Since Duncan was his king, Macbeth owed him loyalty, and since Duncan was staying at his castle, Macbeth owed him a particular debt of hospitality and safety. Likewise, Oedipus, Orestes, and Electra owed their parents some measure of filial devotion. In book one of the *Republic*, Polemarchus repeats this received idea when he says that justice means giving to each person what you owe them. The problems start when you try to specify what this is. Nietzsche speculates on the origins of justice and the law in *On the Genealogy of Morals*. He certainly does not accept any kind of metaphysical framework that would support justice as the balance of nature, but he looks instead at the creditor-debtor relationship as this must have existed at the beginning of human history. Nietzsche argues that our sense of justice is actually a recent development that derives from the very specific claims that our ancestors made against each other:

> Have these genealogists of morals had even the remotest suspicion that . . . the major moral concept Schuld [guilt] has its origin in the very material concept Schulden [debts]? Or that punishment, as requital, evolved quite independently of any presupposition concerning freedom or non-freedom of the will? . . . The idea, now so obvious . . . "the criminal deserves punishment because he could have acted differently"—is in fact an extremely late and subtle form of human judgment and inference.[2]

Even here, then, at the furthest extreme from Platonic idealism, the idea of giving people what they are owed is grasped as the core component of justice from which everything else is consequently derived. And in this regard,

Nietzsche's account convincingly clarifies the material origins of justice at an interpersonal level.

Overall, these basic themes in Shakespeare and the Greek writers express a kind of popular wisdom concerning the nature of justice—and such ideas remain compelling even if they cannot be specified in more detail: What, for example, is the "natural order of things" that justice represents, and how does this help us to understand anything about the nature of justice as the master virtue? How are we to understand justice as a personal virtue? Does it just mean obeying all the laws of the state, or does the deepest commitment to justice go beyond what is legally required? And is what we owe to others based on their legal rights, their needs, or what they deserve?

Thus we begin with three distinct kinds of problems concerning justice that will guide the inquiry that follows. First, justice is often considered the highest of all the virtues, or the master virtue that animates the other virtues and makes them virtues to begin with. Courage without justice really isn't courage, only empty daring, and wisdom without justice is cleverness at best. But justice itself is difficult to describe. In the *Republic*, Socrates elaborates justice in the soul with reference to the just society or the soul writ large. But the final definition of justice in book four is "minding one's business," and this conclusion is unsatisfactory. Indeed, on the face of it, minding one's business seems to be exactly wrong as a description of justice. The just person is not self-involved or afraid to question whatever is done. On the contrary, the just person is someone who is fair and who speaks up for what is right wherever injustice occurs, even when this does not involve his own private interest—like George Orwell, who joined the International Brigade to fight against fascism in the Spanish civil war, not to safeguard his own freedom but to help secure the freedom of others. Hence the first problem with justice: even if it is a master virtue, it is hard to specify since it is so exalted and encompassing. Perhaps this follows from an ambiguity at the heart of justice itself. As Aristotle noted, justice can mean both "according to the law" and "fairness."[3] To pay your taxes, to inherit a fortune or to pay what you owe is justice according to the law. But justice can also mean fairness, and some things can be just in the first sense (or legal) without being just in the second sense (or fair). Likewise, things can also be unfair and unfortunate but this doesn't always mean that they are unjust—dying young, for example, being handicapped, or (arguably) being poor. Part of the problem with justice is to specify the precise distinction between all of these different aspects.

The second set of problems involves the relationship between justice as a personal virtue and justice as a characteristic of society's laws and institutions.

It's often assumed that justice is first and foremost a characteristic of laws and institutions that concerns individuals only in a secondary sense: A judge is just if he or she follows good precedent, doesn't take bribes, and abides by the correct procedures; a citizen is just if he or she obeys the laws and minds her own business. But while there is certainly some relationship between these two levels, justice in the city is by no means the same thing as justice in the soul writ large, and it's not clear whether you could ever derive the one from the other. For example, you could have a society with just laws and institutions in which many people are simply unjust and have to be threatened or punished to ensure compliance. At the same time, good people can continue to endure even in a society whose government and laws have become corrupt and unjust. Take the case of prejudice: discrimination against minorities may be sanctioned by the laws of the state if minorities are not allowed an equal education or if they are effectively denied the right to vote or the right to marry. But public outrage at this perceived injustice, which often begins with the actions of a small group of just people, may ultimately lead to political change, which makes the society more just. Or things may go the other way, with the passing of laws against discrimination or harassment helping to change our sense of what is acceptable and not acceptable on the personal level, too, and in this way individuals become more just. We cannot deny that the two levels are connected and reciprocally affect each other. But at the same time, we cannot assume from the outset that all talk about justice as a personal virtue is a category mistake because it is held that justice is primarily a quality of laws and institutions.

The third issue concerns the content of justice and what it is that we owe to other people. There are several possibilities here, including respect for their rights, or consideration of their needs, or attention to what they deserve given their own particular merits. In what order should we rank these claims? Answering this question will involve arguing for a particular vision of the just society, and this could be a form of socialism, liberalism, libertarianism, conservatism, or communism. But the issue is complicated because each of these different philosophies interprets and evaluates basic ideas like freedom, equality, and community in very different ways.

I will proceed historically. First, an examination of three significant accounts of justice from Plato, Aristotle, and Hume. These accounts have been influential, and they are important for our purposes since they involve three different attempts to figure out the connection between justice as an individual virtue and justice as a feature of societies in general. Next, I will outline justice as a personal virtue and reflect specifically on what it means to be a just person. Finally, returning to the equation of justice in the soul and justice in the ideal society, I will consider the life of George Orwell and his commitment to social justice and democratic socialism. The just individual and the just society are difficult to separate from each other, but this does not mean that one is primary and the other is derived; in fact, both are necessary for moral progress to occur.

Philosophers on Justice

What is justice? And in what sense is it a personal virtue? Or is justice primarily an aspect of policies, laws, and institutions that transcends the individual life? In the history of Western philosophy, there have been several accounts of justice that have been influential in framing the terms of this debate. Here we will focus on Plato, Aristotle, and Hume to grasp some basic features of thinking about justice in our culture, although in each case, these accounts are ultimately associated with the defense of the status quo and a less critical point of view.

In book one of the *Republic*, Cephalus, Polemarchus, and Thrasymachus offer definitions of justice that Socrates challenges and rejects. Like most of the other early dialogues, the discussion of justice in book one is inconclusive. Cephalus is depicted as a representative of traditional religious piety. He argues that justice is just a matter of telling the truth and paying your debts; but this obviously won't do because it identifies justice with some of its legal manifestations and says nothing about its deeper meaning. Polemarchus inherits the argument, and he offers a definition, favored by the poets, that justice is giving to each what they are owed. This is an improvement on Cephalus's position, but it remains indeterminate: What do I owe my friends, for example, and especially those who are no longer in their right mind? Polemarchus's response is problematic: "friends owe it to friends to do something good and nothing bad. . . . And I suppose that an enemy owes his enemy the very thing that is also fitting: some harm."[4] As Socrates points out, this won't do because it means treating justice as if it were a particular craft in the same category as farming or medicine. Crafts can be used for good or evil; the best doctor knows all about poisons and so presumably is also best at the art of poisoning. And if the just person is best at keeping things safe, wouldn't we have to admit by analogy that he is also the best robber? The point here is that justice is not something that can be used as a means to an end. Justice doesn't depend upon our likes or dislikes, and the requirements of justice transcend our particular affections. In fact, justice cannot be used to "harm" anyone. Finally, Thrasymachus bursts on the scene complaining that Socrates has deliberately missed the most obvious point that justice is the advantage of the stronger. This means that every state has its own judicial system but there is no ultimate standard that would allow us to compare them since justice is only an effect of power. In the discussion that follows, it's easy enough for Socrates to show the inconsistency in Thrasymachus's position: whatever his professed definition of justice is, once he starts talking about justice, he can't help describing the splendid *injustice* of the rulers he supposedly admires as opposed to the high-minded innocence of those who favor justice—the rulers couldn't care less about being just. But this means that justice is not simply what the rulers say it is, but something else, which the rulers ignore, and justice returns as a human constant that cannot reasonably be denied. Socrates concludes that anything unjust is divided against itself—there is no honor among thieves—and that justice is the health of the soul.

In book two, Socrates begins to construct the ideal city in speech, using this as a proper analogy for justice within the soul. In such an ideal state, the best people will rule and everyone will be assigned their proper place within the social order. By the end of book four, the construction of the ideal city is complete, and they consider the place of wisdom, courage, temperance, and justice within the regime. Wisdom and courage are easy enough to locate in the rule of the guardians and the obedience of the auxiliaries, respectively. Temperance is not specifically a virtue of the laboring classes but involves the proper arrangement of all three orders and the agreement by each to accept their respective roles of ruling, supporting, and obeying: "We divined pretty accurately a while ago that [temperance] is like a kind of harmony . . . an accord of worse and better, according to nature, as to which must rule in the city and each one."[5] Finally Socrates comes to justice, although at this point his account is quite odd, and not particularly helpful:

> It appears, you blessed man, that it's been rolling around at our feet from the beginning and we couldn't see it after all, but were quite ridiculous. . . . Surely we set down, and often said, if you remember, that each one must practice one of the functions in the city, that one for which his nature made him naturally most fit. . . . Well, then, my friend. . . . This—the practice of minding one's own business—when it comes into being in a certain way, is probably justice.[6]

What is perplexing is that the definition of justice given above really doesn't differ that much from the definition of temperance given earlier. And this is confirmed when Socrates returns to the portrait of the just soul whose inner constitution is supposed to be analogous to that of the just city:

But in truth justice was . . . something of this sort; however, not with respect to a man's minding his external business, but with respect to what is within, with respect to what truly concerns him and his own. He doesn't let each part in him mind other people's business or the three classes in the soul meddle with each other, but really sets his own house in good order and rules himself; he arranges himself, becomes his own friend, and harmonizes the three parts, exactly like three notes in a harmonic scale, lowest, highest and middle.[7]

Once again, there is no real difference between the just soul and the temperate soul, for in each case the ideal is a proper and harmonious attunement of the different aspects of the self. I would suggest that this is precisely Plato's point, for there is no "justice" that goes beyond this ideal arrangement. Justice as the highest social virtue is really an endorsement of the most natural state of affairs, which involves the rule of the few best citizens, just as reason is meant to rule in the soul and everything has its own proper place. No just actions are prescribed for the just man or the just state, but if the soul or state is justly constituted then neither can ever do wrong. And clearly, this is to support the status quo that endorses the rule of a few good men. Some writers have emphasized the irony of the *Republic* and the self-conscious absurdity of the ideal state in which philosophers are kings and men and women exist on terms of equality; but it may well be that this is intended as a parody, which reveals Plato's own commitment to a more traditional hierarchy.

The definition of justice as minding one's business is problematic for another reason. It suggests that just men and women remain completely involved in their own private lives and don't meddle in other people's affairs or concerns. But the concern for justice is surely not a private concern. And if I am moved by the unjust treatment of slaves or women in another society then of course I am going beyond the limited horizon of my own private life and affirming my connection and involvement with others whom I have not even met. At the very end of the *Republic*, in the myth of Er, Plato describes the souls choosing from the collection of lives that are available to them as they are about to be reborn. The soul of Odysseus is the last to choose and we are told: "From memory of its former labors it had recovered from love of honor; it went around for a long time looking for the life of a private man who minds his own business; and with effort it found one lying somewhere, neglected by the others. It said when it saw this life that it would have done the same even if it had drawn the first lot, and was delighted to choose it."[8] On the one hand, this affirms the priority of philosophy over poetry and the Homeric ideal as Odysseus, one of Homer's heroes, repudiates his warrior values in favor of the quiet life endorsed by the philosopher. But at the same time, this is also a final endorsement of justice as minding one's own business—the aristocratic objective is to limit people to the narrow horizon of their lives and to affirm this in the name of justice itself. In the end, the *Republic* is much more partisan than at first is apparent.

Plato's account of justice is prescriptive, not only in terms of the ideal republic constructed in speech, but also in terms of the underlying message of minding one's business, which means accepting your place and not meddling in matters that don't concern you. Aristotle, on the other hand, disdains all reflection on the ideal state, and his comments on justice are deliberately neutral with regard to all the competing conceptions of the good society, including democracy, oligarchy, and aristocracy. In book five of the *Nicomachean Ethics*, he defines the individual virtue of justice in terms of the community interest that establishes laws and the correlative duties of citizens. Aristotle assumes that the state and its laws exist for the well-being of the community and its individual members: "The laws prescribe for all the departments of life, aiming at the common advantage either of all the citizens or of the best of them, or of the ruling class, or on some other such basis. So in one sense we call just anything that tends to produce or conserve the happiness (and the constituents of happiness) of a political association."[9] It follows by definition that the just citizen follows those laws and does whatever he is called on to promote the well-being of the community at large. And in this respect, Aristotle comments, the idea of justice may simply involve the whole of virtue insofar as it relates to others—which would include telling the truth, paying your debts, abstaining from adultery and assault, and so forth. Hence, justice is nothing other than complete virtue; it is the master virtue that includes all other virtues within itself and as the summation of virtue: "neither evening nor morning star is such a wonder."[10] In the *Republic*, Plato also used justice in this exalted and summary sense. But there is a big difference: Plato views justice as an arrangement of the individual soul that precedes all particular actions and responses to others. Aristotle emphasizes that justice concerns the whole of goodness but *only* insofar as it relates to our dealings with others. The problem for Aristotle, though, is that once he derives justice as a personal virtue from what is legally or morally required, he loses an authentic sense of justice as an independent value that would be the measure of particular societies and laws.

In fact, Aristotle argues that justice is an ambiguous term, for it is often used in a more limited sense to describe one particular virtue as opposed to all the others. Thus we wouldn't usually say that neglecting your children or being unfaithful are examples of injustice since other terms would more readily apply in these cases. Following common usage we can therefore distinguish a *particular* sense of justice, as well as injustice, and according to Aristotle, the latter may be characterized as pleonexia, which means having or wanting more than one's fair share. Aristotle puts it this way:

> In all other cases the person who does wrong gains no advantage from his misconduct: e.g. the man who through cowardice throws away his shield, or through bad temper uses abusive language. . . . But when a man takes more than is his share, although he is often actuated by none. . . . of these vices, yet what actuates him is certainly some kind of wickedness (because we blame it) viz., injustice. Therefore there is another kind of injustice which is a part of universal injustice, and there is a kind of "unjust" which is a part of the unjust in general which means "contrary to the law."[11]

The unjust man in the particular sense is a greedy individual who will want to get more than he is entitled to. But Aristotle is deliberately silent as to the question of what my fair share is. He discusses general principles of distributive and corrective justice, but for the most part his account is purely descriptive. In the following comment, for example, he is completely non-committal: "Everyone agrees that justice in distribution must be in accordance with merit in some sense, but they do not all mean the same kind of merit: the democratic view is that the criterion is free birth; the oligarchic that it is wealth or good family; the aristocratic that it is excellence."[12]

Aristotle gives the example of two men who commit adultery. The first does it in order to make money, whereas the second is merely gratifying an unlawful passion. Both men are performing similar actions, but Aristotle argues only the first is unjust because his motive is the desire for unlawful gain, whereas the second is licentious rather than grasping. Other examples are given, but, following Bernard Williams, we should ask whether this desire for gain really could be the motive for every case of particular injustice?[13] For example, a teacher would be unjust in not assigning proper grades out of sheer laziness, and a judge would be unjust if she personally disliked the defendant and decided the case on that basis. In neither of these examples are we dealing with an overweening desire for gain, and yet they are clearly examples of particular injustice. We could more reasonably say that the core of injustice is selfishness and involves self-assertion and an insistence on our own desires even when this means disregarding others and their legitimate claims. It involves not taking the claims of others seriously, or making their legitimate claims secondary to our own selfish pursuits.

Aristotle's account of justice in the *Nicomachean Ethics* is sometimes difficult and fragmentary in character, and there is no unifying perspective that holds the discussion together to show how each part fits into the whole. Also, much of book five is taken up with a formal discussion of corrective and distributive justice, which are less directly related to the nature of justice as a personal virtue. For the most part, Aristotle avoids substantial comments on the nature of the just society. He equates the virtue of justice with adherence to proper proportion: justice consists in treating equals equally and unequals unequally, in proportion to their inequality. But once again, this account remains abstract because he doesn't say what these proportions should be.

In short, Aristotle doesn't give us an account of justice as a personal virtue in any strong sense, but only as a quality that is derived from the existing social order. For Aristotle, being just means being disposed to respect the laws and existing social arrangements as they happen to exist. This may be a valid discussion of the good citizen, but it is not a good account of the just man. He even seems to admit this when he comments, "presumably it is not always the same thing to be a good man and a good citizen."[14] As we have seen, Aristotle is concerned with the difference between justice and equity, and suggests that the latter, which we would think of as fairness, is a necessary supplement to the legal framework that is the basis of justice. But he could quite easily have given us a description of personal justice. Following his discussion of the other virtues, he might have said that the just person is one who is angered by acts of injustice; a just person is careful never to take more than his fair share, but he will also try to help others who have suffered injustice by doing whatever he can to make things right, even if he doesn't know them. Similarly the just man is tolerant of others' views and, like Socrates, he doesn't care about making a nuisance of himself if he feels that an action or a policy is unjustified or unfair.

Finally, though, if we return to Aristotle's point that particular injustice involves grasping or taking more than one's fair share, it seems reasonable to say that from this perspective, justice requires a comparative lack of concern for material goods and a focus on other things—such as the good of the community—as more important and worth pursuing. The unjust person is always seeking more, and this impulse may spill over into unjust actions since he or she is not as committed to the overall good of the community as the most important thing. Later, in the *Politics*, Aristotle complains that the community suffers when money is pursued for its own sake and huge fortunes are amassed. This implies the end of reciprocity and so it is a threat to the justice of the state:

Besides, those who have exceedingly good fortune—strength, wealth, friends and so on—neither wish nor know how to submit to being ruled—indeed, this begins even when they are children at home, since their luxurious upbringing makes them unused to being ruled even at school. On the other hand, the exceedingly needy are excessively abased. And so the needy do not know how to rule but only how to submit to being ruled as slaves, while the fortunate do not know how to submit to any kind of rule but only how to rule as masters over slaves. The result is a city of masters and slaves, not of free citizens, and, moreover, of slaves looking spitefully on their masters and of masters despising their slaves. And this is the furthest of all from friendship and a political community. For community involves friendship; people are unwilling even to share the road with their enemies.[15]

Aristotle concludes that a city benefits by not having such extremes of wealth; we might add that a sense of personal justice is only weakened when there is an undue focus on property relations, whereas another social arrangement, in which the accumulation of property and capital was not so central, would be more just and would also promote personal justice to a much greater extent. The last point is very relevant to David Hume, who restricts considerations of justice almost entirely to the question of property and thereby avoids the deeper problems concerning justice. But Hume, unlike Aristotle, does consider the origins of justice within the individual soul.

David Hume is preoccupied with the psychological origins of the virtue of justice. In human society, people are typically motivated by a strong sense of justice. They feel it is really important to do the right thing and to act in accordance with what justice requires, even though, as sometimes happens, particular determinations of justice actually lead to a negative outcome for the individual or for society in general. The law of inheritance, for example, is a very significant part of our system of laws regarding property. But this means that a wretched person who is already very rich can inherit a fortune while people around him continue to starve. As Hume puts it: "Riches inherited from a parent are in a bad man's hand the instrument of mischief. The right of succession may, in one instance, be hurtful."[16] And again, "When a man of merit, of a beneficent disposition, restores a great fortune to a miser, or a seditious bigot, he has acted justly and laudably, but the public is a real sufferer."[17] These are good examples because they suggest that our concern for justice is not simply based on selfishness—presumably many people would repay a debt even if they could somehow avoid it—but neither is it derived from natural affection or benevolence, for in these examples the outcome is one that conflicts with our sympathies. In A *Treatise of Human Nature*, Hume concludes that justice must be an acquired artificial virtue since it is not a natural sentiment or feeling. In the *Inquiry Concerning the Principles of Morals*, he argues that justice is based on its contribution to public utility—by which he means whatever promotes the interests of humanity, including fellow-feeling, harmony, order, and prosperity—and this is something that has to be learned.

To defend his theory in the *Inquiry*, Hume imagines five extreme situations that would show how justice is grounded in utility because at the very point where justice becomes useless it is no longer binding. This is an intriguing set of thought experiments that also says a lot about Hume's vision of justice. First, he imagines a situation of complete abundance in which "every individual finds himself fully provided with whatever his most voracious appetites can want, or luxurious imagination wish or desire."[18] But in such a situation where there is no scarcity, Hume argues that justice would be useless. No one would insist on having his own property since there would be more than enough for everyone: "Why call this object *mine*, when upon the seizing of it by another, I need but stretch out my hand to possess myself to what is equally valuable?"[19] Hume comments that this situation already exists with regard to air or water, because they are (usually) so plentiful they don't have to belong to anyone: "Justice in that case, being totally useless, would be an idle ceremonial, and could never possibly have place in the catalogue of virtues."[20] The problem with this example is Hume's narrow concern with property relations as the entire focus of justice. He seems to think that without private property justice would be irrelevant since justice is first and foremost the legitimation of property. But what of human rights and entitlements, including liberty, which go beyond property considerations? There are other ways of hurting someone than by taking away what they own. Likewise Hume thinks of justice as the principle that legitimates the distribution of property. But there is no argument to show that such a distribution or property system must be fair before it can receive a legal endorsement. Hume simply assumes that with regard to property, whatever is is right.

The second thought experiment concerns a society in which people are filled with love for their fellow human beings. "Again; suppose, that, though the necessities of the human race continue the same as at present, yet the mind is so enlarged, and so replete with friendship and generosity, that every man has the utmost tenderness for every man, and feels no more concerned for his own interest than for that of his fellows."[21] Hume comments that such a situation may periodically exist in Utopian communities, although the upsurge of benevolence and fellow-feeling usually doesn't last since it derives from an enthusiasm that isn't natural. In such a society, justice becomes irrelevant because everyone would naturally do everything they could for their fellow citizens—they wouldn't need to feel obligated because they would already be motivated out of love. Now perhaps this mutual benevolence rules in families, where insisting on a child's right to a good upbringing is usually irrelevant since the parents naturally want to do all they can for their child. What this emphasizes, however, is the relationship between virtue and love. We need justice because our affections are weak and sometimes we are selfish. In an imperfect world justice is the substitute for love.

The third case is the reverse of the second: "Suppose a society to fall into such want of all common necessaries, that the utmost frugality and industry cannot preserve the greater number from perishing, and the whole from extreme misery."[22] In this situation, Hume argues that the rules of justice would once again be useless because the goal of justice—which is to preserve order and happiness—would be superseded by the stronger motive of self-preservation. In such an extreme situation, people would disregard the ordinary rules of justice concerning property. As proof of this, Hume points out that in these extreme cases, magistrates may throw open private granaries and stocks of food for the public. "But where the society is ready to perish from extreme necessity, no greater evil can be dreaded from violence and injustice; and every man may now provide for himself by all the means, which prudence can dictate, or humanity permit."[23] Hume doesn't specify what these requirements of "humanity" are, but we wish that he had. As it stands, the argument seems to be that when society breaks down, things revert to the underlying need for self-preservation that society is founded on in the first place.

In Elie Wiesel's memoir, *Night*, the block captain tells the prisoners that in Auschwitz all human decency and concern is at an end. The prisoners have nothing except what they can get, and their lives can be snuffed out at any moment. "Don't forget that you're in a concentration camp. Here, every man has to fight for himself and not to think of anyone else. Even of his father. Here, there are no fathers, no brothers, no friends. Everyone lives and dies for himself alone."[24] The interesting thing is that even here in the camps, there is a society of mutual concern that exists between prisoners. Elie Wiesel never abandons his father and does all he can to help him to survive. There are many other stories like this where the extreme situation, like Auschwitz, did not involve the end of personal justice. And this suggests that personal justice or fairness between people may actually be based on something deeper than public utility.

The fourth case is more chilling. Imagine a society in which human beings and some other species of creatures lived side-by-side, but although the latter creatures are rational they are of inferior strength. Hume argues that in this situation we may choose to treat the other creatures kindly but we are under no obligation of justice toward them: "Nor could they possess any right or property, exclusive of such arbitrary lords."[25] According to Hume, justice is useless here because of the great inequality between the two species: "the restraints of justice and property, being totally *useless*, would never have place in so unequal a confederacy."[26] He goes on to talk about our relationship to animals and the relations between civilized Europeans and "barbarous" Indians, as examples of what he's talking about. In this case, Hume seems to assume that established might makes right and justice may ultimately be the advantage of the stronger, as Thrasymachus once claimed. But this seems deeply wrong. The whole point of justice is to ensure that both the strong and the weak are treated fairly and with due regard. A situation where only the privileged species, race, or sex had rights would be completely unjust on the face of it, and only a cynic would say that in such a situation justice was not necessary.

Finally, Hume points out that if each individual were solitary and completely self-sufficient for his own propagation and preservation, then justice would be a pointless consideration. Hume is right on this point: since justice is a social virtue, it orders the relationships between human beings; it's not clear how justice could be relevant to a solitary creature who felt no sense of sympathy or involvement with others. But we are not like this. Human beings are social creatures, and they can only experience fulfillment through interaction, cooperation, and involvement with others; and the circle of concern that sustains us begins with the family and extends along with our sympathy to include the clan, society, and presumably the whole of humankind: "History, experience, reason sufficiently instructs us in this natural progress of human sentiments and in the gradual enlargement of our regards to justice, in proportion as we become acquainted with the extensive utility of that virtue."[27] This would certainly reflect the modern progress toward a concern for international human rights and the idea that we have duties and obligations to poorer people in the world and especially those who were originally enslaved or colonized by our ancestors. But it would also call into question Hume's previous example that implied that justice is beside the point when the disparity between one group and another is extreme.

What is implicit in most of these examples, but which only becomes explicit in the second part of his chapter on justice, is Hume's very conservative and for the most part uncritical attitude toward private property. From his essay, it would appear that the main function of justice is to preserve property relations. Not because these are just—except I think that for him they are just by definition—but because they are the property relations that we have and to undermine or question these in any way would be to call the established order into question, which would be unsettling to everyone. Thus when Hume considers the idea of property, he emphasizes what a completely unnatural and abstract idea it is. Our concept of property is a complex and overdetermined idea involving the right of first possession, the right of inheritance, the right of primogeniture, the right of industry, the right of contract, and so forth: "What is a man's property? Anything which it is lawful for him, and for him alone, to use. But what rules have we, by which we can distinguish these objects? Here we must have recourse to statutes, customs, precedents, analogies, and a hundred other circumstances; some of which are constant and inflexible, some variable and arbitrary."[28] But there is no natural right to property. There are just settled conventions that every society has for deciding these issues, and these differ from one society to the next. Hume's point is that justice requires that whatever rules exist must be upheld for the good of the community in general. But he fully admits these rules are arbitrary. In fact the only society he doesn't seem willing to tolerate would be a society of complete equality of property, as may have existed in Sparta or elsewhere. He argues that in such a society the virtues of industry and freedom would be seriously threatened:

> Render possessions ever so equal, men's different degrees of art, care, and industry will immediately break that equality. Or if you check these virtues, you reduce society to the most extreme indigence; and, instead of preventing want and beggary in a few, render it unavoidable to the whole community. . . . Perfect equality of possessions, destroying all subordination, weakens extremely the authority of magistracy and must reduce all power nearly to a level, as well as property.[29]

But it's not clear that Hume is entitled to make these arguments, and certainly if a society of such complete equality ever existed, where personal property was spurned, he would have no way of condemning it especially if it seemed to advance the well-being of the population. Apart from this one example, however, Hume does not offer a criticism of particular laws or property relations in terms of justice. He has no way of distinguishing good and bad laws, arguing only that whatever laws do exist should be supported since they promote utility.

Hume's discussion of justice is helpful insofar as it describes the complexity of this phenomenon. He shows very clearly how all the attempts to reduce justice to a single principle, such as selfishness, natural altruism, or reason, are bound to fail; and while his own derivation of justice is not without its problems, the overdetermined idea of utility advances the argument considerably. The biggest problem with Hume's account comes from his focus on property as the primary domain of justice. Not only does he neglect other aspects of justice, but in trying to justify the current institution of property, he adopts a conservative point of view that endorses the status quo. At no point does he ask whether particular laws are fair or unfair and at no time does he question whether the whole system is fair or unfair (as opposed to being fair by definition). Hume seems to believe that there is no justice before the institution of justice as a legal form, and this means that it is difficult to criticize particular laws for being unjust. But the fact is, we do criticize our laws as unjust or unfair, and one likely explanation for this is that we have a natural sense of fairness. If a child has something that is taken away by someone else, both he and others would regard it as deeply unfair. Likewise, revenge or the desire to retaliate is most likely one of the original motives behind justice, but it is also an expression of our natural sense of fairness. Someone hurts us and we lash out in response, but this is not a response that we have to learn; in fact in the interests of conventional justice we may have to unlearn it. The advantage of a natural sense of fairness is that it allows us to criticize the justice of policies, laws, and institutions from another level. Our natural sense of fairness may certainly be shaped and affected by justice at the level of society, but it's certainly not conditioned or determined by it. This creates the space for a strong sense of justice as a personal virtue that must be considered separately and for itself

In the history of philosophy, Hume is actually a high point as far as justice as a virtue is concerned. For Hume, justice is an original and important motive for human actions. The desire to act out of duty or because justice requires it isn't secondary even if it's derived from some other set of motives. Hume also argues for the primacy of natural virtues, like benevolence and sympathy, and, significantly, he does not try to uphold the laws or the social structure as the primary ground of justice with individual virtue as its reflected impression. By contrast, John Rawls outlines his philosophical investigation of justice in his essay "Justice as Fairness": "Throughout, I consider justice only as a virtue of social institutions, or what I shall call practices. The principles of justice are regarded as formulating restrictions as to how practices may define positions and opposites, and assigned there are two powers and liabilities, the rights and duties. Justice as a virtue of particular actions or of persons I do not take up at all." But then he adds, "I shall confine my discussion to the sense of justice as applied to practices, since this sense is the basic one. Once it is understood, the other senses should go quite easily."[30] More recent theorists of justice go even further. Rational choice theory, for example, is meant to show the rational necessity of justice as a binding system regardless of individual desires or virtues—for just as long as the law is upheld it does not matter whether this is done willingly, grudgingly, or indifferently.[31] The reconsideration of justice as a strong personal virtue would be to reverse this tendency and give us another point of view for criticizing social arrangements.

Justice as a Personal Virtue

It is the ruling consensus of contemporary social and political theory that individual virtues, including a personal sense of justice, are largely irrelevant to the just society itself. According to this perspective, we should not legislate goodness or support only one particular conception of the good life; we must rather create a system of justice with the necessary rules and procedures that would allow individuals to pursue their own ideas of virtue and living well so long as they don't impose their views on others who decide to pursue virtue in different ways. The final outcome of this whole tendency of thinking would be that justice as a personal virtue is now redundant. It is rather a secondary phenomenon that can be bypassed in favor of the primary manifestation of justice in the overall order of society itself.

I believe this view is mistaken for several reasons. First, we obviously need the individual perspective of justice as fairness in order to criticize the determinations of justice at the higher levels of society. The laws, the policies, and the institutions may simply be unfair and must be criticized accordingly. But if justice as a personal virtue is completely derived from the order of justice in society itself, then there is no way that the first could ever be used to criticize the second. Obviously, there is some relationship between the different levels, but it's one of influence and reciprocity rather than complete determination. A legal decision like that of *Brown vs. Board of Education of Topeka, Kansas* (1954) establishes the law of the land and outlaws racial segregation in American schools; a law is passed by one of the states declaring that gay marriage is without any legal foundation; the country declares war against a foreign power—only a personal sense of justice can allow us to criticize or support these decisions as just or unjust, and this implies a primary manifestation of justice that is finally irreducible to the laws of the land. Our own sense of personal fairness can also be shaped by the determination of the law; making racial discrimination illegal probably caused a lot of people to re-examine their racial prejudices. But this is to underline the fact that jus-

tice at the level of the individual and justice at the level of society are reciprocally related without being reducible to each other.

This leads to the second point that the just society needs people who are
actively just. This is what Rousseau realized in his account of the social contract, and this is what Plato emphasized in his discussion of the *Republic*. For
justice to prevail anywhere, it's not enough to have a perfect legal system or
a set of correct policies in place, for even if the laws are just, it doesn't follow
that the people are just or that they will become just in the course of time.
To achieve the latter, training in personal justice is necessary, and this is why
Plato devotes so much of the *Republic* to the education of the guardians,
which he describes in great detail. The citizens must be diligent or the best
laws will become corrupted; but once again, they can only recognize corruption insofar as they don't identify fairness with whatever the laws require.

The third point involves our admiration of those who struggle for justice
in the world, often against impossible odds. We celebrate those who have in
some way devoted their lives to justice: Nelson Mandela, who refused to give
up his fight against the apartheid society in South Africa and who spent 30
years in prison, many of them in solitary confinement; Ken Sara-Wiwa, who
was hanged in 1995 for his outspoken criticism of mining practices in Nigeria and their effect on the local population; George Orwell and others, who
went to Spain to fight against fascism and for the freedom of people they
didn't even know. We celebrate these heroes who were devoted to justice, as
individual exemplars of virtue whose lives are worthy of imitation. And we
recognize their achievement even if we don't believe that we would be able
to do the same as they did. The important point is the compelling power of
justice as a personal virtue in each of these different lives—mere abstract
principles wouldn't move us so profoundly—and this suggests, once again,
that the two different levels of justice must be viewed as separate even
though they reciprocally enhance each other.

Now it could be argued that the exemplary individuals we have just
considered—Mandela, Sara-Wiwa, Orwell—are moral heroes whose lives
are not models that everyone could be expected to follow. Hence justice
may be a significant presence in the lives of those who are committed to
overcoming oppression and social evil, but it may be urged that it's not an
ordinary virtue in the same sense that we usually require justice in everyday life. Of course, there may be a point where we have to decide whether
to be just or not—whether to return something we found or to refuse a
bribe, for instance—but for the most part, justice doesn't concern us as long
as we do what we are supposed to do and avoid the temptations of injustice. I think this view is mistaken, and in the next few pages, I want to de-

scribe the possibility of justice as a personal virtue as it exists on different levels. Using broad strokes, my aim is to outline a sense of justice as fairness and to show how it operates in the individual's life. We are not dealing with justice as an exalted ideal that stands opposed to everyday life, but justice as fairness as this occurs in ordinary relationships between people— in the parent-child relationship, for example, in the teacher-student relationship, or in the relationship between friends or between people who have been friends, and who ask what they still owe to each other. There are at least three different levels that have to be distinguished.

First, and most basic of all, justice is simply the opposite of injustice; if stealing and killing are unjust actions then it follows that not doing these things is to be just. Following Cephalus, you should tell the truth and pay your debts. But this legal account of personal justice isn't profound, and it isn't clear that someone could be called virtuous and just in any strong sense if all they did was to follow the rules and avoid wrongdoing. The second level of justice as a personal virtue involves fulfilling difficult commitments; being fair with other people and treating them equally insofar as this is appropriate; not relaxing our principles for the sake of what is convenient; and doing the right thing even when this would involve some personal cost. This is justice as an active virtue that involves conscientiousness and the proper measure of devotion to principle. I will examine this active determination of justice as a personal virtue that is based on what we owe to others. Then I will return to the exceptional individuals whose lives involve a commitment to justice and a willingness to speak out against injustice and oppression wherever they occur. This is the third aspect of justice as a personal virtue, and unlike the other two levels, it does not begin with what I owe to others, since it is focused on others and is concerned with what they deserve or need, regardless of my own relationship to them.

One way to begin thinking about justice as an individual virtue would be to examine a particular exemplar or model of justice and then use this as the starting point for a more sustained critical reflection. Let us consider the example of a good judge: such an individual is the very embodiment of justice. He or she is completely impartial and not swayed by emotion, financial reward, personal likes and dislikes, or anything except devotion to the law and its principles. Moreover, the good judge actively cares about justice and strives to see it done so that everyone receives what they deserve. In this respect, being a judge isn't a job like any other that could be done mechanically, lazily, or a without any real involvement. In every way, the good judge is committed to the cause of justice and must put aside, so far as this is possible, all personal interests and desires that would affect her judgment. There is much that is relevant in this model. A just person values being objective and impartial and doesn't play favorites when this would be unfair. As a parent, for example, I owe my children equal consideration and equal treatment; any kind of favoritism would be unjust. As a teacher, I owe it to my students to be impartial and hold them all to the same standard. But there are some things that I owe my children that I don't owe to my students. At the personal level of justice, we are concerned with giving others what we owe them or what they deserve not only in the strictly legal sense of their entitlements as human beings, but also with regard to particular claims that emerge in the context of our everyday relationships with them. Thus it matters that the student deserved an A for his work; the friend deserved another chance; the waiter deserved a big tip for all his help—and the just person, like the judge, is one who is especially mindful of these kinds of considerations, doing everything she can to ensure that she gives other people what they deserve even when this might be difficult. There is no single formula here, as there would be in the case of legal rights, but even at this level, the virtue of justice involves a commitment to a set of principles that underlie our dealings in the world. The just person has reflected on these principles. She is certainly not a slave to principles, but she is prepared to stand by them for as long as they are not proved wrong. This may involve speaking out—for if someone makes a joke about gays or women that is against the individual's beliefs then it would not be just to remain silent. It may involve some kind of action, like joining a protest if the issue is one that is considered important enough, or leaving a lucrative career in a company involved in practices that one deeply disapproves of.

We can say that personal justice on this level is composed of different elements. On the one hand, it involves being very conscientious in dealing with other people and implies a commitment to one's principles that results in action regardless of personal difficulty; but it also involves awareness of the particular situation and a considered evaluation of what is appropriate in any given case. Thus your children deserve different things from you than your students do. You owe consideration to strangers, but you owe much more than consideration to your friends.

Let us consider some of the forms of conscientiousness that constitute personal justice. First, there is honesty, in the sense of a commitment to the truth. It is hard to believe that a student has cheated on a test, and we may try to convince ourselves that we must be mistaken or that it doesn't really matter. But such attempted self-deception is only to make things easier for ourselves. Justice and our commitment to the rules of due process require that we investigate the matter and fail the student if we have to. Likewise, there is consistency: If we really believe that dishonesty is wrong, then we should do something about it whenever we come across it, and we shouldn't be selective about who we confront because we like one person but not another, or feel intimidated by the first person but not the second. In the same way, there is something wrong with legal justice if it is only selectively applied, or if being wealthy allows someone to avoid a prison sentence that would be standard for most people. A commitment to personal justice also involves a desire to discover the correct principles that should govern our dealings with others; it implies openness and a corresponding tolerance for other points of view. It's not enough just to have a rule or a policy that one never deviates from, such as "never being kind to children." This may be an example of consistency, but since it's not a good rule, anyone who adheres to it is not a just person. Likewise, the cultivation of justice as a personal virtue does not involve being a slave to principles or having a fixed set of principles that one applies unreflectively to every situation. In fact, being involved with others will require a frequent challenge to personal principles as we encounter people with different values and principles that we may not initially accept or agree with. A fundamentalist who is deeply committed to traditional beliefs about right and wrong must deal with the child who has decided to come out as gay or lesbian. In this case, a commitment to personal justice doesn't have to involve despising one's child for the sake of one's principles; it should lead one to reconsider those convictions because of the love that one has for one's children.

Returning to the analogy of the judge, however, it has to be said that the judge is typically a distant figure who is supposed to be above and beyond the particular circumstances of the case she is trying. If she admits to any kind of interest or involvement she is allowed to recuse herself. The ideal of the judge emphasizes impersonality and self-overcoming for the sake of justice itself. It also places the very highest value on acting for the sake of principle. Now this is probably not a good model for personal relationships and dealing justly with others. At a personal level, I would say that justice involves caring about other people. It is not disinterested but sometimes even passionately committed; it is important to the just person that people get what they deserve from her, not because of her devotion to an impersonal principle of justice that could be automatic or grudging, but because she values other people and respects them as individual subjects who should be treated with all due consideration. Justice as a virtue concerns our personal relationships with others, and this implies involvement with other people and caring about what they deserve as the subjects of their own lives. The model of the judge is not appropriate here, since it implies remoteness from everyday life and a lack of personal involvement with those one is concerned with. It also suggests that the judge is merely the agent of an impersonal legal necessity that is working through her; and this denies the personal involvement and emotional attachment to justice that exists in the first place because we care about others.

To summarize, justice involves a real commitment to principles and people, which is affirmed by speaking out for whatever is right, even when this may be difficult or inconvenient, and by taking action when words are not enough. So far we have reflected on justice as a personal virtue that one must cultivate in personal dealings with others. The goal of personal justice in this context is always to give people what you owe them, and this involves fairness as the careful attention to justified principles. But this limited concern for one's own debts and obligations is not enough. For even if every debt was paid and every obligation was discharged, there would still be a huge number of people who would not have what they deserve. If we wait for those who are responsible to give the oppressed what they owe them, we will probably be waiting forever.

There are some people, however, whose attention and concern for justice goes beyond their own personal sphere. People like Harriet Tubman, the Trocmes, or Frederick Douglass, who focus not so much on what they personally owe to others but on what other people deserve. This unselfish concern for the well-being of others represents the highest expression of justice as an individual virtue. Take the case of Frederick Douglass: Frederick Douglass was brought up as a slave in the first part of the nineteenth century. Unlike many others who were made to accept their situation as a part of the natural order of things, he came to understand the injustice of his life as a slave, and eventually he was able to escape. Once he made his escape, however, he didn't settle down to enjoy his hard-won freedom and his own private life, but he became an important speaker for the abolitionist cause and dedicated his life to securing the freedom of slaves in all the Southern states. When the Civil War ended, slavery was repealed, but Douglass still continued to fight for the freedom of others, and he became a strong advocate of women's suffrage. The point is, he devoted his whole life to justice, and he viewed all the different kinds of oppression as essentially related to each other. And once he gained his own personal freedom, he continued to fight against injustice even though he was not in any way responsible for it. The focus of his concern with justice was not so much on his own obligations to others but on what other people deserved as human beings. A complete understanding of justice as a personal virtue must include some reference to this standpoint.

It is sometimes said that we are all responsible for each other, and our obligations to other people are therefore without limit. The parable of the Good Samaritan, for instance, may be viewed as an example of giving help that goes beyond what is expected or required: Since the victim was not a Samaritan and the Samaritan had never met the victim, he wasn't expected to help. But the Samaritan felt a deep obligation to assist the man who had been beaten by robbers, and even though he wasn't responsible for this situation, he felt that he had to help him. In this case, obligation was determined by need, and justice involved a response that went beyond paying one's own particular debts. Usually we dwell in the limited sphere of our own personal duties to friends and fellow citizens whose lives intersect with our own, and we try to be fair and just at this level. The deepest commitment to justice, however, would seem to involve an active commitment to other people, like the man left beaten on the side of the road, or the dispossessed in any community, who have been unfairly or unjustly served regardless of who is ultimately responsible. Hence the examples of Frederick Douglass, who fought for the just cause of abolition even after he had won his own freedom, or George Orwell, an Englishman, who risked his own life to fight for the freedom of people in Spain and against the injustice of fascism. In this way, the most complete commitment to justice as a personal virtue leads to a concern with social justice and what other people deserve.

We can now continue the description of justice as a virtue by showing how the theory and practice of social justice can come together in a single life. My example will be the writer George Orwell who lived through the economic misery of the 1930s and protested existing social conditions in works like *The Road to Wigan Pier* and *Down and Out in Paris and London*. Orwell came to loathe his privileged background and rejected imperialism as the most obvious form of injustice. He fought in the Spanish Civil War as an antifascist, and he wrote *Animal Farm* and *1984* against totalitarianism, which destroyed individual freedom in the name of the collective good. Orwell was a democratic socialist, and he became a self-consciously political writer, completely committed to the underlying values of liberty, equality, and fraternity, which are the essential aspects of any radical theory of justice. I will consider the basic meaning of these values and their relation to each other, and then I will show how Orwell remained committed to these values both in his life and in his writings. In this respect he demonstrates how justice as a personal virtue may involve an active concern for other people who suffer unfairly through no fault of their own, as well as an attempt to redress this wrong even at the cost of one's own life.

A Commitment to Social Justice

We can begin with two questions: What is social justice, and what do the supporters of social justice want? The first question is the more difficult one to answer, since there are so many different varieties of radical thought, including egalitarianism, democratic and welfare socialism, anarchism, and Marxism. These groups frequently disagree on tactics, whether violence is ever justified in support of social justice, and whether the ideal society of the future represents a complete break with society as we know it, or involves a progressive transformation of it. In response to the second question, however, I think there would be more agreement, that those who affirm the cause of social justice want a world in which it is possible for everyone to have the best life that it is possible for human beings to have; where the life of everyone matters and everyone matters equally. Hence a world without the hierarchy of classes that severely restricts the possibilities of life for most people, and a world without racism, sexism, and homophobia. It would be a world in which people have a sense of the common good of society and a commitment to the community that supports them, and in which people are free to pursue their own significant life goals because they are not otherwise constrained by economic or cultural forces that require them to serve the needs of others. As things stand, such a world is still a long way off, but it inspires an ideal of social justice that Orwell and many others subscribe to.

Now there is a huge temptation to say that all of this is irrelevant, given the global domination of capitalism with its international markets and multinational corporations affecting the lives of almost everyone on the planet. Likewise it will be said that radical philosophies like socialism simply don't work, and the collapse of the Soviet Union and other former communist states is evidence that capitalism has prevailed as the most efficient system of production and exchange, and there is no reasonable alternative to it. In response we would have to point out that even with globalization steadily increasing, things are getting worse for most people in the world. Thirty million people die of hunger every year, and 800 million live in extreme poverty. The richest one-fifth of the world has well over 90% of the world's income while the poorest one-fifth has only 0.25%. Indeed, the three richest men in the world own as much as the poorest 600 million people combined. Of the 6 billion inhabitants of the planet, barely 500 million live in comfort or anything like it, leaving the rest—the majority of the world's population—in continual distress and need.[32]

What can we do about these distressing statistics and others like them, which reflect the misery of so many individual lives wasted, cut short, or unfulfilled? We all know that "life is unfair," but we would have to say that the situation is also unjust, and anyone who is concerned with social justice should try to change things for the better, either by acting in a limited local way or by working for a more fundamental change in society itself. For in this case, "ought implies can," and to believe that things should be improved implies that one is opposed to any concept of historical necessity, whether this takes the form of global capitalism or communism as the inevitable shape of the future. In what follows, I will not try to defend any particular radical perspective, nor will I propose the blueprint of an ideal society that we can work toward. Rather, I will view socialism in its ethical sense as an outstanding example of the commitment to social justice. George Orwell's understanding of socialism may seem outdated now, since he was primarily concerned with England and Europe in the 1930s, but his life and work involve a commitment to social justice, and it remains an inspiring example for our own very different time.

There are many writers who could be described as "ethical socialists," including Robert Owen, Proudhon, Fourier, Bernstein, and George Orwell. In opposition to Karl Marx, one thing they all have in common is their rejection of the historical inevitability of socialism. For Orwell and all the others, socialism is morally necessary since it is the most obvious manifestation of freedom, justice, and equality. But socialism is not historically necessary—as Orwell puts it, the triumph of Hitler proved that nothing is historically inevitable—and this means that the success or failure of socialism must be more closely tied to the moral character and policies of those who support it. Karl Marx believed that revolutionary violence was inevitable since those in power will never voluntarily relinquish their position, and he viewed the future communist society as the redemption of the nightmare of history that we have had hitherto. But the ethical socialist remains suspicious of an absolute break between the present situation and the future ideal: using violence to end violence or to achieve freedom is problematic, and the experience of the Soviet Union suggests that the revolutionary society that is thereby created will remain violent and opposed to individual freedom.

Marx never emphasizes values, and he does not present himself as an ethical philosopher, partly because he sees values as derivative of the status quo, and partly because he remains deeply suspicious of whatever values are presented as eternal and unchanging. And yet, there is a moral thrust that runs throughout his writings, and the values that he does adhere to are ultimately the same values that the ethical socialist makes explicit. These values can be summarized in terms of the triad of "liberty, equality, and fraternity," and they are the constitutive values of socialism itself. There is both a conceptual and a historical priority to liberty, equality, and fraternity in the reflective understanding of socialism, and we can briefly clarify these values before examining how Orwell uses them in his own work.

First, liberty: In *The Communist Manifesto* and elsewhere, Marx argues that the bourgeois liberal version of freedom is secondary and derived. Certainly, the freedom to vote, the freedom to get a job and the freedom to worship are all significant aspects of individual liberty. But underlying all of these particular liberties is the positive conception of freedom as autonomy or self-determination. True freedom is not just the negative liberty from interference that liberals uphold, but rather, it means being in charge of your own life and being in a position to fulfill your highest potential as a human being. Hence, I am not free if I am uneducated, or unable to afford healthcare, or if I am forced to work long hours just in order to live. I may be entitled to vote, or buy things, or even refuse my labor, but these particular liberties are meaningless and beside the point if I am simply not in a position to cultivate my own human powers because of poverty or prejudice, the lack of education, or some other social handicap.

The liberal notion of equality is affirmed by Kant and other moral philosophers who recognize the moral equivalence of all human beings: Every human being is worthy of respect, and we should not treat others just as a means to our own ends. Once again, however, the socialist understanding of equality involves both a deepening and a clarification of this insight. The point is that true equality requires equal consideration of needs and interests: no one's basic needs are any more or less important than anyone else's, and no one's interests should be taken more or less seriously than those of other people. In a state of nature human beings are basically equal. Some are stronger than others and some have special talents, but all are mortal and even the strongest and most talented people are vulnerable when they are asleep. Following this line of thought, the great inequalities that exist between human beings in our society are not the consequence of natural inequalities that are somehow unavoidable, but the result of social conventions. The question then becomes whether any of these social inequalities can be justified in terms of the common good or some other acceptable measure. The goal of socialism is to remove the unjustifiable inequalities, including the vast inequalities of wealth that typically exist in a capitalist society, and to create a world in which everyone can have the best life that it is possible for human beings to have.

Finally, fraternity is the positive value of community, and it involves the sense of belonging to a society that accepts and affirms each person as a full participant in meaningful projects and practices that transcend the individual life. Marx argues that under capitalism the stress on individual advance-ment and survival has reduced society to a mere collection of individuals who are all absorbed in their own selfish lives—they can only relate indiffer-ently to each other or with hostility as competitors. Hence the negative and atomistic quality of modern life; and hence the socialist desire to instill an authentic sense of community that would enhance our existence by giving us a sense of belonging to something that is real and greater than we are—or the fulfillment of our "species being."

Now it must be allowed that from the socialist perspective, liberty, equal-ity, and fraternity are not completely separable values that can be ranked or ordered in a hierarchy from the most to the least important. Among social-ists at least, there is recognition of the interplay between these different val-ues and the way in which they involve and connect with each other. As Or-well points out, for as long as there are gross inequalities in society, people will never feel a sense of solidarity or belonging to the same social project, for equality is the condition for fraternity or community with others. Hence the importance of apprehending these values in relation to each other and cultivating each of them in a way that best harmonizes with the other two. Or since freedom without equality makes no sense and fraternity without lib-erty is seriously flawed, it may be the case that what we are concerned with here is just *one* value and the creative tension between its different aspects. I suggest that what we are talking about is the ideal of justice, which has these three ineliminable aspects.

With all of this in mind, let us now move directly to George Orwell. Or-well was not a doctrinaire socialist, and he associated socialist theory with the alienated middle class. On the other hand, he viewed socialism as com-mon sense and the expression of basic moral decency; as he wrote in a pref-ace to *Animal Farm*, "I became pro-Socialist more out of disgust with the way the poorer section of the industrial workers were oppressed and neglected than out of any theoretical admiration for a planned society."[33] Orwell had a privileged background and joined the British colonial police in Burma at the age of 19. But he came to realize the intolerable nature of his position as a foreign oppressor in an occupied land, and from that point on, he devoted himself to the fight against injustice and oppression:

I was conscious of an immense weight of guilt that I had got to expiate. I sup-pose that sounds exaggerated; but if you do for five years a job that you thor-oughly disapprove of, you will probably feel the same. I had reduced every-thing to the simple theory that the oppressed are always right and the oppressors are always wrong; a mistaken theory, but the natural result of being one of the oppressors yourself. I felt that I had got to escape not merely from imperialism but from every form of man's dominion over man. I wanted to submerge myself, to get right down among the oppressed, to be one of them and on their side against the tyrants.[34]

Through his service in the Spanish civil war, his experience of being "down and out in Paris and London," and his investigation of poverty in the industrial north of England, Orwell came to have a much deeper understanding of the total nature of society that his privileged origins had previously denied him. He made it his life project to liberate himself from all of the prejudices and received ideas that he had inherited with his upbringing. He was not always successful, but he became an independent thinker who maintained a critical distance from all the great movements of the age, including imperialism, nationalism, fascism, and communism. Orwell developed arguments for social justice and a set of positive proposals for transforming the nature of English society along socialist lines. I begin by reconstructing the main lines of Orwell's ethical socialism through the perspective of liberty, equality, and fraternity that he affirms in all his major writings.

We can start with fraternity: In the Spanish civil war, Orwell experienced a very deep sense of community with his leftist comrades in the Workers' Party of Marxist Unity (POUM). He describes a halcyon time, with no suits and ties or other signs of class distinction, with tipping in restaurants respectfully forbidden, and with many factories, shops, and other businesses collectivized. It was a revolutionary moment of solidarity, unaffected by rank or national origin, which ended only when Stalin's agents hijacked the left and the members of the POUM were arrested as fascist collaborators. He writes in *Homage to Catalonia*:

Up here in Aragon, one was among tens of thousands of people, mainly though not entirely of working-class origin, all living at the same level and mingling on terms of equality. In theory it was perfect equality, and even in practice it was not far from it. There is a sense in which it would be true to say that one was experiencing a foretaste of Socialism, by which I mean that the prevailing mental atmosphere was that of Socialism. Many of the normal motives of civilized life—snobbishness, money-grubbing, fear of the boss, etc.—had simply ceased to exist. The ordinary class-division of society had disappeared to an extent that is almost unthinkable in the money-tainted air of England; there was no one there except the peasants and ourselves, and no one owned anyone else as his master.[35]

This experience, though short lived, gave Orwell the sense that a genuine community of equals was possible and certainly desirable. In *The Road to*

Wigan Pier, he describes the same solidarity that seemed to exist in many working-class families facing hardship and the dole.

Orwell's reflections on equality go back to his experience in Burma as a colonial official, twenty years old and in charge of several thousand people. Looking back on it, it all seems so obviously wrong. But as Orwell notes, imperialism is only the most blatant form of inequality, and he specifically compares colonialism to economic inequality as two versions of the same form of injustice: "Foreign oppression is a much more obvious, understandable evil than economic oppression," he writes. "Thus in England we tamely admit to being robbed in order to keep half a million worthless idlers in luxury, but we would fight to the last man sooner than be ruled by Chinamen; similarly, people who live on unearned dividends without a single qualm of conscience, see clearly enough that it is wrong to go and lord it in a foreign country where you are not wanted."[36] Orwell knew that most of the economic inequality that exists in modern society can never be justified, and he sought to show how our attitudes are shaped by prejudice and a desperate attempt to rationalize the validity of the status quo. Take beggars for example. People complain that beggars don't work. But what is work? Orwell asks. A navvy works by manual labor, and an accountant works by adding up figures. A beggar works by standing outside in all weather and assailing people with requests for money. We might insist that the beggar's "work" is useless, but since when do we care whether work is useful or not? Under capitalism there are many useless occupations, such as advertising, stock-trading, or real estate, but we tend to approve of all of them because we feel that successful money-making is what justifies work and makes it a good thing—and using this standard, the beggar is a failure. We should notice, however, that this does not justify the inequalities of wealth except in a circular way: money is the reward for making money just as poverty is the punishment for not making money, but nothing is thereby shown about whether these arrangements are just. Finally, in his frequent comments on the English educational system, and especially in the memoir of his own schooldays, "Such, Such Were the Joys," Orwell reflects at some length on how inequality in educational opportunity can benefit or ruin a child for life. For years he struggled against the snobbery and class prejudice that had been inculcated at his first private school. His decisions to live as a tramp for some time or to work as a dishwasher suggest an attempt at self-overcoming. But this was not a desire for penance or self-mortification on his part. It expressed the need for a lived connection with the dispossessed, or those who are usually scorned, and this allowed him to experience the common sense of humanity that lies beneath all surface distinctions between people—or the underlying reality of equality.

Writing in the 1930s and 1940s, Orwell was obviously aware of the direct threat to personal freedom being posed by both fascism and Stalinism as the two totalitarian movements of the age. The nightmare of *1984* imagines the complete triumph and fulfillment of totalitarianism in a society in which there is no liberty or equality or fraternity. *Animal Farm* depicts the betrayal of liberty in the name of "equality" and the false fraternity of collectivism that Stalin was able to impose. But Orwell realized the extent to which capitalism was also destructive of individual liberty. The poor are not free, and they certainly don't have the same power of self-determination that is available to the wealthy. And in the absence of any real choices in life, the typical response is one of despair. In *The Road to Wigan Pier*, Orwell uses the full scope of his literary imagination to describe the plight of an ordinary slum woman whom he glimpses briefly from the train. It is a compassionate and compelling portrait, but it is at one with his extended documentary account insofar as it successfully articulates the sense in which poverty is a life sentence that can hardly be endured. He writes:

> At the back of one of the houses a young woman was kneeling on the stones, poking a stick up the leaden waste-pipe which ran from the sink inside and which I suppose was blocked. I had time to see everything about her—her sacking apron, her clumsy clogs, her arms reddened by the cold. She looked up as the train passed, and I was almost near enough to catch her eye. She had a round pale face, the usual exhausted face of the slum girl who is twenty-five and looks forty, thanks to miscarriages and drudgery; and it wore, for the second in which I saw it, the most desolate, hopeless expression I have ever seen. It struck me then that we are mistaken when we say "It isn't the same for them as it would be for us," and that people bred in the slums can imagine nothing but the slums. For what I saw in her face was not the ignorant suffering of an animal. She knew well enough what was happening to her—understood as well as I did how dreadful a destiny it was to be kneeling there in the bitter cold, on the slimy stones of a slum backyard, poking a stick up a foul drainpipe.[37]

Such passages depend upon the novelist's eye for detail, and one could say this hardly constitutes an "argument" for socialism. But Orwell is not an academic philosopher. He wants to make us aware of injustice and misery, and the portrait that he describes here is much more effective and compelling than any statistical study or philosophical analysis could be. Of course, the passage involves an appeal to compassion, but even so it is appropriate, since the concern for justice does not issue from a theoretical reflection on what is just, but from the immediate experience of injustice even when this involves someone else's suffering rather than our own.

Alongside such powerful scenes, Orwell describes in a more prosaic way how unemployment or the threat of unemployment, industrial pollution, bad food, and atrocious housing conditions all serve to undermine the real freedom and self-respect of individual workers and their families. His discussion is full of relevant facts, including the weekly household budgets of families he stayed with, the different levels of unemployment assistance and the real rates of unemployment in the north. Orwell describes working-class homes in documentary detail, down to the number of rooms and their square footage, the number of beds in the house and the number of occupants, the amount of rent paid, and the character of the landlord. This is all calculated to make its appeal to basic "common sense." But at the same time, he realizes the inadequacy of these impersonal facts: "Words are such feeble things. What is the use of a brief phrase like 'roof leaks' or 'four beds for eight people'? It is the kind of thing your eye slides over, registering nothing. And yet what a wealth of misery it can cover!"[38] Orwell protests the squalor of these living conditions that are certainly not "chosen" by those who have to endure them. Indeed, he makes it clear that the workers and their families are not free, but completely and immediately subject to the laws of economic necessity.

Orwell's account of socialism and his underlying reflections on liberty, equality, and fraternity remain compelling. He obviously cared about the workers and the tramps that he knew and sometimes lived with, and his discussions have none of the contempt for the lower classes that you can sometimes glimpse in other socialist writers. Orwell's perspective on socialism is certainly more nuanced than the limited focus on liberty, equality, and fraternity might suggest. But these values are central to all of his writings, and it does not distort his thinking to suggest that Orwell's thought can be grasped in terms of this triad. The ethical perspective on socialism, which involves the promotion of liberty, equality, and fraternity, shapes his understanding of what the just society should be like, and it creates expectations concerning the future. As Orwell writes in his brief essay, "What is Socialism?": "A Socialist is not obliged to believe that human society can actually be made perfect, but almost any Socialist does believe that it could be a great deal better than it is at present, and that most of the evil that men do results from the warping effects of injustice and inequality. The basis of Socialism is humanism."[39]

Both in his life and in his writings, Orwell was preoccupied with the demands of justice, which he regarded as the most important thing. He risked his life for the freedom of others in Spain, and he remained devoted to those who had been dispossessed by unjust social conditions. In this respect, Orwell's commitment to justice goes beyond obedience to the law, or the fulfillment of personal obligations. Looking to the needs and rights of others, it reflects the highest expression of justice as a personal virtue. Obviously, the world that we live in today is quite different from that of Europe in the 1930s. But Orwell's example remains compelling because it still inspires us to challenge the way things are, and work toward a better society for the fulfillment of justice itself.

CHAPTER FOUR

∼

Compassion

Compassion is an ambiguous virtue. In the history of philosophy, there has always been disagreement concerning the value of compassion. It has even been argued that compassion isn't a virtue at all, but an emotional response that cannot be controlled or commanded at will. We are responsible for our actions, it is said, but we don't choose our emotions, and apart from some effort at emotional management, there is not a lot that we can do to change them. Hence compassion isn't good or bad; we should just do the right thing regardless of how we feel about it. Going further, some philosophers, including the Stoics, Nietzsche, and Kant, have claimed that compassion, and more especially pity, is actually a vice, since it can deflect us from our moral purpose, while it also increases the amount of suffering in the world by making us share in the misery of others. No one denies that injustice and misery exist, but only action will help to change things, and our emotional responses are held to be secondary or irrelevant. These kinds of claims are reflected in our everyday thinking about the world, where appeals to compassion and other emotional responses are frequently condemned as forms of weakness or as failures in rational thought. But compassion is sometimes viewed as the highest virtue of all, and thinkers as diverse as Rousseau and Schopenhauer have made it the original virtue of society from which all the other virtues are derived. If we look away from the Western tradition toward Buddhism, we encounter a way of life that is focused on compassion. For Buddhists, a fully developed sense of compassion is the fundamental virtue of human existence and the highest form of moral wisdom, helping to promote the salvation of all sentient beings.

In this chapter, we must therefore determine the value of compassion since it is by no means obvious to everyone that compassion is a virtue or even a good thing. But before we begin that discussion, we must clarify what compassion is. I begin with the following as a working definition: *Compassion is sorrow for the suffering or misfortune of another and the consequent desire to alleviate that suffering which may (or may not) result in action*. The first part of the definition brings out the respect in which compassion involves recognizing the moral standing of another—it is unfortunate that he or she should have to suffer like this. And if compassion for a human being or an animal is possible but not compassion for a chair, then it follows that humans and animals have moral value but chairs do not. The last part of the definition emphasizes that compassion is not passive or just a self-absorbed emotional state. In fact, compassion always involves an impulse to action, insofar as it involves regret for what is happening to the other person and the desire to do something about it. Now other motives, like fear, may be stronger than this compassionate response, but this does not mean that compassion is passive, since compassion will sometimes be stronger than whatever causes us to hesitate, and this will lead to action; a compassionate attitude may also lead to the prevention of suffering before it actually happens.

Compassion can be distinguished from sympathy, empathy, and pity.[1] People often use these terms interchangeably, but the existence of different terms reflects different kinds of experiences that help to specify what compassion is. Sympathy involves a fellow-feeling for others, but it's not specifically directed toward their suffering. Through sympathy we are emotionally linked to another person like a friend or a child, and it means that we will experience their triumphs and failures as fully as if they were our own. Because of the emotional identification involved in sympathy, however, it is difficult to separate what is specifically mine from what belongs to the other. Similarly, empathy implies feeling another person's feelings as if they were our own. Maybe I empathize with you for having to make a speech because I know how nervous you must feel. Or if someone is suffering or in pain, I remember or try hard to imagine what it must be like to suffer like this, and so it could be said that I feel a part of the pain myself. Once again, however, I am focused on my own state of mind and not on the individual who is suffering. Put it this way: Compassion for another person involves recognizing her as an other and giving attention to her as the one who suffers. Sympathy and empathy, on the other hand, tend to reduce the perceived differences between self and other, by mirroring the other's experiences within oneself; but this means that we focus more on our own emotions than the situation of the other person.

Pity is frequently used as a synonym for compassion. The problem is that pity has acquired a negative connotation suggesting condescension and the inferiority of the person who is pitied. Hence we tend to reject pity as an insult. We respond with indignation: I don't want your pity! And we despise self-pity as a kind of servility and abjection. At the same time, however, we may be grateful for the compassionate concern of those who care about us, and sometimes this is the only thing that keeps us going. In *Survival in Auschwitz*, Primo Levi describes just how important it was for him to know that there was someone who saw the extent of his suffering and who still cared about him as a human being: "In concrete terms it amounts to so little," he writes, "an Italian civilian worker [called Lorenzo] brought me a piece of bread and the remainder of his ration every day for six months; he gave me a vest of his, full of patches; he wrote a postcard on my behalf to Italy and brought me the reply. For all this he neither asked nor accepted any reward, because he was good and simple and did not think that one did good for a reward." Lorenzo's compassion and his small acts of kindness kept Levi from falling into despair: "I believe that it was really due to Lorenzo that I am alive today," he writes, "and not so much for his material aid, as for his having constantly reminded me by his presence, by his natural and plain manner of being good, that there still existed a just world outside our own, something and someone still pure and whole, not corrupt. . . . Thanks to Lorenzo, I managed not to forget that I myself was a man."[2] In this regard, even if it only involves a caring look, compassion is a form of recognition that is necessary for our spiritual and emotional well-being. And this suggests that while pity may be related to compassion, it is not at all the same thing, and it would prejudice the discussion to use compassion and pity interchangeably. Sometimes the terms are equivalent, but there is usually a difference. For example, I may pity someone who is about to be executed for committing a terrible crime, but it wouldn't necessarily follow that I also felt compassion for him— for the crime may be too great to even think about his well-being.

More positively, then, we could say that compassion involves feeling with or feeling for another person who suffers some misfortune. The etymology of "com-passion" suggests "feeling with" in a literal way, but one can certainly feel compassion for those who don't realize their own misfortunes and consequently feel no pain. Think about King Lear at the end of Shakespeare's play, when his sufferings have finally made him mad. He may not feel pain anymore, but we feel for him in his plight, even though we probably don't know what it's like to be mad and we can't imagine what it would be like. We also pity those who died before they had a chance to experience much of life, or those who were born with incredible handicaps or disabilities.[3] But these people are unaware of their misfortunes. Thus we may agree that imagination is important for developing compassion, and those who are unable to think of themselves in any other life situation are probably less capable of compassion because they don't understand the possibility of seeing things from another's point of view. But it's not clear that imagination is ever a *necessary* condition for compassion: We encounter someone who is suffering and even before we make an imaginative leap to think of how it must be for that person, we are engaged by her suffering and responsive to it, and it is this that provokes the imaginative leap whenever we make it. And just as it is possible to feel compassion for the insane, or even the dead, it is also possible to feel pity or compassion for the suffering of other creatures with whom we seem to have little in common. Thomas Nagel, in his famous paper, "What is it Like to be a Bat," denies that we could ever use any kind of analogy or imaginative variation to get a sense of what being a bat might be like. We cannot move step by step toward an imaginative identification with the bat for we simply cannot imagine what it would be like to be nocturnal flying creatures living on a diet of insects or fruit.[4] But if compassion for such creatures is possible, and I will argue that it is, then imagination cannot be the precondition for compassion even if it is helpful. And this suggests that compassion involves feeling *for* someone, whereas empathy and sympathy are more readily grasped as modes of feeling *with*.

Compassion is an important moral feeling and a virtue, I will argue, insofar as it brings individuals together into a caring community by making them responsible and involved with each other. In exceptional circumstances, though, such as Nazi Germany, or Cambodia under the Khmer Rouge, the natural response of compassion is mocked or condemned as softness, and this leads to the most terrible cruelty. In fact, compassion and cruelty are opposites. Cruelty delights in the sufferings of others and promotes alienation and the separation of people from each other. Compassion is sorrow at the suffering of another person, and while it may sometimes be weak and ineffectual, it is the recognition of the other in her pain that helps to overcome the distance between people.

In what follows, I consider the arguments of those who condemn compassion as a mere emotion or view it as a vice involving softness or weakness. I focus on the Stoics in the ancient world and Kant and Nietzsche in modern times. On the other hand, I will also consider Buddhism, which celebrates compassion as the most important and appropriate response to the suffering of the world. Next, I give some reasons for the value of compassion as a virtue that can be taught by focusing on compassion as the opposite of cruelty and compassion as the virtue that brings us into a caring community with others. I conclude by looking at the possibility of compassion for animals and how this challenges all of our received ideas about the secondary and instrumental value of animals for human life. The virtue of compassion provides a significant basis for the ethical treatment of animals, or what is usually referred to as "animal rights"—it is only the deliberate blocking of compassion that allows us to accept the inhumane treatment of animals in factory farms, research facilities, slaughterhouses, and circuses. Animal rights may ultimately require attention to justice and the entitlement of all creatures not to be harmed. But without the motivating force of compassion there would be no recognition that justice could be an interest of animals as well as human beings.

Two Perspectives on Compassion

In the history of Western philosophy, the ideal of individual autonomy and self-commandment has often been at odds with the virtues that require responsiveness to others. Taking charge of one's own life, or becoming "authentic," involves a tension with the claims of other people, who may be experienced as a distraction from one's own proper path. Hence the Stoic philosophers Epictetus, Marcus Aurelius, Seneca, and Cicero all emphasize the absolute distinction between those things that are in our power and those things that are not. We cannot do anything about fate, where and when we were born, whether as a slave or as a free individual, or what we encounter in the course of our lives. But we can determine how we are going to act or respond to anything that happens to us. The latter is totally within our control and so we can distinguish absolutely between what is and is not ours. For the Stoic, virtue involves indifference to the play of fortune and acceptance of whatever happens, without rancor, excitement, or regret. For the Stoic, our passions are forms of false judgment, since they involve resistance to what *must* happen, and the wise person is free from such emotions. Thus, according to Cicero, if a Stoic sage is told of the death of his child, he will not be plunged into grief but say something like, "I knew that I had begotten a mortal."[5] Socrates was a hero of the Stoics, and they revalued his life as a demonstration of Stoic virtue. In the last days of his life, for example, Socrates boldly proclaims that nothing is more important than doing what is right, and that all other considerations, including fame, fortune, and even personal safety, are irrelevant. The Stoics believed that health, power, and wealth are secondary goods (or "preferred indifferents") insofar as they allow us to achieve virtue, but they are not in themselves what we should be striving for.

Now none of this is meant to imply that the Stoics were cruel or self-absorbed. For the Stoics, the goal of human life was happiness, or living well, and this meant living in accordance with the inner principle of the universe, which is mind or reason. Cicero, Marcus Aurelius, and others devoted their lives to the community and sought to promote the common good of all, since the latter, along with friendship and family, were among the norms established by nature for human life. Nevertheless, there is still an extreme tension between the self and others in Stoic philosophy, and this leads to the inherent difficulty of friendship or love, which involves opening up to the other person and taking their concerns and goals just as seriously as one's own. If the Stoic distinction between what is in my power and what is not in my power is rigidly maintained, then love, friendship, and compassion all become problematic since they make the well-being of others a conditional aspect of our own well-being, and so they challenge the self-other distinction that the Stoic is bound to maintain. In the case of compassion, for example, the Stoics were clear: give material assistance to help others, if necessary, but to pity the afflicted is to weaken self-mastery by taking one's lead from outside. Seneca, in his plea to Nero, gives us a portrait of the wise man who is always willing to help others, and who is even merciful to those who have offended. But, he says, such a man does not experience pity or any other emotion that would shake his inner composure and rational self-mastery. Hence:

> no sorrow befalls the wise man. His mind is serene and nothing can occur to cloud it over. Again, nothing more befits a man than a great mind. But a mind cannot be both great and also grieving, since grief blunts the wits, debases and shrivels them. And that is something that will not happen to a wise man even in his own misfortunes. On the contrary, he will beat back fortune's anger and break it at his feet. He will always have the same calm, unshaken expression, which he could not do if he were open to sadness.[6]

Seneca also argues that pity is an unmanly vice that can easily lead to the abandonment of whatever is right and good. Indeed, "There are women, senile or silly, so affected by the tears of the nastiest criminals that, if they could, they would break open the prison."[7]

The Stoics were less concerned with developing a philosophical system than with teaching people how to live, and some of the basic ideas that animate Stoicism continue to be popular in everyday life. I might say, for example, that I am free to live my life in whatever way I want; regardless of my education or material circumstances, I possess the power of freedom that allows me to transcend whatever I have been dealt by fate; hence, I have no one to blame but myself, and all my actions belong to me in an absolute sense. But what is true for me is also true for everyone else: We are all sep-arate and free individuals with our own ideas about what it means to live a good life. Of course, it is wrong to violate the rights of another, but that doesn't mean one has to abandon one's own path by responding to what other people want. This might be an exercise in charity, but it would be an example of self-abandonment that cannot be justified.

The Stoic position also underlies later philosophical work by Kant and Nietzsche. In Kant, the absolute distinction between what is in my power and what is not under my control is rephrased in terms of the difference be-tween autonomy and heteronomy. Autonomy, or acting as the lawgiver of one's own existence, is the very foundation of Kantian ethics. It means fol-lowing the rational or higher part of one's own nature and determining, by means of the categorical imperative, whatever is in accordance with the moral law. Kant condemns all heteronomous principles like the will of God, pleasure, inclination, or the needs of others as improper determinations of the will. According to Kant, morality is not a matter of self-abandonment but the highest form of self-fulfillment. And in acting morally we are really most ourselves: "Therefore a free will and a will under moral laws are identi-cal."[8] From this perspective, having compassion for other people is problem-atic if it sways us from our moral purpose and leads us to follow our emotions rather than the appropriate moral principle that applies.

Kant distinguishes between acting from principle and acting out of lov-ing kindness, and typically he affirms the first while disdaining the latter as irrelevant:

> Let us take a man who is guided only by justice and not by charity. He may close his heart to all appeal; he may be utterly indifferent to the misery and misfortune around him; but so long as he conscientiously does his duty in giv-ing to every one what is his due, so long as he respects the rights of other men as the most sacred trust given to us by the ruler of the world, his conduct is righteous. . . . If all of us behaved in this way, if none of us ever did any act of love or charity, but only kept inviolate the rights of every man, there would be no misery in the world except sickness and misfortune and other such suffer-ings as do not spring from the violation of rights.[9]

Kant goes on to affirm "cold-hearted" goodness. The passage suggests his general hostility toward the emotions and it follows from his absolute dis-tinction between reason and the passions, which are supposed to be volatile and unpredictable. In another famous passage, Kant appears to reject com-passion as pointless if there is nothing practical that can be done: "It was a sublime way of thinking that the Stoic ascribed to his wise man when he had him say, 'I wish for a friend, not that he might help me in poverty, sickness, imprisonment etc., but rather that I might stand by him and rescue a man.' But the same wise man, when he could not rescue his friend, said to himself, 'What is that to me?'"[10] Kant even suggests that in this situation, compassion would be a mistake:

> In fact, when another suffers and, although I cannot help him, I let myself be infected by his pain (through my imagination), then two of us suffer, though the evil really (in nature) affects only one. But there cannot be a duty to increase the evil in the world and so to do good from compassion. This would also be an insulting kind of beneficence, since it expresses the kind of benevolence one has toward someone unworthy, called pity; and this has no place in men's relations with one another.[11]

Kant's emphasis is on respect, but without compassion for others, as we will see, respect and the observance of duty may sometimes degenerate into cruelty and adherence to principle for its own sake. There are one or two passages where Kant talks of our duty to cultivate loving kindness: In the section immediately after the one just quoted in *The Metaphysics of Morals*, he writes that it is a duty not to avoid sick rooms or debtors' prisons because such places evoke compassionate feelings that may help us to act morally when the representation of duty is not sufficient. But these passages are quite outnumbered by others, like those quoted above, where Kant says that good-heartedness is not morally relevant.

In Nietzsche's philosophy, the denunciation of pity and compassion becomes more extreme. Through strategies like the eternal recurrence, the overman, and the will to power, Nietzsche encourages us to seize hold of our own existence and resist all the mindless determinations of chance. In *Thus Spoke Zarathustra*, especially, pity emerges as the greatest danger to self-overcoming and the achievement of the sovereign will. Zarathustra counsels us to become hard, for all creators are hard in not succumbing to the emotional appeal of others:

> And if your hardness will not flash and cut and cut to pieces: how can you one day create with me? For creators are hard. And it must seem bliss to you to press your hand upon millennia as upon wax, bliss to write upon the will of millennia as upon metal—harder than metal, nobler than metal. Only the noblest is perfectly hard. This new law-table do I put over you, O my brothers: Become hard![12]

Elsewhere, Nietzsche argues that the Christian impulses of pity and compassion bring us down to the same level as those who are afflicted and sick of life. Zarathustra is definitely a misanthropist; he continually withdraws from the town to the mountain when being with the herd of ordinary people becomes unbearable to him. On the other hand, this does not mean that he doesn't care for other people: Like the Stoics who esteem friendship and public service, or like Kant who emphasizes the absolute value of every person, Zarathustra (and thereby Nietzsche) seeks to inspire the individual soul toward sovereignty and self-mastery; but in the end he can only teach by example: "You had not sought yourselves; and you found me. Thus do all believers; therefore faith amounts to so little. Now I bid you lose me and find yourselves; and only when you have all denied me will I return to you."[13] For Zarathustra, at least, the achievement of personal autonomy must be in total opposition to any kind of involvement with others that would only take us away from ourselves. Later, pity is described as Zarathustra's greatest temptation: In pity we are distracted by the claims of others, but Zarathustra believes that someone who is distracted by others is never capable of living for herself.

We can now review some of the main lines of argument that have emerged from this discussion of Stoicism and its more recent avatars, Nietzsche and Kant. What is wrong with compassion? There are three basic points. First, it is claimed that pity (and likewise compassion) involves a condescending attitude toward the unfortunate person who suffers. Pity and respect are conflicting principles, as in Nietzsche's aphorism, "Being Pitied": "To savages the idea of being pitied evokes a moral shudder: it divests one of all virtue. To offer pity is as good as to offer contempt: one does not want to see a contemptible creature suffer, there is no enjoyment in that."[14] In response, it must be said that the same is not true of compassion. Suffering tends to isolate us, but compassion offers us a bridge that restores us to our place in humanity. This is why we have an absolute need for compassion and consolation when we are grieving or mourning a loss. And the cruelest response is not to take another's suffering seriously, to laugh at her distress, or to withhold compassion in some other way. Without the compassion of others, our emotional recovery becomes much more difficult. As we have seen, Primo Levi claims that Lorenzo's small acts of kindness and compassion were ultimately responsible for his moral (and physical) survival in Auschwitz. Far from being a form of contempt, compassion is really the response of a fellow creature that affirms another's ultimate value in spite of his unfortunate situation. It may even be argued that compassion is the most basic moral response of all, for it is both a natural feeling as well as a particular virtue that we can culti-vate or disdain, and as such, it is the precondition for any concern about oth-ers, the rights they have, and our duties toward them.

The second claim is that pity or compassion is also dangerous for the one who pities, since pity may lead someone away from what is right, by making her act in a purely emotional way. As we have seen, Zarathustra describes pity as his final temptation, the one that prevented him from becoming him-self. But once again, this is begging the question. If our goal is to become completely independent and self-sufficient, then being able to feel for others and feeling moved to respond to them may be a hindrance. But it may also be argued that we are humanized through compassion and this allows us to experience a sense of belonging with other people. Nietzsche, Kant, and the Stoics sometimes seem to assume an opposition between individual develop-ment and involvement with others, but it seems more reasonable to think that these would be reciprocally related to each other. Of course a complete emotional identification with the sufferings of another might lead to paraly-sis and despair, but this would not be compassion, but something more self-involved. Compassion allows us to experience our own humanity through the other person—and this is by no means a contemptible thing.

Finally, from a more utilitarian perspective, pity is also considered ob-jectionable because it seems to increase the amount of suffering in the world. For the Stoics, Kant, and Nietzsche, pity is a useless sentiment. If we are overcome by compassion for others, then not only does this prevent us from taking steps to alleviate their suffering, it also increases suffering, and this is wrong. In response, however, it is by no means obvious that pity is useless. Imagine a world without compassion or pity, and it's not clear that anyone would ever help anyone else or be concerned about their suffering except in a superficial way. The compassionate response to suffering is a ba-sic moral motivation, and once a compassionate attitude becomes more prevalent, it can transform every aspect of society including the way we care for the sick, the poor, and animals. In this respect, it is the very oppo-site of a "useless" sentiment. Nietzsche holds that our preoccupation with the suffering of others must lead to a complete diminution of the human spirit in which the focus is no longer on the achievement of the individual but the well-being of society in general. In *On the Genealogy of Morals*, he even considers whether this could lead to a new European Buddhism: "I un-derstood the ever spreading morality of pity that had seized even on philosophers and made them ill, as the most sinister symptom of a Euro-pean culture that had itself become sinister, perhaps as its by-pass to a new Buddhism? To a Buddhism for Europeans? To—nihilism?"[15] But here again,

Nietzsche assumes the absolute opposition between self and other, the danger of an emotional response, and the particular danger of pity, which squanders our affective resources on others. From another point of view, Nietzsche's insistence on the ideal of personal autonomy is itself the distorting lens that prevents him from grasping the important things in life, which come from the reality of human interdependence.

In the end, we may dispute each of these particular claims in detail, but I think we can only overcome the Stoic perspective by taking another paradigm that rejects individualism and emphasizes the connectedness of all life, and the reality of suffering, which cannot be ignored or rejected as irrelevant. In the history of Western philosophy, Rousseau and Schopenhauer have emphasized the significance of pity or compassion as the foundational virtue that helps to inaugurate society (in the case of Rousseau), or that responds to suffering as the deepest reality of all (in the case of Schopenhauer). But Buddhism is more profound than either of these philosophies. Buddhism offers us an alternative paradigm that challenges the independence of the self, and it suggests a renewed sense of compassion, not as a vice or a questionable virtue, but as the most fundamental virtue that should encompass our existence in the world.

In Buddhism, the four supreme virtues traditionally include compassion (karuna), loving kindness (metta), sympathetic joy (mudita), and equanimity (upekka), and much of Buddhist practice is devoted to cultivating these virtues, which express the wisdom of the bodhicitta or the awakened heart.[16] It would not be wrong to say, however, that out of all these virtues, compassion is the most significant: It is the consummate Buddhist virtue, or as one Tibetan teaching puts it, "Let those who desire Buddhahood not train in many dharmas—but only one. Which one? Great compassion. Those with great compassion possess all the Buddha's teaching as if it were in the palm of their hand."[17] In the Mahayana tradition of Buddhism, the focus on compassion has inspired the powerful ideal of the Bodhisattva: the saint whose compassion is so great he refuses Nirvana until he has helped to release all other creatures from their suffering. The Bodhisattva doesn't stop at private enlightenment, but devotes himself to removing the sufferings of the world through the propagation of wisdom concerning our true nature.

In Buddhist practice, compassion requires feeling for the suffering of others; it is the responsiveness to misery that includes not just the particular sorrows that others experience, but also the underlying reality of suffering that is grasped as the permanent condition of human existence itself. Because of our attachments and desires, suffering is inescapable. But compassion allows us to experience our affinity and our connection with all creatures, and the more we cultivate our sense of compassion, the less preoccupied we are with our own selfish projects. Thus compassion is not just a passive affair since it involves an active response. The goal of compassion that is highlighted by the ideal of the Bodhisattva is to remove suffering, and this precludes being overwhelmed by another's suffering and drowning in their sorrow, as well as the refusal to get involved. It follows that compassion involves an overall attentiveness and availability to the other person. Indeed, Buddhist texts emphasize that the duty to cultivate compassion involves awareness that the other person is more important than our own selfish goals. There are many parables that illustrate this moral point, including one of the Bodhisattva who gave his own body to a hungry tigress who was close to death. In the story, Mahapranada comments: "Yes, self-sacrifice is so difficult!" Mahasattva replied:

> It is difficult for people like us, who are so fond of our lives and bodies, and who have so little intelligence. It is not at all difficult, however, for others, who are true men, intent on benefiting their fellow-creatures, and who long to sacrifice themselves. Holy men are born of compassion. Whatever the bodies they may get, in heaven or on earth, a hundred times will they undo them, joyful in their hearts, so that the lives of others may be saved.[18]

Now of course the Buddhist account of compassion is supported and justified by a very particular view of the nature of things. But we can sketch the underlying Buddhist metaphysics by discussing the doctrine of the four noble truths which are central to Buddhism: According to the first noble truth, the fundamental reality of life is one of suffering. We may not always be in pain, or aware of our suffering condition at any given moment, but the world is continually in flux and everything that exists must eventually pass away. Hence we are doomed to disappointment and loss, not because of bad luck, but because this is part of the very nature of things, which we ignore whenever we strive for some new goal or prize that is meant to satisfy our craving. The second noble truth is that the characteristic suffering of this life derives from our passionate attachment to particular ambitions and people. We cling to people and things, and we tend to love and crave them in a desperate way; so we are doomed to suffer the agony of losing the things that we crave and whatever we achieve for ourselves is always threatened by the possibility of our own death. The third noble truth describes the antidote, which is release from desire and the overcoming of passionate attachment as liberation from the suffering of life. In this respect, one of the illusions that we are most attached to is the idea of a separate and substantial self. Buddhism rejects this idea. It has a no-self (anatman) view of the world, and it endorses the view—similar to the one that was later defended by David Hume—that we are nothing more than a bundle of perceptions without anything that could be regarded as an enduring self. The goal of Nirvana is the overcoming of all selfish projects and the "blowing out" of this insubstantial self so that we can be liberated from the cycle of rebirth. The fourth noble truth describes how this is possible through the eightfold path that involves right views, right resolve, right speech, right conduct, right livelihood, right effort, right mindfulness, and right concentration. I will not explore this in more detail, but these eight different aspects may be viewed as the most significant forms of wisdom, meditation, and ethical action. The eightfold path involves a spiritual discipline and continual self-examination that require us to be present to ourselves and to our experiences in a very focused way. And through this ongoing spiritual cultivation we may approach true wisdom as an appropriate state of mindfulness that corresponds to the ultimate reality of the world.

Now it is certainly the case that Buddhist compassion is founded upon a particular view of the way things are, and a metaphysics that includes karma and reincarnation. But the most important aspect of this view, the fundamental reality of suffering, is one that could be granted by anyone. As we have seen, Western philosophers have often rejected or disdained suffering and derided compassion, which takes suffering seriously. Buddhism gives a central place to compassion because it accepts, realistically I think, that suffering is an unavoidable feature of human life. Notice, then, that with Buddhism it is difficult to disentangle understanding and virtue; compassion is obviously a virtue insofar as it involves responsiveness to the needs of others, but it's also a form of knowledge insofar as it recognizes the illusory nature of our separate existence. In the end, it is not just one person who helps someone else, but life in the service of life.

Buddhist practices are focused on the dissolution of the abyss between that which gives and that which receives. As we have seen, the more committed and involved with others I become, the less I am preoccupied with myself and my own desires. In this way, the deep concerns and anxieties that characterize my everyday existence are removed as I become ever more open to other people and the rhythm of life itself. But the removal of attachment and personal desires does not lead to apathy or the loss of all affect. Instead, once all of these encrustations have been stripped away, we may experience the ultimate joy of enlightenment, which is sometimes called a Buddha nature—a mind with no longings, cravings, or anxieties, an indescribably blissful state of being, which is not the same as complete indifference or lack of concern. The practice of compassion is accordingly a kind of wisdom. Of course, Buddhists insist that both wisdom and compassion are essential for the achievement of salvation or final enlightenment. As Saraha, the teacher of the philosopher Nagarjuna, puts it: "He who clings to the Void / And neglects Compassion / Does not reach the highest stage / But he who practices only compassion / Does not gain release from the toils of existence. / He, however, who is strong in the practice of both / Remains neither in Samsara nor in Nirvana."[19] The Bodhisattva ideal is the expression of an embodied wisdom that can only be achieved through compassion. Hence the Bodhisattva's vow:

> I take upon myself . . . the deeds of all beings, even of those in the hell. . . . I take their suffering upon me. . . . I bear it, I do not draw back from it, I do not tremble at it, I do not lose heart. . . . I must bear the burden of all beings, for I have vowed to save all things living, to bring them safe through the forest of birth, age, disease, death and rebirth. I think not of my own salvation, but strive to bestow on all beings the royalty of supreme wisdom. So I take upon myself all the sorrows of all beings. . . . Truly I will not abandon them. For I have resolved to gain supreme wisdom for the sake of all that lives, to save the world.[20]

In this respect it may be argued that wisdom and compassion are really two aspects of the same thing.

In the *Rhetoric*, Aristotle tells us that we tend to feel compassion for those who suffer undeservedly.[21] He doesn't think we can feel compassion for the evil tyrant, or even that we should, and he also thinks that our compassion is usually limited to those who are somewhat like ourselves. It's not clear whether he would allow that we could feel compassion for an animal. Buddhist compassion is not limited in this way. In Buddhism one is encouraged to feel compassion for all creatures, for all sentient beings, humans and animals, are capable of suffering, pain, and death. And once compassion is promoted without regard to its (sentient) object, it becomes much easier to have an affirmative attitude toward life in all its aspects, and this has a beneficial effect at every level. Buddhists refuse to single out only the good or the poor as deserving objects of compassion. Compassion must be indefinitely extended, for everyone, even the worst criminal and tyrant, is suffering. To insist, like Aristotle, that compassion should be selective is a mistake, for it is to limit the efficacy of compassion and to view the world in terms of separate beings—some deserving and some undeserving—and this challenges the reality of compassion as a power that undermines all of these (illusory) distinctions.

The exiled Dalai Lama of Tibet is held to be the fourteenth manifestation of Avalokiteshvara, the Bodhisattva of compassion. In his autobiography, *Freedom in Exile*, the Dalai Lama emphasizes that Buddhism requires the extension of compassion to all beings, including our enemies; it is remarkable that he has never resorted to violence against or even shown anger at the Chinese who have occupied his country since 1950. At this point, it is estimated that well over a million of his people have been killed, and many others have been imprisoned and tortured. But even though he works tirelessly for the Tibetan cause, he refuses to abandon an attitude of universal compassion: "By living in a society we should share the sufferings of our fellow beings and practice compassion and tolerance, not only toward our loved ones but also toward our enemies."[22]

The Dalai Lama is not a trained philosopher, and his books are free of technical argumentation. In works such as *Ethics for the New Millennium*, *Freedom in Exile*, and *The Compassionate Life*, he provides a thoughtful account of compassion. He writes of the need to cultivate compassion as the primary ethical goal for each individual life, and he describes the Buddhist idea of the great compassion as a moral ideal that testifies to the responsibility that we all have for each other, and for all sentient beings. In *Ethics for the New Millennium*, for example, he points out that people everywhere desire only to be happy, to live decent lives, and to avoid suffering and pain. This is an obvious truth, but it leads to the basic idea that ethics involves sensitivity to others and avoiding everything that might bring harm to them. Hence, as we enhance our sensitivity to the suffering of others, by turning it over and over in our mind rather than blotting it out, we will also develop our ability to connect with others and thereby grow in virtue: "To me, this suggests that by means of sustained reflection on, and familiarization with, compassion, through rehearsal and practice, we can develop our innate ability to connect with others, a fact which is of supreme importance given the approach to ethics I have described. The more we develop compassion, the more genuinely ethical our conduct will be."[23] Buddhists believe that compassion does not have to be conditional; indeed, the feeling can be developed to such a degree that it becomes unconditional, undifferentiated, and universal in scope. This is the "great compassion" that the Dalai Lama describes as an inspiring ideal. It is a form of strength, and not weakness, which shares the suffering of others and offers comfort without being overwhelmed or annihilated by grief. Hence, the serenity and happiness of the Buddhist sage who remains mindful and concerned about all the sorrows of the world. The Dalai Lama comments:

> When we enhance our sensitivity toward others' suffering through deliberately opening ourselves up to it, it is believed that we can gradually extend our compassion to the point where the individual feels so moved by even the

subtlest suffering of others that they come to have an overwhelming sense of responsibility towards those others. This causes the one who is compassionate to dedicate themselves entirely to helping others overcome both their suffering and the causes of their suffering. In Tibetan, this ultimate level of attainment is called *nying je chenmo*, literally "great compassion."[24]

From this perspective, compassion is not a luxury, or just an emotional reaction, but the source of both internal and external peace. In the last part of this chapter, I consider the possibility of compassion for animals in some more detail. But first I will consider the basic value of compassion and its relation to ethical life. I will focus on compassion as the opposite of cruelty, and compassion as the preeminent social virtue.

On the Value of Compassion

The history of the twentieth century may be viewed as a brutal catalogue of cruelties, which began with the Boer war and the first recorded use of concentration camps by the British in South Africa, and ended with the horrors of tribal conflict and massacre in Bosnia, Serbia, Rwanda, and elsewhere. In between these events were the unbelievable horrors of Nazism, Stalinism, the Cultural Revolution of China, and the killing fields of Cambodia. It is difficult to grasp such a mountain of suffering and cruelty; and even though there are countless examples of individual cruelties that could be described, it is difficult to generalize about cruelty as such. However, one theme that does recur in the rise of totalitarian movements, and the pursuit of modern war, is the exhortation to hardness and unflinching firmness, and the consequent denigration of compassion as an unacceptable form of weakness. In his moral history of the twentieth century entitled *Humanity*, Jonathan Glover gives several examples of the deliberate cultivation of hardness as a way of overcoming the more natural human response of sympathy for the sufferings of others: Hitler, for example, consciously desired a new breed of human beings who would be violent, domineering, and cruel. He urged complete ruthlessness toward the enemy, and he boasted: "I am the hardest man the German nation has had for many decades, perhaps centuries."[25] His lieutenant, Heydrich, said, "We must be as hard as granite, otherwise the work of our Fuehrer will perish."[26] Glover comments: "In those carrying out atrocities, hardness was a defence against the horror of what they were doing, like the hardness of soldiers in combat, but Nazi hardness was also something aspired to and deliberately cultivated. Instructions about the need for hardness were passed down the line to those engaged in killing."[27] With such a goal, training must be severe and deliberately calculated to rule out all "sentimental" responses. Glover describes the SS man being encouraged to shoot the dog that he loved or even kill it with his own hands. Being completely hard with oneself means overcoming the weakness of compassion that leaves one open and available to others.

It is interesting that something very similar happened both in Soviet Russia and in Communist China, where compassion was frequently ridiculed and condemned as a remnant of bourgeois individualism. Stalin chose that name for himself because it means "man of steel" and evokes the ideal of firmness and absolute impenetrability. And in Stalin's Russia, as in Nazi Germany, compassion for those arrested or condemned was viewed as a suspect emotion—an unpardonable softness that suggested that one's own commitment to the revolutionary cause was seriously lacking. Likewise in Communist China, during the Cultural Revolution and at other times, compassion and respect for others was completely broken down. People were paraded through the streets with placards around their necks and forced to make public confessions of their "crimes." They were beaten and humiliated, and everyone, including children, was encouraged to participate in these ritual displays of cruelty. Such hardness and ruthlessness became a part of everyday life.

The unfortunate victims of these cruelties were frequently dehumanized and treated scornfully as if they were nothing more than loathsome vermin. During the Holocaust, Jews were systematically starved and forced to live in filthy, overcrowded conditions. This helped to confirm the Nazi teaching of the Jews' subhuman status, and it made it easier for those who were ordered to process and destroy them. Even after the victims' death, the relentless process of dehumanization continued: women's hair from Auschwitz was sold to make mattresses; ashes from the crematoria were used as fertilizer. As Primo Levi puts it, this treatment "was intended to declare that these were not human remains, but indifferent brute matter, in the best of cases good for some industrial use."[28] Considered in this way, cruelty has two aspects. First, it involves deliberately hardening the self and closing the self off from every appeal of the other person. Second, it involves repudiating the other *as* another person: he or she is no longer viewed as a human being but subhuman, or an object without feelings. In other words, cruelty is first made possible by the cancellation of the basic conditions for compassion: cruelty and compassion are completely opposed to each other, and it follows that the virtue of compassion should be cultivated to avoid the horrendous cruelties that have characterized human history up to this point.

At its most extreme, cruelty involves an exultant joy in someone else's suffering. It is not the same as the German idea of Schadenfreude, which means the guilty pleasure in another's misfortune, since cruelty is an open assertion of individual power that tramples the other underfoot solely to delight in her grief and pain. This is frequently a cyclical and cumulative process, for to suffer such cruelty can make one incapable of compassion for other people; recent history in the Balkans, the Middle East, Northern Ireland, and elsewhere provides plenty of examples of men and women who have been so hardened by their own suffering they now feel nothing but joy for the sufferings of those whom they consider their enemies. But a breakthrough is always possible, and it is the personal experience of compassion that allows us to respond to the other person, even in the midst of cruelties, when something different happens to unsettle the usual frame of reference. In the Holocaust, for example, the extermination of Jews soon became a matter of routine that people even joked about. But when, as occasionally happened, someone survived the initial gassing, the ordinary response of caring that had been suppressed briefly reasserted itself. Glover gives an example in which a gas chamber was being cleared and a sixteen-year-old girl was found alive at the bottom of the pile of corpses: "She was given a coat, while Nyiszli [the medical orderly] revived her with injections. . . . [Someone] ran to the kitchen to fetch some tea and warm broth. Everyone wanted to help, as if she were his own child."[29] Of course the same thing happens today when animals occasionally escape on their way to the slaughterhouse. What was just another routine processing of animals for our everyday consumption is suddenly transformed. Now we have to respond to the particular animal that appears to resist its fate, and we experience compassion for its situation. The idea of returning the animal to the slaughterhouse may be repugnant, for the individual has emerged from abstraction to become an object of moral concern. We don't need to limit our examples to the cruelties of war or the treatment of animals. Someone who habitually ridicules or condemns gay people or disabled people may be forced to revalue their ideas if a good friend reveals that he or she is gay, or becomes disabled. In such a case, the habitual and unthinking response may be overwhelmed by the strength of personal connection and the sympathy that exists between the persons concerned. Openness to the other person and the possibility of compassion make ridicule and cruelty much more difficult responses than they had been hitherto.

The second important point is that compassion is the preeminent social virtue. As we have seen, compassion is an individual response to the sufferings of others; but in this way, it helps to build a community of people who care about each other and who are moved to work against evils like prejudice, ignorance, and injustice. Without compassion, society is just a collection of isolated individuals who are only concerned with their own interests and goals. Even Kant recognized this when he argued in the *Foun-*

dations of the Metaphysics of Morals that no one could possibly will to live in a society where everyone was completely self-reliant and no one gave or expected help: "Now although it is possible that a universal law of nature according to that maxim could exist," he writes, "it is nevertheless impossible to will that such a principle should hold everywhere as a law of nature. For a will which resolved this would conflict with itself, since instances can often arise in which he would need the love and sympathy of others, and in which he would have robbed himself, by such a law of nature springing from his own will, of all hope of the aid he desires."[30] Kant doesn't say that a world of independent self-reliant beings would be irrational, only that no one could possibly will to be a member of such a society. We may dispute this reading, but I think the argument serves to emphasize the (unacknowledged) centrality of compassion. We can't even imagine a society where compassion does not exist anymore; and when I feel sorrow at another's suffering and misery, I am to that extent identifying my own well-being with theirs. Their suffering has affected me and makes me aware of my own dependence upon others.

In Rousseau's masterpiece, *Emile*, the tutor uses compassion as a way of bringing his young pupil into correct relations with others. Without denying the pupil's *amour propre*, his natural selfishness (or our own), he directs this toward concern for other people. As far as Rousseau is concerned, no matter what we might say about it, the good fortune of others tends to alienate people; it makes them unhappy with their own lot and makes them want to be in the other person's place. Compassion, on the other hand, inspires a common sense of humanity. But at the same time that we experience the distress of the other person as something that matters, we realize that we may be in a position to offer some assistance, and this makes us aware of our own strength and goodness:

> If the first sight that strikes him is an object of sadness, the first return to himself is a sentiment of pleasure. In seeing how many ills he is exempt from, he feels himself to be happier than he had thought he was. He shares the sufferings of his fellows; but this sharing is voluntary and sweet. At the same time he enjoys both the pity he has for their ills and the happiness that exempts him from those ills. He feels himself to be in that condition of strength which extends us beyond ourselves and leads us to take elsewhere activity superfluous to our well-being. To pity another's misfortune one doubtless needs to know it, but one does not need to feel it.[31]

At this point, the tutor adroitly introduces the stories of Plutarch's noble heroes, including Alexander, Hannibal, and Caesar, who are often represented as the ideal exemplars of human existence. When Emile reads about them, however, their lives seem vain and for the most part failures. He is filled with compassion for them, and he doesn't seek to imitate them since he is content with his own life: "He pities those miserable kings, slaves of all that obey them. He pities those false wise men, chained to their vain reputations. He pities these rich fools, martyrs to their display. . . . He would pity even the enemy who would do him harm, for he would see his misery in his wickedness. He would say to himself, 'in giving himself the need to hurt me, this man has made his fate dependent on mine.'"[32] To reinforce the lesson, and to undercut the possibility of self-satisfaction and vanity, the tutor makes sure that Emile is allowed to make his own mistakes and even tricked in various ways, so he learns to be distrustful of himself and respectful of others. In this way, his overall attitude toward society remains one of concern for other people:

> If he sees discord reigning among his comrades, he seeks to reconcile them; if he sees men afflicted, he informs himself as to the subject of their suffering; if he sees two men who hate each other, he wants to know the cause of their enmity; if he sees an oppressed man groaning under the vexations of the powerful and the rich, he finds out what maneuvers are used to cover over those vexations; and, with the interest he takes in all men who are miserable, the means of ending their ills are never indifferent to him.[33]

In this important text, Rousseau accordingly illustrates the educative role of compassion and the significant part it plays in the moral development of anyone who is to become a citizen of his or her community. More recently, Martha Nussbaum has made similar claims concerning the importance of compassion as the basic social emotion that provides a bridge between the individual and the community and inspires our emergent sense of justice.[34] Going beyond our typically self-centered standards of judgment we ask ourselves how we would feel in the sufferer's situation, and we recognize our own vulnerability to all the misfortunes of life and the evil of others. Hence compassion fosters the sense of a shared humanity. It is the means by which we reach out of ourselves and into the hearts and minds of other people; and in this way it significantly expands the range of humanity over which our altruism may extend.

Now this would seem to be a particularly strong argument for the necessity of compassion, which emphasizes its overall utility for society in general. Both Rousseau and Nussbaum suggest, however, that there are limits to compassion conceived of in this way. In *Emile*, Rousseau argues that when pity and justice come into conflict, it is justice that should prevail since the latter contributes more to the public good. Indeed, he adds that it would be quite wrong to feel compassion or pity for those who are bad:

To prevent pity from degenerating into weakness, it must, therefore, be gener- alized and extended to the whole of mankind. Then one yields to it only in so far as it accords with justice, because of all the virtues justice is the one that contributes most to the common good of men. For the sake of reason, for the sake of love of ourselves, we must have pity for our species still more than for our neighbor, and pity for the wicked is a very great cruelty to men.[35]

In this respect, however, compassion is being treated as an instrumental virtue, and the assignment of proper limits to compassion is to reassert the boundaries between people that compassion undermines.

Nussbaum follows Rousseau and Aristotle by claiming that there are some examples of suffering that we may not sympathize with. Nussbaum follows Aristotle's lead by claiming that there are some examples of suffer- ing that we are unable to sympathize with. Take the case of the Roman sen- ator who is upset because his supply of peacock tongues hasn't arrived in time for his banquet. His values are so alien to us, it seems quite impossi- ble to sympathize with him for his loss. But whether or not it has any so- cial utility, it is by no means obvious that compassion for those who are wicked and compassion for those who worry about things that are unim- portant are inappropriate responses that should be ruled out in advance. Nussbaum is right when she argues that literature expands the moral imag- ination by promoting compassion for those who are vulnerable to the vi- cissitudes of life that we may have escaped for the time being.[36] But what about examples of suffering that derive from a set of values that we might find impossible to embrace? Do we have to say that in these cases compas- sion would be wrong?

I will give two examples. First a work of literature: Chinua Achebe's novel *Things Fall Apart* begins by describing life in traditional Nigerian society be- fore the advent of the British colonial authority.[37] The chief character of the novel—Okonkwo—is the representative of traditional masculine tribal values and, while he is respected by others, he is certainly not blameless: he beats his wives whenever he finds them inattentive, he is domineering, and, to show that he is not weak, he takes part in the murder-sacrifice of Ikemefune, who had come to regard him as a father. In the second part of the novel, the British come, and the traditional order of society is completely shattered. After he kills a policeman in a fit of rage, Okonkwo realizes that no one is going to fight alongside him, and so he hangs himself. When we read this work we certainly feel some compassion for Okonkwo. We realize that he has worked hard to be- come what he is; we understand how things are between men and women in this traditional society; we may even think that sacrificing Ikemefune was somehow justified or at least preferable to an all-out war between rival villages. Likewise, we understand the despair he must feel at the British colonial incursion and the imminent destruction of a traditional way of life. But we don't have to endorse Okonkwo's values or justify everything that he does. The point is, we understand his suffering and his despair, and so we can experience compassion for him. But this does not mean that we approve of his character or his values.

The second example is not from literature but it is related to Achebe's novel insofar as it concerns another clash between two different cultures and the suffering and confusion that this often creates. In recent years, a number of young women in Asia and elsewhere have been disowned or even killed by parents who believe that the family will suffer some kind of collective shame if these women are sexually active or refuse to marry the partners their parents have carefully chosen for them. Such "honor" killings are not at all infrequent, and while they are indefensible, we can also imagine what it's like to have a child who has abandoned a traditional way of life that we remain attached to. And we can feel compassion for the parent whose suffering leads him to disown his child even though we would totally disagree with the values that he espouses, and we would want him to be punished for any crime he commits.

We have seen how compassion is our defense against cruelty, and that compassion is a social virtue insofar it as it leads to moral growth and the challenging of received ideas that we may have inherited from our culture. Compassion, as opposed to pity, involves leaving aside one's own selfish perspective to commiserate in the sufferings of another. Everyone is included in the possible scope of compassion, and so the proper fulfillment of this tendency would be the experience of selflessness and continuity with all sentient creatures. At this level of compassion, loving kindness begins to arise out of our deepest connection to all life; action becomes appropriate to the situation, and generosity is unlimited, because there is no self left to lose. And all of this inspires a powerful sense of the sacred character of life.

Toward Animal Liberation

In his celebrated essay, "Of Cruelty," Montaigne asserts the obvious connection between cruelty to animals and cruelty to human beings. He points out that in ancient Rome people became accustomed to the spectacle of the slaughter of animals, which led to the slaughter of gladiators and criminals as a routine event. And, as if to distance himself from the cruelties of his own age, he admits with some embarrassment to a compassionate nature that can-

not endure the sufferings of any other creature: "Among other of vices, I cru-
elly hate cruelty, both by nature and by judgement, as the extreme of all vices.
But this is to such a point of softness that I do not see a chicken's neck wrung
without distress, and I cannot bear to hear the scream of the hare in the teeth
of my dogs, although the chase is a violent pleasure." And he adds:

> For myself, I have not even been able without distress to see pursued and killed
> an innocent animal which is defenceless and which does us no harm. And as
> it commonly happens that the stag, feeling himself out of breath and strength,
> having no other remedy left, throws himself back and surrenders to ourselves
> who are pursuing him, asking for our mercy by his tears, "Bleeding, with the
> moans / Like some imploring creature," (Virgil)—that has always seemed to me
> a very unpleasant spectacle.[38]

Now it stands to reason that those who are insensitive or cruel to animals are
more than likely to be insensitive or cruel to their fellow human beings. But
this is not an argument for kindness to animals so much as an indirect way of
ensuring kindness to humans. Montaigne concludes that we owe justice to
men, "and mercy and kindness to other creatures that may be capable of receiving it."[39] In his essays, Montaigne always tries to be absolutely honest in
describing the course of his own thoughts and feelings, but he doesn't try to
justify his ideas, and he certainly doesn't write as a philosopher with a thesis
to defend. So we can now ask whether Montaigne's view of compassion for
animals is one that is appropriate and reasonably held; and if so, what follows
with regard to our ordinary treatment of animals?

It isn't hard to see how we can feel compassion for other human beings:
We know the suffering caused by pain, disappointment, and distress, and
when someone else is in obvious anguish we can empathize through an imaginative identification with their situation. But the case of animals is quite different. It could be argued that whatever it is we may be feeling, compassion
itself is not possible in the case of animals, simply because we do not know
what it is like to be an animal. Thus we may experience some feelings of sad-
ness for the cow that is about to be slaughtered, or the calf crammed into a
crate for its whole life just to provide veal for diners. But perhaps it is only a
kind of anthropomorphism to think that in this way we are empathizing with
a nonhuman creature. As we have seen, in "What is it Like to be a Bat,"
Thomas Nagel argues that it is simply impossible to have any idea of what
being a bat or any other animal is like.

> Our own experience provides the basic material for our imagination, whose
> range is therefore limited. . . . I want to know what it is like for a *bat* to be a
> bat. Yet if I try to imagine this, I am restricted to the resources of my own mind,

and those resources are inadequate to the task. I cannot perform it either by imagining additions to my present experience, or by imagining segments gradually subtracted from it, or by imagining some combination of additions, subtractions and modifications.[40]

If imaginative reconstruction of another's experiences is required for compassion, and our ability to imaginatively identify with the inner experience of animals is quite limited, then in fact it would be difficult if not impossible to feel compassion for animals.

In modern Western culture, we tend to use animals as if they were things specifically designed for our use, and we usually ignore the fact that they are sentient beings who are the subjects of their own lives. Every year over 10 billion animals are killed for food in the United States alone; they are crowded together in factory farms to produce cheap food for a fast-food society. Millions of animals—dogs, cats, rats, chimps, etc.—are used in experimental research on new drugs and cosmetics. Of course, the scientist who experiments on animals or the owner of a factory farm would deny that their intention is to be cruel. The scientist might complain that the objections to his research are sentimental in character and therefore not founded on good reasons. But this response assumes, from the outset, that emotions and feelings have no place in science; and this further presupposes an absolute separation between what is rational and what is emotional, and this is questionable. An emotion like compassion is actually a way of knowing the world. To experience compassion is not just a matter of having feelings without any cognitive content. Compassion is a way of orienting ourselves toward other beings. It is to take their own desires seriously, to feel sorrow for their pain, and to be ready and willing to help them insofar as we can. We don't have compassion for non-sentient beings like tables and chairs, but compassion is an appropriate response to anything capable of experience. And our emotions are often the best guide we have to moral understanding: A research assistant feels an impulse of compassion for the suffering of a research animal. She is admonished by the researcher and threatened with the loss of her job. Eventually she becomes inured to the suffering and comes to regard the animals as experiments rather than separate individuals with lives of their own. In other words, scientific objectivity is not a pure and ideal state; for much of the time the use of animals in research and food production is only possible given the complete deadening of authentic human responses.

On the one hand, living with animals allows us to experience their unique personalities and their emotional lives. The complexities of their inner life must remain hidden to us, but the very possibility of an ongoing relationship between creatures of two different species suggests that the burden of proof really lies with the skeptic to prove that what we feel isn't compassion (even though this is what it feels like) or that compassion isn't appropriate in these circumstances. Consider the case of the scientist Claude Bernard, who dissected the family dog while his wife and daughter were out. Bernard insisted that he didn't need to justify what he did and the only responsibility he had was to science. His wife and daughter held a different view, and they founded the first European society for the prevention of cruelty to animals. It is an extreme but telling example. The behavior of the wife and daughter in this case seems quite reasonable; Bernard's seems completely inhumane.[41]

Let us return to the case of the bat. Bats are creatures of the night, associated in Western legends with Dracula and other demonic powers and so perhaps a good example for those who want to argue that compassion for animals is inappropriate or impossible. But bats can become objects of human care and concern, and it is possible to have a meaningful relationship with a bat. In her book *The Bat in My Pocket*, subtitled "A Memorable Friendship," Amanda Lollar describes overcoming revulsion and then beginning to care for Sunshine, the first of many bats she rescued:

> After Sunshine started peeping, she went on to speak the entire bat language. Her different noises seemed to communicate different feelings and needs, and after a few days I began to understand her. A soft chittering noise seemed to convey greeting, affection and happiness. More often than not, she combined the chittering with rubbing her nose softly but vigorously up and down on my finger. The effect was much like a dog happy to see you, licking and nuzzling your hand. She had a reaction to everything: excitement, boredom, happiness, hunger or affection. All of them could be read on her face, and her chitterings took on different notes to match these emotions. Occasionally I could get her to chitter back to me before I picked her up, just by calling her name.[42]

Lollar's compassion for Sunshine allows her to make a connection with the animal that is definitely reciprocated, and her memoir describes the history of their curious relationship. Interestingly enough, it is because of her relationship with Sunshine that she goes on to care for other bats, and eventually she opens a bat sanctuary. Shall we say that this is just sentimentalism on her part? Or isn't there rather something very profound here—an openness and compassion for other beings that isn't limited to one particular species or those who happen to look like us? In this case, compassion and communication are totally bound up with each other, and it seems appropriate to describe the relationship in terms of friendship. All of this has some significant implications for animals and the way we treat them; indeed, the cultivation of compassion as an individual virtue leads to renewed consideration of the welfare of animals and what is collectively referred to as the "animal rights" movement. It is to this that I now wish to turn.

As early as 1781, Jeremy Bentham argued that the mistreatment of animals was completely unjustified and similar in many ways to racial discrimination, which led some people to make slaves of others merely on the basis of the color of their skin. Bentham's reasoning is clear and succinct and deserves to be quoted in full since it is the core position that has inspired later animal activists to argue that we are guilty of speciesism if we justify the infliction of suffering on animals by saying that only human beings have moral worth:

> The day may come when the rest of the animal creation may acquire those rights which never could have been withholden from them but by the hand of tyranny. The French have already discovered that the blackness of the skin is no reason why a human being should be abandoned without redress to the caprice of a tormentor . . . a full-grown horse or dog is beyond comparison a more rational as well as a more conversable animal than an infant of a day, or a week, or at even a month old. But suppose the case were otherwise, what would it avail? The question is not, can they reason? Nor, can they talk? But can they suffer?[43]

All sentient creatures, including humans, cows, dogs, and hens, have an interest in avoiding suffering. And Bentham, like others in the utilitarian tradition, including John Stuart Mill and Peter Singer, can't see any reason for saying that the suffering of humans should be minimized whereas the suffering of animals is unworthy of consideration. It is certainly true that with few exceptions, we only care about the well-being of our fellow human beings; we tend to treat animals as if they existed for our own benefit, and there is a huge amount of animal suffering involved in factory farming, experiments on animals, hunting, and slaughterhouses that is just accepted as an inevitable feature of modern life. Until quite recently, very few people have been concerned about the suffering of animals, and those who have argued for animal liberation or animal rights have been ridiculed as fanatics. The arguments of Bentham and others have gone unheeded, and in philosophy, skeptics have argued that animals can't have rights because they lack the rational capacity to enter into reciprocal relations with other rational beings. All of this begs the question, however, by assuming that rights must be based on some kind of social contract. But apart from this assertion, there is still no good reason for claiming that the suffering of human beings is important while the suffering of animals doesn't matter.

In recent years, the discussion of animal rights has been waged with increasing intensity. Advocates of animal rights think their adversaries are selfish and cruel. Those who oppose animal rights think that the advocates are fanatical and willing to disregard important human interests for the sake of mice and cows. At the same time, the issue of animal liberation has become more central to modern life, both in legal discussions and in popular awareness. Animal liberation can no longer be regarded as a fringe movement, for the welfare of animals is now emerging as a significant public debate whose outcome will probably be an important factor in determining the nature of future society. Indeed the debate is so heated because the two sides represent two fundamentally different paradigms for understanding our place in nature and our relationship to all other sentient beings. I will argue that the virtue of compassion makes us profoundly aware of all the cruelty involved in our ordinary treatment of animals, in the way that we raise animals for food and use them in experiments that are supposed to benefit human beings. And in this way, the development of compassion as a virtue is inherently linked to the movement for animal liberation.

Let us consider some facts and statistics. I don't propose to offer a complete catalogue of human cruelty to animals—that has been done elsewhere—but to show, by using a few significant examples, how many of our dealings with animals produce a huge amount of suffering for the animals involved.[44] In the United States alone, about 10 billion animals die in food production each year; 23 million chickens and 260,000 pigs are slaughtered every 24 hours. The numbers can be tripled if we want to consider the rest of the world. Tens of millions of animals are consumed annually in biomedical research, millions more by hunting and for entertainment purposes (like racing), or the production of fur and other clothing. The sheer numbers of animals involved is staggering, and it points to huge industries employing millions of people who are involved in raising, processing, and killing them.

Even more appalling than the actual numbers are the standard procedures used to process animals raised for food, experimentation, or entertainment. Let us consider some cases: With the growth of factory farm production in recent years, intensive confinement systems have been instituted at every level of the industry. These include the use of the battery cage for laying hens, the gestation crate for breeding pigs, and the veal crate for calves. In the United States, for example, 98% of egg-producing chickens live in battery cages. It is standard practice to put eight hens in a cage of 20" by 19". The birds are unable to spread their wings, and in order to avoid wounds caused by hens fighting, which in such close conditions is inevitable, their beaks are cut off:

> When there are eight birds in a cage this size, the bird barely has room to stand. And even then she is really pressed. There are a lot of birds pressing against

her and turning around is really difficult. And a really important thing about this as well, probably one of the main reasons that crowded hens experience a lot of illness, is there is not enough space for all the birds to eat at the same time. If you're a low-ranking bird—low on the peck order—you tend to get pushed to the back during feeding and you can't get enough food. So often the lowest-ranking bird in that cage gets sick and dies.[45]

Even more notorious is the use of the veal crate, which has now been banned in several European countries: In this system, very young calves are confined in stalls that are so small the animal is unable to turn around or even lie down. To maintain the whiteness of the calves' flesh, they are kept anemic through a diet deficient in iron. Now no one can reasonably deny that such creatures feel pain just as we do. But their interests are ignored as they are treated as nothing more than a food product. The same is true for the millions of animals used in research for medicine and cosmetics each year; or for animals used in sport and entertainment, such as greyhounds who live in small cages stacked on top of each other for up to 22 hours a day. It is strange that we are able to tolerate so much suffering in animals, especially given the care and concern that most people show for their companion animals, such as cats and dogs. But people are often appalled once they become aware of what goes on in slaughterhouses, factory farms, and animal labs; and it may be that people can only work in such places by deliberately desensitizing themselves to the animals' suffering and by rejecting the natural impulse of compassion. This is of course the same emotional suppression that we described in our earlier account of the cruelties that Nazis and others perpetrated by rejecting the natural impulse of caring as a form of weakness.

For the most part, then, our treatment of animals is callous and cruel. But why is it that the animal liberation movement has only become a significant social movement in recent times? The philosophical arguments for animal rights have always been strong, even back in 1781 when Bentham wrote his pioneering essay. But in Western societies at least, it's only recently that people have come to challenge the dominant paradigm that says that the world revolves around us and animals are basically property to use as we see fit. Increasingly, such an anthropocentric point of view is regarded as completely arrogant and self-serving; but it's also self-defeating, since it promotes a sense of alienation from the natural world that leaves us feeling bereft and homeless. Anthropocentrism is both spiritually and morally disastrous. In fact, human beings are one species among countless others inhabiting the planet and even if we possess superior powers, this only creates a corresponding responsibility to care for other creatures and not to make them suffer for our own enjoyment. Consider the furious debate over foxhunting in Britain. Fox-hunting with hounds is a limited example of our cruelty to animals. But it stirs such passions because there is a huge symbolic significance attached to a large group of uniformed riders chasing after a small animal who will be torn limb from limb by the accompanying pack of hounds. It is an image of human triumphalism, the ceremonial display of human might and power over a defenseless creature; and for those who no longer accept the traditional anthropocentric paradigm, it epitomizes our cruelty and callous disregard for the rest of the natural world.

The animal liberation movement is based on the sense that both human beings and animals have inherent value and their lives should not be disregarded or treated without consequence. I will not go into a more detailed discussion of whether animals have rights or not, and the extent to which changes in the law may now be necessary. For example, should we change the legal status of animals as property? It seems to me that such considerations derive from our concern for animal welfare, which is based upon our compassion for their suffering. I will give one final example: Today, increasing numbers of people are becoming vegetarians. For some this may be a dietary choice; while for others it may be a matter of principle, for we know that if everyone became a vegetarian there would be more food to go around and the problem of world hunger might be solved. For many people, vegetarianism is a spiritual choice and an affirmation of our fellowship with other animals. As Cora Diamond argues, in our culture at least, we don't eat people, even after they are dead, because in this way we affirm our fellowship with human beings, and define ourselves as human.[46] But in the same way, we may choose not to eat animals because we don't regard the animal as an inferior to be used and consumed; it is a being whose life has value and significance along with our own. We respect the rights of other animals to live and flourish, and we have compassion for their sufferings. But the basis of our compassion is a sense of fellowship and community with all other sentient beings, and this we can choose to affirm by not eating meat.

Compassion for animals allows us to grasp the significance of compassion as a virtue that is ideally unlimited and universal in scope. At this point, we may be uneasy with the idea of universal compassion, which compassion for animals seems to presuppose, but it is clearly preferable to the rejection of compassion as a foolish response. The problem is not that there is too much compassion in the world, but entirely too much cruelty. And as the Dalai Lama points out, the more we can develop compassion the more genuinely ethical our conduct will be.

CHAPTER FIVE

Wisdom

We think we know what it means to be wise, and there is probably some agreement as to which individuals epitomize wisdom, including Socrates, Confucius, the Buddha, and Jesus. But when we try to articulate the nature of wisdom, we find it hard to describe in any determinate way. Virtues like courage and compassion are more self-evident since they involve specific actions, judgments, and feelings. But to call someone "wise" seems to involve a prior metaphysical commitment concerning the nature of the truth, and this is something about which we can always disagree. Thus according to St. Paul, all the wisdom of the ancient philosophers is only so much foolishness because they don't believe in the word of God: "Where is the wise man? Where is the scribe? Where is the debater of this age? Has not God made foolish the wisdom of the world? For since, in the wisdom of God, the world did not know God through wisdom, it pleased God through the folly of what we preach to save those who believe."[1] On the other hand, philosophers like David Hume or Bertrand Russell would never accept the "wisdom" of those who subscribe to metaphysical or religious beliefs because they regard such ideas as quite groundless speculations.

We could begin with a common-sense perspective, which says that wisdom involves some kind of deep understanding or knowledge. But what kind of knowledge is it? It seems clear, for example, that wisdom is not the same thing as theoretical knowledge. Plato, in the *Laws*, makes the point that sometimes the most sophisticated and knowledgeable people are actually the most foolish, whereas those who are uneducated are frequently the wisest of all. The Athenian says:

> Then let us take it as definitely settled and proclaim our conviction that no function of government may be entrusted to citizens who are foolish in this sense. They must be reprehended for their folly, though they were the most expert of calculators, and laboriously trained in all curious studies and everything that makes for nimbleness of mind, while those of the contrary sort should be styled wise, even though, as the proverb puts it, they can "neither read nor swim," and it is to them, as the men of sense, that our magistracies should be given.[2]

German scientists used their expertise to develop Zyklon B gas, which killed hundreds of thousands of people in World War II; many of the researchers who worked on the atomic bomb gave little thought to the ethics of what they were doing, and Oppenheimer, who was in charge, described the construction of the bomb as a "pretty problem." Would we really want to call these people "wise," even though they were highly intelligent? Likewise, Mr. Casaubon in George Eliot's novel *Middlemarch* is an intelligent man who knows a lot; he has amassed an incredible amount of information in preparing to write his book, "The Key to All Mythologies," but he is not wise because he has no principle of selection or any sense of the impossible nature of his project.

A second possibility would be to suggest that wisdom is equivalent to practical knowledge, which is just the ability and know-how that gets things done. On this view, practical knowledge is a kind of everyday wisdom. But practical knowledge—or know-how—doesn't always have good ends. Iago very skillfully plots Othello's ruin by convincing him that Desdemona is having an adulterous affair; Iago is clever and leaves a trail of false clues that leads Othello to murder his wife. But in the end, this is an example of cunning, not wisdom, for wisdom requires us to pursue only those goals that should be pursued. And if corrupting someone else is not a worthy goal, then it isn't wise to pursue it, even if you can easily achieve it. Of course, Iago could reply that anything apart from the pursuit of self-interest is high-minded stupidity, but even this involves a recognition that the wisdom of an action must be related to one's final goal; without knowing what our final goals should be, no matter how skillful or adept we are, we cannot say that our actions are "wise."

A third possibility would be to say that wisdom is equivalent to philosophical knowledge. But this doesn't get us very far since "philosophical knowledge" is an essentially disputed concept. Pythagoras, who was the first to define philosophy as the love of wisdom, emphasized that the pursuit of wisdom involves a commitment to a complete way of life. Pythagoreans lived in closed communities and cultivated their mathematical and philosophical teachings; their intellectual discoveries were just part of a much broader regimen that included physical and dietary practices that aimed at the liberation of the whole self. Socrates is the archetype of philosophical wisdom and yet he claims that his wisdom has no content, apart from the fact that he knows that he doesn't know anything. Plato defines wisdom as knowledge of the eternal forms, and in the *Republic* the philosopher rules the ideal city by looking toward the form of the Good as his ultimate model. Aristotle rejects the theory of the forms as irrelevant. His own views about wisdom are more complicated because he distinguishes between practical wisdom (phronesis) and theoretical wisdom (sophia). "It is thought to be the mark of a prudent man [phronimos]," he writes, "to be able to deliberate rightly about what is good and advantageous for himself; not in particular respects, e.g. what is good for health or physical strength, but what is conducive to the good life generally."[3] Clearly, phronesis is a virtue; indeed it seems to be the organizing virtue for the whole of our moral life, for without a basic sense of the good life, individual virtues would have no defining context. Wisdom as sophia, on the other hand, involves the knowledge of first principles, as well as the ability to apply them. In the *Metaphysics*, Aristotle summarizes some existing ideas:

> All men suppose what is called Wisdom to deal with the first causes and the principles of things; so that, as has been said before, the man of experience is thought to be wiser than the possessors of any sense-perception whatever. . . . We suppose first, then, that the wise man knows all things, as far as possible, although he has not knowledge of each of them in detail; secondly that he who can learn things that are difficult, and not easy for man to know, is wise . . . also, that which is desirable on its own account, and for the sake of knowing it is more of the nature of Wisdom than that which is desirable on account of its results.[4]

This is a contentious position, however, insofar as it views the highest wisdom as having no other end than itself. At the end of the *Nicomachean Ethics*, Aristotle argues that contemplation is the highest activity of which we are capable, since it is the most godlike, and this suggests that phronesis is only a stepping stone. But Aristotle's account of wisdom as contemplation [theoria] seems remote from ordinary human concerns, and we may wonder about the relevance of such wisdom and its status as a virtue for anyone apart from philosophers. If it is to count as an ethical virtue, its relevance must be demonstrated by its integration into personal life. But a knowledge that had no effect on personal experience and made no difference to the way we live would be distinct from all of our ethical motives. In short, the history of philosophy can offer no consistent perspective on the nature of wisdom; individual thinkers, like Aristotle, appear conflicted; while contemporary philosophers have neglected the subject almost entirely.

Thinking about wisdom is fraught with difficulty, and it may well be the case that we are predisposed to view wisdom through the lens of our own metaphysical commitments. We need a more oblique way of thinking about wisdom, and in what follows my strategy will be to look at three significant literary examples of folly in order to apprehend the nature of wisdom by focusing on its opposite. My examples will be King Lear, Ivan Ilyich, and Don Quixote, chosen in part because they are well known but also because they complement each other in clarifying different aspects of wisdom in its absence.

First, King Lear is a foolish old man who comes up with an absurd test to see which of his daughters loves him the most, and he divides his kingdom accordingly. "Tell me my daughters / (Since now we will divest us both of rule, / Interest of territory, cares of state), / Which of you shall we say doth love us most, / That we our largest bounty may extend / Where nature doth with merit challenge?"[5] As the play makes clear, the ability to praise someone is no real measure of love; Cordelia really does love her father, but she disdains to put that love into words since her love is pure and precious, and to express love for the sake of some material reward is to debase it. This seems so obvious to everyone else, but Lear is filled with a sense of his own importance, and he doesn't really understand other people. He can't see the real devotion of Cordelia because he is vain and self-absorbed. But in the play, he learns the value of what he has lost through suffering and despair. He is driven mad by everything that happens, but at the same time, his madness involves the restoration of wisdom as he comes to understand how precious it is to have others who cherish us and whom we cherish, and not to think of ourselves as the center of everything.

In *The Death of Ivan Ilyich*, Tolstoy describes a man who was the perfect functionary and civil servant. He lived his life according to the book, and he did everything that he was supposed to. But now he is facing his imminent death, and he cannot accept what is about to happen to him because he thinks his suffering is undeserved, as he never did anything wrong: "'Maybe I did not live as I ought to have done,' it suddenly occurred to him. 'But how could that be, when I did everything properly?' he replied, and immediately dismissed from his mind this, the sole solution of all the riddles of life and death, as something quite impossible."[6] When he wasn't working, Ivan squandered his existence on frivolous things, like playing cards and going to dances, and his chief excitement was for objects like the furnishings of his new apartment. Of course, he knew in an intellectual sense that everyone has to die, but he never grasped this on the profound level of his own being, and so he never accepted his mortality until it was too late: "The syllogism he had learnt from Kiezewetter's Logic: 'Caius is a man, men are mortal, therefore Caius is mortal,' had always seemed to him correct as applied to Caius, but certainly not as applied to himself. That Caius—man in the abstract—was mortal, was perfectly correct, but he was not Caius, not an abstract man, but a creature quite, quite separate from all others."[7] And so Ivan lived a frivolous life and never took stock of what was really important until the very end, when reflection became unavoidable. *The Death of Ivan Ilyich* illustrates the absolute importance of critical reflection on one's own life, the wisdom that comes from accepting one's own mortality, and the temptation to lose oneself for the sake of things that are really unimportant.[8]

Don Quixote is another foolish man who takes up the life of a noble knight long after the age of chivalry has ended. Don Quixote is ridiculed by the local people for "tilting at windmills" and pursuing the servant girl Dulcinea as if she were a princess. But even though he is deluded and out of touch with reality, he is a profoundly honorable man, and we understand Sancho Panza's devotion to him. Don Quixote may be out of touch with the real world, but we appreciate him because we greatly prefer the vision of a noble existence that he strives to represent. When Don Quixote finally does awaken from his delusion, it is not a time for rejoicing but a time for sorrow as the rule of ordinary life is reasserted. "Now all profane histories of knight errantry are odious to me. I know my folly now, and the peril I have incurred from the reading of them. Now, by God's mercy, I have learnt from my own bitter experience and I abominate them."[9] The reader is made to realize that Don Quixote's folly derives from the disconnection between his own lofty ideals and the real world that surrounds him. But his inability to live in the real world is actually a sign of his own inherent nobleness.

All of these examples emphasize particular aspects of folly while collectively they suggest a very basic account of the nature of wisdom: that wisdom implies living life in the right way and having a very grounded sense of what is important and what is trivial; it involves making good judgments and choices about how we should live; and it implies having a sense of one's own limits, including the absolute limit of human mortality. To be wise also involves having a sense of one's place in the world and how one fits in with others, and recognizing that they have similar kinds of desires and needs even if their situation is completely different from our own. All of this is still quite general, but we may now extract three basic aspects that should form the core of any more sustained account of wisdom, namely: *reflection*, *integration*, and *the thoughtful awareness of others*. This is not a precise formula of the nature of wisdom, but a very basic attempt to sketch its most important distinguishing features.[10]

The first aspect is *reflection*, which implies the ability and the readiness to stand back or stand apart from what is given to consider its value, its ultimate significance, as well as its strengths and weaknesses. Self-knowledge is an especially important example of this kind of reflection and it is the imperative that is inscribed at the entrance to the temple of Apollo at Delphi: "Know thyself!" which, as Socrates shows, means know your limitations and mortality. Ivan Ilyich seems to be completely lacking in critical reflection about anything. He just accepts the way things are and the part that he is apparently destined to play. He seldom thinks about the value of what he's doing, and he only does what is customary or expected because it is customary or expected. He never considers whether he's really living a good life until the very end when he can no longer avoid the reflection on his life that his imminent death requires. In all of this, he is like Plato's cave dwellers who spend their lives obsessed with shadows and who never think about what lies behind the shadows, or what is important, as opposed to what is just an illusion. Reflection implies detachment or the ability to take a distance from things, including one's self. The interesting thing is that Don Quixote possessed a kind of reflective wisdom insofar as he took up a critical distance from the impoverished world that surrounded him: His retreat into chivalry was based on resistance to his age and the corruption of its values. And hence we could say that even though he is deluded, he is also wise because he rejected this corruption. Earlier we considered whether wisdom could be construed as a kind of knowledge. I think we must conclude that the mere accumulation of information and technical skill can never be considered wisdom, but it is the critical reflection upon knowledge that makes it so, or the questioning that asks, what is the point of all this learning?

The second aspect of wisdom is *integration*, which involves the drive to make sense out of things and to consider how they fit together in the end. Reflection is usually a focused consideration of particular aspects. But with integration one is more concerned with the whole of things, or the different parts in their relationship to each other, which is sometimes referred to as the "big picture." Amongst other things, this means knowing what is ultimately important and what is irrelevant, and how different human projects relate to each other. Thus Don Quixote's return to chivalric values may have been a sort of critical reflection on his age, but he didn't make any explicit connections between his own project and the world that he resisted; in this respect, he lacked an integrative understanding of the world and was limited to heroic folly. More generally, we might say that wisdom as integration involves understanding the place of human beings in the order of nature, and even grasping the significance of our own lives in the ultimate scheme of things. In this regard, one celebrated example of wisdom as integration would be the account that is given in the *Bhagavad Gita*. The text begins with a critical reflection on the part of Arjuna who challenges his duty to fight as a warrior against the opposing clan since this will lead to death and the destruction of those who are in his family. In response Krishna explains Arjuna's moral position, but in terms of the ultimate order of reality that encompasses eons of time and the continual cycle of rebirth toward the ultimate goal of moksha (or salvation). The text celebrates our sense of belonging to the infinite universe, which is personified here by Krishna, and at this point, the marvelous vision is revealed:

> Arjuna saw in that radiance the whole universe in its variety, standing in a vast unity in the body of the God of gods. / Trembling with awe and wonder, Arjuna bowed his head, and joining hands in adoration he thus spoke to his God. / I see in thee all the gods, O my God; and the infinity of the beings of thy creation. . . . / All around I behold thy Infinity: the power of thy innumerable arms, the visions from thy innumerable eyes, the words from thy innumerable mouths, and the fire of life of thy innumerable bodies. Nowhere I see a beginning or middle or end of thee, O God of all, Form Infinite.[11]

The *Bhagavad Gita* is revered as a treasury of wisdom, but it is spiritually appealing because it offers the most profound account of our place in the cosmos as a whole; in this respect, it offers us a vision of complete integration.

I have called the third aspect of wisdom *the thoughtful awareness of others*, and by this I mean a compassionate understanding of others that recognizes the continuity between their lives and our own. No one is completely self-sufficient; we all need each other. To be self-absorbed even in the pursuit of wisdom is not to be wise, since wisdom involves a recognition that the world doesn't revolve around us. And this follows from a compassionate understanding that other people are like ourselves with their own projects and goals, their own strengths and weaknesses. Of course, King Lear was completely lacking in this kind of emotional intelligence. He thought that he was self-sufficient and self-contained and so he had nothing to learn from others. He accepted their existence only insofar as they gratified his own. True wisdom, however, implies humility and the recognition of one's limits, including the final limitation that is imposed by death. This should make us more open to others, and it allows us to accept that sometimes we could even be wrong.

In what follows I will use the three basic aspects of wisdom to clarify the life of Socrates and the Buddha, who are typically regarded as the embodiments of wisdom in the Western and Asian traditions, respectively. If these three basic aspects of wisdom—reflection, integration, and the thoughtful awareness of others—have been correctly identified then we would expect that they could clarify the sense in which the Buddha and Socrates are exemplars of wisdom even though they belong to different cultural contexts. It is more difficult to get a grasp on wisdom in the modern world. Today, many would say that wisdom is a redundant category, since it seems to imply another kind of knowledge that cannot be reduced to calculation, which is the dominant model of knowledge for our age. Wisdom has become a neglected virtue and so we have to rethink its possibility by sketching out some paths in thinking that could be pursued at the present time. Finally, in this chapter, I will focus on multiculturalism, an important aspect of the awareness of others, which leads to the enhancement of wisdom and moral growth.

Two Models of Wisdom: Socrates and the Buddha

There is no question that Socrates embodies the ideal of wisdom in the Western intellectual tradition. He is the archetypal philosopher, the one who loves and reveres the truth more than anything, and he is prepared to sacrifice his life for the sake of doing what is right. In Socrates, there seems to be no separation between theory and practice—as he says, the unexamined life is not worth living—and the life of self-examination that he follows is an essential part of the good life he describes. And yet, the paradox is that Socrates claims to know nothing. He is insistent on the extent of his own ignorance, and he argues that the only difference between himself and the so-called expert authorities is that he at least knows how ignorant he is, whereas they believe foolishly that they have knowledge of ultimate things. His philosophical practice also seems mainly negative and critical, calling into question established ideas and demanding justifications for every opinion given. Socrates does not have a set of fixed teachings that he tries to propagate to others. And to all those who are not completely familiar with his way of life, it may appear that he is just another sophist—

questioning things for the sake of challenging tradition—and so he is condemned for corrupting the Athenian youth.

At his trial, Socrates tells the jury that he has no real interest in the ultimate nature of the cosmos or the kind of metaphysical issues that inspired speculative philosophers like his predecessor Anaxagoras: "I mean no disrespect for such knowledge, if anyone really is versed in it . . . but the fact is, gentlemen, that I take no interest in it."[12] For Socrates, philosophy is practical, and he held that it should lead to personal transformation. He was preoccupied with the meaning of the good life as the most urgent question that should concern us; but he realized that he couldn't tell people how to live their lives, since this would only create followers who couldn't think for themselves. At the same time, Socrates sowed the seeds of dissatisfaction with the received ideas and beliefs that condition all our lives. Plato describes it best in the story of the cave: We spend our lives preoccupied with insignificant things, the pursuit of wealth or fame, which are just shadows of the things that really matter, like virtue and the nature of the good. Finally, the one who finds his way out of the cave feels compelled to return to help others to experience the same enlightenment. He is ridiculed by the cave dwellers for suggesting there could be anything apart from the shadows that enthrall them, but he is insistent, and soon they are ready to kill him. Socrates—or the one who escaped from the cave—does not force people to leave their darkness; he doesn't push them out of the cave because he realizes that self-transformation can only be meaningful if it is something the individual accomplishes for herself. Hence the wisdom of Socrates is the wisdom of the teacher who cares about others and who tries to communicate his enthusiasm while inspiring them to reflection on their own. It is the wisdom of reflection that critically scrutinizes everything in the name of the truth to determine whether it can be justified. And it is the wisdom that seeks to gather everything together to realize a sense of our place in the world, or the relationship between the cave of ordinary experience and the higher realities that transcend it.

This is only an initial sketch, but we can now clarify three aspects of the wisdom of Socrates by looking at three significant incidents in his life—the story of the oracle, his self-identification as a spiritual midwife, and his preparation for death and dying—which emphasize the principles of reflection, the thoughtful awareness of others, and integration, respectively. Obviously, this is somewhat self-fulfilling—we have offered a preliminary account of wisdom in terms of these aspects, and now we are choosing examples that will support the division that we've given. But the analysis must start somewhere, and after discussing Socrates in these terms, I will consider the embodiment of wisdom in an entirely different cultural context by thinking about the wisdom of the Buddha. If the basic structure that I have argued for can also help to make sense out of the Buddha's wisdom, then that would be some evidence for its validity.

We can begin with the story of the oracle that Socrates describes in the *Apology*. When Socrates' friend Chaerephon asked the Delphic oracle whether anyone was wiser than Socrates, the oracle's response was an unequivocal "no." When Socrates was told that, he was seriously perplexed: on the one hand, the oracle was the voice of Apollo so he could not choose to disregard it or consider it wrong; but on the other hand, all of the politicians, poets, and religious experts in Athens seemed to possess a wealth of knowledge about things that he clearly didn't have. So he could neither believe nor disbelieve the oracle, and this impasse leads him to test for himself whether the oracle is mistaken or correct.[13] From a traditional perspective such a response is completely impious since it takes the determination of the truth away from the ultimate religious authority and makes the individual the final judge. But in this way, Socrates begins his career of challenging those who claim to have wisdom. He finds that while some might have specific knowledge or some particular skill, they don't have special wisdom concerning the deeper questions of life; or if they do have wisdom, like the poets, they cannot properly explain the meaning of their words since they are inspired by the gods and didn't reach these conclusions through their own intellectual effort. Eventually, Socrates comes to the conclusion that the oracle was making a more general point about human understanding rather than any specific claim about Socrates himself. Unlike most people, Socrates was fully aware of the extent of his own ignorance; he had no illusions about his limitation as a human being and so the oracle calls Socrates the wisest man in Athens, as a way of underlining the more basic point that true wisdom begins with the recognition of your own ignorance. In his conversations with others, Socrates is often directed by this insight—for if Euthyphro and Thrasymachus claim to know what piety or justice is, they will not be open to any further reflection and discussion about these things until they are made to realize that they don't know what they are talking about.

Wisdom involves an attitude of profound humility. But at the same time it also requires a continual reflection on what is given. Thus it is significant that Socrates begins his philosophical practice by questioning the oracle itself. For in this way, he inaugurates a new model of piety, a new service to the gods, which he continues even after the meaning of the oracle has become clear to him. He pursues this radical reflection in all of his encounters with others, and he regards it as a form of devotion to the gods that was implicitly commanded by the oracle itself. Hence he comes to regard philosophy as a divine mission that he can never abandon, even if it should cost him his life. Socrates practices reflection, then, in the form of continual questioning and the critical scrutiny of whatever is proposed as worthy and good. And this reflection implies a critical distance or detachment from all of the established customs and ideas, and from his own life, insofar as self-examination and self-knowledge are among his most important goals. But reflection is just one of three aspects that are crucial to wisdom. The point of wisdom is not reflection or critical questioning for its own sake. Reflection is balanced by the impulse of integration and conditioned by the thoughtful awareness of others. Socrates' project of the examined life was something he realized for the sake of his fellow Athenians and for human beings in general.

After reflection, then, we may consider the second aspect of Socrates' wisdom, which involves the thoughtful awareness of others. Socrates is not a hermit, and he seems to spend most of his life in the marketplace in discussion with other people. For him, philosophy is an essentially social activity, and it begins and ends with dialogue that embodies the collective pursuit of the good. Socrates' project isn't selfish or self-serving. He doesn't want to win followers for himself, and he says he has nothing to teach them. But in two central metaphors that he uses to describe what it is that he does, the focus on the good of the other person is the determining consideration. In the *Theaetetus*, Socrates describes himself as a kind of spiritual midwife. The image implies care and authentic concern for the other person that cannot be manipulative or controlling. He is first and foremost a teacher, and he assists in the spiritual birth of another. He understands the different kinds of souls and personalities that people have, and he will use different techniques, including relentless criticism or gentle questioning, to guide that person toward self-examination and the meaning of the good life as the most important question of all. Here, we could also mention Socrates' decision not to escape and to accept the decision of the court even though he knew the verdict was wrong. He says in the *Crito* that he doesn't want to do violence to the laws of Athens, which he compares to the parents who gave him life; he cannot disrespect or disregard them because it wouldn't be just, and it would also set an example for resisting the law whenever it doesn't suit you. Socrates' position may be challenged. But the significant point is that in all of this Socrates is most concerned with the possible effect upon others and how escaping or relinquishing philosophy would make philosophy into a conditional good that could be abandoned whenever danger threatened.

Socrates also compares himself to the gadfly. He is like the annoying sting-ing fly who won't let the lazy horse of Athens rest. Nothing would be easier than to rely on the fixed customs that organize Athenian life from one gen-eration to the next, or to assume without question that the rulers and the in-stitutions are decent and needn't be called to account. But this way leads to spiritual torpor and the decline of society in general. And so, for the good of society itself, he practices philosophical questioning that asks for reasons and requires justifications for everything. He realizes the danger he faces: social critics are viewed as subversives and are likely to be slapped down by a gov-ernment that is insecure. But philosophy is Socrates' service to the commu-nity and to his fellow Athenians. For Socrates, philosophy is a basic social good that enhances the life of the individual and helps to strengthen the moral authority of the state through its ongoing critique. Both the gadfly and the midwife derive from the thoughtful consideration of others. And this is an essential aspect of Socratic wisdom: Without it we might admire him as a skilled debater, but I don't think we would consider him a wise man, because his cleverness would all be self-promoting.

Finally, the third aspect of wisdom is integration, and it involves an at-tempt to grasp the big picture. This includes a sense of which things are re-ally important and worth striving for and those that aren't valuable at all; the relationship between the individual and the community that he or she be-longs to; and the relationship between life and death. In the *Republic* Plato has Socrates present us with an integrated vision of the whole of being: In the simile of the divided line and the story of the cave, he offers a compelling metaphysics and an epistemology, an ethics and a political theory that are all interrelated. But this is more Plato's vision than Socrates', and it is certainly inconsistent with Socrates' profession of ignorance. When I say that wisdom involves integration, I don't mean that the wise person must have his or her own systematic philosophy; indeed, we may question whether reality is even open to systematic appropriation at all. Integration in the sense I mean it is the attempt to make sense out of things and to grasp their final significance in the overall context of the whole. It also means taking this understanding and using it to transform one's own life so that it is in attunement with the way things are. Wisdom is not just an intellectual content but something that is affirmed by the whole person who is affected by it. And in Socrates there is a complete integration between theory and practice that shows the fulfillment of this aspect of wisdom.

One example of integration in Socrates' life would be his ongoing reflec-tion on death and its significance for the meaning of life. Beginning with the *Apology*, where he poses the priority between dishonor and death, and later in the *Phaedo*, in which he considers arguments for the immortality of the soul, Socrates offers a sustained reflection on the place of death in human affairs. His thoughtful attitude to death clearly shapes and transforms his attitude to life, his emotional bearing at the trial and afterward when he faces execution. In the *Apology*, Socrates offers the argument that death must be one of two things: oblivion or movement to another realm, where he will be able to meet those who died before him. Neither possibility seems particularly bad—annihilation would be like a long dreamless sleep, whereas the movement to another realm would be exciting, since it would allow him to discuss important questions with all the sages of the past. In either case, death will be an adventure: there is no good reason to fear it, and indeed to be afraid of it is to claim to have knowledge about something that no one can possibly have. Now it may be argued in response to this that it is precisely the unknown aspect of death that makes it so fearsome. Socrates recognizes that death is unknowable with the final words he speaks in the *Apology*: "Now it is time that we were going, I to die and you to live, but which of us has the happier prospect is unknown to anyone but God."[14] We need to put this in perspective, however, for what he emphasizes in this dialogue is that death is not the greatest evil. The theme of the *Apology* is that doing wrong is the worst thing of all, so one should always do the right thing, even when this is dangerous or threatens your life. In this way, Socrates integrates his reflection on death into the course of his own life, and he uses it to strengthen his resolution never to abandon the mission of philosophy that he has been called to. I am not suggesting that Socrates' reflections are somehow self-serving, only that he incorporates his thinking about death into the deepest context of his own life; with him it is never an abstract point of speculation but the reality that he lives by.

In the *Phaedo*, Socrates is portrayed as a guru figure, surrounded by his disciples who are all eager to receive wisdom and reassurance about the fate of their master. Socrates discusses the nature of death, and he offers some arguments for the immortality of the soul. But as Gadamer has pointed out, these arguments are inconclusive because they are really not meant to work.[15] Even to be consistent with the *Apology*, death must remain the great unknown. But what the arguments about immortality do call into question is the idea of the soul as another material thing, like an overcoat, which isn't very different from the rest of the physical world. The arguments don't work because this is not the right way to think about spiritual reality. It is the same point that Socrates makes when his friends ask him how they should dispose of his body: "Any way you like, replied Socrates, that is, if you can catch me and I don't slip through your fingers."[16] Death is radically discontinuous with this life and therefore unimaginable. And just as his dead body has nothing to do with his essential nature, so the latter cannot be grasped as if it were any kind of material thing. We cannot know what death is like, but Socrates insists we can prepare ourselves for death; and this is the whole point of philosophical wisdom: "Ordinary people seem not to realize that those who really apply themselves in the right way to philosophy are directly and of their own accord preparing themselves for dying and death."[17] Montaigne and many others have reflected on this famous line. Socrates explains himself directly by saying that the practice of philosophy involves a separation of the mind from the immediate concerns of the body and in this sense it is an anticipation of the final separation that will occur at death. Underlying this, however, is the idea that wisdom involves coming to terms with one's own mortality. It means being ready to die at any moment; it means living well and being so completely attuned to life that one can accept death without regret as an inevitable part of what makes life meaningful. Socrates has integrated this truth into his own life. It is not just an intellectual possibility but something that he lives by. But in the *Phaedo*, even in his final hours, he is for the most part concerned about his followers who are plunged into gloom and despair since they still haven't grasped this wisdom.

The challenge now is to see whether these three aspects of wisdom in the life of Socrates can also help to clarify the wisdom of the Buddha. Of course, there might be many perspectives on the nature of wisdom that could be pursued. But the schema suggested so far would be more compelling if it could elucidate wisdom in a different cultural context. A broad and imprecise category like wisdom may never be definitively analyzed into its constituent parts. But for as long as our schema continues to be illuminating, it offers a reasonable account of what this virtue involves.

The first aspect, then, is reflection, which implies detachment and the critical scrutiny of accepted truths and values. In many respects, an ongoing reflection and spiritual striving is a constant feature of the Buddha's life, and is especially obvious in the path that he takes toward his eventual enlightenment. According to the standard accounts of his life, Gautama is the cherished prince in a royal household. He lives in a luxurious pleasure palace, but it is an existence based on illusion, in which the realities of sickness, old age, and death are deliberately avoided and hidden from sight. Gautama marries and has a child, and his own personal happiness is complete; but when he drives out in his chariot, he meets an old man, a sick man, and a dead man and in this way finally realizes the reality of suffering that has been kept from him up to that point. These encounters change him, and he makes the decision to leave his palace and live as a spiritual seeker. The suffering of others has profoundly affected him and leaves him indifferent to his own personal success and well-being. As the Buddhist scriptures put it: "When he thus gained insight into the fact that the blemishes of disease, old age, and death vitiate the very core of this world, he lost at the same moment all self-intoxication, which normally arises from pride in one's own strength, youth, and vitality. He now was neither glad nor grieved; all doubt, lassitude, and sleepiness disappeared; sensuous excitements could no longer influence him; and hatred and contempt for others were far from his mind."[18] Gautama could have remained in his palace and lived out a comfortable life in peace, but such a life would be based on a lie; instead, he devotes himself to the meaning of human existence and strives with all his being to discover a solution to the problem of suffering.

According to the Buddhist scriptures, he first becomes a follower of the holy man Alara Kalama, who teaches him meditation and the practice of yoga. Alara Kalama, like other teachers at the time, espoused the old Vedic wisdom in claiming that all suffering ultimately derives from ignorance about the nature of the self and its true relationship to the world. Alara Kalama taught that our attachment to the fleeting pleasures of the world and our desire for personal success and fulfillment are based on a faulty understanding of the way things are: The true reality of things is eternal and absolute, and through meditation and other physical and spiritual disciplines like yoga, one can grasp the absolute and unchanging self as an ultimate reality that underlies all of its fleeting manifestations. In traditional Vedic philosophy, the identification of the self with ultimate reality is expressed in the formula, "Atman is Brahman." Alara Kalama taught Gautama that to experience this insight, it was necessary to overcome the ordinary responses of the body and mind—the basis of our egoism—and retrain the self. This could involve the cultivation of exalted meditative states and physical techniques, which would probably include breathing exercises and the manipulation of the body as practiced by yogis. We are told that Gautama was an adept pupil and even surpassed his teachers, Alara Kalama and later Udakka Ramaputta, by achieving the highest meditative state which is "neither perception nor nonperception." But even though he achieved astonishing personal success, he began to have doubts about this particular spiritual path: for one thing, however blissful the meditative states might be, they were always only temporary and didn't offer a lasting solution to the problem of suffering. Gautama also realized that such a state was dependent on his own personal effort; in this respect, it wasn't a revelation of the self's underlying reality, but an act of will on the part of the individual seeker to escape from the basic reality that ultimately remains the same.

Gautama leaves his teachers and becomes an ascetic. Along with five other monks, he practices the life of extreme austerity to the point of self mortification. Again, as the scriptures put it:

> They greeted him reverently, bowed before him, followed his instructions, and placed themselves as pupils under his control, just as the restless senses serve the mind. He, however, embarked on further austerities, and particularly on starvation as the means which seemed most likely to put an end to birth and death. In his desire for quietude he emaciated his body for six years, and carried out a number of strict methods of fasting, very hard for men to endure. At meal-times he was content with a single jujube fruit, a single sesamum seed, and a single grain of rice—so intent he was on winning the further, the unbounded shore of Samsara. The bulk of his body was greatly reduced by this self-torture, but by way of compensation his psychic power grew correspondingly more and more.[19]

Such asceticism is based on the idea that one can overcome the sufferings of existence by punishing the body with penances that eventually make one oblivious to the allurements of pleasure or the ravages of pain. What Gautama realized, however, was that such self-imposed torments only destroyed the inner sense of calm and physical well-being that was necessary for proper meditation on the problems of life. Likewise, by cultivating such an extreme personal discipline, he was only intensifying and enhancing the feeling of the self that should be overcome. The greedy ego had not been obliterated, but only preserved, and so he turned away from the established forms of spiritual wisdom to cultivate his own spiritual path.

The full story of Gautama the Buddha's final enlightenment needn't be told here. As is well known, he sits down to meditate under the Bodha tree, and he resolves that he will not leave off until he has achieved complete understanding:

> For seven days He dwelt there—his body gave him no trouble, his eyes never closed, and he looked into his own mind. He thought: "Here I have found freedom," and he knew that the longings of his heart had at last come to fulfillment. Now that he had grasped the principle of causation, and finally convinced himself of the lack of self in all that is, he roused himself again from his deep trance, and in his great compassion he surveyed the world with his Buddha-eye, intent on giving it peace.[20]

Soon after this, he delivers the Fire sermon, in which he encapsulates his wisdom in the form of the four noble truths, which have previously been described. Let us note, however, that these basic ideas are not simply given by heaven, but they emerge as basic truths in the context of the Buddha's own experience and are given support by his ongoing engagement with the meaning of existence. In this respect, they suggest a complete integration of his own personal experience and his reflective understanding of life.

I will consider one final story from the Buddha's life that emphasizes both the integration of the Buddha's wisdom, the unity of theory and practice, and the thoughtful consideration of others that is definitive of his mission and his teaching. The various scriptures disagree about when this event took place, whether in Gautama's childhood or after he left the palace; but later he remembers what happened, and it becomes one of the final spurs to his enlightenment:

> The beauties of the landscape and his longing for the forest carried him deep into the countryside. There he saw the soil being ploughed, and its surface, broken with the tracks of the furrows, looked like rippling water. The ploughs had torn up the sprouting grass, scattering tufts of grass here and there, and the land was littered with tiny creatures who had been killed and injured, worms, insects and the like. The sight of all this grieved the prince as deeply as if he had witnessed the slaughter of his own kinsmen. He observed the ploughmen, saw how they suffered from wind, sun, and dust, and how the oxen were worn down by the labour of drawing. And in the supreme nobility of his mind he performed an act of supreme pity. He then alighted from his horse and walked gently and slowly over the ground, overcome with grief. He reflected on the generation and the passing of all living things, and in his distress he said to himself: "How pitiful all this!" . . . He sat down, reflected on the origination and passing away of all that lives, and then he worked on his mind in such a way that, with this theme as a basis, it became stable and concentrated. When he had won through to mental stability, he was suddenly freed from all desire for sense objects and from cares of any kind. . . . He had obtained that concentration of mind which is born of detachment, and is accompanied by the highest rapture and joy, and in this state of trance his mind considered the destiny of the world correctly, as it is. . . . When he thus gained insight into the fact that the blemishes of disease, old age, and death vitiate the very core of this world, he lost at the same moment all self-intoxication, which normally arises from pride in one's own strength, youth and vitality. He now was neither glad nor grieved . . . and hatred and contempt for others were far from his mind.[21]

First, the passage shows a complete attunement to the sufferings of others as the undeniable reality of the world. The profound awareness of these sufferings is what motivated and inspired Gautama on his spiritual quest; he is not so much concerned about his own personal salvation but wants to discover the path that could lead others out of this predicament. This is why he loses all "self intoxication" when he experiences profound compassion for the sufferings of others. Indeed, the experience of compassion is only achieved when one puts aside the ordinary self and its desires. The abandonment of self brings about a kind of tranquility and inner peace that it had been his goal to achieve from the outset, and the doctrine that expresses the ultimate unreality of the self both affirms and is affirmed by the doctrine of compassion, which is the focus of the Buddha's ethical view. All of this is tied to the Buddha's own personal experience and offered to us as the ultimate answer to the question, "How should I live?" not as an absolute prescription—"this is what you have to do!"—but as a path that we can take to determine for ourselves whether this perspective is consistent with human existence as we know it.

As in the earlier discussion of Socrates, then, the nature of wisdom can be grasped in terms of three underlying aspects that are also the necessary conditions of wisdom. Reflection is expressed in the Buddha's relentless striving after the truth and his refusal to accept any teaching that remains doubtful; it is also expressed by the priority that he gives to reflection over other motives including his own physical or spiritual well-being. Integration is achieved with his assimilation of personal experience and his overall philosophy of life; the one informs the other, and he achieves a consistent vision of life that illuminates experience, while it is also grounded in experience itself. Finally, the Buddha is not a solitary seeker after the truth: his mission begins out of concern for fundamental human problems, like suffering and death, and it is driven by his compassion for all people. And when he achieves enlightenment he doesn't withdraw from life; he becomes a teacher and intensifies his efforts to communicate his vision to others. In short, he recognizes that he is human like everyone else, and that wisdom isn't wisdom if it is treated as a private possession to be hoarded for personal use.

In the end, Socrates and the Buddha are quite different from each other. For one thing, Socrates is intensely individual, a real character who stands out against the background of Athenian life and culture. And while he is noble, he also takes some delight in offending the respectable city fathers and making light of his arrogant opponents. But the Buddha isn't like this at all. And once he has achieved enlightenment, he has effectively overcome the separate and selfish part of his being. This is not to say that he has become a blank or an empty personality, but his self-regarding desires and wishes have now been supplanted by his compassionate connection with others, and so he appears inscrutable, and more of a type than a concrete individual. Socrates and the Buddha have different perspectives on life, but their underlying moral wisdom is recognizably the same. I would suggest that other wise persons such as Confucius, Gandhi, Black Elk, or Arjuna are wise because they possess the same essential aspects of wisdom.

So far, this discussion has been a kind of reconstruction, but the fundamental critique of wisdom as an exalted possibility hasn't yet been raised: In the contemporary world we still pay lip service to the wisdom of Socrates, the Buddha, and Confucius, but do we really have any sense of wisdom as a relevant possibility that should be cultivated as a virtue? In the next section, I will consider the contemporary unconcern with wisdom, as well as its status as a neglected virtue. And, I will suggest some ways in which wisdom must still be regarded as a significant possibility of human existence in spite of the accumulation of knowledge and the development of technology that seems to be a defining feature of modern life.

Wisdom in the Modern World

Wisdom has become a problematic virtue. We don't quite know what it means to be wise anymore, and we may be suspicious that wisdom is only an illusory ideal. The reality of contemporary life is that the amount of information that is available to us is growing almost exponentially; people may still be experts and specialists in increasingly restricted fields, but to think that anyone could master the whole of knowledge is now an absurd idea. And so we wonder what wisdom might involve, if it is not just the accumulation of knowledge or an overview of the whole of knowledge, which also presupposes knowledge of the whole of knowledge itself. At the same time, one of the most troubling features of contemporary life is the insistent appeal of so much information as a kind of noise that begins to crowd out the possibility of reflection and a silent return to the self. The more skills we learn, and the more information we acquire, the greater the danger that we will lose ourselves and our sense of what it means to be a human being; and the more likely we are to reject the idea of wisdom as a profound possibility of self-understanding, for this is harder to recognize when it's no longer available to us. In an essay called, "Being I, Being We," Luce Irigaray expresses similar forebodings about the state of contemporary culture. Her analysis would explain not only the skepticism concerning wisdom as a real possibility, but also the oblivion of wisdom in the sense that wisdom has become unthinkable; indeed it hardly registers as an issue that needs to be thought:

> We find ourselves today faced with a new situation with regard to culture: we are witnessing the growth of information into space as well as in time, an

accumulation of knowledge on diverse levels and, at the same time, the loss of human consciousness. We know more things but we return less to ourselves in order to examine the meaning of all these things for a more accomplished human becoming. We are discovering that many realities have remained unknown to us up until now but the discoveries that we are making are so numerous that we forget somewhat the reality and the limits of our own being. And the risk exists of knowing a thousand things, but finally reducing ourselves to an effect of acquisition of knowledge, but of no longer knowing anything about who I am, who you are, who we are. The risk exists that we are becoming computer software with a multitude of stored programs but for which the key for defining the possible unity of these programs is missing, as is the manner of passing from one program to the other, the means of using the whole or a part of it in order to communicate with our self, with the other, between us.[22]

If Irigaray is right, then wisdom remains impossible for as long as reflective self-understanding is stifled by the other imperatives of knowledge. In the society that she describes, the emphasis is on continual becoming and change. Personal achievement is measured in terms of innovation and self-overcoming, and youth is most highly valued because it implies complete openness toward the future. Old age is no longer regarded as a repository of wisdom, but a state of dereliction and decline. And wisdom itself becomes an enigma, because we have grown skeptical of the very idea of an abiding (moral) truth.

So what exactly could wisdom mean for us? And can we provide any new perspectives on the possibility of wisdom that would allow us to grasp its continuing significance for contemporary life? We can now return to the three defining aspects of wisdom—reflection, integration, and the thoughtful awareness of others—that we developed earlier. For if we could find a way of thinking about each of these different aspects in a contemporary range of experience then we might recover the ideal of wisdom as a living possibility that enables us to live wisely and well. The following examples are not intended to be exclusive, nor do they have any kind of priority; other possibilities for wisdom may certainly exist, but the three that I have chosen will demonstrate the basic point.

First, philosophy is the original form of reflection, and true philosophy seems to involve calling everything into question, including the value of philosophy itself. As we have seen, Socrates is the archetypal philosopher. But his effect on people is far from comforting or reassuring. In fact, Socrates unsettles people with his call for self-examination, for it means that we can take nothing for granted anymore and everything must be critically examined. It is not an uncommon complaint that contemporary philosophy has lost some of this critical edge. Philosophy today can certainly be difficult and challenging, but it has also become a kind of expertise in thinking, a skilful analysis of particular problems that needn't affect the thinker in any profound way. As Nietzsche comments in "Schopenhauer as Educator:" "Our academic thinkers are not dangerous, for their thoughts grow as peacefully out of tradition as any tree ever bore its apples; they cause no alarm, they remove nothing from its hinges; and of all their art and aims there could be said what Diogenes said when someone praised a philosopher in his presence: 'How can he be considered great, since he has been a philosopher for so long and has never yet *disturbed* anybody.'"[23]

Perhaps one way to restore the radical reflection that philosophy requires would be to make a sharp distinction between ordinary *calculation*, which involves thought in its everyday activity of processing and organizing the manifold according to fixed rules, and *reflection*, which requires letting things present themselves to thought as they really are, unencumbered by the ordinary presuppositions of the understanding. Of course, this is difficult; but this is what lies behind Socrates' own project of self-examination, and this is why we have come to think of Socrates as the paradigm of reflection. And if philosophy has lost its edge, it can still recover it. Hence, the example of Nietzsche, who offers a profound reflection on everything, including the things that are most taken for granted, like the value of our "values" or the truth about "truth." Later, Heidegger also attempts to return us to the true paths of thinking, which he contrasts with ordinary calculation. With calculation, everything is determined in advance; the categories of the understanding already exist and they drive our thinking along pre-established rails. He writes:

> This calculation is the mark of all thinking that plans and investigates. Such thinking remains calculation even if it neither works with numbers nor uses an adding machine or computer. Calculative thinking computes. It computes ever new, ever more promising and at the same time more economical possibilities. Calculative thinking races from one prospect to the next. Calculative thinking never stops, never collects itself. Calculative thinking is not meditative thinking, nor thinking which contemplates the meaning which reigns in everything that is.[24]

Calculative thinking is organized in terms of the subject-object relationship in which the other, the object, is organized in pre-determined ways by the subject, who remains sovereign and out of play. According to Heidegger, calculation ultimately leads to the domination and control of nature insofar as it precludes the possibility of reverence for that which is other than ourselves: "The world now appears as an object open to the attacks of calculative thought, attacks that nothing is believed able any longer to resist. Nature becomes a gigantic gasoline station, an energy source for modern technology and industry."[25] True thinking, or what Heidegger calls meditative thinking, involves an openness to the outside that allows whatever is given to approach and offer itself to thought. As Lyotard writes in a similar context, "In what we call thinking the mind isn't 'directed' but suspended. You don't give it rules. You teach it to receive. You don't clear the ground to build unobstructed: you make a little clearing where the penumbra of an almost-given will be able to enter and modify its contour."[26] This is thought as openness and readiness to receive. It is the resolution not to be resolute, not to rely on fixed determinations and received ideas, and this causes our discomfiture. "The unthought hurts," Lyotard explains, "because we're comfortable in what's already thought. And thinking, which is accepting this discomfort, is also, to put it bluntly, an attempt to have done with it."[27]

It is interesting to note that this kind of radical reflection and questioning of concepts and experiences also inspires Zen Buddhism. As with Socrates and Nietzsche, one of the goals of Zen is to break apart our routine ways of thinking—to call the established oppositions of thinking into question, and to strip away the encrustations of thought to get back to experience before it is distorted by the mind that organizes and controls it. Zen also uses comedy; many of the Zen koans and stories are informed by a particular kind of irreverence that reminds us of the practice of Socrates and the writings of Nietzsche. Consider, for example, this well-known parable on "Reciting Sutras," which is found in the popular collection, *Zen Flesh, Zen Bones*:

> A farmer requested a Tendai priest to recite sutras for his wife, who had died. After the recitation was over the farmer asked: "Do you think my wife will gain merit from this?" "Not only your wife, but all sentient beings will benefit," said the priest, "My wife may be very weak and others will take advantage of her, getting the benefit she should have. So please recite sutras just for her." The priest explained that it was the desire of a Buddhist to offer blessings and wish merit for every living being. "That is a fine teaching," concluded the farmer, "but please make one exception. I have a neighbor who is rough and mean to me. Just exclude him from all those sentient beings.[28]

Through the parable we grasp the profound community of all beings and the illusory nature of individual reality. We also grasp the unlimited and unconditional nature of true compassion, and the folly involved with particular attachments and grievances. The goal of Zen is enlightenment (sartori), which involves a profound attunement to the way things are. This does not imply a passive acceptance of reality, but an active overcoming of traditional formulations that distort our experience and prevent us from apprehending the actual nature of things. Like philosophy at its best, Zen also inspires reflection, and this is an essential key to the wisdom it provides.

We can now turn to integration. One thing that many wise men and women have in common—including Socrates, the Buddha, Confucius, and Jesus—is their use of parables to make a profound point about the nature of life, or to present a moral truth that would be harder to grasp if it was expressed in a more straightforward way. The parable of the Good Samaritan, for example, is an expression of the unconditional devotion of love, while the story of the cave at the high point of Plato's *Republic* is an attempt to explain the basic nature of the human condition and the relationship between ignorance and enlightenment. The whole point of the parable is that it requires an active response on the part of the reader, or the listener, to make sense out of things. And once the reader, or listener, understands, it means that he or she has been able to integrate this truth at a profound level, which is more than just knowing it intellectually. In fact, one might be able to accept this truth even before one is capable of explaining it to others. In the sense that it "rings true" for us, the parable is an example of the second aspect of wisdom—integration.

I want to suggest here that myth in general involves the same integration of wisdom as parables do; indeed myths are parables that allow us to grasp some enduring truth about human beings that may be hidden from us by the distractions of our everyday life. This is certainly not to deny that there may also be historical or political underpinnings to myth. But the fact is, myths do speak to us on a profound level; we do not typically discount them as irrelevant; different versions of the same myth are often found in completely different cultures; and all of this suggests that the appeal of the myth lies in its ability to clarify underlying patterns of human experience—the reality of birth, coming-of-age, old age, and death, etc.—in a significant symbolic form. Today, as many commentators have remarked, we seem to live in a demythologized society; if we still refer to a contemporary "mythology," we mean the fleeting images and icons of popular culture that don't endure for very long before they are replaced by others that are just as transitory. In this regard, however, we may have lost something that would allow us to integrate the reality of our own lives with the basic order of things, or whatever we choose to call it. The myth is a condensation and clarification of human experience. It is not that the myth provides us with the meaning of life; myths are stories of our search for meaning and significance, but they are

more concerned with "the rapture of being alive," as Joseph Campbell so elo-
quently puts it: "so that our life experiences on the purely physical plane will
have resonances within our own inmost being and reality, so that we actually
feel the rapture of being alive."[29] In *The Power of Myth*, Campbell writes that,
"It [myth] integrates the individual into his society and the society into the
field of nature. It unites the field of nature with my nature. It's a harmonizing force."[30] Myth and the enactment of myth in ritual produce a profound
centering of individual life in relation to the universal themes of human existence like birth, maturity, and death. Where myths have been forgotten,
new myths are crafted or old ones are finally recovered, like the "green man,"
the spirit of the wood, who offers a benign image of masculine spirituality in
harmony with the natural world; or the "white goddess" of birth, love, and
death, another significant figure in contemporary spiritual renewal. In this
way, we are able to gain access to an underlying wisdom through the integration of individual life with profound spiritual realities. This is the source
of the power that lies behind works like the *Bhagavad Gita*; it is also the focus of their wisdom in giving us a sense of our place in the cosmos as a whole.

The third aspect of wisdom involves the thoughtful consideration of others. Wisdom is not something to be hoarded or kept for oneself. It involves
an essential relationship to other people, and it is this that clarifies its standing as a virtue. This aspect of wisdom is present in teaching and also in bringing up children. And it is no accident that all of the world's paradigmatic
sages, including the Buddha, Jesus, and Confucius, were teachers who sought
to communicate their ideas or their way of life to others. They expressed
their wisdom in their manner of teaching and in their understanding of how
to communicate with the individual soul of another person. Socrates, for example, always seemed to understand the basic nature of the person he was
talking to, whether it was someone arrogant and boastful like Euthyphro, a
concerned friend like Crito, or a younger man like Glaucon, and he varied
his way of speaking in each case. Kierkegaard, Nietzsche, and the Zen masters all realized that sometimes teaching has to be subtle and indirect. It is
not enough just to point toward something: if you want the student to grasp
the point for herself, you may have to use paradox or metaphor or even point
away from what is being described to focus attention more fixedly on it.

Of course, we may believe that Jesus was divine and the Buddha was completely enlightened, and so they had nothing further to learn from others.
But in the case of human wisdom, it is clear that the wisest teacher doesn't
just pour received wisdom into the minds of his followers, since teaching is a
reciprocal relationship and the wise teacher is one who remains open to the
possibility of learning from others, including those he is trying to teach. This

is certainly the case in Plato's dialogues, when Socrates is inspired by inter-locutors like Phaedrus or Charmides to go even further in his pursuit of the truth. For Socrates, dialogue and conversation are the key to proper under-standing: the truth is not something that is simply inside of me or out there, but it emerges in the dialectical encounter that exists in the space between us. Putting this differently, I would say that to be truly involved with some-one else implies an ongoing possibility of being affected and transformed by that person. For this is what openness to another person really involves. In short, wisdom presupposes an underlying involvement with others, and the way that we communicate our wisdom is an important part of wisdom itself.

These reflections on three essential aspects of wisdom—reflection, inte-gration, and the thoughtful awareness of others—are not systematic or ex-haustive, but they illustrate the relevance of wisdom for contemporary life and the place for wisdom that still exists. Taken together, they suggest the framework for making wise decisions and living well. In the next section, we will focus our discussion on multiculturalism, which is an obvious manifesta-tion of wisdom as the thoughtful awareness of others: It hardly needs to be said that multiculturalism also involves an ongoing critical reflection and as-pires toward the integration of knowledge. Multiculturalism involves a deep respect for other cultures, which embodies alternative perspectives on the nature of the good life. It also presupposes a basic humility with regard to one's own knowledge and cultural understanding, which means accepting from the outset that one could be wrong. In this regard, the goal of multi-culturalism is knowledge of the other and of the culture that supports her, as well as self-knowledge, which leads to moral wisdom and growth.

Multiculturalism as Wisdom

Until recently, America was regarded as the great "melting pot" of different cultures, and each immigrant group was supposed to assimilate into the American way of life. Likewise, in Britain, France, Australia, and elsewhere, the goal of cultural assimilation was for the most part assumed, although mi-nority groups and former colonial subjects usually found it difficult to achieve acceptance or recognition from the establishment order. But things have changed, and now we are more likely to view diversity as a source of strength than a sign of social fragmentation. Likewise, there is a growing sense that we should teach our children about other cultures and other ways of life, and this is supported by the desire to celebrate individual differences and respect oth-ers who come from different backgrounds. In many ways, multiculturalism has become an important feature of the contemporary scene; and while some would argue that multiculturalism involves the loosening of standards and a preoccupation with what is "politically correct," it has also received considerable intellectual support.

The idea of multiculturalism covers a variety of different movements and theoretical perspectives, but central to all of them is the conviction that people in other cultures are entitled to equal respect and concern. This means that other cultures are to be valued because they represent different ways of promoting human flourishing. The guiding impulse behind multiculturalism is therefore to celebrate cultural diversity and to affirm that we usually do have something to learn from other cultures. Instead of trying to determine the highest form of human existence or the best society in any fixed sense, we should recognize that no single culture has a monopoly on the truth, and different forms of life can be equally good. In recent years, the discussion of multiculturalism has focused on the particular issue of group rights. In *Multiculturalism*, Charles Taylor argues convincingly that personal identity is founded upon recognition by others.[31] At the same time, he points out that the cultural identity of a person, as a Muslim, a Quebecker, or a Native American, is a very significant aspect of who that person is. Misrecognition in this context is therefore a form of oppression and harm, and the conclusion may be drawn that we should respect particular individuals as well as the culture or group they belong to. This may involve passing laws to support or preserve cultures, such as allowing aborigines or Native Americans special rights and entitlements that would not be available to the general population. From an ethical perspective, it also means promoting a system of education in which cultural diversity is a theme of reflection at every level.

In his essay on multiculturalism, Charles Taylor claims that all human cultures that have flourished over a considerable period of time must offer some kind of fulfillment to their members and will most likely have something to offer to all human beings, including ourselves. Thus it would be presumptuous to think that we have nothing to learn from other cultures, or that Western culture is the apogee of all human development. In the nineteenth century, Hegel argued that the history of the world travels from east to west, "for Europe is absolutely the end of history," he wrote. "Asia the beginning."[32] But such an attitude allowed him to ignore the wisdom of other cultures as immature and irrelevant, and it suggests an easy justification for slavery and colonialism as means whereby non-Europeans could be brought into contact with European culture at the vanguard of world history. In this same regard, John Stuart Mill, the father of modern liberalism, assumed that contemporary European society, supposedly composed of independent and autonomous subjects, was the proper model for all human development that should now be imposed on the rest of the world. Ironically, in *On Liberty*, Mill wrote passionately in defense of individual freedom and against the tyranny of public opinion and the state. At the same time he argued: "We may leave out of consideration those backward states of society in which the race itself may be considered as in its nonage," since "despotism is a legitimate mode of government in dealing with barbarians, provided the end be their improvement and the means justified by actually effecting that end."[33] By contrast, the virtue of multiculturalism is that it involves an open, affirmative attitude to different cultures and peoples of the world. It actively resists whatever temptation may exist to judge the other in terms of our own norms, and it recognizes that an authentic encounter with another culture must involve taking their moral practices, customs, and goals just as seriously as we take our own. Bhikhu Parekh makes this point very succinctly when he writes that multiculturalism represents the view that "all cultures are partial and benefit from the insights of others, and that truly universal values can be arrived at only by means of an uncoerced and equal intercultural dialogue."[34]

Now, as a celebration of the diversity and value of different cultures, multiculturalism is unproblematic as long as it involves different festivals or different foods or heroes and heroines from other cultures—including Sacajawea, Harriet Tubman, or Fa Mulan. But when we turn to more troubling issues like polygamy, female circumcision, or those cultures that forbid their members a right of exit, matters are more difficult. It could be argued, for example, that if we really affirmed the value of multiculturalism then it would be inconsistent to accept some cultural practices while condemning others. And this implies that multiculturalism ultimately involves relativism and the refusal to make any judgments. It is therefore necessary to emphasize that cultural relativism is not the same thing as moral relativism, and the one does not imply the other. At the same time, it would also be wrong and not in the spirit of multiculturalism to make judgments about other cultures that are simply the reflection of our own moral beliefs. Indeed, this way of thinking leads us back to Hegel, Mill, and all the others who were convinced of the moral superiority of the West. We must now ask whether there can be a middle path between "monoculturalism," which judges every other culture in terms of itself, and relativism, which refuses to make any judgments at all. Or to put this differently, is there an appropriate model that could help us to understand the possibility of moral growth and understanding through the multicultural perspective?

Before answering this question explicitly, I want to look at three moral issues that can be considered from a multicultural standpoint, and I will describe the process of moral growth for the individual who takes these issues seriously. First, the issue of human rights. On the one hand, it isn't difficult to realize the spirit and importance of the United Nations Declaration of Human Rights and the respect to which its claims are intended as universally valid. On the other hand, other cultural perspectives call into question the Western priority of civil rights over economic rights, and some of them even challenge the whole discourse of rights that is so frequently taken for granted. It may well be the case that the right to free speech is beside the point for someone who cannot read or who is struggling to survive from one day to the next. And, while it is the case that human-rights ideas are very helpful in preventing abuses wherever they occur, it is also apparent, through discussion of different cultural perspectives, that the discourse of "rights" is inherently adversarial in character. The insistence on rights and entitlements, while obviously important, may lead to the separation and alienation of people from each other and from any notion of the community that supports them. Likewise it should be emphasized that the discovery of human rights is a relatively recent development in Western history, and it cannot easily be imposed on those cultures that have traditionally given more of a priority to the needs of the community. In China, the conflict between individual reproductive rights and the state's "one couple one child" policy is an obvious case in point: the desire to have several children is clearly not a vicious desire, but in a situation of economic scarcity, is it right for anyone to have several children? Through these discussions, our own understanding of human rights is deepened. We gain a strong sense of the importance of human rights and their universal application; but at the same time, by looking at other cultural responses to the very idea of human rights, we also become more aware of the internal stresses within the doctrine, the possible problems that arise when one emphasizes an individual-rights perspective, and other ways of thinking about the relationship between the individual and the community.

An example from John Stuart Mill offers a relevant historical parallel. In *On Liberty*, Mill seems to assume, without much argument, that individual flourishing is the final goal of all human development and culture. He also views the relationship between the individual and society in largely oppositional terms. He cannot see how tradition or custom could ever nurture individual development. Thus he dismisses China as a strange land dominated by custom where everyone is basically selfless and identical to each other. He even writes disparagingly of "the Chinese ideal of making all people alike."[35] In this way, he misses the possibility of individual self-determination through involvement with the community itself. In Chinese thought, the concept of *li* includes familial and community rituals and ceremonies, and what we would think of as politeness and manners.[36] Mill might see this as the dead weight of tradition upon the individual soul, but for the Chinese sage it is precisely through such rites and rituals that individuals develop and cultivate themselves through their involvement with the community and others. Not to engage appropriately with others, to refuse to mourn when mourning is called for, or to neglect the customary forms of courtesy suggest anomie rather than autonomy. Of course, there will always be some degree of tension between the life of an individual and the mores of a broader community. But in minimizing the possibility of an authentic relationship to the community, and by dwelling on the supposed despotism of custom, Mill's account of the individual is limited and abstract, while it begs the question of how self-cultivation is to be achieved.

Next, we may consider the issue of female circumcision, which provides us with a traditional cultural practice that is at odds with liberal views about self-determination and individual choice. If we respect the values of the culture, thereby condoning female genital mutilation, then we appear to deny the rights of individual women and girls to choose or reject this practice for themselves. But if we respect the value of individual choice, then we are calling a traditional cultural practice into question, and it is unclear whether this is in the spirit of multiculturalism or just the assertion of the liberal Western perspective, which gives a high priority to personal preference. Many girls may want to undergo circumcision, and older women in the community are frequently the strongest supporters of this practice. But if female circumcision is an injury to women, should we still say that personal choice must be the final arbiter of what should be done? This issue is challenging since it does seem so obviously "wrong" from a Western point of view. But even so, a comprehensive discussion of the issue, emphasizing the history of the practice, and the reasons most typically offered in support of it, should lead to a deeper understanding of the place that it occupies within those societies where it is the norm. In what sense is clitoridectomy a patriarchal practice? Is it a form of community affirmation or just a useless relic? How are women hurt by this practice? And if a girl or woman is exempted, to what extent is she disadvantaged within her society? It would be important to point out that there is often considerable opposition to this practice from the women themselves. Too often we think of other cultures as essentially conservative and monolithic in form, when the fact is that all cultures, and not just our own, are in the process of transformation; we do a disservice to other cultures if we ignore the voices of dissent that they frequently contain. Final attitudes toward female circumcision may not decisively change as a result of our research, but we will learn compassion insofar as we understand the total context that forms the background to this practice. It would also be appropriate to consider related issues within our own culture that would undermine a merely dismissive response—by discussing the subordinate role of women in the church, for example, or the importance of a particular media image of female beauty that is frequently internalized as an ideal. The point of the multicultural approach is to make us more open to other cultures, but also more aware of the possible injustice of our own.

Finally, we can look at attitudes toward the environment. On the one hand, there is the anthropocentric attitude that looks at nature, including animals and plants, as objects that exist for our benefit. Such a view, which seems to epitomize the traditional Western outlook, is supported by the "dominion" theory of creation, as opposed to the "stewardship" view. On the other hand, there is the Native American viewpoint expressed in *Black Elk Speaks*, and other works, that calls for respect and reverence for the whole of nature, which is considered sacred. According to the latter way of thinking, human beings do not stand against the world or in opposition to it. We belong to the world, it does not belong to us. We are all part of a larger family, and this brings us responsibilities to other creatures and the world that we inhabit. Perhaps this issue in particular is one that can illuminate the shortcomings of the traditional Western perspective. For if our anthropocentric worldview has led to serious pollution and damage to the natural world we all depend on, then we obviously require another paradigm, another way of thinking about our relationship to the natural world, and the Native American approach to the environment offers us that.

Altogether, these three examples suggest a general model for understanding moral development that is operative in multicultural inquiry. In essence, multiculturalism involves the promotion of dialogue and understanding within and between different cultures. And so we may ask, what are the true conditions for any authentic dialogue? And how are two people or two cultures to be related to each other if mutual understanding and moral progress are to prevail? The brief answer to this would describe the conditions for mutual respect and reciprocity. The participants in any true dialogue should always affirm each other as subjects since mutual openness does not exist as long as the dialogue is construed in terms of the subject-object relation. And it would not be in the spirit of a true dialogue just to project unreflectively upon the other or to judge the other culture in terms of our own. Authentic dialogue involves an encounter between two subjects or cultures that recognize each other as subjects in their own right. This involves taking the other seriously, not judging the other in terms of one's own values and ideals, but trying to understand the other's point of view and the values that inspire her. After this, the next step in trying to understand another culture would be to project, in a more tentative way, one's own values and beliefs to see what commonalities may exist and to what extent the other culture shares the same moral horizon as one's own. This means accepting that one still has much to learn and remaining open to the possibility that one could be wrong.

In this way, our basic moral beliefs are clarified, realigned, and deepened through the encounter with different cultural perspectives. And there is something like a "fusion of horizons" (to use Gadamer's term), which depends upon openness to the other and a refusal to believe that the truth has already been completely given.[37] The multicultural approach does not require the abandonment of our own values in order to appreciate another culture; but neither does it involve judging other cultures against the established values of our own. What happens is that through the authentic encounter, the self is transformed by the other—not obliterated, but inspired and deepened in trying to understand the other's point of view. The multicultural approach may promote a realignment of our basic moral ideas about the world; it may lead to a more critical and thoughtful perspective on our own culture; or it may promote a more compassionate awareness of the lives and sufferings of others. But in any case, the self cannot remain the same self, something fixed and self-contained, if it is truly open and engaged in an authentic attempt at dialogue and understanding. In this regard, multiculturalism is both the means of achieving wisdom as well as an expression of wisdom itself.

~

Conclusion

We have now looked at five different virtues in detail. We have considered the more traditional ways of thinking about courage, temperance, justice, compassion, and wisdom. We have also dwelt on alternative perspectives that force us to reexamine each of these virtues and make us think about their relationship to social movements like pacifism, environmentalism, socialism, animal liberation, and multiculturalism. I want to return here to a more general level of discussion, and in particular, I want to consider some of the enduring questions concerning virtue, which we are now in a better position to answer. Of course, these questions have remained unresolved since they were first articulated, but I think we are bound to raise them here, since they form such an important part of the framework in which thinking about virtue has always taken place. In no particular order, these questions include: What is the relationship between virtue and happiness? Why should I care about virtue? Are the virtues unified, or are they in conflict with each other? And finally, What is the relationship between the virtuous individual and the good society?

The first question, which seemed to preoccupy many of the ancient philosophers, concerns the relationship between virtue and happiness. In book two of the *Republic*, Glaucon and Adeimantus are portrayed as decent young men. They really want to believe that the life of virtue is the best life of all, and they want Socrates to prove once and for all that the more virtuous you are, the happier you will be. But they also know how the real world works; and between them they offer the most powerful account of justice divorced from happiness, in the case of the unjust man who somehow wins a reputation for justice and becomes successful, and the just man who is unjustly punished for crimes he did not commit: "the just man will have to endure the lash, the rack, chains, the branding iron in his eyes, and finally, after every extremity of suffering, he will be crucified, and so will learn his lesson that not to be but to seem just is what we ought to desire."[1]

The *Republic* is a multi-faceted work, and Glaucon's challenge is the impetus behind Socrates' ongoing discussion of education, ethics, and politics and the metaphysical ultimacy of the good. But it's disputable whether Socrates ever proves that the virtuous man is always happy. In book nine of the *Republic*, Socrates returns to this theme by showing how the tyrant, the most unjust of men, is really the prisoner of his own desires; he can't trust anyone, he lives without friends, and he remains quite miserable, even though he does whatever he wants to do—all of which shows that happiness is more than the satisfaction of desire. This is an interesting perspective on the tyrant whose happiness was routinely celebrated by Greek poets. It serves as a useful corrective to the excesses of poetry and shows the superiority of philosophy, at least on this point. But it doesn't provide a response to the question that Glaucon and Adeimantus had posed. And even if it could be shown that, for the most part and in general, virtue involves happiness and vice leads to misery, it remains to be seen whether there are any necessary connections between these ideas.

Aristotle is more ambivalent about the relationship between virtue and happiness. On the one hand, there are passages in which he suggests that the virtuous man is self-sufficient in his virtue, and to be completely virtuous is just what it means to flourish as a human being. In other passages, however, he adopts a commonsense tone when he points out that there are material conditions for happiness—including good health, and not having to suffer poverty or a great personal loss. He writes:

> It seems clear that happiness needs the addition of external goods, as we have said; for it is difficult if not impossible to do fine deeds without any resources . . . . There are also certain advantages, such as good ancestry or good children, or personal beauty, the lack of which mars our felicity; for a man is scarcely happy if he is very ugly to look at, or of low birth, or solitary and childless; and presumably even less so if he has children and friends who are quite worthless, or if he had good ones who are now dead.[2]

Along these lines, virtue is a necessary condition for happiness although it certainly isn't a sufficient one. The Stoics argued that a life lived completely according to virtue was a happy one, by definition in fact, since the virtuous man has no emotional investment in anything that is not under his control. Others have argued, reasonably enough, that a happy life makes one virtuous, but this may be nothing more than a psychological generalization.

The very frequency of this question in ancient philosophical writings is itself significant, and it suggests a point of global anxiety for ancient philosophy itself. Virtue is exalted above all other things, but does it really lead to happiness on every occasion? And if not, why should we sacrifice ourselves for this impossible ideal? This ties into the second question that we need to consider: Why should I care about virtue? meaning, Why should I be virtuous? Or, Why should I be good? The ancient philosophers realized that there was a connection between living a virtuous life and being worthy of esteem: Whether or not they are honored, the good are simply those who are worthy of praise. This is the same connection that Kant focuses on later when he points out that there appears to be an undeniable link between virtue and happiness because it affronts us when a good man is miserable and it strikes us as totally unreasonable for a bad man to prosper and be happy.[3] Virtue and the *worthiness* to be happy go together. And even though virtue doesn't always lead to happiness, we could still say that virtuous people are "happy" in the sense that they don't suffer any pangs of remorse for having acted badly. They are at peace with themselves, and for the virtuous, this may be the most important thing. As Aristotle puts it:

> We conclude, then, that the happy man will have the required quality [i.e., permanence in happiness], and in fact will be happy throughout his life; because he will spend all his time, or the most time of any man, in virtuous conduct and contemplation. And he will bear his fortunes in the finest spirit and with perfect sureness of touch, as being "good in very truth" and "foursquare without reproach." . . . If . . . the quality of a life is determined by its activities, no man who is truly happy can become miserable; because he will never do things that are hateful and mean.[4]

Perhaps the underlying question that needs to be asked here is, What do we really mean by happiness? And the obvious answer is that it all depends on who you ask. In the *Apology*, Socrates insists that the most important thing is simply to do whatever is right, for against this, all other considerations are really secondary and beside the point: "The truth of the matter is this. . . . Where a man has once taken up his stand, either because it seems best to him or in his obedience to his orders, there I believe he is bound to remain and face the danger, taking no account of death or anything else before dishonor."[5] This suggests a model of the virtuous man who is so concerned about virtue that nothing else is important to him. Hence, if he loses his family or his fortune, he isn't devastated; he stays happy because he was never really attached to those things in the first place. But this does not seem possible, or even desirable as an ultimate ideal. It's not possible, because we do not live in an exclusively moral domain. Certainly, we want to do the right thing, but we also want to find love and friendship, to avoid disease and unnecessary suffering, and to be successful in our chosen path of life. All of these things matter to us, and the whole point of living a virtuous life is to achieve these things in the right way, helping others to get what they deserve and want, and promoting the social conditions for the fulfillment of all. There is something quite limited in being virtuous just for the sake of being virtuous: Perhaps what we should say, then, is that for the virtuous person, the most important thing is to be virtuous and live well; and if she achieves this she is to that extent "happy," avoiding guilt and regret. But this does not mean that she will escape the physical or mental anguish that could be the final consequence for doing whatever is right.

Hence, virtue does not always involve flourishing in the fullest sense, which would include both ethical and non-ethical aspects. The good person confined to a prison for many years is not always "happy," unless we assert, unrealistically, that the truly virtuous person doesn't care about anything except being virtuous. But it is also the case that virtue isn't simply equivalent to whatever is useful in maintaining the social order. Virtue doesn't guarantee the flourishing of the individual (although it may be a necessary condition for it), and virtue doesn't always promote the flourishing of the state: From the perspective of the Athenian government, for example, Socrates' continual questioning of the established authorities, laws, and values is worse than useless insofar as it seems to undermine fixed structures without which society might not survive—especially at this crucial time after the defeat of Athens at the end of the Peloponnesian war. Socrates bases his whole life on self-examination and the commitment to virtue and truth, and he inspires others to live the same way. But there is no guarantee that Socrates' virtuous activity as a gadfly will ultimately strengthen the state—in the short-term it threatens to undermine it, and presumably this is why the charges against him were found to have some merit.

So why should I be virtuous? This question cannot be answered by providing selfish reasons to be virtuous since no one is virtuous if they only act on the basis of rewards or to avoid punishment and censure. What we can say, however, is that the desire to be virtuous is the measure of our commitment to others, and the ideal community that we affirm through living a virtuous life. From this we can derive a commitment to an ideal version of oneself—this is the person that I want to be—as well as the corresponding commitment to all that is good in others. These are things that matter to me; and if I am truly virtuous they will probably matter more than anything else, which doesn't mean that nothing else matters. Something like this is what Kant intended by the kingdom of ends that would be the ultimate product of moral activity; it is also the basis of the Christian community of Thomas Aquinas, or the ideal republic that Plato describes. All of these different ideas express the shared insight that being virtuous requires thinking of oneself, at some level, as the member of an ideal community even when the actual community that we belong to is corrupt and in decay. And to maintain one's commitment to this ideal over a sustained period of time is to live a virtuous life. In the *Republic*, Plato puts it this way: "'But in heaven,' I said, 'perhaps a pattern is laid up for the man who wants to see and found a city within himself on the basis of what he sees. It doesn't make any difference whether it is or will be somewhere. For he would mind the things of this city alone, and of no other.'"[6] Virtuous activity, then, is actually a kind of faith—not faith in a mysterious transcendent ideal such as "the Good," or God—but faith in the moral community that I subscribe to and already belong to through the activity of virtue. In this case, my "faith" helps to create the moral reality that I affirm. I may still be frustrated and unhappy, but by identifying with the ideal community, I am orienting myself in relation to the ethical good. It matters to me that I am doing the right thing; I make a commitment of my whole person, and not just an intellectual commitment, by living a virtuous life.

Turning to the third question, we can now ask about the unity of the virtues. Today it may seem unreasonable to assert the unity or harmony of the virtues as if it was required by moral necessity. We know, for example, that the virtue of patience and the virtue of acting decisively are sometimes at odds with each other, and someone may strongly desire to do the right thing but still lack the virtue of courage. But the unity of the virtues implies that if you have one virtue, then you should have all of them. I don't believe this is an insuperable problem: a virtuous person, by definition, is concerned about doing the right thing, and she wants to do what is best. She will seriously make every effort to bring about what she knows to be right and good. At the very least, being cowardly is something that will matter to her, and she will do everything in her power to overcome that deficiency. She will not be able to say in a spirit of resignation, "I want to be good, but I'm just not brave enough." Even if she realizes that this is the case, this is something she will struggle to overcome, for the commitment and orientation to virtue cannot be partial in the sense of being selective.

In this book, I have focused on five important virtues: courage, temperance, justice, compassion, and wisdom, as the most basic—or "cardinal"— virtues that support all the others. While it may well be the case that some of the secondary virtues could be in tension with each other, I don't believe that these foundational virtues can be in conflict. For one thing, we have remarked on the interconnections between these virtues, and the respect to which they seem to imply each other. Compassion is itself a form of wisdom because it is based on the recognition that everything is interconnected and interdependent; courage requires justice because without it we may achieve evil ends that the faint-hearted would not even dare to attempt; and justice requires having courage because you can't be considered just if you lack the courage to stand by the principles that you support. Other examples could be given, but the point is that all of these are different aspects of the unity of the virtues. And significantly, the harmonious attunement of the virtues is itself an aspect of temperance that has already been described. In this regard, what may seem to be a conflict between the virtues is more likely a failure of temperance, which is the deep wisdom that sustains our place in the order of things and promotes an inner harmony. I recognize that this response is only provisional, and more work needs to be done to confirm this idea. But I am struck by the mutual implication of all of these virtues—the fact that they are defined in terms of each other—and this leads me to anticipate the basic unity of virtue itself.

The remaining question concerns the relationship between individual virtue and the good society. We have noted how in recent years philosophers and other social commentators have become more interested in the virtues that were the focal point of moral understanding in ancient philosophy but then became neglected in the modern period. One reason for the return to virtue is that Kantian and utilitarian ethical philosophies are unable to give us a sense of the real depth of the moral life. They offer no real guidance on the significant question, How should I live? except to say that the individual should follow the principle of utility, the categorical imperative, or some other fixed moral principle, and this promotes a very thin or abstract conception of the self as the moral decision-maker. Reflection on the variety of moral virtues returns us to the complexity of moral life. But at the same time, it is important to note that the return to virtue is not just a return to Aristotle or Aquinas; nor is it a return to a region of "moral experience" that has no connection to the social and cultural movements that surround it. Virtues always develop within a particular community and are shaped by social forces. In reflecting on the virtues, we need to maintain this awareness of social implication, and think about ways in which virtues illuminate the broader social context they belong to.

It seems obvious that our virtues are conditioned by the society in which we live; they are not purely individual goals and achievements since they precede us and inspire us, and their possibility already exists before any philosopher makes them explicit. In this book, I wanted to show how reflection on the virtues can be a lens through which to look at society itself, and how it supports various social movements that are significant in the world today. These movements—pacifism, environmentalism, socialism, animal liberation, and multiculturalism—are the correlatives of the particular virtues we have discussed, and in this respect, this book has been about "radical virtues" that are implicated in the world and force our attention on them. I have shown how the virtuous individual and the good society may be shaped and conditioned by each other in significant ways. But I would deny that the virtue of the individual is simply conditioned by the virtues of society, for both poles must exist separately if moral progress is to ensue.

From a scholarly perspective, the weaknesses of this book are legion: it is too wide-ranging and idiosyncratic, and ultimately it is only a sketch. But these weaknesses may also be its strengths, since the goal is to provoke a renewed understanding of the virtues, to show their relationship to broader social issues, and through a clash of different perspectives, to realign traditional ways of thinking about them. This work is meant to be unsettling, and it is not intended as a complete moral system in which everything finds its own allotted place. In the end, I want to stimulate reflection on the virtues because I think that moral growth follows from the incorporation of these ideas. And in this respect, at least, I believe that virtue can be learned, even if the deeper question remains whether virtue can ever be taught.

~

Notes

Introduction

1. See especially, Elizabeth Anscombe, "Modern Moral Philosophy" (1958), in *Collected Philosophical Papers*, iii (Minneapolis: University of Minnesota Press, 1981), 26–42; Philippa Foot, *Virtues and Vices* (Oxford: Blackwell, 1978); James Wallace, *Virtues and Vices* (Ithaca: Cornell University Press, 1978); Alasdair MacIntyre, *After Virtue*, 2nd ed. (Notre Dame: University of Notre Dame Press, 1984); Edmund Pincoffs, *Quandaries and Virtues* (Lawrence: University of Kansas Press, 1986); Rosalind Hursthouse, *On Virtue Ethics* (Oxford: Oxford University Press, 1999); Michael Slote, *From Morality to Virtue* (Oxford: Oxford University Press, 1995); Christine Swanton, *Virtue Ethics: A Pluralistic View* (Oxford: Oxford University Press, 2005); Thomas Hurka, *Virtue, Vice, and Value* (Oxford: Oxford University Press, 2003). Some representative collections include Roger Crisp and Michael Slote, eds., *Virtue Ethics* (Oxford University Press, 1997); Daniel Statman, ed., *Virtue Ethics: A Critical Reader* (Washington, D.C.: Georgetown University Press, 1997); Ellen Paul, Fred Miller, et al., eds., *Virtue and Vice* (Cambridge: Cambridge University Press, 1995); Peter French et al., eds., *Midwest Studies in Philosophy vol. 13: Ethical Theory: Character and Virtue* (Notre Dame: University of Notre Dame Press, 1988). More popular works include William Bennett, *The Book of Virtues* (New York: Simon and Schuster, 1993); William Bennett, *The Children's Book of Virtues* (New York: Simon and Schuster, 1995); Andre Comte-Sponville, *A Small Treatise on the Great Virtues* (New York: Henry Holt, 2001).

2. Aristotle, *The Ethics of Aristotle*, trans. J. A. K. Thomson (London: Penguin, 1995), 1099a17.

3. Aristotle, *Ethics*, 1106b24.

4. Aristotle, *Ethics*, 1107a1.

5. Aristotle, *Ethics*, 1106a15.

6. John Stuart Mill, *Utilitarianism* (Indianapolis: Hackett, 2001), 38.

7. Friedrich Nietzsche, *Beyond Good and Evil*, trans. Walter Kaufmann (New York: Vintage, 1966), section 199.

8. Friedrich Nietzsche, *The Gay Science*, trans. Walter Kaufmann (New York: Vintage, 1974), section 335.

9. Plato, *Republic*, trans. Allan Bloom (New York: Basic Books, 1991), 509b.

10. Immanuel Kant, *The Metaphysics of Morals*, trans. Mary Gregor (Cambridge: Cambridge University Press, 1991), 197.

11. David Hume, *An Inquiry Concerning the Principles of Morals* (Indianapolis: Bobbs-Merrill, 1957), 83.

12. See MacIntyre, *After Virtue*, especially chapter 10, "The Virtues in Heroic Societies."

Chapter 1: Courage

1. Immanuel Kant, *The Metaphysics of Morals*, trans. Mary Gregor (Cambridge: Cambridge University Press, 1991), 186.

2. See Michel de Montaigne, "Of Honorary Awards," in *The Complete Essays of Montaigne*, trans. D. Frame (Stanford: Stanford University Press, 1958), 277.

3. Immanuel Kant, *Foundations of the Metaphysics of Morals*, trans. L. Beck (Indianapolis: Bobbs-Merrill, 1959), 9.

4. See, for example, R. B. Brandt, "Traits of Character: A Conceptual Analysis," *American Philosophical Quarterly* 7 (1970): 23–37. James Wallace summarizes this view as follows: "Courage and . . . other virtues are privative states. Their polar opposite vices are tendencies to act in certain situations from certain types of motives, while these virtues are the absence of such tendencies." See James Wallace, *Virtues and Vices* (Ithaca: Cornell University Press, 1978), 61.

5. Homer, *The Iliad*, trans. W. Rouse (New York: New American Library, 1938), 244.

6. Homer, *The Iliad*, 218.

7. David Hume, *An Inquiry Concerning the Principles of Morals* (Indianapolis: Bobbs-Merrill, 1957), 77.

8. Hume, *Inquiry*, 82.

9. Aristotle, *The Ethics of Aristotle*, trans. J. A. K. Thomson (London: Penguin, 1995), 1115b22.

10. Aristotle, *Ethics*, 1107b1.

11. Aristotle, *Ethics*, 1115a7.

12. Aristotle, *Ethics*, 1105b10.

13. Aristotle, *Ethics*, 1115a27.

14. Aristotle, *Ethics*, 1115a33.

15. Aristotle, *Ethics*, 1115b21.

16. Aristotle, *Ethics*, 1117a3.

17. Homer, *The Iliad*, 239.

18. This, for example, is the position taken by William Ian Miller in his recent book, *The Mystery of Courage* (Cambridge: Harvard University Press, 2002), 254–70 especially.

19. Thomas Aquinas, *Summa Theologiae* vol. 42 (London: Blackfriars, 1966), 19.

20. Aquinas, *Summa Theologiae*, 19.

21. Aquinas, *Summa Theologiae*, 21.

22. For an excellent discussion of the significance of the paradigm example in Aristotle and Aquinas, see Stanley Hauerwas, "The Difference of Virtue and the Difference it makes," *Modern Theology* 9.3 (1993): 249–64.

23. Aquinas, *Summa Theologiae*, 55.

24. H. Musurillo, ed., *The Acts of the Christian Martyrs* (Oxford: Clarendon Press, 1972), 131. See also the discussion of this and other narratives in Judith Perkins, *The Suffering Self: Pain and Narrative Representation in the Early Christian Era* (London: Routledge, 1995).

25. Musurillo, *Acts*, 119.

26. The idea of "military manliness" is developed in Amelie Rorty's important essay, "Two Faces of Courage," *Philosophy* 61 (1986): 151–76.

27. Robert Graves, *Goodbye to All That* (Harmondsworth: Penguin, 1976), 78.

28. Graves, *Goodbye*, 157.

29. Graves, *Goodbye*, 225.

30. Ralph Waldo Emerson, "Heroism" in *Essays* (New York: Dent, 1978), 139.

31. Emerson, "Heroism," 140.

32. Emerson, "Heroism," 141.

33. Stephen Crane, *The Red Badge of Courage* (New York: Bantam, 1983), 3.

34. Crane, *Red Badge*, 8.

35. Crane, *Red Badge*, 130.

36. Primo Levi, *Survival in Auschwitz*, trans. S. Woolf (New York: Collier, 1973), 22.

37. Levi, *Survival*, 36.

38. Aristotle, *Politics*, in *The Basic Works of Aristotle*, ed. R. McKeown (New York: Random House, 1941), 1277b20.

39. Mohandas Gandhi, *Essential Writings*, ed. John Dear (Maryknoll: Orbis, 2002), 89.

40. Jonathan Glover, *Causing Death and Saving Lives* (Harmondsworth: Penguin, 1979), 259.

41. Gandhi, *Essential Writings*, 95.

Chapter 2: Temperance

1. St. Paul, 1 Corinthians 7:8–9 (RSV) (New York: Collins, 1973).

2. Friedrich Nietzsche, *The Antichrist*, in *The Portable Nietzsche*, ed. W. Kaufmann (London: Chatto, 1971), 59.

3. For an excellent discussion of the history and meaning of temperance, see Alasdair MacIntyre, "Sophrosune: How a Virtue Can Become Socially Disruptive," in P. French et al., eds., *Midwest Studies in Philosophy vol. 13 Ethical Theory: Character and Virtue* (Notre Dame: University of Notre Dame Press, 1988), 1–11.

4. See Cicero, *On Duties (De Officiis)*, trans. W. Miller (Cambridge: Harvard University Press, 1985), I. 4. 11–14.

5. Helen North, *Sophrosyne* (Ithaca: Cornell University Press, 1966).

6. Aeschylus, *The Persians*, in *Aeschylus II*, trans. S. Benardete (New York: Washington Square Press: 1973), 76.

7. Plato, *Symposium*, trans. W. Hamilton (Harmondsworth: Penguin, 1981), 193a.

8. Plato, *Symposium*, 212a.

9. Plato, *Symposium*, 216b.

10. Plato, *Symposium*, 219d.

11. Plato, *Symposium*, 220a.

12. Plato, *Symposium*, 223d.

13. Plato, *Republic*, trans. Allan Bloom (New York: Basic Books, 1991), 579b.

14. See Michel Foucault's discussion in *The History of Sexuality: Volume 2: The Use of Pleasure*, trans. R. Hurley (New York: Vintage, 1986), Pt. I ch. 4, 78–93.

15. Foucault, *History of Sexuality*, 83.

16. Plato, *Republic*, 432a.

17. Plato, *Gorgias*, in *The Collected Dialogues of Plato*, 506e.

18. Plato, *Gorgias*, 508a.

19. Aristotle, *The Ethics of Aristotle*, trans. J. A. K. Thomson (London: Penguin, 1995), 1118b2.

20. Aristotle, *Ethics*, 1118b21.

21. Plato, *Symposium*, 216b.

22. Aristotle, *Ethics*, 1152a20.

23. Aristotle, *Ethics*, 1119b17.

24. Peter Brown, "Late Antiquity," in *A History of Private Life Vol. 1: From Pagan Rome to Byzantium*, ed. P. Aries and G. Duby (Cambridge: Harvard University Press, 1987), 269.

25. St. Augustine, *City of God*, trans. J. O'Meara (London: Penguin, 1984), 582.

26. St. Augustine, *Confessions*, 181.

27. St. Augustine, *City of God*, 578.

28. Thomas Aquinas, *Summa Theologiae* vol. 43 (London: Blackfriars, 1966), 179.

29. Aquinas, *Summa Theologiae*, 185.

30. Aquinas, *Summa Theologiae*, 249.

31. Aquinas, *Summa Theologiae*, 249. The passage quoted from St. Augustine is in *Confessions* Bk. 3 s. 8.

32. See Luce Irigaray's discussion of a spirituality of the body in *Between East and West*, trans. S. Pluhaceck (New York: Columbia University Press, 2002), especially "The Way of Breath," 73–91.

33. Lynn White, "The Historic Roots of our Ecological Crisis" in *Environmental Ethics*, ed. D. Schmidtz and E. Willott (Oxford: Oxford University Press, 2002).

34. J. Baird Callicott, *Earth's Insights: A Survey of Ecological Ethics from the Mediterranean Basin to the Australian Outback* (Berkeley: University of California Press, 1997), 71.

35. Lao Tzu, *Tao te Ch'ing*, trans. D. Lau (Harmondsworth: Penguin, 1972), chapter 81. I refer to this translation hereafter in this chapter.

36. For an excellent collection of essays on Taoism and environmental ethics, see N. Girardot et al., eds., *Daoism and Ecology: Ways Within a Cosmic Landscape* (Cambridge: Harvard University Press, 2001).

37. T. S. Eliot, *The Four Quartets* (San Diego: Harcourt Brace, 1971), 59.

38. Aldo Leopold, *A Sand County Almanac* (New York: Oxford University Press, 1968), 224–25.

39. This example is discussed by Michael Brannigan in *Ethics across Cultures* (New York: McGraw Hill, 2004), 406.

40. Immanuel Kant, *Critique of Judgement*, trans. J. Meredith (Oxford: Oxford University Press, 1982), 110–11.

41. Kant, *Critique*, 127.

Chapter 3: Justice

1. Aeschylus, *The Libation Bearers*, in *The Oresteia Plays of Aeschylus*, trans. P. Roche (New York: New American Library, 1962), 122.

2. Nietzsche, *On the Genealogy of Morals*, trans. W. Kaufmann (New York: Vintage, 1967), second essay, section 4.

3. Aristotle, *The Ethics of Aristotle*, trans. J. A. K. Thomson (London: Penguin, 1995), 1129a26ff.

4. Plato, *Republic*, trans. Allan Bloom (New York: Basic Books, 1991), 332b.

5. Plato, *Republic*, 431e.

6. Plato, *Republic*, 432d–433b.

7. Plato, *Republic*, 443d.

8. Plato, *Republic*, 620c.

9. Aristotle, *Ethics*, 1129b15.

10. Aristotle, *Ethics*, 1129b26.

11. Aristotle, *Ethics*, 1130a22.

12. Aristotle, *Ethics*, 1131a25.

13. See Bernard Williams's essay, "Justice as a Virtue," in A. Rorty, ed., *Essays on Aristotle's Ethics* (Berkeley: University of California Press, 1980), 189–99.

14. Aristotle, *Ethics*, 1130b28.

15. Aristotle, *Politics*, in *The Basic Works of Aristotle*, ed. R. McKeown (New York: Random House, 1941), 1295b14.

16. David Hume, *An Inquiry Concerning the Principles of Morals* (Indianapolis: Bobbs-Merrill, 1957), 121.

17. David Hume, *A Treatise of Human Nature* (Clarendon Press: Oxford, 1965), 497.

18. Hume, *Inquiry*, 15.

19. Hume, *Inquiry*, 15.

20. Hume, *Inquiry*, 15.

21. Hume, *Inquiry*, 16.

22. Hume, *Inquiry*, 17.

23. Hume, *Inquiry*, 17.

24. Elie Wiesel, *Night*, trans. S. Rodway (New York: Bantam, 1982), 105.

25. Hume, *Inquiry*, 21.

26. Hume, *Inquiry*, 22.

27. Hume, *Inquiry*, 23.

28. Hume, *Inquiry*, 28.

29. Hume, *Inquiry*, 25.

30. John Rawls, "Justice as Fairness," *Philosophical Review* 67 (1958): 164–65.

31. See, for example, David Gauthier's account of rational choice theory in *Morals By Agreement* (Oxford: Clarendon Press, 1986).

32. Many of these statistics, and some others, are collected in Kai Nielsen's essay, "Socialism and Egalitarian Justice," in *Social and Political Philosophy: Contemporary Perspectives*, ed. James Sterba (London: Routledge, 2001), 205–30.

33. George Orwell, *Essays*, ed. J. Carey (New York: Random House, 2002), 1211.

34. George Orwell, *The Road to Wigan Pier* (London: Penguin, 1983), 129–30.

35. George Orwell, *Homage to Catalonia* (San Diego: Harcourt, 1980), 104.

36. Orwell, *Road*, 126.

37. Orwell, *Road*, 16.

38. Orwell, *Road*, 203.

39. Orwell, *Essays*, 1005.

Chapter 4: Compassion

1. For a helpful account of the relations between compassion, pity, empathy, and sympathy, see Steven Tudor, *Compassion and Remorse* (Leuven: Peeters, 2001), especially 77–125.

2. Primo Levi, *Survival in Auschwitz*, trans. S. Woolf (New York: Collier, 1973), 109–11.

3. On this point, see Adam Smith, *The Theory of Moral Sentiments* (Amherst: Prometheus Books, 2000), 7–9.

4. Thomas Nagel, "What is it Like to be a Bat," in *Mortal Questions* (Cambridge: Cambridge University Press, 1995), 162.

5. Cicero, *Tusculan Disputations*, trans. J. King (London: Heinemann, 1927), third essay: chapter 14, paragraph 30.

6. Seneca, "On Mercy," in *Seneca's Moral and Political Essays*, ed. J. Cooper and J. Procope (Cambridge: Cambridge University Press, 1995), 162.

7. Seneca, "On Mercy," 161.

8. Immanuel Kant, *Foundations of the Metaphysics of Morals*, trans. L. Beck (Indianapolis: Bobbs-Merrill, 1959), 65.

9. Immanuel Kant, *Lectures on Ethics*, trans. L. Infield (New York: Harper and Row, 1963), 194.

10. Immanuel Kant, *The Metaphysics of Morals*, trans. M. Gregor (Cambridge: Cambridge University Press, 1991), 250.

11. Kant, *Metaphysics*, 250.

12. Friedrich Nietzsche, *Thus Spoke Zarathustra*, in *The Portable Nietzsche*, trans. W. Kaufmann (London: Chatto, 1971), part III: "Of Old and New Tablets," "The Hammer Speaks."

13. Nietzsche, *Zarathustra*, part I: "On the Gift-Giving Virtue," section 3.

14. Friedrich Nietzsche, *Daybreak*, trans. R. Hollingdale (Cambridge: Cambridge University Press, 1982), section 135.

15. Friedrich Nietzsche, *On the Genealogy of Morals*, trans. W. Kaufmann (New York: Vintage, 1967), Preface section 5.

16. For more on Buddhist virtues, see Walpola Rahula, *What the Buddha Taught* (New York: Grove Press, 1974).

17. Quoted by Joseph Goldstein in *One Dharma* (San Francisco: Harper, 2003), 131.

18. Edward Conze, ed., *Buddhist Scriptures* (Harmondsworth: Penguin, 1983), 25.

19. Quoted by Harry Oldmeadow in "Delivering the Last Blade of Grass: Aspects of the Bodhisattva Ideal in the Mahayana," *Asian Philosophy* 7.3 (1997): 193.

20. Oldmeadow, "Delivering," 184. For a more extended version of the bodhisattva's vows, see Shantideva, *The Vow of the Bodhisattva*, trans. Padmakara Translation Group (Boston: Shambhala, 1997).

21. See Aristotle, *Rhetoric*, in *The Basic Works of Aristotle*, ed. R. McKeown (New York: Random House, 1941), 1385b12ff.

22. Dalai Lama, *Freedom in Exile* (San Francisco: Harper, 1991), 81.

23. Dalai Lama, *Ethics for the New Millennium* (New York: Riverhead Books, 1999), 74.

24. Dalai Lama, *Ethics*, 124.

25. Jonathan Glover, *Humanity* (New Haven: Yale University Press, 2000), 344.

26. Glover, *Humanity*, 344.

27. Glover, *Humanity*, 344.

28. Primo Levi, *The Drowned and the Saved*, trans. R. Rosenthal (London: Michael Joseph, 1988), 37.

29. Glover, *Humanity*, 346.

30. Kant, *Foundations*, 41.

31. Rousseau, *Emile*, trans. Allan Bloom (New York: Basic Books, 1979), 229.

32. Rousseau, *Emile*, 244.

33. Rousseau, *Emile*, 251.

34. See Martha Nussbaum, "Compassion: the Basic Social Emotion," *Social Philosophy and Policy* 13.1 (1996): 27–58.

35. Rousseau, *Emile*, 253.

36. On this point, see Jeremiah Conway, "A Buddhist Critique of Nussbaum's Account of Compassion," *Philosophy in the Contemporary World* 8.1 (2001): 7–12.

37. Chinua Achebe, *Things Fall Apart* (Greenwich: Fawcett, 1974).

38. Montaigne, "Of Cruelty," in *The Complete Essays of Montaigne*, trans. D. Frame (Stanford: Stanford University Press, 1958), 316.

39. Montaigne, "Of Cruelty," 318.

40. Nagel, "What is it Like to be a Bat," 169.

41. Mary Midgley discusses this story in *Animals and Why They Matter* (Athens: University of Georgia Press, 1984), 28.

42. Amanda Lollar, *The Bat in My Pocket: A Memorable Friendship* (Santa Barbara: Capra Books, 1992), 16.

43. Jeremy Bentham, *The Principles of Morals and Legislation* (Amherst: Prometheus Books, 1988), 310–11.

44. Most of these examples of animal suffering are drawn from C. Sunnstein and M. Nussbaum, eds., *Animal Rights: Current Debates and New Directions* (Oxford: Oxford University Press, 2004), especially David Wolfson and Mariann Sullivan, "Foxes in the Hen House: Animals, Agribusiness and the Law: A Modern American Fable," 205–33.

45. Dr. Joy Mench of the Department of Animal Science at the University of California, Davis. Quoted by Wolfson and Sullivan, "Foxes," 218.

46. Cora Diamond, "Eating Meat and Eating People" in Sunnstein and Nussbaum, *Animal Rights*, 93–107.

Chapter 5: Wisdom

1. St. Paul, 1 Corinthians 1:20–22 (RSV) (New York: Collins, 1973).

2. Plato, *Laws*, in *Plato: Collected Dialogues*, ed. E. Hamilton and H. Cairns (Princeton: Princeton University Press, 1961), 689c.

3. Aristotle, *The Ethics of Aristotle*, trans. J. A. K. Thomson (London: Penguin, 1995), 1140a24.

4. Aristotle, *Metaphysics*, in *The Basic Works of Aristotle*, ed. R. McKeown (New York: Random House, 1941), 981b27ff.

5. Shakespeare, *King Lear*, Act One, Scene One. *The Riverside Shakespeare* (Boston: Houghton Mifflin, 1974), 1256.

6. Tolstoy, *The Death of Ivan Ilych and Other Stories* (New York: Signet, 1960), 148.

7. Tolstoy, *Ivan Ilych*, 131.

8. Compare John Kekes's discussion of Ivan Ilych in *Moral Wisdom and Good Lives* (Princeton: Princeton University Press, 1993), 152–59.

9. Miguel de Cervantes, *Don Quixote* (Harmondsworth: Penguin, 1967), 936.

10. See the related discussion in Trevor Curnow, *Wisdom, Intuition and Ethics* (Aldershot: Ashgate Publishing, 1999). Curnow specifies the most basic aspects of wisdom as *self-knowledge*, *detachment*, *integration*, and *transcendence*.

11. *Bhagavad Gita*, trans. J. Mascaro (London: Penguin, 1962), 11:13–16.

12. Plato, *Apology*, in *Plato: Collected Dialogues*, 19c.

13. This reading of the oracle story follows John Sallis, *Being and Logos: The Way of the Platonic Dialogue* (Pittsburgh: Duquesne University Press, 1973), 25–63.

14. Plato, *Apology*, 42a.

15. See H. G. Gadamer's essay, "Life and Soul: The Phaedo," in *The Beginning of Philosophy* (New York: Continuum, 1988), 41–49.

16. Plato, *Phaedo*, in *Plato: Collected Dialogues*, 115c.

17. Plato, *Phaedo*, 64a.

18. Edward Conze, ed., *Buddhist Scriptures* (Harmondsworth: Penguin, 1983), 43.

19. Conze, *Buddhist Scriptures*, 46.

20. Conze, *Buddhist Scriptures*, 51–52.

21. Conze, *Buddhist Scriptures*, 42. Karen Armstrong also pays particular attention to this episode in *Buddha* (London: Penguin, 2001), 66ff.

22. Luce Irigaray, "Being I, Being We," in *Between East and West*, trans. S. Pluhaceck (New York: Columbia University Press, 2002), 93.

23. Friedrich Nietzsche, "Schopenhauer as Educator," in *Untimely Meditations*, trans. R. Hollingdale (Cambridge: Cambridge University Press, 1983), section 8.

24. Martin Heidegger, "Memorial Address," in *Discourse on Thinking*, trans. J. Anderson and E. Freund (New York: Harper, 1966), 46.

25. Heidegger, *Memorial*, 50.

26. Jean-François Lyotard, "Can Thought Go On Without a Body," in *The Inhuman: Reflections on Time*, trans. G. Bennington (Stanford: Stanford University Press, 1991), 19.

27. Lyotard, "Thought," 20.

28. P. Reps and N. Senzaki, eds., *Zen Flesh, Zen Bones* (Boston: Tuttle, 1998), 44.

29. Joseph Campbell, *The Power of Myth* (New York: Doubleday, 1988), 5.

30. Campbell, *Power*, 55.

31. Charles Taylor, "The Politics of Recognition" in *Multiculturalism*, ed. A. Gutman (Princeton: Princeton University Press, 1994), 25–73.

32. Georg Wilhelm Friedrich Hegel, *The Philosophy of History*, trans. J. Sibree (New York: Dover, 1956), 103.

33. John Stuart Mill, *On Liberty*, in *Collected Works*, vol. XVIII (Toronto: University of Toronto Press, 1977), 213.

34. Bhikhu Parekh, "A Varied Moral World," in *Is Multiculturalism Bad For Women?*, ed. Susan Okin et al. (Princeton: Princeton University Press, 1999), 74.

35. Mill, *On Liberty*, 274.

36. On the concept of *li*, see Roger Ames, "Rites as Rights: The Confucian Alternative," in *Applied Ethics: A Multicultural Approach*, ed. Larry May et al., 2nd ed. (Upper Saddle River, N.J.: Prentice Hall, 1998), 90–101.

37. See H. G. Gadamer, *Truth and Method* (New York: Crossroad, 1989), for the classic hermeneutical account of understanding.

Conclusion

1. Plato, *Republic*, trans. Allan Bloom (New York: Basic Books, 1999), 362a.

2. Aristotle, *The Ethics of Aristotle*, trans. J. A. K. Thomson (London: Penguin, 1995), 1099a31.

3. Immanuel Kant, *Foundations of the Metaphysics of Morals*, trans. L. Beck (Indianapolis: Bobbs-Merrill, 1957), 9.

4. Aristotle, *Ethics*, 1100b18ff.

5. Plato, *Apology*, in *Plato: Collected Dialogues* (Princeton: Princeton University Press, 1963), 28d.

6. Plato, *Republic*, 592b.

Bibliography

Introduction: General Works on Virtue

Anscombe, Elizabeth. "Modern Moral Philosophy." *Collected Philosophical Papers* 3 (1981): 26–42.

Aristotle. *The Ethics of Aristotle*. Translated by J. A. K. Thomson. London: Penguin, 1995.

Badhwar, Neera. "The Limited Unity of Virtue." *Nous* 30.3 (1996): 306–29.

Bennett, William. *The Book of Virtues*. New York: Simon and Schuster, 1993.

———. *The Children's Book of Virtues*. New York: Simon and Schuster, 1995.

Comte-Sponville, Andre. *A Small Treatise on the Great Virtues*. Translated by C. Temerson. New York: Henry Holt, 2001.

Crisp, Roger, ed. *How Should One Live?: Essays on the Virtues*. Oxford: Oxford University Press, 1996.

Crisp, Roger, and Michael Slote, eds. *Virtue Ethics*. Oxford: Oxford University Press, 1997.

Foot, Philippa. *Virtues and Vices*. Oxford: Blackwell, 1978.

French, Peter, et al., eds. *Midwest Studies in Philosophy: Ethical Theory: Character and Virtue* 13. Notre Dame: University of Notre Dame Press, 1988.

Gottlieb, Paula. "Are the Virtues Remedial?" *Journal of Value Inquiry* 25 (2001): 343–54.

Hume, David. *An Inquiry Concerning the Principles of Morals*. Indianapolis: Bobbs-Merrill, 1957.

Hurka, Thomas. *Virtue, Vice, and Value*. Oxford: Oxford University Press, 2003.

Hursthouse, Rosalind. *On Virtue Ethics*. Oxford: Oxford University Press, 1999.

Kant, Immanuel. *The Metaphysics of Morals*. Translated by Mary Gregor. Cambridge: Cambridge University Press, 1991.

Kruschwitz, Robert, and Robert Roberts, eds. *The Virtues: Contemporary Essays on Moral Character*. Belmont: Wadsworth, 1987.

MacIntyre, Alasdair. *After Virtue*. 2nd ed. Notre Dame: University of Notre Dame Press, 1984.

———. *Dependent Rational Animals*. Chicago: Open Court, 1999.

Mill, John Stuart. *Utilitarianism*. Indianapolis: Hackett, 2001.

Nietzsche, Friedrich. *Beyond Good and Evil*. Translated by Walter Kaufmann. New York: Vintage, 1966.

———. *The Gay Science*. Translated by Walter Kaufmann. New York: Vintage, 1974.

Paul, Ellen, and Fred Miller, et al., eds. *Virtue and Vice*. Cambridge: Cambridge University Press, 1995.

Pieper, Josef. *The Four Cardinal Virtues*. Notre Dame: University of Notre Dame Press, 1990.

Pincoffs, Edmund. *Quandaries and Virtues*. Lawrence: University of Kansas Press, 1986.

Plato. *Republic*. Translated by Allan Bloom. New York: Basic Books, 1991.

Slote, Michael. *From Morality to Virtue*. Oxford: Oxford University Press, 1995.

Statman, Daniel, ed. *Virtue Ethics: A Critical Reader*. Washington, D.C.: Georgetown University Press, 1997.

Swanton, Christine. *Virtue, Ethics: A Pluralistic View*. Oxford: Oxford University Press, 2005.

Taylor, Richard. *Good and Evil: A New Direction*. London: Macmillan, 1970.

Trianosky, Gregory. "What is Virtue Ethics All About?" *American Philosophical Quarterly* (October 1990): 335–44.

Wallace, James. *Virtues and Vices*. Ithaca: Cornell University Press, 1978.

Watson, Gary. "Virtues in Excess." *Philosophical Studies* 46 (1984): 57–74.

Chapter 1: Courage

Aquinas, Thomas. *Summa Theologiae*. vol. 42. London: Blackfriars, 1966.

Aristotle. *The Ethics of Aristotle*. Translated by J. A. K. Thomson. London: Penguin, 1995.

———. "Politics." *The Basic Works of Aristotle*. Edited by R. McKeown. New York: Random House, 1941.

Brandt, R. B. "The Structure of Virtue." *Midwest Studies in Philosophy* 13 (1988): 64–82.

———. "Traits of Character: A Conceptual Analysis." *American Philosophical Quarterly* 7 (1970): 23–37.

Callan, Eamonn. "Patience and Courage." *Philosophy: The Journal of the Royal Institute of Philosophy* 68 (1993): 523–39.

Crane, Stephen. *The Red Badge of Courage*. New York: Bantam, 1983.

Cunningham, Stanley B. "The Courageous Villain: A Needless Paradox." *Modern Schoolman: A Quarterly Journal of Philosophy* 62 (1985): 97–110.

Dent, N. J. H. "The Value of Courage." *Philosophy: The Journal of the Royal Institute of Philosophy* 56 (1981): 574–77.

Emerson, Ralph Waldo. "Heroism." In *Essays*. New York: Dent, 1978.

Gandhi, Mohandas. *An Autobiography: The Story of My Experiments with Truth*. Translated by Mahadev Desai. Boston: Beacon Press, 1993.

———. *Essential Writings*. Edited by John Dear. Maryknoll: Orbis, 2002.

Glover, Jonathan. *Causing Death and Saving Lives*. Harmondsworth: Penguin, 1979.

Graves, Robert. *Goodbye to All That*. Harmondsworth: Penguin, 1976.

Hauerwas, Stanley. "The Difference of Virtue and the Difference it Makes: Courage Exemplified." *Modern Theology* 9 (1993): 249–64.

Hobbs, Angela. "Plato and the Hero: Courage, Manliness and the Impersonal Good." *Ancient Philosophy* 23 (2003): 224–27.

Homer. *The Iliad*. Translated by W. Rouse. New York: New American Library, 1938.

Hume, David. *An Inquiry Concerning the Principles of Morals*. Indianapolis: Bobbs-Merrill, 1957.

Hunt, Lester H. "Courage and Principle." *Canadian Journal of Philosophy* 10 (1980): 281–93.

Kant, Immanuel. *Foundations of the Metaphysics of Morals*. Translated by L. Beck. Indianapolis: Bobbs-Merrill, 1959.

———. *The Metaphysics of Morals*. Translated by M. Gregor. Cambridge: Cambridge University Press, 1991.

Leighton, Stephen. "Aristotle's Courageous Passions." *Phronesis* 53:1 (1988): 76–99.

Levi, Primo. *Survival in Auschwitz*. Translated by S. Woolf. New York: Collier, 1973.

Miller, William Ian. *The Mystery of Courage*. Cambridge: Harvard University Press, 2002.

Montaigne, Michel de. "Of Honorary Awards." In *The Complete Essays of Montaigne*, translated by D. Frame. Stanford: Stanford University Press, 1958.

Musurillo, H., ed. *The Acts of the Christian Martyrs*. Oxford: Clarendon Press, 1972.

Pears, D. F. "Aristotle's Analysis of Courage." *Midwest Studies in Philosophy* 3 (1978): 273–85.

Pears, David. "Courage as a Mean." In *Essays on Aristotle's Ethics*, edited by Amelie Oksenberg Rorty. Berkeley: University of California Press, 1981.

Perkins, Judith. *The Suffering Self: Pain and Narrative Representation in the Early Christian Era*. London: Routledge, 1995.

Porter, Jean. *The Recovery of Virtue: The Relevance of Aquinas for Christian Ethics*. Westminster: John Knox Press, 1990.

Putman, Daniel. "Courage Alone." *Contemporary Philosophy* 18 (1996): 46–49.

———. "The Emotions of Courage." *Journal of Social Philosophy* 23 (2001): 463–70.

———. "Psychological Courage." *Philosophy, Psychiatry, and Psychology* 4 (1997): 1–11.

Pybus, Elizabeth. *Human Goodness: Generosity and Courage*. Buffalo: University of Toronto Press, 1991.

Rogers, Kelly. "Aristotle on the Motive of Courage." *Southern Journal of Philosophy* 32 (1994): 303–13.

Rorty, Amelie. "The Two Faces of Courage." *Philosophy: The Journal of the Royal Institute of Philosophy* 61 (1986): 151–76.

Schedler, George. "Is There Honor in Bravery on Behalf of an Unjust Cause?" *Southwest Philosophy Review: The Journal of the Southwestern Philosophical Society* 14 (1997): 39–46.

Seller, Ann, and Richard Norman. "Pacifism." *Encyclopedia of Applied Ethics*. vol. 3. San Diego: Academic Press, 1998: 399–413.

Wallace, James D. "Cowardice and Courage." *American Philosophical Quarterly* 7 (1973): 97–108.

Walton, Douglas N. *Courage: A Philosophical Investigation*. Berkeley: University of California Press, 1985.

———. "Courage, Relativism and Practical Reasoning." *Philosophia: Philosophical Quarterly of Israel* 22 (1990): 227–40.

Yearley, Lee H. *Mencius and Aquinas: Theories of Virtue and Conceptions of Courage*. Albany: SUNY Press, 1990.

Chapter 2: Temperance

Aeschylus. *The Persians*. In *Aeschylus II*, translated by S. Benardete. New York: Washington Square Press, 1973.

Aquinas, Thomas. *Summa Theologiae*. vol. 43. London: Blackfriars, 1966.

Aristotle. *The Ethics of Aristotle*. Translated by J. A. K. Thomson. London: Penguin, 1995.

Attfield, Robin. "Environmental Ethics." In *Encyclopedia of Environmental Ethics*. vol. 2. San Diego: Academic Press, 1998: 73–81.

Brannigan, Michael. *Ethics Across Cultures*. New York: McGraw-Hill, 2004.

Brown, Peter. "Late Antiquity." In *A History of Private Life: From Pagan Rome to Byzantium* 1. Edited by P. Aries and G. Duby. Cambridge: Harvard University Press, 1987.

Callicott, J. Baird. *Earth's Insights: A Survey of Ecological Ethics from the Mediterranean Basin to the Australian Outback*. Berkeley: University of California Press, 1997.

Campbell, Keith. "Self-Mastery and Stoic Ethics. *Philosophy* 60 (1985): 327–40.

Cicero. *On Duties (De Officiis)*. Translated by W. Miller. Cambridge: Harvard University Press, 1985.

Curzer, Howard J. "Aristotle's Account of the Virtue of Temperance in *Nicomachean Ethics III*." *Journal of the History of Philosophy* 35 (1997): 5–25.

———. "Two Varieties of Temperance in the Gorgias." *International Philosophical Quarterly* (1991): 153–59.

Dorcy, Michael M. "Temperance, the Peregrinations of a Term." *Revue de l'Université d'Ottawa* 35 (1965).

Eliot, T. S. *The Four Quartets*. San Diego: Harcourt Brace, 1971.

Floyd, Shawn. "Aquinas on Temperance." *Modern Schoolman: A Quarterly Journal of Philosophy* 77 (1999): 35–48.

Foucault, Michel. *The History of Sexuality: Volume 2: The Use of Pleasure*. Translated by R. Hurley. New York: Vintage, 1986.

———. *The History of Sexuality: Volume 3: The Care of the Self*. Translated by R. Hurley. New York: Vintage, 1986.

Girardot, N., et al., eds. *Daoism and Ecology: Ways Within a Cosmic Landscape*. Cambridge: Harvard University Press, 2001.

Irigaray, Luce. "The Way of Breath." *Between East and West*. Translated by S. Pluhaceck. New York: Columbia University Press, 2002.

Kant, Immanuel. *Critique of Judgement*. Translated by J. Meredith. Oxford: Oxford University Press, 1982.

Leopold, Aldo. *A Sand County Almanac*. New York: Oxford University Press, 1968.

Lobo, Jennifer Anne. "Theoretical and Practical Dimensions of Sophrosyne in Plato's *Charmides* and *Republic*." *De Philosophia* 19 (2006): 47–58.

MacIntyre, Alasdair. "Sophrosune: How a Virtue Can Become Socially Disruptive." In *Midwest Studies in Philosophy Ethical Theory: Character and Virtue* 13, edited by P. French et al. Notre Dame: University of Notre Dame Press, 1988: 1–11.

Mcghee, Michael. "Temperance." *Philosophical Investigations* 12 (1989): 193–216.

Nietzsche, Friedrich. "The Antichrist." In *The Portable Nietzsche*, edited by W. Kaufmann. London: Chatto, 1971.

North, Helen. *Sophrosyne: Self-Knowledge and Self-Restraint in Greek Literature*. Ithaca: Cornell University Press, 1966.

Pichanick, Alan. "Two Rival Conceptions of Sophrosune." *Polis: The Journal of the Society for the Study of Greek Political Thought* 22 (2005): 249–64.

Plato. "Charmides." In *The Collected Dialogues of Plato*, edited by E. Hamilton and H. Cairns. Princeton: Princeton University Press, 1961.

———. "Gorgias." In *The Collected Dialogues of Plato*, edited by E. Hamilton and H. Cairns. Princeton: Princeton University Press, 1961.

———. *Republic*. Translated by Allan Bloom. New York: Basic Books, 1991.

———. *Symposium*. Translated by W. Hamilton. Harmondsworth: Penguin, 1981.

Schmid, W. Thomas. "Socratic Moderation and Self-Knowledge." *Journal of the History of Philosophy* 21 (1983): 339–348.

St. Augustine. *City of God*. Translated by J. O'Meara. London: Penguin, 1984.

———. *Confessions*. Translated by R. S. Pine-Coffin. Harmondsworth: Penguin, 1974.

St. Paul. 1 Corinthians. *RSV Bible*. New York: Collins, 1973.

Tzu, Lao. *Tao te Ching*. Translated by D. Lau. Harmondsworth: Penguin, 1972.

Van Tongeren, Paul. "Temperance and Environmental Concerns." *Ethical Perspectives: Journal of the European Ethics Network* 10 (2003): 118–28.

Van Wensveen, Louke. "Attunement: An Ecological Spin on the Virtue of Temperance." *Philosophy in the Contemporary World* 8 (2001): 67–78.

———. *Dirty Virtues: The Emergence of Ecological Virtue Ethics*. Amherst: Prometheus Books, 2000.

White, Lynn. "The Historic Roots of Our Ecological Crisis." In *Environmental Ethics: What Really Matters?*, edited by D. Schmidtz and E. Willott. Oxford: Oxford University Press, 2002: 7–15.

Young, Charles M. "Aristotle on Temperance." In *Essays in Ancient Greek Philosophy IV*, edited by John P. Anton. Albany: SUNY Press, 1991.

Chapter 3: Justice

Aeschylus. "The Libation Bearers." In *The Oresteia Plays of Aeschylus*, translated by P. Roche. New York: New American Library, 1962.

Aristotle. *The Ethics of Aristotle*. Translated by J. A. K. Thomson. London: Penguin, 1995.

Aristotle. "Politics." In *The Basic Works of Aristotle*, edited by R. McKeown. New York: Random House, 1941.

Baumrin, Brendan. "Two Concepts of Justice." *Midwest Studies in Philosophy* (1982): 63–72.

Curzer, Howard J. "Aristotle's Account of the Virtue of Justice." *Apeiron: A Journal for Ancient Philosophy and Science* 28 (1995): 207–38.

Drefcinski, Shane. "Aristotle and the Characteristic Desire of Justice." *Apeiron: A Journal for Ancient Philosophy and Science* 33 (2000): 109–23.

Forst, Rainer. "Tolerance as a Virtue of Justice." *Philosophical Explorations: An International Journal for the Philosophy of Mind and Action* 4 (2001): 193–206.

Foster, Susanne. "Justice Is a Virtue." *Philosophia: Philosophical Quarterly of Israel* 31 (2004): 501–12.

———. "Virtues and Material Goods: Aristotle on Justice and Liberality." *American Catholic Philosophical Quarterly* 71 (1997): 607–19.

Gauthier, David. *Morals By Agreement*. Oxford: Clarendon Press, 1986.

Hume, David. *An Inquiry Concerning the Principles of Morals*. Indianapolis: Bobbs-Merrill, 1957.

———. *A Treatise of Human Nature*. Oxford: Clarendon Press, 1965.

Lauzier Stone, Denise. "Justice as a Virtue of Character." *Auslegung: A Journal of Philosophy* 27 (2005): 33–41.

Lutz, Mark J. "Wrath and Justice in Homer's Achilles." *Interpretation: A Journal of Political Philosophy* 33 (2006): 111–31.

Nielsen, Kai. "Socialism and Egalitarian Justice." In *Social and Political Philosophy: Contemporary Perspectives*, edited by James Sterba. London: Routledge, 2001.

Nietzsche, Friedrich. *On the Genealogy of Morals*. Translated by W. Kaufmann. New York: Vintage, 1967.

O'Connor, David K. "Aristotelian Justice as a Personal Virtue." *Midwest Studies in Philosophy* 13 (1988): 417–27.

O'Neill, Onora. "Virtuous Lives and Just Societies." *Journal of Social Philosophy* 20 (1989): 25–30.

Orwell, George. *Essays*. Edited by J. Carey. New York: Random House, 2002.

———. *Homage to Catalonia*. San Diego: Harcourt, 1980.

———. *The Road to Wigan Pier*. London: Penguin, 1983.

Plato. *Republic*. Translated by Allan Bloom. New York: Basic Books, 1991.

Raphael, D. D. *Concepts of Justice*. Oxford: Oxford University Press, 2003.

Rawls, John. "Justice as Fairness." *Philosophical Review* 67 (1958): 164–65.

———. *A Theory of Justice*. Cambridge: Belknap Press, 2005.

Sherman, David. "Aristotle and the Problem of Particular Injustice." *Philosophical Forum* 30 (1999): 235–48.

Slote, Michael. "The Justice of Caring." *Social Philosophy and Policy* 15 (1998): 171–95.

Smith, Tara. "Justice as a Personal Virtue." *Social Theory and Practice: An International and Interdisciplinary Journal of Social Philosophy* 25 (1999): 361–84.

———. "Tolerance & Forgiveness: Virtues or Vices?" *Journal of Applied Philosophy* 14 (1997): 31–41.

Solomon, Robert C. "Justice as a Virtue." In *Social and Political Philosophy: Contemporary Perspectives*, edited by James P. Sterba, 169–86. New York: Routledge, 2001.

Sullivan, Daniel. "Rules, Fairness and Formal Justice." *Ethics* 85:4 (1975): 322–31.

Wein, Sheldon. "Humean Minds and Moral Theory." *Philosophy Research Archives* XIV (1988–89): 229–36.

Weinberger, Ota. "Natural Constituents of Justice." *Law and Philosophy* 13 (1994): 1–25.

Wiesel, Elie. *Night*. Translated by S. Rodway. New York: Bantam, 1982.

Williams, Bernard. "Justice as a Virtue." In *Essays on Aristotle's Ethics*, edited by A. Rorty. Berkeley: University of California Press, 1980.

Young, Charles M. "Aristotle on Justice." *Southern Journal of Philosophy* (1988): 233–49.

Chapter 4: Compassion

Achebe, Chinua. *Things Fall Apart*. Greenwich: Fawcett, 1974.

Aristotle. "Rhetoric." In *The Basic Works of Aristotle*, edited by R. McKeown. New York: Random House, 1941.

Bentham, Jeremy. *The Principles of Morals and Legislation*. Amherst: Prometheus Books, 1988.

Blum, Lawrence A. *Friendship, Altruism, and Morality*. London: Routledge & K. Paul, 1980.

Callan, Eamonn. "The Moral Status of Pity." *Canadian Journal of Philosophy* 18 (1988): 1–12.

Cameron, Frank. "Beyond Pity and Cruelty: Nietzsche's Stoicism." *De Philosophia* 13 (1997): 191–206.

Carr, Brian. "Pity and Compassion As Social Virtues." *Philosophy: The Journal of the Royal Institute of Philosophy* 74 (1999): 411–29.

Cartwright, David. "Kant, Schopenhauer and Nietzsche on the Morality of Pity." *Journal of the History of Ideas* (Jan. 1984): 83–98.

———. "Kant's View of the Moral Significance of Kindhearted Emotions and the Moral Insignificance of Kant's View." *Journal of Value Inquiry* 21 (1987): 291–304.

———. "The Last Temptation of Zarathustra." *Journal of the History of Philosophy* 31 (1993): 49–69.

———. "Schopenhauer's Compassion and Nietzsche's Pity." *Schopenhauer-Jahrbuch* 69 (1988): 557–67.

Cicero. *Tusculan Disputations*. Translated by J. King. London: Heinemann, 1927.

Conway, Jeremiah. "A Buddhist Critique of Nussbaum's Account of Compassion." *Philosophy in the Contemporary World* 8 (2001): 7–12.

Conway, Trudy C. "Compassion: An Aristotelian Approach." *Philosophy in the Contemporary World* 8 (2001): 1–6.

Conze, Edward, ed. *Buddhist Scriptures*. Harmondsworth: Penguin, 1983.

Dalai Lama. *The Compassionate Life*. Boston: Wisdom Publications, 2003.

———. *Ethics for the New Millennium*. New York: Riverhead Books, 1999.

———. *Freedom in Exile*. San Francisco: Harper, 1991.

Deigh, John. "Nussbaum's Account of Compassion." *Philosophy and Phenomenological Research* 68 (2004): 465–72.

Depraz, Natalie. "Empathy and Compassion As Experiential Praxis: Confronting Phenomenological Analysis and Buddhist Teachings." In *Space, Time, and Culture*, edited by David Carr, 189–200. Dordrecht: Kluwer Academic Pub., 2004.

Diamond, Cora. "Eating Meat and Eating People." In *Animal Rights: Current Debates and New Directions*, edited by C. Sunnstein and M. Nussbaum. Oxford: Oxford University Press, 2004.

Dillon, Matthew. "Dialogues with Death: The Last Days of Socrates and the Buddha." *Philosophy East and West* 50 (2000): 525–58.

Donovan, Josephine. "Attention to Suffering: A Feminist Caring Ethic for the Ethical Treatment of Animals." *Journal of Social Philosophy* 27:1 (1996): 81–102.

Glover, Jonathan. *Humanity*. New Haven: Yale University Press, 2000.

Goldstein, Joseph. *One Dharma*. San Francisco: Harper, 2003.

Gowans, Christopher W. *Philosophy of the Buddha*. New York: Routledge, 2003.

Hestevold, H. Scott. "Pity." *Journal of Philosophical Research* 29 (2004): 333–52.

Johnson, Galen A. "Kindness, Justice, and the Good Society." *Journal of the British Society for Phenomenology* 35 (2004): 313–17.

Kant, Immanuel. *Foundations of the Metaphysics of Morals*. Translated by L. Beck. Indianapolis: Bobbs-Merrill, 1959.

———. *Lectures on Ethics*. Translated by L. Infield. New York: Harper and Row, 1963.

———. *The Metaphysics of Morals*. Translated by M. Gregor. Cambridge: Cambridge University Press, 1991.

Levi, Primo. *The Drowned and the Saved*. Translated by R. Rosenthal. London: Michael Joseph, 1988.

———. *Survival in Auschwitz*. Translated by S. Woolf. New York: Collier, 1973.

Lollar, Amanda. *The Bat in My Pocket: A Memorable Friendship*. Santa Barbara: Capra Books, 1992.

Loy, David R. *A Buddhist History of the West: Study in Lack*. Albany: SUNY Press, 2002.

Lutz, Mark J. "Wrath and Justice in Homer's *Achilles*." *Interpretation: A Journal of Political Philosophy* 33 (2006): 111–31.

Midgley, Mary. *Animals and Why They Matter*. Athens: University of Georgia Press, 1984.

Mitchell, Donald W. "The Paradox of Buddhist Wisdom." *Philosophy East and West* 26 (1976): 55–67.

Montaigne. "Of Cruelty." In *The Complete Essays of Montaigne*, translated by D. Frame. Stanford: Stanford University Press, 1958.

Nagel, Thomas. "What is it Like to be a Bat." In *Mortal Questions*. Cambridge: Cambridge University Press, 1995.

Neihardt, J., ed. *Black Elk Speaks*. Lincoln: Bison Books, 2004.

Nichols, Mary P. "Rousseau's Novel Education in the *Emile*." *Political Theory: An International Journal of Political Philosophy* 13 (1985): 535–58.

Nietzsche, Friedrich. *Daybreak*. Translated by R. Hollingdale. Cambridge: Cambridge University Press, 1982.

———. *On the Genealogy of Morals*. Translated by W. Kaufmann. New York: Vintage, 1967.

———. "Thus Spoke Zarathustra." In *The Portable Nietzsche*, translated by W. Kaufmann. London: Chatto, 1971.

Nussbaum, Martha C. "Compassion and Terror." In *Terrorism and International Justice*, edited by James P. Sterba, 229–52. Oxford: Oxford University Press, 2003.

———. "Compassion: The Basic Social Emotion." *Social Philosophy and Policy* 13 (1996): 27–58.

———. "Pity and Mercy: Nietzsche's Stoicism." In *Nietzsche, Genealogy, Morality*, edited by Richard Schacht. Berkeley: University of California Press, 1994.

———. *Upheavals of Thought: The Intelligence of Emotions*. Cambridge: Cambridge University Press, 2001.

Oldmeadow, Harry. "Delivering the Last Blade of Grass: Aspects of the Bodhisattva Ideal in the Mahayana." *Asian Philosophy* 7 (1997): 193.

Pence, Gregory E. "Can Compassion Be Taught." *Journal of Medical Ethics: The Journal of the Institute of Medical Ethics* 9 (1983): 189–91.

Resenbrink, John. "The Dalai Lama on Suffering and Compassion: An Ontological Critique." *Skepsis: A Journal for Philosophy and Interdisciplinary Research* 15 (2004): 225–45.

Rahula, Walpola. *What the Buddha Taught*. New York: Grove Press, 1974.

Rice, Eugene. "Buddhist Compassion As a Foundation for Human Rights." In *Social Philosophy Today: Human Rights, Religion, and Democracy* vol. 21, edited by John R. Rowan, 95–108. Charlottesville: Philosophy Documentation Center, 2005.

Roberts, Lani. "Barriers to Feeling and Actualizing Compassion." *Philosophy in the Contemporary World* 8:1 (2001): 13–19.

Rousseau. *Emile*. Translated by Allan Bloom. New York: Basic Books, 1979.

Schopenhauer, Arthur. *On the Basis of Morality*. Translated by E. F. Payne. Providence: Berghahn, 1995.

Seneca. "On Mercy." In *Seneca's Moral and Political Essays*, edited by J. Cooper and J. Procope. Cambridge: Cambridge University Press, 1995.

Shantideva. *The Vow of the Bodhisattva*. Translated by Padmakara Translation Group. Boston: Shambhala, 1997.

Smith, Adam. *The Theory of Moral Sentiments*. Amherst: Prometheus Books, 2000.

Snow, Nancy E. "Compassion." *American Philosophical Quarterly* (1991): 195–205.

———. "Compassion for Animals." *Between the Species: A Journal of Ethics* 9 (1993): 61–66.

Sprigge, T. L. S. "Is Pity the Basis of Ethics? Nietzsche versus Schopenhauer." In *The Bases of Ethics*, edited by William Sweet, 103–125. Milwaukee: Marquette University Press, 2000.

Tudor, Steven. *Compassion and Remorse: Acknowledging the Suffering Other*. Leuven: Peeters, 2001.

Von Wright, Moira. "Narrative Imagination and Taking the Perspective of Others." *Studies in Philosophy and Education* 21 (2002): 407–16.

Walsh-Frank, Patricia. "Compassion: An East-West Comparison." *Asian Philosophy* 6 (1996): 5–16.

Weber, M. "Compassion and Pity: An Evaluation of Nussbaum's Analysis and Defense." *Ethical Theory and Moral Practice: An International Forum* 7 (2004): 487–511.

Wolfson, David, and Mariann Sullivan. "Foxes in the Hen House: Animals, Agribusiness and the Law: A Modern American Fable." In *Animal Rights: Current Debates and New Directions*, edited by C. Sunnstein and M. Nussbaum. Oxford: Oxford University Press, 2004.

Yao, Fuchuan. "There Are No Degrees in a Bodhisattva's Compassion." *Asian Philosophy* 16 (2006): 189–98.

Chapter 5: Wisdom

Almond, Brenda. "Seeking Wisdom." *Philosophy* 72 (1997): 417–33.

Ames, Roger. "Rites as Rights: The Confucian Alternative." In *Applied Ethics: A Multicultural Approach* 2nd ed., edited by Larry May et al., 90–101. Upper Saddle River, N.J.: Prentice Hall, 1998.

Aristotle. *The Ethics of Aristotle*. Translated by J. A. K. Thomson. London: Penguin, 1995.

———. "Metaphysics." In *The Basic Works of Aristotle*, edited by R. McKeown. New York: Random House, 1941.

Armstrong, Karen. *Buddha*. London: Penguin, 2001.

Campbell, Joseph. *The Power of Myth*. New York: Doubleday, 1988.

Carrithers, Michael. *The Buddha*. Oxford: Oxford University Press, 1996.

Cervantes, Miguel de. *Don Quixote*. Harmondsworth: Penguin, 1967.

Cohen, Maurice. "Dying as Supreme Opportunity: A Comparison of Plato's *Phaedo* and *The Tibetan Book of the Dead.*" *Philosophy East and West* 26.3 (1976): 317–27.

Conze, Edward, ed. *Buddhist Scriptures.* Harmondsworth: Penguin, 1983.

Curnow, Trevor. *Wisdom, Intuition and Ethics.* Aldershot: Ashgate Publishing, 1999.

Dillon, Matthew. "Dialogues with Death: The Last Days of Socrates and the Buddha." *Philosophy East and West* 50 (2000): 525–58.

Gadamer, H. G. "Life and Soul: The Phaedo." In *The Beginning of Philosophy.* New York: Continuum, 1988, 41–49.

———. *Truth and Method.* New York: Crossroad, 1989.

Gilbertson, Mark. "Wisdom: A Forgotten Virtue?" *Contemporary Philosophy* 22 (2000): 53–59.

Godlovitch, S. "On Wisdom." *Canadian Journal of Philosophy* XI:1 (1981): 137–55.

Gowans, Christopher W. *Philosophy of the Buddha.* New York: Routledge, 2003.

Hegel, Georg Wilhelm Friedrich. *The Philosophy of History.* Translated by J. Sibree. New York: Dover, 1956.

Heidegger, Martin. "Memorial Address." In *Discourse on Thinking,* translated by J. Anderson and E. Freund. New York: Harper, 1966.

Irigaray, Luce. *Between East and West.* Translated by S. Pluhaceck. New York: Columbia University Press, 2002.

Kekes, John. *Moral Wisdom and Good Lives.* Princeton: Princeton University Press, 1993.

———. "Wisdom." *American Philosophical Quarterly* 20:3 (1983): 277–86.

Lyotard, Jean-François. *The Inhuman: Reflections on Time.* Translated by G. Bennington. Stanford: Stanford University Press, 1991.

Mascaro, J., trans. *Bhagavad Gita.* London: Penguin, 1962.

Mill, John Stuart. "On Liberty." *Collected Works* 18 (1977).

Mitchell, Donald W. "The Paradox of Buddhist Wisdom." *Philosophy East and West* 26 (1976): 55–67.

Nietzsche, Friedrich. "Schopenhauer as Educator." In *Untimely Meditations,* translated by R. Hollingdale. Cambridge: Cambridge University Press, 1983.

———. "The Twilight of the Idols." In *The Portable Nietzsche,* edited by W. Kaufmann. London: Chatto, 1971.

Parekh, Bhikhu. "A Varied Moral World." In *Is Multiculturalism Bad For Women?* Edited by Susan Okin, et al. Princeton: Princeton University Press, 1999.

Plato. "Apology." In *Plato: Collected Dialogues,* edited by E. Hamilton and H. Cairns. Princeton: Princeton University Press, 1961.

———. "Laws." In *Plato: Collected Dialogues,* edited by E. Hamilton and H. Cairns. Princeton: Princeton University Press, 1961.

———. "Phaedo." In *Plato: Collected Dialogues,* edited by E. Hamilton and H. Cairns. Princeton: Princeton University Press, 1961.

Reps, P., and N. Senzaki. eds. *Zen Flesh, Zen Bones.* Boston: Tuttle, 1998.

Sallis, John. *Being and Logos: The Way of the Platonic Dialogue.* Pittsburgh: Duquesne University Press, 1973.

Shakespeare. *King Lear*. Act One, Scene One. *The Riverside Shakespeare*. Boston: Houghton Mifflin, 1974.

Sherman, Thomas. "Human Happiness and the Role of Philosophical Wisdom in the *Nicomachean Ethics*." *International Philosophical Quarterly* 44:4 (2002).

Singh, R. Raj. "Death Contemplation and Contemplative Living: Socrates and the Katha Upanishad." *Asian Philosophy* 4:1 (1994): 9–16.

Taylor, Charles. "The Politics of Recognition." In *Multiculturalism*, edited by A. Gutman, 25–73. Princeton: Princeton University Press, 1994.

Taylor, Richard. "Ancient Wisdom and Modern Folly." *Midwest Studies in Philosophy* 13 (1988): 54–63.

Tolstoy, Leo. *The Death of Ivan Ilych and Other Stories*. New York: Signet, 1960.

Index

About the Author

Richard White has written widely on the history of philosophy, philosophy and literature, and the philosophy of love and sex. He is the author of *Love's Philosophy* (Rowman & Littlefield) and *Nietzsche and the Problem of Sovereignty* and he is the editor of *Critical and Historical Perspectives on the Philosophy of Nietzsche*. He is a professor of philosophy at Creighton University.

DATE DUE

ACOUSTICAL
HOLOGRAPHY

Volume 1

ACOUSTICAL HOLOGRAPHY

Volume 1

Proceedings of the First International Symposium on
Acoustical Holography, held at the Douglas Advanced
Research Laboratories, Huntington Beach, California
December 14-15, 1967

Edited by

A. F. Metherell
Douglas Advanced Research Laboratories
McDonnell Douglas Corporation
Huntington Beach, California

H. M. A. El-Sum
El-Sum Consultants
Atherton, California

Lewis Larmore
Douglas Advanced Research Laboratories
McDonnell Douglas Corporation
Huntington Beach, California

ℚ PLENUM PRESS • NEW YORK • 1969

Library of Congress Catalog Card Number 69-12533

© 1969 Plenum Press
A Division of Plenum Publishing Corporation
227 West 17 Street, New York, N. Y. 10011

Printed in the United States of America

ACOUSTICAL HOLOGRAPHY
Volume 1

Speakers at the First International Symposium on Acoustical Holography. Reading from the left,
TOP ROW: A. F. Metherell, *Douglas Advanced Research Laboratories*; A. A. DeSousa, *UC Santa
Barbara*; H. Berger, *Argonne National Laboratory*; F. L. Thurstone, *Duke University*; J. W.
Goodman, *Stanford University*; G. Wade, *UC Santa Barbara*. MIDDLE ROW: B. B. Brenden,
Battelle Memorial Research Institute; J. de Klerk, *Westinghouse*; O. K. Mawardi, *Case-Western
Reserve University*; A. Korpel, *Zenith Radio Corporation*; J. L. Kreuzer, *Perkin-Elmer Corpora-
tion*; J. M. Smith, *University of Toronto*; C. J. Landry, *UC Santa Barbara*. FRONT ROW: B. A.
Auld, *Stanford University*; D. Gabor, *Imperial College, University of London*; J. J. Dreher,
Douglas Advanced Research Laboratories; L. Larmore, *Douglas Advanced Research Laboratories*;
H. M. A. El-Sum, *El-Sum Consultants*. Not shown: D. Fritzler and R. K. Mueller, *Bendix
Research Laboratories*, Y. Aoki, *Hokkaido University*, and P. Greguss, *RSRI Ultrasonics
Laboratory*.

PREFACE

Only a space limitation of 115 seats prevented this First International Symposium on Acoustical Holography from having an attendance of over 250. Unfortunately, the size of the auditorium of the Douglas Advanced Research Laboratories required that attendance be by invitation only, and many deserving and interested scientists could not be present. This volume presents the proceedings of the symposium, and hopefully will help compensate those individuals who were unable to attend.

The symposium itself consisted of sixteen formal papers. The seventeenth, by Dr. P. Greguss, was not received in time to be read but is included in these proceedings. The presence of Professor Dennis Gabor considerably enhanced the informal sessions, which frequently became as spirited as one might expect in a new field.

Dr. H. M. A. El-Sum, a consultant to the Douglas Advanced Research Laboratories and a pioneer in the field of holography, set the stage with the first paper. He provided a general introduction to the physical principles and practical methods involved in optical and acoustical holography. His paper also included a summary of various specific techniques currently used in sound holography, with the advantages, disadvantages, and limitations involved for each approach.

Mr. Harold Berger, of the Argonne National Laboratory, concentrated on the various methods for detecting ultrasonic images. He categorized the methods into (1) photographic and chemical, (2) thermal, (3) optical and mechanical, and (4) electronic. Each of the four methods requires a threshold ultrasonic radiation intensity which varies from 1 W/cm^2 for the photographic and chemical to values at least eleven orders of magnitude lower for the electronic techniques.

Bendix Research Laboratories' work on using a liquid–gas interface as a recording medium was reported by Dr. R. K. Mueller. Sound waves impinging on a liquid–gas interface generate a surface deformation consisting of components proportional to linear and quadratic terms in the acoustic amplitude. The quadratic term seems to be the more important for acoustical hologram formation, but the paper discussed the implication of both terms.

vii

Dr. Byron B. Brenden, of Battelle Memorial Research Institute, compared the two principal methods of imaging ultrasound by holography with reconstruction in light. One case employs a scanned acoustical receiver and a modulated light source. The other uses a liquid surface to record the hologram by means of a reflected light beam. He showed several examples of holograms and their reconstructed images produced by both methods.

Mr. Justin L. Kreuzer, of Perkin-Elmer Corporation, discussed the feasibility of applying acoustical holographic techniques to obtain three-dimensional images of opaque objects encountered in nondestructive testing. He found that acoustic wavelengths of 0.3 mm in water provided image detail smaller than 1 mm. Several typical holograms and their reconstructions showed the feasibility of this method, which promises to be an extremely useful tool in the future.

The application of Fourier transforms in assessing the performance of ultrasonic holography systems was reported by Mr. J. M. Smith, of the Institute of Biomedical Electronics, University of Toronto, Canada. He considered the events in the frequency domain, which allows a graphical representation of the effects of system parameters. By using the association between frequency components and resolution he determined the corresponding effects in the spatial domain. This kind of analysis provides an aid to assessing the maximum useful frequency and justifies the use of the spatial frequency of an extreme ray as the maximum frequency of interest.

Dr. F. L. Thurstone, of Duke University, presented some interesting ideas concerning applications of ultrasound holography to biomedical problems. The possibility of using acoustical techniques to replace X rays for certain diagnostic information shows much promise and was also mentioned by other speakers. However, the nature of the propagation of ultrasound in biologic tissue and the resulting image information present in an ultrasound field emanating from such a subject have yet to be fully understood or analyzed.

One of the interesting problems in the field of animal communication concerns the ability of porpoises and dolphins to use echo-location for discrimination between real and false targets. Dr. John Dreher, of the Douglas Advanced Research Laboratories, gave new insight to a possible explanation of this phenomenon. An anatomical description of these animals reveals a possible array of acoustical sensors in the "fatty melon" portion of the animal's head. This array compares with the scanning systems or the liquid–gas interface array used in acoustical holography. Dr. Dreher postulated that these animals possess a neural network which allows them to reconstruct images by means of a holographic process.

Dr. John de Klerk, of Westinghouse Research Laboratories, reviewed the most promising techniques for sound generation as applied to acoustical holography. His presentation covered methods and problems in the frequency range from audio to microwave regions. Special emphasis was placed on the high-frequency spectrum, where sound and optical wavelengths are more nearly comparable.

Although not strictly a holographic technique, acoustical imaging by Bragg diffraction offers promise as an alternate method for producing visual images of a sound source. Mr. A. Korpel, of Zenith Radio Corporation, presented the theory behind this technique and showed some experimental results. In particular, he discussed the property of imaging in depth which is inherent in this process and compared it with optical holographic methods.

Dr. Glen Wade, of the University of California at Santa Barbara, presented the results of the UCSB research utilizing acoustic transparencies for optical imaging and ultrasonic diffraction. This research team illuminates coherent sound in water with either converging or diverging laser light which, in turn, images the cross section of the sound beam. Elastic plates inserted in the sound beam can be rendered acoustically transparent under certain conditions. By treating the back surface of such plates with metal deposits the reconstruction of these deposits appears in the laser beam. Dr. Wade showed examples of line drawings and other figures reconstructed in this manner.

Many workers in acoustical holography have suggested that the reconstruction process be accomplished with a computer instead of the usual optical technique. A study by Dr. J. W. Goodman, of Stanford University, revealed the feasibility of this method. He described in detail the image degradations introduced by scanning errors, insufficient sampling, and digital quantization, as well as reporting on current experimental work in digital reconstruction.

Professor O. K. Mawardi, of Case-Western Reserve University, presented a theoretical analysis of phase distortion due to nonlinear effects in an acoustic field. In particular, he pointed out that the linear superposition concept for weak signals does not apply to strong signals due to harmonic distortion, wave–wave, interaction and induced secondary flow. Besides discussing these nonlinear effects, he gave methods of estimating quantitatively the magnitude of the phase distortions introduced by the second-order effects.

Dr. A. F. Metherell, of the Douglas Advanced Research Laboratories, discussed the relative importance of phase and amplitude in acoustical holography. The technique essentially uses a "variable gamma" recording system to enhance the diffraction fringes at large distances from the axis. His results, illustrated by comparative examples, showed the main effect to be a modification of the overall image intensity but with no effect on the relative intensities of points in the object plane that are visible at all points in the hologram plane. The apparent resolution of the reconstruction appears to improve with this method.

Significant acoustical holography work in Japan was described in a paper by Dr. Yoshinao Aoki, of Hokkaido University, and which was read by Dr. El-Sum. Both theoretical and experimental research were discussed, covering the effects of scanning lines, the hologram-limited aperture, conversion efficiency of the light intensity in the reconstruction, the role of the acoustic frequency on the reconstructed images, and the three-dimensional information storage in acoustical holograms.

Miss D. Fritzler, of Bendix Research Laboratories, described an ultrasonic camera adapted to making holograms. The camera, manufactured by James Electronics, Inc., uses a quartz crystal located at the front window of a cathode ray tube. The crystal is irradiated by the sound beam, and the interference pattern is picked up by the scanning electron beam, which is amplified and displayed on a TV monitor. A photograph of the TV display allows reconstruction by the usual laser technique. Miss Fritzler showed experimental results of this method and discussed some of the limitations.

At the end of the formal presentation, Professor Dennis Gabor summarized the new techniques presented at the symposium. One of the topics which evoked a lively discussion concerned methods of coping with distortion in the reconstructed image due to differences in axial and lateral magnification. Although Dr. Thurstone mentioned a possible solution in his talk by means of a frequency doubling technique, no consensus evolved from the group's comments. However, the participants all agreed that the principal barrier to the acoustical holographic techniques was the lack of a suitable recording array corresponding to the fine-grain film used in optical holography. We would expect to find considerable research and development effort concentrated toward the solution of this problem during the next few years.

Rather than causing unnecessary delay in publication, the editors have allowed the authors to express themselves in their own way. Consequently, different symbols for the same quantity may appear throughout the book. However, this lack of continuity should not cause any confusion, since all symbols are well defined.

A supplementary bibliography at the end of the formal papers contains a compilation of abstracts of nearly all publications on acoustical holography up through 1967. The editors hope new workers in the field will find this collection a useful adjunct to the book as well as a source for references.

The editing of these proceedings has been accomplished with the help and cooperation of all of the authors and many of the staff members of the Douglas Advanced Research Laboratories. The editors are sincerely grateful to all of these individuals and to the McDonnell Douglas Corporation for sponsoring the symposium.

A. F. Metherell
H. M. A. El-Sum
Lewis Larmore

CONTENTS

CHAPTER 4   *by B. B. Brenden*
A Comparison of Acoustical Holography Methods

CHAPTER 5   *by J. L. Kreuzer and P. E. Vogel*
Acoustic Holographic Techniques for Nondestructive Testing

Chapter 1

THE SCOPE OF THE SYMPOSIUM

H. M. A. El-Sum[*]

El-Sum Consultants
Atherton, California

Since interest in the visualization of sound fields is shared by scientists and engineers of a wide range of disciplines, the symposium commences with a broad survey of the subject under discussion. A brief general introduction to the physical principles and practical methods involved in light and sound holography is presented. The rest of the paper dwells upon the various techniques in sound holography, pointing out similarities to and diversities from optical holography, chief advantages of each technique, and limitations or drawbacks of such approaches.

INTRODUCTION

The International Union of Pure and Applied Physics has made an excellent recommendation that a Symposium should commence with a broad survey of the subject under discussion. In the present instance this is more than usually desirable, since interest in visualization of sound fields is shared by scientists and engineers of a wide range of disciplines: physics, geology, metallurgy, mining, biology, medicine, chemistry, nondestructive testing, oceanography, and many other technological subjects. A brief general introduction to the physical principles and practical methods involved in light and sound holography is presented here.

The most important and fundamental contribution of holography to optics is that it provides the means for recording with square law detectors the phase information of an object wave. This is quite a milestone in wave optics, where phase information cannot be recorded by any other technique. On the other hand, linear detectors are available for sound waves (except for extreme ultrasonics, where the wavelength approaches that of visible light), and hence both amplitude and phase information of a sound wave can be meas-

*Concurrently consultant to Douglas Advanced Research Laboratories, McDonnell Douglas Corporation, Huntington Beach, California.

ured without the need of the technique of holography. One may then ponder the reasons for extending holography, as it is known in optics, to sound.

The reasons for using acoustical holography ([1]) rather than other conventional techniques to form visual images in insonified objects are its simplicity and flexibility, ability of real-time visualization of three-dimensional images, rapid extraction and processing of acoustic information, enormous depth of field, insensitivity (under certain conditions) to turbulence and turbidity of the environment, capability of retrieving the information about the target from discrete sampling points, localization of targets or defects in such targets, nondestructive testing utilizing the unique interaction of sound with the object and/or three-dimensional interferometry, and capability of detecting extremely low powers that could not be otherwise detected ([2–4]).

Before the development of the laser the need for coherent optical sources, was the main hurdle in the advancement of optical holography. On the other hand, coherent sound sources have always been with us, and it seems that acoustical holograms should have been made well before the optical ones. They probably have been made, but discarded as useless out-of-focus images. Even if they have not been discarded, they could not have been reconstructed optically because of the lack of strong coherent light sources.

The difficulties in making sound holograms are rather different from those encountered in making optical ones. The fundamental problems in sound holography are in the recording technique. Other serious problems are due to the nature of the nonlinear propagation of sound, the relatively long wavelength resulting in limited-aperture holograms, and reconstruction with much shorter wavelength radiation.

DEFINITIONS

Like optical holography, acoustical holography is a two-stage process in which the diffraction pattern of an object irradiated by sound waves is biased by a coherent reference wave and recorded, either permanently, such as on a photographic film, or temporarily on an appropriate medium. This recording may be on the surface of a recorder or throughout its volume. A realistic, three-dimensional visual image is created when the acoustical hologram is interrogated with a suitable coherent light source. From a surface-type recording two twin images are reconstructed simultaneously; they are mirror images of each other. The terminology used for these images is rather confusing, and thus I prefer and urge the use of the terminology originally introduced by Gabor. This terminology is rephrased below.

Hologram. A recording (permanent or semipermanent, surface or volume) of the diffraction pattern of an object biased by a coherent background radiation. This biasing radiation may be referred to as reference wave.

Reconstructed Image. An image reconstructed from a hologram when illuminated by the reference wave alone.

Twin Images. The two images reconstructed from a surface-type hologram.

True Image. The reconstructed image which exactly duplicates the original object. Mathematically it is described by a wave function identical to that of the object.

Conjugate Image. The reconstructed image which is described by a wave function conjugate to that describing the object. This image is a mirror image of the original object, or its true image, in all directions (i.e., axially as well as in any transverse plane). Depending on the reconstruction arrangement, both or either of the twin images can be real or virtual with respect to the hologram.

Sonoptography.* Synonymous with acoustical holography.

Sonoptigram.* A hologram made with sound.

GENERALIZED PRINCIPLES OF HOLOGRAPHY

The following discussion is restricted to those holographic formulas that are relevant to scalar wave fields ([1]). When two monochromatic and mutually coherent waves U_0 and U_r are superimposed at plane H [Fig. 1(a)] the resultant wave,

$$U = U_r + U_0$$

when detected by a square law detector, results in a recorded intensity:

$$I = UU^* = U_rU_r^* + U_0U_0^* + U_rU_0^* + U_r^*U_0 \qquad (1)$$

where the asterisk denotes complex conjugate.

The first two terms in the above equation represent the intensities of the waves U_r and U_0, respectively, while the last two terms represent additional intensities due to the interference between U_r and U_0. The recording in the plane H is the hologram of the two waves U_r and U_0, one of which may be considered the reference wave while the other is the object wave. Notice the symmetry of the four terms in Eq. (1). Assuming linear recording of the intensity I and that the hologram response t to an illuminating wave U_0 or U_r is also linear (e.g., t is the wave amplitude transmission of the hologram

*Term first introduced by Larmore ([33]).

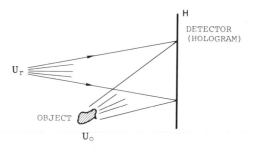

a. Construction of hologram
(U_r and U_o are coherent)

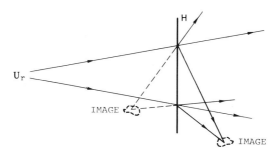

b. Wavefront reconstruction of images

Fig. 1. General principle of the construction of a
hologram and reconstruction of the object images.
(a) The object wave U_0 and reference wave U_r interfere
coherently on the hologram plane H. (b) Illuminating
the hologram with the reference wave alone reconstructs
twin images of the object. In this arrangement the true
image is virtual and the conjugate image is real.

recorded on a transparency), then it is easy to prove that illuminating the
hologram with either U_r or U_0 will result in the creation or reconstruction of
the other wave and its complex conjugate ([1]) (Fig. 1(b)). The hologram H is a
surface-type, and hence no information is recorded in depth. The two reconstructed waves are the twin images of the original object. The location of
these images depends upon the geometrical arrangement in making the
hologram, the arrangement of the reconstruction process, the change in the
magnification of the hologram before its reconstruction, and the ratio
between the wavelengths of the radiation used in making and reconstructing

the hologram. In general, if there is an angular separation between U_r and U_0, the twin reconstructed images are angularly separated ([5]) and each can be viewed without interference from the other (depending of course on the bandwidth of the object and the angular separation between U_r and U_0. On the other hand, if U_r and U_0 are coaxial ([6-9]), the two reconstructed images are also coaxial and their interference can be minimized or eliminated under certain conditions ([10-12]).

The hologram (surface-type) may be considered as a compound zone plate with a built-in object. Thus it has an equivalent focal length f which is, to a first approximation, given by

$$1/f = (1/v) - (1/u) \qquad (2)$$

where v and u are the distances measured from the point of intersection of the hologram with the line joining the reference source to the object. All distances are positive when measured in the direction toward the reference source.

If the hologram's linear dimension x is changed to x' (i.e., by a factor $m = x'/x$) and the reconstructing wavelength λ' is different from the original wavelength λ used to record the hologram such that $\lambda'/\lambda = \mu$, then in the reconstruction process the hologram acts like a lens having a focal length f' given by $f' = m^2/\mu f$ and

$$\frac{1}{f'} = \pm \left(\frac{1}{v'} - \frac{1}{u'} \right) \qquad (3)$$

where the $+$ sign gives the position of the true image and the $-$ sign gives the position of the conjugate image. In the above equation v' and u' refer to the distances of the reconstructed image and the illuminating source in the reconstruction process, respectively. This equation results from the fundamental property of the hologram:

$$x^2 \propto f\lambda = \text{const.}$$

Equation (3) reveals the first and the unsurmountable difficulty in reconstructing acoustical holograms with visible light: $1/\mu$ is of the order of magnitude of 1000, and it can be easily shown that unless $m = 1/\mu$ the reconstructed image will suffer from aberration (mainly spherical) ([10,11]), and, more important, from distortion caused by the difference between the axial and transverse magnifications, M_L and M_T respectively,

$$M_L = \frac{(\mu/m^2)(1/v^2)}{\{ \pm (\mu/m^2)[(1/v) - (1/u)] + 1/u' \}^2} \qquad (4)$$

and

$$M_T = m \left(\frac{u}{u - v} \right) \left(1 - \frac{v'}{u'} \right) \tag{5}$$

The deviation from the rule that m must be equal to $1/\mu$ may be tolerated in planar objects, but not for producing an undistorted and faithful image of a three-dimensional object.

There are many ideas for partially overcoming this difficulty, but none has yet been proven satisfactory. For example, Thurstone recently proposed ([12]) a frequency multiplication approach, where the hologram will appear as if it was made with a frequency higher than the acoustic frequency actually used. This may introduce a reduction factor of 10 at most, which is still two orders of magnitude less than the needed reduction. A paper by Dr. Thurstone appears as Chapter 7 in this volume. Another technique is to increase the hologram aperture by intensifying the far off-axis faint unrecorded fringes, as will be described by Metherell in Chapter 14.

Another problem that is usually encountered in acoustical holography is that of the specular reflection. Most surfaces which are considered rough in the visible region are quite smooth when insonified, since the wavelength of sound is considerably long. Consequently, these surfaces act as mirrors for acoustic waves, with the result that cylinders, for example, may appear as straight lines, and hence accurate interpretation of the image will be difficult. As an illustration, Fig. 2 shows the reconstruction from an optical hologram of a statue of the Three Graces. The front view of the Three Graces is reconstructed from one side of the hologram, while the back view is reconstructed when the hologram is viewed from the back. Notice the strong and undesirable reflection from the curved surfaces of the object.

It seems that the only way to avoid this type of mirror reflection is to roughen the surface relative to the wavelength to be used in the hologram recording.

Other difficulties encountered in acoustical holography are peculiar to the technique used, the interaction of the sound with the object, and the nonlinear propagation of sound wave. I shall briefly deal with these topics, leaving many gaps and details to be filled in other chapters.

SOUND RECORDING

Sound can be detected and recorded either directly, such as on photographic films, or indirectly, by converting its energy to another type of energy before detection and then to optical energy if it is to be recorded on a photographic emulsion. Actually, nearly all sound detectors are of the second type. One may even look upon holography as a means for detecting sound energy.

(a)

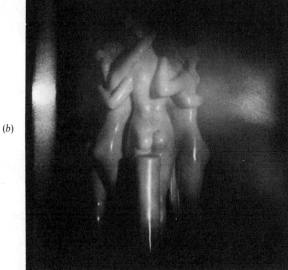

(b)

Fig. 2. Reconstructed image of a statue of the Three Graces. (a) Reconstruction from one side of the hologram. (b) Reconstruction from the other side of the same hologram. Both the hologram and the reconstruction were made with 6328-Å He–Ne laser. Notice the strong specular reflection referred to in the text. Photos courtesy of M. Lehmann, Stanford Electronics Laboratory.

The threshold of detectable acoustic power by different detectors varies from about 1 W/cm^2 for photographic emulsion and other chemical detectors to not less than 0.1 W/cm^2 for thermoplastic recording. These are rather high levels, and account for the reason no one has yet attempted to record sound

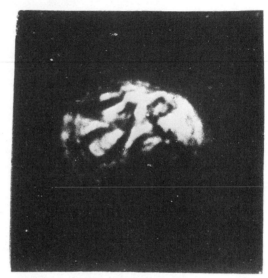

Fig. 3. Optical reconstruction (right) of an object (left) from 5-MHz underwater acoustical hologram recorded on thermoplastic layer spread on the water surface. The object was made of copper wire 0.020 in. in diameter, with the outside diameter of the object being 5/8 in. From Young and Wolfe ([13]).

Fig. 4. Optical reconstruction of a frog pelvis from an acoustical hologram on thermoplastic film. An underwater 5-MHz sound source insonified the frog, and the thermoplastic film was spread on the water surface. The white lines in the view at right are made to aid in viewing the reconstructed image (middle), while the left view is an X-ray picture for comparison. Notice the tail bone at the bottom of the reconstructed image. From Young and Wolfe ([13]).

holograms directly on a photographic film. However, Young and Wolfe ([13]) at General Electric have very recently published reconstructions from acoustical phase holograms on thermoplastic material (Figs. 3 and 4).

Thermal detectors, luminescent detectors, and liquid crystals have a threshold of about 0.1 W/cm^2.

Interaction of light waves with pressure-sensitive properties of a fluid, such as density and acoustically induced surface deformation, can be used to detect acoustic power of the order of 10^{-3} W/cm^2. The next section will elaborate on the technique of such detection and recording.

For very low power, of the order of 10^{-8} W/cm^2 and less, one has to resort to either piezoelectric materials and electron beam scanning or to direct laser beam scanning ([14]) of an acoustically deformed surface, which will be discussed further in a later section. It is desirable to push this limit still further down.

Detectors are discussed in more detail in Chapter 2 of this volume.

I now proceed to discuss various arrangements for making acoustical holograms, starting with the liquid surface deformation method pioneered by R. K. Mueller [see ([15])], P. S. Green, and B. B. Brenden.

LIQUID SURFACE DEFORMATION

An object is submerged in a liquid and insonified, as shown in Fig. 5. A coherent sound source provides a reference beam which interferes coherently with the scattered wave from the object. When the resultant wave impinges on the free and calm surface of the liquid it will be deformed and the deformation, to a first degree of approximation, is a function of the impinging resultant sound pressure. Obviously, the arrangement is analogous to making an ordinary optical hologram, Fig. 1a, with a sound source replacing the light source and the free surface of the liquid replacing the recording film. Hence

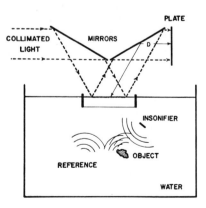

Figure 5. Principle of the liquid deformation method. The insonified object and the reference source are in a quiet water tank. A 12-μ Mylar membrane at the top of the tank holds a 6% Triron X-100 wetting agent, on the surface of which ripples are formed and viewed by the collimated light. From Green ([34]).

the free surface actually records a phase-type hologram (analogous to a bleached optical hologram) which will directly reconstruct the object when illuminated with a coherent light source, or which can be transformed onto a photographic film to produce a permanent record of the hologram that can in turn be appropriately reconstructed. The arrangement is suitable for making on- or off-axis holograms using either the same source to provide the object and the reference waves or two coherent sources for the two waves (which cannot be done yet with lasers). The technique is obviously capable of producing real-time reconstruction.

The sound wave has three effects on the free liquid surface on which it impinges: (1) a uniform levitation, (2) deformation superimposed on the levitation (this is the main holographic information), and (3) small vibrations of the deformed surface (these vibrations are very small and could be ignored in the first approximation of our analysis).

The vertical surface deformation h of the liquid surface is a function of the perpendicular acoustic pressure P, the density ρ of the liquid, its surface tension γ, and the acceleration of gravity g. These factors are related by the pressure equilibrium equation:

$$\rho g h - \gamma \nabla^2 h = 2P \tag{6}$$

where $P = |p|^2/2\rho v$, with p the acoustic pressure amplitude and v the velocity of the sound in the liquid.

Green [34] calculated the transfer function $G_1(f)$ relating the acoustic radiation pressure to the liquid surface deformation height.

$$G_1(\omega) = \frac{2/\rho g}{1 - (\gamma \omega^2/\rho g)} \tag{7}$$

where

$$\omega^2 = \omega_x^2 + \omega_y^2, \qquad \omega_x = 2\pi f_x, \qquad \omega_y = 2\pi f_y$$

with f_x and f_y the x and y spatial frequency components. This transfer function $G_1(f)$ distribution (Fig. 6) shows that the liquid surface interaction with the sound field acts as a low-pass filter with a 50% cutoff frequency f_0 inversely proportional to the surface tension:

$$f_0 = (1/2\pi)(\rho g/\gamma)^{\frac{1}{2}} \tag{8}$$

For pure water γ is about 75 dyn/cm, and hence the 50% cutoff frequency is about 0.6 cycles/cm.

This means that this liquid surface deformation technique is best suited for on-axis or Gabor-type hologram, and not for far off-axis holography, where fine fringes are produced. To increase the cutoff frequency, the surface of the liquid may be wetted by a wetting agent, such as Triten X-100, which has a surface tension less than that of the water.

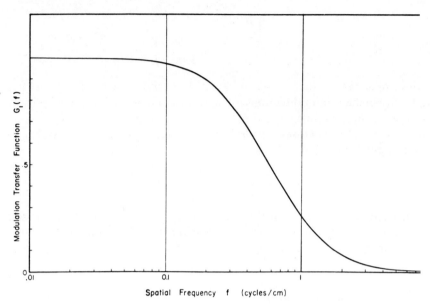

Fig. 6. Transfer function relating pure water displacement to acoustic radiation pressure. From Green ([34]).

In the reconstruction process or for recording the surface deformation on a photographic film the interaction of the illuminating light wave with the deformed liquid surface should be investigated. Naturally, one would expect that since the reflecting power from the surface depends upon the slope of the ripples, the reflection should be higher for higher spatial frequency, and hence the light–surface interaction will act as a high-pass filter. This can be easily shown by considering the reflection of a plane wave of coherent light of wavelength λ from the deformed surface. Assuming normal incidence for simplicity, the reflected beam $\mathbf{U}_0$ at the surface plane is

$$\mathbf{U}_0 = \exp i(4\pi h/\lambda) \qquad (9)$$

where h is again the small deformation height and it is assumed that the incident light wave has a unit amplitude. At a distance D above the surface the reflected wave will then be given by the convolution:

$$\mathbf{U}_D = (1/i\lambda D)(\mathbf{U}_0 * \mathbf{G}) \qquad (10)$$

where $\mathbf{G} \approx \exp i(\pi/\lambda D)(x^2 + y^2)$. From Eq. (10) the recorded intensity at distance D above the liquid surface is $I_D = \mathbf{U}_D\mathbf{U}_D^*$. Carrying on the normal Fourier transformation of I_D and with some approximation, the transfer function $G_2(f)$ relating surface-height deviation and recording plane intensity is:

$$G_2(\omega) = \frac{8\pi}{\lambda} \sin\left(\frac{D\lambda}{4\pi}\omega^2\right) \qquad (11)$$

where ω is again equal to $[4\pi^2(f_x^2 + f_y^2)]^{\frac{1}{2}}$, f_x and f_y being the spatial frequencies in the x and y directions. In order to avoid distortion in the optically reconstructed twin images and for reconstruction of high-order diffraction images the surface deformation h should be small relative to the wavelength of the light, in which case Eq. (11) can be approximated as:

$$G_2(\omega) \approx \frac{16\pi}{\lambda} \frac{1}{\rho g} \frac{1}{1 + (\gamma/\rho g)\omega^2} \sin\left(\frac{D\lambda}{4\pi}\omega^2\right) \qquad (12)$$

which is plotted in Fig. 7 for the case where $D\lambda/4\pi$ is equal to 10^{-4} cm^2 and $\gamma/\rho g$ is equal to 0.0765 cm^2. The lowest frequency f' at which the function $G_2(\omega)$ drops to zero is given by

$$f' = 1/(\lambda D)^{\frac{1}{2}} \qquad (13)$$

Combining the effect of sound–liquid surface and deformed surface–light interactions, it is then seen that this technique acts like a bandpass filter extending from about 1 to 20 cycles/cm. This imposes limitation on the angle subtended at the liquid surface by the reference source and the point on

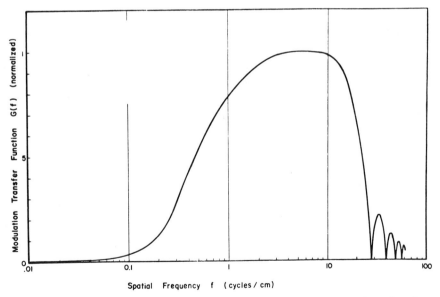

Fig. 7. Transfer function for complete conversion process for pure water and small surface displacement. From Green (^{34}).

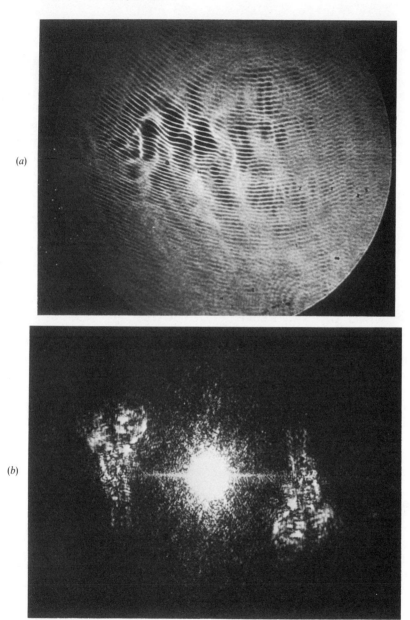

(a)

(b)

Fig. 8. Optical reconstruction (b) of a car key from an acoustical hologram (a) recorded with fluid surface deformation arrangement shown in Fig. 5. Hologram was made with the reference source in the same plane as the insonified key; 5-MHz acoustic frequency; 6328-Å reconstructing optical wavelength; hologram demagnified 18 × before reconstruction; object 14 cm below surface. From Green ([34]).

the object most distant from the reference. For example, for an acoustic frequency of 5 MHz this angle could not exceed 36°.

Figs. 8a and 8b show an example of a hologram and reconstruction taken with the arrangement shown in Fig. 5. The acoustic frequency of 5 MHz formed the hologram, with the object and reference source placed equidistant (at a distance of 14 cm) below the surface, thus forming a Fourier-type hologram. The reconstruction, Fig. 8b, shows the true reconstructed images simultaneously in focus; the reconstruction was made with He–Ne CW laser (wavelength 6328 Å), after the hologram had been demagnified by a factor of 18. The cell in Fig. 5 at the top of the water surface is filled with 6% Triton X-100 wetting agent on a 12-μ Mylar membrane. The transducer illuminating the object was a 3-mm PZT disk with a cemented divergent steel lens, while the reference wave was provided by a 25-mm disk with a polystyrene lens.

Other arrangements and detailed analysis of liquid surface deformation technique for acoustical holography are further discussed in Chapters 3 and 4.

SCANNING OR SAMPLING TECHNIQUE

Basically, this is a technique by which the hologram plane is appropriately sampled. The detected energy is converted to light and recorded in a synchronous manner on a photographic film. A reduction of the hologram size may be achieved by adjusting the mapping ratio between the actual hologram plane and the photographic recording. This technique is obviously limited to making a surface-type hologram. However, it can be applied to any sound propagating medium: gas, liquid, or solid.

There are three types of scanning: mechanical, electronic, and laser beam.

Mechanical Scanning

An appropriate transducer scans a plane in the medium where a hologram is made. In one arrangement the signal from the transducer is amplified, and modulates a small light bulb which is focused, in a dark room, on a photographic plate. This has been done for objects submerged in water [16, 17], as discussed further in Chapters 4 and 5, or in air [1, 18 – 22], as is described in Chapter 14.

In another arrangement the detected signal modulates the scanning spot, of a CRT, the face of which is photographed. Darkness of the laboratory in this case is not necessary. By adjusting the ratio between the speed of the scanning transducer and that of the flying spot scanner and by adjusting the camera demagnification of the face of the CRT a high reduction of the acoustical hologram is obtained. The linear response and stabilization of the CRT are of utmost importance.

Since acoustic waves can be detected by linear transducers, it is not necessary to use a reference beam as in optical holography. Such a reference beam can be simulated electronically in a way to imitate either a plane or a spherical wave falling at any angle on the hologram ([21, 22]). Figure 9 shows a hologram of a cutout of a letter "R" 6 ft high by 4 ft wide with a stroke width of 12 in. insonified in air with a 18-kHz sound beam, corresponding to 0.75 in. wavelength. The reference beam electronically simulated a plane reference wave falling perpendicular to the hologram. Hence the resultant hologram was an on-axis, Fresnel type. Furthermore, the fringes far off-

Fig. 9. Acoustical hologram made in air with 0.75 in. wavelength insonifier placed 15 ft behind the object. Electronic reference beam was added after the object wave amplitude was normalized across the hologram plane. From unpublished work by A. F. Metherell, Douglas Advanced Research Laboratories.

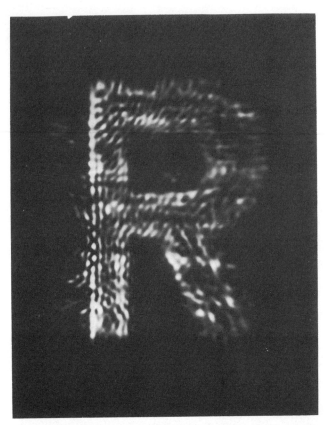

Fig. 10. Optical reconstruction with 6328-Å converging laser beam of the hologram of Fig. 9 after it was demagnified to 0.2 in. The original object was a letter "R" 6 ft high by 4 ft wide and 12-in. stroke width. The conjugate images of the "R" and the source were filtered out. From unpublished work by A. F. Metherell, Douglas Advanced Research Laboratories.

center were enhanced by using the phase lock technique described by Metherell in Chapter 14. The scanned plane was 8 ft × 10 ft, and the resultant hologram was reconstructed after it had been demagnified by a total factor of 50 to about (2/10) in. with a 6328-Å He–Ne laser. The reconstruction was done with a converging light beam resulting in the formation of real-time images of both real and conjugate waves of the letter "R" and the insonifier. By proper filtering ([23]) the conjugate images of the object and the insonifier were eliminated, rendering a clean good reconstruction, as shown in Fig. 10.

Apart from the speckle effect due to the small aperture of the hologram and the coherent illumination the resolution of the reconstructed image

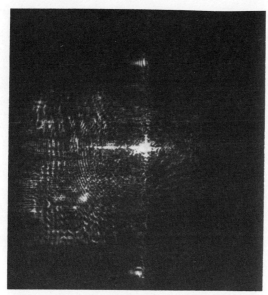

Fig. 11. Optical reconstruction of the insonifying source of the letter "R" of Fig. 9 and 10. The source is at the center of the picture. Spurious points above and below the reconstructed source are not positively identified. From unpublished work by A. F. Metherell, Douglas Advanced Research Laboratories.

approaches that of the wavelength used, as evidenced from the stroke width of the letter, which is only 16 wavelengths. In another plane the insonifier is clearly reconstructed, as shown in Fig. 11, which illustrates the three-dimensional imaging property of holography.

The main drawback of mechanical scanning is the slow recording speed of the hologram. This requires great stability of both the system and the environment. For example, small thermal variation or frequency drift can be ruinous, as shown in Fig. 12, which should be the same as Fig. 9 if the air conditioner of the room did not cause periodic room temperature fluctuation of 1°C during the exposure. It has been estimated that at the normal room temperature of about 25°C temperature fluctuation should not exceed 0.05°C, which is quite a severe restriction. One solution to this difficulty is to either record the hologram in the shortest time possible or use a reference wave which propagates through the same medium ([24]).

Electronic Scanning

A hologram is projected on a piezoelectric crystal, creating an electric potential pattern of the hologram. An electronic beam scanning the crystal

Fig. 12. Effect of temperature variation of the environment. This hologram should be the same as Fig. 9 were it not for the 1°C periodic fluctuation of the room temperature. From unpublished work by A. F. Metherell, Douglas Advanced Research Laboratories.

produces modulated secondary emission, which records the hologram either directly on a photographic film or projects it on the face of a CRT. The advantage of this technique lies in both the sensitivity of the detected signal and the speed of scanning. On the other hand, it has a limited angular field of view and a limited resolution. For high resolution the transducer should be as thin as possible; but the thinner it is, the weaker it will be mechanically, and hence the smaller will be its aperture. Moreover, the transducer should operate at its resonance frequency, which means that the transducer thickness should be of the order of half the acoustic wavelength impinging upon it. It has been shown [25] that the minimum resolvable distance δ on such transducer is

$$\delta \text{ (in mm)} = 2.86/\text{Acoustic frequency} \quad \text{(in MHz)} \qquad (14)$$

Another limitation in this technique is the sensitivity of the transducer to the angle of incidence of the radiation; the angle of incidence should not exceed 5°–10° from the perpendicular. This creates a severe limitation on the angular field of view of the object and the angular separation between the object and the reference waves. To overcome such difficulties, the object wave should be adjusted to fall as close as possible to the perpendicular to the transducer and an electronic reference wave ([22]) should be used, which can be simulated to have any angle of incidence as well as any shape.

Laser Beam Scanning

Mechanical scanning is too slow, and electronic scanning cannot be used with high acoustic frequencies because of the limitation on the thickness of the transducer. On the other hand, laser beam scanning combines fast scanning with the high acoustic frequencies. There are two main methods for utilizing a laser beam to record the ripples on a liquid or a solid surface on which acoustic waves impinge. The two methods vary mainly in the deflecting schemes of the laser beam. One method proposed by Gabor ([26]) is to use mechanical deflection of the beam to detect the frequency modulation imposed on a sampling laser beam as it is reflected from a thin membrane in the sound field. The other method, after Korpel and co-workers ([14, 27, 28]), uses Bragg reflection from frequency-modulated ultrasonic waves in a water cell to deflect the scanning laser beam ([29]). It has been used to visualize sound fields in both liquids and solids. Figure 13a shows a hologram of a thin sheet of neoprene with 5 holes each 1.25 mm in diameter. The sheet was placed in a small cavity machined in a solid block of Lucite through which sound propagated. The standing wave on the surface of the Lucite was detected by the laser beam scanner. The sound frequency was 9 MHz. The hologram produced is equivalent to an object wave propagating in the direction of the Lucite surface and a reference beam perpendicular to it. The reconstruction is shown in Fig. 13b.

Adler et al. ([28]) reported that laser scanning technique is capable of detecting power as slow as 1 μW/cm^2, corresponding to amplitudes less than 0.1 Å. The theoretical limit of the technique may be pushed to 10^{-8} W/cm^2 ([27]). Thus it is not only a fast scanning technique but quite a sensitive one too.

On the other hand, it has a limitation on angular field of view due mainly to the limitation on the laser beam deflection technique.

EFFECT OF SCANNING ON HOLOGRAM RECONSTRUCTION

The number of scanning lines depends on the highest frequency to be recorded. The width of the scanning line should be less than $\frac{1}{4}$ the width of the finest fringe to be recorded. The scanning effect on a hologram is the same as

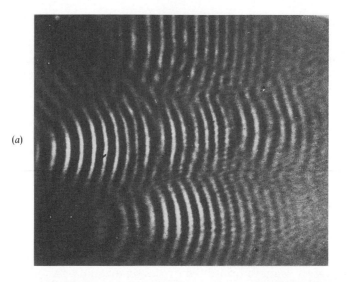

(a)

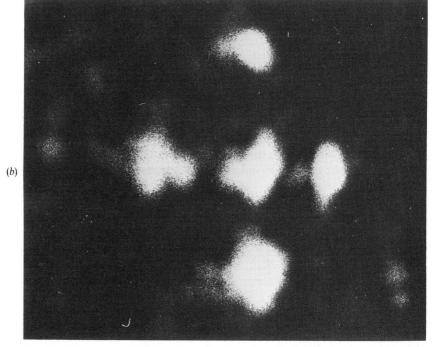

(b)

Fig. 13. (a) Hologram of five holes in a thin sheet of neoprene. The sheet was inserted in a cavity machined in a lucite block. A 9-MHz acoustic wave was used and a laser beam scanned a 10 × 7.5 mm area of the Lucite face to form this hologram. (b) Optical reconstruction of the hologram. The holes were 1.25 mm in diameter ($\frac{1}{4}$ the acoustic wavelength in lucite), and placed at the corners and center of a 4.5 × 4.5 mm square. Photos courtesy of A. Korpel, Zenith Radio Corp.

that of a diffraction grating (one- or two-dimensional grating, depending on whether a linear scan or a two-dimensional sampling, as by using a detection mosaic, is used), superimposed on the hologram. This results in multiplication of each of the reconstructed images. These images may or may not interfere with one another depending upon the number of the scanning lines and the bandwidth of the object.

The simplest way to analyze the scanning or sampling effect is by studying the Moiré pattern of Fresnel plate (hologram of a point object) and a linear diffraction grating. It can be easily shown that secondary zone plates are produced, with their centers separated by a distance $n/2\pi a$, where n is $\pm 1, 2, 3, \ldots$, the order of the Moiré pattern, and a is the spacing between

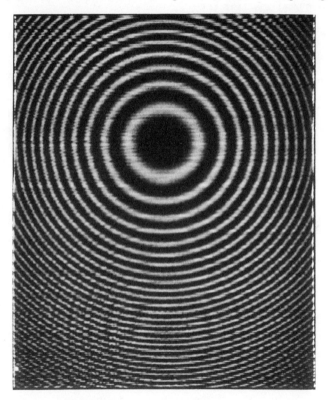

Fig. 14. Acoustical hologram of a point source made in air by phase locking and scanning technique. The scanning lines produced the Moiré pattern duplication of the hologram (a Fresnel zone plate configuration). Using the same scanning frequency an extended object should not extend more than half the distance between the two zone plate patterns. Photo courtesy of A. F. Metherell, Douglas Advanced Research Laboratories.

the scanning lines, assuming the area of the central zone of the zone plate is unity. This separation should be greater than twice the object linear dimension in that direction in order to prevent overlapping and interference between the images. Figure 14 is an acoustical hologram of a point object. Although the scanning lines are too close to be seen, their effect can be seen in producing the first-order Moiré pattern at the bottom (a secondary zone plate). Thus with the arrangement used to record Fig. 14 the extent of the object perpendicular to the scanning lines should be less than half the distance between the centers of the original and the secondary zone plates.

DIRECT VISUALIZATION OF SOUND FIELD BY BRAGG DIFFRACTION OF LIGHT

Although this technique does not belong to acoustical holography in the true sense (because of the absence of a reference wave), it is so close and important that it deserves inclusion here.

Korpel [30] successfully produced visual shadows of insonified objects by direct interaction of light waves with the sound field. Referring to Fig. 15, coherent light diverging from a point source O intersects the sound rays originating from the point sound source S. The light and sound rays intersect at points such as A, B, and C, such that the light rays form an angle ϕ_B with the sound wavefronts (perpendicular to the sound rays). If this angle satisfies the Bragg condition:

$$\sin \phi_B = \lambda/2\Lambda \tag{15}$$

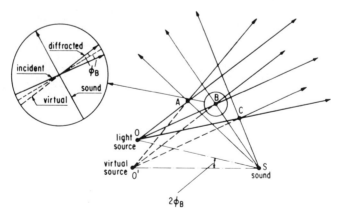

Fig. 15. Imaging of a point sound source S at point O' by Bragg reflection of light emitted from the point O. From Korpel [30].

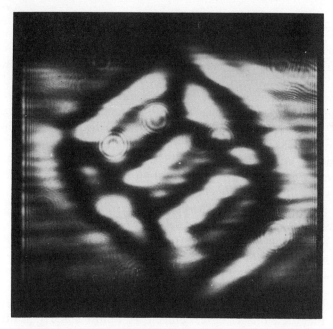

Fig. 16. Direct imaging by the Korpel technique (Bragg reflection) of Fig. 15. The object was a cube 5 mm on the side, made of soldering iron wire insonified with 22-MHz sound wave and imaged by a 6328-Å light. Photo courtesy of A. Korpel, Zenith Radio Corp.

where λ and Λ are the light and sound wavelengths, respectively, then the light will be reflected and all the rays will meet at a point O', which could be considered as the image of the sound source S. Since the Bragg angle ϕ_B is very small, it is obvious that the light illumination should be nearly perpendicular to the direction of propagation of the sound wave.

If S is an extended object, then the image O' is a demagnified image of S. The demagnification factor is the ratio between the light and sound wavelengths. The resolution δ of the optical image formed is determined by the size of the light source multiplied by the ratio Λ/λ.

Figure 16 is an example of an image formed by this technique. The object is a cube 5 mm on the side made of soldering iron wire insonified with a 22-MHz sound wave, and the sound field was illuminated perpendicularly with a 6328-Å coherent light beam. This technique is now extensively used using ultrasonics in the giga-Hertz range propagating in solids (such as quartz crystals[31]) for ultrasonic microscopy. Korpel, the pioneer of this technique, discusses this subject in Chapter 10, and Wade et al. discuss their activities in this field in Chapter 11.

GENERAL REMARKS

Some of the problem areas which I have not touched upon are related to the propagation of sound, its attenuation, and its interaction with objects.

Sound propagates nonlinearly. This nonlinearity becomes more serious as the amplitude and frequency of the sound increase. Mawardi has shown [32], for example, that the phase of a plane wave reflected from a plane mirror can be distorted by as much as 3° in air for a fluctuating pressure sound wave of amplitude 0.01 atm and of 10^4 Hz frequency, while the phase distortion is 1° in water for a wave having an amplitude of 1 atm and 10 MHz frequency.

In Chapter 11 Wade *et al.* show that at certain angles of incidence opaque sound objects may become transparent, a fact which one should be aware of in order to avoid misinterpretation of the reconstructed images.

Again, I would like to emphasize that recording media deserve serious attention, since fast recording can solve many of the other problems in this area.

Finally, with regard to the quality of the reconstructed images, it should be noted that these images never compete with those made optically, simply because the resolution is determined by the acoustic wavelength (making the hologram), which is much larger than the optical wavelength, and also because of the specular reflection.

The successes attained in the short active years of this subscience of acoustical holography is indeed quite encouraging. Although it is clear that future progress will depend heavily on technological advances, pure scientific investigation in many areas should not be ignored.

REFERENCES

1. A. F. Metherell, H. M. A. El-Sum, J. J. Dreher, L. Larmore, *J. Acoust. Soc. Am.* **42**:733–742 (1967).
2. D. Gabor, in: *Progress in Optics*, Vol. I (Emil Wolf, ed.), North-Holland Publishing Co., Amsterdam, 1961, pp. 122–124.
3. D. Gabor and W. P. Goss, *J. Opt. Soc. Am.*, **56**:849 (1966).
4. J. W. Goodman, R. B. Miles, and R. B. Kimball, *J. Opt. Soc. Am.* **58**:609–614 (1968).
5. E. N. Leith and J. Upatnieks, *J. Opt. Sci. Am.* **52**:1123–1130 (1962); **53**:1377 (1963).
6. D. Gabor, *Proc. Roy. Soc. (London)* **A197**:454–487 (1949); *Proc. Phys. Soc.* **B64**:449–469 (1951).
7. H. M. A. El-Sum, Ph.D. Thesis, Stanford University (1952).
8. P. Kirkpatrick and H. M. A. El-Sum, *J. Opt. Soc. Am.*, **46**:825–831 (1956).
9. G. L. Rogers, *Proc. Roy. Soc. (Edinburgh)* **A63**:193–221 (1952).
10. R. W. Meier, *J. Opt. Soc. Am.* **55**:987–992 (1965).
11. E. N. Leith, J. Upatnieks, and K. A. Haines, *J. Opt. Soc. Am.* **55**:981–986 (1965).

12. F. L. Thurstone, paper presented at the 74th Meeting of the Acoustical Society of America, Miami, Florida, 1967.

13. J. D. Young and J. E. Wolfe, *Appl. Phys. Letters* **11** : 294–296 (1967).

14. A. Korpel, paper No. I2 presented at the IEEE Symposium on Sonics and Ultrasonics, Vancouver, Canada, Oct. 1967.

15. R. K. Mueller and N. K. Sheridan, *Appl. Phys. Letters* **9** : 328–329 (1966).

16. K. Preston, Jr. and J. L. Kreuzer, *Appl. Phys. Letters* **10** : 150–152 (1967).

17. R. B. Smith, paper No. I7 presented at the IEEE Symposium on Sonics and Ultrasonics, Vancouver, Canada, Oct. 1967.

18. A. F. Metherell, H. M. A. El-Sum, J. J. Dreher, and L. Larmore, *Phys. Letters* **24A** : 547–548 (1967).

19. A. F. Metherell, H. M. A. El-Sum, J. J. Dreher, and L. Larmore, *Appl. Phys. Letters* **10** : 277–279 (1967).

20. G. E. Massey, *Proc. IEEE* **55** : 1115–1117 (1967).

21. A. F. Metherell and H. M. A. El-Sum, *Appl. Phys. Letters* **11** : 20–22 (1967).

22. A. F. Metherell and H. M. A. El-Sum, paper presented at the 74th Meeting of the Acoustical Society of America, Miami, Fla., 1967a ; *J. Acoust. Soc. Am.* **42** : 1169 (1967).

23. L. Larmore, H. M. A. El-Sum, and A. F. Metherell, *J. Opt. Soc. Am.* **58** : 730 (1968).

24. J. W. Goodman, *Appl. Phys. Letters* **8** : 311–313 (1966).

25. J. E. Jacobs, paper No. I1 presented at the IEEE Symposium on Sonics and Ultrasonics, Vancouver, Canada, Oct. 1967.

26. D. Gabor, French Patent No. 1,479,712 (March 28, 1967).

27. A. Korpel and P. Desmares, *J. Acoust. Soc. Am.* (Sept. 1968).

28. R. Adler, A. Korpel, and P. Desmares, paper No. N3 presented at the IEEE Symposium on Sonics and Ultrasonics, Vancouver, Canada, Oct. 1967.

29. A. Korpel, R. Adler, P. Desmares, and W. Watson, *Appl. Optics* **5** : 1667–1675 (1967).

30. A. Korpel, *Appl. Phys. Letters* **9** : 425–427 (1966).

31. C. Quate, paper No. 1 presented at the IEEE Symposium on Sonics and Ultrasonics, Vancouver, Canada, Oct. 1967.

32. O. K. Mawardi, *Rept. Progr. Phys.* **21** : 156 (1956).

33. A. F. Metherell, H. M. A. El-Sum, J. J. Dreher, and L. Larmore, "Sonoptography," DARL Research Communication No. 25 ; *Phys. Letters* **24A** : 547–548 (1967).

34. P. S. Green, Lockheed interval report No. 6–77–67–42 (Sept. 1967).

Chapter 2

A SURVEY OF ULTRASONIC IMAGE DETECTION METHODS*

Harold Berger

Argonne National Laboratory, Argonne, Illinois

Methods for detecting ultrasonic images are reviewed. The basic ideas behind each technique are discussed, and indications are given of the threshold ultrasonic radiation exposure required to produce useful images. The review includes discussions of four categories of detection methods. These are (1) photographic and chemical, (2) thermal, (3) optical and mechanical, and (4) electronic. Although various reviewers have used different methods for categorization, this one has the advantage of grouping the detection methods approximately according to the lower threshold ultrasonic radiation intensity required to produce images. For the four groups mentioned the threshold ultrasonic intensities required vary from about 1 W/cm² for the photographic and chemical methods to values at least 11 orders of magnitude lower for the electronic techniques. The thermal techniques require ultrasonic intensities on the order of 0.1 W/cm²; the optical and mechanical methods require an average intensity of about 10^{-4} W/cm². Examples of images produced by many of the detection techniques are given.

INTRODUCTION

A great many phenomena have been employed to detect ultrasonic images. The methods vary not only in technique, but also in sensitivity, required exposure time, complexity, and general image quality. There are a number of methods for categorizing these techniques[1-6]. One that offers an advantage in grouping the techniques approximately in terms of threshold sensitivity, or the minimum ultrasonic intensity needed for image detection, involves four basic mechanisms. These are (1) photographic and chemical, (2) thermal, (3) optical and mechanical, and (4) electronic.

This review is limited to the ultrasonic frequency range, i.e., to mechanical vibrations having a frequency of about 20 kHz or higher. For the most part the review emphasizes the frequency range 0.5–30 MHz, where transmission by means of a liquid or solid material is normally required. Frequencies closer to the lower limit of the ultrasonic range can be transmitted

*Work performed under the auspices of the U.S. Atomic Energy Commission.

Table I
Ultrasonic Image Detection Methods

	Approximate threshold sensitivity (W/cm^2)	Reference for sensitivity value
Photographic and chemical methods		
Direct action on film	1–5	(^{90})
Photographic paper in developer	1.0	(^{11})
	0.1*	(^{12})
Starch plate in iodine solution	1	(^{13})
Film in iodine solution	1	(^{14})
Color change effects	0.5–1†	(^{15})
Thermal techniques		
Phosphor persistence changes	0.05–0.1	(^{16})
Extinction of luminescence	1	(^{6})
Stimulation of luminescence	—	—
Thermosensitive color changes	1	(^{3})
Change in photoemission	0.1	(^{17})
Change in electrical conductivity	0.1	(^{18})
Thermocouple and thermistor detectors	0.1	(^{19,20})
Optical and mechanical methods		
Optical detection of density variations	10^{-3}	(^{21})
	3×10^{-4}	(^{5})
Liquid surface deformation	10^{-3}	(^{3,22})
	10^{-5}	(^{5})
Solid surface deformation	10^{-6}	(**)
Mechanical alignment of flakes in liquid	2.8×10^{-7}	(^{10})
Acoustic birefringence	10^{-1}	(^{3,23})
Electronic methods		
Piezoelectric detector—mechanical movement of transducer or object, or use of an array of transducers to form an image	10^{-11} 5×10^{-12}	(‡) (^{24})
Probe detection of potential on back of piezoelectric receiver	($^{\#}$)	—
Electron scan of piezoelectric receiver	2×10^{-11}	(^{5})
Electron scan of piezoresistive receiver	10^{-7} §	(^{6})
Piezoelectric—electroluminescent phosphor detector	10^{-6}	(^{29})

*This value is given for a "satisfactory picture quality." It is indicated in (^{12}) that the lower threshold intensity can be as low as 0.05 W/cm^2.

†Under special conditions (^{15}) indicates that this method can respond to intensities as low as 0.07 W/cm^2.

**This technique was brought up during the discussion at the 74th Meeting of the Acoustical Society of America, Miami Beach, Fla., Nov. 13–17, 1967, by A. Korpel, Zenith Radio Corp., Chicago, Ill.

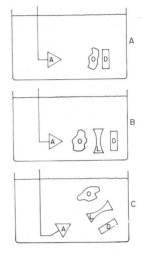

Fig. 1. Several arrangements for preparing ultrasound images by immersion techniques are shown in these three side views of water tanks. In each view A is the ultrasound generator (in the arrow head direction), O is the object being viewed, and D is the detector. In views (B) and (C) L is an ultrasound lens. View (A) represents a direct-shadow, through-transmission technique. View (B) shows through-transmission with a lens. View (C) represents a reflection arrangement.

through air or other gaseous media; in that case microphone-type detectors can be used ([7]). The author is not aware of ultrasonic imaging investigations at frequencies greater than 30 MHz, although some such studies have been proposed ([8,9]).

The geometries used to prepare ultrasonic images vary with the application. Some typical arrangements are shown for immersion methods in Fig. 1. These arrangements are typical for most of the detectors to be discussed. In some cases the detector might be situated in the tank wall rather than inside the tank, so that it would be accessible as needed. In the Pohlman cell ([10]), for example, this would be a convenient means for directing light at the cell in order to complete the detection process.

The arrangements shown in Fig. 1 generally do not apply to the optical and mechanical methods, the group which includes the Pohlman cell. Geometrical arrangements for those methods will be discussed in a later section of this report.

The threshold sensitivities required for the various detection methods vary from about $1 \, W/cm^2$ for the photographic and chemical methods, $0.1 \, W/cm^2$ for the thermal methods, an average of about $10^{-4} \, W/cm^2$ for the optical and mechanical methods, to values at least as low as $10^{-11} \, W/cm^2$ for the electronic techniques. A list of methods and threshold sensitivities is given in Table I.

---

‡The estimate of $10^{-11} \, W/cm$ for the threshold sensitivity of an array of piezoelectric detectors, each followed by an amplifier, was made by Jacobs, abstract A5, 74th Meeting of the Acoustical Society of America, Miami Beach, Florida, Nov. 13–17, 1967. See also ([82]).

#A capacitance probe should provide a sensitivity improvement of 6 dB over that of an electron scan of a piezoelectric receiver at the same scanning speed. See ([25]).

§A piezoresistive camera tube with a CdS target has been demonstrated in work at Northwestern University under the direction of J. E. Jacobs. See ([26–28]).

PHOTOGRAPHIC AND CHEMICAL METHODS

Ultrasound can be detected by means of the direct action of ultrasound energy on a photographic emulsion and because ultrasound accelerates or causes some chemical reactions. The fact that ultrasonic radiation influences a photographic emulsion was reported in 1933 by Marinesco and Truillet ([30]). Subsequent studies by other investigators still have not clearly revealed the exact mechanism involved ([31,32]). The analysis by Bennett ([32]), in which he showed that luminescence and pressure effects did not appear to explain all the existing facts, remains a good discussion of this situation. Although Bennett indicated rather conclusively that the softness of the photographic emulsion was a very important factor in its response to ultrasound, he stated in his conclusion that "there is not sufficient evidence to delineate clearly the mechanism, whether thermal, mechanical or otherwise". Bennett's work did indicate that the photographic speed of the film emulsion had little effect on the result (his tests included film speeds for tungsten from less than 10 to 160).

The softness of the emulsion has been shown to be a significant factor for the film detection of ultrasound. Film exposed in the dark to ultrasound and developed in the normal manner will yield a useful image with an exposure time of about 4 hr for an ultrasonic intensity of 1 W/cm². If the temperature of the film is raised from 20° to 28°C, a significant exposure improvement factor can be obtained ([32]). If the emulsion is soaked in water at room temperature prior to exposure, a factor of about four times less exposure can be used ([14]). Both these improvements were reported to be based on the fact that the emulsion was softened.

These photographic film methods of course require darkroom techniques. There are other photographic methods which do not. One involves the ultrasound exposure of film in an iodine solution ([14]). The effect of the ultrasound exposure on the emulsion is to render the emulsion resistant to fixing to an extent proportional to the exposure. The image becomes visible during the exposure because the emulsion turns a darker yellow color.

The image can be made visible more easily after completion of the exposure by fixing the film for a short time (for example, 1 min in Kodak liquid X-ray fixer and replenisher) in order to clear the unirradiated emulsion. The remaining emulsion then displays the sound pattern by a yellow color against the clear background. Those areas of greatest exposure remain essentially yellow, while in areas of intermediate exposure the emulsion is partially cleared. There is therefore some grey scale in the image. This detection method can be used in the light since the exposed film is not developed and light appears to have little influence on the fixing of the emulsion. A typical field pattern picture taken by this method is shown in Fig. 2.

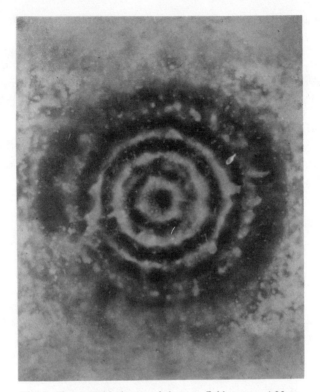

Fig. 2. Photographic image of the near-field pattern 1.25 cm
from a 6.3-cm diameter barium titanate transducer. The frequency was 420 kHz. The exposure was taken using Royal
Ortho sheet film (emulsion toward the transducer) in an iodine–
water solution (7.75 ml stock iodine solution per gal of water).
The exposure was 1 hr. The dark areas on this print represent
areas in which the emulsion remained after fixing, and therefore represent areas of ultrasonic exposure.

The speed of this method appears to be independent of photographic
film speed at least over the measured tungsten speed range from 6 to 150.
Optimum iodine concentrations appear to be in the order of 1 to 10 ml/gal.*
Ultrasonic exposure times in these iodine concentrations are from 30 min
to 1 hr.

A second photographic method which can be performed in the light
involves the ultrasound exposure of photographic film or paper in a developer
solution ([11,12]). The uniformly light-exposed emulsion develops more

*The iodine solution was made by adding known amounts of stock solution to the water in the
exposure tank. The stock solution contained 30 g of iodine in 1 l of methyl alcohol. Typical
concentrations varied from 0.5 to 50 ml of stock iodine solution per gallon of water.

quickly in areas where the ultrasonic intensity, and therefore agitation of the developer, is highest.

A thorough study of this technique with photographic paper has been made and reported by Arkhangel'skii and Afanas'ev ([12]). They found that one could obtain a maximum paper density contrast in the exposed areas for a developer concentration of 0.2, an exposure time of 90–110 sec, and an ultrasonic intensity of 0.15–0.25 W/cm^2 for photographic paper No. 6. The threshold sensitivity was reported to be 0.05 W/cm^2 for a high developer concentration and an exposure time of 40 sec. Exposure times could not be too long or the paper would develop completely. An example of an ultrasonic image produced by this method is shown in Fig. 3.

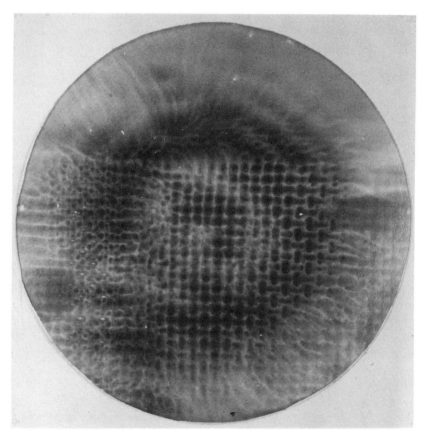

Fig. 3. An ultrasonic image of a 16-mesh wire screen taken by photographic paper in a developer solution. The near-field pattern from the barium titanate transducer is also shown. Exposure time was 30 sec.

A practical aspect of the developer and photographic paper study by Arkhangel'skii and Afanas'ev is that they devised a thin detector cell containing developer solution and paper. The cell had ultrasound transmitting windows of thin (0.15 mm) rubber and allowed a space of 2 mm inside the cell for the paper and developer solution. In this manner the need for a large tank containing developer solution as the exposure tank was eliminated.

The same authors also studied the resolution characteristics of the photographic paper method. The resolution is determined by the transverse diffusion of the developing solution in the photolayer and by the presence of nonuniform streaming. This latter effect leads to distorted images because fresh developer is directed along the ultrasonic field by the acoustic wind. The rubber-covered detector cell tended to eliminate some of this problem. Assuming that the streaming problem could be eliminated, the authors indicated that the resolution of the detector could be in the range of 0.01 mm. Some of the resolution potential of this technique is demonstrated in Fig. 4.

One chemical detection method that has been studied by a number of investigators involves potassium iodide–starch solutions ([13,15,33–35]). Under ultrasonic irradiation air-filled water undergoes an oxidizing reaction to form H_2O_2, which tends to discolor organic dyes. For example, the potassium iodide–starch solution tends to turn blue. Rust et al. ([33]) used this phenomenon to detect ultrasound images by making an array of boxes containing this solution. Each liquid-filled box tended to darken depending upon the ultrasonic intensity. Darkening also depended upon the iodine concentration and the exposure time.

The individual liquid-filled boxes had to be at least one wavelength in depth for optimum results. The threshold ultrasonic intensity was reported to be 0.5–1.0 W/cm². At that intensity exposure times were only about 2 min. The threshold intensity could be lowered to a value as low as 0.07 W/cm² if small amounts of aliphatic chlorides such as CCl_4 or chloroform were added to the solution ([15]).

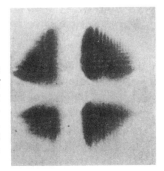

Fig. 4. A photograph of a sound-absorbing cross taken by ultrasound at a frequency of 3 MHz, an intensity of 0.3 W/cm², and with a photographic paper in developer technique is shown. The cross was 3 mm from the photographic paper and 4 cm from the ultrasonic transmitter. Note the diffraction patterns within the dark transmission areas on the photograph. From Arkhangel'skii and Afanas'ev ([12]).

A similar method suggested by Bennett [13] called for the exposure of films of starch on glass plates in an iodine solution. Here too a blue color was produced in areas of higher ultrasound intensity. Exposure times of about 2 min at 1 W/cm^2 were common.

A number of other chemical techniques involving more complicated organic dyes have also been investigated [3,36].

THERMAL TECHNIQUES

The mechanical vibrations produced by ultrasound yield some heating effects. A variety of image detection methods which make use of this effect have been described in the literature. One can simply scan a thermocouple or thermistor probe across the image area to produce an image signal [19,20]. An array of thermocouple detectors could also be used [8], as shown in Fig. 5. Thermocouple junctions as small as 5 μ have been reported to be possible [8]. Image techniques such as this have been reported. The thermistor work indicated that ultrasound intensities as low as 0.1 W/cm^2 could be detected [20]. Similar values, on an average basis, are obtained for the thermocouple work. The use of a thermopile, of course, improves sensitivity, probably at the expense of spatial resolution. Richards [37] reports the detection of ultrasonic intensities as low as 0.01 W/cm^2 with a thermopile detector. In terms of temperature sensitivity, Fry and Dunn [8] report that the detection of temperature rises due to ultrasound as small as 10^{-4}°C should be possible.

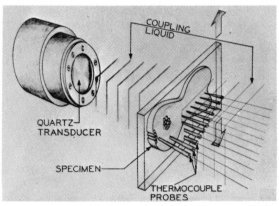

Fig. 5. A thermocouple array system for detecting ultrasonic images as proposed by Fry and Dunn [8]. The spacing could be much closer than shown in order to take advantage of the potential spatial resolution represented by thermocouple junctions as small as 5 μ. From Fry and Dunn [8].

Semiconductor materials have shown some response to the heating effects of ultrasound ([38,39]). Sulfides of zinc and cadmium have been shown to change conductivity with ultrasonic exposure, an effect attributed to heating. Ultrasonic intensities as low as 0.1 W/cm^2 were detectable.

A similar threshold limitation was theorized in a report by von Ardenne ([40]). A camera tube which would derive signals from changes in tube target photoemission caused by heating as a result of ultrasound exposure was proposed. The sensitivity calculation involved an ultrasonic frequency of 5 MHz.

Another thermal detection method for ultrasound involves compounds which change color as a function of temperature ([3,36,41]). Several iodine, chloride, and organic thermal color change materials have been studied ([41]). Mercury silver iodide appears to be one of the best of these compounds. This reversibly chromotropic compound has been studied for ultrasound image detection by several investigators. When prepared in a thin screen Ernst and Hoffman ([36]) report that the yellow material instantly changes to a bright red color when placed at the focus of an ultrasonic transducer.* The material was most sensitive at about 50°C, and Ernst and Hoffman found it desirable to expose the material in a water bath at about that temperature. Good results were also obtained in transformer oil even at room temperature. Best results with reported work on thermal color changes involve an exposure time of the order of 1 sec at an ultrasonic intensity of 1 W/cm^2 ([1,3]).

One could speculate that superior results could now be obtained by taking advantage of the recent development of temperature-sensitive liquid crystal materials. These materials, described by Fergason ([42]) and by Wood-mansee ([43]), can be developed to operate within various temperature ranges; they display a color change over the entire visible spectrum (red to blue) for temperature variations of only 1 to 2°C. Woodmansee and Southworth have indicated that this color change could be accomplished with a tempera-ture variation as small as 0.1°C.†

A number of luminescent techniques have been described as ultrasound image detectors. The methods include those in which ultrasound-induced heating stimulates luminescence ([36,45,46]) or extinguishes luminescence stimulated by another radiation such as ultraviolet ([36,47,48]). It is interesting that ZnS stimulated by ultraviolet can be made to show a decrease in luminescence with ultrasound excitation for silver-activated material or an increase in luminescence under similar conditions if ZnS(Cu) is used ([45]).

*Methods for preparing screens are given in ([36]).
†The very small temperature range possible was brought up during the discussion of ([44]) at the Fifth International Conference on Nondestructive Testing, Montreal, Canada, May 1967. The discussion will be published in the Proceedings of this conference.

Heat-induced phosphor persistence changes have also been investigated for ultrasound image detection in rather extensive studies by Peterman ([49]) and Peterman and Oncley ([50]). The phosphor Ca–SrS was stimulated by ultraviolet and was then exposed to ultrasound. Ultrasonic exposure increased persistence, so these areas were brighter and could be photographed. Ultrasound exposure times as short as 1 min at an intensity of 0.1 W/cm² yielded good results. The reported threshold sensitivity was 0.05 W/cm². A spatial resolution of 0.2 mm was achieved.

OPTICAL AND MECHANICAL METHODS

Two of the methods described in this section differ from the remaining techniques in that these normally provide visual images obtained by passing light through a sample in a direction perpendicular to the ultrasonic beam direction. Therefore one obtains side-view photographs of the ultrasound beam as opposed to the ultrasound area photographs obtained by the methods shown in Fig. 1.

A diagram of one such method, a schlieren system ([51]), is shown in Fig. 6. Parallel light passing through the water tank is diffracted by the ultrasound beam as a result of the periodic changes in the water index of refraction. An example of a schlieren ultrasound photograph is shown in Fig. 7. A striking side view of an ultrasound beam is displayed. Schlieren methods have been widely used to display ultrasound and other vibrational phenomena in transparent media ([51–55]). For ultrasound, systems which display beam patterns of continuous-wave ([51]) and pulsed systems ([56]) have been described, as have color schlieren techniques ([55]). Threshold ultrasound

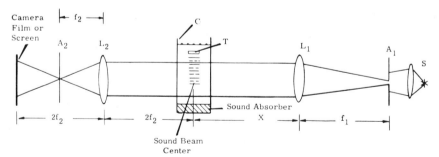

Fig. 6. Diagram of a schlieren optical system for visualizing ultrasound. Parallel light passing through the water tank is diffracted because of the periodic change in the index of refraction of the water; this is caused by the ultrasonic vibrations. The central, undiffracted light beam can be stopped by an opaque stop located at A_2; A_2 can also be an aperture moved off-axis to intercept diffracted light. The image is viewed on a frosted glass screen or detected on film. From Fitch ([51]).

Fig. 7. A schlieren photograph of a continuous-wave ultrasound beam from a 5-MHz, 1.87-cm diameter, zirconate titanate transducer (beam enters from the right). The RF power was 20 W. The ultrasound beam is shown striking a thin sheet of aluminum. Reflected and transmitted ultrasound beams can be readily observed. Evidence of conversion of the longitudinal beam to shear waves in the aluminum and subsequent reirradiation as longitudinal waves into the water can also be observed. Photograph is through the courtesy of B. Cross and G. J. Posakony, Automation Industries, Inc., Boulder, Colorado.

intensities as low as 3×10^{-4} W/cm^2 have been claimed to provide useful results for schlieren ultrasound imaging ([5]).

A similar type of ultrasonic photographic technique depends on the fact that some transparent media become temporarily birefringent when stressed. Polarized light passing through the medium will be partially depolarized in regions of high ultrasonic intensity. Photographs taken by this method in a medium of fused quartz show good contrast and clearly

picture details such as the Fresnel region of a 10-MHz x-cut quartz transducer and beam sidelobes. This work by McNamara and Rogers ([23]),
indicates that useful results can be obtained at ultrasonic intensities ([3]) as
low as 0.1 W/cm^2; this value is not necessarily a lower limit.

A relatively sensitive technique for detecting ultrasound depends on the
fact that a material surface will deform due to the pressure of an acoustic
beam. Most work with this technique has involved liquid surface deformation
and the viewing of this deformation by reflected light from the surface. Some
early work ([57]) was done by transmitting the viewing light through the
liquid and deformed surface, but this seems to be less sensitive than the
reflection method ([3]). Many of the characteristics of this technique have been
studied by Pigulevskii ([22]), who found that the sensitivity of the technique is
inversely proportional to the coefficient of surface tension and to the density
of the liquid. At high ultrasonic frequencies (above 10 MHz) the surface
tension forces are predominant, while at low frequencies (0.5 MHz) the
capillary forces give way to gravitational forces. Between these two extremes
both effects play a role. The threshold sensitivity ([22]) for a water medium was
reported to be 1.5×10^{-3} W/cm^2; threshold sensitivity values as low as
10^{-5} W/cm^2 have been mentioned ([5]).

Most work with liquid surface deformation has been done with large
water tanks which contained the ultrasound transducer, the inspection
object, and the necessary mirrors and/or lenses. A modification reported by
Gericke and Grubinskas ([58]) is of interest, since it uses only a liquid-filled
detector cell. The ultrasound beam is introduced into a shallow, liquid-filled
dish by direct coupling of the ultrasonic transducer or a flat inspection object.
The detector cell arrangement is shown in Fig. 8. The ultrasound window at
the bottom of the cell is thin plastic. The liquid used in most of the described
work is oil (SAE-20). Experimentally it was found that a liquid depth of
about 5 mm gave best results. The complete imaging system is shown in the

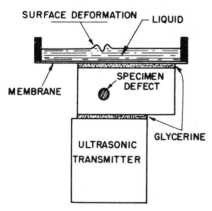

Fig. 8. Detector cell arrangement for liquid
surface levitation method for preparation of
ultrasonic images of flat inspection samples.
After Gericke and Grubinskas ([58]). Photo
courtesy Army Materials and Mechanics
Research Center.

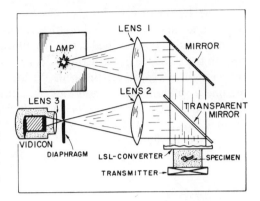

Fig. 9. Diagram of the liquid surface levitation detection arrangement for real-time television presentation of ultrasonic images. After Gericke and Grubinskas ([58]). Photo courtesy Army Materials and Mechanics Research Center.

diagram in Fig. 9. Reflected light from the deformed liquid surface is imaged by television techniques. The real-time system was shown to be capable of imaging continuous-wave, frequency-modulated, and pulsed ultrasound. An example of a near-field pattern as photographed from the television presentation is shown in Fig. 10.

Recent work indicates that one need not use a liquid in order to observe surface deformation due to ultrasound energy. Korpel ([59]) has discussed the detection of deformation of a metal surface by reflecting laser light from the surface.* Indications are that at an ultrasound frequency of 2 MHz the threshold sensitivity of the technique would approach 10^{-6} W/cm^2.

Another novel variation of the surface deformation method of detecting ultrasound images has recently been reported by Young and Wolfe ([60]). A deformable film on a solid substrate placed on the liquid surface can detect the deformation either on a dynamic basis for a warmed detector or as an integrating detector. In the latter case it was reported that useful ultrasonic images could be obtained for ultrasonic intensities in the range 0.1–1.0 W/cm^2 with exposure times of one to several seconds. The ultrasonic frequency range studied was 5–30 MHz.

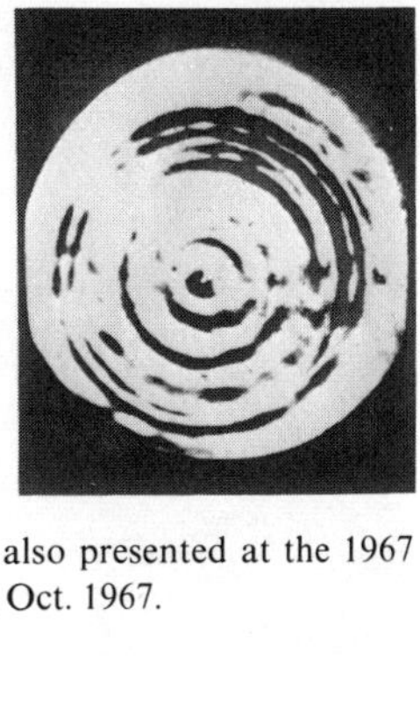

Fig. 10. A surface-relief ultrasound photograph of the near-field pattern of a 7.5-cm diameter, 1-MHz ceramic transducer operated continuous wave obtained by the method shown in Fig. 9. After Gericke and Grubinskas ([58]). Photo courtesy Army Materials and Mechanics Research Center.

*See Table I, footnote (**). Some discussion of this technique was also presented at the 1967 IEEE Symposium on Sonics and Ultrasonics, Vancouver, Canada, Oct. 1967.

The Pohlman cell ([10]) also has been used as a method for detecting ultrasound images. This method, described by Pohlman ([61]) in 1939, makes use of a liquid (xylene) filled cell in which small aluminum flakes are suspended. In the presence of ultrasound the flakes tend to become aligned so they reflect light incident on the cell. With no ultrasound present the flakes assume a random orientation and present a grey background by reflected light. Improved contrast results if a small bias voltage, typically 25–30 V AC, is put across the cell ([62]). The voltage tends to align the flakes so that no light is reflected in the absence of ultrasound. Examples of some Pohlman cell images are shown in Fig. 11.

Fig. 11. Pohlman cell ultrasound images. The top view is the reflected light from the randomly oriented aluminum flakes. The second view shows the improved background which results from the application of an AC voltage. The third view shows an ultrasound beam. The fourth and fifth views show 5-MHz ultrasound images of an ultrasound absorbing cross with and without acoustic enlargement, respectively. Photos courtesy of H. E. Van Valkenburg, Sperry Products Div., Automation Industries, Inc.

The threshold sensitivity of the Pohlman cell has been reported ([10]) to be 2.8×10^{-7} W/cm^2. At such low ultrasound intensities one would anticipate a reaction time of the order of minutes for this detector. At intensities of the order 10^{-1}–10^{-3} W/cm^2 the reported reaction time is 1 sec or less ([62]). One major problem with the Pohlman cell is the limited dynamic range, 20 dB ([63]).

ELECTRONIC METHODS

The electronic method of detecting ultrasound images can provide the best sensitivity of all the categories discussed, and for this reason it is the detection method used most. Piezoelectric or electrostrictive transducers have been widely used to detect ultrasound images either on the transducer itself, by mechanically scanning the transducer(s) or object, or by making use of an array of transducers. A great number of materials, including quartz, lithium sulfate, and ceramic materials such as barium titanate, lead zirconate–titanate, and lead metaniobate, have been shown to be useful as ultrasound generators or receivers. Each material has some characteristics— for example, receiving or transmitting constant or Curie temperature—which may make a given transducer material most useful in a special application. The reader is referred to Goldman ([64]) for further discussion of these transducer materials and properties. However, since this discussion is concerned with detection, it should be noted that lithium sulfate has a very high receiving constant. Therefore this material is particularly useful as an ultrasound detector.

The mechanical movement of a transducer or object provides an imaging method which has been applied a great deal in medical ([65,66]) and industrial ([67,68]) nondestructive testing applications. Scanning methods ([69]) such as B and C scan, and complicated motions over curved surfaces have been used to generate images. The image can be presented by recording in sympathy with the mechanical movement of the transducer. Image readout can be on an oscilloscope, film or paper recording. An example ([70]) of the latter type of record for a through-transmission ultrasonic image of a human hand and forearm is shown in Fig. 12.

Fig. 12. An ultrasound, through-transmission image of a human adult hand and forearm. The two transducers scanned a saw-tooth pattern across the object. The recording shows areas of high ultrasound transmission in the dark lines, and low transmission (the bone images) in the white areas. The ultrasound frequency was 1 MHz. From Beck ([70]).

It is difficult to comment on the threshold sensitivity or resolution of such systems because of the many variations which are possible. Most reported systems are pulse-echo types, in the frequency range from 1 to 10 MHz, and make use of quartz or ceramic transducers. Resolution capabilities of the order of one to a few mm and threshold sensitivities of 10^{-11} W/cm^2 or less seem readily achievable with such techniques. In the case of the array systems threshold sensitivities of that order, and as low as 5×10^{-12} W/cm^2, have been reported ([24]).

Since a piezoelectric transducer actually acts as a mosaic ([71]), in that the voltage signal at any location on the piezoelectric detector is proportional to the incident ultrasonic intensity at that point, images can be prepared without moving the object or detector by suitably recording the voltage variations on a number of locations on a piezoelectric detector of reasonable size. This has been done by mechanically moving a small probe ([72,73]) across the back of a piezoelectric material. A faster approach is to scan the piezoelectric target with an electron beam and generate a television-type signal.

Television methods for detecting ultrasound images have been described by several investigators ([4,5,9,21,26,74–77]). Television camera tube systems have been shown to provide a linear response ([21]) over a wide range of ultrasonic intensities (3×10^{-9} to 3×10^{-3} W/cm^2), and a threshold sensitivity ([5]) as low as 2×10^{-11} W/cm^2 has been discussed.

Ultrasound television camera tubes have included continuously evacuated and sealed tubes, with ultrasound targets of barium titanate or quartz. Only quartz has been used in the sealed tubes. Figure 13 shows a photograph of such a tube. Tubes of this type built into the sidewall of an immersion tank provide television images of incident ultrasound images by all three approaches illustrated in Fig. 1, direct shadow, through-transmission with lenses, and reflection methods ([78]). Continuous-wave and pulsed systems ([76]) have been described.

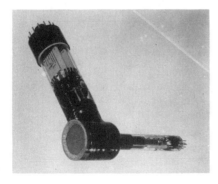

Fig. 13. The photograph shows a sealed ultrasound camera tube for 2-MHz ultrasonic frequency operation. The 5-cm diameter quartz faceplate and target (left) is scanned by high-velocity electrons from the electron gun on the right. Secondary electrons modulated by the piezoelectric voltages generated by the ultrasound irradiated quartz are collected and amplified in the electron multiplier structure (large upper arm of the tube).

Image areas which have been described with these tubes are dependent upon the ultrasonic frequency of operation. Since the piezoelectric target serves as the tube faceplate in most tubes, one must compromise between resonant frequency and physical size. Some typical sizes ([79]) include 1 MHz, 10 cm diameter; 2 MHz, 5 cm diameter; and 5 MHz, 2.5 cm diameter. If the target is physically supported, as by a metal grid ([9]), somewhat larger sizes can be used. Some work has also been reported on the use of the piezoelectric target cemented inside a vacuum window ([75,80]). In that case large physical sizes can be used for high-frequency ultrasound operation.

This latter approach does degrade the resolution characteristics of the system. The resolution properties of the television method in general are such that one can resolve a distance about equal to the thickness of the resonant detecting target for the normally used quartz and barium titanate transducer materials. Jacobs ([81]) has shown that the minimum image diameter, R, which can be resolved is:

$$R \quad (\text{in mm}) = 2.86/\text{Frequency} \quad (\text{in MHz})$$

Ultrasound incident on the tube at angles other than perpendicular will be imaged with poorer resolution. If the angle of incidence is greater than about 5°, then most of the ultrasonic energy will be converted to shear waves and images will not be observed.

An example of a continuous-wave ultrasound television image is shown in Fig. 14. This image was obtained with a 30 frame/sec, 525-line television system ([79]).

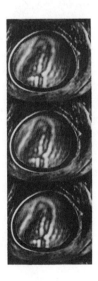

Fig. 14. Three frames of a kinescope motion picture record of the ultrasonic image of a finger tip (adult, index finger). The ultrasonic camera tube, containing a 5-cm-diameter barium titanate target, is overscanned; only the central round area of each frame represents ultrasound image area. The side view of the finger was obtained by a direct-shadow, through-transmission method; the ultrasonic frequency was 1.9 MHz. Note the transmission through the tissue (right side of finger) and attenuation (dark areas) in the bone area. Note also the fringes around the finger image; these represent interference between the direct ultrasound beam and ultrasound reflected from the finger.

The piezoelectric camera tube provides useful ultrasound images on a real-time basis. One difficulty with this method concerns the lack of extended grey scale in the image. It is difficult to present more than five to ten distinct shades of grey. The recent development of a color television system ([82,83]) to display continuous-wave ultrasound images may ease this problem and lead to greater reliability in the interpretation of ultrasound images. In this new system differences in ultrasonic intensity continue to be displayed as differences in brightness. Differences in phase of the ultrasound incident on the camera tube are displayed as color differences. Acoustic impedance variations as small as one part in 10^8 are reported to be detectable by taking advantage of the color sensitivity of the human eye.

Another approach to ultrasound television involves the electron scan of a piezoresistive target ([26-28]). A high electrical resistivity target which would change conductivity with incident ultrasound would offer a number of advantages. This vidicon-like camera tube would respond to a wide range of ultrasonic frequencies as opposed to the resonant frequency and odd harmonic response of the piezoelectric target tubes, and, most important, it would offer the advantage of information storage. The present piezoelectric target tubes present to the electron return beam a signal proportional to the ultrasonic intensity incident at the moment of scan. A storage system, on the other hand, would present all the accumulated signals since the last scan. This can lead to significant improvements in sensitivity. A tube of this type has been described and demonstrated. The initial tube, employing a CdS(Cu) target ([27]), responded to ultrasonic intensities ([6]) of the order of 10^{-7} W/cm^2.

Another interesting possibility for electronic ultrasound image detection involves a combined piezoelectric and electroluminescent detector. A diagram of such a detector is shown in Fig. 15. Proper choice of electroluminescent material and thickness, along with perhaps some additional stimulation for luminescence such as a bias voltage or ultraviolet illumination, would yield a phosphor which could be stimulated by the piezoelectric voltages generated in a reasonable ultrasonic intensity. Methods of preparing thin phosphor

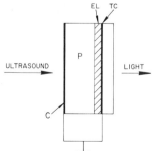

Fig. 15. Diagram of a piezoelectric electroluminescent ultrasound image detector. The voltage generated across a thin electroluminescent phosphor layer (EL) by the action of ultrasound on a piezoelectric material (P) would stimulate light emission which could be observed through the transparent electrode (TC) and a glass support plate. The TC electrode on the phosphor is connected to the C electrode on the piezoelectric material; voltages generated on the piezoelectric material appear at the interface with the electroluminescent layer.

layers by vacuum evaporation ([84]) and by vapor deposition ([85]) are well developed. Electroluminescent layers as thin as 1 μ have been described ([86]).

It is reported that an active program to develop such a detector for ultrasound images ([29]) is in progress at Imperial College in London. Initial thoughts are that electroluminescent phosphors which will be stimulated by voltages of the order of millivolts seem possible. If this is true, then threshold sensitivities in the order of 10^{-6}–10^{-7} W/cm^2 seem feasible.

CONCLUSIONS

An obvious conclusion is that a potential user of ultrasonic image detection methods has a choice of a great number of methods. The categorization method chosen in this review may be of some assistance in this regard because of the relationship of the threshold sensitivity with each category.

For the particular problem of image detection in acoustical holography, it is recognized that only a few of these detection methods have been applied ([7,60,87,88]). The review may provide a useful service by drawing attention to other potentially useful detection techniques. It also serves to draw attention to previous reviews of ultrasonic image detection methods in which the varied emphasis may be useful for suggesting other image detection methods.

For the acoustical holography detection problem one is drawn to those techniques which provide film or film-like images, since these can readily be applied to the holography reconstruction process. Many of the photographic and phosphor methods do provide simplicity and attractive resolution capability. The one major disadvantage of most of these methods is the relatively poor threshold sensitivity. The electroluminescent phosphor approach, when fully developed, promises to ease that difficulty and yet retain the other advantages of the film and phosphor technique. The liquid-crystal thermal detection technique also shows promise.

The television detection method offers a number of advantages, such as low threshold sensitivity, good resolution, and real-time presentation. The recently described real-time holography presentation technique ([89]) lends itself to the Sokolov-type tube, to laser scanning of a water surface, and to any technique which can yield an electronic scanning signal. The real-time holography approach will undoubtedly be useful in many application areas.

REFERENCES

1. G. Spengler, *Nachrichtentechnik* 3:399–402, (1953).
2. L. Bergmann, *Der Ultraschall*, 6th ed., S. Hinzel, Stuttgart, 1954.
3. L. D. Rozenberg, *Soviet Phys.—Acoustics* 1:105–116 (1955).

4. W. R. Turner, An Evaluation of Image Techniques in the Ultrasonic Inspection of Material, Naval Ordnance Laboratory, Silver Spring, Md., Report NAVORD-4090 (July 2, 1956).

5. C. N. Smyth, F. Y. Poynton, and J. F. Sayers, *Proc. IEE* **110**:16–28 (1963).

6. H. Berger and R. E. Dickens, A Review of Ultrasonic Imaging Methods, With A Selected Annotated Bibliography, Argonne National Laboratory, Argonne, Ill., Report ANL-6680 (1963).

7. A. F. Metherell, H. M. A. El-Sum, J. J. Dreher, and L. Larmore, *Appl. Phys. Letters* **10**(10): 277–279 (May 15, 1967).

8. W. J. Fry and F. Dunn, Ultrasonic Absorption Microscopy and Spectroscopy, in: Proc. Symposium on Physics and Nondestructive Testing, Southwest Research Institute, San Antonio, Texas, 1962, pp. 33–57.

9. J. E. Jacobs, *Science Journal* pp. 60–65 (April 1965).

10. R. Pohlman, *Z. Angew. Physik* **1**:181–187 (1948).

11. Y. Torkikai and K. Negishi, *J. Phys. Soc. Japan* **10**:1110–1113 (1955).

12. M. E. Arkhangel'skii and V. Ia. Afanas'ev, *Soviet Phys.—Acoustics* **3**:230–235 (1957).

13. G. S. Bennett, *J. Acoust. Soc. Am.* **24**:470–474 (1952).

14. H. Berger and I. R. Kraska, *J. Acoust. Soc. Am.* **34**:518–519 (1962).

15. R. Haul, H. J. Studt, and H. H. Rust, *Angew. Chemie* **62**:186–188 (1950).

16. L. A. Peterman and P. B. Oncley, *IRE Trans. on Ultrasonic Eng.* **4**:42–52 (Aug. 1956).

17. M. von Ardenne, *Nachrichtentechnik* **5**:49–51 (1955).

18. L. Herforth and J. Krumbiegel, *Naturwissenschaften* **42**:39 (1955).

19. F. Dunn and W. J. Fry, *J. Acoust. Soc. Am.* **31**:632–633 (1959).

20. E. K. Labartkava, *Soviet Phys.—Acoustics* **6**:468–471 (1960).

21. P. K. Oshchepkov, L. D. Rozenberg, and Iu. B. Semmenikov, *Soviet Phys.—Acoustics* **1**:362–365 (1955).

22. E. D. Pigulevskii, *Soviet Phys.—Acoustics* **4**:359–365 (1958).

23. F. L. McNamara and T. F. Rogers, *J. Acoust. Soc. Am.* **25**:338 (1953).

24. P. S. Green, Final Report on Underwater Acoustic Imaging, Underwater Electronics Group, Lockheed Research Laboratory, Palo Alto, Calif. (June 29, 1967); available as Report AD-656-091.

25. C. N. Smyth, *Ultrasonics* **4**:15–20 (1966).

26. J. E. Jacobs, D. W. Cugell, and N. U. Phan, Application of T.V. Scanning Techniques to the Problem of Visualizing Ultrasound Images, in Proc. of the International Conference on Medical Electronics (P. L. Frommer, ed.), New York, 1961, p. 21.

27. N. U. Phan, The Application of Television Scanning Techniques to the Problem of Visualizing Ultrasound Images, unpublished M.S. Thesis, Northwestern University, Evanston, Ill. (1961).

28. J. E. Jacobs, U.S. Patent 3,236,944 (Feb. 22, 1966).

29. E. Neppiras, Bournemouth, England, private communication (Nov. 1967).

30. N. Marinesco and J. J. Truillet, *Compt. Rend.* **196**:858–860 (1933).

31. P. J. Ernst, *J. Acoust. Soc. Am.* **23**:80–83 (1951).

32. G. S. Bennett, *J. Acoust. Soc. Am.* **25**:1149–1151 (1953).

33. H. H. Rust, R. Haul, and H. J. Studt, *Naturwissenschaften* **36**:374–375 (1949).

34. H. H. Rust, *Angew. Chemie* **64**:308–311 (1952).

35. P. Renaud, *J. Chim. Phys.* **52**:339 (1955).

36. P. J. Ernst and C. W. Hoffman, *J. Acoust. Soc. Am.* **24**:207–211 (1952).

37. W. T. Richards, *Science* **76**:36–37 (1932).

38. L. Herforth and J. Krumbiegel, *Naturwissenschaften* **42**:39 (1955).

39. V. A. Zhuralev and M. I. Kozak, *Soviet Phys.—JETP* **36**:236 (1959).

40. M. von Ardenne, *Nachrichtentechnik* **5**:49–51 (1955).

41. H. Tielsch and A. Boczek, *Z. Angew. Physik* **7**:213–218 (1955).
42. J. L. Fergason, *Sci. Am.* **211**:76 (August 1964).
43. W. E. Woodmansee, *Materials Evaluation* **24**:564–572 (1966).
44. W. E. Woodmansee and H. L. Southworth, Thermal Nondestructive Testing With Cholesteric Liquid Crystals, in: Fifth International Conference on Nondestructive Testing, Montreal, Canada, May 1967, to be published.
45. M. Leistner and L. Herforth, *Naturwissenschaften* **44**:59 (1957).
46. P. Jarman, *J. Acoust. Soc. Am.* **32**:1459–1462 (1960).
47. H. Schreiber and W. Degner, *Naturwissenschaften* **37**:358–359 (1950).
48. H. Chomse, W. Hoffman, and P. Seidel, *Naturwissenschaften* **40**:288–289 (1953).
49. L. Peterman, *J. Acoust. Soc. Am.* **24**:416–417 (1952).
50. L. A. Peterman and P. B. Oncley, *IRE Trans. on Ultrasonic Eng.* **4**:42–52 (Aug. 1956).
51. C. E. Fitch, *Materials Evaluation* **22**:124–127 (1964).
52. W. G. Mayer, *Ultrasonic News* (Branson Instruments, Stamford, Conn.) **5**(10):9–11, 14–15 (Spring 1961).
53. D. W. Holder and R. J. North, Schlieren Methods, National Physical Laboratory Notes on Applied Science No. 31, 1963; available from Her Majesty's Stationery Office, London, 98 pages (includes 269 references).
54. F. R. Rollins, *J. Acoust. Soc. Am.* **35**:616–617 (1963).
55. T. J. Kessler and W. G. Hill, Jr., A Color Schlieren System, Tech. Report 105-ME-F, Rutgers—The State Univ. College of Eng., Dept. of Mech. Eng., New Brunswick, N.J. (Nov., 1965).
56. D. Ensminger, Battelle Memorial Institute, Columbus, Ohio, private communication (July 1964).
57. K. Schuster, *Jenaer Jahrbuch*, 1951, p. 217.
58. O. R. Gericke and R. C. Grubinskas, Utilization of the Liquid Surface Levitation Effect As A Means of Ultrasonic Image Conversion For Materials Inspection, Abstract U6, 74th Meeting of the Acoustical Society of America, Miami Beach, Fla., 1967; complete paper to be published.
59. A. Korpel, Zenith Radio Corp., Chicago, Ill., private communication, 1967.
60. J. D. Young and J. E. Wolfe, *Appl. Phys. Letters* **11**(9):294–296 (Nov. 1, 1967).
61. R. Pohlman, *Z. Physik* **113**:697–707 (1939).
62. H. E. Van Valkenburg, abstract U8, 74th Meeting of the Acoustical Society of America, Miami Beach, Fla., 1967.
63. T. F. Hueter and R. H. Bolt, *Sonics*, J. Wiley and Sons, New York, 1965, pp. 352–354.
64. R. Goldman, *Ultrasonic Technology*, Reinhold Publishing Corp., New York, 1962, pp. 37–56.
65. J. H. Holmes, *Ultrasonics* **6**:60–66 (1967).
66. T. G. Brown, *Ultrasonics* **6**:118–124 (1967).
67. G. Martin, *Brit. J. Nondestructive Testing* **9**:27–60 (1967).
68. R. H. Selner and H. Berger, *Materials Evaluation* **25**:91–95 (1967).
69. R. C. McMaster (ed.), *Nondestructive Testing Handbook*, Ronald Press, New York, 1959, Vol. II, Sec. 43, pp. 26–37.
70. W. N. Beck, *J. Acoust. Soc. Am.* **29**:865 (1957).
71. S. Sokolov, U.S. Patent 2,164,125 (June 27, 1939).
72. E. E. Suckling and W. R. MacLean, *J. Acoust. Soc. Am.* **27**:297–301 (1955).
73. E. E. Suckling and S. Ben-Zvi, *J. Acoust. Soc. Am.* **34**:1277–1278 (1962).
74. W. Freitag, H. J. Martin, and G. Schellbach, Descriptions and Results of Investigations of an Electronic Ultrasonic Image Converter, in: Proc. 2nd Annual Conference on Medical Electronics, Charles C. Thomas, Springfield, Ill., 1959, pp. 373–379.
75. W. E. Lawrie and K. E. Feith, *J. Acoust. Soc. Am.* **34**:719 (1962).

76. J. E. Jacobs, H. Berger, and W. J. Collis, *IEEE Trans. on Ultrasonic Eng.* **10**:83–88 (1963).

77. W. R. Turner, *J. Acoust. Soc. Am.* **36**:2016 (1964).

78. J. E. Jacobs, W. J. Collis, and H. Berger, *Materials Evaluation* **22**:209–212 (1964).

79. H. Berger, A Television System For Ultrasonic Imaging, Argonne National Laboratory, Argonne, Ill., Report ANL-7042 (1966).

80. H. B. Karplus, Face Plates For Image Converters, Abstract K6, 74th Meeting of the Acoustical Society of America, Miami Beach, Fla., 1967.

81. J. E. Jacobs, *Materials Evaluation* **25**:41–45 (1967).

82. J. E. Jacobs, Ultrasound Image Converters, presented at the 1967 IEEE Symposium on Sonics and Ultrasonics, Vancouver, Canada, Oct., 1967, to be published.

83. J. E. Jacobs, K. Reiman, and L. Buss, The Use of Color Display Techniques To Enhance The Sensitivity of the Ultrasonic Camera, *Materials Evaluation*, to be published.

84. G. A. Antcliffe, *Brit. J. Appl. Phys.* **17**:327 (1966).

85. D. A. Cusano, Cathode-Photo- and D.C. Electroluminescence in Zinc Sulfide Layers, in: *Luminescence of Organic and Inorganic Materials*, (H. Kallmann and G. M. Spruch, eds.), John Wiley and Sons, New York, 1962, pp. 494–522.

86. P. Goldberg and J. W. Nickerson, *J. Appl. Phys.* **34**:1601–1608 (1963).

87. R. K. Mueller and N. K. Sheridon, *Appl. Phys. Letters* **9**(9):328–329 (Nov. 1, 1966).

88. K. Preston, Jr., and J. L. Kreuzer, *Appl. Phys. Letters* **10**(5):150–152 (March 1, 1967).

89. H. Boutin, E. Maron, and R. K. Mueller, Real Time Display of Sound Holograms by KD*P Modulation of a Coherent Light Source, Abstract K4, 74th Meeting of the Acoustical Society of America, Miami Beach, Fla., 1967.

Chapter 3

THE LIQUID–GAS INTERFACE AS A RECORDING MEDIUM FOR ACOUSTICAL HOLOGRAPHY

R. K. Mueller and P. N. Keating

Bendix Research Laboratories
Southfield, Michigan

Sound waves impinging on a gas–liquid interface generate a surface deformation consisting of components proportional to linear and quadratic terms in the acoustic amplitude. The quadratic term, which can be related to the radiation pressure of the acoustic waves, is most important for hologram formation. This paper discusses the implication of both the linear and quadratic terms.

INTRODUCTION

It is well known that any wave or particle field is amenable to holographic techniques. In the early days of holography, X rays and electrons occupied the center of interest ([1–3]), and it was primarily the advent of the laser, providing a highly coherent light source, that brought light-to-light holography to its present prominent place. Acoustical holography, which requires laser light for effective optical display, also owes to this device much of the rapid development that we are witnessing at present.

In light-to-light holography the hologram is essentially an information storage device. Its usefulness lies in providing a more or less permanent record of the spatial modulation of a light field. In acoustical (or other non-light-to-light) holography the information storage aspect is, if present, incidental. The main objective is to transfer the spatial modulation of a sound field onto a light field, whereupon imaging and other information processing can be done optically.

A very simple and rather effective acoustooptical transducer which performs this transfer operation in real time is a liquid–gas interface ([4]). The interface reflects light and deforms under an impinging sound wave, the deformation being roughly proportional to the incident acoustic intensity. A light wave reflected from such a deformed surface therefore receives a spatial modulation that corresponds under appropriate circumstances to the spatial modulation of the acoustic field in the liquid. It is the purpose of this paper to discuss this surface deformation pattern in some detail.

THE WAVE EQUATION

Sound propagation in a liquid is an inherently nonlinear process. However, if we take only second-order quantities into account, an approximation that is sufficient for our purposes, the surface deformation can be expressed in terms of solutions of the linearized sound equation

$$\left(\Delta - \frac{1}{c^2}\frac{\partial^2}{\partial t^2}\right)\phi = 0 \tag{1}$$

where ϕ is the velocity potential and c the sound velocity. The velocity $\mathbf{v}$ in the sound field is given by

$$\mathbf{v} = \operatorname{grad} \phi \tag{2}$$

and the pressure due to the acoustic field is

$$p' = p - p_0 = \rho\,\partial\phi/\partial t \tag{3}$$

where p_0 is the hydrostatic pressure in the liquid and ρ is the density.

From these quantities one can derive the energy density, energy flux, and momentum flux in the sound field ([5]), the time averages of which are the nonlinear quantities dominating the surface deformation effect.

In order to avoid difficulties of interpretation, we shall in the following equations write all quantities as real functions. We obtain then for the energy density in the acoustic field

$$E = (\rho/2)(\operatorname{grad} \phi)^2 + (\rho/2c^2)(\partial\phi/\partial t)^2 \tag{4}$$

for the energy flux density $\mathbf{F}$

$$\mathbf{F} = \rho(\partial\phi/\partial t)\operatorname{grad} \phi \tag{5}$$

and for the momentum flux density tensor Π

$$\Pi_{ik} = \frac{\rho}{2}\left\{\frac{\partial\phi}{\partial x_i}\frac{\partial\phi}{\partial x_k} + \frac{1}{c^2}\left(\frac{\partial\phi}{\partial t}\right)^2\delta_{ik}\right\} \tag{6}$$

A plane wave solution of Eq. (1), on which we shall base much of our later discussion, is

$$\phi = A\sin(\mathbf{kr} - \omega t) \tag{7}$$

where $\mathbf{k}$ is the propagation vector with the magnitude k:

$$k = 2\pi/\lambda = \omega/c \tag{8}$$

With Eq. (5) we can relate the amplitude A of the plane wave, Eq. (7), to the time-averaged energy flux density F and obtain

$$A = (1/\omega)(2Fc/\rho)^{1/2} \tag{9}$$

For a typical frequency of 10 MHz and an energy flux density F of 10^7 erg/cm^2-sec ($= 1$ W/cm^2) one obtains in water a velocity potential amplitude of

$$A \approx 2 \cdot 10^{-2} \quad cm^2/sec \tag{10}$$

which we shall use as a reference for numerical values of characteristic quantities later on.

THE BOUNDARY CONDITIONS

In order to avoid complications that are immaterial to the interface deformation, we assume a liquid-filled half-space $z < z_0$ bounded by a planar interface $z = z_0$ under hydrostatic conditions. We assume further that no acoustic energy is transmitted through the interface. This assumption, which simplifies the following considerations drastically, is well justified since the energy transfer through a gas–liquid interface is extremely small.

If a sound field is present in the liquid, the interface deviates from its hydrostatic state. We describe this deviation by a function $h(x, y, t)$ defined as

$$h(x, y, t) = z_{\text{interface}} - z_0 \tag{11}$$

The velocity of the liquid normal to the hydrostatic interface is then

$$v_z = \partial h/\partial t \tag{12}$$

which, in view of Eq. (2), gives the following relation between the surface deformation $h(x, y, t)$ and the acoustic field:

$$(\partial\phi/\partial z)_{z=z_0} = \partial h/\partial t \tag{13}$$

The acoustic field ϕ is determined by its sources and a boundary condition at the interface. Our assumption of zero energy transfer through the interface implies that the energy flux component normal to the interface vanishes at the interface. This is in our approximation, which includes terms up to second-order, equivalent to the condition that the z component of the energy flux vanishes at $z = z_0$:

$$(F_z)_{z=z_0} = \rho \left(\frac{\partial\phi}{\partial t}\right)_{z=z_0} \left(\frac{\partial\phi}{\partial z}\right)_{z=z_0} = 0 \tag{14}$$

Since $(\partial\phi/\partial z)_{z=z_0}$ is, according to Eq. (13), not equal to zero, we find from Eq. (14) that

$$\partial\phi/\partial t = 0 \qquad \text{at} \quad z = z_0 \tag{15}$$

This boundary condition, together with the source distribution, uniquely defines the acoustic field in the liquid.

THE SURFACE DEFORMATION

Equation (13) relates the surface deformation to the acoustic field ϕ. Integrating Eq. (13), we obtain

$$h(x, y, t) = h_0(x, y) + h_1(x, y, t) \tag{16}$$

with

$$h_1 = \int (\partial\phi/\partial z)_{z=z_0}\, dt \tag{17}$$

The time-independent function h_0 is an "integration constant" that we shall now determine.

If a liquid–gas interface in a gravitational field deviates from equilibrium, gravitation and surface tension tend to restore a planar interface. The restoring forces act normal to the interface, and can therefore be expressed as an equivalent pressure p_s. The relation between p_s and the surface deformation is given by

$$p_s = -\rho g h + \gamma\left(\frac{\partial^2}{\partial x^2} + \frac{\partial^2}{\partial y^2}\right)h \tag{18}$$

where g is the gravitational acceleration and γ the surface tension of the interface.

A time-independent deformation on the interface can therefore exist only if the acoustic field exerts a corresponding pressure on the interface which counteracts p_s.

Such a pressure is indeed present at the interface because of the discontinuity of the acoustic energy density that exists there. The magnitude of this pressure is equal to the time-averaged energy density differential across the surface. Because we have assumed zero energy transfer, this differential is equal to the energy density at the interface. We therefore obtain from Eq. (4) and from the boundary conditions Eq. (15) the following equation for the radiation pressure p_r:

$$p_r = (\rho/2)(\partial\phi/\partial z)_{z=z_0}^2 \tag{19}$$

The equilibrium condition $p_s + p_r = 0$ then yields a relation between the stationary surface deformation h_0 and the acoustic field, from which h_0 can be determined for any given field configuration. We obtain

$$\left(\frac{\partial^2}{\partial x^2} + \frac{\partial^2}{\partial y^2} - \frac{\rho g}{\gamma}\right) h_0 = -\frac{\rho}{2\gamma} \overline{\left(\frac{\partial \phi}{\partial z}\right)^2}\Bigg|_{z=z_0} \tag{20}$$

THE SURFACE UNDER PLANE WAVE EXCITATION

Most characteristic features of surface deformation important for holography are already present if the surface is exposed to two interfering plane waves. Consider an acoustic field which fulfills our boundary condition, Eq. (15), and consists of a signal wave with amplitude A incident on the surface under an angle θ and a reference wave with amplitude B impinging normal to the surface:

$$\phi = 2A \sin(k_1 x - \omega t) \sin[k_2(z - z_0)] + 2B \sin \omega t \sin[k(z - z_0)] \tag{21}$$

with

$$k_1 = k \sin \theta, \qquad k_2 = k \cos \theta, \qquad \text{and} \qquad k = \omega/c$$

The normal velocity component $v_z = \partial\phi/\partial z$ at the surface is

$$\left(\frac{\partial \phi}{\partial z}\right)_{z=z_0} = 2Ak_2 \sin(k_1 x - \omega t) + 2Bk \sin \omega t \tag{22}$$

With Eq. (17) and (22) we obtain for the time-dependent component of the surface deformation h_1

$$h_1 = 2(A/C) \cos \theta \cos(k_1 x - \omega t) - 2(B/c) \cos \omega t \tag{23}$$

The stationary surface deformation h_0 must be determined from Eq. (20). The acoustic field quantity in Eq. (20) is the time-averaged energy density at the surface, which in the present case is

$$\bar{E}_{z=z_0} = \frac{\rho}{2} \overline{\left(\frac{\partial \phi}{\partial z}\right)^2}\Bigg|_{z=z_0} = \rho(A^2 k_2^2 + B^2 k^2 + ABk_2 k \cos k_1 x) \tag{24}$$

Introducing Eq. (24) into Eq. (20), we obtain

$$\left(\frac{\partial^2}{\partial x^2} + \frac{\partial^2}{\partial y^2} - \frac{\rho g}{\gamma}\right) h_0 = -\frac{\rho}{\gamma}\{A^2 k_2^2 + B^2 k^2 + ABkk_2 \cos k_1 x\} \tag{25}$$

with the solution

$$h_0 = (A^2 k_2^2/g) + (B^2 k^2/g) + \{ABkk_2 \cos k_1 x/[g + \gamma k_1^2/\rho]\} \tag{26}$$

Since γk_1^2 is very large compared to ρg under typical operating conditions, we can simplify Eq. (26) to

$$h_0 = \text{const} + [AB\rho \cos \theta \cos k_1 x/(\gamma \sin^2 \theta)] \tag{27}$$

and we obtain for the total surface deformation

$$h = \text{const} + \frac{2A \cos \theta \cos(k_1 x - \omega t)}{c} + \frac{\rho AB \cos \theta \cos k_1 x}{(\gamma \sin^2 \theta)} \tag{28}$$

The largest term in Eq. (28) is the constant "levitation" term. This term is a constant only because we have assumed an unbounded plane wave. In the more realistic case of ultrasonic beams of limited lateral extension this term causes a surface deformation over the extension of the beam which is in general of low symmetry and causes aberration in the optical playback in addition to the unavoidable aberration resulting from the difference between the acoustic and the optical wavelengths. This aberration can be minimized by allowing the reference beam to impinge normal to the surface (as we did in this example) and increasing the reference beam intensity relative to the signal beam. Under this condition the asymmetry of the levitation term is minimized. For a reference beam intensity of 1 W/cm^2 and a frequency of 10 MHz the levitation in the center of the beam is about 80 μ. In addition to the levitation term, we have two periodic terms—one stationary and one periodic in space and time—both of which can be used to transfer spatial modulation from the acoustic field onto the light field. Their relative importance depends on the intensity of the reference beam. We obtain for the ratio of their amplitudes

$$R = \rho Bc/(2\gamma \sin^2 \theta) \tag{29}$$

which for water and a 30° offset angle gives

$$R = 110(\bar{F}_B)^{1/2} \tag{30}$$

where F_B is the energy flux density of the reference beam in W/cm^2.
    The amplitude of the linear term in water is of the order

$$A_{\text{linear}} \approx 2 \cdot 10^{-7} (\bar{F}_A)^{1/2} \tag{31}$$

where F_A is the energy flux density of the signal beam in W/cm^2. With a typical value of 10 mW/cm^2 for the signal beam one obtains an amplitude for the linear term of 2 Å, which is too small for effective playback. With the same signal beam and a reference beam of 1 W/cm^2 one obtains for the stationary term an amplitude of 160 Å, which is adequate for optical reconstruction. One can improve the situation further by increasing the intensity of the reference beam up to a surface modulation depth of about 1000 Å. At higher energies, however, it is necessary to pulse the reference beam in order to avoid serious surface distortions due to the streaming effect resulting from transfer of momentum from the beam to the fluid in a lossy medium.

GENERAL SURFACE EXCITATIONS

We have shown in the foregoing sections that the stationary surface deformation is the dominant information-carrying process. If the signal beam is a plane wave, the stationary periodic surface deformation is proportional to the interference term in the time-averaged energy density at the surface. This is no longer the case if this interference term is not a simple harmonic function. With an interference term $u(x, y)$ the corresponding surface deformation h_0 is

$$h_0(x, y) = (1/\gamma) \int u(\xi \zeta) \ln(1/r) \, d\xi \, d\zeta \tag{32}$$

where

$$r^2 = (x - \xi)^2 + (y - \zeta)^2$$

if we neglect, as discussed earlier, the effect of gravitation in Eq. (20).

The surface deformation, as Eq. (32) shows, is not a true image of the interference pattern of the signal with the reference beam, but is rather the image seen through a system with an impulse response of $\ln(1/r)$. The convolution with $\ln(1/r)$ in Eq. (32) has the effect of suppressing high spatial frequencies, thus decreasing the resolution and giving rise to image distortion. The distortion can be minimized by increasing the offset angle as much as the system permits.

CONCLUSION

The liquid–gas interface as an acoustooptical transducer for ultrasonic holography recommends itself because of its inherent simplicity and real-time capability. The foregoing discussion, however, shows that these advantages are partially offset by the relatively high intensity levels (at least of the reference beam) which are required for successful direct playback as well as by the aberrations introduced by this method as a result of the nature of the physical processes involved.

REFERENCES

1. D. Gabor, A New Microscopic Principle, *Nature* **161**:777 (1948).
2. D. Gabor, Microscopy by Reconstructed Wavefronts I, *Proc. Roy. Soc.* (*London*) **A197**:454 (1949).
3. H. M. A. El-Sum, Reconstructed Wave-Front Microscopy, Ph.D. Thesis, Stanford University (1952).
4. R. K. Mueller and N. K. Sheridon, Sound Holograms and Optical Reconstruction, *Appl. Phys. Letters* **9**:328 (1966).
5. L. D. Landau and E. M. Lifshitz, *Fluid Mechanics Course of Theoretical Physics*, Vol. VI, Pergamon Press, London, 1959.

Chapter 4

A COMPARISON OF ACOUSTICAL HOLOGRAPHY METHODS

Byron B. Brenden

Battelle Memorial Institute, Pacific Northwest Laboratory
Richland, Washington

A comparison is made between two methods of imaging ultrasound by holography with reconstruction in light. One method employs a scanned acoustical receiver, an electronic reference, and a modulated light source which is moved in synchronism with the acoustical receiver. A photographic transparency is produced which serves as the hologram for reconstruction of the acoustic field in the optical domain. A second method employs a liquid surface to record the acoustical hologram of transilluminated objects. Reflection of quasicoherent light from the hologram produces real-time acoustical imaging. The interaction of ultrasound and light with the liquid surface is discussed. Examples of images produced by both methods confirm that both are capable of achieving the resolution expected on the basis of the wavelengths and hologram apertures used. The sensitivity of the scanned hologram method greatly exceeds that of the liquid surface method but this advantage is offset by the capability for real-time imaging of the liquid surface method.

INTRODUCTION

Two methods of performing acoustical holography with reconstruction in light have been reported. One method described recently by Smith [1], which is similar to the methods of Preston and Kreuzer [2], Metherell *et al.* [3], and Massey [4], employs a scanned acoustical receiver, an electronic reference, and a modulated light source which is moved in synchronism with the acoustical receiver. A photographic transparency is produced which serves as the hologram for reconstruction of the acoustic field in optical space.

The other method is similar to that of Mueller and Sheridon [5] and employs a liquid surface to record the acoustical hologram of transilluminated objects. Reflection of quasicoherent light from the hologram produces real-time acoustical imaging.

A major difference between the two methods is the energy density required to form the hologram. The energy density required for liquid surface holography is several orders of magnitude greater than for scanned holography. The advantage of liquid surface holography is that it can be used as part of a real-time viewing system, whereas scanned holography is a two-step process requiring the formation of a photographic transparency. Objects must remain stationary during the scan time, which may be quite long. No such limitation is imposed in the use of real-time liquid surface holography, where the object may be in motion.

We have been limited in liquid surface holography to imaging only transilluminated objects. On the other hand, in the investigation of scanned holography at Battelle-Northwest only diffuse reflecting objects have been used.

ACOUSTICAL HOLOGRAPHY EMPLOYING A LIQUID SURFACE

Experimental Arrangement

Liquid surface holography as carried out at Battelle-Northwest employs the arrangement shown in Fig. 1. The liquid surface serves as the square law detector upon which the hologram is formed. A hologram so formed may be used in either of two ways. It may be photographed so that the resulting transparency may later be illuminated by monochromatic light from a point source to reconstruct an image, or it may be directly illuminated and the image viewed in real time.

We have successfully imaged at frequencies of 3, 5, 9, 10, 15, 20, 30, and 50 MHz using air-backed x-cut quartz crystals at their fundamental frequencies of 3, 5, 10, and 20 MHz and at their odd harmonic frequencies. At the present time it appears that absorption of acoustic energy in the liquid has prevented successful imaging at frequencies above 50 MHz. Frequencies

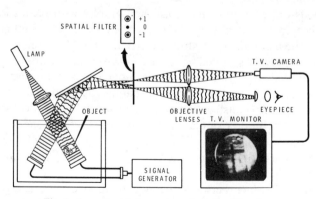

Fig. 1. Acoustical holography using a liquid surface.

less than 3 MHz are also of interest, and there appears to be no reason why the method will not work at lower frequencies, although the hologram becomes very coarse-structured for direct real-time imaging, and at some lower frequency it will probably become advantageous to use the two-step process whereby the hologram is photographed and reduced in size before reconstruction of the image.

Although it would seem that a continuous acoustic wave should be used for this type of imaging, we have found that pulses of approximately 80 μsec duration repeated every 2 or 3 msec produce the best results.

Before showing the results of our work an analysis of the interaction between the acoustic waves, the liquid surface, and the light used to reconstruct the images will be presented.

Analysis

Two ultrasonic waves having plane wavefronts are generated by two air-backed x-cut quartz crystals, T_0 and T_r, each $2\frac{1}{4}$ in. in diameter. These waves are usually directed toward the liquid surface at equal but opposite angles θ_s to the normal and may be characterized by the expressions

$$u_0(x, y, z) = p_0 \exp i(-\eta_s y + \zeta_s z) \qquad (1)$$

and

$$u_r(x, y, z) = p_r \exp i(\eta_s y + \zeta_s z) \qquad (2)$$

where

$$\eta_s = (2\pi/\Lambda) \sin \theta_s \qquad (3)$$

$$\zeta_s = (2\pi/\Lambda) \cos \theta_s \qquad (4)$$

and Λ is the wavelength of acoustic vibration in the liquid. At the liquid surface, $z = 0$, where the two waves intersect to form a hologram Eq. (1) and (2) are modified to

$$u_0(x, y) = p_0(x, y) \exp i[-\eta_s y - \phi(x, y)] \qquad (5)$$

and

$$u_r(x, y) = p_r \exp i\eta_s y \qquad (6)$$

i.e., the transmission of the object beam through and around the object produces x and y variations in the pressure amplitude p_0 and introduces a phase change ϕ which is also a function of x and y.

Interference of the acoustic beams defined by Eqs. (5) and (6) produces an intensity distribution given by

$$I(x, y) = |u_0 + u_r|^2/2\rho c \qquad (7)$$

where ρ is the density of the liquid and c is the velocity of ultrasound in the liquid. Reflection of the ultrasonic waves at the surface produces a radiation pressure P given by ([6])

$$P(x, y) = 2 I(x, y)/c \tag{8}$$

Pressures due to gravity and surface tension oppose the radiation pressure, so that for a unit area the local force balance equation becomes

$$P(x, y) = \rho g z' - \gamma \left(\frac{\partial^2 z'}{\partial x^2} + \frac{\partial^2 z'}{\partial y^2} \right) \tag{9}$$

where g is the acceleration of gravity and γ is the surface tension. Using Eqs. (5)–(8) to define the radiation pressure P, and assuming a stationary solution for z' of the form

$$z'(x, y) = A[\exp i(2\eta_s y + \phi) + \exp -i(2\eta_s y + \phi)] + B \tag{10}$$

yields

$$A(x, y) = \frac{P_r P_0(x, y)}{\rho c^2 [\rho g + 4\gamma \eta_s^2 + \gamma(\partial^2 \phi/\partial x^2 + \partial^2 \phi/\partial y^2)]} \tag{11}$$

and

$$B(x, y) = \frac{P_r^2 + [P_0(x, y)]^2}{g \rho^2 c^2} \tag{12}$$

The prime on $z'(x, y)$ distinguishes this analytic expression for the liquid surface from the z coordinate. In Eq. (11) the term $4\gamma \eta^2$ predominates, so that we may normally write without much loss of accuracy

$$A(x, y) = (P_r/4\rho\gamma c^2 \eta_s^2) P_0(x, y) \tag{13}$$

Equation (10) characterizes the hologram. It indicates that the liquid surface will have the configuration shown in Fig. 2. Conjectured edge contours have been added since the effects of acoustic beams of finite cross-sectional area are not included in the analysis.

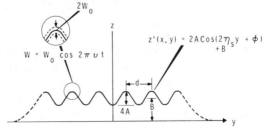

Fig. 2. Configuration of the liquid surface.

One should not assume that the ripples on the liquid surface vibrate appreciably at the frequency of the acoustic waves generating them. The only vibration of the liquid surface at the frequency of the acoustic waves occurs on the crests of the ripples and is several orders of magnitude smaller in amplitude than the amplitude of the ripple pattern. Furthermore, the ripples are very shallow, having a crest to valley distance of about two orders of magnitude less than the overall liquid elevation B when the acoustic frequency and intensity are 1 MHz and 0.1 W/cm^2, respectively, in water.

If the hologram is illuminated by a monochromatic homocentric source of light incident at an angle θ_l to the normal to the surface, the light experiences a change in phase which for sufficiently small values of $z'(x, y)$ may be taken as $2\zeta_l z'$, where

$$\zeta_l = (2\pi/\lambda)\cos\theta_l \tag{14}$$

The reflected beam of light may be characterized by

$$U(x, y, z) = D\exp i\{\eta_l y + \zeta_l[z + 2z'(x, y)]\} \tag{15}$$

or according to Eq. (10),

$$U(x, y, z) = D\exp(2i\zeta_l B)\exp[4i\zeta_l A\cos(2\eta_s y + \phi)] \times \exp i(\eta_l y + \zeta_l z) \tag{16}$$

Better physical interpretation of Eq. (16) is achieved if use is made of the identity ([7])

$$\exp(i\sigma\cos\alpha) \equiv \sum_{n=-\infty}^{\infty} i^n J_n(\sigma)e^{-in\alpha} \tag{17}$$

where $J_n(\sigma)$ is the nth order Bessel function. Let

$$\sigma = 4\zeta_l A(x, y) \tag{18}$$

and

$$\alpha = 2\eta_s y + \phi(x, y) \tag{19}$$

so that Eq. (16) becomes

$$U(x, y, z) = D\exp i\zeta_l[z + 2B(x, y)]\sum_{n=-\infty}^{\infty} i^n J_n[4\zeta_l A(x, y)]$$

$$\times \exp i[(\eta_l - 2n\eta_s)y - n\phi(x, y)] \tag{20}$$

Each value of n corresponds to a diffracted order of light. For $4\zeta_l A(x, y)$ sufficiently small we may use the approximation

$$U(x, y) = D\exp i\zeta_l[z + 2B(x, y)] \times \{\exp(i\eta_l y)$$

$$+ 2i\zeta_l A(x, y)\exp i[(\eta_l - 2\eta_s)y - \phi(x, y)]$$

$$+ 2i\zeta_l A(x, y)\exp i[(\eta_l + 2\eta_s)y + \phi(x, y)]\}$$

$$\equiv U_0(x, y) + iU_{+1}(x, y) + iU_{-1}(x, y) \tag{21}$$

The second term on the right-hand side of Eq. (21) is similar to the expression given previously to characterize the acoustic pressure distribution at the hologram surface. In fact, at the surface $z = 0$ if the angle of incidence of the light is chosen so that $\eta_l = \eta_s$, the intensity $U_{+1}U^*_{+1}$ of light is identical to the intensity $u_0u^*_0$ of the acoustic wave except for a constant multiplier.

We can write

$$[U_{+1}(x, y)]^2 = \left[\frac{\zeta_l D p_r}{2\rho\gamma c^2 \eta_s^2} u_0(x, y) \right]^2 \tag{22}$$

which shows that the light wave reflected from the hologram into the first order is a scaled replica of the acoustic wave emanating from the object and suggests that a virtual image of the object may be seen in this light. Similarly, the term $U_{-1}(x, y)$ forms a real image. The condition $\eta_l = \eta_s$ is not critical. Good images with only slight distortion are produced at almost any reasonable value of η_l.

Two-Step Holography Using a Liquid Surface

Direct photography of the hologram is possible if continuous acoustic waves are used and if the structure of the hologram is sufficiently coarse. If the acoustic waves are pulsed, the light must be pulsed in synchronism with the acoustic pulses. A more ideal arrangement for photographing the liquid surface hologram would involve pulsing the light source and acoustical transducers in synchronism, attenuating the zero-order light to reduce its

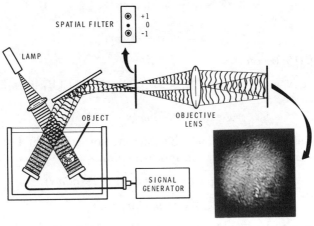

Fig. 3. Method of recording a liquid surface hologram.

intensity to that of the first-order light, and forming and photographing an image of the liquid surface in zero- and first-order light.

The necessity for chopping or pulsing the light source is eliminated by use of the arrangement shown in Fig. 3, in which the image of the liquid surface is formed and photographed in the light of the two first orders. This results in a hologram which acts as though it had been formed by acoustic waves of half the wavelength actually used except that contrast is greatly increased in the image. Figure 4 shows a reconstruction produced from a hologram made in this way using 5-MHz ultrasound and a He–Ne light source. The object is a wire screen with $\frac{1}{8}$ in. spacing between wires which are 0.050 in. in diameter. A fringe system exists in the hologram but is too fine-structured to be seen. Actual fringe separation on the liquid surface was about 0.015 cm.

The image was reconstructed by illuminating the hologram with convergent light from a helium–neon laser, a method which is described in more detail later in this paper.

Real-Time Holography with a Liquid Surface

The chief advantage of liquid surface holography, the capability for real-time imaging, is lost in two-step holography. Real-time imaging is demonstrated in Fig. 5, which shows photographs of reconstructed images of the same screen as shown in Fig. 4 and which, in the real-time imaging arrangement of Fig. 1, were displayed on a closed-circuit television monitor. The images seen here were produced using 9-MHz ultrasound making an angle θ_s of 15° to the normal of the water surface. A 100-W superpressure mercury vapor lamp was used as a light source in reconstruction. The angle of incidence θ_l of the light on the hologram surface was 30°. Figure 5 also

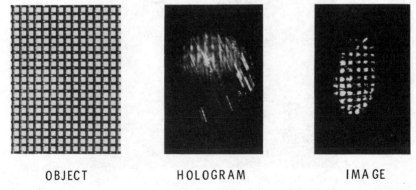

OBJECT   HOLOGRAM   IMAGE

Fig. 4. Two-step ultrasonic holography using a liquid surface (2/15/66—Frequency: 5 MHz Type V-F Plate).

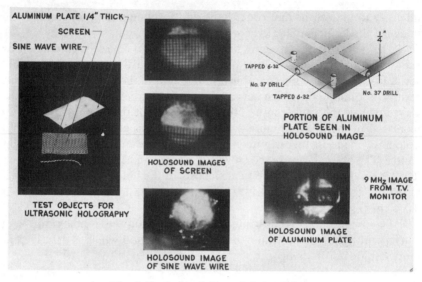

Fig. 5. Examples of ultrasonic holography.

demonstrates the imaging of the internal structure of a $\frac{1}{4}$ in. thick aluminum plate. The holes drilled in the plate are all approximately 0.105 in. in diameter. Figure 6 is an image of the same aluminum plate used to produce Fig. 5 except that it was photographed through the eyepiece rather than off the television monitor. The contours of the holes drilled in from the edges of the plate are more sharply defined. Both corners on the edge of the plate are clearly imaged. The acoustic frequency for this and all succeeding figures is 10-MHz.

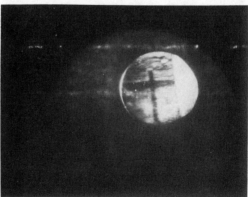

Fig. 6. Real-time liquid surface holographic image. Object: $\frac{1}{4}$-in. thick aluminum plate. Frequency: 10 MHz. Hole diameters: 0.0106 in.

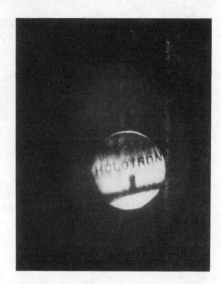

Fig. 7. Real-time liquid surface holographic image. Object: milled letters in aluminum plate. Frequency: 10 MHz. Letter size: $\frac{3}{16}$-in. high, milled 0.010-in. deep, with 0.020 in. linewidth.

The same plate has the name of the sponsor of this research milled in one side. The real-time image is recorded in Fig. 7. The letters are $\frac{3}{16}$ in. high, milled 0.010 in. deep, with a 0.020 in. linewidth. The field of view is $1\frac{1}{2}$ in. in diameter.

Figure 8 shows the real-time acoustic image of a penny showing the image of Lincoln produced from a liquid surface hologram.

ULTRASONIC HOLOGRAPHY USING A SCANNED HOLOGRAM METHOD

Construction of the Hologram

The scanned hologram method of ultrasonic holography has been investigated at Battelle-Northwest by R. B. Smith. He uses the arrangement shown in Fig. 9 for construction of the hologram. Objects in a tank of water are illuminated by 10-MHz ultrasound. The objects for which holograms and reconstructed images are shown in figures cut from styrofoam, which acts as a good diffuse scatterer of ultrasound. The figures were placed on the tank bottom which was a $\frac{1}{2}$-in. thick slab of absorbing rubber. The object-to-hologram distance was typically 25 cm.

A small receiving transducer is used to scan a plane in the field of ultrasound scattered by the objects. The area scanned, 4.2×5.3 cm or 280×350 wavelengths, is almost identically the same as used for the previously described work with liquid surface holography. A raster-type scan was made at line frequencies of 16, 32, or 63 lines/cm. The latter has a spacing quite close to one wavelength.

Fig. 8. Real-time liquid surface holographic image.
Object: penny. Frequency: 10 MHz.

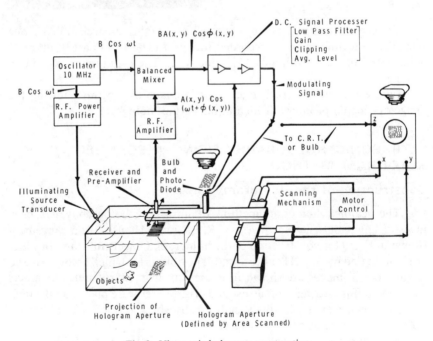

Fig. 9. Ultrasonic hologram construction.

The transducer most commonly used as a receiver was 0.63 mm or about 4 wavelengths in diameter and resonant at 10 MHz. The amplified signal from the transducer provides an electrical analog in amplitude and phase of the sound field at every point in the scanned plane.

A reference signal derived from the same oscillator as is used to drive the illuminating transducer is combined with the signal from the receiver transducer in a balanced mixer.

The output of the mixer is subjected to some tailoring before its intensity modulates the recording light source. The signal is amplified, some larger transient peaks are clipped, and the average level is shifted to center on the dynamic range of the light source and film sensitivity. Two types of light sources have been used. One of these is a cathode ray tube (CRT). Signals to position the spot of light on the CRT are derived from linear potentiometers on each of the two axes of the scanning mechanism. It is important that the x, y positioning on the CRT be strictly proportional to that of the scanner; otherwise astigmatism will exist in the hologram.

The other type of light source is a tungsten lamp mounted on the scanner. No problem of x, y positioning is encountered with this arrangement. The bulb has mounted to it a photodiode which serves two purposes. It monitors the bulb brightness and is thus helpful in judging exposure during the recording time. It is also used in a feedback circuit to make the bulb brightness a linear function of the signal from the balanced mixer.

Reconstruction of the Image

Figure 10 shows the reconstruction geometry. The beam of light from a helium–neon laser is expanded by the microscope objective to fill the aperture of a lens of about 60 cm focal length which images the focus of the microscope objective at an image distance of about 7 meters. Holograms placed close to the lens diffract light to form two conjugate images. Effects of variations in film thickness are eliminated by immersing the hologram in an index-matching liquid between plate glass flats.

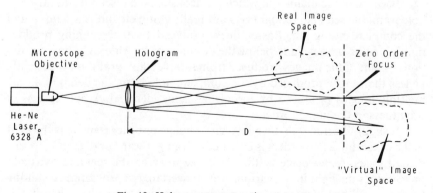

Fig. 10. Hologram reconstruction geometry.

Fig. 11. Some of the objects used for imaging.

Holograms and Reconstructions

Figure 11 is a picture of some of the objects which have been used for imaging. The holograms and reconstructions to be shown use the "9" as the object. The holograms are positive enlargements of the original polaroid transparency.

Figure 12 is a hologram produced using the CRT light source with a raster frequency of 15.7 lines/cm.

The corresponding images produced by this hologram are shown in Figure 13. These images were recorded by placing photographic film about 7 meters away from the 60 cm focal length lens used in the reconstruction arrangement of Fig. 10 and moving the lens to bring first the "virtual" image, then zero-order, and finally the real image into focus. The term "virtual" is used here merely to identify that image which would be virtual if collimated rather than converging light were used to illuminate the hologram. Actually, in this case both images are real.

Because of the manner in which the acoustic field is scanned to form the hologram, the scanned hologram is not really complete but is a sampling of the complete hologram. Raster lines produced by the scanning produce multiple images above and below the desired image. Although the information content of the images produced from sampled holograms must certainly be less than those produced by the complete hologram, the detail in all the multiple images produced by the raster seems identical except for loss of brightness in the higher orders.

It should be noted that where a given image or order is in focus the light in the other diffracted orders is either converging toward or diverging from a distant focus. At no place within the space between the real and "virtual" images does the light in the various orders overlap. No programmed shifting in phase of the electronic reference signal is needed to produce the off-axis

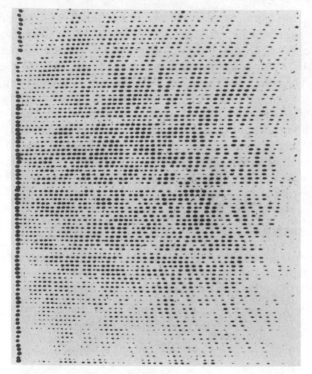

Fig. 12. Hologram (70519.1).

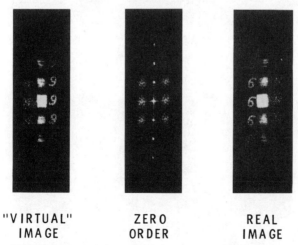

"VIRTUAL"   ZERO   REAL
IMAGE   ORDER   IMAGE

Fig. 13. Reconstruction (70519.1). Object; the numeral "6",
2.3 × 4 cm, linewidth 5 mm. Distance: 25 cm. Raster: 15.7
lines/cm. Recording: CRT.

image. It is only necessary that the objects be outside the space defined by projecting the area of the scan plane in the direction of the normal to the plane.

Figure 14 was produced using a tungsten filament lamp mounted on the scanner. The raster frequency is now about double that of the previous hologram. This is especially apparent in the reconstructions shown in Fig. 15. The multiple images produced by the raster are now about twice as far apart. An interesting phenomenon is noted in the zero-order focus, where faint half-order points of light are formed. These occur when the forward scan lines form one uniformly spaced raster and the backward or retrace scan lines form a second set which is not perfectly intermeshed with the first set. The brightness of this intermediate-order focused light is a measure of the degree of raster spacing error.

CONCLUSIONS

Acoustical holography using either scanned or liquid surface holograms is capable of producing images with detail approaching the resolution expected on the basis of the wavelengths and hologram apertures used.

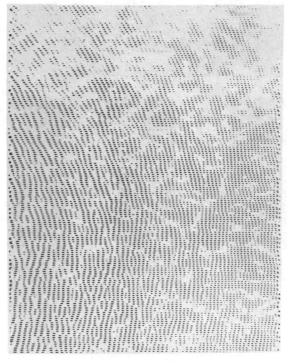

Fig. 14. Hologram (70621.A).

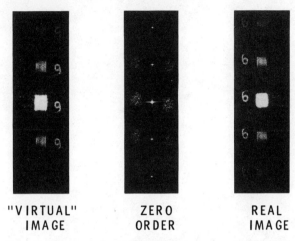

"VIRTUAL"   ZERO   REAL
IMAGE   ORDER   IMAGE

Fig. 15. Reconstruction (70621.A). Object: the numeral "6," 24 × 4 cm, linewidth 5 mm. Distance: 25 cm. Raster: 31.5 lines/ cm. Recording: scanner mounted bulb.

The sensitivity of the scanned hologram method greatly exceeds that of the liquid surface method, but this advantage is offset by the capability for real-time imaging of the liquid surface method.

ACKNOWLEDGMENTS

The author wishes to thank D. R. Hoegger, G. N. Langlois, V. I. Neeley, J. L. Stringer, R. B. Smith, S. C. Keeton, and many others at Battelle-Northwest for assistance given in work leading to the results reported in this paper.

REFERENCES

1. R. B. Smith, *Ultrasonic Imaging Using a Scanned Hologram Method*, BNWL-SA-1362, October, 1967.
2. K. Preston, Jr., and J. L. Kreuzer, *Appl. Phys. Letters* **10**(5):150–152 (1967).
3. A. F. Metherell, H. M. A. El-Sum, J. J. Dreher, and L. Larmore, *Appl. Phys. Letters* **10**(10): 277–279 (1967).
4. G. A. Massey, *Proc. IEEE* **55**(6):1115–1117 (1967).
5. R. K. Mueller and N. K. Sheridon, *Appl. Phys. Letters* **9**:328–329 (1966).
6. T. F. Hueter and R. H. Bolt, *Sonics*, John Wiley and Sons, New York, 1966, pp. 42–44.
7. J. A. Stratton, *Electromagnetic Theory*, McGraw-Hill Book Co., 1941, p. 372.

Chapter 5

ACOUSTIC HOLOGRAPHIC TECHNIQUES FOR NONDESTRUCTIVE TESTING*

Justin L. Kreuzer

The Perkin-Elmer Corporation
Norwalk, Connecticut

Paul E. Vogel

U.S. Army Materials and Mechanics Research Center
Watertown, Massachusetts

The first part of this paper reports progress to date on an experimental investigation of the feasibility of applying holographic techniques to acoustical imaging to obtain three-dimensional images of opaque objects as encountered in nondestructive testing. Equipment was fabricated to make acoustical holograms of objects in water. Acoustical holograms were recorded by mechanically scanning an acoustical point transducer over the water's surface in a TV-like raster. The acoustic frequency was 5 MHz. The resulting holograms were then used to make visible images. Holograms of objects examined in water, where the ultrasonic wavelength was 0.3 mm, show image detail smaller than 1 mm. A variety of acoustical holograms and their corresponding images (including one of a hole in an aluminum block) are presented and discussed. The second part of this paper presents a simplified theoretical analysis of these acoustical holograms. The effects of nonlinearities, sampling rates and pulse duration, coherent sound, and wavelength scaling on the acoustical image are discussed. The problem of three-dimensional visualization of the acoustical image is considered in detail. The third part of this paper discusses some potential uses of acoustical holographic techniques in nondestructive testing.

INTRODUCTION

The application of holographic techniques to acoustical (ultrasonic) imaging offers several advantages over other imaging techniques used in ultrasonic nondestructive testing. A hologram provides a permanent two-dimensional record of a three-dimensional object. An acoustical (ultrasonic) hologram

*This research program was carried out at the Perkin-Elmer Corporation, Norwalk, Connecticut under contracts DA-19-066-AMC-286 (x) and DAAG46-67-C-0132 (x) from the U.S. Army Materials and Mechanics Research Center, Watertown, Massachusetts.

73

provides good lateral resolution without the need for complex ultrasonic imaging optics and good depth resolution without the need for very short pulses of ultrasonic energy. The ability to use a large number of moderately long ultrasonic pulses which are coherently recorded permits the detection of very weak ultrasonic scattering regions. Thus very small faults that transmit most of the incident sound should be detectable. A transmission acoustical hologram of an object is an interferogram and thus indicates the degree of material uniformity. As an application, acoustical holograms can be used to measure uniformity before and after heat treatment.

This paper is divided into three parts: (1) experiments, (2) theoretical analysis and discussion of some properties of acoustical holograms, and (3) potential uses of acoustical holographic techniques in nondestructive testing.

EXPERIMENTS

The Acoustical Hologram

We shall give a definition of an acoustical hologram as it applies to this research program. An acoustical hologram is a two-dimensional record of the amplitude and phase of a coherent (single-frequency) ultrasonic radiation field which is generally dispersed by the stationary object to be holographed. The acoustical hologram can be used to form a three-dimensional image of the dispersing object.

The record is made in a plane which is free of radiation-dispersing (scattering) objects. Our acoustical holograms are records of coherent ultrasonic radiation recorded as photographic transparencies. When coherent light from a laser is properly incident on the acoustical hologram the original amplitude and phase pattern will be impressed on the transmitted radiation and a visible image of the object will be formed.

The ultrasonic amplitude and phase are recorded on our holograms by recording the time-averaged square of the sum of the radiation field and a mutually coherent electrical reference. This electrical reference is equivalent to the reference wave that is usually formed with a beamsplitter in conventional optical holography ([1]). Our electrical reference is equivalent to an ultrasonic plane wave propagating in a direction perpendicular to the acoustical hologram plane.

Acoustical Hologram Recorder

The acoustical hologram is recorded as shown in Figs. 1–4 ([2]). The object under observation is immersed in water and illuminated with 100-μsec pulses (repeated at a rate of 40 to 200 Hz) of 5-MHz ultrasonic radiation from a

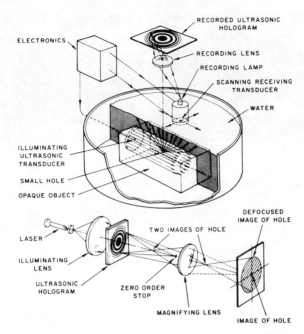

Fig. 1. Sketch of the acoustical hologram recorder and visible image formation. Top: acoustical hologram recorder. Bottom: Visible image formation.

Fig. 2. Photograph of acoustical hologram recording equipment.

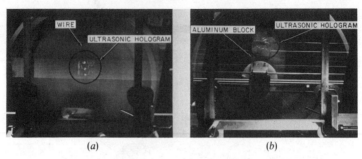

(a)   (b)

Fig. 3. Acoustical hologram recording equipment in operation. These photo-graphs show preliminary ultrasonic holograms superimposed on a view of the object being holographed, and were taken by the camera which looks into the mirror as shown in Fig. 2. (a) An ultrasonic hologram of a wire at 45° to the hologram plane superimposed on a photograph of the wire. (b) An ultra-sonic hologram of an air-filled hole at about 45° to the hologram plane super-imposed on a photograph of the block of aluminum containing the hole. The hologram is not centered over the aluminum block probably either because the block was not exactly parallel to the scan plane or the transmitting transducer was not uniformly bonded to the aluminum.

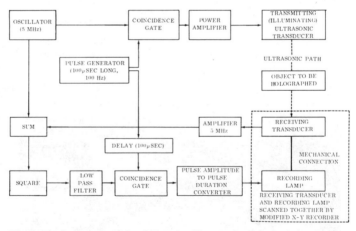

Fig. 4. Block diagram of the electronics. The numbers shown in parentheses are nominal values. Actual values were adjusted for each object holographed.

stationary, flat, 5-cm-diameter transducer. The ultrasonic illumination signal is derived from a continuously operating oscillator. The sound reflected back from the object is received by an air-backed ceramic transducer with an effec-tive diameter of approximately 0.4 mm. The receiver transducer is nominally resonant at 5 MHz. The receiver is operated with a delayed gate to isolate sound from the desired range of observation from other-sound reflecting regions. The receiving transducer is scanned in an approximate TV raster scan horizontally over the object by a modified $X-Y$ recorder. The area scanned is 30×30 cm. A complete scan takes from 15 to 90 min. This is as fast as the scanner would scan.

The reference beam for the acoustical hologram is synthesized (Fig. 4) by adding electrically to the received sound signal a portion of the signal from the 5-MHz oscillator. This sum is then squared, filtered, and used to modulate the duration of a pulse of light from a miniature tungsten filament lamp over the range from about 2 to 10 msec. The lamp is fastened to the top of the receiving transducer so that the pair maps the amplitude and phase of the sound reflected from the object to be holographed. A time exposure photograph is made of the lamp as it scans. This converts the invisible sound field into a visible hologram. The hologram is photographed at one-tenth actual size on Polaroid 55P/N film, which produces a transparent negative. This transparency is the acoustical hologram used to form the three-dimensional visible image.

The electronics, which operate over a limited dynamic range of about five to one, and the Polaroid film introduce some nonlinearities into the hologram. It is shown later that nonlinearities increase the background illumination or noise, but this is found to be unimportant in this work.

Visible Image Formation from the Acoustical Hologram

A visible image is formed from the ultrasonic hologram as shown in the lower part of Fig. 1. A helium–neon laser which produces about $\frac{1}{2}$ mW of coherent 6328 Å (red) light in the fundamental transverse mode provides enough light for convenient viewing of the image.

The hologram (Polaroid negative) is wetted with tetrahydronaphthalene and sandwiched between two optical flats to minimize phase variations due to film thickness irregularities. If the negative does not exhibit reticulation, an image can be formed without sandwiching the negative. However, this image has reduced resolution and the background has more scattered light. In general the optics shown in Fig. 1 are ordinary lenses such as small telescope objectives and thin simple senses. The three-dimensional property is readily observed by continuously moving the magnifying lens along the optical axis to focus on one part of the image or another. The effect is quite dramatic in the case of the wire (Fig. 6) and the hole in aluminum (Fig. 12) both of which were at 45° to the hologram plane. Unfortunately, the effect is not as dramatic in these still photographs taken in several planes of focus because one cannot move continuously through the plane of focus as is possible in real life or in a movie.

The images formed from the holograms can be found by merely moving the imaging lens until the image appears. Of course the position of the image can also be calculated.

When viewing the visible image formed by an acoustical hologram one generally focuses on planes parallel to the hologram plane. In conventional pulse-echo ultrasonic imaging one records an image at right angles to this plane.

Some Acoustical Holograms and Images

This section contains copies of some acoustical holograms and the images they formed. Some photographs made in coherent and incoherent light are included for comparison. The images are shown in circles which are approximately the diameter of the ultrasonic illumination. The scales shown on the ultrasonic holograms refer to the sonic field, which is ten times the size of the holograms used to form the images. Black areas on the holograms were produced when the recording lamp was on. The holographed objects were approximately 10 cm below the heavy dashed line or X drawn on the acoustical holograms. White areas in the image reflected sound.

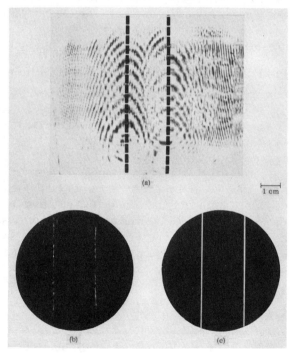

Fig. 5. Two wires parallel to the hologram plane. (a) Acoustical hologram of two wires separated by 20 mm. The wires are parallel to the hologram plane and are 1.6 mm in diameter. (b) Acoustical hologram formed image. (c) Conventional photograph.

Figures 5–12 illustrate typical resolution, three-dimensional properties, and the effect of coherent acoustical images for objects in water and a hole in an aluminum block. Compare Figs. 10–12 (the hole at 45° in aluminum) with Figs. 6 and 7 (the wire in water at 45°).

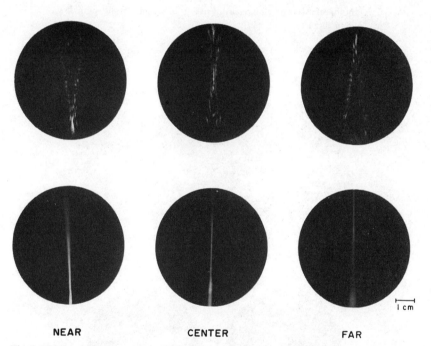

| NEAR | CENTER | FAR |

Fig. 6. The image in three planes of focus. The object is a 1.6-mm diameter wire at 45° to the hologram plane. The three images were made from the one acoustical hologram shown in Fig. 7. These images illustrate the three-dimensional properties of the acoustical hologram. Top: Acoustical hologram image of the wire in three different planes of focus: near, center, and far end of the wire, respectively. The out-of-focus pattern produced by the wire is due to the coherent sound and high numerical aperture (0.40) of the ultrasonic hologram. Bottom: Conventional photographs of the same wire to simulate the ultrasonic hologram images. The numerical aperture (0.05) was smaller, and thus the out-of-focus blur is less. Incoherent radiation gives a different out-of-focus image than coherent radiation.

Fig. 7. Acoustical hologram of a wire at 45° to the hologram plane. The near end of the wire is at the bottom. Corresponding images are shown in Fig. 6. This hologram is similar to the hologram shown being recorded in Fig. 3a except that the sound is incident from a slightly different direction.

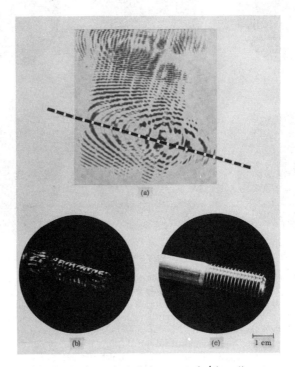

Fig. 8. (a) Acoustical hologram of $\frac{1}{2}$-in. diameter 13-threads/in. bolt. (b) Acoustical hologram image. (c) Conventional photo. The bolt was ultrasonically and optically illuminated in a similar manner with radiation incident perpendicular to the bolt axis as indicated by the highlights.

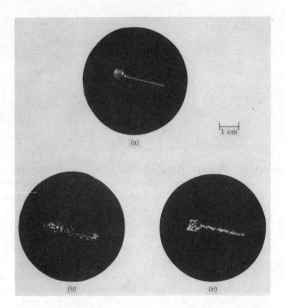

Fig. 9. Comparison of acoustical hologram images, conventional photographs, and coherent light photographs. One-inch-long bolt with knurled head, $\frac{1}{4}$-in. diameter with 20 threads/in. (a) conventional photograph made with incoherent light. (b) image made from acoustical hologram. (c) Photograph made with coherent light at a smaller numerical aperture to provide resolution approximately equal to the acoustical hologram image (b). These illustrate the speckle-like nature of images made in coherent radiation ([1,3]).

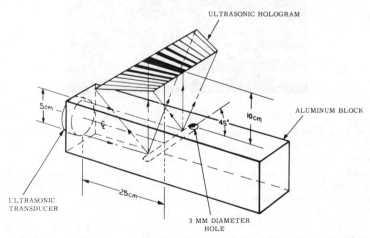

Fig. 10. Sketch of an acoustical hologram superimposed over a cylindrical hole in an aluminum block. The aluminum block is the opaque object in the water in Fig. 1. A cylindrical hole has replaced the spherical hole. This produces the cylindrical zone plate acoustical hologram shown instead of the spherical zone plate shown in Fig. 1.

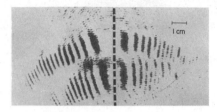

Fig. 11. Acoustical hologram of the cylindrical hole in an aluminum block. The diameter of the hole is about 3 mm. The hole is at 45° to the hologram plane. The near end of the hole is at the bottom. The relative location of the hole and acoustical hologram is shown in Fig. 10. The hole was filled with air. This hologram was made approximately as shown in Fig. 3b except that the aluminum block is not parallel to the hologram plane in Fig. 3. The comment on asymmetry for Fig. 3 also applies. The void across the center of the zone plate was produced because the center of the hole was not illuminated with sound. This happened because the hole was inadvertently drilled with its center at the last axial pressure null of the illuminating transducer ([4]). The transmitting transducer diameter is 5 cm; the ultrasonic wavelength is 1.3 mm in aluminum (at a frequency of 5 MHz) and the center of the hole is 25 cm from the illuminating transducer.

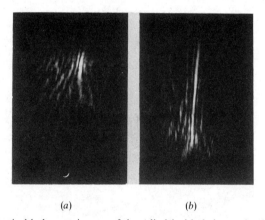

(a)   (b)

Fig. 12. Acoustical hologram images of the cylindrical hole in an aluminum block. These acoustical hologram images of the hole were made from the hologram shown in Fig. 11 with the void filled in. Ultrasonic imagery in aluminum has reduced resolution when compared to imagery in water because the ultrasonic wavelength is larger in aluminum. (a) Image of the hole in a plane parallel to the acoustical hologram plane. Only one end of the hole is in focus, corresponding to the wire shown in Fig. 6. The actual image appears quite lifelike as one continuously focuses first on one end and then the other. (b) Life-sized image of the entire cylindrical hole made by remagnifying at 45° to the hologram plane the reduced image of the hole, which is at 45° to the hologram plane. The reduced image was scaled by the acoustic-to-optical wavelength ratio. The entire cylindrical hole is now in focus at one time.

THEORETICAL ANALYSIS AND DISCUSSION OF SOME PROPERTIES OF ACOUSTICAL HOLOGRAMS

General Theory

This section presents a theoretical and numerical analysis of the acoustical holograms and the images produced in our experiments.

Let the acoustic radiation signal as received by the receiving transducer that is to be recorded as a hologram be expressed in complex form as follows:

$$p(x, y)e^{j\omega t} \tag{1}$$

where ω is the radian temporal frequency and t is time. The hologram is to be recorded in the plane $z = 0$.

Let the electrical reference, which is equivalent to a plane wave propagating perpendicular to the hologram plane, be

$$re^{j\omega t} \tag{2}$$

where r is a complex constant.

The desired complex light amplitude transmittance, $a(x, y)$, of the photographic recording of the hologram is

$$a(x, y) = |r + p(x, y)|^2 \tag{3}$$

Let the amplitude of the reference be much larger than the signal, i.e.,

$$r \gg |p(x, y)| \tag{4}$$

then

$$a(x, y) \approx |r|^2 + r^*p(x, y) + rp^*(x, y) \tag{5}$$

When this recording is illuminated by collimated coherent light the transmitted field immediately beyond the hologram consists of a plane wave with amplitude $|r|^2$, the signal field with amplitude $r^*p(x, y)$, and its complex conjugate $rp^*(x, y)$. The signal field and its complex conjugate each produce an image of the object. We will now describe these two images.

We shall illustrate the formation of an image by an acoustical hologram by an example in one dimension. Let the object consist of N points which do not obscure each other. Each point is located a moderate distance from the hologram plane at (x_n, z_n), where z_n is the depth or distance from the hologram plane. Let each point have amplitude and phase reflectivity b_n, which we will assume to be real and positive since this produces no reduction in the generality of our result. The acoustic field consists of spherical waves which will produce, to a first approximation, a signal in the plane $z = 0$

given by

$$p(x) \approx \sum_{n=1}^{N} b_n \exp j \left[\frac{\pi}{\Lambda} \frac{(x - x_n)^2}{z_n} \right] \tag{6}$$

where Λ is the wavelength of sound. Let

$$r = |r|e^{j\varphi} \tag{7}$$

then from Eq. (5)

$$a(x) = |r|^2 + 2|r| \sum_{n=1}^{N} b_n \cos \left(\frac{\pi}{\Lambda} \frac{(x - x_n)^2}{z_n} - \varphi \right) \tag{8}$$

Thus the hologram consists of a constant term which produces the undiffracted (zero order) and a sum of conventional zone plates of different amplitudes, phases, scales, and centers ([5]).

Let us consider one of these zone plates. When illuminated with collimated coherent light of wavelength Λ one zone plate produces the usual pair of diffracted orders representing real and virtual point images at (x_n, z_n) and $(x_n, -z_n)$, respectively, in addition to the zero order (undiffracted light). The zone plate produces only one pair of diffracted orders because the fringes are sinusoidal fringes and not merely the alternate transparent and opaque regions usually shown in textbooks ([5]).

In the real image plane the real image is superimposed on the zero order and the defocused virtual image. The real image will be essentially free (by geometric theory) from the superimposed defocused virtual image and zero order if the region on the hologram directly above the object which contains all the $x = x_n$ is made opaque so that the real image is formed in the shadow of the opaque region. It was found experimentally that the out-of-focus virtual image was not very objectionable. There was a noticeable loss of image quality when the center of the hologram was blocked; therefore the center was not blocked. However, the presence of the zero order which was strong because the reference was much larger than the signal, was objectionable. The zero order was removed by the stop shown in Fig. 1. The detrimental effects of the virtual image may be minimized by placing the hologram plane far from the object and increasing the hologram size by a corresponding amount to keep the angle subtended by zone plates in the hologram constant to preserve resolution.

Next we shall consider some of the effects of nonlinearities of the equipment on the image. Let us consider the difference between a "positive" and "negative" hologram, which is the difference between a positive and negative photographic print of a zone plate. From Eq. (8) we see that a negative and positive hologram can be said to differ only by $\varphi = \pi$, which is merely a relative phase shift of the reference. With the zero order removed a positive hologram and a negative hologram produce the same intensity image.

In practice the recorded hologram may not have the desired transmittance given by Eq. (3), but a nonlinear transmittance $a'(x, y)$. Let the nonlinear transmittance be expressed as a power series

$$a'(x, y) = \sum_{n=0}^{\infty} C_n [A(x, y)]^n \tag{9}$$

where the C_n are constants. The magnitudes and signs of C_0 and C_1 determine whether the hologram is a positive or negative. The terms with $n \geqslant 2$ are the nonlinear terms. By substituting Eq. (8) into the one-dimensional version of Eq. (9) we find that the effect of nonlinearities is to produce undesired zone plates which will add an undesired background to the image. Successful formation of an image from a hologram implies that the nonlinearities mentioned may be neglected. Fairly large nonlinearities were found to be tolerable.

The resolution of small detail for a specified wavelength produced by a zone plate of diameter d in the hologram is the same as a lens of the same diameter. By the Rayleigh criterion the angular resolution α is

$$\alpha = 1.22(\Lambda/d) \tag{10}$$

and the linear resolution δ is

$$\delta = 0.61\Lambda/\sin(\theta/2) \tag{11}$$

where θ is the total angle subtended from the point to the zone plate.

In our work the receiving transducer is made of a piezoelectric ceramic in which the ultrasonic longitudinal velocity is about 3.8 km/sec. Sound incident from water, where the ultrasonic velocity is 0.4 of the sonic velocity in the ceramic, is not transmitted into the receiving transducer in the longitudinal mode if β, the angle of incidence, satisfies

$$\sin \beta > 0.4, \qquad \beta > 24° \tag{12}$$

Thus the zone plates subtended a maximum total angle of 48°. The corresponding optimum resolution according to the Rayleigh criterion as given by Eq. (11) is

$$\delta = 0.5 \, \text{mm} \tag{13}$$

for an ultrasonic wavelength of 0.3 mm. The diameter of a point image measured between the first dark rings of the Airy pattern is 2δ or about 1.0 mm.

In two dimensions a point a distance z from the hologram plane produces a spherical ultrasonic wave which produces a signal with phase expressed in radians that is given exactly by

$$\gamma = \frac{2\pi z}{\Lambda}\left\{\left[1 + \left(\frac{x}{z}\right)^2\right]^{1/2} - 1\right\} \tag{14}$$

This phase was approximated in Eq. (6).

If the hologram is scaled by an arbitrary factor m so that

$$x = mx' \tag{15}$$

the resulting zone plate gives an image a distance

$$z' = \frac{\Lambda}{\lambda}\frac{z}{m^2} \tag{16}$$

from the scaled zone plate. In general, the imaging is not perfect. There is spherical aberration associated with the image. The spherical wavefront phase aberration in radians associated with the scaled image is the phase difference between a spherical wavefront and the scaled zone plate and is approximately

$$\Delta\gamma \approx \frac{\pi x^4}{4\Lambda z^3}\left[\left(\frac{\lambda m}{\Lambda}\right)^2 - 1\right] \tag{17}$$

for small phase errors. The spherical aberration is zero for perfect scaling, which is given by

$$m = \Lambda/\lambda \tag{18}$$

Correct scaling produces the same numerical aperture at both wavelengths. A three-dimensional object that was a certain number of ultrasonic wavelengths long will thus be perfectly imaged as an optical image the same number of light wavelengths long. From Eq. (18) we find

$$m = 475 \tag{19}$$

for $\Lambda = 0.3$ mm and $\lambda = 0.633\ \mu$. The reduction by 475 times made a hologram too small to remove the zero order conveniently. It was found experimentally that the holograms made directly from the scanner with $m = 10$ gave satisfactory images and were more convenient to use. In addition, one can see in Eq. (17) that slight scaling is of little value in reducing spherical aberration.

If two different wavelengths are used and the ultrasonic hologram is not scaled ($m = 1$) or if the optical image from a scaled hologram is enlarged to be life size in the x–y plane, a magnification in depth (z axis) results. From Eq. (16) a life-sized image ($m = 1$) in the x–y plane is found to be magnified in the z direction by the ratio of the ultrasonic to optical wavelengths. In our experiments the depth magnification is 475 times for the ultrasonic wavelength of 0.3 mm in water and 2000 times for the corresponding wavelength of 1.3 mm in aluminum. Depth magnification also results from conventional optical magnification and can be derived from the thin-lens formula relating image and object distance to the focal length and magnification. This depth magnification is a result of the use of two different wavelengths. The image in the $x–y$ plane is not affected by the change of wavelengths (except for the scale if the incident light is not collimated).

The following are typical parameters for our experiments:

$$z = 100 \text{ mm}, \qquad \theta = 48°, \qquad x = 40 \text{ mm}, \qquad \Lambda = 0.3 \text{ mm},$$

$$\lambda = 6.33 \times 10^{-4} \text{ mm} \tag{20}$$

The phase error given by Eq. (17) is about one wavelength or 6 radians. The major effect of this error is to increase the sidelobe amplitude. Experimentally this was found to be tolerable.

Effects of Sampling the Acoustical Hologram

Our holograms consist of discrete (although sometimes overlapping) samples taken in two spatial dimensions and in time. The effect of spatial sampling the hologram plane is similar to placing two crossed gratings with periods equal to the two spatial sampling rates over a continuously recorded hologram. When a hologram covered by crossed gratings is viewed light diffracted by the hologram is diffracted again by the gratings. The gratings must be fine enough so that undesired light diffracted by the grating remains outside of the desired beam diffracted by the hologram.

An alternative way to study the effect of sampling is to use the sampling theorem for band-limited functions. The sampling theorem says that to preserve a frequency band-limited function, samples are needed at spacings of half the smallest fringe spacing. For an acoustical hologram the finest fringe spacing is one-half an acoustic wave. The finest fringes are produced by two waves traveling in opposite directions parallel to the hologram plane. For this extreme case four samples per acoustic wavelength are required. In our experiment the finest fringe spacing is about 0.8 mm, produced by interference between sound at the angle $\beta = 24°$ measured from the normal to the hologram plane and the (strong) reference. Thus samples are taken at least every 0.4 mm.

If the acoustical hologram is scaled by the ratio of the wavelength of light to the wavelength of sound, no light will be diffracted by the sampling grating if the samples are spaced closer than every half acoustic wavelength. If the sampling is coarse or if the hologram is not scaled, light is diffracted by the sampling process. This additional light forms additional images away from the central or main image if samples are recorded as points. These extra images will generally exhibit greater optical aberrations than the main image even for evenly spaced samples. The brightness of these extra images depends upon the shape of the recorded samples. The quality of the main image is not altered significantly if the sampling rate varies slightly over the hologram plane. The effect of nonuniform sampling on the main image is similar to the effect of optical apodization or amplitude shading of an optical aperture. The effect of nonuniform sampling on the additional sampling diffracted images is more severe. Aberrations will be significant (in the images nearest the main image) if the sample spacing drifts by one half of the mean sample spacing. This drift corresponds to a diffraction grating with one half-wavelength of grating spacing error. Such a grating will produce a good "zero order" (corresponding to the main image) but produces badly aberrated "first orders" (corresponding to the sampling diffracted images).

The acoustical hologram is sampled in time because we operate the acoustical hologram recorder with pulsed acoustical illumination and a gated receiver. The pulsed mode of operation eliminates undesired acoustical reflections. The pulsed illumination is coherent with respect to the reference because the reference and illumination pulse are derived from the same oscillator. The illumination pulse is likely to be distorted because of the difficulty of generating the high power desired. However, any nonlinearly-generated acoustic frequencies present in the illumination are mostly filtered out during the generation of the hologram recording lamp signal because the nonlinearly-generated acoustic frequencies are not present in the reference.

The main effects of short illumination pulse and receiver gate durations correspond to recording a conventional optical hologram in light of a limited temporal coherence length corresponding to the overlapping portion of the pulse and gate durations. Figure 13 shows how short acoustical illumination and receiver gate durations reduce resolution by reducing the angle subtended by the zone plate recorded from a point defect. This is

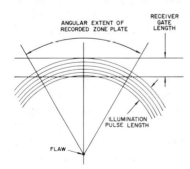

Fig. 13. The effect of range gating on the acoustical hologram. The main effect of short illumination pulse and receiver gate durations (range gating to eliminate reflections) is to limit the angle subtended by a zone plate and hence limit resolution.

exactly what happens when we record conventional optical holograms in light of limited coherence.

Properties of the Image Formed by an Acoustical Hologram

In order to understand some of the properties of the visible image formed by an acoustical hologram, we must first review some basic principles of acoustical holography. In forming the visible image from an acoustical hologram we are coherently mapping the amplitude and phase of the acoustic field into an optical field. We generally assume that the acoustic and optical fields are solutions to similar three-dimensional wave equations. Both types of waves are generally treated as scalar waves. Under these assumptions the optical field propagates exactly like the acoustic field in regions free from sources if we scale the optical field by the ratio of the acoustic wavelength to the optical wavelength. Essentially, we have a unique boundary value problem for a source-free region. The acoustical hologram is a map of the acoustical boundary values. The hologram plane is the boundary. When we illuminate the acoustical hologram we impress the acoustical boundary values onto an optical field. It is possible to show that an arbitrary optical field and acoustic field cannot be similar (except for linear scaling) throughout a volume unless their relative scales are in the ratio of their two wavelengths.

The preceding paragraph places stress on recreating an optical map of the acoustic field in a source-free region. The acoustical hologram does not and cannot know anything about the sources that originally scattered the acoustic field. For example, the acoustical hologram cannot tell if the spherical acoustic wave was scattered by a point or by a concave or convex spherical reflector (at appropriate distances). The determination of the origin of the acoustic source is made by the viewer when he "recognizes" a familiar object. When one views the image of a coherently acoustically illuminated cylinder one can move the focus from the plane of the cylinder to its center and change the image of the cylinder into a line. We cannot tell if the object is a line or a cylinder from the acoustical hologram alone.

People have a preconceived idea of what a "natural" image is. A natural image is what we are used to seeing with the unaided eye. A conventional three-dimensional optical hologram makes a natural image. A natural image is characterized by a range of depth of focus, resolution, and three-dimensional effect which we associate with an object of known size. The wavelength of the visible light plays a dominant role in determining the characteristics of a natural image. Thus the visible image made from an acoustic field for which the acoustic wavelength is much larger than the wavelength of visible light will not have the characteristics of a natural image. The differences (discussed below) are a property of the wavelength, not the application of holography. Most of the following discussion pertains to the case where the acoustical hologram wavelength is larger than the visible wavelength. We should also note that an acoustical or any other hologram (such as X-ray) for which the hologram wavelength is smaller than the optical wavelength presents a situation that is the reverse of most of the following discussion.

If we could "see" the large-wavelength acoustical image directly with our eyes, we would see natural images of low resolution. The resolution is low because of the large wavelength and low numerical aperture of the eye. But we cannot see the large acoustic wavelength and must map the image into the smaller wavelength of visible light. If we view the mapped image so that the lateral scale (in planes perpendicular to the eye's optical axis) is one-to-one, we now see an image with depth magnification which is greater than one to one. The depth magnification may be linear or a function of the depth, depending upon the optics used in viewing. We will consider primarily linear depth magnification. This is discussed in more detail later. Although the visible wavelength is smaller than the acoustic wavelength, the resolution is still low because the best normal resolution is of the order of one wavelength of the acoustic wavelength, which is readily resolved by the eye. If the optical image is scaled (reduced) by the ratio of the acoustic to the optical wavelength, an image is formed whose scale is the same in three dimensions and whose properties would be similar to the natural image if we ignore scale. The smallest resolvable detail, which was of the order of one acoustic wavelength, is now of the order of one optical wavelength in the reduced image.

We wish to view the visible image formed by an acoustical hologram in a manner that presents the most information. We feel that the most important parameter of the image is resolution, because the acoustic wavelength is already large. The image should be scaled (in the plane perpendicular to the viewer's eyes) enough so that detail as small as one acoustic wavelength can be seen. A scale of one-to-one often satisfies this requirement and presents a natural scale for the object in one plane. The one-to-one scale produces a depth magnification.

This depth magnification is objectionable because it prevents us from "seeing" the acoustical image as we see three-dimensional optical images. We will discuss how depth magnification originates and what we can and cannot do about it. The origin of the depth magnification is the change from the large acoustic wavelength to the small optical wavelength. Previously we have considered this from a mathematical viewpoint. Here we will discuss the depth magnification to gain some insight into the problem. High resolution in the acoustical domain of the order of one acoustic wavelength is mapped into similar linear resolution in the optical domain. High resolution in the acoustical domain is low resolution in the optical domain. The high numerical aperture (a large solid angle of a spherical wave for each point in the image) acoustical image becomes a low numerical aperture (small-angle) optical image. Geometric optics can now be used to show that for both the acoustical and optical domains to exhibit the same depth of focus characteristics the lower numerical aperture optical domain must have the observed depth magnification. Another way of observing the origin of depth magnification is to study the image seen in a conventional microscope with a magnification equal to the ratio of the acoustic to the optical wavelength. The image appears to have the same depth magnification that the acoustical hologram produces. Depth magnification is associated with any ordinary microscope. Depth magnification may be considered to arise because we convert a high numerical aperture image into a low numerical aperture image so that the eye may "see" the high resolution produced by the high numerical aperture. The depth of focus is preserved. For example, we cannot see along a depth of 1 mm at once under a high power microscope, although we can easily see this depth without the microscope. Thus we see that depth magnification arises from the change in wavelength and numerical aperture between the acoustical and optical domains. This change is necessary if we are to utilize the maximum acoustical resolution, because the numerical aperture of the unaided eye is low.

Next we will show that we cannot reduce depth magnification and make a perfect one-to-one visible three-dimensional image from an arbitrary acoustical image if the acoustic and optical wavelengths differ. In the previous paragraphs we have shown that a one-to-one three-dimensional image cannot be formed with optics. One can also show by wave and geometric optics that if one plane is perfectly imaged one-to-one no other plane is perfectly imaged if the wavelengths differ.

The use of lenses can be considered to be a linear operation. We will show that all attempts, even nonlinear techniques, will fail. We know the acoustic field in the hologram plane; hence we know the acoustic field everywhere in a source-free region. We ask, why can't we merely recalculate what the field would have been there if the acoustic wavelength was equal to the optical wavelength? We can recalculate what the acoustic field would have been for a new wavelength in any one plane (or other smooth curve). However, the nature of the recalculated field throughout the entire region depends upon the plane we choose for the recalculation. The chosen plane represents the source of the acoustic field. The correct plane can only be chosen if the acoustic sources (or some special properties) are known. In general, we do not know the acoustic sources (i.e., where flaws are located).

In summary, we see that the general reasons we cannot recompute a general acoustical hologram to change the wavelength are (1) we cannot have the same acoustic field throughout a volume for different wavelengths, (2) an acoustical hologram can be used to recreate an acoustic field throughout an (apparent) source-free region, and (3) we could recompute the acoustical hologram only if the locations of the sources are known, but the acoustical hologram cannot tell the source plane from any other plane (except with external information).

We have just discussed why an acoustical (hologram) image of an object appears the way it does and what one can and cannot do about it. In the light of this previous discussion we will discuss ways to view the acoustical (hologram) image. We should use optics to make an aberration-free one-to-one image (in a plane perpendicular to the viewer's optical axis) (Fig. 12). The image can be a real image projected on a screen or a virtual image projected directly into the viewer's eye. A virtual image might be viewed in an optical instrument similar to a microscope. The optics should be designed by modern computer lens-design methods to compensate for any optical aberrations that might result from the use of acoustical hologram technique ([6]). The viewer focuses on different planes by moving suitable lenses and/or the acoustical hologram. It is possible to arrange the focusing so that the hand moves through a proper one-to-one depth corresponding to the change in focus. The focused image plane (real or virtual) could also be moved an amount corresponding to the change in focus. If the planes of focus and image are moved together rapidly, a pseudo three-dimensional image will result. A beam splitter or second hologram could be used to insert a three-dimensional visible scale (in the same or another color light) to allow measurements to be made. The previous techniques could be combined in a binocular microscope in which each eye sees (predominantly) the image formed by one half of the acoustical hologram. This will produce some parallax with only a little loss of resolution. The purpose of these viewing techniques is to make it easier for the viewer to interpret the acoustical image. For example, we wish to make it easy for the viewer to identify and locate flaws in a noisy environment.

POTENTIAL USES OF ACOUSTICAL HOLOGRAPHIC TECHNIQUES IN NONDESTRUCTIVE TESTING

A number of techniques employing a variety of different types of energy have been used to image the interior of optically opaque objects for the purpose of nondestructive testing. Possibly the first widely accepted method of industrial nondestructive testing, radiography, was begun in 1924 at the Watertown Arsenal under Dr. H. H. Lester as a hard application of medical X-ray techniques. Nondestructive testing rapidly grew to be an indispensable tool in quality control, embracing other generalized imaging techniques including those using magnetic particles, penetrants, ultrasonics, eddy currents, microwaves, and within the last five years or so, infrared and thermal imaging techniques. Each of these approaches has an optimum application, and many of these techniques can augment or reinforce the findings of other methods. No one technique has yet been developed that is universal in application, but with each advance more small gaps are closed in the state of the art.

But there are more gaps to be filled, and one is the inability to actually "see" inside an optically opaque specimen to evaluate the internal structure in terms of its various possible good or bad characteristics.

Much has been accomplished only in very recent years in the field of imagery, even though the basic concepts of Sokolov and others date back to the 1920's. Most recently, Gericke and Grubinskas ([7]) reported the development of an ultrasonic imaging technique using the liquid surface levitation effect, which does not require the specimen itself to be immersed.

In the materials testing field the newest and most sophisticated imaging system, acoustical holography, now shows promise. The theory is sound, the promise is high, but the art is in its infancy. Present experimental methods are slow and require immobility of the system components while making the hologram. However, these and other limitations are not considered to be insurmountable, and in view of the potential benefits developmental work should continue.

In conventional ultrasonic testing a small flaw can be in the shadow of a larger flaw (or deliberately made void) and will go undetected. The term "flaw" in this instance may be misleading because it might suggest that the larger flaw would be sufficient cause for rejection, so that the presence of a hidden smaller flaw would be only of academic interest. This is not necessarily so.

For example, in a specimen consisting of two materials bonded together (Fig. 14) one material could contain a void that is acceptable. But if a perfect bond is necessary and an area of lack of adhesive smaller than the void is located behind the void, it is unlikely that the bond flaw would be detected

Fig. 14. An application of acoustical holography to nondestructive testing. A conventional pulse-echo ultrasonic transducer receives no signal from the flaw because the flaw is in the shadow of the (narrow angular) ultrasonic beam. The acoustical hologram recording transducer receives a signal from the flaw because of the large angular response of the point transducer used. The viewer can focus the acoustical hologram image to provide resolution equal to or greater than that which the larger conventional transducer provides.

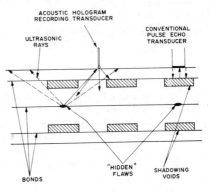

using conventional ultrasonic test methods. The concealed flaw would be expected to stand out readily in the holographic image, having been recorded in the hologram by the scattering of the ultrasound from behind the shadow area of the larger flaw.

The application of holographic techniques to ultrasonic imaging appears to be useful for several other reasons. Holographic techniques provide a permanent two-dimensional record of a three-dimensional object. Very weakly reflecting defects located throughout a large volume should be detectable with good lateral and depth resolution. This is possible because holographic techniques permit the use of a large number of moderately long ultrasonic pulses from a range of positions. The pulses are coherently recorded. This is opposed to pulse-echo techniques, which, in general, can use only very short pulses from one position. These pulses are incoherently recorded.

One acoustical hologram provides high resolution throughout a depth determined by the maximum permissible time-gated range. This is in contrast to direct ultrasonic imaging with ultrasonic optics, which must be accurately focused to form a high-resolution image. For example, with one hologram one can look with high resolution throughout a 100 mm (or greater) depth instead of only a 1 or 2 mm depth as with one direct ultrasonic image.

A transmission acoustical hologram of an object is an interferogram and thus indicates the degree of material uniformity.

A problem is caused by the refraction and reflection of sound at curved surfaces and by internal defects. This is similar to viewing optically several air bubbles inside of a thick piece of curved transparent nonuniform glass. One can usually see the bubbles, but their shape is distorted and some may be obscured. Time-gating to select the range of interest will minimize the detrimental effects of reflections and extraneous scattered sound.

In conclusion, we feel that the application of holographic techniques to the field of ultrasonic nondestructive testing shows a potential of improved sensitivity and resolution as compared to direct ultrasonic imaging. We expect that (after further research) ultrasonic holographic imaging techniques will be profitably applied to nondestructive testing.

REFERENCES

1. E. M. Leith and J. Upatnieks, Photography by Laser, *Sci. Am.* **212**:6, June 1965.
2. K. Preston, Jr. and J. L. Kreuzer, Ultrasonic Imaging Using a Synthetic Holographic Technique, *Appl. Phys. Letters* **10**:150–152 (Mar. 1967).
3. B. M. Oliver, Sparkling Spots and Random Diffraction, *Proc. IEEE* **51**(1):220–221 (Jan. 1963).
4. L. E. Kinsler and A. R. Frey, *Fundamentals of Acoustics*, 2nd ed., John Wiley and Sons, New York, 1962, pp. 175–177.

5. F. A. Jenkins and H. E. White, *Fundamentals of Optics*, McGraw-Hill Book Co., New York, 1957, pp. 360–361.
6. A. Offner, Ray Tracing Through a Holographic System, *J. Opt. Soc. Am.* **56**:1509–12 (1966).
7. O. Gericke and R. Grubinskas, Utilization of the Liquid Surface Levitation Effect as a Means of Ultrasonic Image Conversion for Materials Inspection, presented at the 74th Meeting of the Acoustical Society of America, Miami Beach, Fla., Nov. 1967.

Chapter 6

APPLICATION OF FOURIER TRANSFORMS IN ASSESSING THE PERFORMANCE OF AN ULTRASONIC HOLOGRAPHY SYSTEM

J. M. Smith and N. F. Moody

Institute of Bio-Medical Electronics
University of Toronto, Ontario, Canada

It has been found that the Fourier transform is a useful tool for determining some of the properties of ultrasonic holograms and of the scanning systems which are used to generate them. Consideration of events in the frequency domain allows graphical representations of the effect of system parameters to be made, and using the association between frequency components and resolution the corresponding effects in the spatial domain can be appreciated. Calculation of the impulse response of an ultrasonic holography system and evaluation of the Fourier transform of the hologram indicate criteria which may be used for assessing the maximum useful frequency passing through an aperture from a point source. Experimental results show that the observed attenuation of high-frequency components in the Fourier transform agrees reasonably well with the above criteria. They also justify the use of the spatial frequency of an extreme ray as the maximum frequency of interest. Applying these concepts to an extended object allows us to describe it by a spatial frequency spectrum. Its bandwidth in any particular hologram can be determined from a study of the Fourier transform, which makes it possible to visualize each component of the hologram in terms of a characteristic spatial frequency. For faithful reproduction the image spectra should be isolated, thus specifying the necessary carrier frequency and sampling rate. Other disturbances to which the Fourier transform is subject as it is processed by the scanning and recording system have been calculated. The operations upon the signal from the time it is detected in the sound plane to the stage where it is recorded on film are considered, and the effects of such parameters as detector and light-source apertures, scanning frequency, and scaling ratio are discussed in terms of the frequency domain.

INTRODUCTION

A good many of the ultrasonic holography systems described in the literature ([1-5]) have employed a scanning system to produce the hologram, the process being used to replace the exposure of a photographic plate in conventional optical holography. Scanning introduces another degree of freedom to ultrasonic holography which is not present in its optical counterpart. It allows, for instance, the introduction of electrical reference beams and other data processing techniques, such as analog-to-digital conversion, for computer reconstruction. Although scanning is time consuming, it is apparent that it will continue to be used to investigate the holographic process.

In this chapter we consider some of the effects of the scanning system on the final hologram and attempt to provide some answers as to how the resolution and image quality will be affected. Quite often a more penetrating insight into this aspect of the subject can be gained by working in the frequency domain rather than in the spatial domain, and consequently we will begin by establishing a criterion by which an estimate of the maximum frequency in a hologram can be obtained.

A CRITERION FOR THE MAXIMUM FREQUENCY IN A HOLOGRAM

Consider the simple ultrasonic holographic system shown in Fig. 1, which uses for an object a small diameter hole. If this hole has a diameter of the order of one wavelength, the emerging wavefront can be considered spherical with constant amplitude over an aperture which is small compared to the object–H-plane distance. Based on the above assumptions, the phase

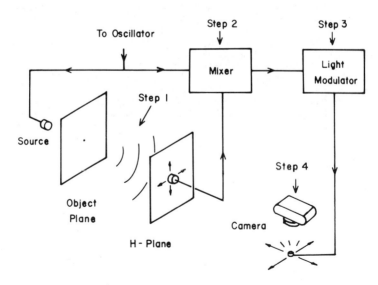

Fig. 1. A basic scanned hologram system.

at any point on the H-plane with respect to the origin may be written as

$$\varphi(x, y) = k[(x^2 + y^2 + R^2)^{\frac{1}{2}} - R]$$

$$= k\left[\frac{x^2 + y^2}{2R} - \frac{(x^2 + y^2)^2}{8R^3} + \cdots\right]$$

where the origin of the coordinate system (x, y, z) is at the hole in the object plane and the H-plane is located at $z = R$. Here $k = 2\pi/\lambda$. In the practical case to be studied $(x^2 + y^2)_{max} = 193$ cm^2 and $R = 42$ cm, which makes the second and subsequent terms negligible with respect to the first.

Assuming the obliquity factor to be negligible, the amplitude distribution across the H-plane becomes

$$h(x, y) = h_0 \exp[-jk(x^2 + y^2)/2R] \tag{1}$$

This is added to an electrical signal which simulates a plane parallel reference beam, $f(x, y) = f_0$. The sum is then a signal the amplitude of which is used to modulate the intensity of a light source. The equation of the holo- gram obtained by photographing this light source as it moves in synchronism with the scanner may be written in the form

$$t(x, y) = f_0^2 + |h(x, y)|^2 + f_0 h_0 \exp\left[-jk\frac{(x^2 + y^2)}{2R}\right]$$

$$+ f_0 h_0 \exp\left[+jk\frac{(x^2 + y^2)}{2R}\right]$$

$$= f_0^2 + |h(x, y)|^2 + 2f_0 h_0 \cos k\frac{(x^2 + y^2)}{2R} \tag{2}$$

No aperture restrictions have yet been imposed. In order to do this, the function $t(x, y)$ must be multiplied by another function $a(x, y)$, where

$$a(x, y) = 1, \qquad |x| \leqslant x_0, \qquad |y| \leqslant y_0$$
$$a(x, y) = 0, \qquad |x| > x_0, \qquad |y| > y_0 \tag{3}$$

the coordinates $\pm x_0, \pm y_0$ defining the extremities of the aperture. For this to be a valid experiment the aperture must be the limiting factor (not system parameters, whose effect will be discussed later). The dimensions of the aperture then limit the final theoretical resolution in the reconstructed image. Thus the hologram equation becomes

$$t_a(x, y) = a(x, y)f_0^2 + a(x, y)|h(x, y)|^2 + 2f_0 h_0 a(x, y) \cos k\frac{(x^2 + y^2)}{2R} \tag{4}$$

The hologram corresponding to this equation is shown in Fig. 2a, where the characteristic Fresnel zone plate structure is evident. Some irregularities

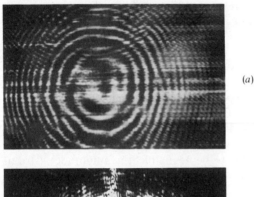

(a)

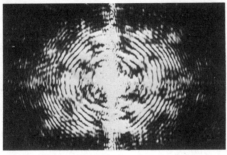

(b)

Fig. 2. (a) Hologram of a pinhole with a parallel reference beam. (b) The Fourier transform of the hologram shown in (a).

can be detected in the central area, due to the nature of the illuminating source. A small amount of backlash in the scanning mechanism caused the relative horizontal displacement of adjacent scanning lines.

Taking the Fourier transform of Eq. (2) according to

$$T(\xi, \eta) = \int\limits_{-\infty}^{+\infty}\!\!\int t(x, y) \exp[-jk(\xi x + \eta y)] \, dx \, dy$$

where ξ and η are spatial frequency variables, we find that

$$T(\xi, \eta) = T_1 \sin \frac{\lambda R}{4\pi}(\xi^2 + \eta^2) + T_0 \, \delta(\xi, \eta) \tag{5}$$

where $T_0 \, \delta(\xi, \eta)$ represents the DC term, i.e., an impulse at the origin. Using the convolution theorem with Eq. (4), the Fourier transform of the third term, i.e., the image term, of the aperture-limited hologram can now be described as

$$T_A(\xi, \eta) = A(\xi, \eta) * T_1 \sin \frac{\lambda R}{4\pi}(\xi^2 + \eta^2) \tag{6}$$

where

$$A(\xi, \eta) = F\{a(x, y)\} = 4x_0 y_0 \left(\frac{\sin \xi x_0}{\xi x_0}\right)\left(\frac{\sin \eta y_0}{\eta y_0}\right)$$

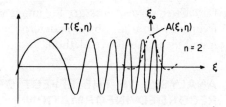

Fig. 3. Illustration of the convolution described by Eq. (6). In this case the number of "cycles" under the aperture function is given by $n = 2$.

The physical implications of this convolution can be best understood by the representation in Fig. 3, where for simplicity the problem has been reproduced in one dimension. As ξ becomes large the value of the convolution decreases because the number of "cycles" of the hologram function occurring beneath the aperture function becomes larger, resulting in a reduced net sum. The periodicity, however, remains the same. It is convenient to assign a number n, to the number of "cycles" included under the aperture function when the magnitude of $T_A(\xi, \eta)$ is sufficiently small. This places an upper bound ξ_0 on the frequency spectrum, which may be written as a function of n by calculating the period at ξ_0 as the inverse of the instantaneous frequency, multiplying by n, and equating to the width of the main lobe of the aperture function. Then

$$\xi_0 = 2\pi n x_0 / \lambda R \tag{7}$$

To obtain a practical value for n the Fourier Transform of the hologram of Fig. 2a was optically generated in the conventional manner ([7]). This is shown in Fig. 2b.

Note that the higher frequency components do decay in amplitude as expected. Measurement of the frequency corresponding to negligible intensity in the outer areas gives a value for $n = 0.94$. Thus in this particular case the value of ξ_0 becomes

$$\xi_0 = 2\pi(0.94)x_0 / \lambda R$$

One criterion that has been used for maximum frequency is the frequency of an extreme ray, i.e.,

$$\xi_0 = \max\left(\frac{2\pi x_0}{\lambda R}, \frac{2\pi y_0}{\lambda R}\right) \qquad y_0 \ll R, \quad x_0 \ll R \tag{8}$$

Note that this corresponds to $n = 1$, which represents a frequency slightly higher than that actually measured, and is thus a justifiably useful criterion.

Any object may be regarded as a series of points, and the hologram of it is the superposition of many Fresnel zone plates. Thus the maximum useful frequency in the hologram is the maximum frequency through the aperture coming from an extreme point. Note that the point concept does not allow for carrier waves necessary for image separation. Thus when the maximum frequency from an object is determined this carrier must be added to that found using the above method.

ANALYSIS OF THE EFFECT OF SCANNING SYSTEM ON RECORDED INFORMATION

So far the discussion has been centered around the frequency components of the final hologram and how an estimate of the maximum values can be assessed. A basic assumption was a perfect recording system, transition from the sound plane to the final hologram being effected without loss of information. Usually, however, an ultrasonic hologram is made in a series of steps and it is useful to understand how each of these steps affects the final frequency spectrum. Consider the system of Fig. 1, where the process has been divided into four steps: Step 1: Recording of the sound signal in the H-plane. Step 2: Addition of an electrical reference beam. Step 3: Modulation of a light source. Step 4: Recording of light source movements on film to give the final hologram. A quantitative approach to the problem of system analysis falls into these four categories and each will be treated in turn.

Step 1. Recording of the Sound Signal in the H-Plane. First some assumptions and observations:

1. The detector has a circular aperture which is sufficiently small to accept sound waves from all angles of interest.
2. Scanning is continuous in the x direction and discrete in the y direction.
3. The electrical signal produced by the detector will be the average of the function in the H-plane over the detector aperture.
4. The H-plane function $h(x, y)$ is considered to be aperture-limited. Resolution caused by finite apertures may be readily calculated using Rayleigh's criterion ([6]), which gives the theoretical limit. Our present concern is with practical limitations caused by system parameters.

If the signal produced by the detector when positioned at (x, y) is $d(x, y)$, statement (3) says in effect

$$d(x, y) \propto \underset{\substack{\text{Detector} \\ \text{aperture}}}{\int \int} h(\alpha, \beta) \, d\alpha \, d\beta \qquad (9)$$

At any point (x, y) the detector aperture may be described by the function

$$r_1(\alpha - x, \beta - y) = 1, \qquad (\alpha - x)^2 + (\beta - y)^2 \leqslant C_1^2$$
$$= 0, \qquad (\alpha - x)^2 + (\beta - y)^2 > C_1^2 \qquad (10)$$

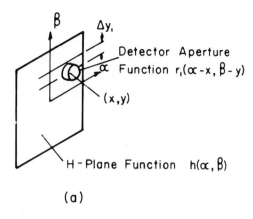

(a)

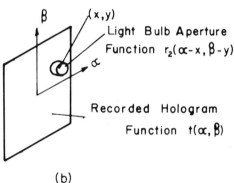

(b)

Fig. 4. (a) Derivation of the electrical signal $d(x, y)$ from a finite-aperture detector scanning the H-plane. The final signal is a function of (x, y), the coordinates (α, β) being dummy variables. (b) The final hologram is produced by a scanning light source, which produces an intensity distribution over an area described by $r_2(\alpha - x, \beta - y)$ for the signal corresponding to each point (x, y) in the H-plane.

where C_1 is the radius of the detector aperture as shown in Fig. 4a. Now $d(x, y)$ becomes

$$d(x, y) \propto \int\int_{-\infty}^{+\infty} h(\alpha, \beta)r_1(\alpha - x, \beta - y)d\alpha \, d\beta \qquad (11)$$

One other thing to remember is that due to scanning $d(x, y)$ is defined for only discrete values of y. Hence the above integral must be multiplied by a function $\delta_{\Delta y_1}(y)$ which represents a series of sampling planes $y = m \Delta y_1$ ($m = 0, \pm 1, \dots \pm n$), i.e.,

$$d(x, y) \propto \delta_{\Delta y_1}(y) \int\int_{-\infty}^{+\infty} h(\alpha, \beta)r_1(\alpha - x, \beta - y) \, d\alpha \, d\beta$$

Since $r_1(x, y)$ is an even function, this may be rewritten as a convolution

$$d(x, y) \propto \delta_{\Delta y_1}(y)[h(x, y) * r_1(x, y)] \qquad (12)$$

The result of Step 1 then is an electrical signal which is a function of x and is defined only for discrete values of y.

Step 2. Addition of an Electrical Reference Beam. The result of this step is to produce a new signal

$$s(x, y) = f(x, y) + d(x, y) \tag{13}$$

where $f(x, y)$ is the electrical reference beam.

Step 3. Modulation of the Light Source. It must be remembered that the quantities $d(x, y)$ and $f(x, y)$ have associated with them a time-dependent component $e^{j\omega t}$ which, as is normal practice, has been suppressed in the calculation. The signal $s(x, y)$ is the sum of two phasors $f(x, y)$ and $d(x, y)$, and the amplitude of the resultant phasor may be written

$$[s(x, y)s(x, y)^*]^{1/2} = \{[f(x, y) + d(x, y)][f(x, y) + d(x, y)]^*\}^{1/2} \tag{14}$$

Note the amplitude of this phasor is a function of (x, y) only, and in practice this signal may be realized by rectifying the signal $s(x, y)$, thus removing the

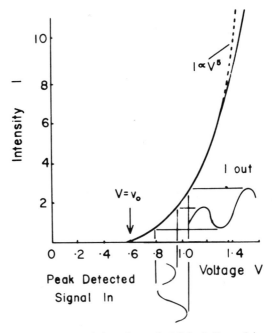

Fig. 5. Characteristics of a typical light bulb used in practice. The curve $I \propto V^5$ is superimposed for comparison. The output due to a rectified input signal $(ss^*)^{1/2}$ is shown. Intensity is designated in arbitrary units.

understood time dependence $e^{j\omega t}$. This signal, after any necessary amplification, is used to modulate the intensity of a light source.

Before continuing it is appropriate to consider some light-bulb characteristics. The measured characteristics of a bulb used in practice are shown in Fig. 5. These characteristics were found to agree very closely with the equation $I \propto V^5$, which is shown superimposed. In addition, it is assumed that the response of the light intensity is sufficiently good to follow variations in $[s(x, y)s(x, y)^*]^{1/2}$. This is of course a criterion of its usefulness. The characteristics show that considerable voltage is necessary to reach a threshold of zero intensity, and rather than waste signal here an external bias $V = v_0$ is supplied.

Thus the signal across the bulb is $[s(x, y)s(x, y)^*]^{1/2} + v_0$, which is converted to an intensity

$$I(x, y) \propto [[s(x, y)s(x, y)^*]^{1/2} + v_0]^5$$

$$\propto v_0^5 + 5v_0^4(ss^*)^{1/2} + 10v_0^3(ss^*) + 10v_0^2(ss^*)^{3/2}$$

$$+ 5v_0(ss^*)^2 + (ss^*)^{5/2} \tag{15}$$

If $|f(x, y)| \gg |d(x, y)|$, i.e., the depth of modulation is low, then using practical values, as indicated in Fig. 5, v_0^5 is relatively small compared to other terms and may be neglected. The remaining terms are each of the form

$$\text{const}(ss^*)^{n/2} = \text{const}(|f|^2 + dd^* + fd^* + f^*d)^{n/2} \qquad n = 1, 2, 3, 4, 5$$

Once again, if $|f(x, y)| \gg |d(x, y)|$, then regardless of the value of n this may be written in the form*

$$b_0|f|^2 + b_1 dd^* + b_2 fd^* + b_3 f^*d$$

where the b_i are constants which are dependent on n.

Thus $I(x, y)$ may be written in the form

$$I(x, y) \propto b_0'|f|^2 + b_2' dd^* + b_2' fd^* + b_3' f^*d \tag{16}$$

where the b_i' are redefined constants.

The net result of Step 3 then is to produce, via the light bulb, an intensity $I(x, y)$ which contains data about the function $h(x, y)$ at the point (x, y). It is also noted at this stage that the intensity function has a form similar to the equation describing an optical hologram.

---

*Other methods of detection have been used, one of particular interest being phase detection([5]). Here the two product terms only are generated, which means the restriction $|f(x, y)| \gg |d(x, y)|$ is no longer meaningful. Use of feedback ([5]) to obtain a linear intensity–voltage characteristic means that the product terms, $fd^* + f^*d$, only will be produced at the output. The elimination of spurious terms means a much purer hologram, to which the present analysis applies equally well.

Step 4. Recording of Light Source Movements on Film to Give the Final Hologram. This final step is achieved by placing the light source behind an aperture and causing it to scan in synchronism with the detector, a camera being used to photograph both movements and intensity variations. Assuming the film plane is the same size as the *H*-plane (if this is not so, the film plane may be referred to the *H*-plane using suitable scaling factors), at a given detector location (x, y) the film will be illuminated by a circle of light with intensity $I(x, y)$, and as a function of the film plane coordinates (α, β), the intensity may be described as

$$I_1(\alpha, \beta) = I(x, y)r_2(\alpha - x, \beta - y) \tag{17}$$

where

$$r_2(\alpha - x, \beta - y) = 1, \qquad (\alpha - x)^2 + (\beta - y)^2 \leqslant C_2^2$$
$$= 0, \qquad (\alpha - x)^2 + (\beta - y)^2 > C_2^2 \tag{18}$$

where C_2 is the radius of the light source aperture. The transmittance function, $t(\alpha, \beta)$, of the developed film can be written in terms of the intensity incident upon the film and the γ of the process,

$$t(\alpha, \beta) \propto I_1(\alpha, \beta)^\gamma$$

As x varies across one line of the scan the transmittance function will be

$$t(\alpha, \beta) \propto \int_{1\,\text{line}} I_1(\alpha, \beta)^\gamma \, dx \tag{19}$$

and adding the effect of all lines,

$$t(\alpha, \beta) \propto \iint_{H\text{-plane}} I_1(\alpha, \beta)^\gamma \, dx \, dy \tag{20}$$

Substituting Eq. (17)

$$t(\alpha, \beta) \propto \int\!\!\int_{-\infty}^{+\infty} I(x, y)^\gamma r_2(\alpha - x, \beta - y)^\gamma \, dx \, dy$$

$$\propto I(\alpha, \beta)^\gamma * r_2(\alpha, \beta)^\gamma \tag{21}$$

the change in limits being allowable since $I(x, y)$ is zero outside the *H*-plane. It is assumed here that the transmittance function is cumulative in an additive fashion upon successive exposures.* In addition, if $|f(x, y)| \gg |d(x, y)|$,

$$I(\alpha, \beta)^\gamma \propto b_0''|f|^2 + b_1''dd^* + b_2''fd^* + b_3''f^*d$$

---

*This is true if the film is operated in a linear region of its transmittance–exposure curve, in which case $\gamma = 1$.

and since $r_2(\alpha, \beta)$ is a constant, $r_2(\alpha, \beta)^\gamma$ is also constant, $\therefore$

$$t(\alpha, \beta) \propto (b_0''|f|^2 + b_1''dd^* + b_2''fd^* + b_3''f^*d) * r_2(\alpha, \beta) \qquad (22)$$

which describes the transmittance of the total recorded hologram. This completes Step. 4.

ANALYSIS IN THE FOURIER TRANSFORM DOMAIN

So far all calculations have been carried out in the spatial domain. The effect of the various convolutions is difficult to visualize. Interpretation is made somewhat easier by treatment in the frequency domain. The transition can be effected smoothly by taking the Fourier transforms of important results. These are summarized step by step in Table 1 and illustrated in Figs. 6 and 7.

Table I
Transformation of Results into the Frequency Domain

	Space domain	Frequency domain†
Step 1:		
Functions	$r_1(x, y)$	$R_1(\xi, \eta) = \dfrac{2J_1[C_1(\xi^2 + \eta^2)^{1/2}]}{C_1(\xi^2 + \eta^2)^{1/2}}$
	$h(x, y)$	$H(\xi, \eta)$
	$\delta_{\Delta y_1}(y)$	$\delta_{2\pi/\Delta y_1}(\eta)$
Result	$d(x, y) \propto \delta_{\Delta y_1}(y)[h(x, y) * r_1(x, y)]$	$D(\xi, \eta) \propto \delta_{2\pi/\Delta y_1}(\eta) * [H(\xi, \eta)R_1(\xi, \eta)]$
		(see Fig. 6)
Step 2:		
Result	$s(x, y) = f(x, y) + d(x, y)$	$S(\xi, \eta) = F(\xi, \eta) + D(\xi, \eta)$
Step 3:		
Result	$I(x, y) \propto b_0'|f|^2 + b_1'dd^*$	$I(\xi, \eta) \propto b_0'\delta + b_1'D * D_-^*$
	$+ b_2'fd^* + b_3'f^*d$	$+ b_2'F * D_-^* + b_3'F_-^* * D$
Step 4:		
Function	$r_2(x, y)$	$R_2(\xi, \eta) = \dfrac{2J_1[C_2(\xi^2 + \eta^2)^{1/2}]}{C_2(\xi^2 + \eta^2)^{1/2}}$
Result	$t(\alpha, \beta) \propto (b_0''|f|^2 + b_1''dd^*$	$T(\xi, \eta) \propto [\underbrace{b_0''\delta + b_1''D * D_-^*}_{\text{zero order}}$
	$+ b_2''fd^* + b_3''f^*d) * r_2(\alpha, \beta)$	$+ \underbrace{b_2''F * D_-^*}_{\text{conjugate}} + \underbrace{b_3''F_-^* * D}_{\text{virtual}}]R_2(\xi, \eta)$
		(see Fig. 7)

†Note: $\delta = \delta(\xi, \eta) =$ DC (zero-frequency) term; $D_-^* = D^*(-\xi, -\eta)$; $F_-^* = F^*(-\xi, -\eta)$. Aperture functions have been normalized with respect to the aperture area.

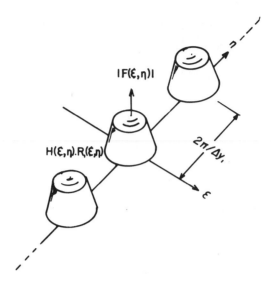

Fig. 6. The function $D(\xi, \eta)$ represents the original object spectrum $H(\xi, \eta)$ attenuated by the detector aperture function $R(\xi, \eta)$. The multiplicity is due to scanning, and for separation of the spectra $2\pi/\Delta y_1$ must be greater than the bandwidth of the object spectrum.

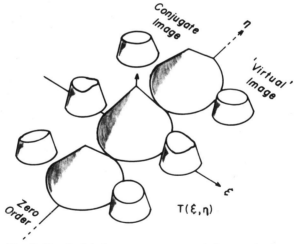

Fig. 7. The final hologram spectrum according to the last frequency-domain equation of Table I. In this case the zero-order component due to intermodulation terms is shown. This term, which has twice the spectral bandwidth of the object, determines the carrier frequency. Note the attenuation of the image terms along the ξ axis due to the finite light-bulb aperture function.

It is now evident that the function $D(\xi, \eta)$ reproduces the object spectrum with an attenuation caused by multiplication with the detector aperture function. A multiplicity of spectra will be produced due to scanning in the horizontal direction (Fig. 6). Further processing introduces second-order terms which may be suppressed if $|f(x, y)| \gg |d(x, y)|$. Intermodulation terms are also introduced which may be spatially separated from the object spectrum components by the use of a carrier, either on the object beam or on the electrical reference beam (Fig. 7). The light-bulb aperture causes some further attenuation according to the last frequency-domain equation in Table I, the overall effect being displayed in Fig. 7.

Some interesting conclusions may be drawn from this:

1. In deciding upon a detector aperture, a compromise must be made between sensitivity and frequency spectrum requirements. To utilize the available spectrum space as efficiently as possible, the object should be recorded about zero frequency (Fig. 8).

2. The scanning frequency must be sufficiently large that spectral components due to sampling will be separated (Fig. 6). This will depend on the nature of the object to be recorded.

3. The peak detection of the sum signal leading to intermodulation terms $|f|^2 + dd^*$ puts a constraint upon the carrier frequency. It must have a value at least $(3/2)W$, where W is the spectral bandwidth of the object. If phase detection is used, the zero-order terms are eliminated, but the DC (zero-frequency) component exists. The carrier need only be slightly greater than $\frac{1}{2}W$. This allows more spectral space for the final image spectra, which is especially important in view of the effect of the light-bulb aperture.

4. Ideally, the light-bulb aperture should be made as small as possible as this affects the image spectra after they have been placed upon a carrier (Fig. 7). Thus the lower the carrier can be made without interfering with the other components, the better.

PRACTICAL APPLICATIONS

Conclusions made so far have been of qualitative nature, and an attempt will now be made to assign some numbers. For any given object the maximum frequency striking the hologram plane can be described by

$$\xi_{max} = (2\pi/\lambda) \sin \theta_{max}$$

where θ_{max} is the maximum angle between the horizontal and the line joining an object point and a point on the hologram plane. The result is restricted to one dimension only. As the carrier is usually a function of ξ only, this direction is most critical. The bandwidth product $\xi_{max}\lambda$ is then solely a function of the geometry. The aperture functions of interest

$$R_1(\xi) = 2J_1(\xi C_1)/\xi C_1, \qquad R_2(\xi) = 2J_1(\xi C_2)/\xi C_2$$

can also be written as a function of $\xi\lambda$,

$$R_1(\xi\lambda) = \frac{2J_1[\xi\lambda(C_1/\lambda)]}{\xi\lambda(C_1/\lambda)}$$

$$R_2(\xi\lambda) = \frac{2J_1[\xi\lambda(C_2/\lambda)]}{\xi\lambda(C_2/\lambda)} \tag{23}$$

There are three ways of recording a hologram : (1) With the object axis on the hologram axis (in-line), the carrier being added with an electrical reference beam. (2) With the carrier superimposed upon the object beam (off-axis holography), with square law detection of the sum signal. (3) As in (2) but with phase detection, thus eliminating the zero order.

These conditions are illustrated in Fig. 8. The object bandwidth that can be recorded under each of these conditions will now be considered. First, it is necessary to establish a criterion as to how much attenuation (in frequency space) due to the apertures can be tolerated. No experiments have been carried out to assess this, but a figure of 0.6 has been arbitrarily chosen. This will be caused by the combined contributions of the apertures.

Curves for the above three cases have been calculated as follows: (1) The maximum allowable object bandwidth product for a given attenuation of the highest component is calculated as a function of C_1/λ using Eq. (23).

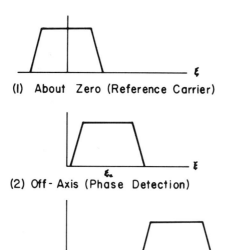

(I)   About   Zero   (Reference   Carrier)

(2) Off - Axis   (Phase   Detection)

(3) Off - Axis (Square   Law   Detection)

Fig. 8. Three possible ways of recording an ultrasonic hologram. In the final analysis a combination of (1) and (2) is most efficient, as the effect of both apertures is then minimized.

(2) Assuming we already know the attenuation due to the detector, the attenuation due to the light-bulb aperture referred to the hologram plane is calculated, making the total attenuation equal to 0.6, and this value is used to determine C_2/λ, which is then a parameter on the curve described in (1). Note that the value of C_2/λ will depend on the magnitude of the carrier introduced to give image separation.

The curves may be used as follows : (1) From system geometry determine the bandwidth product $\xi_{max}\lambda = 2\pi \sin \theta_{max}$. (2) Use this figure to determine a detector aperture and light-bulb aperture, using the curve applicable to the recording method. If a total attenuation of 0.6 is too large, curves may be redrawn using any other desired figure. Note that as detector aperture is reduced, so is the sensitivity, and thus a compromise must be made.

An example is shown in Fig. 9. Three curves have been drawn corresponding to the three recording methods. In all cases the detector aperture

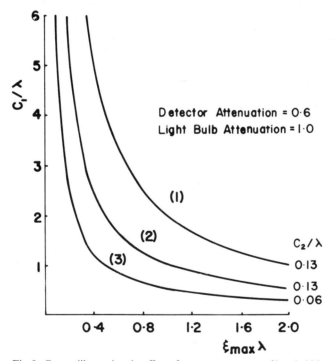

Fig. 9. Curves illustrating the effect of system parameters of bandwidth product $\xi_{max}\lambda$ for the three cases of Fig. 8. In case (1) the parameter C_2/λ is calculated for the insertion of a carrier according to the requirements of phase detection (i.e., no zero-order terms). The relationship between recording method and sensitivity (C_1/λ) for a given $\xi_{max}\lambda$ is readily apparent.

attenuation is 0.6 and the light-bulb aperture is made sufficiently small that virtually no attenuation results. However, if conditions warrant, the attenuation may be divided between the two apertures in any desired ratio.

SUMMARY

An experiment for establishing that the maximum frequency of an aperture-limited hologram may be represented approximately by the frequency of an extreme ray has been described. This can be used to find the maximum frequency of a given object in a given holographic situation.

A method has been presented whereby the characteristics of a scanning system in terms of its physical parameters may be determined. It has been shown that the two main factors affecting the fidelity in recording the aperture-limited frequency spectrum discussed above are the detector and light-source apertures. Some curves have been drawn which establish values for these in terms of wavelength for a given allowable attenuation of the aperture-limited frequency spectrum. The treatment also verifies the restrictions on carrier frequency and scanning frequency which have been previously discussed in the literature.

REFERENCES

1. F. L. Thurstone, in: *Proceedings of the Symposium on Biomedical Engineering*, Vol. 1, Marquette University, Milwaukee, Wisconsin, 1966, p. 12.
2. K. Preston, Jr. and J. L. Kreuzer, *Appl. Phys. Letters* **10**: 150 (1967).
3. G. A. Massey, *Proc. IEEE* **55**: 1115 (1967).
4. A. F. Metherell, H. M. A. El-Sum, J. J. Dreher, and L. Larmore, *Appl. Phys. Letters* **10**: 277 (1967).
5. R. B. Smith, paper presented at the 1967 IEEE Symposium on Sonics and Ultrasonics, Vancouver, Canada, Oct. 1967.
6. G. W. Stroke, *An Introduction to Coherent Optics and Holography*, Academic Press, New York, 1966.
7. L. J. Cutrona, E. N. Leith, C. T. Palermo, and L. J. Porcello, *IRE Trans. on Information Theory* **6**(3): 386 (1960).

Chapter 7

BIOMEDICAL PROSPECTS FOR ULTRASOUND HOLOGRAPHY

F. L. Thurstone

Division of Biomedical Engineering, Duke University
Durham, North Carolina

The basic problems associated with ultrasonic imaging by holographic methods are presented and the implications relative to possible diagnostic application are discussed. Several possible techniques for recording the magnitude and phase of sonic fields are analyzed and recent results obtained with a mechanical scanning system are presented. The distortion and aberration of the reconstructed images which are associated with wavelength scaling present a technological obstacle to be overcome. The nature of image presentation that has been used in the reconstruction of visible images has neither used the entire information contained in the hologram nor achieved desirable image geometry. An intermediate image processing scheme may provide a useful approach toward the solution of these problems. The nature of propagation of ultrasound in biologic tissue and the resulting image information present in an ultrasound field emanating from such a subject have yet to be fully understood or analyzed. There is little doubt, however, that given a suitably rapid detection and image presentation system, very considerable diagnostic information can be obtained by this method.

INTRODUCTION

Interest in acoustical holography and in the generation by this method of visible images corresponding to sound field configurations has increased at a rapid rate. Since the earliest demonstration of visible images generated by wavefront reconstruction from acoustical holograms numerous techniques and procedures have been employed (see Appendix). Acoustical holography offers two basic advantages as an imaging technique. First, holography offers the possibility of recording and utilizing more of the information contained in a coherent sound field than do the more conventional amplitude detection systems ([1]). Second, holography offers the possibility of recording and presenting three-dimensional image information.

One application of holographic imaging with ultrasound which holds some promise and which would be of considerable value is the use of this technique to visualize internal structures to assist in medical diagnosis. Ultrasonic energy in certain frequency ranges passes quite readily through living tissue, while appreciable amounts of this energy are reflected from the various tissue interfaces. Although the exact mechanisms of propagation and reflection in tissue are not well understood, pulse-echo imaging techniques have been widely investigated for diagnostic application. Most of these techniques have not been entirely satisfactory, but this has not been because of any lack of available echo information. Ultrasound propagates at a fairly constant velocity of about 1500 meters/sec in soft tissue structures, and wavelengths in the range of 0.1 to 1.0 mm propagate with reasonable levels of attenuation. Given wavelengths of this magnitude and appreciable echo information, there is every reason to expect that excellent images of the structural geometry can be produced. Two basic limitations on the application of ultrasound holography to medical diagnosis are apparent. First, since all living tissue is dynamic in nature due to cardiac activity, respiration, etc., the time required to obtain the recorded hologram must be small. To date systems have not been developed which will record a sufficient amount of information in a short period of time. Second, in order to have the greatest diagnostic usefulness, the image presentation must provide the three-dimensional subjective character produced in optical holography. To date images reconstructed from acoustical holograms have not achieved this three-dimensional character because of the image anomalies associated with the difference in wavelengths between the investigating acoustic field and the reconstructing light field.

Thus the biomedical prospects for ultrasound holography are almost wholly dependent upon the development of ultrasound holographic imaging techniques in general. If acoustical holography can be developed to the point where image resolution approaches the acoustic wavelength and if detection systems can be made capable of recording large amounts of information from low-intensity ultrasound fields in short periods of time, then the biomedical applications of this technique might be very great indeed.

In order for ultrasound holography to be widely accepted as a diagnostic procedure, the technique will have to be developed so that: (1) it produces good high-resolution images of the anatomical structure, (2) the images have a three-dimensional character, (3) the time required for the procedure is small, (4) the instrumentation is reliable and relatively simple to operate, and (5) the cost is not prohibitive.

Since the holographic imaging of viable tissue structures has not yet been investigated, the remainder of this chapter will deal with the problems of acoustical holography in general. That a sampling procedure using a synthesized reference signal can be used to generate acoustical holograms for subsequent image generation has been reported by the author, and these techniques have been extended by numerous other groups. The appendix to this chapter contains a reprint of the paper presented by the author at the Symposium on Biomedical Engineering in Milwaukee, Wisconsin together with illustrations of results presented at that time. Since the basic procedures are outlined in this appendix, this chapter will proceed with a discussion of the information detection and image presentation problems.

Since the hologram is a recording of the interference between two coherent fields, the recording system must be capable of resolving the minimum interference fringe spacing produced. Thus the detection and recording system should ideally be capable of detecting and plotting an interference pattern which may have fringe spacings approaching the acoustic wavelength. Sampling techniques in which a small transducer is scanned through the two dimensions of the hologram plane must use a detector which has an effective area which is small enough to resolve the minimum fringe spacing present in the acoustic field. If the reference signal is not actually present in the acoustic field but is introduced after the detection of the field intensity, then the detector must be capable of preserving the phase information present in the coherent object signal. Scanning techniques which involve electronically sampling the potential generated on the surface of a large piezoelectric element are capable of quite satisfactory fringe resolution. However, the acoustic impedance of piezoelectric transducers commonly used to detect ultrasonic energy is generally very much greater than that of the coupling media, and consequently the critical angle of incidence is very restricted. The fact that energy must impinge on the transducer in a direction essentially normal to the transducer face imposes an

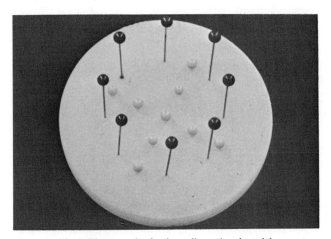

Fig. 1 Photograph of a three-dimensional model.

effective limitation on the optical aperture of the detecting system. The nonuniform directional sensitivity of piezoelectric transducers has severely limited the results obtained to date with this type of system.

Nonuniform directional sensitivity of the detection system may also lead to image anomalies in addition to a simple loss of image resolution. An example of such an anomaly is present in the following illustrations, which are presented here to show the three-dimensional imaging available with acoustical holography. Figure 1 shows a three-dimensional model consisting of roughly spherical glass pinheads placed in the form of an X in one plane and in the form of an ○ at a plane 2 cm above the plane of the X. The pinheads are roughly 1.9 mm in diameter and are placed on 1-cm centers in the plane of the X. An ultrasound hologram 8-cm square was recorded at a distance of 13 cm from the plane of the ○ and 15 cm from the plane of the X at a frequency of 5 MHz. Images reconstructed using a He–Ne laser were recorded at two different planes in space and are shown in Figs. 2 and 3. The image planes are quite distinctly focused; however, each object pin appears as two distinct points. Although a single point source was used for ultrasonic illumination, the detecting transducer had two major lobes in the directional sensitivity pattern, which produces a multiple image. Thus an additional requirement for an ideal information detection system is that it have relatively uniform directional sensitivity throughout a large aperture angle.

The acoustic field information detected in a sampling process may be processed before being stored in the form of a hologram transparency. Specifically, the nonlinearity of the overall recording process, including the film used for the hologram transparency, can be adjusted to any arbitrary

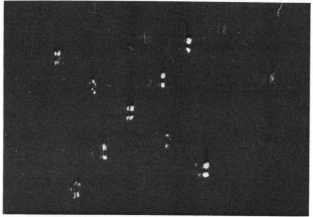

Fig. 2. A single image plane in the reconstructed image obtained from a sampled acoustical hologram recording of the object shown in Fig. 1.

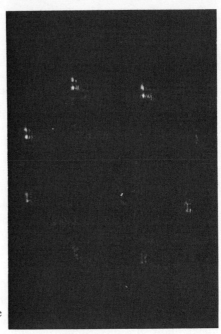

Fig. 3. A second image plane from the same hologram as that used in Fig. 2.

characteristic. The overall square-law characteristic frequently desired in holographic recording is easily achieved. It is also possible to combine the object and reference signals in other than a simple linear summation. Thus one can record only phase information or any arbitrary combination of amplitude and phase information.

There are associated image distortions and aberrations in any holographic imaging process where the information is obtained at one wavelength for subsequent image reconstruction at a different wavelength. The nature of these geometrical distortions and aberrations is dependent upon the ratio of the wavelengths and the recording and reconstructing geometry. When the reconstruction geometry is optimally analogous to the recording configuration the primary image aberration is in the form of spherical aberration. The extent to which image aberration degrades the reconstructed images has yet to be determined. Aside from limited efforts at a nonlinear scaling of the hologram recording little has been reported with regard to this problem. The primary image distortion associated with the change in wavelength has largely masked any image aberrations present.

The primary image distortion associated with reconstructing images from holograms obtained with ultrasound fields is that of longitudinal or axial magnification. Recognizing that variations in the curvature of the reference field between the recording and reconstructing processes is analogous to the use of a simple lens, it is convenient to assume a plane-wave reference field for both recording and reconstruction. The resulting equations can be modified by means of simple lens equations if nonplanar reference fields are used. With this condition the longitudinal magnification is simply the ratio of the wavelengths of recording to reconstructing fields, whereas the lateral or azimuthal magnification is unity. To illustrate the significance of this distortion, an ultrasound frequency of 5 MHz has a wavelength in water of 0.3 mm. Using coherent light at a wavelength of 6328 Å, the reconstructed image would be magnified longitudinally by this wavelength ratio of 500:1.

In addition to the image aberrations and distortion just described, there may be significant amounts of optical noise superimposed on the reconstructed image. Depending upon the nature of the recording system and the recording geometry, this noise may include information from the unwanted or twin image produced in the reconstruction process and it may include any or all of the following: light energy diffracted by the grating nature of a uniform sampling interval used in recording the hologram; energy leakage through or diffracted around a zero-order stop used to eliminate light not diffracted by the hologram; and out-of-focus information when a single image plane of a three-dimensional image is recorded. Because of the large longitudinal distortion of images reconstructed from ultrasound holograms it has not been possible to present realistic three-dimensional virtual images. For planar objects this poses no problem, but for three-dimensional objects considerable optical noise is associated with recording an individual image plane.

The basic objective of schemes directed toward the reduction of the longitudinal image distortion inherent in the ultrasound holographic imaging process is the generation of realistically sized and proportioned three-dimensional virtual images similar to those which can be obtained with optical holography. There are several techniques available for reduction of this distortion, and a practical image processing system may involve their simultaneous application.

One procedure for reducing image distortion which has been used in essentially all acoustical holography involves a linear reduction in size of the recorded hologram. If the recorded hologram is reduced by a factor L, the magnification factors are modified so that the lateral magnification is reduced by L and the longitudinal magnifaction is reduced by the square of this factor. Thus if the hologram is scaled by a factor equal to the wavelength ratio, the recording geometry is exactly reproduced in the reconstructed image with a reduction in size equal to this ratio. Under this condition all aberration and distortion factors can be made to disappear. However, with the relatively large wavelength ratios involved in acoustical holography the image size would be too small for direct visualization. If optical magnification is used to increase the image size, there is a consequent introduction of longitudinal distortion exactly analogous to that which is being eliminated by the scaling process. Since the resolution limitation imposed by the wavelength of the acoustic field may be greater than the resolving ability of the unaided eye, this difference in resolution can be translated into a reduction in image size without loss of visible information or subjective quality of the image. However, reduction in image size beyond this amount will result in a loss of visible information unless the object size makes a lesser reduction impractical.

Another approach to the reduction of this image distortion involves synthesizing a hologram from the acoustic field information, but a hologram which has the characteristics of being recorded at a shorter wavelength. Except for the fundamental limitation on image resolution imposed by the actual wavelength of the investigating field, such a hologram can be made to have all the characteristics of having been recorded at a shorter wavelength, including the consequent reduction of image distortion. This might be accomplished by computer processing of the information contained in the recorded hologram and subsequent synthesis of a new hologram. A first approximation to this procedure can be accomplished by multiplying the phase of both object and reference signals before combining them for the generation of the hologram.

In order to reduce the longitudinal distortion factor still further, still other techniques must be developed which will produce a lateral magnification without concurrent greater longitudinal magnification. Although this cannot be done optically, it can be accomplished by properly scaling the hologram in a nonlinear manner. By a technique somewhat analogous to the bandwidth reduction scheme proposed by Kock [2] for optical holography, the limited information available from an acoustic field can be used to generate a hologram which does not provide the resolution capability inherent in the wavelength of the reconstructing field. Thus, rather than using the fragmented aperture for the purpose of reducing the information content of an optical hologram as suggested by Kock, it is possible to maintain the information content and reduce the effective wavelength characteristic of the recorded hologram by compressing the information into fragmented sections [3].

In conclusion, acoustical imaging by ultrasound holography may have very widespread application for presenting images of opaque structures which are at least partially transparent to ultrasound. The technique has been used to present three-dimensional images of model structures by both through transmission and reflection of ultrasonic energy. To date these images have not been readily visualized because of the severe image distortions inherent in the holographic process when applied to long-wavelength fields. However, image processing techniques may reduce these distortions for more effective visualization of three-dimensional subjects. In addition to the problems of image reconstruction and presentation there remain fundamental limitations on the acoustic signal detection process. These limitations have either restricted the amount of image information detected or have imposed long periods of time for the signal detection process. The development of a large-area detection system sensitive to acoustic energy through a large angle of incidence would obviate this problem.

REFERENCES

1. P. Greguss, Techniques and Information Content of Sonoholograms, *J. Photo. Sci.* **14**: 329–332 (Nov. 1966).
2. W. E. Kock, Use of Lens Arrays in Holograms, *Proc. IEEE* **55**:1103–1104 (L) (June 1967).
3. F. L. Thurstone, On Holographic Imaging with Long Wavelength Fields, *Proc. IEEE* **56**: 768–9 (Apr. 1968).

APPENDIX. ULTRASOUND HOLOGRAPHY AND VISUAL RECONSTRUCTION*

INTRODUCTION

The use of sonic energy as a means of detecting the location and nature of structures not normally visible would be greatly enhanced if it would be possible to provide a direct conversion of sonic energy into electromagnetic energy in the visible spectrum. If the magnitude and direction of propagation could be simultaneously converted, it would be possible to see the object under study as if it were at least partially transparent. One method of recording a complex acoustic wave distribution and reproducing an analogous wave distribution with light is the method of holography and wavefront reconstruction. Sonic holography offers the possibility of obtaining and utilizing a greater portion of the information contained in a sonic field configuration produced by the reflection or absorption of sonic energy than do the more usual methods of ultrasonic imaging. This method will provide a more meaningful display of the sonic information, including the presentation of vivid three-dimensional images including parallax effects and other features peculiar to holography. This method may be applicable both in medical diagnosis and in the area of nondestructive analysis in industry and research.

The use of radiant ultrasonic energy in research and diagnostic medicine has increased rapidly because of the unique features of the propagation of energy in this form. This energy form has been used in a number of techniques for presenting optical images corresponding to the structure and geometry of biologic tissue ([1,2]). These techniques have either attempted to present a single cross-sectional plane of the subject under study or have compressed the three-dimensional subject into the two-dimensional image presented. It is the purpose of this paper

*In: *Proceedings of the Symposium on Biomedical Engineering*, Vol. 1, Marquette University, Milwaukee, Wisconsin, 1966, pp. 12–15.

to present a different approach to the problem of imaging by the use of a wavefront reconstruction method.

The method of storing information contained in a complex monochromatic field and subsequently reproducing this field configuration was first described by Gabor ([3-5]). This method involves the use of a coherent reference field or carrier which, together with the field emanating from the object under study, produces a complex field configuration due to the constructive and destructive interference effects. Using monochromatic fields of light, this interference pattern can be recorded directly on photographic film. Such an optical image of the interference pattern is called a hologram. The hologram will, when illuminated with a coherent monochromatic field similar to the original reference field, produce a complex field. This field can be shown to be the sum of the original field pattern and its complex conjugate field ([4,6]). Thus a virtual image is produced corresponding to the field emanating from the original object together with a conjugate field which will produce a real image of the object. These images are created by the reproduction of the original field configuration, and the process is called wavefront reconstruction.

Two images are produced in the wavefront reconstruction process, and these can be described as the sidebands on the modulated carrier or reference field ([4]). These images arise from the fact that the complex field configuration is recorded in the two dimensions of the hologram with the real variable optical density. Thus there is a phase difference ambiguity resulting in the production of conjugate images. In an optical sense, the hologram can be described as a generalized zone-plate, having both positive and negative focal length ([6]). Several methods have been described which can reduce or eliminate the unwanted twin image ([7,8]), including the technique of recording two holograms at different spatial positions.

With the development of the laser as a source of coherent monochromatic light a major obstacle to the development of holography was overcome. Since that time considerable interest has developed in the use of hologram images, both for photography and for visualizing other radiant energy field configurations ([9]). Coherent monochromatic light from a laser can be used to illuminate a hologram transparency in order to produce a visible reconstructed field distribution corresponding to the energy field from which the hologram was obtained.

It is not necessary that the reconstructed field have the same wavelength as the original field because the interference patterns can be photographically and optically scaled. Indeed, Gabor's earliest work was toward the scaling of electron wavelengths up to visible light for use in electron microscopy. More recently microwave holograms have been recorded and the wavelength scaled down to the visible range ([10,11]). Although previously reported holograms have been optical images of the defraction patterns present in electromagnetic energy fields for subsequent illumination with electromagnetic energy of visible wavelengths, there is no reason that the technique should not be applied to sonic fields for conversion to visual images, provided a suitable conversion from acoustic energy to optical density can be accomplished in generating the hologram.

In scaling the linear dimensions of the hologram together with a change in the wavelength the images reconstructed are correspondingly magnified or minified. This factor can be offset by proper optical scaling in the reconstruction process. The focal lengths of a hologram considered as a zone-plate lens ([6]) has been shown to be proportional to the linear scale L on which the hologram is reduced and to the wavelength according to the relationship

$$f \propto L^2/\lambda \tag{A1}$$

Thus with a reduction of the wavelength from ultrasound to visible light, combined with a similar reduction in linear dimension of the hologram, the focal length of the hologram and the image size are reduced in the same ratio. Since this change in wavelength may be on the order of 1000 to 1, a fairly considerable optical magnification will be desirable in the reconstruction.

The amount of useful magnification would be limited only by the resolving capability of the hologram itself.

The resolving capability of a sonic hologram can be determined from the Rayleigh criterion, which gives the minimum resolvable separation between two point sources as

$$D = 0.61\lambda/\sin\alpha \qquad (A2)$$

where α is the half-angle of the hologram aperture. Thus for reasonably large apertures the limit of resolution approximates the sonic wavelength. In addition to providing improved resolution, a large aperture is desirable in order to more fully develop a three-dimensional image with parallax effects. The image resolution obtainable from a hologram can also be expressed in terms of the smallest interference fringe spacing which can be obtained in the hologram [12], the limit of resolution being one-half the minimum fringe spacing.

An interesting feature of holography is that each portion of the hologram contains information obtained from the entire subject under study. Hence any portion of the hologram is capable of reproducing the entire image with a degradation of resolution determined by the effective aperture of the portion used in reconstruction. This characteristic of holography gives rise to the possibility of obtaining a large apparent aperture for three-dimensional imaging by means of multiple small-aperture holograms. This technique has been demonstrated by masking a large hologram with a grid of small apertures, which resulted in a minimal degradation of the re-constructed image [11].

The basic requirements for converting a sonic field into an analogous visible field by means of holography are that sonic fields must be produced which have both spatial and temporal coherence and that a satisfactory system can be obtained for generating the photographic hologram. Temporal coherence or monochromaticity of the sonic fields can be readily obtained by driving the ultrasonic transducers at constant frequency and within their limits of reasonably linear operation. The requirement for spatial coherence can be met by focusing the reference field through a point or by using a very small point source. Alternatively, if the hologram is produced by a scanning process, the reference signal need not be produced in the sound field but can be injected into the detecting system. The sonic energy used to illuminate the object under study need only be coherent in a temporal sense, and this can be accomplished by driving the illuminating transducers from the same source as that which provides the reference signal. Aside from questions of desirable geometry and optical magnification, the basic problem becomes the conversion of sonic field intensity into optical density or light intensity for the generation of the hologram itself. Once obtained the hologram can be illuminated with the coherent monochromatic light available from a laser and will produce visible images corresponding to the original sound field configuration.

Numerous methods are available for measuring and recording sonic field intensities. Kossoff [13] has reviewed these methods and classified them into the categories of thermal, mechanical, optical electrical and chemical techniques. Thermal and mechanical techniques are at present limited to the measurement of sonic intensity at a point, and hence would have to be swept through the desired hologram plane in a scanning operation. Optical techniques utilizing a direct acoustical optical interaction such as the Schlieren technique have the restriction that information is generally obtained in the plane of propagation rather than in a plane relatively normal to the propagation path. A direct electrical technique such as scanning the potential generated on a piezoelectric crystal could record the interference pattern in the plane of the crystal. The limited aperture restriction imposed on such a system could be obviated by recording several holographic images each of small aperture and subsequently combining them in the reconstruction process. Direct chemical processes which are affected by ultrasound perhaps offer the simplest and the most direct form of conversion. An example of such a technique would be the starch–iodine reaction investigated by Bennett [14] and by Kossoff [13]. A limitation on this method would appear to be the available resolution determined by the grain size in the image. It is likely that with investigation a chemical emulsion can be obtained which will be sensitive to sonic energy and which will provide a permanent record in optical density or reflectivity with good resolution. Until such a process is available, the direct electrical techniques and mechanical scanning methods hold the greatest promise.

A technique for synthesizing ultrasonic holograms by mechanically scanning a detecting probe is presently under study. In this method (Fig. A1) a small piezoelectric detector is scanned through the sonic field in two dimensions corresponding to the plane of the hologram. The field intensity detected by the probe is used to control a small light source which is focused onto a photographic film plate so that a permanent hologram is recorded (Fig. A2). With the present system the hologram size can be as large as 40-cm square. The detecting crystal has a minimum effective aperture of approximately 1 mm. This, together with the optical recording device, limits the resolution obtained in the hologram to approximately 2 mm per fringe. Holograms produced in this manner can be photographically scaled and subsequently illuminated with a continuous wave helium–neon gas laser for wavefront reconstruction. This illumination is in the visible spectrum at a wavelength of 6328 Å (Fig. A3).

One feature of ultrasound holography is the ease with which the phase of the reference beam can be controlled. At frequencies in the megacycle region the phase of a driving signal can easily be controlled with a high degree of precision. This gives rise to the possibility of obtaining more than one hologram of the same object with the same geometry but with different reference signal phase. From a communication theory standpoint, this gives rise to the ability to eliminate the phase ambiguity that results from recording a complex interference pattern with a single real variable (optical density) in two dimensions.

With the scanning method under study the reference beam need not exist in the sound field. It can instead be induced directly into the detector amplifier. Here the description of the reference signal as a carrier is in the more obvious sense. Injection of a constant reference signal phase yields the same results that would be obtained with a perfectly coherent plane wave reference. If the

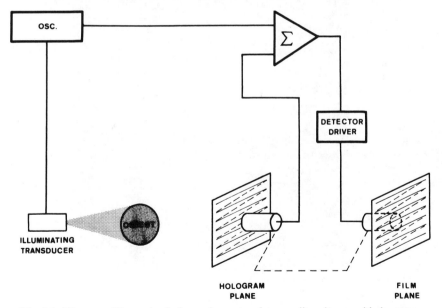

Fig. A.1. Diagram of the mechanical scanning system for recording ultrasound holograms.

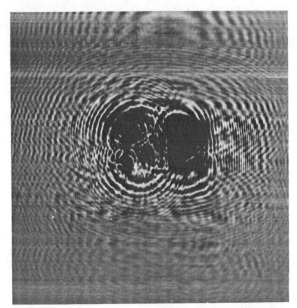

Fig. A2. Through-transmission hologram obtained with the
scanning system of an ultrasound transparency at an object
distance of 10 cm.

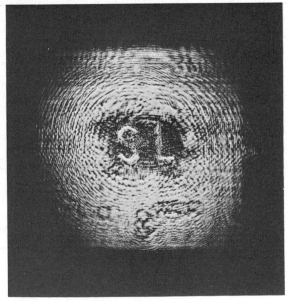

Fig. A3. Reconstructed real image of the letters SL stenciled in
the object transparency. Letter size 1.9 cm, reconstructing wavelength 6328 Å. Central area of hologram masked for zero-order
stop.

reference source were present in the sonic field, this would correspond to an infinite distance between the source and the hologram plane.

The usefulness of the technique may depend greatly on the relative attenuation and dispersion of sonic energy within the subject under test; that is, the degree of transparency of the subject to sound. With the finite and manageable propagation velocity of sonic energy it will be possible to record holographic information from selected volumes by means of time-gated circuitry. Such a time-gating system may be required if the surface reflectivity of the object under study is very high and tends to mask information emanating from internal structures.

CONCLUSIONS

A new investigative technique has been presented which utilizes the information contained in an ultrasonic field configuration to develop an analogous visible field for direct observation of the subject or material responsible for the original sonic configuration. This visible reconstructed field may have application in diagnosis and in material testing. The process involves the recording of sonic Fresnel diffraction patterns or point-by-point intensity levels and is dependent upon this acoustical-to-optical conversion process.

ACKNOWLEDGMENTS

This project has been aided by grants from The National Foundation, The American Cancer Society, and The North Carolina Heart Association.

REFERENCES

1. D. Gordon, Ultrasonic Rays in Medical Diagnosis—A Survey, *Med. Electron. Biol. Eng.* **1**:51 (1963).
2. F. L. Thurstone, N. I. Kjosnes, and W. M. McKinney, Ultrasonic Scanning of Biologic Tissue by a New Technique, *Science* **149**:302 (1965).
3. D. Gabor, A New Microscopic Principle, *Nautre* **161**:777 (1948).
4. D. Gabor, Microscopy by Reconstructed Wave-Fronts, *Proc. Roy. Soc. London* **A197**:454 (1949).
5. D. Gabor, Microscopy by Reconstructed Wave Fronts: II, *Proc. Phys. Soc.* **B64**:449 (1951).
6. G. L. Rogers, Gabor Diffraction Microscopy: the Hologram as a Generalized Zone-Plate, *Nature* **166**:237 (1950).
7. E. N. Leigh and J. Upatnieks, Reconstructed Wavefronts and Communication Theory, *J. Opt. Soc. Am.* **52**:1123 (1962).
8. G. L. Rogers, Elimination of the Unwanted Image in Diffraction Microscopy, *Nature* **167**:190 (1951).
9. E. N. Leith and J. Upatnieks, Photography by Laser, *Sci. Am.* **212**:24 (1965).
10. R. P. Dooley, X-Band Holography, *Proc. IEEE* **53**:1733 (1965).
11. W. E. Kock, Hologram Television, *Proc. IEEE* **54**:331 (1966).
12. M. E. Haine and J. Dyson, A Modification to Gabor's Proposed Diffraction Microscope, *Nature* **166**:315 (1950).
13. G. Kossoff, Calibration of Ultrasonic Therapeutic Equipment, *Acustica* **12**:84 (1962).
14. G. S. Bennett, A New Method for the Visualization and Measurement of Ultrasonic Fields, *J. Acoust. Soc. Am.* **24**:470 (1952).

Chapter 8

ACOUSTICAL HOLOGRAPHIC MODEL OF CETACEAN ECHO-LOCATION

John J. Dreher

Douglas Advanced Research Laboratories
McDonnell-Douglas Corporation, Huntington Beach, California

The echo-location signal of *Odontocetes* and its characteristics are discussed, with an anatomical description of the cetacean systems responsible. Extant theories on cetacean hearing are briefly reviewed, with reference to areas of performance unexplained by present knowledge. A possible construct employing holographic techniques, or a neural analog thereof, is presented as an alternate explanation.

Delphinos audire manifestum est quanum audiant mirum.

Pliny

INTRODUCTION

The last decade has been marked by intense interest in signal processing. Much of our ignorance concerning animal systems is being surmounted by the interdisciplinary attack as evidenced, for instance, by the 1966 Frescati Conference on Animal Sonars ([17]), which synthesized electronics, physics, mathematics, and biology. Communication among such alien species is never easy. Generalizations repugnant to the specialist are a necessary evil. For our purposes here the consideration of an acoustical holographic animal processing system runs this risk as well. Most of the following statements regarding cetacean hearing, sound production, and behavior have many qualifications introduced by many investigators. A synthesis of what seems generally verifiable, therefore, may be the most useful introduction for those for whom this presentation is intended.

It is well known that dolphins emit at least two separate types of sounds ([1,2]). One sound, a frequency-modulated whistle, is radiated laterally from the animal's neck and may have a communicative function ([3,4]). The other sound, a short-duration broadband click, is used for echo-location ([5,6]).

127

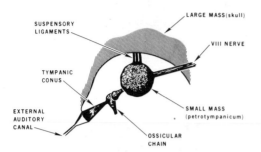

Fig. 1. Schematic of cetacean ear.
From Reysenbach de Haan ([7]).

The nature of the hearing mechanism, essentially a mammalian ear modified to accept ultrasonic frequencies, constitutes one of the questions examined in this chapter. Our model here subsumes another sensing mechanism.

The structure of the cetacean ear has been exhaustively described ([7, 8]). Figure 1 shows a schematic representation of the middle ear according to Reysenbach de Haan ([7]). Here the petrotympanicum is seen isolated from the skull by a system of suspensory ligaments. The critical frequency of this suspension in the smaller whales is approximately 50 Hz, thereby allowing the boney process to act as a seismic mass to frequencies above this value. The two massive petrotympanica are thus isolated from the skull, and hence, physically, from each other. Since the Organ of Corti and semicircular canals are enclosed in this bony mass, it is clear that sound coming directly from the water *via* the skull would suffer enormous attenuation from the tissue–air–tissue interfaces, a value we would calculate to be near 60 dB, re 0.0002 μbar.

The base of the tympanic conus, stretched out in the sulcus tympanicus, evidently connects external acoustic signals with the inner ear *via* the ossicular chain suspended in the tympanic cavity. Sound energy in the water is transmitted via the blubber, the tissue, or the water to the tympanic conus, and in turn to the petrotympanicum, and thus into the inner ear of the whale. Just how the signals are transmitted to the conus is not yet clear. First of all, it would appear certain that the external meatus is useless in the sense that it serves land mammals. Dissections show that the canal runs a more or less S-shaped course over a distance of about 10 cm, starting at the opening of the external auditory meatus, which is about 0.5 mm in diameter. The canal remains narrow, with a diameter of 0.5–1 mm and a somewhat oval shape. After the first bend it begins to widen, funnel-like, at the end to a diameter of about 5 mm. The wall of the auditory canal is formed by the epidermis, and contains neither sudoriferous, sebaceous glands, nor cerumenous glands ([7]). There is no cerumen plug closing off the canal in odontocetes as in the Baleen whale, although examination has shown the canal to be obstructed by desquaminated tissue, a serious impairment if it is to serve as a sound conductor. The external meatus is generally closed, and of such a size that it must be located by a dissection pick. All this, of course, tends strongly to preclude hearing by methods normal to land animals.

If, however, we trace the involvement of the tympanic conus, we note that there are some connecting ligaments that could serve to transmit sound incident upon the winglike structures of the lower jaw. The possibility arises, therefore, in view of the very light, hollow jaw structure and the fact that it contains a lipoid substance remarkably like that of the melon, that these jaws could serve as antennas for passive sensing of the acoustical environment. As attractive and logical as this might appear, we should like to examine some other evidence that might lead to consideration of an alternative explanation, if not of hearing *per se* as we know it, then of the animal's perceived analog of his environment.

We may draw on a number of observed facts of cetacean activity and structure to make our construct. First, it is clear that Delphinidae can navigate, find food, and discriminate targets by acoustical means alone. The instrument here, the echo-ranging click common to all genera, can apparently furnish both geometric and target strength information.

Analyses of these sounds ([1, 9]) show them to be typically short (approximately 1 msec), with a repetition rate from 0.01 to 400 sec^{-1}. Dependent upon the species, the pulse duration may vary as shown in Fig. 2, *Globicephela* showing the ability to use both a long and short pulse if desired. This may not be unexpected, since estuarine and pelagic varieties of Delphinidae have different sonar requirements, depending upon whether they are cruising, maneuvering, or hunting. Whatever may be the characteristics of clicks peculiar to various species, we are still intrigued by the mechanism of production. Alternate explanations of this have been advanced, one being pneumo-mechanical in nature ([1,6,10−12]) and another involving action of the larynx ([13−16]). An experimental investigation into the directional characteristics of the delphinid skull ([12]), has shown that these forward-emanating clicks, transduced to the water *via* the fatty melon, can be quite precisely beamed, with beamwidth a function of frequency. This is illustrated in Fig. 3.

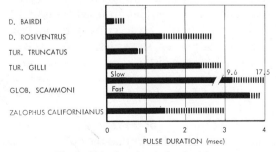

Fig. 2. Echo-location pulse durations.

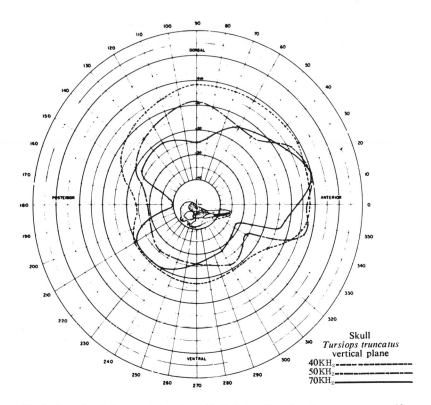

Fig. 3. Directional characteristics of delphinid skull reflectivity. From Evans *et al.* ([12]).

The signal itself, while broadband as one consequence of its relatively short duration, shows definite harmonic structure derived from the geometry of the skull. In the dolphin the skull reflector consists of three intersecting paraboloid faces, with the major dish facing forward. It has been noted that *Tursiops*, an estuarine animal, has considerable latitude for neck movement and regularly scans the forward field in locating his targets. On the other hand, pelagic species (e.g., *Stenella*) due to fused third and fourth cervical vertebrae, lack this mobility. Figure 4, a spectrographic analysis of a simultaneous whistle and echo-location run, shows respectively as *A*, *B*, *C*, and *D* the frequency–amplitude plots of whistle, returning echo, whistle, and active pulse. The harmonic nature of the latter may be also observed in signals emitted by *Delphinus* and *Globicephela*. Clearly, then, the animal is emitting a signal with a tonal structure.

We now come to the question of the returned echo. Experimental work done by Evans and Powell ([17]) indicates that the dolphin can both discriminate form and detect target strength. Looking at the subject quite clinically, it is

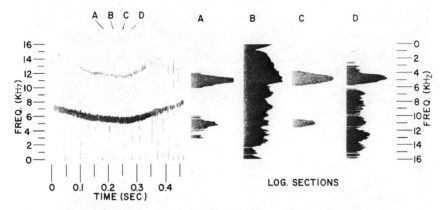

Fig. 4. Sound spectrogram showing simultaneous whistle and echo-location.

logical to say that if we were designing the animal it would be convenient and efficient if it had monostatic reception apparatus—ideally an array. Such a scheme, shown in Fig. 5, indicates the surface of the melon to be the ideal location, as suggested by Evans and Dreher in 1961 ([18]).

A. D. Grinnell, in an *ad hoc* critique of K. S. Norris and his co-workers during the Frescati Conference, noted melon sensitivity of anesthetized *Stenella* to sounds of 15–100 kHz and to clicks. It is also interesting to note that dolphin trainers' experience has shown dolphins submit cheerfully to eye-covers, but resent violently any covering of the melon.

Some histologies of *Tursiops* melon were done by Kenneth Bloome at Lockheed in 1960 (unpublished work), and although innervation studies were not performed, a definite possibility of an array seemed to exist.

As on other areas of the animal's body, the tegument of the melon is anchored to the supporting tissue by structures called rete pegs. Although the formation of these on the remainder of the body is irregular, an adaptation in the melon has rendered them quite different. Figure 6 shows a slice of the melon surface at 375 × enlargement. It will be seen from this view that we are

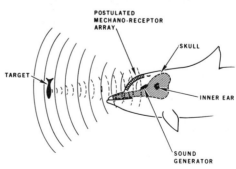

Fig. 5. Schematic of possible melon array.

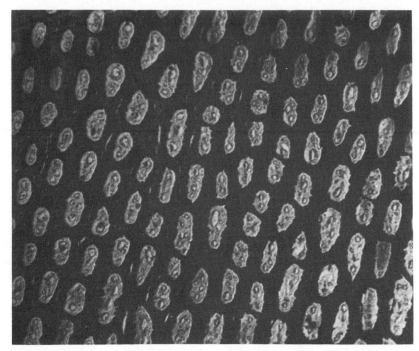

Fig. 6. Histological section of melon structure showing array of tubules normal to melon surface. (Magnification approximately 375×.)

looking down a remarkably regular array of tiny tubles, most of them oval in cross section, with an average diameter of 0.0004 in., spaced in longitudinal columns with an 0.0004-in. separation between columns. These dimensions would set the maximum activating frequency in water at 4.2×10^7 Hz. Such an array could approximate the performance of a medium-resolution photographic emulsion, or about 100 lines/mm, apparently exceeding the animal's requirements for targets of his interest, which in general are small to medium fish.

This matrix of electrolyte-filled tubules might well serve a number of purposes, including the sensing of velocity and temperature, as well as interception of acoustic signals whose interpretation requires phase information. Assuming for the moment that such a mechanism exists, we can hypothesize a construct somewhat like the following: during the off-duty cycle of the echo-location pulse the returning echo with both phase and amplitude information impinges on the melon as a traveling wave. The geometry of the target will, of course, modulate the return wave into a unique pattern of condensations and rarefactions which will sweep across the melon surface.

Successive echo-location pulses will furnish a redundant series of these returns, which are then neurally processed to retrieve the desired information.

There are also some extremely interesting observations to be made regarding the animal's sonar pulse itself that are not incompatible with such a theory. Figure 7 shows a face-on plot of the intensity of the click signal elicited mechanically from a cadaver. We are looking not at a symmetrical envelope, but at one which has a more powerful sound field on the right side, which is in accord with cetacean "right-headedness." This is to say that on animals so far observed the right side of the head invariably shows a larger structural development. No previous explanation for this had been advanced, although Purves ([13]) attributes the sound field asymmetry to the experimental techniques under which it was produced and the skull asymmetry to respiration requirements. A second point of interest lies in the evidence that under careful signal processing it can be shown that double pulses exist ([8]).

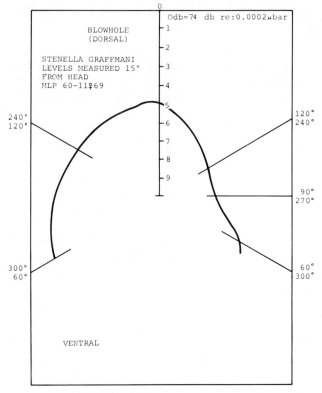

Fig. 7. Polar plot of sound pressure around *Tursiops* cadaver head while emitting echo-location clicks stimulated by pressurized air in trachea. Head is pointing toward reader.

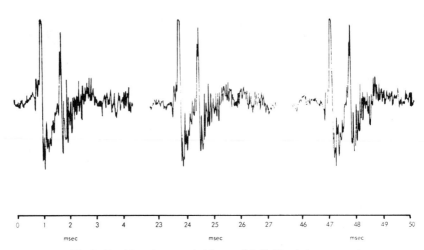

Fig. 8. Double pulse recorded from wild *Globicephela scammoni.*

Figure 8 illustrates such a double pulse recorded from a wild *Globicephela scammoni.* In this particular signal the interval between pulses was approximately 2 msec and may be the result of sequential action of the two nasal plugs being pulsed by a semicircular sac. This double pulsing has been reported for *D. bairdi, D. rosiventrus, T. truncatus,* and *G. scammoni* [8].

We thus may envision a double pulse, out of synchrony in both amplitude and phase, that could be compared upon return by the animal's nervous system.

At this juncture we can point to no certainty of a holographic construct. There are, however, some physical circumstances that might allow us to entertain such a possibility.

First of all, the animal seems to have some equipment capability for such a system; second, he customarily works with a weak signal-to-noise ratio in the echo returns. Let us consider these in turn. We observe the following in regard to capability:

1. An array-like structure of tubules.
2. A monostatic location of the array.
3. Cranial nerve VIII (acoustic) dominating all other cranial nerves in size.
4. Trigeminal and facial nerves the next two largest nerves.
5. Extensive branching of facial nerves throughout the forward head area.
6. Correlation beds around auditory cortex [19].

In regard to signal strength and the nature of the signal available, we observe the following: It seems obvious that the short echo pulses are a tradeoff made by the animal to gain power, and hence range. What is the maximum range of detection or recognition? At present no systematic studies are available; however, some inferences can be made. Evans and Dreher ([20]) reported on scouting behavior of *Tursiops gilli* observed during a cruise in Scammon's Lagoon. Here a pod of dolphins swimming down the lagoon stopped short some 400 yards of a 50-ft boat and an acoustic barrier comprised of 2-in. diameter upright aluminum tubes moored 20 ft apart and in line with the boat. After immediate schooling the animals proceeded to make several echo-location runs to investigate this barrier. It was clear from their initial behavior that they had detected some obstruction which they had picked up with their routine navigational sonar.

Assuming a sound pressure level of 120 dB re. 0.0002 μbar, the author having observed 110 dB ranges at one meter produced in captivity by *T. truncatus*, we may get some idea of a theoretical limit that might be expected. Much of the energy measured with unfiltered equipment is accounted for by the very wide bandwidth of the pulse, conservatively 100 kHz. Figure 4, while not a complete frequency record, shows a spectral reinforcement of 2 kHz width at about 14 kHz. Assuming this one band contains half the power, we are entering the problem with a signal of 117 dB at one meter's distance from the animal. According to Fig. 9, propagation loss contours according to Horton, the signal would suffer about 51.5 dB attenuation before ever reaching the 400-yard distant target, and with perfect reflection suffer the same amount in returning, a total of 103 dB. This would result in a net signal of 14 dB available for processing. Further, assuming a critical band filtering (as exists in the human ear), we see from the Knudsen ([22]) curves in Fig. 10 that in sea state 1, the least perturbation above flat calm, the ambient interference in the frequency range around 14 kHz amounts to a spectrum level of about 10 dB. For a 2-kHz bandwidth this would mean approximately 43 dB, or a situation in which the animal must operate on a − 29 dB signal-to-noise ratio. This, of course, is not an impossible condition to work with, but the usual hearing physiology cannot give us the answer. It would seem obvious from

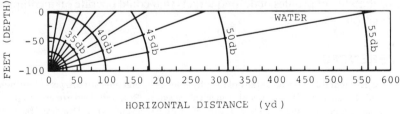

Fig. 9. Underwater propagation loss contours. After Horton ([21]).

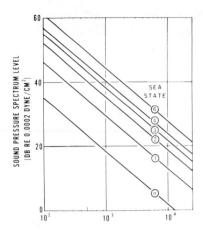

Fig. 10. Sea state curves. After V. O. Knudsen. (^{22}).

our own signal processing experience that some sophisticated form of retrieval is required, with the holographic technique being one possibility, cross-correlation being another.

Were this latter to be the case, we might postulate a (near) simultaneous reception of both lobes of the asymmetric signal of Fig. 7, with some correlation operation being performed in the two lobes of the auditory cortex. Being humans, not dolphins, we are hardly in a position to say that such a scheme would be less satisfactory than sensing a diffraction pattern over the whole array, which intuitively seems the more attractive concept. With our own familiar algorithmic method of matching analog signatures, it might seem an almost insurmountable task to store comparison templates of the mix of false targets which must continually occupy the animal's target space. A representation of three-dimensional space, therefore, however interpreted or reconstructed, would allow selective focus of the animal's attention on certain target features. Recovery of phase information over the area of the melon is thereby necessary, and according to our present state of ignorance might be effected by a neurally stored reference pulse, or, more conceivably, by referencing the phase of adjacent sensors as a function of time of echo return. In this fashion we might even conjecture a prebiasing mechanism based on the probability of profiles of desired targets that could operate on incomplete information.

REFERENCES

1. W. E. Evans and J. J. Dreher, Study of the Physiological Communicative Aspect of Porpoise Sound Production, Physical and Chemical Sciences Research Department Research Memorandum No. 1979 Lockheed Aircraft Company, California Division, Burbank, California (1960).

2. R. G. Busnel and Albin Dziedzic, Acoustic Signals of the Pilot Whale *Globicephela Melaena* and of the Porpoises *Delphinos Delphis* and *Phocaena Phocena*, in: *Whales, Dolphins and Porpoises* (K. Norris, ed.), University of California Press, 1966.

3. J. J. Dreher, Linguistic Considerations of Cetacean Sound Production, *J. Acoust. Soc. Am.* **33**: 12 (Dec. 1961).

4. J. J. Dreher, Cetacean Communication; Small Group Experiment, in: *Whales, Dolphins, and Porpoises* (K. Norris, ed.), University of California Press, 1966.

5. W. N. Kellogg, Auditory Perception of Submerged Objects by Porpoises, *J. Acoust. Soc. Am.* Vol. **31**, No. 1 (Jan. 1959).

6. W. N. Kellogg, *Porpoises and Sonar*, University of Chicago Press, Chicago, 1961.

7. F. W. Reysenbach de Haan, Hearing in Whales, *Acta Otolaryngologica*, Suppl. 134 (1956).

8. P. E. Purves, The Anatomy and Physiology of the Outer and Middle Ear in Cetaceans, in: *Whales, Dolphins and Porpoises* (K. Norris, ed.), University of California Press, 1966.

9. J. J. Dreher, W. W. Sutherland, and W. Evans, Instrumentation Techniques for Analysis of Characteristics of Animal Sonar Pulses, LF18525, Office of Naval Research, Contract No. Nonr 3680 (00) (14 Jan. 1965).

10. W. E. Evans and J. H. Prescott, Observations of the Sound Production Capabilities of the Bottlenose Porpoise. A Study of Whistles and Clicks, *Zoologica* **47**: 121–128 (1962).

11. K. S. Norris, Some Problems of Echolocation in Cetaceans, in: *Marine Bioacoustics* (W. Tavolga, ed.), Pergamon Press, New York, 1964.

12. W. E. Evans, W. W. Sutherland, and R. G. Beil, Directional Characteristics of Delphinid Sounds, in: *Marine Bioacoustics* (W. Tavolga, ed.), Pergamon Press, London, 1964.

13. P. E. Purves, Anatomical and Experimental Observations on the Cetacean Sonar System, in: *Animal Sonar Systems* (R. G. Busnel, ed.), Laboratoire de Physiologic Acoustique, Jouy-en-Josas, 1967.

14. B. Lawrence and W. E. Schevill, Gular Musculature in Delphinids, *Bull. Mus. Comp. Zoologica* **133**: 5–58 (1965).

15. E. I. Griffin, Making Friends with a Killer Whale, *National Geographic* **129**: 418–446 (1966).

16. J. C. Lilly, *Man and Dolphin*, Gollancz, London, 1962.

17. W. E. Evans and B. A. Powell, Discrimination of Different Metallic Plates by an Echolocating Delphinid, in: *Animal Sonar Systems* (R. G. Busnel, ed.), Laboratoire de Physiologic Acoustique, Jouy-en-Josas, 1967.

18. W. E. Evans and J. J. Dreher, Hearing in Cetacea, Lockheed Technical Memorandum 50017 (Feb. 1961).

19. F. A. Ries and O. R. A. Langworth, A Study of the Surface Structure of the Brain of the Whale (*Baleanoptera Physalus* and *Physetu Catadon*), *J. Comp. Neurol.* Vol. **68**, No. 1 (1937).

20. W. E. Evans and J. J. Dreher, Observations on Scouting Behavior and Associated Sound Production by the Pacific Bottlenosed Porpoise (*Tursiops gilli Dall*), *Bull. So. Cal. Acad. Sci.* **61**:4 (Oct. 1962).

21. J. W. Horton, *Fundamentals of Sonar*, U.S. Naval Institute, 1957.

22. V. O. Knudsen, R. S. Alford, and J. W. Emling, Underwater Ambient Noise, *J. Mar. Res.* **7**: 410–429 (1948).

Chapter 9

THE GENERATION OF SOUND*

J. de Klerk

Westinghouse Research Laboratories
Pittsburgh, Pennsylvania

Methods and problems in sound generation from audio to microwave frequencies are reviewed. Special emphasis is placed on the high end of the frequency spectrum, where sound and optical wavelength are comparable.

INTRODUCTION

Acoustical holography consists in essence of observing and storing the shadow of an object which is being irradiated with sound. The irradiation process concerns the generation and propagation of sound in the medium in which the object is immersed. The observation process concerns the detection and intensity measurement of the sound arriving at some chosen plane on the remote side of the object from the irradiation source. While this chapter is mainly concerned with the irradiation source, i.e., the generation of sound, a brief description of some of the physical properties of the transmission media will be necessary.

The resolution that can be achieved in such a system is dependent upon the sound wavelength, which is determined by the frequency and the acoustic velocity in the medium. The relation between these parameters is given by the equation

$$v = f\lambda \tag{1}$$

where v is velocity, f is frequency, and λ is the wavelength; alternatively,

$$\lambda = v/f \tag{2}$$

For the observation of any appreciable detail of the object being observed the sound wavelength must be smaller than the dimensions of such details. As the sound transmission medium can consist of a solid, a liquid, or a gas,

*The work reported here has been partially supported by the U.S. Air Force under Contract AF 19(628)-4372.

Eq. (2) has been used to compute the sound wavelength as a function of frequency for each of the three possible states. These calculations have been plotted as shown in Fig. 1 for typical velocities, 0.5, 1.0, and 5.0×10^5 cm/sec for a gas, a liquid, and a solid, respectively.

From Fig. 1 it is clear that at a particular frequency λ is smallest for propagation in a gas and largest in a solid. However, the practical upper frequency limit of sound propagation in the medium is determined by the

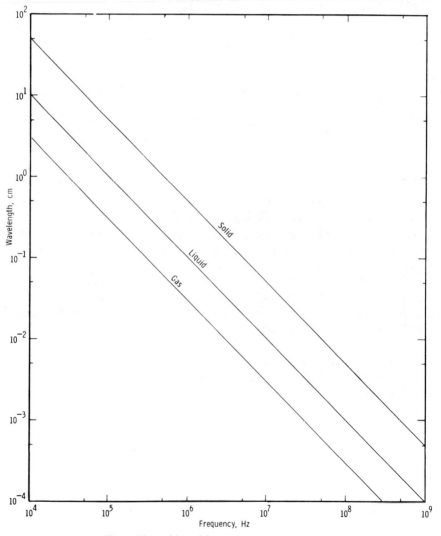

Fig. 1. Plots of λ vs. f, for a gas, a liquid, and a solid.

rate at which the energy is attenuated. The sound intensity I decreases with distance x according to ([1])

$$I_x = I_0 e^{-2\alpha x} \qquad (3)$$

where α, the absorption coefficient, is largest for a gas and smallest for a solid. The attenuation rate is proportional to the square of the frequency.

These considerations place approximate practical upper frequency and wavelength limits of useful propagation as given in Table I.

Table I

Medium	Frequency, f	Wavelength, λ (cm)
Gas	~ 100 kHz	0.5
Liquid	~ 100 MHz	0.001
Solid	~ 1000 MHz	0.0005 (Compressional) 0.00025 (shear)

SOUND GENERATION

Sound Generation in a Gas

Sound generation in a gas at audible frequencies is generally achieved by means of a moving piston or diaphragm, while at ultrasonic frequencies whistles capable of generating very high intensities are generally employed. The moving piston, in the form of a conventional cone loudspeaker, is driven by the interaction between an alternating current flowing in a coil at the driving frequency and a magnetic field passing through the coil. The latter is placed in a gap between the poles of a permanent magnet as shown in Fig. 2. Moving diaphragms are usually employed in horn loudspeakers ([2]), which are capable of much higher acoustic power output than cone loudspeakers. Ultrasonic frequencies can also be generated by making use of the magnetostrictive properties of ferromagnetic materials. In this method ([3]) a bar of magnetic material is magnetized by an electric current flowing in a coil wound around the bar. When the direction of current flow in the coil is reversed the direction of magnetization is reversed. During magnetization the length of the bar is altered. The magnitude of change and the sense, i.e., whether the length increases or decreases, depends upon the magnetostrictive constant of the material from which the bar has been made.

Such a bar can be made to resonate in a compressional mode at a frequency f given by the equation

$$L = (n/2f)(E/\rho)^{1/2} \qquad (4)$$

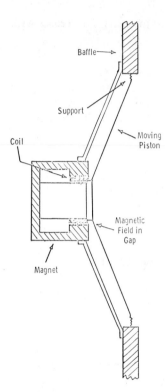

Fig. 2. Cone loudspeaker.

where L is the length of bar, n the order of harmonic, E Young's modulus, and ρ the density. This method is suitable for generating sound in either a gas or a liquid.

In each case the generated sound beam diverges when the generating surface is a plane or a point source. The angle of divergence is proportional to the ratio of the wavelength to the diameter of the diaphragm or cone, λ/D. Various forms of whistles and sirens are also capable of generating intense sound at frequencies ranging from sonic up to 100 kHz [3].

Sound Generation in a Liquid

The two most frequently used methods of sound generation in liquids employ magnetostriction or piezoelectricity. The former method, as described above, is capable of generating high acoustic powers, but is limited to frequencies below 100 kHz. Piezoelectric generators, however, are capable of useful acoustic outputs up to frequencies far beyond the limits imposed by the acoustic attenuation of the liquid medium. This limit for liquids is in the vicinity of 100 MHz, where the wavelength is of the order of 10^{-3} cm.

The attenuation in a liquid at a chosen frequency is three to four orders of magnitude smaller than that in a gas, thus allowing operation at much higher frequencies and shorter wavelengths in the liquid.

When a piezoelectric material is placed in an electric field the material becomes strained, the type and direction of the strain being determined by both the direction of the electric field and the crystal structure of the piezo-electric material. As an example, when an electric field is applied parallel to the X_1 direction in α-quartz this material suffers either a compressive or a tensile strain along this axis, depending upon the direction of the electric field along the X_1 axis. Thus a quartz plate can be made to vibrate in a thickness extensional, or compressional, mode when the thickness dimension of the plate and the direction of the electric field are along the X_1 axis. Such plates vibrate at their fundamental frequencies when their thickness is equivalent to half an acoustic wavelength ($\lambda/2$) for the particular mode of vibration. High acoustic powers can also be generated by a suitable mosaic structure of smaller transducers as used in sonar applications. Some of the ferroelectric ceramic materials, such as barium titanate and PZT, are also able to generate high acoustic powers, but are limited in frequency to the order of approximately one MHz. These materials, however, have an advantage in that they can easily be fabricated into odd shapes and then polarized in the desired direction.

Sound Generation in a Solid

Unlike gases and liquids, which can only support compressional waves, solids are capable of supporting both compressional and shear waves. Whereas gaseous and liquid media are directly coupled to the sound generator, solids must be coupled to the generator by some kind of liquid or solid coupling medium, usually called a bond. At ultrasonic frequencies the most commonly used sound generator is a quartz disk, which is generally cemented directly onto the solid transmission medium. The cement or bond could be an epoxy resin, a low melting point crystalline solid, such as salol, or a viscous oil capable of supporting shear waves, when sufficiently thin, as well as compressional waves. The type of wave generated by the transducer is determined by its orientation with respect to the crystallographic axes of the quartz.

From Eq. (2) it will be seen that as the frequency increases the wavelength λ decreases. Since transducers which resonate at their fundamental frequency are $\lambda/2$ thick, the maximum fundamental frequency attainable with disk transducers, which are normally ground and polished to the desired thickness, is determined by their mechanical strength. These transducers become too thin to handle at frequencies greater than 100 MHz. When they are excited at harmonic frequencies much higher frequencies can be attained.

However, at these higher frequencies the acoustic bond between the transducer and solid medium becomes the major problem.

At frequencies in excess of 100 MHz thin-film piezoelectric transducers[4] which have been deposited from the vapors directly onto the solid avoid all the bonding problems. Furthermore, they can be made sufficiently thin and efficient to operate at fundamental resonance up to 100 GHz. The method used by the author for depositing such transducers is illustrated in Fig. 3. In this method the component elements of the piezoelectric material, such as CdS or ZnS, are evaporated from separate crucibles to provide the necessary vapors from which the films are condensed. The solid sample being coated is maintained at an elevated temperature, usually near 200°C, to obtain epitaxial stoichiometric film growth of the desired hexagonal structure. A baffle plate is placed between the crucibles and the sample housing to prevent direct molecular beams from the crucibles from striking the sample surface. An inner glasswalled furnace surrounding the crucibles, baffle, and

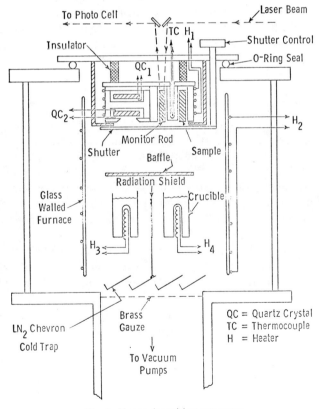

Fig. 3. Vapor-deposition apparatus.

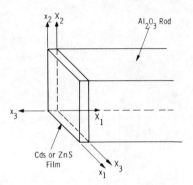

Fig. 4. Orientation of CdS or ZnS on Al_2O_3.

sample housing is maintained at a temperature slightly below the sample temperature to ensure the desired vapor pressure of each element during deposition. The film thickness is monitored during deposition by means of a quartz crystal microbalance and by optical interference using a laser beam. The piezoelectric films resulting from this deposition process are highly oriented and stoichiometric. When deposited on an amorphous surface the CdS or ZnS c or X_3 axes are normal to the surface, while the X_1 and X_2 axes are fairly randomly oriented. On single-crystal samples, however, the X_1 and X_2 axes also become highly oriented. Figure 4 shows the orientation of a CdS or ZnS film with respect to the sapphire substrate. With this type of piezoelectric film it is possible to generate compressional or shear waves as shown in Fig. 5. Shown at the lower left is the piezoelectric matrix for the crystal class 6 mm to which CdS and ZnS belong. The definitions of the crystallographic directions in ZnS and Al_2O_3 used in the diagram are given in the symmetry elements for hexagonal and trigonal crystals. Referring to the piezoelectric matrix at the bottom left, it will be seen that when an electric field is applied normal to the ZnS transducer, i.e., along its X_3 axis, compressional waves will be generated by the ZnS and consequently propagate along the X_1 axis of the Al_2O_3. If the electric field is directed along the ZnS X_1 axis, a shearing strain will be generated about the ZnS X_2 axis resulting in the T_2 or slow shear mode in the Al_2O_3. The T_1 or fast shear mode is generated when the electric field is directed along the ZnS X_2 axis, which results in a shearing strain about the ZnS X_1 axis. The characteristic velocities of the three acoustic waves in the Al_2O_3 are indicated by the shaded planes in the sample. Their positions along the sample represent the appropriate distances traveled after unit time, while the polarization diagrams at the top of Fig. 5 indicate the displacement vectors or directions of particle motion for the different modes. The values of attenuation shown in the body of the Al_2O_3 sample were measured in one of the samples at 4°K at 1 GHz ([5]).

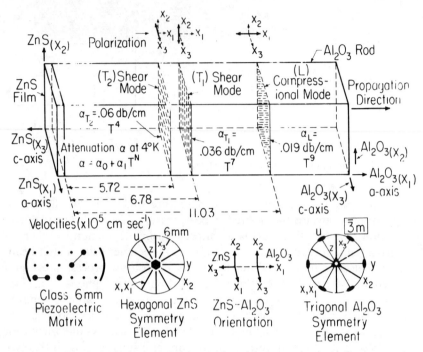

Fig. 5. Acoustic pure mode generation and propagation in Al_2O_3.

The manner in which compressional and shear wave generation is achieved in samples like that shown in Fig. 5 is indicated in Figs. 6 and 7. These broadband microwave cavities direct the electric field in the desired directions. Figure 6 shows a cavity with disk electrodes suitable for directing

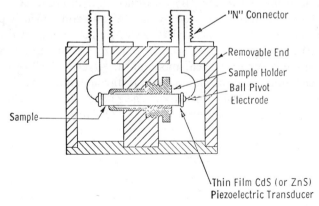

Fig. 6. Compressional mode cavity.

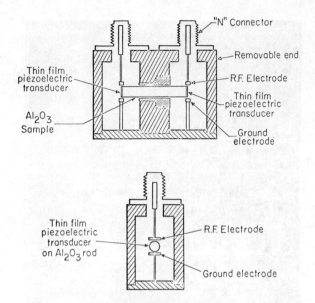

Fig. 7. Shear mode cavity.

the electric field perpendicular to the piezoelectric film, resulting in compressional waves. Figure 7 shows how the line electrodes generate an electric field in the plane of the film transducer. The sample is rotated about its longitudinal axis to find the correct crystallographic direction for the desired shear wave, as indicated in Fig. 4. When a pulsed AC electric field is applied to the piezoelectric transducer sound pulses propagate along the sample and reverberate between the ends until all the sound energy has been dissipated ([6]). Figure 8 shows how the sound pulses of the compressional and shear modes generated in Al_2O_3 by the above technique attenuate with distance. The upper oscilloscope trace represents compressional waves in Al_2O_3 at 1 GHz at room temperature, while the center trace represents the fast shear mode and the lower trace the slow shear mode.

DETECTION OF SOUND

In sound detectors the reverse of the generation process usually occurs. Resolution of detail in the sound picture being detected is determined by the sound wavelength and the dimensions of the detector active element. If the sound picture is allowed to impinge upon a screen upon which a thin piezoelectric film has been deposited, the surface of the film will become charged. The charge density will be proportional to the intensity of the impinging sound. The charged surface could then be scanned by well-known electron

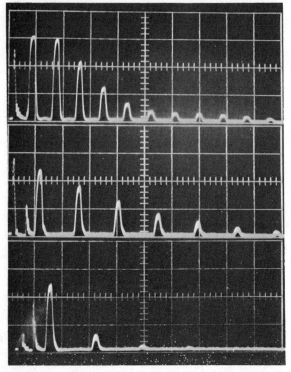

Fig. 8. L, T_1, and T_2 modes in Al_2O_3 at room temperature as observed on an oscilloscope.

beam techniques. The vapor-deposition technique described [4] could be used for uniform deposition of the piezoelectric material on the surface of the screen.

REFERENCES

1. L. Bergman, *Ultrasonics*, John Wiley and Sons, New York, 1948.
2. H. F. Olson, *Acoustical Engineering*, D. Van Nostrand Co., New York, 1957.
3. B. Carlin, *Ultrasonics*, McGraw-Hill Book Co., New York, 1960.
4. J. de Klerk and E. F. Kelly, *Rev. Sci. Instr.* **36**:506 (1965); J. de Klerk, in *Physical Acoustics*, Vol. 4A (W. P. Mason, ed.), Academic Press, New York, 1966.
5. J. de Klerk, *Phys. Rev.* **139**:A1635 (1965).
6. J. de Klerk, *Ultrasonics* **2**:137 (1964).

Chapter 10

ACOUSTICAL IMAGING BY DIFFRACTED LIGHT—TWO-DIMENSIONAL INTERACTION*

A. Korpel

Zenith Radio Corporation
Chicago, Illinois

A formalism is developed describing quantitatively in terms of plane waves the weak interaction of two-dimensional sound and light fields of arbitrary cross-section. This formalism is applied to the analysis of the phenomenon of acoustical imaging by diffracted light demonstrated previously by the author ([4]).

INTRODUCTION

In analyzing the interaction of arbitrary fields of sound and light, it is convenient to represent these fields by their plane wave distributions, as there exist some very simple rules defining and restricting the possible relative directions at which plane waves can interact. These rules are conveniently derived on the basis of quantum-mechanical wave–particle equivalence combined with the theorem of momentum conservation ([1]). Figure 1 illustrates the condition of momentum (or wave vector) conservation in two dimensions:

$$\mathbf{k} \pm \mathbf{K} = \mathbf{k}_{\pm 1} \qquad (1)$$

where $\mathbf{k}$ is the wave vector of the incident light, $\mathbf{K}$ that of the sound, and $\mathbf{k}_{\pm 1}$ that of the scattered light. A similar relation holds for the frequencies:

$$\omega \pm \Omega = \omega_{\pm 1} \qquad (2)$$

where ω is the frequency of the incident light, Ω that of the sound, and $\omega_{\pm 1}$ that of the scattered light. In the usual experimental conditions $\Omega \ll \omega$ and hence $k \approx k_{\pm 1}$.

*This chapter was originally published in *IEEE Transactions on Sonics and Ultrasonics*, Volume SU-15, Number 3, July 1968, and is reprinted here by courtesy of the editors.

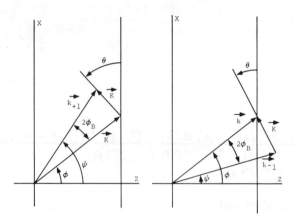

Fig. 1. Momentum or wave vector conservation in Bragg diffraction.

As shown in Fig. 1, for a given **k** only two directions of diffracted light are possible, corresponding to generation of the $+1$ order (k_{+1}) and the -1 order (k_{-1}). If the interaction is weak, so that rescattering can be neglected, these are the only orders of interest. Defining θ as the (counterclockwise) angle between **K** and the X axis, ϕ as that between **k** and the Z axis, and ψ that between either $\mathbf{k}_{+1}$ or $\mathbf{k}_{-1}$ and the Z axis, we find

$$\theta = \psi \mp \phi_B \tag{3}$$

and

$$\phi = \psi \mp 2\phi_B \tag{4}$$

where the upper and lower signs refer to the generation of the $+1$ and -1 orders, respectively. The angle ϕ_B is called the Bragg angle and is given by:

$$\sin \phi_B = K/2k \tag{5}$$

We shall in what follows use the concept of angular spectrum, i.e., the various fields will be characterized by their plane wave distributions $E_0(\phi)$, $E_{\pm 1}(\psi)$, and $S(\theta)$, these quantities specifying, respectively, the complex amplitude of the plane wave component of incident light (E_0) in the direction ϕ, that of the diffracted light $(E_{\pm 1})$ in the direction ψ, and that of the sound (S) in the direction θ. A precise definition of the amplitudes will be given later.

In classical terms the Bragg diffraction process is one of parametric mixing $(^2)$, and [with (3) and (4)] one expects the plane wave amplitudes to be related by $(^3)$

$$E_{+1}(\psi) = -jCS(\psi - \phi_B)E_0(\psi - 2\phi_B) \tag{6}$$

and

$$E_{-1}(\psi) = -jCS^*(\psi + \phi_B)E_0(\psi + 2\phi_B) \tag{7}$$

where C is an interaction constant, the magnitude of which depends on the medium in which the interaction takes place and (as will be shown later) on the ratio k/K. The complex conjugate sign (asterisk) in (7) indicates the phase inversion inherent in frequency-difference (lower-sideband) generation. The coefficient $-j$ expresses the fact that the interaction process is basically one of phase modulation of the incident light by the refractive index variations caused by the sound. This leads to "sidebands" (i.e., diffracted orders $E_{\pm 1}$) in quadrature with the "carrier" E_0.

In order to bring out the imaging properties of Bragg diffraction, let $E_0(\phi)$ be constant independent of ϕ, representing the field of a line source. Inspection of (6) and (7) then shows that the plane wave distribution of the diffracted light is identical to that of the sound or its conjugate. Hence the diffracted light should carry an image of the sound field. That this is indeed the case has been made plausible by ray tracing and has been demonstrated experimentally ([4]). In the present chapter the imaging process will be analyzed more rigorously using a plane wave interaction approach along the lines indicated above. It will be shown that this method confirms the results obtained by ray tracing. In addition, it provides quantitative information concerning the interaction strength and may be used to calculate resolution, aberrations, etc. For the present the analysis is limited to two dimensions.

PLANE WAVE INTERACTION FORMALISM

In this section we shall define more precisely the amplitudes used in (6) and (7) and derive the interaction constant C. In the coordinate system of Fig. 1 we shall take the light to be polarized perpendicular to the plane of the paper. We shall also consider the interacting medium to be a liquid and hence the strain S to be a scalar quantity more properly called the condensation ([5]). The various fields may then be represented by their angular plane wave spectra ([6]):

$$S(z, x) = \int_{-\infty}^{+\infty} S(\theta) \exp\{jK(z \sin \theta - x \cos \theta)\} \, d\{\sin(\theta - \theta_0)\} \tag{8}$$

$$E_0(z, x) = \int_{-\infty}^{+\infty} E_0(\phi) \exp\{-jk(z \cos \phi + x \sin \phi)\} \, d\{\sin(\phi - \phi_0)\} \tag{9}$$

and

$$E_{\pm 1}(z, x) = \int_{-\infty}^{+\infty} E_{\pm 1}(\psi) \exp\{-jk(z \cos \psi + x \sin \psi)\} \, d\{\sin(\psi - \psi_{0\pm})\} \tag{10}$$

where the time dependence of the field is suppressed for simplicity. For mathematical convenience (this will become clear later) we write $d\{\sin(\phi - \phi_0)\}$ rather than $d\phi$. Thus the resultant complex amplitude of those plane waves whose wave normals are between ϕ and $\phi + d\phi$ is defined as $E_0(\phi)\,d\{\sin(\phi - \phi_0)\}$ in this formulation, with a similar interpretation of $S(\theta)$ and $E_{\pm 1}(\psi)$. Note that ϕ and ψ are taken counterclockwise from the Z axis and θ from the X axis.

Neglecting evanescent waves ([6]), the total angular range of plane waves in the angular spectra $E_0(\phi)$, $E_{\pm 1}(\psi)$, and $S(\theta)$ is assumed not to exceed 180°. The angles ϕ_0, $\psi_{0\pm}$, and θ_0 are to a certain extent arbitrary provided the following condition is satisfied:

$$-\pi/2 < \phi - \phi_0, \qquad \psi - \psi_{0\pm}, \qquad \theta - \theta_0, \qquad <\pi/2 \qquad (11)$$

Thus ϕ_0, $\psi_{0\pm}$, and θ_0 may conveniently be taken as the center of the corresponding plane wave distribution indicating the "average" direction of propagation. For the sound field this direction is taken along the X axis:

$$\theta_0 = 0 \qquad (12)$$

The spectra $E_0(\phi)$, $E_{\pm 1}(\psi)$, and $S(\theta)$ may be derived from the complex value of the fields $E_0(z, x)$, $E_{\pm 1}(z, x)$, and $S(z, x)$ along any cross section by a simple Fourier transform ([6]). Consider the configuration of Fig. 2, which is of particular interest to the discussion.

The incident light field is a beam of light of width D, the amplitude of which is accurately known along a cross section through z_0, x_0 with the

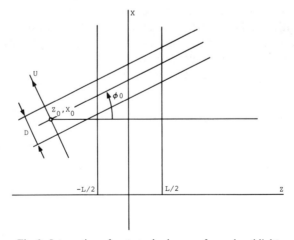

Fig. 2. Interaction of rectangular beams of sound and light.

normal to the cross section making an angle ϕ_0 with the Z axis:

$$E_0(u) = A_0 \qquad |u| < D/2 \tag{13}$$

$$E_0(u) = 0 \qquad |u| > D/2 \tag{14}$$

where u is the coordinate along the cross section:

$$z = z_0 - u \sin \phi_0 \tag{15}$$

and

$$x = x_0 + u \cos \phi_0 \tag{16}$$

Substituting (15) and (16) into (9), we find

$$E_0(u) = \int_{-\infty}^{+\infty} E_0(\phi) \exp\{-jk(z_0 \cos \phi + x_0 \sin \phi)\}$$

$$\times \exp\{-jku \sin(\phi - \phi_0)\} \, d\{\sin(\phi - \phi_0)\} \tag{17}$$

The second exponential term will be recognized as a Fourier transform between ku and $\sin(\phi - \phi_0)$. The inverse transform gives

$$E_0(\phi) = (k/2\pi) \exp\{+jk(z_0 \cos \phi + x_0 \sin \phi)\}$$

$$\times \int_{-\infty}^{+\infty} E_0(u) \exp\{+jku \sin(\phi - \phi_0)\} \, du \tag{18}$$

Substituting (13) and (14) into (18), we find

$$E_0(\phi) = (kA_0D/2\pi) \exp\{+jk(z_0 \cos \phi + x_0 \sin \phi)\}$$

$$\times \mathrm{sinc}\{\tfrac{1}{2}kD \sin(\phi - \phi_0)\} \tag{19}$$

where we have used the notation $\mathrm{sinc}\, X = \sin X / X$.

The sound field interacting with $E_0(\phi)$ is a beam of sound of width L accurately known along the z axis:

$$S(z) = S_0 \qquad |z| < L/2 \tag{20}$$

$$S(z) = 0 \qquad |z| > L/2 \tag{21}$$

By a similar calculation as before we find

$$S(\theta) = (KS_0L/2\pi) \, \mathrm{sinc}\{\tfrac{1}{2}KL \sin \theta\} \tag{22}$$

In order to derive the interaction constant C we will consider a specific case for which the answer is well known, that of a plane wave of light incident at the Bragg angle on a sound column of width L. Let us restrict ourselves to the $+1$ order. Thus we shall take $\phi_0 = -\phi_B$ and let $D \to \infty$. From (19) we have:

$$E_0(\phi) = A_0 \exp\{+jk(z_0 \cos \phi_B - x_0 \sin \phi_B)\} \, \delta\{\sin(\phi + \phi_B)\} \tag{23}$$

where δ denotes the Dirac delta function. Substituting (23) and (22) into (6), we find

$$E_{+1}(\psi) = (-jCA_0KS_0L/2\pi)\exp\{+jk(z_0\cos\phi_B - x_0\sin\phi_B)\}\,\delta\{\sin(\psi - \phi_B)\} \tag{24}$$

As expected, the diffracted light is a plane wave propagating at angle $\psi = \phi_B$. The ratio R of diffracted to incident light intensity is given by

$$R = (CKS_0L/2\pi)^2 \tag{25}$$

According to a calculation by Phariseau ([7]) this ratio, for weak interaction at the Bragg angle, is given by

$$R = (\tfrac{1}{2}k_0\,\Delta n\,L)^2/\cos^2\phi_B \tag{26}$$

where k_0 is the light propagation constant in vacuum and Δn the peak refractive index variation caused by the strain in the sound field.

For an isotropic medium the following relation holds ([8])

$$\Delta n = -\tfrac{1}{2}n^3pS_0 \tag{27}$$

where n is the refractive index of the medium and p the elastooptic strain coefficient. Equating (25) with (26) and (27), we find

$$C = \tfrac{1}{2}\pi(k_0/K)(n^3p/\cos\phi_B) \tag{28}$$

ACOUSTICAL IMAGING

We shall now show the existence of a spatial image of the sound field in the diffracted light and derive the imaging rules. We will assume the sound field to be illuminated by a quasi-line source located at z_0, x_0. The prefix "quasi" is used in the sense that the angular spectrum of the source is subject to condition (11), where we will choose $\phi_0 = -\phi_B$. The angular spectrum may be obtained from (19) by letting $D \to 0$, while A_0D remains finite. The sinc term then becomes unity, independent of ϕ, and we find

$$E_0(\phi) = (kA_0D/2\pi)\exp\{+jk(z_0\cos\phi + x_0\sin\phi)\} \tag{29}$$

In deriving the angular spectrum of the diffracted light we will again limit ourselves to the $+1$ order. From (29) and (6) we have:

$$E_{+1}(\psi) = (-jCkA_0D/2\pi)\exp[jk\{z_0\cos(\psi - 2\phi_B) + x_0\sin(\psi - 2\phi_B)\}]$$
$$\times S(\psi - \phi_B) \tag{30}$$

We now calculate the field $E_{+1}(z, x)$ from (30) and (10), setting ψ_{0+} equal to ϕ_B, the latter being the average direction of scattered light:

$$E_{+1}(z, x) = \frac{-jCkA_0D}{2\pi} \int_{-\infty}^{+\infty} \exp[jk\{z_0 \cos(\psi - 2\phi_B) + x_0 \sin(\psi - 2\phi_B)\}]$$

$$\times \exp\{-jk(z \cos \psi + x \sin \psi)\} \, S(\psi - \phi_B) \, d\{\sin(\psi - \phi_B)\} \quad (31)$$

With the notation $\theta = \psi - \phi_B$ we may rewrite (31) as follows:

$$E_{+1}(z, x) = \frac{-jCkA_0D}{2\pi} \int_{-\infty}^{+\infty} \exp(jKz' \sin \theta - jKx' \cos \theta)S(\theta) \, d(\sin \theta) \quad (32)$$

where

$$z' = (k/K)(x_0 - x) \cos \phi_B + (k/K)(z_0 + z) \sin \phi_B \quad (33)$$

and

$$x' = (k/K)(x_0 + x) \sin \phi_B - (k/K)(z_0 - z) \cos \phi_B \quad (34)$$

Comparing (32) with (8), we find:

$$E_{+1}(z, x) = (-jCkA_0D/2\pi)S(z', x') \quad (35)$$

Hence the diffracted light carries an image of the sound field, the imaging rules being given by (33) and (34)

In order to bring out the essential features of the image transformation, we introduce a new coordinate system for the sound by rotating the ZX axes counterclockwise over an angle $(\pi/2) - \phi_B$ to new axes ξ and ζ as indicated in Fig. 3:

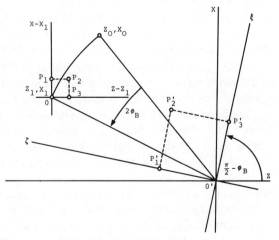

Fig. 3. Illustration of imaging rules.

$$\xi = z \sin \phi_B + x \cos \phi_B \tag{36}$$

$$\zeta = -z \cos \phi_B + x \sin \phi_B \tag{37}$$

We may then rewrite (35):

$$E_{+1}(z, x) = (-jCkA_0D/2\pi)S(\xi', \zeta') \tag{38}$$

From (33) and (34) we find:

$$(K/k)\xi' = z - z_1 \tag{39}$$

and

$$(K/k)\zeta' = x - x_1, \tag{40}$$

where

$$z_1 = z_0 \cos 2\phi_B - x_0 \sin 2\phi_B \tag{41}$$

and

$$x_1 = x_0 \cos 2\phi_B + z_0 \sin 2\phi_B \tag{42}$$

Thus the imaging involves a rotation by $(\pi/2) - \phi_B$, a translation of the origin to the point z_1, x_1 and a uniform demagnification by a ratio K/k. As indicated in Fig. 3, the point z_1, x_1 may be found by rotating the point z_0, x_0 (the location of the original line source) counterclockwise about the Y axis through an angle $2\phi_B$. The demagnification ratio K/k guarantees physical consistency of the imaging process with known laws of wave propagation, i.e., K/k is the ratio by which a field at wavelength Λ ($=2\pi/K$) has to be scaled down if it is to be faithfully reproduced at wavelength λ ($=2\pi/k$) and if both fields are to satisfy the wave equation.

As an example, consider in Fig. 3 a sound field generated by four quasi-line sources O', P'_1, P'_2, and P'_3. The optical image will consist of the field generated by the four quasi-line sources of diffracted light O, P_1, P_2, and P_3, where $\overline{OP_1} = (K/k)\overline{O'P'_1}$, etc. The complex amplitudes of the light sources may be derived from the complex amplitudes of the sound sources by application of (35), taking A_0 as the complex amplitude of the illuminating line source at z_0, x_0. The amplitude of any non-source point in the light field may be similarly derived from the corresponding non-source point in the sound field or by directly applying the optical wave equation to the system of sources O, P, P_2, and P_3. The scaling factor K/k guarantees that the results of these two calculations will be identical.

For a simple interpretation of the imaging rules, consider the intuitively plausible geometric ray construction shown in Fig. 4. Draw the ray pencil OP from the source of light O at z_0, x_0 to the point P of the sound field at z', x'. Construct the diffracted ray PR at an angle $2\phi_B$ relative to OP. Extend PR

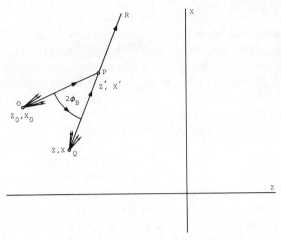

Fig. 4. Derivation of imaging rules by ray tracing.

back by a length $\overline{PQ} = \overline{OP}$. The point Q at z, x is then the image of P; its coordinates satisfy (33) and (34), as may be shown by simple analytic geometry.

Although the discussion has been limited to the $+1$ order, it will be clear that a quite similar analysis can be given for the -1 order. In that case the resulting imaging rules will correspond to a rotation by $-2\phi_B$ in Fig. 4, while in (35) we have to replace S by S^*.

Because of the assumption of an ideal line source for E_0, the imaging process as expressed by (35) does not produce any loss in resolution. For an arbitrary illumination $E_0(\phi)$ the resulting finite resolution and aberration may be calculated in a straightforward manner. As an example, consider the practical case of illumination by a nonideal line source, for which D is finite. In that case the sinc term in (19) has to be carried along in the calculation and instead of (32) we find

$$E'_{+1}(z, x) = \frac{-jCkA_0D}{2\pi} \int\limits_{-\infty}^{+\infty} \exp(jKz' \sin\theta - jKx' \cos\theta)$$

$$\times\ S(\theta)\,\mathrm{sinc}\{\tfrac{1}{2}kD \sin\theta\}\,d\{\sin\theta\} \tag{43}$$

with z' and x' as defined before. Hence

$$E'_{+1}(z, x) = (-jCkA_0D/2\pi)S'(z', x') \tag{44}$$

where

$$S'(\theta) = S(\theta)\,\mathrm{sinc}\{\tfrac{1}{2}kD \sin\theta\} \tag{45}$$

Thus the resulting image is that of a fictitious sound field S', which may be thought of as derived from the original field S through spatial frequency filtering as expressed by the sinc term. This term restricts the angular spectrum of S to an angular width of $2\arcsin(\pi/kD)$ or a numerical aperture of π/kD, thereby limiting the minimum resolvable detail. In the general case too, the angular spectrum of the illuminating field $E_0(\phi)$ may be represented by a spatial filtering operation on $S(\theta)$, thus expressing resolution and aberration conveniently in terms of spatial frequency response.

In conclusion, the plane wave interaction formalism developed in this chapter may be used in a straightforward way to calculate in detail the interaction of complex field configurations in two dimensions. Applied to the case of acoustical imaging, it confirms the intuitive ray tracing method and readily provides information about the intensity and spatial frequency content of the image. The extension of the theory to three dimensions is in preparation and will be published at a later date.

REFERENCES

1. E. I. Gordon, A Review of Acoustooptical Deflection and Modulation Devices, *Proc. IEEE* **54**: 1391–1401 (Oct. 1966).
2. P. K. Tien, Parametric Amplification and Frequency Mixing in Propagating Circuits, *J. Appl. Phys.* **29**: 1347 (1958).
3. A. Korpel, Interaction of Sound and Light Fields of Arbitrarily Prescribed Cross Section I, Zenith Radio Corporation Research Report No. 66–2 (Sept. 7, 1966).
4. A. Korpel, Visualization of the Cross-Section of a Sound Beam by Bragg Diffraction of Light, *Appl. Phys. Letters* **9**: 425 (1966).
5. A. Wood, *Acoustics*, 1st ed., Interscience Publishers, New York, 1941, p. 56.
6. J. A. Ratcliffe, Aspects of Diffraction Theory, *Rep. Progr. Phys.* **XIX**: 188–267.
7. P. Phariseau, On the Diffraction of Light by Progressive Supersonic Waves, *Proc. Indian Acad. Sci.* **44**: 165 (1956).
8. T. M. Smith and A. Korpel, Measurement of Light–Sound Interaction Efficiencies in Solids, *IEEE J. of Quantum Electronics* **QE-1**: 283–284 (Sept. 1965).

Chapter 11

ACOUSTICAL TRANSPARENCIES FOR OPTICAL IMAGING AND ULTRASONIC DIFFRACTION

G. Wade, C. J. Landry, and A. A. de Souza

University of California
Santa Barbara, California

Illuminating coherent sound in water with either converging or diverging laser light makes the imaging of the cross section of the sound beam possible. In this fashion an acoustic beam of rectangular cross section shows up as a rectangular patch of light on a screen. Silhouettes of paper clips and other objects placed in the path of the beam can be imaged and made to appear as sharply delineated dark regions within the patch. If we place in the beam path a plate made from an elastic material of uniform thickness, we immediately notice that the sharpness of the silhouette depends upon the angle of incidence of the sound. In fact, by rotating the plate in the water we can generally find a number of orientations for which the silhouette completely disappears. The plate is then transparent to the sound. If we treat one of the surfaces of such a plate by scratching the surface or by depositing various thicknesses of material on it, the scratches or deposits will show up on the screen sharply silhouetted. For example, aluminum deposited on a glass plate gives a silhouette whose opacity depends on the thickness of the deposit. By arranging a pattern of deposits of varying thickness we can produce what we might call an acoustical transparency, from which we can construct an image on the screen. In principle, the deposited pattern can correspond to a printed page, a line drawing, a photograph, or almost any other arrangement desired.

INTRODUCTION

A number of methods have recently been developed for acoustical imaging. Among these is a technique which utilizes the phenomenon of Bragg diffraction from acoustic wavefronts. The principle of the technique bears a great deal of similarity to the behavior of a "thick" hologram, although in a strict sense it is not holographic because no reference beam or reference signal is used. Even so, acoustic phase information is retained in the method and direct three-dimensional imaging is theoretically possible. Since the technique has been well explained in papers by Korpel ([1]) and by Adler ([2]), we will not describe it here in any detail.

While in theory the Bragg imaging technique is usable with any acoustic wavelength, it is practically realizable only for wavelengths within two or three orders of magnitude of that of the interacting light. Because of the attenuating properties of gases for acoustic waves at high frequencies the method is thus limited to the imaging of objects enclosed in either liquid or solid media. Even in these cases the object to be imaged cannot be located more than a few inches from the light–sound interaction region. For this reason the technique may find its greatest application in the form of an acoustical microscope for producing visual images of small acoustic scattering centers which cannot be imaged with light alone.

Most of the experiments carried out to date have utilized an "acoustical cell," a small box measuring typically 3 in. × 2 in. × 5 in. and containing filtered and distilled water as an acoustical medium (Fig. 1). A quartz transducer is mounted at one end of the cell and driven by an RF generator at perhaps 10 or 20 MHz. The resulting longitudinal acoustic waves travel through the water and are absorbed at the end of the cell opposite the transducer. Glass windows are provided in the sides of the cell and typically a converging beam of coherent light is allowed to pass through the acoustic beam (Fig. 2). (Diverging light could also be used, but some difficulty would then be encountered in isolating the portion of light containing image information.) Because of the directional selectivity of Bragg diffraction the

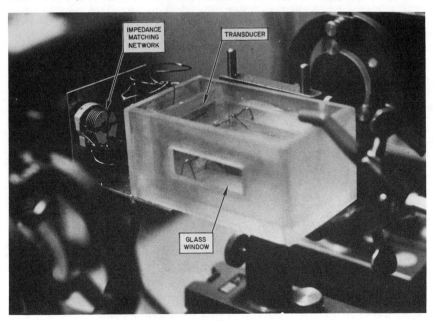

Fig. 1. Acoustical cell.

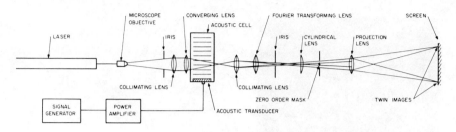

Fig. 2. Diagram of experimental setup for acoustical imaging.

diffracted light emerges with an angular spectrum which is similar to that of the acoustic beam. For this reason the emerging light can be focused by a system of lenses to produce an optical image of the acoustic beam cross section on a screen. The experimental setup used to accomplish this is shown in Fig. 3.

If small objects are then placed in the path of the acoustic waves, but not in the light beam, their silhouette can be visibly observed on the screen. As one would expect, the contrast of the silhouette depends on the extent to which the object either absorbs or reflects the acoustic energy. Figure 4 is a

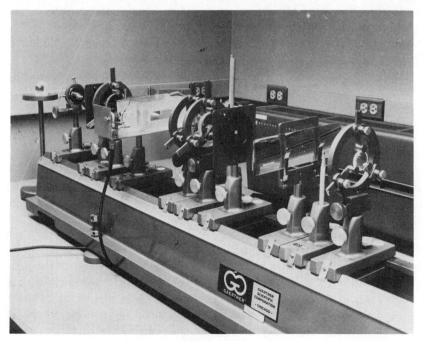

Fig. 3. Experimental setup for acoustical imaging.

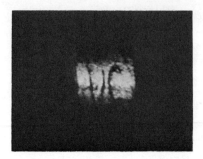

Fig. 4. Image of wire letters.

photograph of the image produced by a wire object in the shape of the letters "UC." For the case shown the transducer was driven at 18 MHz, which corresponds to an acoustic wavelength of 83 μ in water. The wire from which the object was made had a diameter of about 1 mm. The rather poor quality of the image is primarily due to the lenses used and to suspended particles in the water. In subsequent experiments the image quality has been greatly improved.

In experimenting with this imaging technique it was soon noticed that certain objects, particularly strips of glass or sheet metal, appeared to be acoustically transparent for certain angles of incidence of the acoustic waves. While this behavior points out certain limitations of the method when imaging generalized objects, it also leads to considerations of possible uses for the phenomenon.

Furthermore, it is possible to use this approach to make diffracting screens. The opaque portion of such a screen would be produced by a deposited layer of material of proper thickness and the aperture by a region on the plate containing no deposit. A pattern consisting of a series of parallel lines properly spaced would give a diffraction grating for use in ultrasonic spectral analysis. Diffracting screens involving various other special patterns could be used experimentally to test diffraction theory.

The plate itself without any deposit is useful in measuring compressional and shear-wave velocities within the plate material. At certain selected angles of incidence it is possible to excite either pure compressional or pure shear waves. Ordinarily, combinations of both kinds exist in the plate. When only one kind is present, by measuring the light intensity on the screen we can determine the plate opacity and hence the acoustical thickness of the plate for that kind of wave. Knowing this and the actual plate thickness we can obtain the velocity.

A related concept involves the use of acoustically transparent plates as spatial filters. For a coherent acoustic beam, in which the entire spatial spectrum is very narrow, there will be only one angle of incidence of the sound upon a thin plate for which the transmission through the plate is complete. Hence only a narrow portion of the spatial spectrum of any acoustic beam can be transmitted through the plate without back reflection. Such a plate can serve as a band-pass spatial filter.

If the object is a properly designed plate of acoustically lossless material with a pattern deposited or scratched on one of its surfaces, the acoustic waves will pass through the object and be processed in a manner similar to the processing of light waves by means of a photographic transparency. The plate with its surface pattern can then logically be called an "acoustical transparency." When the transparency is placed in the acoustical cell an image corresponding to the deposited pattern on the plate will be produced. In principle, the pattern could be printed characters, a line drawing, a continuous tone photograph, etc.

A number of possible uses for acoustical transparencies come to mind. This paper describes the principles and details of such transparencies and, in addition, suggests some of these possible uses.

ACOUSTICAL TRANSPARENCIES

Consider a plate of elastic material of uniform thickness immersed in an acoustical medium. Assume that the elastic material is acoustically lossless. For purposes of illustration, also assume for the moment that the plate material is glass and that the acoustical medium is water, as in Fig. 5. The behavior associated with wave propagation from the water into the plate and then back into the water on the other side of the plate is generally quite complicated. Analyses of this kind of situation have appeared in the literature over a long period of time ([3]). In general, sound propagating from one acoustical medium to another is partially reflected and partially transmitted in accordance with relationships which by now are well understood.

Under the proper conditions a sound beam impinging upon a plate immersed in water may cause a motion of the particles in the plate such that

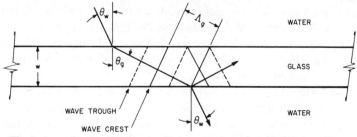

Fig. 5. Acoustic wave propagation from water through a glass plate and back into water.

a large fraction of the sound energy is transmitted through the plate. The particle motion is built up by virtue of successive reflections of the sound from the surfaces of the plate. An example of this phenomenon is the transmission of sound at normal incidence through a plate whose thickness is an exact number of half wavelengths. Under these conditions if the plate is acoustically lossless, all of the sound energy is transmitted and none of it is reflected back. At oblique incidence the situation is more complicated. The particle motion in the plate is generally made up of both compressional waves and shear waves. Analysis of this general case tends to be involved, and the solutions are not very tractable. However, even when both kinds of waves are present, if the angle of incidence and the plate thickness are in the proper relationship, the plate can again become transparent or almost transparent to the sound.

Under certain circumstances only one of the two kinds of waves is propagated, and the solution is simplified. When this is so the behavior is similar to that of an electromagnetic wave propagating along analogous sections of transmission line. Assume that two similar sections of transmission line (corresponding to the water) are separated by a short section of a dissimilar transmission line with a different characteristic impedance (corresponding to the plate). Wave transmission through the middle section will be complete (that is, the middle section will look transparent) if its length is a multiple of a half phase wavelength, where the phase wavelength is given by

$$\Lambda_p = \Lambda_g/\cos\theta_g \tag{1}$$

Hence the glass will appear transparent to the sound when

$$W = N\Lambda_p/2 = N\Lambda_g/(2\cos\theta_g) \tag{2}$$

As previously stated the above reasoning is too simple for the general case as it leaves out the fact that ordinarily both compressional and shear waves get excited in the plate and not just one of these two kinds. Regardless of the complexities involved it is quickly observed in experimenting with thin plates that for a number of angles of incidence the plate becomes very nearly transparent to the sound. We first noticed this effect when we tried to image letter-shaped cuts in thin sheets of metal. Some difficulty was encountered in producing images this way because the metal sheet itself frequently appeared to be acoustically transparent.

It was noticed that by placing a glass sheet (in this case a glass microscope slide) in the acoustic beam and rotating it about an axis perpendicular to the beam direction various positions could again be found where the sheet would become almost totally transparent to the acoustic energy. Similarly, for other positions it was almost totally opaque.

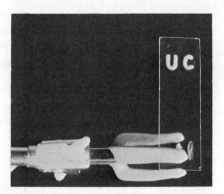

Fig. 6. Lettered glass slide.

These observations led to the concept of the acoustical transparency as a simple means of fabricating objects for acoustical illumination. Pieces of masking tape in the form of letters were placed on a glass slide, on the side of the slide away from the transducer. The slide was then positioned in the sound beam and rotated to a point where the clear portion became acoustically transparent. The silhouetted letters could be imaged clearly since the tape absorbed the acoustic energy. Figure 6 shows the prepared glass slide, and Fig. 7 is a photograph of the image produced by it. The relative contrast of the letters against the background depends on the orientation of the slide with respect to the sound beam (that is, the effective acoustical thickness of the slide).

We could also treat the back surface of a sheet of elastic material by depositing layers of additional material of the proper thickness on it. The deposits could then be made to show up on a screen as sharp silhouettes. For example, aluminum deposited on a glass plate will give a silhouette whose opacity depends on the thickness of the deposit. This can be seen by considering the transmission line analogy. The aluminum deposits comprise

Fig. 7. Image of letters on slide.

additional sections of mismatched transmission line. These sections reflect an amount of acoustic energy in accordance with their thickness, thus leading to variation in opacity. By providing a pattern of deposits of varying thickness we can produce a complicated acoustical transparency and from it construct a given image on the screen.

TRANSPARENCIES AS DIFFRACTING SCREENS

The transparency principle can be put to use in fabricating diffracting screens. One interest we currently have for a diffracting screen is to produce evanescent waves. Diffraction theory shows that an illuminated diffracting screen can generate so-called evanescent or "creeping" wave components which travel along the screen's back surface. As these components move away from a diffracting aperture they cling to the screen with shorter wavelengths than for the incident radiation, and transport no energy in the direction perpendicular to the screen. In fact, their amplitudes attenuate exponentially in that direction.

An experiment we are undertaking is one which will check for the physical existence of evanescent-wave components generated by diffracting screens. It should be possible to detect these components by probing with laser light and observing Bragg diffraction of light. A measurement of the intensity of the diffracted light would then determine the amplitude of the corresponding evanescent acoustic-wave components.

A screen with a suitable diffracting aperture, such as a slit or a grating, is more difficult to produce for sound than for light. Ideally, the "black portion" of the screen should completely prevent the passage of sound (either by absorption or reflection) and the aperture portion should permit passage without attenuation. As described before, if an elastic sheet of arbitrary thickness is used to provide the "black portion," some of the incident sound will generally be able to pass through. This problem can be circumvented and an effective diffractive aperture can be designed by using the concept of the acoustical transparency. One of the simplest diffracting screens is one in which the aperture is a single diffracting slit. This would be easy to fabricate using the transparency principle. The slit portion could be produced by the proper thickness of elastic material, and the black portion by an additional deposit of such thickness that total reflection or absorption is obtained. Although simple to build, such a diffracting screen will not produce evanescent-wave components which are detectable in the experiment described above. We quickly checked this by placing slits of various widths in the acoustical cell and visually searching for the corresponding diffracted light. None was found. Although much of the pattern of the angular spectrum of the scattered sound could be seen clearly in the Bragg-diffracted light,

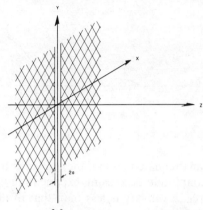

Fig. 8. Acoustical diffraction screen with a long slit as the diffracting aperture.

there was no evidence of diffraction for any evanescent-wave component in the sound. To get diffracted light from an evanescent-wave component we are planning to use an acoustical diffraction grating which will also be fabricated on the acoustical transparency principle. Theoretical considerations of the behavior of the diffracting slit and the grating are given below.

Consider the angular spectrum of waves emerging from a long slit in an acoustical diffracting screen irradiated from behind by a normally incident, planar sound beam. The screen and a set of axes are shown in Fig. 8. As illustrated, the screen occupies the $z = 0$ plane. The incident radiation travels in the $+z$ direction. Let the angular spectrum of the diffracted waves be represented by the complex function $\mathbf{U}'(f_x)$, where f_x is the x-directed spatial frequency in cycles per unit length. The value of f_x for any planewave component is given by the x-axis direction cosine for that component divided by the wavelength Λ of the incident sound. The function $\mathbf{U}'(f_x)$ can be calculated from the Fourier transform of the complex wave-distribution function $\mathbf{U}(x, z)$ evaluated at $z = 0^+$. Thus

$$\mathbf{U}'(f_x) = \int_{-\infty}^{\infty} \mathbf{U}(x, 0^+) \exp(-j2\pi f_x x)\, dx$$

$$= 2a \frac{\sin(2\pi f_x a)}{2\pi f_x a} \tag{3}$$

Here we have assumed that the intensity of the incident radiation is unity. If $2a$ is significantly smaller than Λ, then a substantial portion of the angular spectrum, represented by the cross-hatched region in Fig. 9, will correspond to evanescent-wave components. For this condition the evanescent components in the region $f_x \gtrsim 1/\Lambda$ are relatively large. These components travel

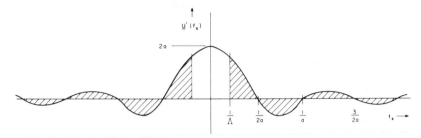

Fig. 9. Plot of $U'(f_x)$ vs. f_x for a slit whose width is substantially less than a wavelength.

unattenuated along the screen's back surface in the x direction, their amplitude decreasing exponentially with distance in the z direction. Their phase velocity is less than that of normally propagating sound waves and hence their wavelengths are shorter.

Evanescent components from such a slit are not detectable by means of a light–sound interaction system. In order to detect the presence of any sound wave, there must be a variation of refractive index in the sound cell which corresponds to the wave in question. It is this variation which permits Bragg diffraction of the light and makes the detection possible. Because of destructive interference among all the wave components present on the back surface of the screen there is no variation of refractive index in that region. The cancellation is complete at the surface and nearly so at any short distance away from the surface. We do not have to consider longer distances since the evanescent components attenuate rapidly with distance.

From a mathematical point of view, the above cancellation takes place because the entire spectrum of components in the curve of Fig. 9 is present. If by some means we could arrange to eliminate all components except those within a small selected region of the evanescent portion, the cancellation would not take place and an actual variation of refractive index would exist. Elimination of the interfering components can be accomplished by using a grating of closely-spaced parallel slits in place of the single slit. For $2N$ such slits the Fourier angular spectrum is given by

$$U'(f_x) = 4a \frac{\sin(2\pi f_x a)}{(2\pi f_x a)} \sum_{m=1,3,5,\ldots}^{2N-1} \cos \pi f_x mh \qquad (4)$$

where $2a$ is the slit width and h the periodicity of the grating.

Equation (4) is similar to Eq. (3) except that a finite series of cosine terms multiplies the $(\sin x)/x$ term. The series has positive or negative peaks at $f_x = m/h$, where m is an integer; positive, if m is even, and negative if m is odd. Between the peaks the series stays close to zero. The larger the value of N the sharper and narrower the peaks. Thus the role of the grating is to intensify certain regions of the $(\sin x)/x$ curve and to attenuate other regions.

Assume that N is large, that Λ is greater than twice the slit width (that is, $\Lambda > 4a$), and that the slit width is equal to half the periodicity (that is, $4a = h$). Then sharp positive or negative peaks will exist at 0, $\frac{1}{4a}$, $\frac{1}{2a}$, etc. By examining the curve of Fig. 9 we can see that essentially only one propagating wave emerges from the grating (traveling directly along the z axis), and only the one large evanescent component (traveling along the x axis). For the evanescent component $f_x = \frac{1}{4a}$. The other emerging waves (all evanescent) are small because they correspond to the values of f_x which coincide with nulls of the $(\sin x)/x$ curve or with portions of the curve having small amplitude. Thus the effect of the grating is to isolate in space a particular evanescent component by eliminating the components corresponding to adjacent portions of the $(\sin x)/x$ curve. By illuminating the back side of the grating with light incident at the Bragg angle with respect to the evanescent component we should be able to observe Bragg diffraction of the light and thus detect the presence of the evanescent component.

TRANSPARENT PLATES AS BAND-PASS SPATIAL FILTERS

As we have seen, a thin elastic plate of uniform thickness with no deposits or marks on the surfaces can appear transparent as far as a planar beam of incident sound is concerned. This does not mean that such a transparent plate is a perfect window. This point was made evident in a simple experiment in which a steel plate was placed between an object to be imaged and the illuminating laser light. The positions of the various components in the acoustical cell are illustrated by Fig. 10. The object to be imaged in this case was the acoustical transparency with the letters "UC" which was described before. Although the image produced was clearly recognizable (see Fig. 11), there was some deterioration (compare with Fig. 7). The steel plate was oriented so that it was relatively transparent to a large spectrum of the spatial components in the sound, but it could not be transparent to all. For a coherent acoustic beam in which the entire spectrum is very narrow there will be only one angle of incidence of the sound upon any thin elastic plate for which the transmission through the plate is complete. Even where the plate is thick there will be at most a finite number of such angles of incidence. All other angles are incorrect for complete transmission. This means that only narrow portions of the spatial spectrum of any acoustic beam can be transmitted through the steel plate without back reflection. The spatial components corresponding to incorrect angles will therefore be transmitted incompletely. In the previously described experiment the transmission for certain components was better than for the remainder of the spectrum and the steel plate therefore constituted a band-pass spatial filter, thus lowering the quality of the image.

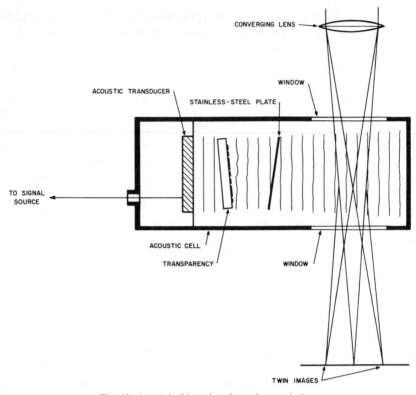

Fig. 10. Acoustical imaging through a steel plate.

Studies of the filtering characteristics and the general wave propagation through a plate of uniform thickness have bearing on how sound propagates through surfaces. This in turn is associated with the practical matter of

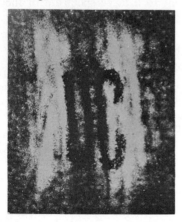

Fig. 11. Letters imaged through steel plate.

imaging sound-scattering centers within a material opaque to light. To image such centers the sound would have to be transmitted through a surface of the material in order for it to pass into an optically transparent medium. One useful application for this kind of system could be in locating imperfections in manufactured parts made from optically opaque material.

TRANSPARENT PLATES FOR VELOCITY MEASUREMENT

A number of experiments involving the transparency principle have been performed in which compressional and shear-wave velocities for various materials were readily measured. As was explained before, in general whenever an elastic plate in an acoustical cell is irradiated with sound combinations of both compressional and shear waves are actually launched. However, at certain selected angles of incidence of the sound upon the plate only pure compressional waves or pure shear waves are produced ([3]). For example, at normal incidence only the compressional waves are excited. When only one kind of wave is present we can compare the light intensity within the image silhouette with that just outside the silhouette, and get data from which to calculate the corresponding velocity. By varying the frequency of the sound we can readily find a frequency for which the silhouette disappears. As shown in the preceding paragraphs, under these circumstances the acoustical thickness of the plate is equal to an integral number of half phase wavelengths. Knowing the acoustical thickness and the actual plate thickness we can determine the velocity. We have tried this procedure for both stainless steel and glass and find that we can obtain accurate measurements of compressional and shear-wave velocities.

A conventional method of velocity measurement, which is in frequent use, requires attaching acoustical transducers to both sides of such a plate and adjusting the frequency of the sound until the phase of both transducers is the same. Our method described above appears to be advantageous in that there is no necessity for attaching the transducers, and there is no source of possible error due to phase shift within these transducers.

The theoretical basis for the technique can be understood by recalling the previous analogy to transmission line theory. The compressional wave velocities were measured by irradiating the plate at normal incidence. Under these circumstances if the plate is laterally infinite, only a compressional wave can be excited. Even in the noninfinite plate, for all practical purposes, only a compressional wave gets excited if the lateral dimension of the plate is much larger than the thickness.

For the angle of incidence at which only shear waves are excited the wave motion induced in the plate is made up of two equal waves traveling at right angles to each other and each having an angle of refraction of 45°.

By finding the correct angle of incidence experimentally we are able to set up pure shear waves in the plate and measure the shear-wave velocity. Determining the correct angle of incidence involves a simple graphical solution (experimentally determined) of two simultaneous equations based on Snell's law and Eq. (1) (⁴).

CONCLUSION

We have demonstrated that properly designed transparencies can be illuminated by sound waves and used to produce visual images. Some applications for these transparencies are found in fabricating acoustical diffracting screens and band-pass spatial filters. A diffracting screen of this type is presently being constructed for the purpose of studying evanescent waves in liquids.

An additional application for the acoustical transparency concept is that of direct visualization of inhomogeneities in prepared samples of solid materials. A quantitative determination of such inhomogeneities could be made by finding the acoustic velocity (and the acoustic attenuation constant if desired) at specific points in the sample. This is accomplished simply by measuring light intensities in the optical image plane. In this respect the acoustical imaging technique offers an advantage over other velocity measurement methods, since localized measurements can be made with a minimum of effort.

The fact that a solid elastic plate of uniform thickness can be made to appear completely transparent is evidence that some unexpected and perhaps undesirable effects may arise in producing images of acoustically irradiated objects. For example, with objects having certain ranges of size, portions of them may appear transparent, thus making their images unrecognizable in some cases.

Although the feasibility of making acoustical transparencies is now established, only elementary transparencies have so far been made and little is known of the ultimate quality and character of their imaging potentialities or of their practical applications. Other possible uses should be explored.

REFERENCES

1. A. Korpel, Visualization of the Cross Section of a Sound Beam by Bragg Diffraction of Light, *Appl. Phys. Letters* **9**:425 (1966).
2. R. Adler, Interaction between Sound and Light, *IEEE Spectrum* **4**(5):42 (1967).
3. R. D. Fay and O. V. Fortier, Transmission of Sound Through Steel Plates Immersed in Water, *J. Acoust. Soc. Am.* **23**(3):339 (May 1951).
4. G. Wade, J. P. Powers, and A. A. de Souza, Acoustic Velocity Measurements with an Ultrasonic Cell, submitted for publication.

Chapter 12

DIGITAL IMAGE FORMATION FROM DETECTED HOLOGRAPHIC DATA*

J. W. Goodman

Department of Electrical Engineering
Stanford University, Stanford, California

Digital imaging techniques, which have been successfully used to reconstruct images from optical holograms, are equally well suited to forming images from acoustical data. For objects of modest space-bandwidth product (e.g., 256 × 256 resolution cells) computation times can be acceptably short and significant gains in simplicity and flexibility can be achieved by digital rather than optical reconstruction. Image degradations introduced by scanning errors, insufficient sampling, and quantization are discussed, and current experimental work in digital reconstruction from optical holograms is described.

INTRODUCTION

Holography in its usual form is a *two-step* imaging process ([1,2]). The first step requires detection of the pattern of interference between a wave scattered by an object of interest and an additional wave which serves as a phase reference. The second step requires reconstruction of an image from the previously detected data. When the object is illuminated with optical radiation then for reasons of convenience it is usually also desirable to carry out the second step with optical radiation, using a single photographic transparency for three separate tasks: (1) detection, (2) storage, and (3) spatial modulation of light during the reconstruction process. However, when the original illumination is nonoptical (e.g., acoustic or microwave radiation), then the conveniences associated with photographic detection are no longer available, and the desirability of carrying out the second step of the process optically requires reexamination. We are concerned here with the possibility of *digital* image formation from detected holographic data, and we shall attempt to outline the advantages and limitations of such an approach.

*The work reported here was sponsored by the Office of Naval Research.

OPTICAL IMAGE RECONSTRUCTION FROM NONOPTICAL DATA

Production of a Photographic Transparency

There are a number of methods by means of which nonoptical detected data may be transferred to a photographic transparency, thus allowing optical image reconstruction to be carried out in the usual manner. One approach, which has been used by several workers in acoustical and microwave holography ([3-6]), is to attach a small light bulb directly to the scanning detector. The brightness of the bulb is modulated in accord with the intensity of the radiation at each point along the scanning raster. A time-exposed photograph of the moving, modulated bulb yields a photographic transparency from which an optical image may be reconstructed.

A second approach, which has also been used in acoustical holography ([7]), is to display the detected data on a CRT monitor, which may then be photographed to yield a hologram transparency.

Sources of Image Degradation

There are a number of possible sources of image degradation in either of the above procedures. These sources may be broadly classified into four categories as follows:

1. Those associated with the original (nonoptical) sensing process (e.g., noise and nonlinearities of the detector, the finite size of the detector, and non-uniformities of the scanning raster).

2. Those peculiar to the particular method used to transfer data to photographic film (e.g., light bulb response nonlinearities, CRT response nonlinearities, CRT scan nonuniformities, and aberrations of the photographic optics).

3. Those arising from the large difference in wavelengths used for recording and reconstructing (e.g., unequal transverse and longitudinal magnifications, and possibly severe spherical aberration).

4. Those associated with the optical reconstruction equipment (e.g., film-grain noise, film nonlinearities, scattering from imperfections and dust particles in the reconstruction apparatus, and aberrations of the reconstruction optics).

In principle, it is possible to eliminate or correct for all sources of degradation that are nonrandom (deterministic) in nature. Unfortunately, it is very difficult, from a practical point of view, to achieve perfection in this respect. Much of the blame must often be assigned to the problem of transferring the detected data to a photographic transparency with a high degree of fidelity. In addition, optical reconstruction techniques are highly inflexible (in comparison with digital techniques), making compensation of all but the simplest degradations very difficult.

Advantages of Optical Image Reconstruction

In spite of these difficulties there are two respects in which optical techniques are far superior to digital methods of image reconstruction. First is the ability to present three-dimensional virtual images. While digital techniques are capable of preserving and displaying all of the three-dimensional properties of an image, there is to date no method of display which yields as satisfying and pleasing results as a three-dimensional virtual image.

A second advantage of optical reconstruction techniques is their ability to handle very large amounts of data. Thus if we imagine holograms consisting of more and more independent resolvable elements, eventually we reach a point beyond which digital techniques require unacceptably large amounts of storage and/or computation time. Exactly when digital techniques become unfeasible is a complicated question. To indicate the general order of magnitude, however, it is safe to say that data consisting of more than a 1000×1000 array of points are more than we would care to process digitally, given the present state of computer technology.

For the remainder we shall assume that there *do* exist nonoptical imaging problems for which the display of a three-dimensional virtual image is not essential and for which holograms with only a modest number of resolvable elements are of concern.

DIGITAL IMAGE RECONSTRUCTION

General Procedure

The goal of the digital image reconstruction process is to duplicate with high precision on a digital computer the analog operations performed by the more conventional optical system. To accomplish this goal, it is first necessary to sample the data collected by the sensor. The sampled data are then quantized to a certain predetermined number of grey levels and stored in computer memory. The image is formed by appropriate digital manipulations of the stored data (to be described in more detail shortly) and may be displayed optically on a CRT or may be printed out directly in numerical form.

All image degradations associated with the production of a photographic transparency (i.e., category 2 above) are eliminated by this process, as are likewise the degradations associated with the optical processor (i.e., category 4 above). In their place, however, are new degradations introduced by the sampling and quantization processes. The nature of these new degradations, as well as precautions for minimizing them, will be discussed in a later section.

The Required Digital Operations

The digital operations required to form an image depend upon the relative positions of the object plane of interest and the point of origin of the reference wave. (If the reference is supplied internally by an electronic signal of constant phase, then the reference point is effectively at infinity.) The simplest case occurs when the reference point is coplanar with the object; the mathematical operations required are then a simple two-dimensional Fourier transformation followed by a squared-modulus operation to yield intensity. Thus if $I_d(\xi, \eta)$ represents the intensity distribution measured by the detector, then the image intensity distribution may be found by the discrete analog of the operation

$$I_i(x, y) = \left| \int\int_{-\infty}^{\infty} I_d(\xi, \eta) \exp[-j2\pi(x\xi + y\eta)] \, d\xi \, d\eta \right|^2 \tag{1}$$

In discrete notation the required manipulation is

$$I_i(r, l) = \left| \sum_{k,m=0}^{N-1} I_d(k, m) W^{rk+lm} \right|^2 \qquad r, l = 0, 1, \ldots, N-1 \tag{2}$$

where (k, m) are sample-point indices in the $N \times N$ array, (r, l) are image point indices, and

$$W = \exp\left(-j\frac{2\pi}{N}\right) \tag{3}$$

When the reference and object are not coplanar the mathematical transformation required to obtain an image is a *Fresnel* transform followed by a squared-modulus operation. The Fresnel transform can be realized by first multiplying the detected holographic data by an appropriate quadratic phase factor and then Fourier transforming the product. Thus if z_r is the distance from the reference point to the detection plane and if we wish to "focus" the digital imaging system on a plane at distance z_0 from the detection plane, the required calculation is the discrete analog of

$$I_i(x, y) = \left| \int\int_{-\infty}^{\infty} I_d(\xi, \eta) \exp[j(\pi/\lambda\Delta)(\xi^2 + \eta^2)] \exp[-j2\pi(x\xi + y\eta)] \, d\xi \, d\eta \right|^2 \tag{4}$$

where

$$\Delta = z_r z_0/(z_r - z_0)$$

The discrete form of this operation is

$$I_i(r, l) = \left| \sum_{k,m=0}^{N-1} I_d(k, m) \exp[j\pi\alpha^2(k^2 + m^2)] W^{rk+lm} \right|^2 \tag{5}$$

$$r, l = 0, 1, \ldots, N - 1$$

where if $\delta\xi$ and $\delta\eta$ are the sampling increments (assumed equal) in the holo-gram plane and λ is the wavelength of the original radiation, then the para-meter α is given by

$$\alpha = \delta\xi/(\lambda\Delta)^{1/2} = \delta\eta/(\lambda\Delta)^{1/2} \tag{6}$$

The Fast Fourier Transform

An enormous change in the economy of digital Fourier-transform opera-tions has occurred with the development of the so-called "fast Fourier transform" by Cooley and Tukey [8, 9]. The basic philosophy underlying the fast Fourier transform technique may be understood by considering the simple one-dimensional discrete Fourier transform

$$F(r) = \sum_{k=0}^{N-1} f(k)W^{rk} \qquad r = 0, 1, \ldots, N - 1 \tag{7}$$

To determine $F(r)$ by the direct method we must perform N multiplications and additions for each value of r. Thus to calculate $F(r)$ at N points a total of N^2 multiplications and additions are required.

The improved economy of the Cooley–Tukey technique may be under-stood by viewing Eq. (7) as a matrix multiplication [10]

$$[F] = [W][f]$$

where

$$[F] = \begin{bmatrix} F(0) \\ F(1) \\ \vdots \\ F(N-1) \end{bmatrix}, \qquad [f] = \begin{bmatrix} f(0) \\ f(1) \\ \vdots \\ f(N-1) \end{bmatrix}, \tag{9}$$

and

$$[W] = \begin{bmatrix} 1 & 1 & 1 & \cdots & 1 \\ 1 & W & W^2 & \cdots & W^{N-1} \\ 1 & W^2 & W^4 & \cdots & W^{2(N-1)} \\ \vdots & & & & \\ 1 & W^{N-1} & W^{2(N-1)} & \cdots & W^{(N-1)^2} \end{bmatrix} \tag{10}$$

Now, if $N = \beta_1 \cdot \beta_2 \cdot \cdots \cdot \beta_n$, where the β's are positive integers, then the $N \times N$ matrix $[W]$ may be factored into n matrices,

$$[W] = [W_1][W_2] \cdots [W_n] \tag{11}$$

where the $N \times N$ matrix W_i has only $\beta_i N$ nonzero elements. It follows that Eq. (8) may be rewritten

$$[F] = [W_1][W_2] \cdots [W_n][f] \tag{12}$$

If the matrix multiplication is performed step by step, multiplying $[W_n]$ and $[f]$ first, then multiplying $[W_{n-1}]$ and the product $[W_n][f]$, etc., the total number of multiplications and additions required is $(\beta_1 + \beta_2 + \cdots + \beta_n)N$. When $\beta_1 = \beta_2 = \cdots = \beta_n = 2$, this number reduces to $2N \log N$. For large N far fewer operations are required with the Cooley–Tukey method than with the direct method.

Estimates of the computation times required for various sized arrays with an IBM 7094 computer have been made by Huang and Kasnitz ([10]) and are listed in Table I.

TABLE I

Array size, N	Direct computation, T	Fast Fourier transform, T
64 × 64	8 min	3 sec
256 × 256	30 hr	1 min
512 × 512	20 days	5 min
1024 × 1024	1 yr	20 min

The estimates in Table I were made on the assumption that the core memory is sufficiently large to store all of the data. For large arrays the storage requirements can become enormous. Just how much storage is required depends on a number of factors. First, the number of grey levels of input data is an important parameter. Perhaps more important, the two-dimensional transform is performed by first executing one-dimensional transforms across the rows of the input data and then executing one-dimensional transforms down the columns of the results. A crucial storage decision concerns the precision with which the results of the first transformations must be retained before executing the second set of transformations. We know of no hard-and-fast rules in this respect, and can only refer the reader to the particular experiments that we have performed, as described in a later section.

EFFECTS OF QUANTIZATION, SAMPLING, AND SCAN NONUNIFORMITIES

Quantization

When the output of an analog detector is quantized by an A/D converter a nonmonotonic and irreversible nonlinear distortion of the detected data is introduced. As indicated in Fig. 1, the effective response curve of the detector then takes the appearance of a "staircase." Such a nonlinearity has two effects on the reconstructed image: higher-order (distorted) images are generated, and distortions appear in the first-order image. The chief effect of these latter distortions is a reduction of image contrast, although it is also possible for false image detail to be introduced ([11]).

Previously developed methods ([12, 13]) of analyzing the effects of non-linearities in holography can be applied to quantization nonlinearities. We briefly outline the method of analysis and present the important results. Attention is restricted to diffuse objects, i.e., objects consisting of a multitude of independent scatterers. In addition, the ratio of reference intensity to object intensity at the recording plane is assumed to be considerably greater than unity. With these assumptions the detected pattern of intensity obeys the statistics of a narrowband Gaussian process. The power spectrum of this process can be shown (using the Van Cittert–Zernike theorem) to be proportional to the intensity distribution across the object. The average intensity distribution in the reconstructed image is similarly proportional to the power spectrum of the process *after quantization*. Thus the effects of quantization on the intensity distribution in the first-order image are exactly analogous to the effects of quantization on the power spectrum of a narrowband Gaussian random process.

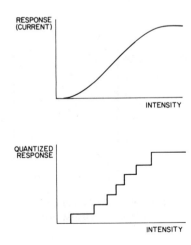

Fig. 1. Detector response curve before and after quantization.

The power spectra of quantized narrowband Gaussian random processes have been studied in the communication theory literature. Most relevant are the works of van Vleck and Middleton ([14]) and Hurd ([15]), whose results we adapt here. Figure 2 shows the predicted intensity distributions in the first-order image of a uniformly bright, diffuse patch for various numbers of quantization levels. Note that for an "ideal limiter," which quantizes to only two levels, the "tails" introduced by the quantization reduce the contrast by about 5%. On the other hand, when eight grey levels are used the maximum intensity of the tails is about 25 dB below that of the desired image.

Sampling

The discrete Fourier transform operation is in actuality a Fourier series calculation. As such, the results of the computation are periodic, with a period which is inversely proportional to the sampling increment in the hologram plane. Consequently, if the interference pattern is sampled too infrequently, aliasing components will appear in the computed image.

For reasonably small numerical apertures the maximum spatial frequency contained in the intensity pattern incident on the detector is

$$f_{max} \approx (\sin \phi_{max})/\lambda \qquad (13)$$

where ϕ_{max} is the maximum angular separation of the reference and object.

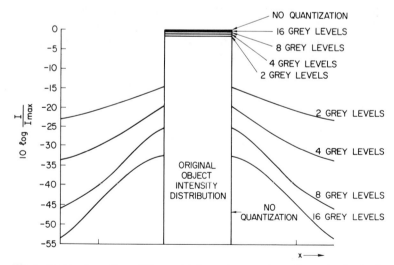

Fig. 2. Images of a uniform diffuse patch for various numbers of quantization levels (quantization levels assumed here are those minimizing the mean-square quantization error).

To avoid aliasing errors, it is therefore necessary to sample at intervals $\delta\xi$ which satisfy

$$\delta\xi < 1/2f_{max} = \lambda/(2 \sin \phi_{max}) \tag{14}$$

Equation (14) is not a sufficient condition to guarantee freedom from aliasing effects, however. If the detector is driven over such a large dynamic range that its response is not linearly proportional to changes of incident intensity, then the bandwidth of the detected data will exceed f_{max}. Similarly, quantization introduces higher-frequency components. If the response characteristics of the detector are monotonic and known in advance, then these nonlinearities can be compensated by appropriate modification of the quantization levels on the A/D converter. However, the nonlinearities inherent in quantization are irreversible and therefore cannot be compensated.

Scan Nonuniformities

Scanning devices invariably suffer some degree of error in their conversion of spatial position into temporal position. Such effects result in errors of the relative positions of detected fringes, and lead directly to "wavefront aberrations" across the exit pupil of the simulated optical system. One of the attractions of the digital method of image formation is that the effects of such aberrations can be removed without great difficulty. To do so, it is only necessary to include a known, isolated point-source as part of the object. When the detected data are Fourier transformed, twin aberrated images of the point source appear. If one of these aberrated images is isolated and *inverse* Fourier transformed, a phase-modulated complex function $\exp[j\phi(\xi, \eta)]$ is obtained. If the detected hologram is multiplied by the conjugate function $\exp[-j\phi(\xi, \eta)]$, then one of the twin images of the entire object will be aberration free (the other image will be doubly aberrated).

EXPERIMENTAL RESULTS

A number of experiments have been performed to demonstrate the feasibility of forming images digitally from detected holographic data. In all experiments to date the object has been a transparency, backlighted through a diffuser by a He–Ne laser. The reference is supplied as a point-source coplanar with the object, and the resulting interference pattern may be recorded on photographic film. If the hologram transparency is imaged onto the photosensitive surface of a vidicon, as shown in Fig. 3, the electronic signal so produced serves as a convenient input to an analog-to-digital converter. As an alternative approach, the original interference pattern may

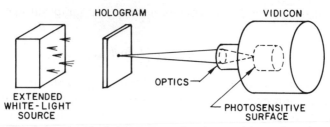

Fig. 3. Imaging the hologram onto the photosensitive surface of a vidicon.

be directly sensed on the photosensitive surface of the vidicon (with the optics removed), as shown in Fig. 4.

In the experiments of concern here the vidicon output was sampled to form a 256 × 256 array of intensities, each of which was quantized to eight grey levels. A PDP-6 computer was used, images being obtained with 5 min of computation time. Approximately 52,000 36-bit words of core storage were required. The majority of core storage was utilized to save the results of the one-dimensional transformations across the rows of data (i.e., before transforming down the columns), with 18 bits of storage being used for each complex Fourier coefficient. The results of the computation were quantized to eight grey levels and presented on a scope display.

Figure 5 shows a scope display of hologram after quantization, storage, and recall from memory. In this case the original hologram was photographic. Figure 6 shows the twin images obtained with 5 min of computation. For comparison purposes Fig. 7 shows the twin images obtained optically from the same hologram. The granular nature of the digitally formed image can to a large extent be attributed to the so-called "speckle effect" ([16]) that is always associated with images of diffuse objects illuminated by coherent light; granularity can also be seen in the optical reconstruction of Fig. 7, but due to the heavier exposure it is not quite as noticeable.

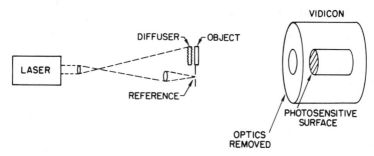

Fig. 4. Direct detection of the pattern of interference.

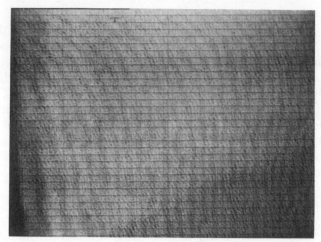

Fig. 5. Hologram recalled from computer memory and displayed on a CRT (the horizontal lines are not present in the stored data, but instead are a consequence of the method of display).

Fig. 6. Digitally computed image.

Fig. 7. Optical reconstruction.

Of particular interest in the digitally formed image is the information about the *vidicon* which is evident. First, the drop off of intensity of the image points furthest from the reference is a direct indication that the modulation transfer function of the vidicon is beginning to fall off at correspondingly high frequencies in the hologram. Of equal interest is the bright cross in the middle of the digital images (but not present in the optical reconstruction), with the horizontal portion of the cross being particularly extended and intense. The cross indicates the presence of an unexpected interference which remains "coherent" from scan to scan in the hologram plane. This interference is believed to arise from the periodic wire mesh or grid through which the electron beam in the vidicon passes just before striking the photoconductive surface.

Experiments are now underway to demonstrate the possibility of "focusing" the digital computations on various image planes. In addition, future experimental work will include phase microscopy, for which the computer calculates the *phase* distribution across the original object and displays contours of constant phase shift.

SUMMARY AND CONCLUSIONS

When holograms are formed with nonoptical radiation the possibility of digital reconstruction must be seriously considered. If a pleasing three-dimensional virtual image is the ultimate goal, then optical reconstruction is definitely called for. In addition, for holograms containing more than a certain critical number of resolvable points optical techniques are to be preferred. Just where the crossover point occurs depends on the particular computer available and on the computation time that can feasibly be invested. With the present state of computer technology holograms consisting of up to 1000×1000 resolvable points are not unfeasible for digital image formation. As computer technology advances digital techniques will undoubtedly become more and more important in acoustical and microwave holography, as well as in certain specialized applications of optical holography. With the present state of technology holograms which are simple enough to be displayed on a CRT and photographed are in most cases within the realm of digital capability.

REFERENCES

1. D. Gabor, *Nature* **161**:777 (1948); *Proc. Roy. Soc.* **A197**:454 (1949); *Proc. Phys. Soc.* **B64**: 449 (1951).
2. E. N. Leith and J. Upatnieks, *J. Opt. Soc. Am.* **52**:1123 (1962); **53**:1377 (1963); **54**:1295 (1964).
3. F. L. Thurstone, *Proc. Symp. on Biomed. Eng.* **1**:12 (1966).

4. K. Preston, Jr. and J. L. Kreuzer, *Appl. Phys. Letters* **10**:150 (1967).
5. G. A. Massey, *Proc. IEEE* **55**:1115 (1967).
6. Y. Aoki, *Appl. Opt.* **6**:1943 (1967).
7. A. F. Metherell, H. M. A. El-Sum, J. J. Dreher, and L. Larmore, *J. Acoust. Soc. Am.* **42**: 733 (1967).
8. J. W. Cooley and J. W. Tukey, *Math. Comp.* **19**:297 (1965).
9. W. T. Cochran, J. W. Cooley, D. L. Faum, H. D. Helms, R. A. Kaenel, W. W. Lang, G. C. Maling, Jr., D. E. Nelson, C. M. Rader, and P. D. Welch, *Proc. IEEE* **55**: 1664 (1967).
10. T. S. Huang and H. L. Kasnitz, *Proceedings of the Computerized Imaging Techniques Seminar*, Society for Photo-Optical Instrumentation Engineers, XVII-1 (1967).
11. A. A. Friesem and J. S. Zelenka, *Appl. Opt.* **6**:1755 (1967).
12. J. W. Goodman, *J. Opt. Soc. Am.* **57**:560 (1967).
13. G. R. Knight, *J. Opt. Soc. Am.* **57**:1413 (1967).
14. J. H. Van Vleck and D. Middleton, *Proc. IEEE* **54**:2 (1966).
15. W. J. Hurd, *IEEE Trans. on Information Theory* **IT-13**:65 (1967).
16. T. J. Skinner, *J. Opt. Soc. Am.* **53**:1350A (1963).

Chapter 13

PHASE DISTORTIONS DUE TO NONLINEAR EFFECTS IN AN ACOUSTIC FIELD

O. K. Mawardi

Case Western Reserve University
Cleveland, Ohio

Linear superposition theory is commonly used to obtain acoustical diffraction patterns for weak acoustic signals. As the sound intensity is increased nonlinear effects set in. These can be responsible for amplitude as well as phase distortions of the primary interfering waves. The present chapter discusses quantitatively the magnitude of the phase distortion introduced by the second-order effects of wave–wave interaction for a system of two monochromatic interfering two-dimensional beams.

INTRODUCTION

The subject matter of this chapter is nonlinear phase distortion suffered by an acoustic plane wave. The interest in phase distortion in acoustic waves has been instigated in part by the important role this geometric property of wavefronts plays in the transmission of communication signals by acoustical means.

The general question of nonlinear acoustical distortions in a fluid is quite old. Lamb [1] in 1910 had already obtained theoretically an estimate of the magnitude of the second harmonic generated in a sound wave. This prediction appears to be in substantial agreement with experiments which were performed much later [2]. Although a survey of the literature reveals that amplitude distortion in sound waves has been studied often, very little information can be had on nonlinear phase distortion.

The necessary mathematical techniques needed to treat this complex problem, however, were developed some time ago by Lighthill [3]. This formulation, which was initially used by him to study sounds of aerodynamic origin, can be adapted to the topic of this chapter.

The present chapter is divided in a number of parts. In the first three the formalism needed to discuss nonlinear distortion is summarized. The

187

fourth section is devoted to the derivation of the interference pattern needed in the study of wave–wave interactions. In the remaining sections calculations pertaining to the estimate of phase distortions are developed.

FORMULATION OF THE PROBLEM

Several results of acoustical investigations are derived on the tacit assumption that the fluctuating amplitudes (or velocities) in the sound field are small. The smallness parameter is the ratio of the amplitude of the fluctuation to the wavelength of sound. In a standing wave the amplitudes may become large enough to violate this fundamental smallness criterion. As a result nonlinear distortions set in.

The problem posed here can be briefly stated this way: Given a wave interference pattern which is produced by a number of incident plane waves and which extends over a finite region of space, to find the phase distortion suffered by the waves emerging out of the interference region.

The first-order interactions of the incident waves will obviously yield the interference pattern predicted by conventional acoustical theory. Higher-order interactions, on the other hand, must lead to the generation of waves with wave numbers different from those associated with the incident waves. If the interfering waves have all the same wave number k, the nonlinear interaction will lead to the appearance of wave numbers nk, $n = 0, 2, 3, \ldots$. Now one can argue that reradiation of acoustic energy at the wave numbers nk must be equivalent to an attenuation of the incident or primary waves. This must be reflected as a correction in the dispersion relation for the primary waves and this in turn probably introduces a phase shift. Hence the clue to the solution of the problem lies in a careful study of the higher-order wave interactions.

It has been known for some time that the dynamical behavior of a viscous compressible fluid can be represented by a number of subsidiary coupled fields [4–6]. Indeed, to a first order one can identify three modes: a vorticity, a dilatation (or compression), and an entropy field associated with the flow. Formally, if ω, S, and ρ are, respectively, the vorticity, entropy, and fluctuating density, it can be shown that

$$O_1(\omega) = \varepsilon f_{1,1}(\omega, S, \rho) + \varepsilon^2 f_{1,2}(\omega, S, \rho) + \cdots$$

$$O_2(S) = \varepsilon f_{2,1}(\omega, S, \rho) + \varepsilon^2 f_{2,2}(\omega, S, \rho) + \cdots \tag{1}$$

$$O_3(\rho) = \varepsilon f_{3,1}(\omega, S, \rho) + \varepsilon^2 f_{3,2}(\omega, S, \rho) + \cdots$$

where the O's are linear differential operators, the ε is a smallness parameter, and the $f_{i,j}$ are the interactions between the component fields. For example, $f_{1,1}$ can be visualized as the rate of vorticity created by the combined action of the three modes, $f_{2,1}$ the rate of entropy fluctuation produced by the weak interactions between the fields, and so on.

This procedure, although very useful in clarifying the interaction processes, is extremely laborious and lacks generality. To circumviate these difficulties, Lighthill developed a very powerful technique which is very well suited to treat the question discussed here.

The starting point of the discussion is the equations of motion for the fluid. When no sources (or sinks) are present in the flow field the relation for the conservation of mass and momentum for a Stokesian fluid are given by

$$\partial \rho / \partial t + \nabla \cdot (\rho \mathbf{u}) = 0 \tag{2}$$

and by

$$\rho(\partial \mathbf{u}/\partial t + \mathbf{u} \cdot \nabla \mathbf{u}) = -\nabla p + \mu(\nabla^2 \mathbf{u} + \tfrac{1}{3}\nabla\nabla \cdot \mathbf{u}) \tag{3}$$

In (2) and (3) ρ stands for the density of the fluid, p for the scalar pressure, $\mathbf{u}$ for the local velocity, and μ for the viscosity of the fluid. Rewriting the foregoing relations for the sake of conciseness in tensor notation, we find

$$\frac{\partial(\rho u_i)}{\partial t} + \frac{\partial(\rho u_i u_j)}{\partial x_j} = -\frac{\partial p_{ij}}{\partial x_i} \tag{4}$$

and

$$\partial \rho / \partial t + \partial(\rho u_i)/\partial x_i = 0 \tag{5}$$

where

$$p_{ij} = [p - c_0^2(\rho_0 + \rho)]\delta_{ij} - \mu\left(\frac{\partial u_i}{\partial x_j} + \frac{\partial u_j}{\partial x_i} - \frac{2}{3}\delta_{ij}\frac{\partial u_k}{\partial x_k}\right)$$
$$= [p - c_0^2(\rho_0 + \rho)]\delta_{ij} + \eta_{ij} \tag{6}$$

The symbol δ_{ij} used above is Kronecker's delta.

The formulation used by Lighthill follows at once by manipulating Eqs. (4)–(6). It is found that

$$\frac{\partial^2 \rho}{\partial t^2} - \nabla^2 p = \frac{\partial^2 T_{ij}}{\partial x_i \, \partial x_j} \tag{7}$$

where

$$T_{ij} = (\rho_0 + \rho)u_i u_j + p_{ij} \tag{8}$$

Now in several applications of interest the strong interaction between the modes of the fluid alluded to above takes place in a finite region of space, say R, and it is required to find the effect of these interactions far away. In

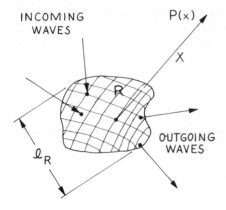

INCOMING WAVES

P(x)

X

R

OUTGOING WAVES

l_R

Fig. 1. General arrangement for system of interacting waves. The characteristic length associated with the region of interference R is l_R. Here $P(x)$ is a test point.

acoustical parlance, it is required to find the signal which originated in R and which will be sensed at a distance $x \gg l_R$, where l_R is the characteristic dimension of R (Fig. 1).

Outside R the acoustical approximation

$$p = \rho c_0^2 \tag{9}$$

is valid. The symbol c_0 stands for the velocity of sound *outside* R. Consequently, Lighthill's relation reduces to

$$\nabla^2 \rho - \frac{1}{c_0^2} \frac{\partial^2 \rho}{\partial t^2} = -\frac{1}{c_0^2} \frac{\partial^2 T_{ij}}{\partial x_i \partial x_j} \tag{10}$$

This equation is rigorously correct. The aforementioned relation demonstrates in a striking manner the physical meaning of the nonlinear terms on the right-hand side of this equation. First of all, from the theory of differential equations these terms play the role of acoustical sources. Secondly, by inspection of (6) and (8) these terms can be broken up into three groups. One group, containing $[p - c_0^2(\rho + \rho_0)]\delta_{ij}$, is related to the nonlinearity effects induced by the change of local compressibility. The other, $(\rho_0 + \rho)u_iu_j$, describes the convection with the flow of changes in momentum, and, as was demonstrated by Lighthill, the effect of $\partial^2(\rho_0 + \rho)u_iu_j/\partial x_i \partial x_j$ is akin to an acoustical quadripole. Finally, the group described by the η_{ij} terms is connected with viscous effects and it contributes a preponderant part to the distortion whenever the influence of boundaries on the flow field is appreciable.

Lighthill's Eq. (10) is very well suited to formulate in a precise manner the problem of harmonic generation. If now one considers the density ρ to be the sum of the densities of the primary waves, ρ_p, and of the reradiated wave, ρ_r, then (10) transforms into the pair

$$\nabla^2 \rho_p - \frac{1}{c_0^2} \frac{\partial^2 \rho_p}{\partial t^2} = 0 \tag{11}$$

and

$$\nabla^2 \rho_r - \frac{1}{c_0^2} \frac{\partial^2 \rho_r}{\partial t^2} = -\frac{1}{c_0^2} \frac{\partial^2 T_{ij}}{\partial x_i \partial x_j} \tag{12}$$

The first relation (11) is to be used in obtaining the interference pattern, while (12) of course yields the waves due to the nonlinear interaction.

In the case which will be discussed here, viz., phase distortions produced in a wave interference pattern, the viscous terms play a minimal role. Accordingly, they will be dropped from the analysis and only the first two groups of terms of T_{ij} will be considered. We now turn our attention to the explicit evaluation of these terms.

THE INTERACTION TERMS

The detailed discussion of the appropriate equivalent sound sources was given by Westervelt ([7]). For the sake of convenience the essential points of his arguments will be duplicated. The source terms are now given by

$$T_{ij} = (\rho_0 + \rho)u_i u_j + [p - c_0^2(\rho_0 + \rho)]\delta_{ij} \tag{13}$$

The density ρ really should have been written ρ_p; the subscript is dropped for simplicity of notation, but with the understanding that it refers to values of the primary waves. The pressure is now expanded by a Taylor's series

$$p = \sum \frac{1}{n!} \left(\frac{d^n p}{d\rho^n} \right)_{\rho = \rho_0} \rho^n$$

$$= c_0^2 \rho + \sum_{n=2}^{\infty} \frac{1}{n!} \left(\frac{d^n p}{d\rho^n} \right)_{\rho = \rho_0} \rho^n \tag{14}$$

Hence

$$T_{ij} = (\rho_0 + \rho)u_i u_j + \left[\sum_{n=2}^{\infty} \frac{1}{n!} \left(\frac{d^n p}{d\rho^n} \right)_{\rho = \rho_0} \rho^n \right] \delta_{ij} \tag{15}$$

Retaining terms up to the second order, it is shown that for an irrotational field, i.e., for $\nabla \times \mathbf{u} = 0$, the right-hand side of Eq. (12) reduces to

$$\frac{\partial^2 T_{ij}}{\partial x_i \partial x_j} = -\frac{\rho_0}{c_0^2} \left[(\nabla \cdot \mathbf{u})^2 + \mathbf{u} \cdot \nabla^2 \mathbf{u} + \nabla \frac{1}{2} u^2 - \frac{1}{2c_0^2} \left(\frac{d^2 p}{d\rho^2} \right)_{\rho = \rho_0} \nabla^2 \rho^2 \right] \tag{16}$$

But the fluctuating velocity $\mathbf{u}$ and density ρ which appear in (16) are those for the primary waves. By virtue of (11) they are described by the conventional linearized acoustics relations, viz.,

$$\partial\rho/\partial t + \rho_0 \nabla \cdot \mathbf{u} = 0 \tag{17}$$

and

$$\frac{\partial u}{\partial t} = (c_0^2/\rho_0) \nabla^2 \rho \tag{18}$$

Combining (16), (17), and (18), it can be demonstrated that explicitly

$$\frac{\partial^2 T_{ij}}{\partial x_i \, \partial x_j} = \Box^2\left(E + p - \frac{\rho}{c_0^2}\right) - \frac{1}{\rho_0 c_0^2}\left[1 + \frac{1}{2}\frac{\rho_0}{c_0^2}\left(\frac{d^2 p}{d\rho^2}\right)_{\rho = \rho_0}\right]\frac{\partial^2}{\partial t^2}\rho^2 \tag{19}$$

where $E = \frac{1}{2}[\rho_0 u^2 + c_0^2(\rho^2/\rho_0)]$.

But it was pointed out by Westervelt that the portion of the source function containing the d'Alembertian $\Box^2$ will not contribute anything to the radiation field since it vanishes identically outside the region R. Consequently, it can be dropped out in the subsequent discussion.

DESCRIPTION OF INTERFERENCE PATTERN

In order to demonstrate the concepts discussed in the previous sections, the case of the interference pattern formed by a collimated two-dimensional beam and its reflection from a perfectly reflecting mirror is investigated. The mirror is assumed to be located in the xy plane. The direction of propagation of the incoming beam, taken to be in the yz plane, makes an angle γ with the normal (Fig. 2).

The first-order solution of (11), i.e., the interference pattern, is classical [8]. It is very convenient to describe the interference field by a means of a velocity potential ϕ. The definition of ϕ is such that

$$\mathbf{u} = -\nabla\phi \tag{20}$$

All other acoustical quantities are easily derivable from this potential. For instance, using (17) one obtains for a harmonic variation for the time

$$\rho = (i\rho_0/\omega)\nabla^2\phi \tag{21}$$

Let the amplitude of the potential of the incident sound wave be A and let k be its wave number. The interference pattern is given by

$$\phi(y, z, t) = 2A \cos(kz \cos \gamma) \exp[i(ky \sin \gamma - \omega t)] \tag{22}$$

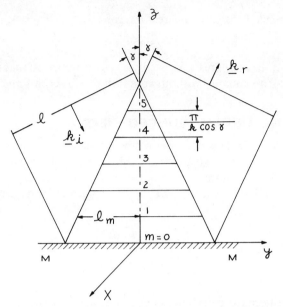

Fig. 2. Corresponding interference pattern for the system of an incident and reflected beam. The width of beam is l, the angle of incidence is γ, and wave vectors $\mathbf{k}_i$ and $\mathbf{k}_r$ are for incident and reflected waves, respectively.

for a rigid mirror, while it is

$$\phi(y, z, t) = 2iA \sin(kz \cos \gamma) \exp[i(ky \sin \gamma - \omega t)] \tag{23}$$

for a pressure release surface.

In liquids the latter case is quite frequent, so the discussion will center around the pressure release mirror. The solution of (23) indicates that the potential vanishes at all planes $z = m\pi/(k \cos \gamma)$, $m = 0, 1, 2, 3, \ldots$. Consequently, it is possible to subdivide the whole interference pattern by infinitely thin, impervious (to the sound) partitions parallel to the xy plane and situated $\pi/(k \cos \gamma)$ apart. Since the pattern cross section is triangular, these partitions are of unequal lengths, being in fact $2[l \sin \gamma - (m\pi/k \cos \gamma)] \tan \gamma$ wide, where l is the width of the incident beam. It is readily checked that these partitions do not affect in any way the dynamical relations between the incident and reflected beam.

When $kl \ll 1$ it is obvious that the potential does not vanish anywhere other than on the plane $z = 0$. The functional dependence $\sin(kz \cos \gamma) \approx kz \cos \gamma$, the velocity component parallel to z, is constant everywhere in the interference region. For $kl \gg 1$ the number of times the potential will vanish in the interference field is the nearest integer to

$$(kl \cos \gamma \sin \gamma)/\pi \doteq n \tag{24}$$

In the applications of interest n is usually a large number, so that it is possible to consider (24) an equality without committing too serious an error.

THE SECOND-ORDER INDUCED FIELD

The induced field is now evaluated by subdividing the interference region R into elementary strips outlined by the parallel partitions referred to above and then obtaining the sound intensity radiated from each section. Using the approximate relation (24), the half-length of each strip is

$$l_m = \left(\frac{n\pi}{k \cos \gamma} - \frac{m\pi}{k \cos \gamma} \right) \tan \gamma$$

$$= \frac{\pi \sin \gamma}{k \cos^2 \gamma}(n - m) \tag{25}$$

The fluctuating density emanating from any one section will be at a frequency 2ω and wave number $2k$. It is formally given by

$$\rho_{r,m}(\mathbf{r}_0) = \int_V \frac{\partial^2 T_{ij}(\mathbf{r}')}{\partial x_i' \partial x_j'} \frac{\exp(i2k|\mathbf{r}_0 + \mathbf{\Delta}_m - \mathbf{r}'|)}{4\pi|\mathbf{r}_0 + \mathbf{\Delta}_m - \mathbf{r}'|} d\mathbf{r}'$$

$$+ \int_V \frac{\partial^2 T_{ij}(\mathbf{r}'')}{\partial x_i'' \partial x_j''} \frac{\exp(i2k|\mathbf{r}_0 - \mathbf{\Delta}_m - \mathbf{r}''|)}{4\pi|\mathbf{r}_0 - \mathbf{\Delta}_m - \mathbf{r}''|} d\mathbf{r}'' \tag{26}$$

The volume of integration extends over the region occupied by the mth section. The position vectors $\mathbf{r}_0$, $\mathbf{r}'$, and $\mathbf{r}''$ are as shown in Fig. 3. The vector $\mathbf{\Delta}_m$ is along the positive z axis and its magnitude is $(2m - 1)\pi/(2k \cos \gamma)$.

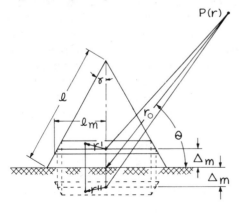

Fig. 3. Schematic representation of position vectors associated with an equivalent source for the mth section.

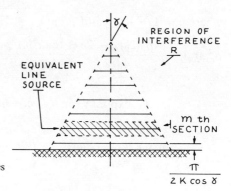

Fig. 4. Arrangement for array of line sources for describing the interference pattern.

From Fig. 3 $\mathbf{r}''$ is the image of $\mathbf{r}'$ in the mirror. Consequently,

$$\frac{\partial^2 T_{ij}(\mathbf{r}')}{\partial x_i \, \partial x_j} = \frac{\partial^2 T_{ij}(\mathbf{r}'')}{\partial x_i'' \, \partial x_j''} \tag{27}$$

If $|\mathbf{r}_0|$ is much greater than $|\mathbf{r}'|$ and $|\Delta_m|$, i.e., one examines the Fraunhoffer region of the radiation field, both denominators of the integrands of (26) become r_0.

A further approximation of the estimate of the integral (26) can be obtained by substituting for the equivalent array of primary sources that rigorously describes the interference pattern an assembly of sources spread on planes as shown in Fig. 4. In this approximate representation the width of the mth strip is reduced to a line and it is located at a height $(2m - 1)\pi/(2k \cos \gamma)$. The spatial dependence of the sources in the y direction is kept unchanged. As a result of these modifications the integral of (26) now simplifies to

$$\rho_{r,m}(\mathbf{r}_0) = \frac{(\exp i2kr_0)b}{4\pi r_0} \cos(2k\Delta_m \cos \theta)$$

$$\times \int_{-l_m}^{l_m} \frac{\partial^2 T_{ij}(\mathbf{r}')}{\partial x_i' \, \partial x_j'} \exp(-2iky' \cos \theta) \, dy' \tag{28}$$

In the above formula $b = \pi/(k \cos \gamma)$.

Using Eqs. (19) and (21), the equivalent strength for the source density contributing to the radiation is computed to be

$$\frac{\partial^2 T_{ij}}{\partial x_i \, \partial x_j} = -\frac{1}{\rho_0 c^2}\left[1 + \frac{1}{2}\frac{\rho_0}{c_0^2}\left(\frac{d^2 p}{d\rho_0^2}\right)_{\rho = \rho_0}\right]\frac{\partial^2}{\partial t^2}\rho^2$$

$$= -\frac{h}{\rho_0 c_0^2}\frac{\partial^2}{\partial t^2}\left[A\frac{2\rho_0}{\omega}k^2 \exp\{i(ky' \sin \gamma - \omega t)\}\right]^2 \tag{29}$$

where $h = 1 + \frac{1}{2}(\rho_0/c_0^2)(d^2p/\partial\rho^2)_{\rho=\rho_0}$. Hence from (28) and (29)

$$\rho_{r,m}(\mathbf{r}_0) = \frac{\exp i(2kr_0 - 2\omega t)}{4\pi r_0} \frac{16\pi k^3 h A^2 \rho_0}{c_0^2 \cos\gamma} \cos\left(\frac{(2m-1)\pi \cos\theta}{\cos\gamma}\right)$$

$$\times \int_{-l_m}^{l_m} \exp[i2ky'(\sin\gamma - \cos\theta)]\, dy'$$

$$= \frac{\exp i(2kr_0 - 2\omega t)}{4\pi r_0} B \cos\left(\frac{(2m-1)\pi\cos\theta}{\cos\gamma}\right) \frac{\sin[2kl_m(\sin\gamma - \cos\theta)]}{k(\sin\gamma - \cos\theta)}$$

$$\tag{30}$$

where $B = 16k^3 h A^2 \rho_0 (c_0^2 \cos\gamma)^{-1}$.

The corresponding acoustic intensity due to $\rho_{r,m}$ is

$$I_{r,m} = \frac{c_0^3}{\rho_0}|\rho_{r,m}|^2$$

$$= \left(\frac{B}{4\pi r_0}\right)^2 \frac{c_0^3}{\rho_0} \cos^2\left(\frac{(2m-1)\pi\cos\theta}{\cos\gamma}\right)\left\{\frac{\sin[2kl_m(\sin\gamma - \cos\theta)]}{k(\sin\gamma - \cos\theta)}\right\}^2 \tag{31}$$

while the power radiated is

$$P_{r,m} = 2\pi \int_0^\pi I_{r,m} r_0^2 \sin\theta\, d\theta$$

$$= \frac{B^2}{8\pi}\frac{c_0^3}{\rho_0} \int_0^\pi \cos^2\left(\frac{(2m-1)\pi\cos\theta}{\cos\gamma}\right)\left\{\frac{\sin^2[2kl_m(\sin\gamma - \cos\theta)]}{k(\sin\gamma - \cos\theta)}\right\}^2 \sin\theta\, d\theta$$

$$\tag{32}$$

For small angles of incidence γ and $kl_m \gg 1$ the above integral is computed to be (see Appendix)

$$P_{r,m} \doteq \frac{c^3}{\rho_0}\frac{B^2}{8\pi}\frac{l_m}{k}\left(\frac{\pi}{2} + \mathrm{Si}(kl_m \sin\gamma) - \frac{\sin^2(2kl_m \sin\gamma)}{2kl_m \sin\gamma}\right)$$

$$= \frac{32\omega^4 A^4 \rho_0}{c_0^5} \xi\left(\frac{\pi}{2} + \mathrm{Si}(\xi) - \frac{\sin^2 2\xi}{2\xi}\right) \tag{33}$$

where Si stands for the sine integral and $\xi = kl(\sin^2\gamma/\cos\gamma)[(n-m)/n]$. Now, the power flux for the primary waves out of any one section is

$$P_{p,m} = 2\pi\rho_p^2 \frac{c_0^3}{\rho_0}\frac{\pi}{k\cos\gamma} = 2\pi\omega A^2 \rho_0 \frac{1}{\cos\gamma} \tag{34}$$

Since the acoustic power reradiated at the 2ω frequency is at the expense of the incoming primary wave, the harmonic power can be considered as a damping, reducing the primary flux by the fraction

$$\frac{P_{r,m}}{P_{p,m}} = \left(\frac{16}{\pi}\frac{\omega^3 A^2}{c_0^5}\right)\xi\left[\frac{\pi}{2} + \text{Si}(\xi) - \frac{\sin^2 2\xi}{2\xi}\right] \tag{35}$$

To fix the ideas, a few representative numbers are given. In air the magnitude of $P_{r,m}/P_{p,m}$ can be as high as 20% for a fluctuating pressure amplitude of 0.01 atm and for a frequency of 10^4 Hz. In water for the pressure amplitude a hundred times larger and a frequency of 10 MHz the fraction is only 1.0%.

The functional behavior of $\psi = \xi\{\frac{1}{2}\pi + \text{Si}(\xi) - [(\sin^2 2\xi)/2\xi]\}$ as a function of position m is shown in graphical form in Fig. 5 for different values of kl ranging from 10^3 to 10 and for a fixed value of the incidence angle $\gamma = 0.1$ rad. The beam is assumed to be made of 10 sections, i.e., $n = 10$.

PHASE DISTORTION IN WAVEFRONT

The nonuniformity of the amplitude in the reflected primary wave front will lead to a phase distortion which is readily demonstrated as follows.

The normal mode representation for the sound pressure propagating down the beam is given by

$$p = -\rho_0\frac{\partial\phi}{\partial t} = +i\omega\rho_0 \sum_n (\exp ik_n y)\left(a_n \cos\frac{n\pi z}{l} + b_n \sin\frac{n\pi z}{l}\right) \tag{36}$$

Here the y axis is along the direction of propagation of the beam. The two-dimensional beam is defined by the region between two planes a distance l

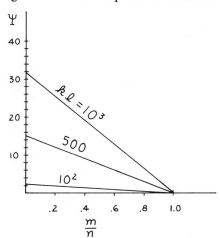

Fig. 5. Functional representation of
$\psi = \xi\{\frac{1}{2}\pi + \text{Si}(\xi) - [(\sin^2 2\xi)/2\xi]$
versus the position m/n.

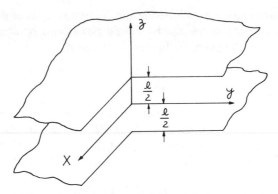

Fig. 6. Orientation of reflected beam with respect to new
set of axis as described in text.

apart and parallel to the xy plane (Fig. 6). The beam has been idealized by assuming it is sharply outlined by the planes $z = \pm l/2$. Actually, it is not, and the edges are described by diffraction pattern occuring there. The k_n are obtained from

$$k_n^2 = k^2 - (n\pi/l)^2 \tag{37}$$

All modes with an order n such as $k^2 > (n\pi/l)^2$ will propagate. The modes with an order higher than this critical value will be damped.

The coefficients a_n and b_n occurring in (36) are obtained from the Fourier expansion for the pressure at $y = 0$. The pressure at the origin is given by

$$p(z, 0) = \sum_n a_n \cos(n\pi z/l) + b_n \sin(n\pi z/l) \tag{38}$$

But it was shown that this distribution is

$$p(z, 0) = \omega\rho_0 A\left(1 - \frac{P_{r,m}}{P_{p,m}}\right)^{1/2}$$

$$\doteq \omega\rho_0 A\left(1 - \frac{1}{2}\frac{P_{r,m}}{P_{p,m}}\right) \tag{39}$$

Since the above relation is almost linear with z, we can express the pressure by a mean constant value $p_0 = \omega\rho_0 A(1 - \frac{1}{4}|P_{r,m}/P_{p,m}|_{\max})$ plus a part oddly symmetric about the origin. Consequently, the a_n vanish and

$$b_{(2n+1)} = (2/n\pi)(-1)^{(2n+1)}, \qquad n = 0, 1, 2, \ldots \tag{40}$$

The expansion (36) is thus

$$p = i\omega\rho_0 \left(1 - \frac{1}{4}\frac{P_{r,m}}{P_{p,m}}\right) e^{iky} \left[\frac{2}{(2n+1)\pi}\right] \sum_{n=0}^{\infty} (\exp ik_{2n+1}y)\frac{i\omega\rho_0}{4}\left|\frac{P_{r,m}}{P_{p,m}}\right|$$

$$\times (-1)^{n+2}\sin\frac{(2n+1)\pi z}{l} \tag{41}$$

The expression (37) is still valid, except that $(2n+1)$ replaces the index n. It is now easy to obtain the required result.

Indeed, Eq. (40) can be rewritten as

$$p/i\omega\rho_0 = a_0 e^{iky}[1 + \alpha \exp[i(k_1 - k)y]\sin(\pi z/l)$$
$$-\tfrac{1}{3}\alpha \exp[i(k_3 - k)y]\sin(3\pi z/l) + \cdots] \tag{42}$$

where $a_0 = 1 - \tfrac{1}{4}|P_{r,m}/P_{p,m}|$ and $\alpha = (1/2\pi a_0)|P_{r,m}/P_{p,m}|$. The phase of the acoustic pressure thus appears to vary from point to point over the beam cross section. For $kl \gg n\pi$ the phase distortion on a wavefront is derived from

$$p/i\omega\rho_0 \doteq a_0 e^{iky}[1 + \alpha \exp(-i\pi y/kl^2)\sin(\pi z/l)$$
$$-\tfrac{1}{3}\alpha \exp(-i3\pi y/kl^2)\sin(3\pi z/l) + \cdots] \tag{43}$$

The maximum deviation of the phase angle with respect to the phase at the axis $(z = 0)$ occurs at the edges, i.e., at $z = \pm l/2$. This deviation for a distance (from $y = 0$) equal to any integer number of wavelengths is given by

$$\beta = \pm\tan^{-1}\frac{\alpha[\sin(\tfrac{1}{2}\lambda^2/l^2) + \tfrac{1}{3}\sin(\tfrac{3}{2}\lambda/l)^2 + \cdots]}{1 + \alpha[\cos(\tfrac{1}{2}\lambda/l)^2 + \tfrac{1}{3}\cos(\tfrac{3}{2}\lambda/l)^2 + \cdots]} \tag{44}$$

Now the series in the numerator and the denominator are finite, since the acoustic pressure for modes $n\pi/l > k$ are attenuated. For large values of kl, however, many terms are taken and the sum of the sequences is approximately that of the series. Now, the series are identified with those for the so-called square sine and cosine ([9]). Hence

$$\sin[\tfrac{1}{2}(\lambda/l)^2] + \tfrac{1}{3}\sin[\tfrac{3}{2}(\lambda/l)^2] + \cdots = \pi/4 \qquad \pi > \tfrac{1}{2}\lambda^2/l^2 > 0$$

$$= 0 \qquad \lambda^2/l^2 = 2n\pi, \qquad n = 0, 1, 2, \ldots$$

and similarly the cosine series sums to $\pi/4$ for $\pi/2 > \tfrac{1}{2}\lambda^2/l^2 > -\pi/2$ and vanishes for $\lambda^2/l^2 = n\pi, n = \pm 1, 2, 3, \ldots$.

Since the quantity α is much smaller than unity, the maximum deviation for the phase is

$$\beta = 2\tan^{-1}\left(\frac{\tfrac{1}{4}\pi\alpha}{1 + \tfrac{1}{4}\pi\alpha}\right) \tag{45}$$

Since $2\pi\alpha$ was estimated to vary from 1% to 20%, β will then range from $1'$ to $3°$ for the same conditions.

CONCLUSION

The previous discussion has demonstrated that as a result of the non-linearity of the medium wave–wave interactions phase distortions will sense in the interacting waves. The resulting phase distortions in the example discussed here appear small because only the Fraunhoffer region of the diffraction field is examined.

If for any reason the measurement of the primary wave in the arriving front is important, the effect of the phase distortion can be minimized by correlation techniques. This is because the fluctuations appear to have different signs on different portions of the incident front. The measure for the distortion β varies with the frequency. In fact for small angles β as observed by inspection of (45) and (35) is proportional to the square of the amplitude of the signal and the cube of the frequency and varies linearly with kl. Explicitly, the maximum magnitude of the excursion is

$$\beta = \pm \left(\frac{16\omega^3 A^2}{\pi c_0^5} \right) kl \frac{\sin^2 \gamma}{\cos \gamma} \left[\frac{\pi}{2} + \text{Si} \left(\frac{kl \sin^2 \gamma}{\cos \gamma} \right) - \sin^{-2} \left(\frac{2kl \sin^2 \gamma}{\cos \gamma} \right) \right]$$

The arguments in this paper were centered around the case of a single frequency. When a spectrum of frequencies is dealt with the same procedure outlined here can be used, but the algebra becomes more laborious. However, an order-of-magnitude idea of the effect can be obtained from the estimates obtained from the simple case of the single frequency.

APPENDIX

To calculate the integral in Eq. (32),

$$I = \int_0^\pi \cos^2 \left(\frac{(2m-1)\pi \cos \theta}{\cos \gamma} \right) \left\{ \frac{\sin^2[2kl_m(\sin \gamma - \cos \theta)]}{k(\sin \gamma - \cos \theta)} \right\}^2 \sin \theta \, d\theta$$

we introduce the transformation $\zeta = 2kl_m(\sin \gamma - \cos \theta)$ and notice that since

$$\cos^2 \left(\frac{(2m-1)\pi \cos \theta}{\cos \gamma} \right) = \frac{1}{2} \left\{ 1 + \cos \left(\frac{2\pi(2m-1)\cos \theta}{\cos \gamma} \right) \right\},$$

the integrand of I will consist of two terms, one of which contains $\cos(2\pi(2m-1)\cos \theta/\cos \gamma)$. Since this term fluctuates very rapidly it can be neglected. Then for $\sin \gamma \ll 1$, I reduces to

$$I = \frac{l_m}{k} \int_{2kl_m \sin \gamma}^{2kl_m} \frac{\sin^2 \zeta}{\zeta^2} d\zeta$$

But it is known (^{10}) that the above integral is

$$I = \frac{l_m}{k}\left[-\frac{\sin^2 \zeta}{\zeta}\bigg|_{2kl_m \sin \gamma}^{2kl_m} + \int_{2kl_m \sin \gamma}^{2kl_m} \frac{\sin 2\zeta}{\zeta}d\zeta \right]$$

for very large values of kl_m

$$I \to \frac{l_m}{k}\left[\frac{\pi}{2} + \text{Si}(\xi) - \frac{\sin^2 2\xi}{2\xi} \right]$$

which is the value used in the text.

REFERENCES

1. H. Lamb, *The Dynamical Theory of Sound*, Edward Arnold, London, 1910, p. 174 ff.
2. A. L. Thuras, R. T. Jenkins, and H. T. O'Neill, *J. Acoust. Soc. Am.* **6**: 173 (1935).
3. M. J. Lighthill, *Proc. Roy. Soc.* (London) **A222**:1 (1952).
4. P. Moyal, *Proc. Camb. Phil. Soc.* **48**:329 (1952).
5. L. S. G. Kovaznay, *J. Aero. Sci.* **20**:657 (1953).
6. O. K. Mawardi, *Rept. Progr. Phys.* **21**:156 (1956).
7. P. J. Westervelt, *J. Acoust. Soc. Am.* **29**:199, (1957).
8. L. Brillouin, *Les Tenseurs en Mécanique et en Elasticité*, Dover Publications, New York, 1946, p. 268 ff.
9. R. Courant, *Differential and Integral Calculus*, 2nd ed., Blackie and Sons Ltd., London, 1943, p. 443.
10. G. Watson, *A Treatise on the Theory of Bessel Functions*, 2nd. ed., Macmillan, New York, 1948, p. 152.

Chapter 14

THE RELATIVE IMPORTANCE OF PHASE AND AMPLITUDE IN ACOUSTICAL HOLOGRAPHY*

A. F. Metherell

Douglas Advanced Research Laboratories
McDonnell Douglas Corporation, Huntington Beach, California

This chapter describes an investigation to determine qualitatively the effect of recording a hologram by detecting only the phase of the object wave rather than both the phase and the amplitude, as in conventional holography. The "phase-only" hologram offers three advantages over a conventional hologram in acoustical or microwave holography: first, the amount of data to be acquired is reduced because only the phase needs to be measured; second, the full dynamic range of the recording equipment can be used over the entire hologram aperture; and finally, there is a possibility that image resolution may be better. In experiments conducted with sound using a frequency of 18 kHz (0.75-in. wavelength) in air, holograms were made using both "phase-only" and conventional techniques. Objects used were (1) a cutout of the letter "R," and (2) three point sound sources at different relative intensities. Reconstructed images of the objects made from both types of holograms did not show any noticeable differences either in image geometry or in image grey scale. For the geometry and relative intensity levels in the object image to be preserved it appears that the following two conditions are necessary: the surface of the object should be made up of points which radiate spherical waves; and all the points on the object surface that are visible at one point in the hologram plane should also be visible at all other points in the hologram plane. Unless these conditions are satisfied, the reconstructed image from a "phase-only" hologram will still be geometrically correct, but the grey scale, though still in evidence, will appear distorted. A new technique for completely eliminating the conjugate image in reconstructing a true image of the object in the Gabor (on-axis) type of arrangement is also discussed. This consists of (1) blocking the defocused conjugate image with an aperture placed at the focus of the true image of the source which "illuminates" the object, and (2) blocking the zero-order wave with a stop.

INTRODUCTION

A hologram is a recording of the phase and amplitude of an object wave in an arbitrary plane known as the plane of the hologram. In optical hologra-

*This work was conducted at the Douglas Advanced Research Laboratories, McDonnell Douglas Corporation, under company sponsored funds.

phy ($^{1,\,2}$) experimenters go to great lengths to assure that both the amplitude and phase of the object wave are recorded linearly. When holography was carried over into the long wavelengths, such as acoustical ($^{3-6}$) or microwave (^{7}) holography, where hologram data are detected electronically, it was assumed that both the amplitude and phase would have to be linearly detected and recorded.

In our experiments we originally used the scanning method, which was very time-consuming. As a result we sought means for reducing the recording time. In so doing we examined the relative importance of the amplitude and phase and decided that by reducing the amount of recorded data in the hologram we might achieve our goal. Although we still have not achieved a reduction in recording time, we have found the answer to the question: Is it necessary to record both the phase and the amplitude of the object wave, or can we record the phase only and assume a constant value for amplitude? The results of the investigation reported here suggest that for acoustical holography the phase alone may suffice.

The following section contains a description of experiments in which conventional holograms are compared with "phase-only" holograms in which the object wave amplitude was normalized to a constant quantity. These experiments revealed that there is no significant difference between the quality of the reconstructed images from the two types of holograms. To explain these results, mathematical consideration is then given to the question of the relative importance of phase alone versus phase plus amplitude. It is shown that the amplitude term in the hologram plane acts only on the overall amplitude of the object points and not on their relative amplitudes. The same result is seen from a qualitative physical argument.

The significance of this finding as it applies to acoustical (or microwave) holography is this: First, since only the phase of the object wave, rather than both the phase and the amplitude, need be measured at each point on the hologram, the data acquisition requirement is appreciably reduced. Second, the recording system, which has only a limited (linear) dynamic range, can be adjusted so that the "phase-only" hologram fills the available dynamic range not only at localized positions on the hologram but across its whole area, whereas the conventional hologram can utilize the full dynamic range only in those parts of the hologram where the object wave intensity is at a maximum. Third, there may even be an improvement in image resolution, which is a consequence of using the whole hologram area to its maximum dynamic range, and hence effectively increases the hologram aperture available.

EXPERIMENTS

General Instrumentation

The basic experimental arrangement shown in Fig. 1 was used in all the

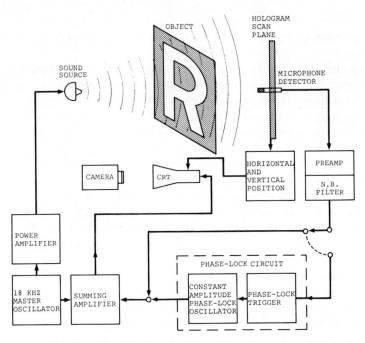

Fig. 1. Layout of sound source, object letter "R," and scanning microphone with associated electronic components.

experiments but one, in which the object consisted of three point sound sources instead of the letter "R." The frequency was 18 kHz, which gave a wavelength of $\frac{3}{4}$ in. in air. A master oscillator provided the 18-kHz signal, which was amplified by a McIntosh amplifier to drive a JBL Lansing high-frequency tweeter sound source. The sound source was placed approximately 19 ft from the microphone scanning rig. An 8-ft by 8-ft masonite board with a large letter "R" cut out of it provided the object. The "R" measured 6 ft high by 4 ft wide with 1-ft lettering width. This "R" was placed approximately 6 ft from the scanning rig. For resolution considerations the size of the "R" was made large because of the $\frac{3}{4}$-in. wavelength that was used. Even at this size the lettering stroke width was only 16 wavelengths.

An Altec 175A microphone, which had a frontal detection aperture diameter of $\frac{3}{4}$ in. (which is a large sampling area relative to the wavelength), was used to scan a plane 8 ft horizontally in vertical increments of $\frac{1}{2}$ in. over a total height of 10 ft. The vertical and horizontal positions of the microphone were electrically synchronized with the horizontal and vertical positions of the spot on the CRT. The microphone output was amplified and filtered to eliminate rig and room noise. The signal could then either be passed directly into one channel of a summing amplifier (which was done when recording a conventional hologram) or be passed through the phase lock circuit and then into the summing amplifier (which was done when recording a "phase-only" hologram).

An electronic reference signal derived from the same signal generator which provided the sound source signal was passed into the second input to the summing amplifier. Unlike some of our earlier experiments [8], the phase of this electronic reference was not changed; it therefore simulated a plane acoustic reference wave falling perpendicularly onto the scanning plane. The output from the summing amplifier was connected to the cathode input of the CRT to modulate the spot intensity. As the microphone scanned the hologram plane a Polaroid oscilloscope camera on time exposure recorded the acoustical hologram written on the face of the CRT.

The phase-lock circuit consisted of a Hewlett-Packard 3300A function generator with the 3302A Trigger/Phase Lock Plug-In Unit. This device contained its own oscillator, which was set to approximately the experimental frequency being used. The phase-lock trigger circuit was used to lock the oscillator frequency to the trigger signal. The microphone signal was connected to the trigger input. The output from the phase-lock circuit was thus derived from the oscillator, so that its amplitude was always a constant value (no matter how much the microphone signal level varied), but its phase was always locked to that of the microphone signal. Hence the microphone and phase-lock circuit together may be considered to constitute a phase-sensitive detector independent of amplitude. With the phase lock in the circuit the output from the summing amplifier is the sum of the reference wave and a constant-amplitude wave whose phase is locked to that of the detected acoustical object wave. Without the phase lock in the circuit the output from the summing amplifier is the sum of the reference wave and the object wave.

Reconstruction Technique

The acoustical hologram was reduced photographically on a transparency so that the 8-ft width of the scanning plane was reduced to 0.2 in. This gave a linear reduction of 480:1. Since the acoustic-to-optical-wavelength ratio was 30,105:1, this photographic reduction was not sufficient to eliminate the longitudinal distortion in the reconstruction images. However, this was not important in our experiment because the "R" was two-dimensional.

The reconstruction was then made by placing the demagnified acoustical hologram in front of a He-Ne laser (Fig. 2). The beam from the laser (6328 Å) was expanded and then focused to a point beyond the hologram; in other words, the reconstruction was done with a converging beam, in order to obtain two real reconstructed images. A zero-order stop was placed at the zero-order beam focus. The true images of the "R" and tweeter formed a

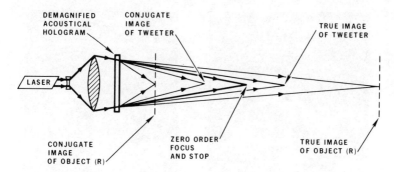

Fig. 2. Arrangement used to reconstruct the acoustical holograms.

three-dimensional image to the right of the zero-order stop, while the conjugate images were to the left. To record the image of the "R" or tweeter, a photographic film was placed in the respective image planes.

First Experiments with the Letter "R"

Figure 3 shows the results of the first comparative experiments conducted with and without the phase-lock technique. The hologram of Fig. 3b, is the conventional hologram made in the conventional manner. Notice that the fringe contrast, which is the object wave amplitude, decreases toward the edge of the hologram. The hologram of Fig. 3a is the "phase-only" hologram made with the phase lock in the circuit. Notice that the fringe contrast is constant over the hologram. The fringe positions, however, are the same for both holograms, indicating that the object wave phase is the same in both.

The reconstructions from the two holograms are shown in Fig. 3c. These reconstructed images were made simultaneously, with both demagnified holograms placed side by side in the reconstructing arrangement (Fig. 2).

The quality of the holograms is not very good, as can be seen from the horizontal bars running through the reconstructed images. These bars were subsequently found to be mainly due to temperature fluctuations in the laboratory, which caused changes in the acoustic path length during scanning. Apart from these defects both images appear about equal in quality. The speckled backgrounds surrounding the reconstructed "R" are the out-of-focus conjugate images superimposed on the image.

The Three Point-source Experiments

The preceding experiments showed that the geometry of the object can be reconstructed as well with the "phase-only" hologram as with the conventional hologram, but did not indicate anything about the reconstructibility of grey scales. To test reconstructibility of grey scales, the object "R"

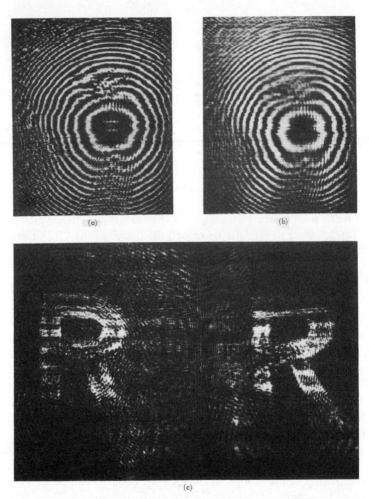

Fig. 3. The first experiments comparing the conventional acoustical hologram
(*b*) with the "phase only" acoustical hologram (*a*). The reconstructed images of
the respective holograms are shown in (*c*). The poor quality (horizontal
streaking) of the reconstructed "R" in both cases was due to temperature
changes during scanning.

was removed from the field and three point sources, or tweeters, were
placed 14 ft in front of the microphone scanning rig in a plane parallel to the
scanning plane. Two were placed 48 in. apart to form the base of an isosceles
triangle and the other was placed 48 in. above the base to form the apex. All
the tweeters were driven from separate amplifiers set at different levels but
supplied from the same oscillator, so that all the tweeters were coherent. A
conventional acoustical hologram was then recorded without the phase lock

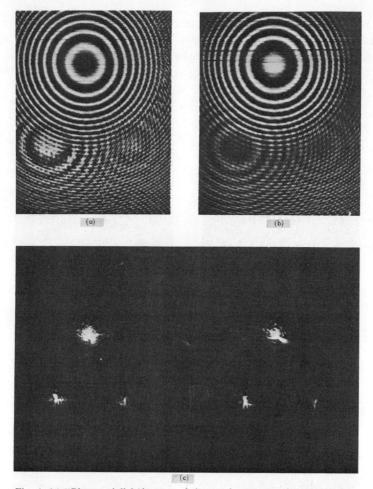

Fig. 4. (a) "Phase-only" hologram of three coherent sound sources set at different amplitudes. (b) Conventional hologram of same experimental setup. Both are positives. The difference in the hologram zone-plate centers is due to a small change in temperature between the two experiments that changed the total acoustic path length. (c) The reconstructed images of the three sound sources from each of the respective holograms, showing that the relative intensities in the object image are preserved in the "phase-only" hologram.

in the circuit, with the result shown in Fig. 4b. A "phase-only" acoustical hologram was then recorded with the phase lock in the circuit under the same conditions, with the result shown in Fig. 4a. Notice again that the fringe contrast varies in the conventional hologram, whereas the contrast is constant in the "phase-only" hologram.

The reconstructed images obtained by simultaneously reconstructing the two holograms are shown in Fig. 4c. The relative intensities of the reconstructed tweeter images from the two holograms agreed with each other

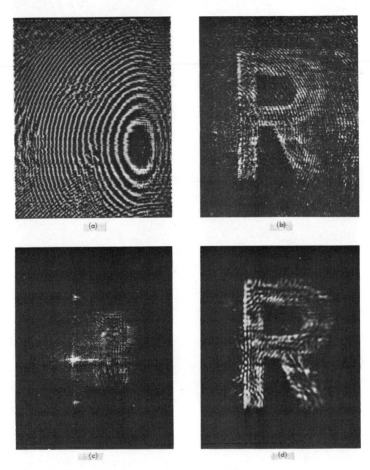

Fig. 5. (a) The recorded acoustical hologram. (b) The reconstructed true image of the "R" recorded by placing a photographic film at the focus of the true "R" image (Fig. 2). The background speckle is the out-of-focus conjugate images of the tweeter and "R." (c) The bright dot is the reconstructed true image of the sound source recorded by placing a photographic film at the focus of the true sound source (tweeter) image (Fig. 2). The out-of-focus conjugate "R" can be seen to the right of the sound source. (d) The reconstructed true image of the "R" [similar to (b)] with the conjugate images removed by spatial filtering. The spatial filter in this case was an aperture placed in the focal plane of the true sound source (tweeter) image (see Fig. 2), which allowed only the light from the sound source (c) to pass through.

within the accuracy of the spot light intensity meter used to measure them (readings were 1:2.2:4.3).

Elimination of the Conjugate Images*

Figure 5a shows another hologram of the letter "R" using the arrangement similar to that described earlier. This is a "phase-only" hologram—one of the better ones that we have produced. The reconstructed true image of the "R" is shown in Fig. 5b. The circular fringe pattern superimposed on the "R" is the out-of-focus true tweeter image; the surrounding background light is the combination of the out-of-focus conjugate tweeter and "R" images.

The reconstructed tweeter image (the brightest dot) is shown in Fig. 5c, which illustrates the three-dimensional nature of the acoustical hologram. The horizontal and vertical streaks through the tweeter image are due to diffraction of the edges of the rectangular aperture of the hologram. The bright dot above the tweeter image is the first-order diffracted image of the true tweeter image due to the microphone raster line effect. At an equal distance below the true tweeter image is the conjugate diffracted image, almost too weak to be seen in the figure. The other bright dot below the true tweeter image is unexplained. To the right of the reconstructed true tweeter image are the out-of-focus conjugate "R" and tweeter images.

In the acoustical arrangement (Fig. 1) the sound radiating from the tweeter passed through the cutout of the letter "R." This acoustic field is reproduced optically in the reconstruction process. By blocking all the light in the true tweeter image plane (Figs. 2 and 5c) except for the reconstructed true tweeter image, the entire conjugate image field, noise, and diffracted images due to the raster line effect are blocked. Blocking was accomplished by placing a small aperture in the true image plane to allow only the tweeter image to pass through the aperture. The result can be seen in the reconstructed true "R" image plane (Fig. 5d), where the background has been removed.

Essentially the same result can be obtained by placing a stop to block the conjugate tweeter image in the conjugate tweeter image plane instead of placing the aperture in the true tweeter image plane. This alternative method does not block out general noise in the image, although the aperture method does to some extent.

THE PHASE AND AMPLITUDE OF AN OBJECT WAVE

Qualitative mathematical and physical explanations of the experimental results presented in the preceding sections are offered in the following para-

---

*This technique for eliminating the conjugate image was first suggested by Mr. Sid Spinak of the Douglas Advanced Research Laboratories, McDonnell Douglas Corporation.

graphs. A rigorous mathematical analysis of the process has yet to be developed.

Qualitative Mathematical Explanation

A Point Object

In this section attention is given to the wave U_0 radiated from an object which is illuminated with coherent radiation. To begin with, we shall not consider the effect of biasing U_0 with a reference U_r to record a hologram. The basic concept presented here applies to a coherent object wave in general and hence may prove useful in certain practical types of holography.

Consider the point-source object j radiating a coherent spherical wave of amplitude a_j (measured one wavelength from the point), as shown in Fig. 6. The point is located at coordinates x_j, y_j, z_j. The wave at a point P in the xy plane can be expressed by

$$U_j = A_j \exp(i\omega t + i\phi_j) \tag{1}$$

where A_j and ϕ_j are the amplitude and phase, respectively, of the object wave at $P(x, y)$. The $i\omega t$ term is the time-varying carrier frequency of the wave, which may be dropped from the equation. Thus

$$U_j(x, y) = A_j(x, y) \exp[i\phi_j(x, y)] \tag{2}$$

From Fig. 6 we see that the distance $|r_j|$ between point j and point P is

$$|r_j| = [z_j^2 + (x - x_j)^2 + (y - y_j)^2]^{1/2} \tag{3}$$

$$A_j = a_j[z_j^2 + (x - x_j)^2 + (y - y_j)^2]^{-1/2} \tag{4}$$

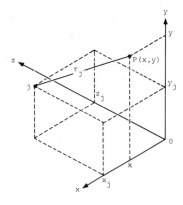

Fig. 6. Coordinate system for a point object j and a point p in the xy plane.

If ψ_j (a constant) is the phase of the source (with respect to whatever reference is chosen), we have

$$\phi_j = (2\pi|r_j|/\lambda) + \psi_j \quad \text{radians}$$

$$\phi_j = \{2\pi[z_j^2 + (x - x_j)^2 + (y - y_j)^2]^{1/2}/\lambda\} + \psi_j \tag{5}$$

where λ is the wavelength of the coherent radiation.

Thus the point j is uniquely defined by the five parameters $x_j, y_j, z_j, a_j, \psi_j$.

An Extended Object

Suppose the object is an extended three-dimensional object as shown in Fig. 7. Assume that the object is such that the surface which is visible at an arbitrary point P in the plane xy (which later will be taken to be a hologram plane) is also visible at all other points P in the xy plane. When the surface of the object is diffusely reflecting the surface may be considered to be made up of many point scatterers which radiate spherical waves, as shown for the single jth point in Fig. 1. It follows that the total contribution of the object wave at the given point $P(x, y)$ can be expressed as

$$\mathbf{U}_0 = \sum_{j=1}^{j=n} \mathbf{U}_j = \sum_{j=1}^{j=n} A_j \exp i\phi_j \tag{6}$$

As this is the summation of harmonic waves of the same frequency, Eq. (6) can be expressed as a single harmonic wave of amplitude A_0 and phase ϕ_0 due to the total contribution of the object, namely,

$$\mathbf{U}_0 = A_0 \exp i\phi_0 \tag{7}$$

where

$$A_0 = \left[\left(\sum_{j=1}^{j=n} A_j \sin \phi_j \right)^2 + \left(\sum_{j=1}^{j=n} A_j \cos \phi_j \right)^2 \right]^{1/2} \tag{8}$$

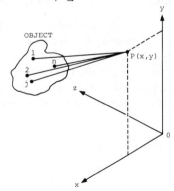

Fig. 7. An object whose surface may be represented by point scatterers 1, 2, j, n.

and

$$\tan \phi_0 = \left[\left(\sum_{j=1}^{j=n} A_j \sin \phi_j\right) \Big/ \left(\sum_{j=1}^{j=n} A_j \cos \phi_j\right)\right] \qquad (9)$$

At a given point P in the xy plane Eqs. (8) and (9) are functions only of the same object parameters $x_j, y_j, z_j, a_j, \psi_j$. Hence

$$A_0 = f_1(x_j, y_j, z_j, a_j, \psi_j) \qquad (10)$$

and

$$\exp i\phi_0 = f_2(x_j, y_j, z_j, a_j, \psi_j) \qquad (11)$$

Equation (7) may therefore be written

$$U_0 = f_1 \cdot f_2 \qquad (12)$$

The fundamental purpose of holography and imaging in general is usually to be able to retrieve the object parameters $x_j, y_j, z_j, a_j, \psi_j$. If none of these parameters is already known and if there is no one point on the object brighter than all the others to act as a reference wave, we know from experience that the product of f_1 and f_2 gives retrievable information about the object parameters (because both f_1 and f_2 are recorded in the hologram process when U_r is added). On the other hand, we do know from experience that nothing can be retrieved from f_1 alone. (This is like exposing a photographic plate to light reflected from a scene without a known reference.) Since both f_1 and f_2 are functions of the same object parameters, it is possible that the function f_2 alone may be responsible for the retrievability of the parameters $(x_j, y_j, z_j, a_j, \psi_j)$. If this be so, the function f_1 operates only on the overall amplitude. The experiments described in the previous section indicate that if we take f_2 alone, all the object parameters can be retrieved except that, since the amplitude operator f_1 is removed, only the relative amplitudes $a_1 : a_2 : \cdots : a_j : \cdots : a_n$ are retrievable instead of the absolute values of a_j.

Qualitative Physical Explanation

The same result can be expected from a purely physical viewpoint.

Consider the object wave U_0 at one point P_1 in the xy plane. The object wave contains contributions from each of the object points, as can be seen from Eqs. (7)–(9). The same is true for a second point $P_2(x_2, y_2)$ in the xy plane. Suppose the amplitude (but not the phase) of the object wave at P_2 is changed by a factor M. Then the object wave at P_2 will be

$$MU_0 = MA_0 \exp i\phi_0 \qquad (13)$$

From Eq. (8)

$$MA_0 = \left[\left(\sum_{j=1}^{j=n} MA_j \sin \phi_j\right)^2 + \left(\sum_{j=1}^{j=n} MA_j \cos \phi_j\right)^2\right]^{1/2} \qquad (14)$$

and from Eq. (4)

$$MA_j = (Ma_j)/[z_j^2 + (x - x_j)^2 + (y - y_j)^2]^{1/2} \qquad (15)$$

Thus, modifying the object wave amplitude at a given point is equivalent to modifying the object source amplitudes by the same factor, with the result that the relative amplitudes of one object point with respect to any other is preserved and only their absolute values are changed.

Thus if the object wave amplitude is factored by a different amount M at another point $P(x, y)$, the relative amplitudes in the object plane will be preserved. The total effect on the object image of doing this over the entire surface of the xy plane will be to sum the effects from each of the points $P(x, y)$, and hence affect only the overall image intensity. The relative intensities on the object image surface will be preserved.

The factor M cannot be allowed to vary widely from point to point in the xy plane without destroying the geometry or relative intensities from point to point in the object. Only if the function $M(x, y)$ does not also affect the reconstructed wave phase ϕ_0 can M vary over the surface of the hologram.

The linear detection of an acoustical (or microwave) field allows independent measurement of its amplitude as well as its phase. This enables the detected object wave to be processed prior to summation with the reference wave. In the experiments described earlier in this chapter the object wave amplitude was modified without changing the phase, which satisfies the requirement for $M(x, y)$ stated above.

The particular case of interest in this chapter is where $M(x, y) = A_0^{-1}$, so that instead of the object wave U_0 being linearly recorded, as in conventional holography, the modified object wave is linearly recorded, where

$$MU_0 = A_0^{-1}U_0 = \exp(i\phi_0) \qquad (16)$$

In other words, only the phase information in the object wave is recorded, and the amplitude of the object wave is normalized to unity. This modified object wave is then summed with a reference wave, and the intensity is then recorded in the usual manner. The resulting "phase-only" hologram is therefore a linear recording of only the phase of the object wave rather than both the phase and the amplitude, as in the conventional hologram.

This means that a detector which is sensitive to the phase only and is insensitive to the amplitude of the object wave can be used to record a "phase-only" hologram. Yet in the reconstruction the original object appears geometrically correct and with relative surface intensities reproduced in their correct proportions to each other. The inference is therefore that the intensities in the object plane (a_1, a_2, a_j, etc.) must be contained in the phase of the object wave. This is seen to be the case, as is clear in Eq. (9), where ϕ_0 is a function of a_j as well as of x_j, y_j, z_j, and ψ_j.

Conventional and "Phase-only" Hologram Fringe Patterns

It is worthwhile to illustrate the differences in the appearance of fringe patterns in conventional and "phase-only" holograms for a number of simple cases.

Case 1. Consider a single point object located at coordinates (Fig. 6) $x = 0, y = 0, z = 30\lambda$, with an amplitude 3 (at $x = y = z = 0$). The intensity A_0^2 of the object wave falls off radially from the origin of xy as shown in Fig. 8a. The phase of the object wave ϕ_0 continuously increases radially from $x = y = 0$ in the xy plane (Fig. 8b). When a plane reference wave $\mathbf{U}_r$ is added which falls perpendicularly onto the xy plane the intensity of the sum of the object and reference waves $|\mathbf{U}_r + \mathbf{U}_0|^2$ (which is what the conventional hologram records) forms a zone-plate pattern. The intensity as it varies radially from the center of the zone is shown in Fig. 8c. Physically, the positions of the fringe peaks and troughs can be interpreted as the object wave

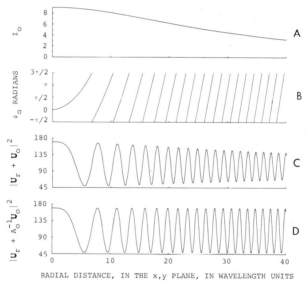

RADIAL DISTANCE, IN THE x,y PLANE, IN WAVELENGTH UNITS

Fig. 8. Curves for a point object situated at a distance 30 wavelengths on the z axis of an xyz coordinate system. The ordinate is the radius in the xy plane from the origin $x = y = z = 0$. (a) Intensity A_0^2 of the wave $\mathbf{U}_0$ from the object. (b) Phase ϕ_0 of the object wave $\mathbf{U}_0$. (c) Intensity $|\mathbf{U}_r + \mathbf{U}_0|^2$ of the object wave plus a plane reference wave of amplitude 10 and wavefront parallel to the xy plane. This curve is equivalent to a conventional hologram fringe pattern. (d) Intensity $|\mathbf{U}_r + A^{-1}\mathbf{U}_0|^2$ of the sum of the reference wave and the constant-amplitude object wave. This curve is the "phase-only" hologram fringe pattern.

phase information; the difference in height between the peaks and troughs (the fringe contrast) is the object wave amplitude information. Figure 8c is a trace of a conventional hologram of a point object.

If the object wave intensity (Fig. 8a) is normalized to a constant value before summing with the reference wave, the result $|U_r + A_0^{-1}U_0|^2$ appears as shown in Fig. 8d. The ordinate (intensity) value of this curve is thus directly related to the object-wave phase. This is a trace of the "phase-only" hologram.

Case 2. The arrangement for case 2 is similar to that for case 1 except that an additional object point is present, situated at $z = 40\lambda$ ($x = y = 0$). The amplitude of each point object wave alone at $x = y = z = 0$ is 1.5. Figures 9a and 9b show the intensity and phase, respectively, of the total object wave in the xy plane as it varies radially from $x = y = 0$. The addition of a perpendicular plane reference wave results in the conventional hologram intensity pattern, the trace of which is shown in Fig. 9c, which is in fact the superposition of two zone-plate patterns.

If the object wave intensity (Fig. 9a) is normalized and the "phase-only" hologram intensity $|U_r + A_0^{-1}U_0|^2$ is calculated, the result is as shown in

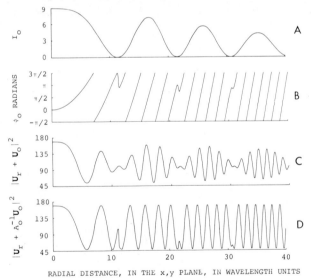

Fig. 9. Curves for a two-point object. One point is located at $x = 0$, $y = 0$, $z = 30$ wavelengths and the other at $x = 0$, $y = 0$, $z = 40$ wavelengths, both with amplitudes 1.5 at $x = y = z = 0$. (a) Intensity A_0^2 of the object wave. (b) Phase ϕ_0 of the object wave. (c) Intensity $|U_r + U_0|^2$ (conventional hologram) of the object plus reference waves (same reference as Fig. 8). (d) Intensity $|U_r + A^{-1}U_0|^2$ ("phase-only" hologram).

Fig. 9d. Note that this is not equivalent to "clipping" the curve shown in Fig. 9c. The amplitude of the curve in Fig. 9d is directly related to the object wave phase. The curve does not go to a maximum at $x \approx 11.3$, $x \approx 21.3$, and $x \approx 30.7$ because the phase of the object wave at these points decreases momentarily as x increases instead of continuously increasing with x, as can be seen in Fig. 9b. That is, $d\phi_0/dx$ was negative for $11.2 < x < 11.7$, $21.4 < x < 21.8$, and $30.6 < x < 30.9$.

Case 3. The object wave is composed of two plane waves. One plane wave has an amplitude of 1.4 and impinges on the xy plane with its normal making an angle of 60° with the z axis, 30° with the y axis, and 90° with the x axis. The second plane wave has an amplitude of 1.6 and its normal makes an angle of 75° with the z axis and 25° with the y axis. The intensity of the total object wave in the xy plane varies in the x direction as shown in Fig. 10a. The phase of the total object wave varies as shown in Fig. 10b. When a plane reference wave impinging perpendicularly onto the xy plane is added to the object wave the resulting conventional hologram fringe pattern is as shown in Fig. 10c. The "phase-only" hologram of the same object wave is shown in Fig. 10d.

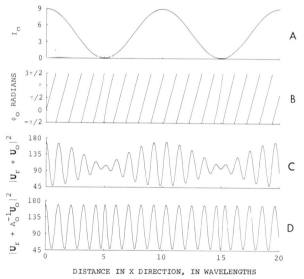

DISTANCE IN X DIRECTION, IN WAVELENGTHS

Fig. 10. Plane waves of amplitudes 1.4 and 1.6 fall on the xy plane at angles 60° and 75° from the z axis, respectively, making up the object wave. A reference wave, amplitude 10, falls on the xy plane in the z direction. (a) Intensity A_0^2 of the object wave. (b) Phase ϕ_0 of the object wave. (c) Intensity $|U_r + U_0|^2$ (conventional hologram). (d) Intensity $|U_r + A^{-1}U_0|^2$ ("phase-only" hologram).

At first glance it appears that information has been lost in Fig. 10*d* because the "beating" in the fringe amplitude (seen in Fig. 10*c*) has been removed. It looks almost as though the fringe frequency in Fig. 10*d* were constant, which would imply that a reconstruction from a hologram of the type in Fig. 10*d* would produce only a single-component object wave instead of the two components, one at 60° and the other at 75° to the *z* axis. Closer examination of the curve shows that this is not the case because the spatial fringe frequency is not constant but varies in step with the "beat" in the conventional curve shown in Fig. 10*c*. Thus the information has not been lost.

The Hologram as a Spatial Frequency Carrier

A hologram is a spatial frequency carrier of spatial information, just as a radio broadcast is a temporal frequency carrier of temporal information. A conventional hologram is a combination amplitude-modulated (AM) and frequency-modulated (FM) spatial carrier wave. A "phase-only" hologram, however, is a strictly frequency-modulated (FM) spatial carrier wave, as seen in Figs. 10*c* and 10*d*.

No electrical engineer would design a radio broadcast system as a combination AM/FM system because the FM signal will carry all the necessary information and the addition of AM to the FM would be redundant. The anology to the hologram as a spatial frequency carrier is not total, however, since we know that an FM radio signal can transmit absolute amplitudes, whereas the "phase-only" (FM) hologram will record relative amplitudes only.

Effect on Image Resolution

One important point which has not been considered in this chapter is the question of the effect that the "phase-only" technique has upon image resolution. Undoubtedly, the resolution must be affected in some way. However, it is apparently not affected very adversely, because the resolution of the reconstructed images such as Fig. 5*b*, is less than two wavelengths (as seen by the edge sharpness of the legs of the "R") and therefore cannot be significantly improved.

Intuitively, we can see that the resolution of a "phase-only" hologram may perhaps be better than that of a conventional hologram. Consider a hologram of a point object where the hologram aperture is infinite. The hologram will resemble a zone-plate pattern (Fig. 8*a*–8*b*). As the distance from the center of the zone-plate increases, the fringe contrast of the conventional hologram (Fig. 8*c*) decreases. Thus at a large distance from the center of the zone-plate pattern the fringe contrast will be effectively zero, and hence we will be utilizing only that part of the hologram aperture where the fringes are visible, and not the full available aperture. However, in the "phase-only" hologram (Fig. 8d) the fringe contrast is kept constant; thus the full available aperture of the hologram plane will be utilized. Since resolution is a direct function of effective aperture, the inference is that the "phase-only" hologram may give better resolution. This argument is only intuitive, however, and the whole question of resolution is still open.

CONCLUDING REMARKS

Within the accuracy limits of the experiments that we conducted, our results indicated that a hologram made with object wave phase information only gives a reconstructed image of the original object in which the geometry is correct and the grey scale is preserved, provided the following conditions are satisfied:

1. The surface of the object must be composed of points which radiate spherical waves.

2. All the points on the object surface that are visible from one point in the hologram plane must also be visible at all other points in the hologram plane.

The mathematical explanation given in the previous section is just that—an explanation but not a proof—and hence a conclusive mathematical study of the "phase-only" imaging process would be desirable.

Further work is required to investigate the effect of "phase-only" holography on image resolution. Intuitively, it seems that a "phase-only" hologram may produce a better resolution in the reconstructed image.

The method of eliminating the conjugate image in the in-line Gabor type of hologram has proved useful. The technique is limited to certain arrangements that can yield a point focus in the reconstructed image, and therefore may not be useful in diffusely illuminated scenes.

ACKNOWLEDGMENTS

The author wishes to thank Dr. H. M. A. El-Sum for many helpful discussions and Mr. Sid Spinak for suggesting the method for eliminating the conjugate image, as described on p. 211, and for assisting with the experiments.

REFERENCES

1. D. Gabor, *Proc. Roy. Soc.* (London) **A197**: 454–487 (1949); *Proc. Phys. Soc.* **B64**: 449–469 (1951).
2. E. N. Leith and J. Upatnieks, Jr., *J. Opt. Soc. Am.* **52**: 1123–1130 (1962); **53**: 1377 (1963).

3. F. L. Thurstone, *Proc. Symp. Biomed. Eng.* **1**:12–15 (1966).
4. R. K. Mueller and N. K. Sheridon, *Appl. Phys. Letters* **9**:328–329 (1966).
5. K. Preston, Jr. and J. L. Kreuzer, *Appl. Phys. Letters* **10**:150–152 (1967).
6. A. F. Metherell, H. M. A. El-Sum, J. J. Dreher, and L. Larmore, *J. Acoust. Soc. Am.* **42**:733–742 (1967).
7. R. P. Dooley, *Proc. IEEE* **53**:1733–1735 (1965).
8. A. F. Metherell and H. M. A. El-Sum, *Appl. Phys. Letters* **11**:20–22 (1967).

Chapter 15

ACOUSTICAL HOLOGRAMS AND OPTICAL RECONSTRUCTION

Yoshinao Aoki

Department of Electronics Engineering
Hokkaido University, Sapporo, Japan

Theoretical and experimental investigations of the construction of acoustical holograms and the optical reconstruction of their images are described. The matrix representation of Gabor's hologram is presented, and the matrix method is used to analyze the experimental results obtained. The acoustical holograms are constructed through use of sound waves of 10 kHz and 20 kHz frequency, and the virtual and conjugate images are reconstructed using laser light of 6328 Å wavelength. The effect on the reconstructed image of the scanning lines produced by the scanning of a recording microphone is discussed. An improvement of the image is obtained by eliminating the spectra of the scanning lines. Furthermore, the reconstructed images are investigated as functions of the following conditions involved in constructing their acoustical holograms: (1) the level of the resultant light intensity converted from the acoustic fields, (2) the limitation of the scanning plane, and (3) the wavelength of the sound wave. The detection by use of holographic techniques of objects buried in a model of a turbid and turbulent medium is described. Three-dimensional information storage in acoustical holograms is also discussed.

INTRODUCTION

Acoustical holography is a new technique for imagery which uses sound waves. It promises new possibilities and applications which cannot be achieved with optical holography. Recently several investigations ([1-8]) have been reported in which this technique has been further developed with the help of advanced techniques of optical holography.

This paper describes theoretical and experimental investigations of acoustical holography. The technique of holography used in the experiment reported is Gabor's coherent background holography ([9,10]). The principle of this holographic technique is analyzed by the matrix method. Acoustical holograms are constructed by scanning the hologram plane with a microphone; the optical reconstruction of the images is accomplished in a manner similar to that used in conventional optical holography.

223

The scanning technique is one of the important aspects of this experiment. The effect on the reconstructed images of the method used for scanning is discussed both theoretically and experimentally. The reconstructed images are improved in the process of the optical reconstruction by eliminating the spectra of the scanning lines. The reconstructed images are investigated under three different conditions: (1) changes in the intensity level of the light converted from the acoustic fields (2) the case where the scanning plane has limited aperture and (3) different wavelengths of the sound waves. In addition, the detection of objects buried in a model of a turbid and turbulent medium, and the three-dimensional information storage in acoustical holograms are discussed to show some of the properties of acoustical holograms which are applicable to various types of apparatus and systems.

MATRIX REPRESENTATION OF HOLOGRAPHIC SYSTEMS

Scalar Sound Waves

If we consider a sound wave as a scalar wave, we can treat sound in the same manner as the scalar light wave. We can use the theories ([11-14]) developed in optical holography for analyzing acoustical holography by replacing the amplitude of optical fields with the amplitude of the sound pressure. Therefore we may explain acoustical holography in exactly the same way as we explain optical holography.

Matrix of a Lens

Imaging systems, including holographic systems, can be considered as transformers of light rays from the object points to the image points. Hence the matrix method is a convenient way of treating these imaging systems. Although the matrix method is well known in the analysis of ordinary lens systems ([15,16]), we derive the matrix representation of a lens in this section

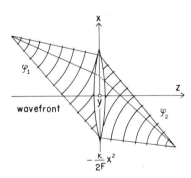

Fig. 1. A convex lens as an optical phase shifter.

preparatory to showing the application of the matrix method to holographic systems.

A lens is an optical phase shifter which shifts the incident phase ϕ_1 to the exit phase ϕ_2, as shown in Fig. 1. Let $(-\phi_f)$ be the amount of the phase shifted by the lens; then

$$\phi_2 = \phi_1 - \phi_f \tag{1}$$

We introduce the following vectors:

$$\mathbf{K}_1 = \text{grad } \phi_1$$

$$\mathbf{K}_2 = \text{grad } \phi_2 \tag{2}$$

$$\mathbf{F} = \text{grad}_t \, \phi_f$$

for a plane or a spherical wave ([17]) $|\mathbf{K}|_1 = |\mathbf{K}|_2 = k = 2\pi/\lambda$, where k is the wave number and λ is the wavelength of light. In other words, $\mathbf{K}_1$ and $\mathbf{K}_2$ are the wave vectors. The partial differential grad_t is concerned with the variables x and y on the plane perpendicular to the optical axis (z axis), and $\mathbf{F}$ is defined as a localized spatial frequency vector. Equation (1) can now be rewritten: using Eq. (2), Eq. (1) becomes

$$\mathbf{K}_2 - \mathbf{K}_1 = -\mathbf{F} \tag{3}$$

The lens formulas expressed in Eqs. (1) and (2) are concerned, respectively, with the wavefront and the light rays perpendicular to the wavefront of the optical fields. For a convex lens with focal length F we can, using the paraxial ray approximation, express ϕ_f as follows:

$$\phi_f = \frac{k(x^2 + y^2)}{2F} = \frac{kr^2}{2F} \tag{4}$$

The formula of a convex lens is obtained from Eqs. (3) and (4) as follows:

$$\frac{\mathbf{K}_2}{k} - \frac{\mathbf{K}_1}{k} = -\frac{\mathbf{r}}{F} \tag{5}$$

where $\mathbf{r}$ is the position vector of a ray on the lens. Equation (5) can be expressed with the x components of the vectors as

$$m_2 - m_1 = -x/F \tag{6}$$

where m_1 and m_2 are the directional cosines of the incident and exit rays on the lens with respect to the x axis. In the paraxial ray approximation we can replace m_1 and m_2 by the slopes x_1' and x_2', which are defined as

$$x_1' = \frac{dx}{dz}\bigg|_{x=x_1} \qquad x_2' = \frac{dx}{dz}\bigg|_{x=x_2} \tag{7}$$

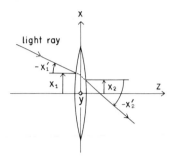

Fig. 2. Definition of the position and slope of a ray.

where x_1 and x_2 are the positions of, respectively, the incident and exit rays on the lens, as shown in Fig. 2. We obtain the matrix of the lens which transforms the position x_1 and the slope x'_1 of a ray to x_2 and x'_2 from Eq. (6) under the condition that the lens is thin, the positions x_1 and x_2 of the incident and refracted rays are equal. The resultant matrix is as follows:

$$\begin{bmatrix} x^2 \\ x'_2 \end{bmatrix} = \begin{bmatrix} 1 & 0 \\ -1/F & 1 \end{bmatrix} \begin{bmatrix} x_1 \\ x'_1 \end{bmatrix} \tag{8}$$

The same matrix representation of the convex lens can be obtained with respect to the y axis. The matrix of a concave lens with focal length F is also obtained by replacing F by $-F$ in Eq. (8).

Matrix of a Diffraction Grating

A diffraction grating and its transmittance function $f(r)$ are shown in Fig. 3. The function $f(r)$ has a period $4a$ and is expressed by Fourier series as

$$f(r) = \frac{1}{2}\left[1 + \sum_{n=1}^{\infty} \frac{\sin(n\pi/2)}{(n\pi/2)} \{\exp(i2\pi n v r) + \exp(-i2\pi n v r)\} \right] \tag{9}$$

where v is the fundamental space frequency, and

$$v = 1/4a \tag{10}$$

We illuminate the diffraction grating with coherent light and consider only the diffracted beam of nth order. Then the ϕ_f in Eq. (1) can be obtained from Eq. (9) as

$$\phi_f = 2\pi n v r \tag{11}$$

From Eqs. (3) and (11) we can obtain the equation of the diffracted light rays as follows:

$$\mathbf{K}_2 - \mathbf{K}_1 = \mp 2\pi n v \mathbf{r}_0 \tag{12}$$

where $\mathbf{r}_0$ is a unit vector of r direction. The vector on the right side of Eq. (12)

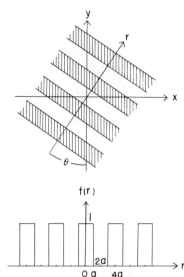

Fig. 3. A diffraction grating expressed by the transmittance function $f(r)$.

is proportional to the nth-order space frequency of the grating, and the direction of the vector is oriented in the direction of the gradient of the transmittance function of the grating. Therefore we define this vector as the spatial frequency vector. In a general interference pattern the vector $\mathbf{F}$ defined in Eq. (2) is proportional to the localized spatial frequency, and it is defined as the localized spatial frequency vector. We rewrite Eq. (12) with x components of the vectors as follows:

$$m_2 - m_1 = \mp \lambda n v \cos \theta \tag{13}$$

where θ is defined in Fig. 3 and m_1 and m_2 are the directional cosines with respect to the x axis of the incident and exit rays. Taking the paraxial ray approximation, we can replace m_1 and m_2 by the ray slopes x'_1 and x'_2. Then the matrix representation of the diffraction grating is obtained from Eq. (13) as follows:

$$\begin{bmatrix} x_2 \\ x'_2 \end{bmatrix} = \begin{bmatrix} 1 & 0 \\ 0 & 1 \end{bmatrix} \begin{bmatrix} x_1 \\ x'_1 \end{bmatrix} + \begin{bmatrix} 0 \\ \pm \lambda n v \cos \theta \end{bmatrix} \tag{14}$$

Equation (14) is the same as the matrix representation of a thin prism, and we can express the diffraction grating by a group of thin prisms.

Matrix of a Zone-Plate

The zone-plate is the hologram of a point object. The zone-plate is constructed by illuminating a point object by coherent light, as shown in

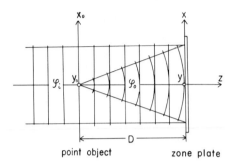

Fig. 4, where ϕ_i and ϕ_0 describe the phases of the coherent illumination and the object wave, respectively. If the zone-plate is recorded by means of a photographic film which is a square-law detector of optical fields, the zone-plate consists of following components: $(\phi_i - \phi_i)$, $(\phi_0 - \phi_0)$, $(\phi_i - \phi_0)$, and $(-\phi_i + \phi_0)$. For simplicity of analysis, the illuminating light consists of parallel rays. The phases ϕ_i and ϕ_0 relative to the phase at the (x_0-y_0) plane in Fig. 4 are obtained as follows:

$$\phi_i = kD, \qquad \phi_0 = k\left(D + \frac{x^2 + y^2}{2D}\right) \tag{15}$$

When the zone-plate is illuminated by light of the same wavelength as that of the constructing light the equation for rays diffracted by the components $(\phi_i - \phi_0)$ and $(\phi_0 - \phi_i)$ is obtained from Eqs. (3) and (15) as follows:

$$\frac{\mathbf{K}_2}{k} - \frac{\mathbf{K}_1}{k} = \mp \frac{\mathbf{r}}{D} \tag{16}$$

where $\mathbf{r}$ is a position vector of a ray on the zone-plate. Equation (16) is the same as Eq. (5), and we can write the matrix representation of the zone-plate as follows:

$$\begin{bmatrix} x_2 \\ x_2' \end{bmatrix} = \begin{bmatrix} 1 & 0 \\ \mp 1/D & 1 \end{bmatrix} \begin{bmatrix} x_1 \\ x_1' \end{bmatrix} \tag{17}$$

Equation (17) shows that we can express the zone-plate by the combination of a convex and a concave lens of focal length D.

Matrix of Gabor's Hologram

The hologram produced in Gabor's coherent background holography is a collection of zone plates which are constructed by the diffracted waves from each object point. Figure 5 shows the construction of Gabor's hologram. For simplicity of analysis we consider the diffracted wave from one point on the object, and we express the phase of this diffracted wave as ϕ_0 and

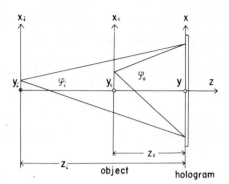

Fig. 5. Construction of Gabor's hologram.

that of the illuminating wave as ϕ_i. These phases at the xy plane of Fig. 5 are obtained with paraxial ray approximation as follows:

$$\phi_i = k_1 \left[z_i + \frac{(x - x_i)^2 + (y - y_i)^2}{2z_i} \right]$$

$$\phi_0 = k_1 \left[z_0 + \frac{(x - x_0)^2 + (y - y_0)^2}{2z_0} \right]$$

(18)

where $k_1 = 2\pi/\lambda_1$, with λ_1 the wavelength of the coherent wave used to construct the hologram. Let us assume the recording of the hologram to be done by square-law detection and the ray transformation to be accomplished with respect to the components $(\phi_i - \phi_0)$ and $(\phi_0 - \phi_i)$ as described in the preceding section. We define the following vectors:

$$\mathbf{F}_i = \text{grad}_t \, \phi_i = \frac{k_1(x - x_i)}{z_i}\mathbf{x}_0 + \frac{k_1(y - y_i)}{z_i}\mathbf{y}_0$$

$$\mathbf{F}_0 = \text{grad}_t \, \phi_0 = \frac{k_1(x - x_0)}{z_0}\mathbf{x}_0 + \frac{k_1(y - y_0)}{z_0}\mathbf{y}_0$$

(19)

where $\mathbf{x}_0$ and $\mathbf{y}_0$ are the unit vectors in the x and y directions on the hologram. The equation for rays diffracted by the components $(\phi_i - \phi_0)$ and $(\phi_0 - \phi_i)$ is obtained from Eqs. (3) and (19) as follows:

$$\frac{\mathbf{K}_2}{k_2} - \frac{\mathbf{K}_1}{k_2} = \mp \frac{(\mathbf{F}_0 - \mathbf{F}_i)}{k_2}$$

(20)

where $|\mathbf{K}_1| = |\mathbf{K}_2| = k_2 = 2\pi/\lambda_2$, with λ_2 the wavelength of the reconstructing light wave. When we construct the hologram using a wave of wavelength long compared with the light wave, it is necessary to reduce the hologram for optical reconstruction. Let m be the reduction rate of the hologram, and change the variables x and y in Eq. (18) to mx and my to reduce the hologram. Then we obtain the following equation from Eq. (20), taking the paraxial ray approximation,

$$x'_2 = x'_1 \mp \left[\frac{m^2}{\mu}\left(\frac{1}{z_0} - \frac{1}{z_i}\right)x_i - \frac{m}{\mu}\left(\frac{1}{z_0} - \frac{1}{z_i}\right) \right] \tag{21}$$

where $\mu = \lambda_1/\lambda_2$. From Eq. (21) we obtain the following matrix representation of Gabor's hologram under the condition that the hologram is thin and the incident and exit positions of the rays coincide on the hologram:

$$\begin{bmatrix} x_2 \\ x'_2 \end{bmatrix} = \begin{bmatrix} 1 & 0 \\ \mp\frac{m^2}{\mu}\left(\frac{1}{z_0} - \frac{1}{z_i}\right) & 1 \end{bmatrix}\begin{bmatrix} x_1 \\ x'_1 \end{bmatrix} + \begin{bmatrix} 0 \\ \mp\frac{m}{\mu}\left(\frac{x_0}{z_0} - \frac{x_i}{z_i}\right) \end{bmatrix} \tag{22}$$

Equation (22) can be obtained from the cascade product of the matrices of a lens and a thin prism. Therefore we can consider that Gabor's hologram consists of a convex or concave lens with focal length $\frac{1}{F} = \frac{m^2}{\mu}\left(\frac{1}{z_0} - \frac{1}{z_i}\right)$ and a group of thin prisms which refract the light beam according to the coordinate x_0 of the object points. Figure 6 shows this interpretation schematically.

CONSTRUCTION OF ACOUSTICAL HOLOGRAMS

Experimental Arrangement

The principle of acoustical holography is the same as that of optical holography. We replace the coherent optical source with a coherent sound wave source in order to construct acoustical holograms. However, there is a technical difficulty in acoustical holography; namely, there is no photo-

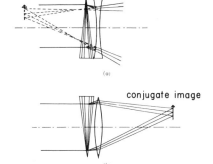

virtual image

(a)

conjugate image

(b)

Fig. 6. Expression of Gabor's hologram by the combination of a lens and a group of thin prisms. (a) reconstruction of conjugate image. (b) reconstruction of virtual image.

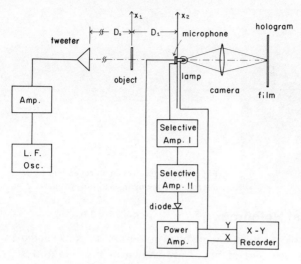

Fig. 7. Block diagram of experimental arrangement for constructing acoustical holograms.

graphic film or equivalent displaying apparatus applicable for sound waves. Therefore we must contrive some means of recording acoustic field patterns. In radio wave holography the situation is the same as in acoustical holography, and the techniques developed in acoustical holography may contribute to radio wave holography ([18–21]). In like manner we may apply techniques developed in radio wave holography to acoustical holography. The surface of water, CRT, a lamp, etc., may be used to obtain acoustical holograms. In our experiment the acoustic field pattern is converted to light intensity patterns by a lamp and recorded on films as acoustical holograms. The block diagram of an experimental arrangement for constructing acoustical holograms is shown in Fig. 7. The tweeter radiates sound waves which are applied to an object; the object radiates the secondary wave. The interference between the primary wave from the tweeter and the secondary wave from the object is received by a microphone, which mechanically scans the acoustic fields at the hologram plane. The output signals from the microphone are amplified by two selective amplifiers and detected by a diode. The detected signals are amplified by a power amplifier which in turn lights a lamp. The scanning of the lamp is synchronous with the scanning of the microphone. The light intensity pattern converted from the acoustic field pattern is recorded on a film by a camera as an acoustical hologram. The X–Y recorder is a monitor of the signal level to the lamp. Figure 8 is the photograph of an object and the experimental equipment for receiving and displaying the acoustic fields.

Fig. 8. Photograph of an object and the experimental equipment for constructing acoustical holograms.

Acoustical Hologram

The object and its acoustical hologram as constructed in the experimental arrangement of Fig. 7 are shown in Figs. 9*a* and 9*b*, respectively. The object is made of aluminum plate measuring 17 cm × 21 cm. The hologram is constructed under the condition that the distance D_0 from the tweeter to the object is 356 cm, the distance D_1 from the object to the microphone is 70 cm, and the frequency of the sound wave is chosen as 18 kHz. The experiment is conducted in a soundproof chamber. The lines on the hologram show the scanning lines of the microphone and the lamp.

OPTICAL RECONSTRUCTION OF IMAGES

Reconstruction Condition

The optical reconstruction of images using laser light is accomplished with the optical system shown in Fig. 10. The acoustical holograms obtained

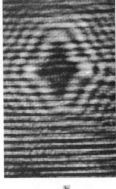

a

b

Fig. 9. (*a*) Object. (*b*) Acoustical Hologram.

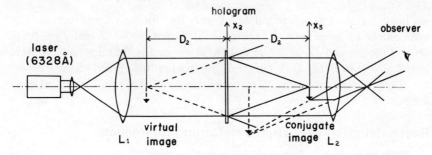

Fig. 10. Optical system for constructing original images from acoustical holograms.

in this experiment are Gabor's holograms, as described above. Now let $x_i = 0$, $z_0 = D_1$, and $z_1 = D_1 + D_0$ in Eq. (22); we can now obtain the matrix representation of the acoustical hologram obtained with the experimental arrangement shown in Fig. 7. The acoustical hologram illuminated by the parallel rays of laser light (slope of ray $x' = 0$) reconstructs the virtual and conjugate images at a distance D_2 from the hologram, as shown in Fig. 10. The transformation of rays of the incident laser light to the image points is then obtained by the cascade product of the matrices of the free space of length D_2 and of the hologram:

$$
\begin{bmatrix} x_3 \\ x_3' \end{bmatrix} = \begin{bmatrix} 1 & D_2 \\ 0 & 1 \end{bmatrix} \left[\begin{bmatrix} 1 & 0 \\ \mp \dfrac{m^2}{\mu}\dfrac{D_0}{D_1(D_0 + D_1)} & 1 \end{bmatrix} \begin{bmatrix} x_2 \\ 0 \end{bmatrix} + \begin{bmatrix} 0 \\ \pm \dfrac{mx_1}{\mu D_1} \end{bmatrix} \right]
$$

$$
= \begin{bmatrix} 1 \mp \dfrac{m^2}{\mu}\dfrac{D_0 D_2}{D_1(D_0 + D_1)} & D_2 \\ \mp \dfrac{m^2}{\mu}\dfrac{D_0}{D_1(D_0 + D_1)} & 1 \end{bmatrix} \begin{bmatrix} x_2 \\ 0 \end{bmatrix} + \begin{bmatrix} \pm \dfrac{m}{\mu}\dfrac{D_2}{D_1}x_1 \\ \pm \dfrac{m}{\mu}\dfrac{x_1}{D_1} \end{bmatrix} \qquad (23)
$$

In Eq. (23) x_2 and x_3 represent the coordinates of the hologram and the image plane. In the image plane the diffracted rays from the holograms come to one point on the image, and the position x_3 of the image point is determined independently of position x_2. The reconstruction condition can therefore be obtained from the matrix element of Eq. (23), i.e., by setting it equal to zero at the image plane, and the reconstruction condition is obtained as follows:

$$
D_2 = \pm \frac{\mu}{m}\frac{D_1(D_0 + D_1)}{D_0} \qquad (24)
$$

where the $+$ and $-$ signs correspond to the conjugate and virtual images, respectively. In Eq. (23) the reduction rate m of the hologram is large and we must reduce the acoustical holograms for optical reconstruction. For example, if we take typical experimental values, $\lambda_1 = 1.5$ cm, $\lambda_2 = 0.6\,\mu$, $D_1 = 1$ meter, and $D_2 = 10$ cm (where $D_0 = \infty$ for simplicity), we obtain $m = 5 \times 10^2$ from Eq. (23). This result shows that for optical reconstruction we must reduce an acoustical hologram of 1 meter $\times$ 1 meter size to 2 mm $\times$ 2 mm.

Reconstruction of Virtual and Conjugate Images

The reconstructed images are small because of the small size of the reduced hologram, and it is difficult to observe the images directly. Therefore we observe the reconstructed conjugate image after magnifying it by lens L_2 in the optical system shown in Fig. 10. But we cannot magnify the virtual image in this optical system. We use the optical system shown in Fig. 11 for observing both virtual and conjugate images. In Fig. 11 the lens L_2 with focal length F produces the real images of the reconstructed virtual and conjugate images, and we can observe these images after magnifying them by convex lens L_3. The transformation of rays through the hologram to the image plane in Fig. 11 can be obtained from the cascade product of the matrices of free space, of the lens, and of the hologram:

$$
\begin{bmatrix} x_3 \\ x_3' \end{bmatrix} = \begin{bmatrix} 1 & D_2 \\ 0 & 1 \end{bmatrix} \begin{bmatrix} 1 & 0 \\ -1/F & 1 \end{bmatrix} \left(\begin{bmatrix} 1 & 0 \\ \mp \dfrac{m^2}{\mu} \dfrac{D_0}{D_1(D_0 + D_1)} & 1 \end{bmatrix} \begin{bmatrix} x_2 \\ 0 \end{bmatrix} \right.
$$

$$
\left. + \begin{bmatrix} 0 \\ \pm \dfrac{m}{\mu} \dfrac{x_1}{D_1} \end{bmatrix} \right)
$$

$$
= \begin{bmatrix} 1 - \dfrac{D_2}{F} \mp \dfrac{m^2}{\mu} \dfrac{D_0 D_2}{D_1(D_0 + D_1)} & D_2 \\ -\dfrac{1}{F} \mp \dfrac{m^2}{\mu} \dfrac{D_0}{D_1(D_0 + D_1)} & 1 \end{bmatrix} \begin{bmatrix} x_2 \\ 1 \end{bmatrix} + \begin{bmatrix} \pm \dfrac{m}{\mu} \dfrac{D_2}{D_1} x_1 \\ \pm \dfrac{m}{\mu} \dfrac{x_1}{D_1} \end{bmatrix} \tag{25}
$$

The reconstructed condition for each image can be obtained from the matrix element of Eq. (25) in a manner similar to that in the preceding section:

$$
\frac{1}{F} = \frac{1}{D_2} \mp \frac{m^2}{\mu} \frac{D_0}{D_1(D_0 + D_1)} \tag{26}
$$

where the $+$ and $-$ signs correspond to the virtual and conjugate images, respectively. Equation (26) shows that for the virtual image $F < D_2$ and for

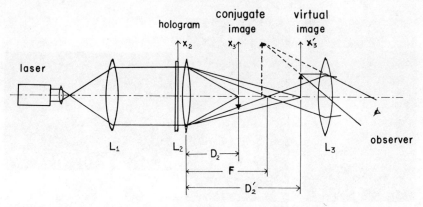

Fig. 11. Optical system for observing the virtual and conjugate images reconstructed from acoustical holograms.

the conjugate image $F > D_2$. The dimension of the reconstructed images can be obtained from Eq. (25) using Eq. (26) as follows:

$$x_3 = \mp \frac{m}{\mu} \frac{D_2}{D_1} = \frac{mF(D_0 + D_1)}{m^2 D_0 F - \mu D_1(D_0 + D_1)} x_1 \qquad \text{For virtual image} \qquad (27)$$

$$= \frac{mF(D_0 + D_1)}{m^2 D_0 F + \mu D_1(D_0 + D_1)} x_1 \qquad \text{For conjugate image} \qquad (28)$$

The value of x_3 of Eq. (27) is larger than that of Eq. (28), i.e., the dimension of the virtual image is larger than that of the conjugate image. The coordinate x_3 of the images has a negative value in Eq. (27) and a positive value in Eq. (28) when the coordinate x_1 of the object is positive. This means that the reconstructed images have an inverse relationship.

Experimental Results

The optical reconstruction is done using laser light at a wavelength $\lambda_2 = 6328$ Å in the optical system shown in Fig. 11. The acoustical hologram used (shown in Fig. 9b) is reduced to dimensions of 2.5 mm × 3.8 mm for optical reconstruction. The reconstructed conjugate and virtual images from the acoustical hologram are shown in Figs. 12a and 12b, respectively. The virtual image is reconstructed at a greater distance from the hologram than is the conjugate image, and the dimensions of the virtual image are larger than those of the conjugate image, as described in the preceding section. The arrows show that these images are reconstructed with inverse relationship. Figure 12c shows the spectra of the transmitting light from the hologram taken at the focal plane of lens L_2. We can recognize the spectra of the scanning lines in Fig. 12c.

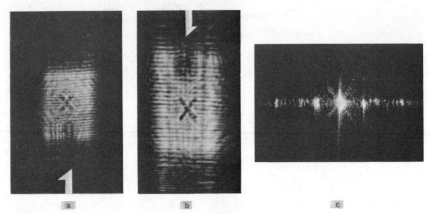

Fig. 12. (*a*) Reconstructed conjugate image. (*b*) Reconstructed virtual image. (*c*) Spectra of the acoustical hologram taken at the focal plane of lens L_2 in Fig. 11.

EFFECT OF SCANNING LINES ON THE RECONSTRUCTED IMAGES

Scanning Lines as a Diffraction Grating

In this experiment the acoustical holograms are constructed by scanning the acoustic field with a microphone. If the scanning is done closely and no scanning lines appear on the hologram, there is little effect of the scanning on the reconstructed images. However, in this experiment the scanning is not done closely, and hence the scanning lines do appear on the hologram. On the other hand, it is necessary that the acoustical hologram constructed from the sampled information of the acoustic fields reproduce the image with the proper resolution. In other words, the method of scanning is determined by the required resolution in the images.

When the hologram with the scanning lines is reconstructed in the optical system shown in Fig. 10 the scanning lines diffract the laser beam, and we can consider that the hologram with scanning lines is composed of a hologram without scanning lines and a diffraction grating. Therefore the transformation of rays from the hologram with the scanning lines to the image plane in the optical system of Fig. 10 can be obtained for the nth order diffracted beam through the use of Eqs. (14) and (22) as follows:

$$
\begin{bmatrix} x_3 \\ x_3' \end{bmatrix} = \begin{bmatrix} 1 & D_2 \\ 0 & 1 \end{bmatrix} \left[\begin{bmatrix} 1 & 0 \\ \mp \dfrac{m^2}{\mu} \dfrac{D_0}{D_1(D_0 + D_1)} & 1 \end{bmatrix} \begin{bmatrix} x_2 \\ 0 \end{bmatrix} + \begin{bmatrix} 0 \\ \pm \dfrac{m}{\mu} \dfrac{x_1}{D_1} \end{bmatrix} + \begin{bmatrix} 0 \\ (\pm)\lambda_2 n v \end{bmatrix} \right]
$$

$$= \begin{bmatrix} 1 \mp \dfrac{m^2}{\mu} \dfrac{D_0 D_2}{D_1(D_0 + D_1)} & D_2 \\ \mp \dfrac{m^2}{\mu} \dfrac{D_0}{D_1(D_0 + D_1)} & 1 \end{bmatrix} \begin{bmatrix} x_2 \\ 0 \end{bmatrix} + \begin{bmatrix} \pm \dfrac{m}{\mu} \dfrac{D_2}{D_1} x_1 (\pm) \lambda_2 n v D_2 \\ \pm \dfrac{m}{\mu} \dfrac{x_1}{D_1} (\pm) \lambda_2 n v \end{bmatrix} \qquad (29)$$

The reconstruction condition is obtained from the matrix element of Eq. (29), which is the same condition as for Eq. (24). The coordinate x_3 of the reconstructed images is obtained from Eq. (29) as follows:

$$x_3 = \frac{D_0 + D_1}{m D_0} \left(x_1 \pm \frac{\lambda^1 n v D_1}{m} \right) \qquad (30)$$

Equation (30) shows that the laser beam, diffracted by the scanning lines, reconstructs images, and if the period $4a$ of the scanning lines is large (i.e., the fundamental spatial frequency v of the scanning lines is small), the images reconstructed by each diffracted laser beam overlap and the resolving power of the reconstructed images falls. On the other hand, if $4a$ is small (i.e., if v is large enough), the diffracted higher-order images do not overlap and the effect of the scanning lines on the reconstructed image is not serious. This does not mean that the virtual and conjugate images are separated; each diffracted beam carries both images.

Effect of Scanning Lines on the Reconstructed Images

Acoustical holograms are constructed for different periods of the scanning lines. Figures 13a and 13b are the acoustical holograms of the object shown in Fig. 9a when the scanning is done with average frequency $v = 0.8$ lines/cm (Fig. 13a) and $v = 0.6$ lines/cm (Fig. 13b). The frequency of the sound wave chosen was 18 kHz.

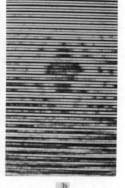

Fig. 13. Acoustical holograms constructed for different periods of the scanning lines. Here v is the fundamental spatial frequency derived from the scanning period $4a$ as $v = 1/4a$. (a) $v = 0.8$ lines/cm. (b) $v = 0.6$ lines/cm.

a   b

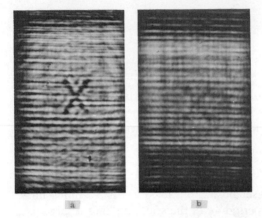

a   b

Fig. 14. Reconstructed images from holograms of Fig. 13 in the optical system of Fig. 10. Here (a) and (b) correspond to Figs. 13a and b, respectively.

The optical reconstruction of images is done in the optical system shown in Fig. 10. Figures 14a and 14b show the reconstructed images which correspond to the holograms in Figs. 13a and 13b, respectively. Figures 14a and 14b show that the rough scanning deteriorates the reconstructed image, and that the resolution in the image depends largely on the method of scanning.

Improvement of Reconstructed Images

The scanning lines affect the resolution of the reconstructed images. Now, we would like to improve the reconstructed images to eliminate the scanning lines arising in the process of the optical reconstruction. The spectra shown in Fig. 12c of light transmitted through the acoustical hologram appear at the focal plane of lens L_2 in the optical system shown in Fig. 15. In Fig. 12c the bright lines at both sides are the spectra of the scanning lines. We cut out the spectra of the scanning lines with a slit, as shown in

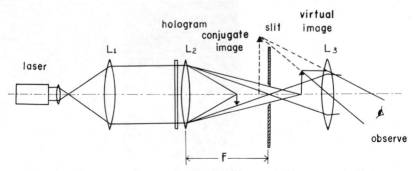

Fig. 15. Optical system for improvement of images reconstructed from acoustical holograms on which the scanning lines appear. The slit cuts the spectra of the scanning lines.

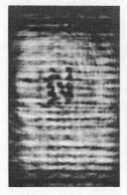
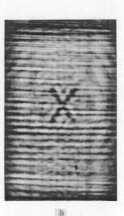

Fig. 16. Reconstructed images with the optical system shown in Fig. 10. The frequency of the sound wave is chosen as 14 kHz for object N and 18 kHz for object X.

a   b

Fig. 15. This slit prevents transmission not only of the diffracted light by the scanning lines, but also of part of the light from the conjugate image. Figures 16a and 16b are the reconstructed images with the optical system shown in Fig. 10; the frequency of the sound wave chosen is 14 kHz for the object "N" and 18 kHz for the object "X". Figures 17a and 17b show the reconstructed images, with the optical system shown in Fig. 15, corresponding to the images of Fig. 16. Comparing the images of Fig. 16 and Fig. 17, we recognize that the reconstructed images of Fig. 17 are improved by the elimination of the effect of the scanning lines.

When the object spectra overlap the spectra of the scanning lines this method of improving the images is not available. For such a case we must change the scanning direction or scan closely to improve the reconstructed images.

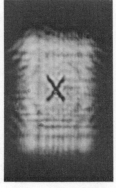

Fig. 17. Reconstructed images with the optical system shown in Fig. 15.

a   b

EFFECTS OF HOLOGRAM CONSTRUCTION CONDITION ON THE RECONSTRUCTED IMAGES

Effect of Light Intensity Level on the Reconstructed Images

It is desirable to hold linearity in recording the acoustic field intensity used to construct holograms. However, the electrical circuit, the lamp, and the film show nonlinear characteristics for both weak and strong signals. In this section we examine how the electrical signals converted from the acoustic fields are recorded on the films and discuss the effect of the light intensity level on the reconstructed images. Figure 18 shows the variation of the signal voltage to the lamp caused by the scanning of the microphone. The signal voltage monitored by the $X-Y$ recorder shown in Fig. 7 corresponds to the light intensity of the lamp. Figures 19a and 19b are acoustical holograms constructed by changing the level of the signal voltage by means of the gain control of the amplifiers. The arrows in Fig. 19 indicate where electrical signal variations shown in Fig. 18 are monitored. In Fig. 19 we recognize that the film records the variation of electrical signals fairly faithfully, but the details of the variation are not clear and there are saturated parts on the film. This causes deterioration of the reconstructed images. The frequency of the sound wave chosen is 15 kHz.

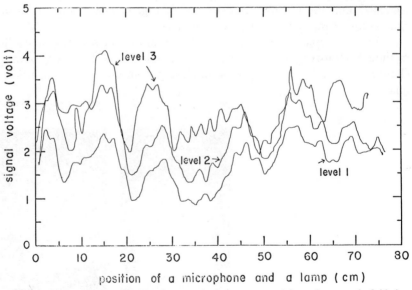

Fig. 18. Variation of the signal voltage to the lamp converted from the acoustic fields by the scanning of the microphone. The level of the signal voltage is changed by the gain control of the amplifier.

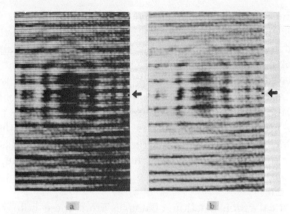

Fig. 19. Acoustical holograms constructed by changing the level of the light intensity. The arrows show where the signal voltage is monitored to plot Fig. 18; (a) Level 1; (b) Level 3.

The optical reconstruction of images is done in the optical system shown in Fig. 10. The reconstructed images shown in Figs. 20a and 20b correspond to levels 1 and 3, respectively. There is little difference in these reconstructed images because within these levels the lamp and the film are not strongly saturated and the DC component of the film transmission is adjusted in the developing process.

Effect of Limited Scanning Plane on Reconstructed Images

The wavelength of the 10 kHz sound wave is about 6×10^4 times longer than that of the laser light used in this experiment. This suggests that

Fig. 20. Reconstructed images from acoustical holograms of Fig. 19 with the optical system of Fig. 10. Here (a) and (b) correspond to levels 1 and 3, respectively.

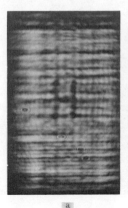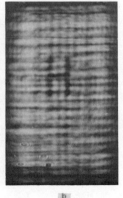

the hologram plane to be scanned by a microphone must be very large to obtain sufficient information for image reconstruction from the hologram plane as is done in optical holography. Actually, we cannot scan such a large hologram plane; however, the objects used in this experiment are not very large compared with the wavelength of the sound wave, and we can obtain reasonable size acoustical holograms in the planes to be scanned. To investigate the effect of the limited scanning plane on the reconstructed images, the acoustical holograms are constructed so that the holograms obtained can be covered with apertures of various sizes. The holograms obtained are shown in Figs. 21a, 21b, and 21c which correspond, respectively, to the actual scanning planes of 70 cm × 85 cm, 50 cm × 60 cm, and 40 cm × 55 cm.

The optical reconstruction of images from these holograms is done with the optical system shown in Fig. 10. Figures 22a, 22b, and 22c are the reconstructed images obtained, and they show that the reconstructed images become worse as the holograms become smaller.

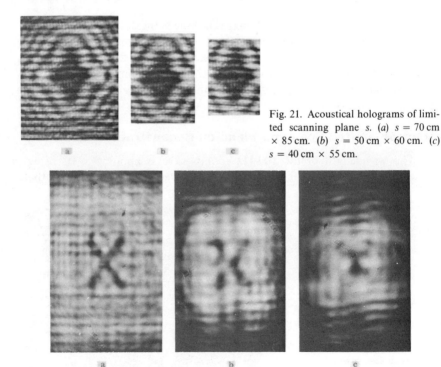

Fig. 21. Acoustical holograms of limited scanning plane s. (a) s = 70 cm × 85 cm. (b) s = 50 cm × 60 cm. (c) s = 40 cm × 55 cm.

Fig. 22. Reconstructed images from the acoustical holograms of Fig. 21 with the optical system of Fig. 10. Here (a), (b), and (c) correspond to (a), (b), and (c) of Fig. 21.

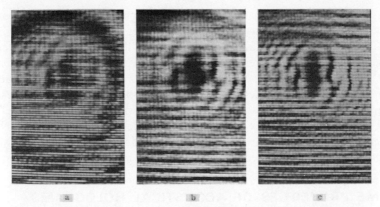

Fig. 23. Acoustical holograms constructed with different frequencies f of the sound wave. (a) $f = 12$ kHz. (b) $f = 14$ kHz. (c) $f = 18$ kHz.

Effect of Frequency of Sound Wave on Reconstructed Images

The stroke width of the letters used as the objects in this experiment is comparable to the wavelength of the sound wave. This suggests that the effect of changing the wavelength (i.e., the frequency of the sound wave) on the reconstructed images is remarkable. Acoustical holograms were constructed with various sound frequencies from about 10 kHz to 20 kHz. The acoustical holograms obtained are shown in Figs. 23a, 23b, and 23c. In these figures we recognize that the interference stripes become clearer as the frequency increases.

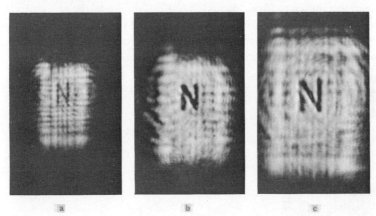

Fig. 24. Reconstructed images from the acoustical holograms of Fig. 23 with the optical system of Fig. 15. Here (a), (b), and (c) correspond to (a), (b), and (c) of Fig. 23.

The optical reconstruction of images is done with the optical system shown in Fig. 15. The reconstructed virtual images are shown in Figs. 24a, 24b, and 24c, where the images are reconstructed at different places, with different magnitudes, and for different frequencies. This is explained by Eqs. (26) and (27). The resolution of the reconstructed images increases as the frequency of the sound waves increases. We obtain fairly good reconstructed images at a frequency of 12 kHz. The sound wave has a wavelength of about 2.8 cm at the frequency of 12 kHz in air, and the stroke width of the letter "N" is 2.5 cm. This indicates than an object of the order of magnitude of a wavelength can be reconstructed in the holographic imaging system.

SOME PROPERTIES OF ACOUSTICAL HOLOGRAMS

Detection of Objects in a Turbid and Turbulent Medium

The holographic technique is excellent for imagery in a turbulent medium. Especially when the medium is opaque or turbid, acoustical holography permits imaging of an object which cannot be imaged by optical holography. This characteristic of acoustical holography is applicable to the detection and imagery of objects in opaque gaseous media, turbid fluids, solids, the human body, under the sea, and under the earth's surface. To examine these characteristics, a model of a turbid and turbulent medium was made and objects buried in the medium were detected.

Figure 25 shows the medium, which is made of fragments of light synthetic resins. The object—the letter "X"—is constructed of aluminum plate, and is buried in the medium and cannot be seen. The acoustical holograms obtained are shown in Figs. 26a and 26b; Fig. 26a shows the object immersed in the medium of Fig. 25 with light turbidity and turbulence; Fig. 26b shows the object in the same medium with heavy turbidity and turbulence. The frequency of the sound wave chosen was 18 kHz.

Fig. 25. Model of a turbid and turbulent medium in which an object (the letter "X") is placed.

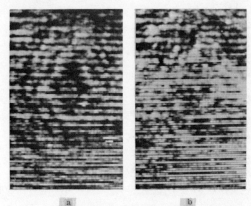

Fig. 26. Acoustical holograms of the object placed in the medium of Fig. 25. The degree of the turbidity and turbulence of the medium is lighter in (a) than in (b).

The optical reconstruction is accomplished in the optical system shown in Fig. 10. The reconstructed images are shown in Figs. 26a and 26b. Although the reconstructed image is not obvious, the image obtained of the object "X" is discernible in Fig. 27a. We cannot recognize a perfect image in Fig. 27b, but we can detect a figure similar to the object.

Three-Dimensional Information Storage in Acoustical Holograms

Three-dimensional information storage is one of the important properties of holograms. Using this property, we can obtain the stereo-image using the sound wave and focus the image of the arbitrary plane where the desired object exists.

An acoustical hologram is constructed in an arrangement where two objects, the letters "S" and "N", are placed some distance apart; the distance

Fig. 27. Reconstructed images from the acoustical holograms of Fig. 26 with the optical system of Fig. 10. Here (a) and (b) correspond to (a) and (b) of Fig. 26.

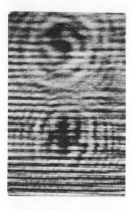

Fig. 28. Acoustical hologram.

a   b

Fig. 29. Two different images reconstructed from a single acoustical hologram of Fig. 28 with the optical system
of Fig. 15.

from the tweeter to the letter "S" is 354 cm, from the letter "S" to the letter
"N" is 27 cm, and from the letter "N" to the microphone is 45 cm. The
frequency of the sound wave chosen is 18 kHz. The resulting hologram is
shown in Fig. 28.

The optical reconstruction is done with the optical system of Fig. 15.
Two images reconstructed from the single hologram of Fig. 28 are shown in
Figs. 29a and 29b. Figures 29a and 29b show that on the image plane of the
letter "S" the image of the letter "N" is out of focus, and on the image plane
of the letter "N" the image of the letter "S" is out of focus. The image planes
and the magnitudes of the images are determined from Eqs. (26) and (27).
This shows that we can extract three-dimensional information from the
coherent light from the hologram, which is only a two-dimensional pattern
under incoherent light.

ACKNOWLEDGMENT

The author wishes to thank Dr. M. Suzuki of the Hokkaido University for giving him the opportunity to conduct experiments related to the present work. He also wishes to thank Dr. T. Asakura for his discussion on holography and N. Tsukamoto for his help in the experiments.

The author wishes to express his gratitude to Dr. A. F. Metherell and Dr. H. M. A. El-Sum for their kind arrangements for the presentation at the First International Symposium on Acoustical Holography of the paper on which this chapter is based.

REFERENCES

1. R. K. Mueller and N. K. Sheridon, *Appl. Phys. Letters* **9**:328 (1966).
2. K. Preston, Jr and J. L. Kreuzer, *Appl. Phys. Letters* **10**:150 (1967).
3. A. F. Metherell, H. M. A. El-Sum, J. J. Dreher, and L. Larmore, DARL Research Communication No. 25, Douglas Paper No. 4491, (1967).
4. A. F. Metherell, H. M. A. El-Sum, J. J. Dreher, and L. Larmore, *Phys. Letters* **24A**:547 (1967).
5. A. F. Metherell, H. M. A. El-Sum, J. J. Dreher, and L. Larmore, *Appl. Phys. Letters* **10**:277 (1967).
6. A. F. Metherell and H. M. A. El-Sum, *Appl. Phys. Letters* **11**:20 (1967).
7. G. A. Massey, *Proc. IEEE* **55**:1115 (1967).
8. Y. Aoki, N. Yoshida, N. Tsukamoto, and M. Suzuki, *Proc. IEEE* **55**:1622 (1967).
9. D. Gabor, *Nature* **161**:777 (1948).
10. M. Born and E. Wolf, *Principles of Optics*, 3rd ed., Pergamon Press, New York, 1965, p. 453.
11. E. N. Leith and J. Upatnieks, *J. Opt. Soc. Am.* **52**:1123 (1962).
12. J. A. Armstrong, *IBM J. of Res. Develop.* **9**:171 (1965).
13. R. W. Meier, *J. Opt. Soc. Am.* **55**:987 (1965).
14. A. Offner, *J. Opt. Soc. Am.* **56**:1509 (1966).
15. W. Brouwer, *Matrix Methods in Optical Instrument Design*, Benjamin, New York, 1964.
16. E. L. O'Neill, *Introduction to Statistical Optics*, Addison-Wesley, Massachusetts, 1963, p. 30.
17. Y. Aoki, *J. Opt. Soc. Am.* **56**:1648 (1966).
18. R. P. Dooley, *Proc. IEEE* **53**:1733 (1965).
19. W. E. Kock, *Proc. IEEE* **54**:331 (1966).
20. L. J. Cutrona, E. N. Leith, L. J. Porcello, and W. E. Vivian, *Proc. IEEE* **54**:1026 (1966).
21. Y. Aoki, *Appl. Opt.* (to be published).
22. E. N. Leith and J. Upatnieks, *J. Opt. Soc. Am.* **54**:1295 (1964).

Chapter 16

ULTRASONIC HOLOGRAPHY *VIA* THE ULTRASONIC CAMERA

D. Fritzler, E. Marom, and R. K. Mueller

Bendix Research Laboratories
Southfield, Michigan

Various ways of recording the interference patterns of ultrasonic waves have recently been described. These methods include real-time reconstructions obtained by the reflection of a laser beam from the interference patterns set on the interface between two materials, as well as the use of a delayed sonic hologram in which the ultrasonic interference pattern is recorded photographically after being obtained point by point by scanning techniques. We wish to report a new way of obtaining a hologram, by recording the interference pattern as displayed by a commercially available ultrasonic camera. A quartz crystal located at the front window of a cathode ray tube is irradiated by a sound beam scattered from an object and by a second unscattered reference beam. The interference pattern picked up by the scanning electron beam is amplified and displayed on a TV monitor and photographed conventionally. The processed photograph is viewed in laser light, and the two reconstructed images are thus obtained. Experimental results, as well as limitations of the method and possible real-time holographic viewing, are discussed.

INTRODUCTION

Several means of obtaining ultrasonic holograms have recently been reported in the literature ([1–3]). These include real-time reconstructions obtained by reflection of a laser beam from the interference pattern generated on the interface between two materials, as well as the use of delayed sonic holograms for which the interference pattern was recorded photographically after being obtained point by point from mechanical or laser scanning techniques. We wish to report a means of obtaining immediate displays of ultrasonic holograms by electronic scanning of a piezoelectric crystal on which two interfering sound beams impinge. Thus with a proper readout system the photographic process can be eliminated entirely, opening another way to real-time holographic displays and reconstructions.

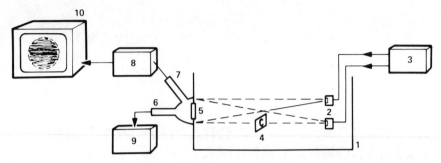

Fig. 1. Experimental setup. Immersed in the water tank (1) are two ultrasonic transducers (2) fed by generator (3). The beams are impinging upon quartz target (5) after one of the beams was scattered by target (4). The electron beam in cathode ray tube (6) induces secondary emission multiplied by electron multiplier (7) and carrier amplifier (8) and finally displayed on TV monitor (10). Box (9) includes the electronic circuits for beam generation and deflection.

The apparatus used was an ultrasonic camera,* a schematic diagram of which is shown in Fig. 1. It is an improved version of the system described by Sokolov in 1930.† A quartz crystal located at the front window of a cathode ray tube is irradiated by a 7-MHz ultrasonic beam scattered from an object immersed in a water tank and by a second unscattered reference beam, both beams obtained from the same generator. The ultrasonic waves impinging on the piezoelectric crystal induce a voltage whose magnitude at any point varies linearly with the instantaneous ultrasonic amplitude of that point. This voltage distribution modulates the intensity of the secondary emission generated by the scanning electron beam. The resulting signal is then amplified by the electron multiplier and video amplifier and displayed on the television monitor after square-law detection in the electronics. The ultrasonic hologram displayed on the television screen is photographed and, as for conventional holograms, two reconstructed images are obtained by placing the processed photographic plate in a laser beam.

The ultrasonic object and reference beam were generated by two $\frac{1}{4}$-in.-diameter 7-MHz transducers apertured to $\frac{1}{8}$ in. to obtain a uniform far-field pattern at the receiving crystal. To ensure angular separation of the reconstructed images from the zero-order diffracted light, the object and reference beam subtended an angle of 10°.

Figure 2 shows a photograph of a hologram of the letter "C" (right) placed 20 cm from the receiving crystal, as well as the original letter (left). The width of the lettering was 3 mm cut from a $1\frac{1}{2} \times 1$ cm brass plate. The reconstructions obtained for each of the two images together with their

*Manufactured by James Electronics Inc., 4050 N. Rockwell St., Chicago, Illinois.
†See, for instance, S. Sokolov, Means for Indicating Flaws in Materials, U.S. Patent 2,164,125.

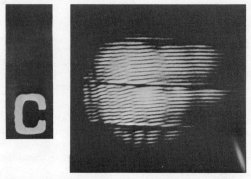

Fig. 2. Object (left) and interference pattern (right) as displayed on TV monitor.

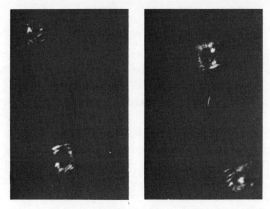

Fig. 3. Reconstructed images. The picture consists of two exposures; left, focused on the vertical image, and right, on the conjugate one. In each instance the twin image is blurred and the center undiffracted light was mechanically obstructed.

unfocused conjugate images are shown in Fig. 3. The images obtained in the figure were reconstructed by placing a negative transparency of the hologram displayed on the television screen inside a liquid gate and illuminating it with a convergent He–Ne laser beam as shown in Fig. 4. The liquid gate minimizes phase variations due to film thickness irregularities, thus reducing the noise in the reconstructed images. Since the object was positioned less than its far-field distance away from the receiver, the two images are reconstructed in separate planes equidistant from the focus of the reconstruction beam, their position being determined by the conventional holographic

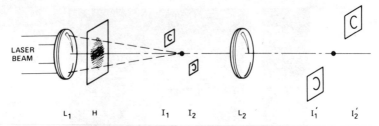

Fig. 4. In the reconstruction process converging laser light is diffracted by the hologram H. The real (I_1) and conjugate (I_2) images are thus obtained very near the optical axis. Lens L_2 then images the two images on the output screen in a convenient size (I_1' and I_2').

image equation,

$$\frac{1}{\lambda_l D_2} \mp \frac{1}{\lambda_s m^2 D_1} \pm \frac{1}{\lambda_s m^2 R_1} + \frac{1}{\lambda_l R_2} = 0 \tag{1}$$

where λ_s and λ_l are the acoustic and laser beam wavelengths, respectively, D_1 and D_2 are the object and image distances, respectively, R_1 and R_2 are the radii of curvature of the reference and reconstruction beams, respectively, and m is the size reduction scaling factor introduced in the recording of the hologram.

Since in our experiment the acoustic wavelength is a factor of 300 larger than that of the laser beam, the second and third terms of Eq. (1) are small compared to the first and last term if the hologram is not demagnified considerably, and the images will therefore be reconstructed very close to the focus of the reconstruction beam.

The lateral magnification of the images is given by

$$M_{\text{lat}} = \frac{1}{m} \frac{\lambda_l D_2}{\lambda_s D_1} \tag{2}$$

and the longitudinal magnification by

$$M_{\text{long}} = (\lambda_s/\lambda_l) M_{\text{lat}}^2 \tag{3}$$

Unless the hologram is scaled, the reconstructed images are demagnified proportional to the ratio of the light to sound wavelength, and optical means of magnifications have to be employed to obtain usable images.

In addition, three-dimensional reconstructions will be distorted unless the longitudinal and lateral magnifications are equal and independent of the object and image distances. This condition is fulfilled only if the hologram is scaled by a factor equal to the wavelength ratio λ_l/λ_s and the lateral magnification is equal to λ_l/λ_s.

The main limitation of this system, as well as of previously described scanning techniques, is the limited resolution obtainable. The maximum resolution is determined by the acoustic wavelength as well as by the aperture and maximum angle of detection of the receiving material (15° for quartz). The smallest resolvable transverse distance between any two points on the object as given by the Rayleigh criterion as $1.2D_1\lambda_s/a$, where a is the aperture of the receiver. The 2-in. aperture with a frequency of 7-MHz and an object distance of 20 cm gave a resolution of about 1 mm. Large angles of incidence cannot be used, since ultrasonic waves at angles of incidence greater than 15° are not detected by the quartz crystal receiver. This limitation is due to the fact that a crystal operated at the resonance point (its thickness is half the wavelength of the ultrasound in quartz) is equivalent to an array (mosaic) of receivers with apertures equal to approximately three times the wavelength of the ultrasound in water. These rather large apertures of the individual receivers limit the maximum angle of incidence of the detectable ultrasound. The size of the object that can be investigated is limited by the aperture and by the maximum angle of detection of the receiver; however, it can be extended by using a larger crystal or multiple receivers.

The sensitivity and the resolution of the system as well as the angular separation of the images can be increased by using an electronically generated reference beam in the construction of the hologram instead of the acoustic reference, since it is then possible to place the object closer to the receiver without obstructing the reference beam and use normal incidence of the object beam on the receiver, thus avoiding losses due to reflection of the acoustic beam at the crystal. The electronic scanning techniques provides a very simple means to add an electronic reference beam, which is completely equivalent to a sonic plane wave incident at an angle θ_x with the normal to the hologram plane.

Such a plane wave is represented at the receiving plane by

$$R_{\text{ref}} = \exp i[k_s(\sin \theta_x)x + \omega_s t] \tag{4}$$

where $k_s = 2\pi/\lambda_s$ and ω_s is the frequency of the acoustic beam.

Since the x direction (vertical, in our case) of the receiver is scanned with speed V_x, Eq. (4) can be rewritten as

$$R_{\text{ref}} = \exp i[k_s(\sin \theta_x)v_x t + \omega_s t]$$

$$= \exp i[(\omega_s + \Delta\omega)t]$$

Thus an electronic reference equivalent to an acoustic plane wave at an angle θ_x can be generated by a signal of frequency $\omega_s + \Delta\omega$. The control of the frequency difference $\Delta\omega$ determines the interference fringe spacing, or, equivalently, the reference offset angle.

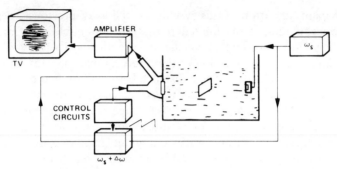

Fig. 5. Schematic diagram of electronic reference beam insertion. The reference oscillator provides a constant frequency ($\omega_s + \Delta\omega$) during the vertical sweep of the electron beam and is locked to the ultrasound generator (ω_s) during the blanking period of each displayed frame. Signals from the quartz receiving tube as well as from the reference oscillator are fed to the video amplifier and then displayed on the TV monitor. The control circuits determine the locking period of the reference oscillator as well as the scanning of the electron beam.

Fig. 6. Reconstructed image from hologram made with the use of the electronic beam. The object, the letter "C," was the negative of that shown on the left of Fig. 2. It thus obstructed the sound beam (bright background).

The apparatus used in the hologram generation using an electronic reference is shown in Fig. 5. The experimental arrangement is essentially the same as that shown in Fig. 1, except that the object beam is incident normally on the crystal and the acoustical reference is replaced by a signal from an oscillator added to the output of the electron multiplier prior to amplification by the video amplifier. Care is taken in locking the phase of the reference synthesized beam during the blanking period of each frame.

Figure 6 shows the reconstructed image of the letter "C," which in this case was a negative of the "C" used previously.

Electronic scanning provides several advantages compared to previously described techniques of ultrasonic holography. The main advantage is the greater scanning speed and simplicity in operation, resulting in an immediate display of holograms.

While water turbulence degrades the images obtained from ultrasonic holograms displayed on the water surface, it has very little effect in the electronic scanning method.

The capability of the system to immediately display a hologram leads to a new way of obtaining real-time holographic reconstructions by phase modulating a laser beam with the holographic signal from the video amplifier (using electrooptical effects, for instance) and then process the beam as shown in Fig. 4. These possibilities are presently being investigated at this laboratory [5, 6].

ACKNOWLEDGMENTS

The authors acknowledge the skillful help of Mr. Harold Chambers with the electronic instrumentation and of Mr. J. Kelly during all the phases of this experiment.

REFERENCES

1. R. K. Mueller and N. K. Sheridon, *Appl. Phys. Letters* **9**:328–329 (1966).
2. K. Preston and J. L. Kreuzer, *Appl. Phys. Letters* **10**:150–152 (1967).
3. A. F. Metherell, H. M. A. El-Sum, J. J. Dreher, and L. Larmore, *Appl. Phys. Letters* **17**:277–279 (1967).
4. R. W. Meier, *J. Opt. Soc. Am.* **55**:987 (1965).
5. G. Marie, *Phillips Res. Repts.* **22**:110–132 (1967).
6. E. Marom, H. Boutin, and R. K. Mueller, *J. Acoust. Soc. Am.* **42**:1169 (A) (1967); **43**:384 (1968).

Chapter 17

ACOUSTICAL FILTERING WITH HOLOGRAPHICALLY MATCHED SPATIAL FILTERS

Pal Greguss, Jr.

RSRI Ultrasonics Laboratory
Budapest, Hungary

The reconstruction of ultrasonic holograms with ultrasonic waves is hampered by the fact that the thickness of the recording element is not on the order of the ultrasonic wavelength. However, using, e.g., typographical methods, it would be possible to produce such print from ultrasonic holograms. This may open a new field in ultrasonics: "correlation filtering" comparable in principle to the filtering methods used in optics. Some preliminary results are demonstrated, and it is shown that this method could be used for flaw recognition.

INTRODUCTION

Wavefront reconstruction imagery [first described by Gabor [1,2]] using ultrasonic waves is creating considerable interest. As we have demonstrated [3-6], there is no fundamental difference in principle between holograms taken with laser light and those taken with ultrasonic waves. Consequently, all holography procedures which can be performed with electromagnetic or electron waves can also be carried out with ultrasonic waves. It should be noted, however, that ultrasonic wavelengths are several orders of magnitude larger than those used for wavefront reconstructions by visible light, and so an acoustical hologram reconstructed with visible light produces an image reduced by the ratio of the wavelengths. Fortunately, there are several ways overcome this drawback of ultrasonic holography. One is to reduce the ultrasonic hologram transparency and then illuminate it with a He–Ne laser; the reconstructed image will be formed at the theoretical image plane as calculated by the formulas for conventional holography [7-9]. The ultrasonic hologram can be considered as a large-scale mask of an optical transform whose diffraction pattern is the original object, since the Fourier transform of a Fourier transform is the original object again. We have demonstrated (^{10}) that an optical diffraction picture with a relatively simple addition permits the reconstruction of the original ultrasonic hologram.

This method requires visible light for the read-out of the holograms. Therefore the question arises: why not reconstruct the ultrasonic holograms with ultrasonic waves? The main objection to this is that ultrasonic waves cannot be seen without image converters and so all phase information of the ultrasonic waves will be lost. The purpose of this chapter is to show that this is not always the case.

EXTENDING SPATIAL FILTERING TO ACOUSTIC WAVES

One of the most exciting problems in ultrasonic nondestructive testing is the identification of flaws. Basically the same problems also arise in sonar applications and in ultrasonic diagnostics. From the viewpoint of information theory these problems can be considered as spatial filtering tasks.

Spatial filtering in optics was first described almost sixty years ago by Abbe (^{11}), and recently a special type of a spatial filter, the so-called matched filter, has been used for character recognition and signal detection (^{12}). The basic principles of optical correlation filtering with matched filters may be readily understood in terms of Fig. 1. The object to be investigated is placed in the plane P_1 and illuminated with coherent light. At plane P_2 the Fraunhofer diffraction pattern of the object is displayed. The complex amplitude of this wave distribution represents a Fourier transform of the object. The lens L_2 takes a second Fourier transform, thus restoring the original object, since an imaging process can be formulated as two successive Fourier transformations. If now a mask of the Fourier transform of a given picture detail is placed in the plane P_2, it is possible to selectively filter this picture detail out of the image O, in a way quite similar in principle to the filtering methods used in electrical communication systems. In other words, it is possible to determine whether or not the object under investigation has this sort of picture detail, because the output image at plane P_3 will have maxima in the places where the correlation between the picture detail and the object has a maxima. The correlation filtering process thus provides a graphical answer in the photographic output to the otherwise rather involved

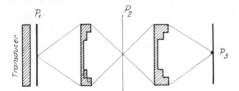

Fig. 1. Principle of the correlation filtering arrangement.

problem concerning the degree of correlation of the picture detail with other resembling picture details of the object. The level of brightness can be interpreted as a degree of correlation.

It is evident that in the whole filtering process only the wave character of the light is exploited, and so this process could also be accomplished with acoustic, i.e., ultrasonic waves if suitable lenses, filters, and recording techniques are at one's disposal. So we have only to find a way of implementing the desired complex filter function. Without holography this would be much more difficult to produce, since the complex filter function might vary widely both in amplitude and phase. It has been shown ([13]) that such a filter can be obtained by recording the diffraction pattern of the desired picture detail together with a coherent background in the Fourier transform arrangement illustrated in Fig. 2. The similarity between a complex filter and a Fourier transform hologram is readily recognized.

One basic requirement in applying this technique to ultrasonic waves is to have acoustical lenses with good optical properties. Acoustical lens theory, however, has not evolved very far, nor has much experimental work been done with other than single elements for power applications (energy concentration). Nor is it true that acoustical lens design is strictly analogous to optical lens design. We have found, however, that the so-called zone-lenses designed by Tarnoczy ([14]) on the basis of waveguides are very suitable not only for ultrasonic Fourier holography but also for complex spatial filtering with ultrasonic waves.

Using this concept, the first interesting result is that curvature of lens surfaces is unnecessary to produce a lens effect. The zone thus consists of a series of flat rings differing in thickness by $\lambda/2$. The focal length is given by

$$F = \frac{r_n^2}{n\lambda[1 - (c_1/c_2)]} + \frac{n\lambda}{4}\left[1 + \frac{c_1}{c_2}\right] \qquad (1)$$

where r_n is the radius of ring n, c_1 the sound velocity in the liquid medium, c_2 the sound velocity in the material of the lens, and λ the acoustic wavelength.

The radii of the individual rings are determined for a given focus. If we reduce the lens diameter or the number of the transmitting rings by circular diaphragms of different diameters, the focus migrates, contrary to expectation, toward the lens as the diaphragm aperture gets smaller.

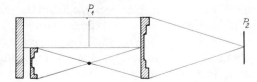

Fig. 2. Fourier-transform hologram recording of a complex filter.

The second problem in acoustical filtering with holographically matched spatial filters is connected with the ultrasonic detection methods. In this case, the problem is (a) to record the ultrasonic field distribution in the plane P_2 of Fig. 2, (b) to obtain the complex filter, and (c) to determine the correlation between the picture detail and the object in the plane P_3 of Fig. 1. Of the several possible solutions to this problem, the best, in our opinion, is to use the same sonosensitive plate technique we have used in our previous investigation ([15]). The so-called sampled acoustical hologram technique could perhaps also be considered, but we feel that at present it gives very poor ultrasonic holograms compared to the ultrasonic holograms recorded on sonosensitive plates. This is not the only reason we have chosen the sonosensitive plate technique, especially for recording the complex filter. Our complex filter must have the ability to diffract the ultrasonic waves, since without this the correlation between the picture detail we are interested in and the object as a whole could not be determined in the arrangement of Fig. 1. Ordinary ultrasonic holograms, however, do not diffract ultrasonic waves as laser light holograms (or reduced ultrasonic holograms) do light waves, because the thickness of the ultrasonic recording element is not on the order of the ultrasonic wavelength. Therefore we have to transform the obtained ultrasonic hologram—the complex filter—in a form which satisfies the diffraction laws for the ultrasonic waves. Such a transformation, however, involves unavoidable loss in the information content, and so if the original ultrasonic hologram is of poor quality, we do not expect the transformed complex filter to fulfill its duty as a complex spatial filter with ultrasonic waves.

PRELIMINARY EXPERIMENTS

The acoustical lenses used in the arrangements indicated schematically in Figs. 1 and 2 and implemented as shown in Fig. 3 have been designed according to Eq. (1), and were made of synthetic resin. The diameters and the focal lengths of the lenses varied from 40 to 70 mm and from 35 to 150 mm, respectively.

To obtain the Fourier transform hologram of the picture detail we were interested in, the picture detail was placed in the focal plane P_1 of the smaller acoustical lens (half lens). This plane P_1 was at the same time also the focal plane of the large lens, which formed the diffraction pattern of the picture detail with the coherent background in the plane P_2, where the sonosensitive plate was placed to record the ultrasonic field intensity distribution.

After processing the sonosensitive plate the Fourier transform hologram obtained was regarded as a mask for printed circuits. To overcome the difficult problem of greytone control, we replaced the continuous intensity

Fig. 3. Lenses used in the experiments, and experimental apparatus for recording the complex filter.

factor by hachures, somewhat similar to the halftone simulation used in the printing industry. We used etching and engraving techniques well known in typography. One of these filters can be seen in Fig. 4.

Several trials were also made to achieve ultrasonic holograms which could be reconstructed with ultrasonic waves, by using a monomer methyl-methacrylate and polymerizing it with ultraviolet light only where the film (in the original ultrasonic hologram) was transparent. This method, however, gave only poor results. Nevertheless, we think this could be a

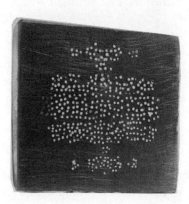

Fig. 4. Ultrasonic spatial filter.

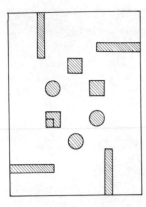

Fig. 5. Flaw distribution in a plate.

promising way to get a "thick" ultrasonic hologram, and we are trying to improve it.

Since the scope of our preliminary investigations included the determination of whether or not the complex spatial filtering technique could be also used in ultrasonic nondestructive testing for flaw configuration recognition, and perhaps in diagnostics too, we made complex filters from different types of artificial flaws such as bore holes of 5 mm diameter and 300 mm long, spheres with 5 mm diameter, and squares 5 × 5 mm. The object to be investigated was a 90 × 120 × 20 steel plate in which these types of flaws were distributed as shown in Fig. 5.

During the period in which we were conducting our investigations we discovered the paper of Brown and Lohmann ([16]) dealing with complex spatial filtering with binary masks, and we had the feeling that this method could be very useful for our purpose. Therefore we copied their matched filter for the letter "E" taking into account however, the fact that we are using ultrasonic and not light waves.

RESULTS

In spite of the fact that the quality of ultrasonic holograms, and especially ultrasonic complex filters, leaves much to be desired, the results we have obtained with the technique described above are really very encouraging, as can be seen from Figs. 6–8.

In Fig. 6 the very dark dots of light correspond to the bore holes, since the ultrasonic complex filter of a bore hole was placed in the plane P_2 of the arrangement of Fig. 1. The dots, which are barely visible in the center, however, correspond to spheres and squares when the ultrasonic complex filter of the sphere was used. However, the difference is quite distinguishable.

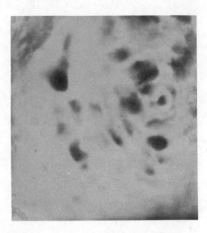

Fig. 6. Very dark dots correspond to bore holes.

In Fig. 7 the very dark dots correspond to spheres and squares when the ultrasonic complex filter of the sphere is used. No differences can be seen between spheres and squares, and the situation does not change if the complex filter of the square is used.

Finally, results of the experiment with the filter made according to the method of Brown and Lohman is shown in Fig. 8. The more or less dark dots are not as pronounced as in the experiments mentioned above. The object we investigated in this experiment contains nine engraved letters as seen in Fig. 9.

GENERAL REMARKS

Our preliminary investigations have shown that the application of acoustical spatial filtering using filters based on ultrasonic holography may

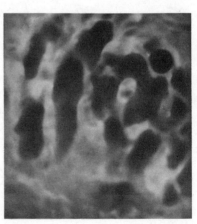

Fig. 7. Very dark dots correspond to spheres and squares.

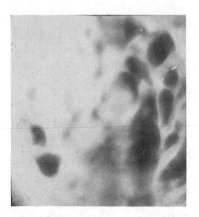

Fig. 8. Results obtained with filter made according to Brown and Lohmann. Dark dot should correspond to the letter "E."

Fig. 9. Letters embedded in plastic.

be important not only as a pure scientific curiosity, but also in nondestructive testing, where the shape of the flaw and its characteristics are important. New opportunities may arise in the medical field, too, since ultrasonic methods could not only replace X ray diagnosis but by using the spatial filtering technique they may give more specific information. The practical possibilities are at present, however, limited not only by the problems arising from wavelength differences, but also by the fact that the preparation of suitable filters leaves much to be desired. Research, however, continues and the real success, we hope, will not fail to come.

REFERENCES

1. D. Gabor, *Nature* **161**: 77 (1948).
2. D. Gabor, *Proc. Roy. Soc.* London **A197**: 545 (1949).

3. P. Greguss, paper presented at the 2nd International Conference on Ultrasonics, Prague, 1965.
4. P. Greguss, paper presented at the Symposium on Techniques in Applied Photography, London, 1965.
5. P. Greguss, *Research Film* **5**:330 (1965).
6. P. Greguss, *Science Journal* **2**:83 (1966).
7. P. Kirkpatrick and H. M. A. El-Sum, *J. Opt. Soc. Am.* **46**:825 (1956).
8. G. W. Stroke, *An Introduction to Coherent Optics and Holography*, Academic Press, New York, 1966.
9. G. L. Rogers, *J. Sci. Instr.* **43**:677 (1966).
10. P. Greguss and V. Bugdahl, *Research Film*, to be published.
11. E. Abbe, *Die Lehre von der Bildentstehung im Mikroskop* (O. Lummer and F. Reiche, eds.), Friedrich Vieweg, Braunschweig, 1910. (Available from University Microfilm, Ann Arbor, Michigan, catalog No. OP 10744.)
12. A. Vander Lugt, *Proc. IEEE* **IT-LO**:139 (1964).
13. D. Gabor, G. W. Stroke, R. Restrick, A. Funkhouser, and D. Brumm, *Phys. Letters* **18**:116 (1965).
14. T. Tarnoczy, *Ultrasonics* **3**:115 (1965).
15. P. Greguss, *Perspective* **8**:287 (1966).
16. B. R. Brown and A. W. Lohmann, *Appl. Optics* **5**:967 (1966).

Chapter 18

SUMMARY AND DIRECTIONS FOR FUTURE PROGRESS*

Dennis Gabor

Imperial College, London, England, and
CBS Laboratories, Stamford, Connecticut

I want to say how thrilled I was by this Symposium. I am quite sure it is the beginning of greater things. The reconstructions shown are still mostly in the stage that mine were in, in 1947, before I dared to publish them. I should say, though, that the last one by Metherell (Chapter 14) was better, and that the bolt shown by Kreuzer and Vogel (Chapter 5) and one picture by Brenden (Chapter 4) were also good. After 1948 it took us almost 15 years before holography started to give really good pictures. Now, we won't have to wait another 15 years. The reason for this is that at that time we couldn't see any real application for holography. The only important one that I could see then was improving the electron microscope; but now we can visualize two colossally important groups of applications: One is ultrasonic holography, to produce small-scale high-definition pictures, chiefly and most importantly for medical purposes, and perhaps also for fault-finding in materials investigations. The other objective is, of course, underwater imaging for oceanography. In this Symposium the short-wave aspect has been greatly emphasized, but I am sure that the other aspect is also receiving attention. The situation of sound holography now as compared with that of light holography in 1947–48 is that we did not at that time possess highly coherent sources. With sound we have almost unlimited coherence. However, although sound sources are perfectly coherent because they operate in the classical or electrical engineer's range, we might lose some coherence at considerable distances in the ocean. This loss of coherence is serious only when the path length in the ocean is large; there are some measurements at 500 kHz that show complete coherence over 35-meters path length. We have powerful coherent sources, too, and we have various other advantages over light holography.

*This chapter is based on the summary talk given by Dr. Dennis Gabor, F.R.S., at the end of the First International Symposium on Acoustical Holography. Eds.

With light the only thing we can measure is intensity—that is the only physical reading we have. But with sound the amplitude becomes a reality. With light it wouldn't be difficult at all to take a whole recording which contains amplitude and phase in two pictures. All we would have to do would be to beat the object wave with two local oscillators in quadrature, registering the sine and cosine components, and in two pictures we would then have a complete record of the amplitude and phase of the object wave. However, this isn't necessary because we have other means for getting rid of the ambiguity caused by the recording of intensities only. The ambiguity is, of course, in the "twin" or "conjugate" image. In 1950 I saw that the best possibility for getting rid of this ambiguity was through the use of two "quadrature" pictures for eliminating the conjugate image. Nowadays we have various simpler methods, and I congratulate Metherell on his last method. It ought to have occurred to me 20 years ago, but it didn't. (I went only part way, by using "dark-field" reconstructions, in which the direct beam was cut off by a small black patch.) Another method, of course, is to skew the reference beam. Another is to take a *bad* picture and correct it optically, to produce *twice* the aberrations in the twin image, which then become almost invisible. So there is no need to take two pictures; but we could easily do this with sound, and we can do various other tricks. In optics the intensity in the hologram is given by the well-known equation

$$I = A_0^2 + A_1^2 + 2A_0A_1\cos(\theta_1 - \theta_0)$$

where $A_1\exp(i\theta_1)$ and $A_0\exp(i\theta_0)$ are the object and reference beams, respectively.

An optical camera can't do anything but record intensity. But this is not the case in sound holography. We can just as well form $A_1A_0\exp i(\theta_1 - \theta_0)$ directly, which is the average or "wattmetric" product of the two amplitudes $A_1\exp(i\theta_1)$ and $A_2\exp(i\theta_2)$, and thereby we get rid of the background. We get also rid of the third and higher powers of the cosine term, which are a nuisance in light holography. However, the cosine will be positive and negative, and we cannot record negative quantities on an ordinary photographic plate, although we could record them in a (bleached) phase hologram. But even if we take transmission-contrast photographic plates for simplicity, we still can make certain improvements. One, as explained by Metherell, is to make the interference fringes always go from a zero to a maximum. I am not so sure that is the best method. (Incidentally, I want to

Fig. 1. "Bottoming" hologram. Minimum background for true amplitudes and non-negative transmission.

mention that when I started thinking of holography 20 years ago I started exactly this way—with phases alone.) The best way, in my opinion, is probably to let the bottom of the fringes (the minima) go to complete blackness. Any electrical engineer can make an amplifier such that the output "bottoms" at zero (see Fig. 1). This gives *true* amplitudes but a minimum background and therefore minimum noise.

What about noise? Why are the pictures we obtain today so poor and noisy? One of the factors affecting these pictures is obviously that the scanning aperture produces a certain spurious line structure, a vertical "aperture error." But I must admit that I couldn't see any difference between horizontal and vertical resolution in these pictures. I should say that the jitter in the horizontal scanning was about as strong as the vertical aperture error, except in the pictures of Kreuzer and Vogel (Chapter 5), where I could hardly see any effect of the jitter.

The aperture error was discussed by Smith and Moody (Chapter 6) and was also touched upon by Aoki (Chapter 15). Eliminating it completely is not that simple. If we have a scanned picture, then in any one of these lines we get only one datum. What is the best we can do with this situation? The best in my opinion is to cut down the vertical frequencies to a minimum, by using, from the Shannon–Whittaker sampling theorem, an aperture of the shape of a $(\sin x)/x$ or "slit" function (see Fig. 2). If we then add up these lines, we get the "cardinal function," which contains no frequencies higher than the line frequency. Unfortunately, this "slit-type" aperture function is not easy to produce. It has positive and negative values, and extends far to both sides of the line. It would be fairly easy to produce digitally because there is nothing that fundamentally limits the algorithm, but it would further complicate the already fairly complicated synthesis which Goodman has explained (Chapter 12). There may be, however, a possibility of producing it optically, because "negative light" can be produced with coherent light. If we have a coherent background, we can add to it positive or negative amplitudes by means of a stepped filter which has a step of half a wavelength in it. This will add and subtract, and in this way we can produce the effect of positive and negative light. This may be worth remembering at a further stage of sound holography once the vertical resolution becomes noticeably worse than the horizontal resolution. This isn't the case as yet, as noted above.

Fig. 2. "Slit" or "sinc" function, $(\sin x)/x$. Optimum vertical aperture for avoiding unreal, high frequencies. With this aperture the vertical distribution is the Shannon–Whittaker "cardinal function." The line spacing is π.

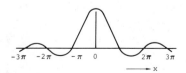

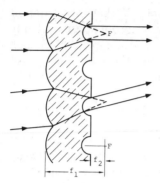

Fig. 3. Arnulf's "afocal plate" for depth correction. The effect is (approximately) as if the refractive index at the right were a fraction f_2/f_1 of the refractive index at the left. In the example $f_1 : f_2 = 3 : 1$. Several afocal plates can be used in tandem.

A disadvantage of acoustical holography which has been much emphasized here is that we would like to see three-dimensional pictures, but that unless we reduce the hologram to a ridiculously small size, we cannot see the correct depth proportions. This is a point worth thinking about. There exists, probably unknown to many, an optical method for overcoming this, devised by the French inventor, Professor Arnulf, of the Institut d'Optique, Paris, about 30 years ago. It consists of taking a lenticular plate consisting of afocal lens pairs. A convex positive lens and a concave negative lens have their foci at exactly the same point. The beam comes out thinner, and the angle is increased in the inverse ratio, that is to say, it will be multiplied by the ratio of the focal lengths. This is a trick to circumvent Lagrange's theorem. We are up against the fact that the longitudinal magnification is the square of the transverse magnification. This is Maxwell's formulation of Lagrange's theorem, which in its original form states that the product of width and angle is an invariant in an optical system. In modern language, this means nothing other than that the information is an invariant in the system—an obvious and fundamental property. One cannot get around it except by Arnulf's trick. This gives us a bigger angle but no gain in resolution, because the resolution will be automatically limited by the size of the lenticules. (This feature also occurs in Thurstone's suggestion of "breaking up the hologram.") I do not think, though, that Arnulf's trick will be of much value for reducing the depth by a factor of more than about five or so, and what we need may be something of the order of 20 or even more.

Let us now consider some of the other difficulties of acoustical holography. We have not discussed the influence of the media, except for turbulence, and, as Mawardi has pointed out, we have not yet really come up against turbulence. There is no turbulence in these quiet devices, but we may have convection. Heat may be transferred from the bottom to the top by rising vortices, a process which is inherently inhomogeneous. This, however, could be very easily overcome in tank experiments by having the top warmer and the bottom of the devices cooler, because this stops the convection. Of course, turbulence will come up in ocean problems and there will also be other effects, such as strong distortion by heat gradients. The velocity of sound varies steeply with temperature, and therefore temperature gradients will bend sound very strongly. But that, of course, is something which cannot be helped. A mitigating circumstance would be if we could have the reference source at about the same distance as the object, and near it. Then turbulence would not matter very much because though the phases would vary in a random manner, they would vary together. This arrangement is feasible in a good many cases, though not always.

Scanning, of course, is not a final solution, because in most practical applications we cannot wait long enough for the scanning hologram to be completed. What has been done so far are merely feasibility experiments. When it comes to good pictures with a 1000×1000 definition the time will increase by a very considerable factor, and it may take a day to take a reasonable picture. So, undoubtedly, more hydrophones will have to be used simultaneously in some economical manner.

Of the methods other than scanning, the oldest, I think, is either Sokolov's method or Pohlman's (I'm not certain which), but I think Sokolov's can be considered as the better of the old methods. I studied this problem some years ago and my conclusion was then and still is that the Sokolov tube will never give good holograms. The best I have seen so far is what Fritzler showed (Chapter 16), and it has about a hundred lines. We just can't get a decent hologram with a hundred lines, even for very modest purposes. One might think that with a hundred lines we could reconstruct a reasonable picture with 10,000 picture points. But the fact is that even with photographic plates we can never manage to get good holographic reconstructions with the bare minimum of information. Theoretically, information in the hologram need not be better than that of the image. But in all cases in which we introduce a rather complicated intermediate process we also introduce a considerable noise factor. It appears that we want about an order of magnitude more resolution in the holograms than would be sufficient to get a picture of the same size. I don't know why this should be so, but this seems to be the experience even with rather good photographic plates. It is quite possible that the situation will be better in acoustical holography because here we really have some advantages over the photographic process. We can, for instance, keep exactly to the $\gamma = -2$ rule, and avoid certain "crosstalk" terms which arise from the nonlinearity of the photographic process. When I made my first hologram I had to be very careful because there was only minimum coherence; and I kept very strictly to the $\gamma = -2$ rule. Nowadays this is not important—now we can take an almost black and white hologram because the higher harmonics all fall outside the first-order diffraction pattern, but it appears that we pay for this with a certain amount of noise. Ultimately, it may be possible to get 100×100 picture points with something like a 100×100 hologram, but hardly with the Sokolov tube.

The other most successful method for the time being is the free-surface method which is the ingenious idea of Mueller and Brenden. This, for the time being, is only about as good as the scanning method, except, of course, that it is instantaneous. What prevents it from being better are really secondary effects. One of the deficiencies is evidently the mismatch between the optical wavelengths and the acoustic wavelengths. Others are the properties of a very soft recording surface, where we have the surface tension as the only restoring force. The soft surface will deform in a macroscopic way during the taking of the pictures. So, for the time being, the quality of these pictures is about the same as that of the scanning pictures, though not quite as good as the picture taken by Metherell and several of Kreuzer and Vogel. The only defect in some of the pictures of Kreuzer and Vogel was something which is in the nature of things. Practically everything is a mirror in ultrasound and one can see nothing but "glare." Illuminated by a central light, the "three disgraces" which were presented would show nothing but a few glare spots in their convexities. No photographer would, of course, operate under such conditions. The trick to eliminate the glare is sideways illumination. Sonar pictures are excellent because they show shadows. One can also use diffuse illumination—or at least illumination from many points. I realize that in the method of Mueller and Brenden this isn't quite so easy, because there the illumination is fairly fixed by the condition that there be no streaming on the surface. The pressure tensor here must not have a horizontal component. The illumination and the object beam must be fairly well balanced here and this will probably make it difficult to use very diffuse illumination.

Let us now discuss some of the contributions; if I unintentionally forget a few people, I apologize in advance.

El-Sum's summary (Chapter 1) was absolutely excellent. Berger's review (Chapter 2) of all the methods at our disposal was also excellent; he covered a good many which are not generally known. I was very surprised to note how promising are some of the methods based on the color change of liquid crystals, which are highly sensitive to temperature differences. I do not think, though, that it is advisable to use very high sensitivities. If there is a noticeable change in color with 10^{-4} degrees, I just wouldn't touch that material because if you want to do an experiment with something which requires a temperature regulation to 10^{-3} degrees, then you might have to wait a month before the temperature has equalized to the point at which we could start the experiment. I regret that though Berger has given the sensitivities, he has not given the wavebands of the various methods. The most promising method from 5 MHz downward appears to be to use single hydrophones. Beyond that there is a possibility of constructing matrices of hydrophones as almost continuous sheets of piezoelectric surfaces, in other words, a variation of the Sokolov tube. The only difference would then be that we would have to attach amplifiers to each of the elements of that piezoelectric matrix instead of scanning them electronically. That may be a difficult thing because even with modern techniques it is not easy to equalize 10,000 or more amplifiers.

I was very much interested in Thurstone's brilliant review of medical applications (Chapter 7). The conclusion is that this is a very important field. He hasn't emphasized it very much, but one of the greatest promises of ultrasonic holography is, of course, the detection of soft tumors. There is no doubt that there will be sufficient contrast once we can make a proper viewing device, because ultrasonic echo methods have already shown us soft tumors with remarkable contrast. The Proceedings of the Chicago Conference on the Medical Applications of Ultrasound contain a number of excellent pictures of very small tumors which could be well detected by essentially radio-echo methods. There is sufficient contrast; all we need is a good viewing device. As Thurstone emphasized, this must be instantaneous and it must give three-dimensional views with correct depth to get the proper three-dimensional proportion. May I suggest going ahead seriously with efforts to produce holograms using the 10.5-μ line of the CO_2 laser. This would be a colossal step in bridging the gap between acoustic and light wavelengths, and would bring us much nearer the condition of equal depth magnification and lateral magnification. I have already mentioned Arnulf's trick, which is good for a factor of five or so. A third trick would be, of course, to use a lens before making the hologram. This is, though, something we should like to avoid, since the great advantage of holography is just that it short-circuits the very difficult problem of acoustical imaging. An acoustical lens which is useful in holography need not be a flat-field objective lens; it can be something far more primitive because errors can be corrected on the light-optical side, but an acoustical lens of any sort is a complication which we would prefer to avoid. After all, the greatest advantage of holography is that *any* surface can replace a lens system and realize the third dimension.

As regards the instantaneous display of reconstruction, there are now various methods, but I don't think that the Sokolov tube is very promising. The thickness of the crystal cannot be very small and the voltage on it is quite considerable. It seems to me that the hydrophone is a much more promising solution because with the hydrophone there is a possibility of combination with display devices such as the Eidophor, thermoplastic recording, photo-plastic recording, etc. These are methods for instantaneous and high-definition holography. Another important medical application of ultrasonic holography is in pregnancies—absolutely ideal, because there are hardly any air cavities in the abdomen. It is an ideal subject and, of course, there is no genetic damage, while radiographers still have a bad conscience—they still don't know what genetic damage they may be doing.

Dreher's presentation (Chapter 8) is an extremely fascinating one. Is sonar involved or is it holography? A crucial question is this: "Does the porpoise distinguish from the right to left or also up and down?" Because if it is just right and left, then I should say sonar is sufficient. Dreher noted in discussion that it is apparently up and down. If it's up and down, then there is a strong suspicion that the beast has invented holography before me. I wouldn't be surprised.

As regards de Klerk's contribution (Chapter 9), I suppose it is a surprise that sound generation can now be pushed to such high frequencies. But I must say that perhaps it is a little early still to hope for correspondingly high definitions. We shall be able to use such high definitions only when we have something like the equivalent of a photographic plate. The wavelengths he mentions are coming nearer to those which are recorded on a photographic plate, and we are really very far from having anything as fine as that in our recording mechanisms. For the time being we will probably have to be satisfied with about 20 MHz maximum. A 15-MHz, 0.1-mm wavelength would be ample for most purposes, and we would not need to go higher.

Korpel's method (Chapter 10) is in a class by itself, because it isn't holography. But I should say that it opens some interesting possibilities. What I consider very interesting is that it is a new method for looking into a three-dimensional medium. In this ingenious method a light source, in this case a linear light source, will have images which will correspond to the sound sources. This is really a new method of crystal analysis or medium analysis; instead of plane waves we have spherical waves. I don't think it is very applicable to X rays. This is because a linear *focus* with X rays is much more difficult to produce than a parallel beam. Perhaps the nearest possibility is, as in the Kossel–Moellenstedt method, to focus an electron beam right on the crystal as a surface source. Then maybe we can see something with the X rays produced by this source.

Another line which interested me very much is the possibility of using holography for seismic waves or earth waves. That is to say, instead of the explosion waves used at present, use coherent oscillations, measure the field at the surface of the earth, and then conclude what's below. This is again the point at which we know too little. It is a problem of quite a different order from ordinary holography because a hologram does not really give an image of three-dimensional space. If x, y, and z are the three coordinates, it doesn't give the optical density of the medium at any point x, y, z. It is a two-dimensional record, an integral over the depth dimension, and we can use it for "three-dimensional vision" only because our space is limited by objects, by surfaces. Holography can sort out these surfaces, but it cannot find, for instance, striations in front of us. This is, of course, the type of problem for which radar echo methods are exactly appropriate. Altogether, holography and sonar (or radar, or echo sounding) are exactly complimentary, because radar and sonar are absolutely wonderful for looking sideways—the only thing they cannot do is to look forward. And holography can do exactly that.

As regards the digital reconstruction of holograms (Goodman, Chapter 12), with all admiration for the brilliant Cooley–Tukey algorithm, I still prefer the apparatus which does it exactly with the speed of light instead of in twenty minutes. And it seems to me that the reconstructions by this method, I don't know for what reason, are still not as good as we would expect from a 256×256 picture.

Mawardi (Chapter 13) gave a brilliant contribution on nonlinear effects in sound fields, and it was shown, perhaps somewhat to the surprise of some, that there is no such thing as a linear monochromatic sound wave. As soon as there is anything in its way, a second harmonic will be generated, because in the mass conservation equation there is a second-order term which we always neglected in school. I was surprised to see how considerable those effects can be. They wouldn't hurt us very much at the moment, because all we would notice is that, for instance, the mirror in Mawardi's example appears a little inclined to its true position, and at the present stage of sound holography the error would be negligible.

And now I hope I have said enough controversial things to stir thoughts up in a few of these areas.

Chapter 19

SUPPLEMENTARY BIBLIOGRAPHY

Compiled by A. F. Metherell

Following is an alphabetical list of references and abstracts of papers specifically devoted to *acoustical* holography which may prove useful to the reader. These are all the references that I have on the subject, but they do not necessarily represent everything that has been published. The notation "abstract" following an entry indicates that only the abstract has been published.

There are many related papers which are not included, such as those on holography in general and on acoustic imaging and detection. For a bibliography on holography in general, the reader may refer to the *Journal of the SMPTE* **75**:373–435 (Apr. 1966); **75**:759–809 (Aug. 1966); and **76**:392–395 (Apr. 1967).

E. E. Alderidge, Ultrasonic Holography as an Extension to C-Scan, presented at the conference on Holography–Recent Advances and Applications held at the National Physical Laboratory, Teddington, England, Jan. 17–18, 1968.

After analyzing the Reference Beam and Gabor holograms from a geometric view point corresponding to thin lens and ray theory, an instrumentation of an Ultrasonic Reference Beam hologram, using synthetic aperture technique and electronic signal processing, is described. This arrangement is so similar to that used for C-Scan that the Ultrasonic hologram can be regarded as a natural extension of C-scan. Its optical reproduction and its possible application to a particular nondestructive testing problem are briefly discussed.

Y. Aoki, N. Yoshida, N. Tsukamoto, and M. Suzuki, Sound Wave Hologram and Optical Reconstruction, *Proc. IEEE* **55**:1622–1623 (Sept. 1967).

An acoustical hologram is constructed using a sound wave (20 kHz), scanning the acoustical fields by a microphone, and lighting a lamp by amplified electrical signals from the microphone. The original image is reconstructed to illuminate the sound wave hologram of reduced size by laser light (6328 Å), and observed by a microscope.

Y. Aoki, N. Yoshida, N. Tsukamoto, and M. Suzuki, Sound Wave Hologram and Optical Reconstruction, *Oyo Butsuri* **36**(9): 701–704 (1967) (in Japanese).

An experiment to construct holograms using sound wave (20 kc) and to reconstruct the original images using laser light (6328 Å) is conducted. The acoustical fields are detected by a microphone which scans the fields mechanically. The electric signals from the microphone are amplified and light a lamp fixed on the back of the microphone. The light intensity distributions converted from the acoustical field distributions are recorded on film by a camera as sound wave holograms. The original images are reconstructed to illuminate the obtained sound wave holograms of reduced size by laser light.

H. M. A. El-Sum, Acoustic Holography, Presented to the SPIE Seminar-in-depth on Holography, San Francisco, May 23–24, 1968.

The visualization of sound fields has recently attracted the attention of scientists and engineers of a wide range of disciplines. A brief introduction to the physical principles and practical methods involved in both light and sound holography will serve to point out similarities and differences.

The two proven methods for forming acoustical holograms, the "free surface" method and the "scanning" method, will be discussed in detail. Other, less perfected, methods will also be included in the discussion; most of these require rather high acoustical intensities, and this will lead to a number of nonlinear effects, which result finally in phase distortion. Time allowed, such effects will also be discussed.

The last part of the paper will discuss various applications of acoustical holography.

P. S. Green, Acoustic Holography, LMSC Tech. Rept. 6-77-67-11 (Dec. 1966), Lockheed Missiles and Space Company, Palo Alto, California.

P. S. Green, Acoustic Holography, LMSC Tech. Rept. 6-77-67-42 (Sept. 1967), Lockheed Missiles and Space Company, Palo Alto, California.

The liquid surface deformation method of acousto-optical image conversion is a convenient aid in the formation of acoustic holograms suitable for optical reconstruction. Furthermore, the fact that surface deformation is proportional to the intensity of acoustical waves impinging on the surface enables one to employ the liquid surface directly as a reflecting, phase hologram, obviating the conventional process of photographing the surface deformation for holographic purposes. However, both the instantaneous and the photographic forms of the liquid surface conversion method have limited spatial frequency response, which restricts the angle that may be subtended (at the liquid surface) by the object field. A derivation is presented here of the spatial frequency transfer function associated with each of the two conversion techniques.

In the case of direct reconstruction, the transfer function relating surface-height deviation to intensity of the incident acoustic field is found to be that of a low-pass spatial filter with a cut-off spatial frequency inversely proportional to the square root of surface tension. For pure water this frequency is approximately $f_0 = 0.6$ cycles/cm. Since spatial frequencies well in excess of this are typical in offset-reference holography, compensatory spatial filtering of the optical field may be required.

An analysis is made of the transformation relating acoustic intensity and recording-plane light intensity in the "self-interference" method for photographing the surface relief. For surface displacements that are small with respect to an optical wavelength, the transformation has the characteristics of a linear, bandpass spatial filter. The pass band typically extends from about 1 to 20 cycles/cm. However, some difficulty was encountered in attempting to meet this "small displacement" condition simultaneously for all regions of the hologram, particularly with objects having a considerable specular component in their reflected field.

For spatial frequencies well above f_0, the acoustic intensity (at the liquid surface) which effects a surface-height deviation of one sixteenth an optical wavelength is found to be proportional to surface tension and to the square of spatial frequency. For pure water an intensity of 8.5×10^{-3} W/cm^2 is required for a spatial frequency of 10 cycles/cm. The sensitivity of this conversion method was found to be marginal for forming holograms of three-dimensional backscattering objects.

Acoustic holograms have been produced of several three-dimensional objects using the "self interference" method for photographing the fluid surface. Optical reconstructions made from photoreduced copies of these holograms are presented.

P. Greguss, Ultraschallhologramme, *Research Film* **5**(4):330–337 (1965) (in German).

Within the framework of his attempts to achieve cinematography by ultrasound waves, the author discusses the possibilities of applying Gabor's Hologramme method to image-formation by means of ultrasound, and describes some attempts made by him along these lines.

P. Greguss, Pictures by Sound, *Perspectives* **8**(4):287–302 (1966).

The geometric similarity of sound and light waves has stimulated numerous attempts at creating visible sound images. The physical nature of sound waves enables them to pick up new kinds of information.

P. Greguss, Techniques and Information Content of Sonoholograms, *J. of Phot. Sci.* **14**(6):329–332 (Nov.–Dec. 1966).

Some attempts have been made to apply ultrasonography to metrology, from which sonophotometry has evolved. The information content of this method is, however, not sufficient since the sonosensitive films record only amplitude of the U.S. waves and do not give any information about phase variation. It is shown that using the holography method, discovered in 1947 by D. Gabor, and using sonosensitive plates, holograms can be obtained by U.S. waves. Drawing a parallel between these holograms, termed sonoholograms, and those of Leith and Upatnieks, taken with laser, it is not possible to establish any principal differences.

P. Greguss, Possibility and Limitations in Sonoholography (Abstract), *J. Acoust. Soc. Am.* **42**(5):1186 (Nov. 1967).

The geometric similarity of sound and light waves has stimulated numerous attempts at visible sound images. Since 1964, efforts have been made to produce and to reconstruct holograms by ultrasonic waves. Sometimes there is a chance to get information from a hologram without wavefront reconstruction by using Moire fringes techniques. Wavefront reconstruction by ultrasonic waves promises a new way to overcome the difficulties issuing from the wavelength differences. Using a new acoustical–optical lens system, ultrasonoholograms can be obtained that can be treated as an ordinary laser hologram. Ultrasonoholography has its future not only in the nondestructive testing of materials, but also in ultrasonic diagnostics. Possibilities and limitations will be discussed.

J. Halstead, Ultrasound Holography, *Ultrasonics*, No. 6, part 2, 79–87 (Apr. 1968); paper presented to the conference on Ultrasonics for Industry, London, Nov. 1, 1967.

Ultrasound–optical image converters can visualize objects by ultrasonic waves in optically opaque media. Ultrasound holography displaces the difficult production of conventional images by ultrasound lenses. Five examples of ultrasound object-image relations are derived from the principles of holography.

The absence of a suitable ultrasound image converter restricts practical applications. Possible ultrasound detectors are outlined; for example, a potentially useful ultrasound camera with a wide aperture modification. Also, current literature of ultrasound holography is reviewed.

A. Korpel, Acoustic Imaging and Holography, IEEE Symposium on Sonics and Ultrasonics, Vancouver, Canada, Oct. 5, 1967.

The purpose of this paper is to discuss and compare various methods of acoustic imaging which have the property of providing both phase and amplitude information about a sound field, thus making it possible to image this field in three dimensions. Most of these methods rely on the holographic technique developed for optical fields, in which phase and amplitude are recorded on a photographic film as modulations in density and spacing of a spatial reference carrier. This is accomplished by photographing in some plane the interference pattern between a reference beam and the light scattered from the object under study. Sound waves will not, of course, register directly on a photographic plate, but several methods are available for making visible the distribution of sound intensity in a particular plane.

A. Korpel and P. Desmares, Rapid Sampling of Acoustic Holograms by Laser Scanning Techniques, *J. Acoust. Soc. Am.* (to be published).

The paper discusses a technique in which a laser flying spot scanner is used to record an acoustical hologram by reading out the periodic deformations of a solid surface caused by an incident sound field. The technique is compared with the Sokolov tube method and shown to have comparable sensitivity while not being restricted to low frequencies and small areas. A description is given of experiments using sound frequencies of 2 and 9 MHz, and photographs are presented showing holograms and reconstructions obtained with this technique.

J. L. Kreuzer, Ultrasonic Three-Dimensional Imaging Using Holographic Techniques, Symposium on Modern Optics (Mar. 22–24 1967), New York, New York.

L. Larmore, H. M. A. El-Sum, and A. F. Metherell, Acoustical Holograms Using Phase Information Only (Abstract), *J. Opt. Soc. Am.* **58**:730 (May 1968).

Optical signals require square law detectors and hence direct phase measurement is not feasible without the use of a coherent reference beam. On the other hand, acoustical beams can be converted to useful electrical signals directly with linear transducers. Consequently, an external reference beam can be provided electronically rather than acoustically to form an acoustical hologram. A scheme is described where such an external reference beam, phase locked with the signal beam, is used to record only the phase of the signal in an acoustical hologram. All fringes in such a hologram have the same visibility and the resulting hologram reconstructs the original object with its same gray scale and apparent better resolution.

Particularly, these results apply to reconstruction made with the appropriate spatial filtering which eliminates the interference from the conjugate image in a narrow field, coaxial (Gabor) type hologram. The optical analog of this scheme is to record an optical hologram on a photographic film having linear characteristics and variable gamma, depending on the signal intensity. Discussion of this technique will be illustrated with some recent results.

R. B. MacAnally, Inclined Reference Acoustic Holography, *Appl. Phys. Letters* 11:266–268 (Oct. 1967).

Acoustical Holographic experiments of the Leith–Upatnieks type, in which the inclined planar reference is simulated electrically by a simple technique, are described. The results graphically illustrate that finite "film" resolution introduces ambiguities into acoustical and optical holograms. The experiments were performed at 1 MHz, a frequency suitable for long-range underwater imaging and detection.

E. Marom, H. Boutin, and R. K. Mueller, Real-Time Display of Sound Holograms (Abstract), *J. Acoust. Soc. Am.* 42(5):1169 (Nov. 1967).

It is possible to reconstruct optically a sound hologram by reflecting a laser beam from the pattern formed on the water surface. The acoustically illuminated object is then viewed in real time but the quality of the reconstruction is poor because of aberrations due to streaming and oscillatory surface disturbances. A way of improving the real time reconstruction process is presented, in which the holographic pattern is recorded on the surface of a piezoelectric crystal, immersed in the water, and then forms the end wall of a Sokolov-type electron tube. A scanning electron beam reads off the corresponding voltage pattern obtained on the surface of the piezoelectric crystal. It produces an output signal that is then applied to a deuterated KDP crystal scanned by an electron beam synchronized with that of the first tube. It is therefore possible to modulate the index of refraction of KD*P and obtain phase modulation corresponding point by point to the holographic pattern recorded on the quartz surface. Illumination of the crystal with laser light will permit optical reconstruction of acoustically illuminated objects.

G. A. Massey, Acoustic Holography in Air with an Electronic Reference, *Proc. IEEE* 55(6):1115–1117 (June 1967).

This letter describes the formation of acoustical holograms retaining the properties of holograms made by the Leith–Upatnieks method without requiring the use of an acoustical reference wave. Holograms are recorded by scanning a linear transducer over an inclined plane; the phase reference is synthesized electronically in the receiver. Experimental results in air at 25 kHz are described.

G. A. Massey, Applications of Holography to Acoustic Imaging, IEEE Symposium on Sonics and Ultrasonics, Vancouver, Canada, Oct. 5, 1967.

This paper outlines the theory of holographic acoustical imaging without an acoustic reference beam, and presents the results of several experiments. The process of acoustical hologram formation using an electronic reference is described briefly. The tolerance of this imaging technique to changes in the speed of sound in the medium due to thermal variations, as well as phase changes due to motion of the medium in the acoustical path, are considered. The effect of oscillator drift and the advantages of using directional scanning transducers are discussed.

A. F. Metherell, H. M. A. El-Sum, J. J. Dreher, and L. Larmore, Sonoptography, DARL Research Communication No. 25 (Jan. 1967), Douglas Advanced Research Laboratories, Huntington Beach, California.

The principle of reconstructed wavefronts is extended to the formation of visual pictures of acoustical waves, a process hereafter termed sonoptography. A sonoptigram is equivalent to a hologram in optics. Sonoptography yields better results than conventional lens systems, particularly in the presence of turbulence and turbidity. Sampled sonoptigrams have successfully reconstructed images of acceptable quality. The signal-to-noise ratio in a sampled sonoptigram increases with the number of sampled points as well as with the reduction in the size of the sampling probe.

Applications of sonoptography to various problems in different fields are discussed, and preliminary results of experimental work are presented. Proposed future work on sonoptography at the Douglas Advanced Research Laboratories is outlined.

A. F. Metherell, H. M. A. El-Sum, J. J. Dreher, and L. Larmore, Optical Reconstruction from Sampled Holograms Made with Sound Waves, *Phys. Letters* **24A**(10):547–548 (May 8, 1967).

Experiments are described in which a reconstructed image was formed from a sampled hologram. The hologram is called a sonoptigram because it was made using sound instead of light.

A. F. Metherell, H. M. A. El-Sum, J. J. Dreher, and L. Larmore, Image Reconstruction from Sampled Acoustical Holograms, *Appl. Phys. Letters* **10**(10):277–279 (May 15, 1967).

The wavefront reconstruction technique has been used to reconstruct an optical image from a sampled hologram. The hologram was made using sound waves at 21 kHz instead of light. This was done by sampling the acoustical field with an ordinary microphone.

A. F. Metherell, H. M. A. El-Sum, Simulated Reference in a Coarsely Sampled Acoustical Hologram, *Appl. Phys. Letters* **11**(1):20–22 (July 1, 1967).

Four real images were reconstructed from a coarsely sampled acoustical hologram made with an ordinary microphone. An internal reference was used which electronically simulated two-plane reference waves impinging on the acoustical hologram plane at an angle of + and − 42.55° from the perpendicular. The sound frequency was 20 kHz, with a wavelength of 0.676 in. in air.

A. F. Metherell, H. M. A. El-Sum, J. J. Dreher, and L. Larmore, Introduction to Acoustical Holography, *J. Acoust. Soc. Am.* **42**(4):733–742 (Oct. 1967).

The principle of reconstructed wavefronts is extended to the formation of visual pictures of acoustical waves. The important relationships used in conventional optical holography that also apply to acoustics are briefly reviewed. It is shown that image formation using the principles of acoustical holography yields better results than conventional acoustical lens systems, particularly in the presence of turbulence and turbidity. Experiments are described in which coarsely sampled acoustical holograms, made with sound wavelengths of 0.64 in. and longer, have successfully reconstructed images of acceptable quality. The signal-to-noise ratio in a sampled acoustical hologram is shown to increase with the number of sampled points as well as with the reduction in the size of the sampling probe. Applications of acoustical holography in different fields are discussed.

A. F. Metherell and H. M. A. El-Sum, Reference Waves in Synthesized Acoustical Holograms (Abstract), *J. Acoust. Soc. Am.* **42**(5):1169 (Nov. 1967).

The reference wave necessary for recording a hologram of an object irradiated with acoustical waves [A. Metherell and H. El-Sum, *Appl. Phys. Letters* (July 1967)] can be provided externally by appropriately controlling the phase between two coherent signals, the one that derives the sound source, and the other which is used as a reference by summing it electronically with the signal diffracted from the object. The shape of the wavefront of the reference wave and the angle it makes with the object wave are determined by the phase shift between the two waves on the recording plane. This in turn depends on the wavelength, the recording technique (continuous or sampled) (A. Metherell, H. El-Sum, J. Dreher, and L. Larmore, *Appl. Phys. Letters* **10**:277, (1967); *J. Acoust. Soc. Am.* (Oct. 1967)), the type of hologram sought (narrow or wide angle, Fourier, Fresnel, etc.), and the final optical reconstruction. These and other factors affecting the choice and control of the reference beam will be discussed. Experimental results of acoustical holograms taken with various sound frequencies (9–21 kHZ) will be presented.

A. F. Metherell, Seeing with Sound, *Oceanology International* pp. 22–25 (Mar.–Apr. 1968).

The new technique of "sonoptography" translates sound into three-dimensional visual images. Although still a laboratory curiosity, this acoustical form of holography shows promise of replacing sonar, and accelerating ocean exploration.

A. F. Metherell and S. Spinak, Acoustical Holography of Nonexistent Wavefronts Detected at a Single point in Space, *Appl. Phys. Letters* **13**(1): 22–24 (July 1968).

An experiment is described in which a hologram is recorded by scanning the source and having the detector stationary. The resulting "scanned source" hologram is shown to be identical to the conventional "scanned detector" hologram. The significance of this experiment is that it demonstrates that sampled holograms of an object can be recorded at a single point in space with either a scanning source or an array of sources; that the object wavefront need not actually exist in space but may be geometrically synthesized; and that the object may be illuminated by a changing rather than stationary wave field. The interesting possibilities to which this configuration gives rise are briefly discussed.

R. K. Mueller and N. K. Sheridon, Sound Holograms and Optical Reconstruction, *Appl. Phys. Letters* **9**(9):328–329 (Nov. 1, 1966).

A hologram has been made of an object illuminated by ultrasound, using the deformation of the water surface by radiation pressure. An optical reconstruction of this sound hologram with laser light has been achieved.

R. K. Mueller and N. K. Sheridon, Formation of Ultrasonic Images by Holographic Techniques (Abstract), *J. Acoust. Soc. Am.* **40**(5):1284 (Nov. 1966).

Experiments demonstrating the formation of optical images of objects immersed in sound-propagating media (water, in our case) and illuminated by ultrasonic waves are described. The image formation is achieved via a sound-diffraction pattern that is used as an optical hologram. A visible diffraction pattern due to sound waves diffracted off an acoustically illuminated object and an acoustical reference beam is produced at the surface of the water by the balance of the radiation pressure of the sound waves with the surface tension of the water. Since the radiation pressure is proportional to the sound intensity, the surface deformation produced in this manner has all the characteristics of a hologram. Coherent light reflected off this surface, therefore, forms a conjugate pair of optical images of the acoustically illuminated object. The optical reconstruction is reduced in size in the ratio of acoustical to optical wavelength and has to be viewed with magnifying optics. Objects transparent to sound waves appear transparent in the optical reconstruction, and thus, internal features of the objects can be viewed or recorded.

R. K. Mueller, Sound Holography and Optical Reconstruction (Abstract), *J. Acoust. Soc. Am.* **41**(6):1601 (June 1967).

Image formation and sound holography for general wave fields are discussed to provide the background for the discussion of acoustical holography, which covers the following aspects: acoustical holography by scanning methods, nonacoustical recording of acoustical holograms, the surface as a recording medium, surface response to sonic radiation pressure and its application to real-time holography. Problems connected with optical reconstruction of acoustical holograms and potential applications of acoustic holography are considered.

R. K. Mueller, E. Marom, and D. Fritzler, Ultrasonic Holography by Electronic Scanning of a Piezoelectric Crystal, *Appl. Phys. Letters* **12**(2): 26–28 (Jan. 15, 1968).

Images have been optically reconstructed from acoustical holograms displayed by electronic scanning of a piezoelectric crystal, irradiated by the sonic beams.

K. Preston, Jr. and J. L. Kreuzer, Ultrasonic Imaging Using a Synthetic Holographic Technique, *Appl. Phys. Letters* **10**(5):150–152 (Mar. 1, 1967).

Visible three-dimensional ultrasonic imaging of the interior and exterior of optically opaque objects has been achieved using a synthetic holographic technique at a frequency of 5 MHz. An ultrasonic hologram and the corresponding visible image are presented.

J. M. Smith and N. F. Moody, Factors Affecting Image Quality in Ultrasonic Holography, IEEE Symposium on Sonics and Ultrasonics, Vancouver, Canada, Oct. 5, 1967.

Advances in the field of holography since the invention of the laser have stimulated extensions of the principle using other forms of radiation. Ultrasonic waves in particular have been shown to be adaptable to the process. A system recently designed and at present in use at the University of Toronto employs a scanning device to detect the amplitude and phase of the sound pressure across the hologram plane, which is then mixed with an electrical reference beam to produce the hologram signal. This is converted to a light intensity and recorded on photographic film.

R. B. Smith, Ultrasonic Imaging Using a Scanned Hologram Method, Battelle Memorial Institute Report BNWL-SA-1362, presented at IEEE Symposium on Sonics and Ultrasonics, Vancouver, Canada, Oct. 5, 1967.

Holograms of ultrasonic sound fields in water have been recorded on film using a scanning technique. Reconstruction of the hologram in a coherent light beam forms the optical analog of the original sound field and permits the imaging of objects as seen by ultrasound. Using techniques similar to some previously reported, we have obtained holograms of diffusely reflecting objects in water by scanning a point transducer over a plane portion of the scattered sound field. An electronic reference signal is used rather than an ultrasonic reference beam. The received signal and reference are combined in a balanced mixer to obtain the phase-amplitude signal. By analog methods, this signal intensity modulates a point light source moving in synchronism with the scanning transducer.

F. L. Thurstone, Ultrasound Holography and Visual Reconstruction, *Proc. Symp. Biomed. Eng.* **1**:12–15 (1966). (Reprinted in Ch. 7, pp. 120–125.)

This paper presents a new technique for the utilization of sonic energy for the purpose of visualizing opaque objects which are transparent with respect to sound. With this technique, internal structures in an opaque body can be presented optically and visualized in three dimensions.

F. L. Thurstone, Ultrasound Holograms for the Visualization of Sonic Fields, in the Proceedings of the 19th Annual Conference on Engineering in Medicine and Biology, Nov. 17, 1966, p. 222.

F. L. Thurstone, Three-Dimensional Imaging by Ultrasound Holography, *Digest of 7th International Conference of Medical and Biological Engineering,* Stockholm, Sweden (1967), p. 313.

F. L. Thurstone, Holographic Imaging with Ultrasound, (Abstract) *J. Acoust. Soc. Am.* **42**(5):1148 (Nov. 1967).

Ultrasound fields, having both spatial and temporal coherence, have been used to produce sonic holograms that can produce three-dimensional images in a visible light field. The sound field is detected by mechanically or electronically scanning a piezoelectric element and determining both magnitude and phase of the sonic field. The information thus obtained is processed sequentially by electronic, optical, and photographic techniques to produce a hologram transparency. The generation of the images by wavefront reconstruction is accomplished with the coherent light produced by a laser.

F. L. Thurstone, On Holographic Imaging with Long Wavelength Fields, *Proc. IEEE* **56**(4):768–769 (1968).

Holograms recorded at microwave, acoustic, and other long wavelengths inherently produce image distortion when reconstruction is accomplished at visible wavelengths. A technique is presented for the reduction or elimination of this primary distortion.

Leonard Weiss and E. Douglas Holyoke, The Examination of Soft Tumors in the Rat by Ultrasonic Holography (Abstract), *Biophys. J.* Vol. 8, No. A-43 (1968).

Two separated ultrasonic transducers were immersed in water and oriented so that their radiations converged at a liquid/air interface, to form an interference pattern. The specimen was inserted in the path of one of the beams, to create an ultrasonic hologram at the liquid/air interface. The hologram was illuminated by a monochromatic, quasi-coherent light source, which was reflected from the liquid surface, and diffracted by the interference at the liquid/air interface, to give rise to diffracted orders containing the reconstructed holographic image. The orders of the diffracted light beam were then separated, and one of the orders, carrying the reconstruction information from the surface of the ultrasonic hologram, was photographed.

We have explored the use of this technique in detecting implanted tumors and inflammatory lesions in skin-flaps raised from rats. It is possible to detect discrete spherical lesions of down to 2 mm diameter, under conditions where they are not visualized by standard soft-tissue X-ray techniques.

J. D. Young and J. E. Wolfe, A New Technique for Acoustic Holography, *Appl. Phys. Letters* **11**:294–296 (Nov. 1, 1967).

A new method of recording ultrasonic holograms using deformable films on solid substrates is described. The films have been used to phase-modulate laser light for image reconstruction.

INDEX

Three different fonts are used in connection with author listings. Plain characters indicate direct mention of the author's name or work. Page numbers in italics refer to citations of his publications. Boldface number ranges show authorship of chapters in this book.